The Law of Remedies for Torts or Private Wrongs

By

Francis Hillard

BeardBooks

Washington, D.C.

Reprinted 2000 by Beard Books, Washington, D.C.

ISBN 1-893122-77-8

Printed in the United States of America

Remedies for Torts

PREFACE.

The following work is specially designed to be a sequel or supplement to another book which has been received with some favor by the profession, — "The Law of Torts or Private Wrongs." This explanation is necessary, in order to save the present treatise from the charge of being more desultory and disconnected than any legal text-book ought to be. Had my original plan been more comprehensive, the contents of the following pages might, without marked impropriety, have been scattered among the successive chapters of the former work. Constituting, therefore, as they now do, the material of a separate book, they require to be read in connection with the former one, before the question of their pertinency, utility, and methodical propriety can be fairly passed upon. A few remarks will explain the plan of the present book.

In treating of *remedies for torts,* of course it is not proposed to enter into a consideration of those matters of mere *process* or *practice,* which are for the most part common to all suits at law, whether founded upon contracts or upon wrongs; and which are generally and variously regulated in the several States by express statute. In such a plan would be included the writ, service, entry, trial, verdict, judgment, execution, and numerous other incidental points, all of great practical importance, but having no special connection with the main subject of this work, and the law pertaining to which depends so extensively upon positive legislation.

Another limitation of the plan of the present work, depending on somewhat different considerations, is, that it omits those *remedies* which are directed to the recovery of *compensation;* and is confined to that restricted class, which claims specifically the property, personal or real, alleged to be wrongfully taken or detained; including *replevin*, and *real action* or *ejectment;* — the action of *detinue*, though it belongs to the same class, being now substantially obsolete. With reference to *actions for damages*, the *remedy* has to some extent unavoidably been treated, in the work to which the present is a supplement, in connection with the wrong itself. Thus it would be impossible to treat of the *wrong* of conversion, without at the same time treating of the *remedy* of *trover*. And so with the wrong and remedy, both entitled *trespass*, and the wrong of *negligence*, redressed by the *action on the case*. But, with regard to the *specific* remedies, which we are about to consider, it is far otherwise. There is no particular wrong for which replevin is the appropriated remedy. And, in reference to the unlawful withholding of real property, the wrong of *disseisin* and the remedy of *ejectment* are so inseparably connected together, or rather the remedy so far regulates and controls the wrong, that to treat of the subject at all was found inconsistent with the plan of the former work, and the whole was reserved for future consideration.

There are, however, three topics, applicable alike to all torts, and still strictly coming under the head of *remedies*, which will be found fully treated in the present work.

CHAPTER III.

CHAPTER IV.

CHAPTER V.

CHAPTER VI.

CHAPTER VII.

CHAPTER VIII.

CHAPTER IX.

CHAPTER X.

CHAPTER XI.

BOOK IV.

EVIDENCE.

CHAPTER I.

CHAPTER II.

CHAPTER III.

CHAPTER IV.

CHAPTER V.

CHAPTER VI.

CHAPTER VII.

CHAPTER VIII.

CHAPTER IX.

CHAPTER X.

CHAPTER XI.

CHAPTER XII.

BOOK V.

DAMAGES.

CHAPTER I.

CHAPTER II.

CHAPTER III.

CHAPTER IV.

CHAPTER V.

CHAPTER VI.

CHAPTER VII.

CHAPTER VIII.

CHAPTER IX.

CHAPTER X.

CHAPTER XI.

CHAPTER XII.

CHAPTER XIII.

CHAPTER XIV.

CHAPTER XV.

CHAPTER XVI.

CHAPTER XVII.

CHAPTER XVIII.

CHAPTER XIX.

INDEX TO CASES CITED.

A.

D.

G.

H.

I.

J

K.

T.

U.

V.

THE LAW OF REMEDIES FOR TORTS,

OR

PRIVATE WRONGS.

BOOK I.

REPLEVIN.

CHAPTER I.

GENERAL NATURE AND OBJECTS OF THE ACTION.

1. Definition and general nature of the action.
2. Delivery of the goods to the plaintiff.
3. Tortious taking, whether necessary — *cepit* and *detinet*; practice in different States.
11. Lies, in general, only for personal property; — things pertaining to the realty; choses in action.
14. A local action.
16. In what courts.
17. Successive replevins of the same property.

§ 1. THE action of replevin is thus described by an elementary writer of authority. By replevin, the owner of goods unjustly taken and detained from him, may regain possession through the medium of, and upon application to, the sheriff, upon giving him security to prosecute an action against the person who seized. It is principally used in cases of distress; but it seems that it may be brought in any case where the owner has goods taken from him.[1] And the action is said to be founded on a taking, and the right which the party from whom the goods are taken has to have them restored to him until the question of title to the goods is determined.[2] (*a*)

[1] 3 Steph. N. P. 2482; 1 Chit. Pl. 162.

[2] Per Lord Redesdale, Shannon *v.* Shannon, 1 Sch. & L. 327.

(*a*) It is held that a plaintiff in replevin is bound by the same rule with other plaintiffs, when similarly situated. Rodericks *v.* Payne, 1 McC. 407. The action is held not to involve a prohibition to inferior tribunals. Lynah *v.* Commis. Harp. 336; Gist *v.* Cole, 2 N. & M'C. 456. In Pennsylvania, as modified by statute, replevin seems to

§ 2. As we have seen, the action of replevin contemplates delivery, in the first instance, to the plaintiff. It is held, that symbolical delivery to the plaintiff is not sufficient without his consent, which is a question for the jury. But a return, that the goods were replevied and delivered, is *primâ facie* evidence of delivery.[1] (*a*)

§ 3. The restricted propositions are sometimes found, that replevin lies for any *tortious or unlawful taking* of goods, and not merely in cases of a *distress*.[2] (See ch. 2.) That replevin in the *detinet* may be brought when the taking was tortious; and that form of action does not admit the original possession of the defendant to have been lawful.[3] That at common law replevin lies only where there has been a tortious taking; and where, under a statute, replevin is brought for an unlawful detention simply, the plaintiff must strictly follow the statute.[4] Hence, where the slave of A, a resident of New Orleans, ran away, and was afterwards sold at auction in Natchez, and bought by B, who sent him to Little Rock, and sold him afterwards to C, who had no knowledge of A's title; it was held that A could not maintain replevin against C for un-

[1] Hayes *v.* Lusby, 5 Har. & J. 485.

[2] Pangburn *v.* Patridge, 7 Johns. 140; Cummings *v.* M'Gill, 2 Tayl. 98; Drummond *v.* Hopper, 4 Har. 327; Rector *v.* Chevalier, 1 Mis. 345; Wright *v.* Armstrong, Bre. 130; Vaiden *v.* Bell, 3 Rand. 448; Dickson *v.* Mathers, 1 Hemp. 65; Galloway *v.* Bird, 12 Moo. 547; 4 Bing. 299; Pangburn *v.* Patridge, 7 John. 140; Hopkins *v.* Hopkins, 10 ib. 373; Boulton *v.* Thompson, 14 ib. 87; Bruce *v.* Ogden, 6 Halst. 370. See Smith *v.* Crockett, Minor, 277.

[3] Zachrisson *v.* Ahman, 2 Sandf. 68.

[4] Trapnall *v.* Hattier, 1 Eng. 18; Drummond *v.* Hopper, 4 Harring. 327. See Johnson *v.* Johnson, ib. 171.

be an action for damages. Thus, where the taking was accompanied with wrong and outrage, the plaintiff may recover damages beyond the value of the property, without allegations of special damage, or of such aggravating circumstances. Otherwise with consequential damages, not necessarily or naturally resulting from the tortious act. Schofield *v.* Ferrers, 46 Penn. 438. Where goods are not replevied, (restored) but detained by the defendant, and judgment in replevin is rendered against him; he cannot satisfy such judgment by giving up the goods and paying the damages assessed for the taking and detention. *Retorno habendo* has no existence, except where the goods have been replevied, and the verdict is for the defendant. Hence, it is no ground of error, that the verdict did not sever the damages given for the value from those given for the tortious taking. Schofield *v.* Ferrers, 46 . enn. 438. In Vermont, it has been held that replevin does not lie except under the statute. Miller *v.* Warner, Brayt. 168. Not to try title. Taggart *v.* Hart, ib. 215. Replevin is not superseded, in Indiana, by the remedy for trial of the right of property. (2 Rev. Sts., ch. 5, p. 493). Firestone *v.* Mishler, 18 Ind. 439. In Kentucky, replevin does not lie where property is held adversely. Dillon *v.* Wright, 7 J. J. Mar. 10.

(*a*) In Pennsylvania the plaintiff is entitled to recover, although the sheriff is prevented by the defendant from replevying the property and delivering it to the plaintiff. But judgment rendered only for the property actually replevied will, while unreversed, be a bar to an action of trover for the value of the rest. Bower *v.* Tallman, 5 W. & S. 556. In Massachusetts, a defendant in replevin, who has prevented the officer from delivering the property to the plaintiff by himself attaching it, cannot object to the prosecution of the replevin on

lawfully detaining the slave. So a person receiving property, knowing it to have been obtained by a trespass, is held not liable to an action of replevin.[1]

§ 4. The same rule is sometimes expressed by the proposition, that "in general, when *trespass* will lie, replevin will also;"[2] or in all cases where trespass lies.[3] (*a*)

§ 5. But, even upon this restricted view of the remedy in question, it is held, that an *unlawful intermeddling* with, or an *exercise or claim of dominion* over property, without authority or right, will render the party liable to trespass or replevin.[4] So a taking, under color of a contract with a drunken bailee, may be regarded as a *tortious* taking;[5] or obtaining goods by fraudulent pretences; and replevin will lie for them without a demand.[6] So, in replevin, any evidence, which shows that the defendants obtained possession from one not authorized to sell, is sufficient evidence of an unlawful taking.[7] So where A, having the possession and management of a farm, forbade B to take his horse therefrom; held a sufficient taking to support replevin.[8]

§ 6. These distinctions, however, as to what constitutes a tortious taking, have become comparatively unimportant, because the prevailing and almost universal rule now is, that replevin lies for the recovery of any personal chattel *unlawfully detained*

[1] 1 Eng. 18; Harper *v.* Baker, 3 Mon. 421.

[2] Per Shaw, C. J., Esson *v.* Tarbell, 9 Cush. 415.

[3] Marshall *v.* Davis, 1 Wend. 109; Hopkins *v.* Hopkins, 10 John. 369; Bruen *v.* Ogden, 6 Halst. 370.

[4] Haythorn *v.* Rushforth, 4 Harr. 160.

[5] Drummond *v.* Hopper, 4 Harr. 327.

[6] Ayers *v.* Hewett, 1 App. 281.

[7] Gray *v.* Nations, 1 Pike, 557; Eggleston *v.* Mundy, 4 Mich. 295.

[8] Moore *v.* Moore, 4 Mis. 421.

the ground of such non-delivery. Pomeroy *v.* Trimper, 8 Allen, 398. In Michigan, replevin does not lie if the goods are in the plaintiff's possession, though an officer claims them by a levy. Hickey *v.* Hinsdale, 12 Mich. 99.

(*a*) By a late decision in England, replevin is not maintainable, unless there has been a taking of the goods out of the possession of the owner. Thus A, being indebted to the plaintiff, brought him 15*l.* towards payment, but requested and obtained permission to lay the money out in the purchase of a horse and cart, which were to be the plaintiff's, but of which A was to have the possession and use, subject to such occasional use as the plaintiff might require to have of them, and to their being given up to the plaintiff when he should demand them. After A had purchased the horse and cart, and had the possession and use of them for some time, he determined to emigrate. They were used in transporting his effects to the pier at which he was to embark, and the defendant, to whom he owed money for fodder supplied to the horse, went with him, to procure payment if he could. At parting, A delivered the horse and cart to him, telling him to take them for the debt, but adding, that he owed the plaintiff money also, and that, if he would discharge the debt due to the defendant, which was much less than their value, he was to give them up to him. The plaintiff for some time remained in ignorance of what had passed, and, afterwards coming to the knowledge of it, demanded them, but the defendant refused to deliver them unless his debt was paid; whereupon the plaintiff replevied. On the plea of *non cepit*, held, there was no taking which would

from the owner, although there may have been no tortious taking.[1] The reasons for this more liberal application of the action are well explained by the court in Massachusetts. "It is a general remark in the books, that, where there has been a tortious taking, replevin will lie . . . Where the taking was originally without wrong, but the party detains the goods wrongfully, the owner should have some remedy for them specifically, if to be found. The defendant contends that *detinue*, in such case, is the only remedy. . . . This is certainly not so effectual a remedy, if, indeed, it be not entirely obsolete. The judgment in *detinue* is to recover the thing, or the value of it, if it cannot be found, with the damages for the taking. In replevin, the thing is immediately seized; but in *detinue* the possession is not changed until after judgment; and this being conditional, the value, as estimated by the jury, may be but a poor compensation. After a judgment in *detinue*, a *distringas* goes to the defendant, *ad deliberanda bona;* and if he will not deliver them, the plaintiff shall have the value, as ascertained by the jury. So that it is at the defendant's election to deliver the goods or the value. Replevin is, then, the only certain remedy, and it may be maintained where the taking was lawful, but the detention unlawful." This extended application of the remedy is further justified, by a statutory provision for it, where goods are taken, *distrained*, or *attached*.[2] In a later case, argued for the defendant by very eminent counsel, the same learned judge re-affirms the former decision, upon a full examination of the English and American authorities on both sides of the question.[3] And, in still another case, Mr. Justice Wilde holds that "such is clearly the law of Massachusetts, whatever may be the law of England," referring to the terms of the writ prescribed by statute, — "taken, detained, or attached" (as the case may be).[4] And, in a comparatively recent case, it is said, "By our statute replevin will lie for a wrongful detention only."[5]

§ 7. And as, upon the theory of a wrongful *taking*, replevin is held a concurrent remedy with trespass, so, upon the ground of

maintain replevin. Mennie *v.* Blake, 37 Eng. L. & Eq. 169.

[1] Marston *v.* Baldwin, 17 Mass. 606; Baker, *et al.* *v.* Fales, 16 Pick. 147; Badger *v.* Phinney, 15 Mass. 359.

[2] Per Putnam, J., Badger *v.* Phinney, 15 Mass. 362, 363.

[3] Baker *v.* Fales, 16 Mass. 147.

[4] Marston *v.* Baldwin, 17 Mass. 610.

[5] Esson *v.* Tarbell, 9 Cush. 415; acc. Weaver *v.* Lawrence, 1 Dall. 156; Shearick *v.* Huber, 6 Bin. 3; Stoughton *v.* Rappalo, 3 S. & R. 562; Cullum *v.* Bevans, 6 Har. & J. 469; Daggett *v.* Robbins, 2 Blackf. 415; Waterman *v.* Matteson, 4 R. I. 539; Seaver *v.* Dingley, 4 Greenl. 306.

wrongful *detainer* only, it is concurrent with the other action for damages, of *trover*.[1]

§ 8. The prevailing doctrine in relation to replevin, in still another aspect, is stated by a writer of high authority, as follows: "Replevin may be brought to recover goods which are still detained by the person who took them, and this is called replevin in the *detinet*, which has been long since obsolete. But the modern action is in the *detinuit*, which is so called, because, as the word imports, it is brought when the goods have been delivered to the party, which is done by the sheriff upon a writ of replevin, or plaint, levied before him. The plaintiff in replevin in the *detinet* was entitled to recover as well the value of the goods as damages for taking them. But in the present action in the *detinuit* he can only recover damages for the taking."[2] (*a*)

[1] Eggleston *v.* Mundy, 4 Mich. 295.

[2] Potter *v.* Worth, 1 Wms. Saun. 347 b, n. 2.

(*a*) The law upon this subject in the different States is variously modified by express statute and local usage. In New Hampshire it is held, that, at common law, and before the statute in relation to replevin, replevin could be maintained for the wrongful *detention* of a distress. Osgood *v.* Green, 10 Fost. 210.

In Pennsylvania, replevin lies, wherever one man claims goods in the possession of another. Boyle *v.* Rankin, 22 Penn. 168.

In Indiana, it is necessary to prove either an unlawful taking or an unlawful detainer. Baer *v.* Martin, 2 Cart. 229.

In Arkansas, to maintain replevin in the *detinet*, the plaintiff is not bound to prove a bailment by himself or some person for him to the defendant. Phelan *v.* Bonham, 4 Eng. 389.

In Missouri, replevin will lie, although no trespass has been committed by the defendant in taking the property. Skinner *v.* Stense, 4 Mis. 93.

In Georgia, the action of replevin is confined to cases of *wrongful distress*. Hewitson *v.* Hunt, 8 Rich. 106.

In Ohio, it has been held that replevin lies in all cases, unless specially excepted by statute. Stone *v.* Wilson, Wright, 159.

But by a late decision, it is wrongful detention, verified by affidavit, that gives the right of action. A tortious taking is insufficient. State, &c. *v.* Jennings, 14 Ohio St. 73.

In North Carolina, a power of distress, given to a navigation company, upon a refusal to pay their tolls, is constitutional, and replevin lies for its abuse. The State *v.* Patrick, 3 Dev. 478.

The act of North Carolina in relation to replevin (Rev. Sts. ch. 101) does not repeal or supersede the common-law remedy. Duffy *v.* Murrill, 9 Ired. 46.

In Pennsylvania, replevin is not altogether a proceeding *in rem*, but against the defendant in the writ personally, with a summons to appear. Bower *v.* Tallman, 5 W. & S. 556.

In Delaware, replevin is not confined to distress for rent in arrear, but may be used wherever one claims property in another's possession. Clark *v.* Adair, 3 Harring. 113.

In Wisconsin, a verdict, that the property detained is that of the plaintiff, and awarding damages for the detention, is defective, and must be set aside, unless it be also found that the detention was unjust. Swain *v.* Roys, 4 Wis. 150.

But in replevin in the *cepit*, a verdict of "unjust detention" does not dispose of the material issue raised by the allegation of taking, and is therefore bad. Replevin in the *cepit*, under the Code, resembles the old trespass *vi et armis*, and only puts the taking in issue. Replevin in the *detinet* is a substitute for the old action of detinue, where the injury is only in the keeping. Ronge *v.* Dawson, 9 Wis. 246.

In Minnesota, under the statute, the plaintiff must allege that the defendant "wrongfully" took the property. Coit *v.* Waples, 1 Min. 134.

The statute of Wisconsin, adopted in Minnesota, retains the common-law action

§ 9. A somewhat intermediate view of the point in question is, that replevin lies against a possessor of property unlawfully taken (except officers of the law).[1] Thus, in New York, a declaration in replevin in the *cepit* must show a wrongful taking. But it is sufficient to allege that the defendant took the property of the plaintiff, and unjustly detains the same. Such an allegation imports a tortious taking.[2] (*a*)

§ 10. The following case illustrates the nature of the title and demand which are necessary to constitute a *wrongful detention*, and justify an action of replevin upon that ground. After the deacons of a church had seceded from it, the church elected trustees, authorizing them to demand, receive, and recover of the deacons, of whom the defendant, A, was one, all the church property. The communion plate, which was under A's care, was kept at the house of B, who lived near the meeting-house. The trustees showed A a copy of the vote, and requested him to deliver them the plate. He replied that he would consult his counsel, and, if the trustees had a right to the plate, he would deliver it to them. After a few days, the trustees made a demand on B, who refused, saying, that A had directed her not to deliver it to any one without an order from him. The church then elected the plaintiff a deacon; and he showed B the certifi-

[1] Murphy *v.* Tindall, 1 Hemp. 10.

[2] Childs *v.* Hart, 7 Barb. 370.

of replevin, and also gives it in lieu of detinue, where only the detention is wrongful. Ib.

In Mississippi, replevin lies only in case of distress for rent. Wheelock *v.* Cozzens, 6 How. Miss. 279.

In New York, the "claim or delivery of personal property," under the Code, is a substitute for replevin as it was regulated by the Revised Statutes. That action was a possessory action for the recovery of specific property in the defendant's possession or control, with damages for the detention. If the property were removed or concealed (in fraud of the replevin) so that the sheriff could not find it, and only in such case, the Revised Statutes added the remedy of arrest and bail. Replevin could not be maintained against a party who had neither the possession nor control of the chattels claimed, and had not parted with them in fraud of the action. The plaintiff's remedy was in trespass or trover. The assumption of the court in Cary *v.* Hotaling, and Olmstead *v.* Hotaling, 1 Hill, 311, that replevin was a concurrent remedy in all cases with trespass *de bonis asportatis*, was not well founded. Roberts *v.* Randel, 3 Sandf. 707.

The replevin statute of Arkansas, which provides for putting the plaintiff in possession of property before his title is adjudicated, is constitutional. Fleeman *v.* Haren, 3 Eng. 136; Prater *v.* Frazier, 6 Eng. 249.

In order to maintain a bill in equity under the (Mass.) Rev. Sts. c. 81, § 8, to compel the delivery of property detained, &c., so that it cannot be replevied, the plaintiff must show that he has a legal right to maintain an action of replevin, and that such action cannot be effectually prosecuted by reason of the concealment, &c., of the property of the defendant. Clapp *v.* Sheppard, 2 Met. 127.

(*a*) Counts in the *cepit* and in the *detinet* may be joined in replevin; but in such case, in Arkansas, the plaintiff must support each count by affidavit. Cox *v.* Grace, 5 Eng. 86.

cate of his election, and demanded the plate; but B refused to deliver it, assigning the same reason as before; whereupon the plaintiff forthwith replevied it. Held, the trustees were not authorized to receive and recover the property; that A's refusal, until he could ask advice, was not unreasonable, and their demand, if valid, could not avail the plaintiff, suing in his capacity of deacon; that the plaintiff's demand on B could not affect A before he had notice of it; and consequently there was no evidence of a tortious detention.[1]

§ 11. A writ of replevin is, in general, effectual for the delivery of *goods* or *personal property* only.[2] Thus, it does not lie for crops cut and removed by a disseisor.[3] Nor for a freehold, or a house built on leased land, illegally distrained.[4] Nor for things fixed to the freehold; as in case of fixtures separated from a mill.[5] Though it is otherwise if, after the sheriff has levied on them, they are severed.[6] (*a*) Nor against the actual, *bonâ fide* owner of land, for taking slates out of it.[7] So the original owner of land sold for taxes cannot bring replevin for timber cut by the purchaser before redemption.[8] (*b*) So, in New York, the purchaser of land sold on execution, after receiving the sheriff's deed, cannot maintain replevin in the *cepit* for timber which had been cut by the defendant while he remained in possession, during the fifteen months subsequent to the sale.[9] But replevin may be maintained for trees cut down, though made into posts and rails.[10] Or, by a mortgagee against a mortgagor in possession, for wood and timber cut, in waste of the estate, and substantial diminution of the security.[11] (*c*) Or for " mills, barns, steam-engines, offices, and sheds," which may or may not be fixtures. This is matter of evidence, unnecessary to be stated in pleading.[12] And where title to real estate is incidentally

[1] Page *v.* Crosby, 24 Pick. 211.
[2] Roberts *v.* The Dauphin, &c. 19 Penn. 71; Rex *v.* Leeds, 4 T. R. 584; 2 Saun. 84.
[3] De Mott *v.* Hagerman, 8 Cow. 220.
[4] Vausse *v.* Russel, 2 M'Cord, 329.
[5] Powell *v.* Smith, 2 Watts, 126.
[6] Cresson *v.* Stout, 17 Johns. 116.
[7] Brown *v.* Caldwell, 10 S. & R. 114.
[8] Cromelien *v.* Brink, 29 Penn. 522.
[9] Rich *v.* Baker, 3 Denio, 79.
[10] Snyder *v.* Vaux, 2 Rawle, 423.
[11] Waterman *v.* Matteson, 4 R. I. 539.
[12] Brearly *v.* Cox, 4 Zabr. 287.

(*a*) In Arkansas, replevin lies for a slave, notwithstanding the act of 1840, making slaves real estate. Gullett *v.* Lamberton, 1 Eng. 109.

(*b*) One claiming land as a preëmptor cannot maintain replevin for timber cut thereon, till his right has been proved. Bower *v.* Higbee, 9 Mis. 259.

(*c*) Replevin does not lie by the assignee of a mortgage, for a house erected by the mortgagor after the mortgage, and sold to the defendant. Clark *v.* Reyburn, 1 Kans 281.

brought in question in replevin, evidence as to such title is admissible. Thus, in replevin for logs cut upon land of the defendant's vendor, and seized by the plaintiff, it was material for the defendant to prove that the logs were not taken from land in the plaintiff's possession. Held, evidence of title was admissible, to prove possession in the rightful owners, which possession the defendant had purchased, the law casting the possession of wild timber lands on the owner, in the absence of any actual adverse possession.[1]

§ 12. The record book of a corporation may be replevied.[2] So a deed, by the grantee.[3]

§ 13. An equitable assignee of a chose in action cannot replevy it from the legal owner.[4]

§ 14. Replevin is *local*, and must be brought in the county where the goods are taken or distrained.[5] So, although brought for a cause of action for which trespass *de bonis asportatis* would lie.[6] And the venue will not be changed from the county where the cause of action arose.[7] Upon this point, it is stated by a writer of high authority: "Replevin differs from trespass *clausum fregit.* In the latter it is held to be sufficient for the plaintiff to allege the trespass to have been done in a vill or parish only, without mentioning any *place*, for it is not material; and if the plaintiff do mention a place, the defendant may justify in another place without a traverse, and the plaintiff must ascertain the place in a new assignment. But as there can be no new assignment in replevin,[8] and it is also an action which requires greater certainty in the declaration, the plaintiff is bound to mention the place of taking at first in his declaration.[9]"

§ 15. But the *plea* of the plaintiff need not mention the place of taking, but only refer to the property mentioned in the previous pleadings.[10]

§ 16. The *courts*, in which the action of replevin may be brought, are, of course, prescribed by statute in the different States. (*a*)

[1] Clement *v.* Wright, 40 Penn. 250.
[2] Southern, &c. *v.* Hixon, 5 Ind. 165.
[3] King *v.* Gilson, 32 Ill. 348.
[4] Clapp *v.* Shepard, 2 Met. 127.
[5] Robinson *v.* Mead, 7 Mass. 353. But see Crocker *v.* Mann, 3 Mis. 472.
[6] Williams *v.* Welch, 5 Wend. 290.
[7] Atkinson *v.* Holcomb, 4 Cow. 45.
[8] Cockley *v.* Pagrave, Freeman, 238.
[9] Potter *v.* North, 1 Wms. Saun. 347 *a*, note.
[10] Judd *v.* Fox, 9 Cow. 259. See Gardner *v.* Humphrey, 10 John. 53.

(*a*) In Massachusetts, it is held that a justice of the peace has no jurisdiction, nor the Court of Common Pleas any appellate jurisdiction, in an action of replevin, except

§ 17. Questions have sometimes arisen in reference to *successive writs* of replevin of the same property.[1] The owner of personal property, left in possession of A, may, by his own act, repossess himself of such property, although taken from A by virtue of a writ of replevin.[2] So it is no sufficient plea to a writ of replevin, that the chattels had been before delivered to the defendant, upon his writ of replevin against A; nor that the same officer from whom they were taken by such writ executed the writ of replevin against the defendant.[3] So, at common law, if the plaintiff, in an action of replevin, be nonsuited, he is not thereby barred from bringing another action of replevin, the merits of the cause not having been tried; and the statute of Edw. I., prohibiting a second replevin after a nonsuit, is not in force in Indiana.[4] But, in general, one cannot replevy replevied property.[5] And the wrongful detainer of a chattel, who has had judgment for its value against the owner in replevin, cannot himself recover in replevin, after judgment in trover against himself for its value.[6]

§ 18. A party who recovers in replevin, and gets a return from one party, cannot afterwards sue the same and another party in

[1] See Hackett *v.* Bonnell, 16 Wis. 471.
[2] Spencer *v.* McGowen, 13 Wend. 256.
[3] Ilsley *v.* Stubbs, 5 Mass. 280.
[4] Daggett *v.* Robbins, 2 Blackf. 415.
[5] Dearmon *v.* Blackburn, 1 Sneed, 390.
[6] Hoag *v.* Bremar, 3 Mich. 160.

for beasts distrained for going at large, or impounded for doing damage. Jordan *v.* Dennis, 7 Met. 590. See Gen. Sts.; Riddon *v.* Emory, 6 Greenl. 261; McKnight *v.* Crinnion, 22 Mis. 559.

Where an action of replevin for goods, commenced before a justice of the peace, was carried to the Court of Common Pleas by appeal; and that court rendered judgment for the defendant for a return, with damages and costs; and the plaintiff brought a writ of error, for want of jurisdiction: so much of the judgment as awarded a return and damages was reversed, and so much as awarded costs was affirmed. Jordan *v.* Dennis, 7 Met. 590.

In Vermont, a justice has no jurisdiction in replevin, except for beasts distrained or impounded, even where the value of the property is less than seven dollars. Glover *v.* Chase, 1 Williams, 533.

In Indiana, replevin lies before any justice of the peace in the county, though the defendant and the justice reside in different townships. Beddinger *v.* Jocelyn, 18 Ind. 325; Test *v.* Small, 21 ib. 127.

In Wisconsin, the territorial statute on the subject requires the process in replevin to be issued in the name of the United States; if not so issued, no jurisdiction is acquired. Roach *v.* Moulton, 1 Chand. 187.

It is held, in Massachusetts, that replevin lies, in a State court, against a marshal of the United States, for property attached by him on mesne process from a United States court against a third person. Howe *v.* Freeman, 14 Gray, 566. But see 24 How. 450.

The jurisdiction conferred by statute upon the St. Louis Law Commissioner's Court, in actions in the nature of actions of replevin, where the value of the property claimed does not exceed $150, is regulated by the value of the property, and not by the damages. Annis *v.* Bigney, 28 Mis. 247.

In Minnesota, a justice has no jurisdiction in replevin under the statute, as at common law, until the property has been found and replevied. St. Martin *v.* Desnoyer, 1 Min. 41.

trespass for the same transaction, whether the damages awarded in replevin had been recovered or not.[1] If all the goods described in the plaint in replevin were not found, trover lies for the residue.[2]

§ 19. The delivering, to the plaintiff in replevin, of the goods sued for, does not tend to prove property in him. Therefore, where replevin is brought by A against B and C for a boat, and they plead specially that B had previously brought replevin against A for the same boat, and the sheriff had replevied it; the former record, consisting of the writ and return, is not competent evidence, though admissible under a plea of property, and the plea may properly be struck off, on motion, as frivolous and tendering an impertinent issue. The court repudiate the argument that, by this proceeding, the defendant in replevin loses his title to the property, and can only look to the plaintiff's bond given to the sheriff, and refer to the following distinction: "It has been said, in one case, that if a defendant retain the property, and give a property-bond, he becomes the owner as against the plaintiff, whatever his title may have been before; but his case is unlike that of a plaintiff to whom the property has been replevied. A verdict against a defendant retaining the goods is for their value, and there is no judgment against him *pro retorno habendo*. A verdict against the plaintiff, to whom the goods have been delivered, cannot be for their value, and the defendant is entitled to his writ of *retorno habendo*, even when the plaintiff becomes nonsuit."[3]

§ 20. Goods belonging to A, having been levied on, were replevied by B, to whom they were delivered, and who died pending the suit; whereupon the sheriff retook the goods from the possession of B's executors, claiming to hold them by virtue of the original levy, and they brought replevin against him. Held, the replevin by B gave him only a temporary right of possession, which expired when the suit abated, and the retaking by the sheriff was lawful.[4]

[1] Karr *v.* Barstow, 24 Ill. 580.

[2] Ibid.

[3] Lorett *v.* Burkhardt, 44 Penn. 173, per Strong, J. 174.

[4] Burkle *v.* Luce, 6 Hill, 558, 1 Comst. 163. See Bradyll *v.* Ball, 1 Bro. Ch. 427; Woglam *v.* Cowperthwaite, 2 Dall. 68; Frey *v.* Leeper, ib. 131; Acker *v.* White, 25 Wend. 614.

CHAPTER II.

REPLEVIN IN CASE OF DISTRESS, IMPOUNDING, ETC.

1. Originally limited to this class of cases.
2. Trespass *ab initio*.
3. Practice in different States as to cattle, impounding, fences, &c.

§ THE remedy of replevin is more especially applicable in cases of *distress*. Indeed it was originally confined exclusively to this class of cases. Blackstone says, "this (replevin) obtains only in one instance of an unlawful taking, that of a wrongful distress. . . . For things personal are looked upon by the law as of a nature so transitory and perishable, that it is, for the most part, impossible either to ascertain their identity, or to restore them in the same condition as when they came to the hands of the wrongful possessor. . . . But, in the case of a distress, the goods are, from the first taking, in the custody of the law; . . . and therefore they may not only be identified, but also restored, . . . without any material change."[1]

§ 2. In replevin, where the defendant justifies the taking of the beasts as a distress *damage feasant*, the plaintiff may reply, that the avowant, after making the distress, abused it, so as to render him a trespasser *ab initio;* as (in New York) if he impounds the cattle after making the distress, without having the damages previously assessed by the *fence-viewers*, according to the direction of the act. (Sess. 24, ch. 78, § 16.) And he shall recover damages for the unlawful taking.[2] But replevin in the *cepit*, as for trespass *ab initio*, will not lie for beasts taken *damage feasant*, although the distrainor has omitted to have his damages appraised within twenty-four hours, the time limited by the statute. It seems, however, that replevin in the *detinet* would lie. So, also, the owner may after such neglect retake his property, or bring trover, after demand and refusal.[3]

[1] 3 Bl. Comm. 146.

[2] Hopkins *v.* Hopkins, 10 Johns. 369.

[3] Hale *v.* Clark, 19 Wend. 498.

§ 3. In New Hampshire, where, after notice, cattle have escaped on to an adjoining close, through defect of the fence of such adjoining owner, and have been taken *damage feasant*, replevin will lie to reclaim them.[1]

§ 4. In Massachusetts, the action of replevin, given by the Rev. Sts. ch. 113, § 17, to one whose beasts are unlawfully distrained or impounded, does not exclude all other remedies at common law. Trespass will still lie. The distinction is taken, that, "when a statute confers some new right, or prescribes a remedy for a violation of that right, then the remedy thus prescribed, and no other, is to be pursued. But where a remedy existed at common law, and a statute creates a new remedy in the affirmative, without a negative, express or necessarily implied, a party may still seek his remedy at common law."[2]

§ 5. The owner of a posted animal cannot maintain replevin therefor, in Arkansas, until he has proved his property before a justice, and paid, or tendered, the costs to the taker-up, as required by the Digest, ch. 65, § 25–29.[3]

§ 6. In Michigan, replevin for cattle impounded will not lie under the general replevin law of the State.[4]

§ 7. Where the ownership of cattle, impounded at a certain time, is in question, and evidence has been introduced tending to show that the same, together with other cattle described, were at that time in the possession of the plaintiff in replevin; evidence of a sale by the plaintiff of such other cattle at a subsequent time is not competent to prove ownership of the cattle impounded at the time of impounding.[5]

§ 8. In Massachusetts, a pound-keeper, who receives and impounds beasts for going at large, and refuses to deliver them to the owner, on demand, unless his fees and those of the field-driver are paid, is not, in any case, liable therefor in an action of replevin.[6] The statute provisions, requiring such payment, apply to the *alleged* cause of distress and impounding, without reference to the legality of such proceeding. "Whether" the animals "were at large contrary to law," was a question "which the plaintiff had a right to bring into judgment in a proper action

[1] 11 N. H. 241.
[2] Coffin *v.* Field, 7 Cush. 355. Per Bigelow, J., 358.
[3] Phelan *v.* Bonham, 4 Eng. 389.
[4] Johnson *v.* Wing, 3 Mich. 163.
[5] Edmunds *v.* Leavitt, 7 Fost. 198.
[6] Folger *v.* Hinckley, 5 Cush. 263.

against the proper party. The proper party was the field-driver, who was the actor in the seizure of the sheep, and not the pound-keeper, who was bound to receive them, and who was forbidden by law to deliver them except as above stated."[1] On the other hand, in Connecticut, replevin cannot be sustained against the impounder for animals lawfully impounded, under the act relating to the restraining of swine (Rev. Sts. tit. 3, ch. 7, § 97), but which, without his knowledge, the pound-keeper, after a tender of the poundage fees, unlawfully detains. The pound-keeper, in such case, is not the agent of the impounder.[2]

§ 9. A tender of the lawful costs of impounding cattle, made after a writ of replevin has been unconditionally put into the hands of the sheriff for service, will not sustain the action.[3]

§ 9 *a*. The certificate left with the pound-keeper determines the impounder, and replevin may be brought against the person who signs the certificate.[4]

§ 10. Avowry (*a*) in replevin. Plea, that the defendant drove the cattle three miles to the town pound, and that it was his duty to have restrained them in some other place more convenient for relieving them with meat and water. Held, the plea was bad, because it did not allege that the defendant had another convenient place; and, if he had, he had an election to restrain them in the town pound.[5]

§ 11. Plea, that the defendant detained the plaintiff's milch cows in a pound, from seven o'clock in the morning till five o'clock in the afternoon, in warm weather, and did not relieve them with any meat and water, whereby they became greatly injured by shrinking of their milk and in other respects. Held, on general demurrer, a sufficient averment that the cattle needed relief, notwithstanding the objections that the plea set forth the evidence itself, instead of its legal result, and did not expressly aver that the cattle needed relief.[6] "It was the duty of the party impounding to furnish suitable food for the creatures. It was not done. The party impounding should, as nearly as might be reasonably done, keep and feed the cattle, and give water to them as

[1] Per Metcalf, J., 5 Cush. 266.
[2] Hall *v.* Hall, 24 Conn. 358.
[3] Bills *v.* Vose, 7 Fost. 212.
[4] Eastman *v.* Hills, 6 Shep. 247.
[5] Adams *v.* Adams, 13 Pick. 384.
[6] Ibid

(*a*) See *Avowry*

often as was required according to the usage of the country and of good husbandry." [1]

§ 12. In Massachusetts, if a writ of replevin is filled up within twenty-four hours after impounding, with the intent, at all events, to have it served, whether the defendant shall give notice of the impounding within twenty-four hours or not; the action is thereby commenced, although the writ is not served nor given to an officer for service, and no bond is executed, within twenty-four hours.[2] In such case, the plaintiff waives the statutory notice, and cannot rely, in support of his action, on the want of such notice.[3]

§ 13. In answer to the avowry in replevin of cattle impounded, the plaintiff pleaded tender of a certain sum as costs, and issue was joined. The replication alleged a pound breach, recaption, and additional costs thereof, amounting to a sum stated not included in the tender, and the rejoinder alleged that the lawful additional costs were so included, whereupon issue was joined. Held, the affirmative of both issues was on the plaintiff, and he was entitled to open and close.[4] The defendant alleged that the lawful additional costs of a recaption were a sum stated, and they were not included in the tender. Rejoinder, that they were so included, but not denying that they were the sum so stated. Held, the plaintiff was estopped to deny that such lawful costs amounted to that sum.[5]

§ 14. In replevin against a field-driver for cattle impounded by him for going at large, the defendant may show, not only that he gave the plaintiff the notice required by (Mass.) Rev. Sts. ch. 113, § 8, but also that he posted notices according to the provisions of § 9; but not that the cattle were not suitably provided for, or were ill-treated in the pound; the statute imposing this responsibility upon the pound-keeper, not the field-driver.[6]

§ 15. In Massachusetts, the Rev. Sts. ch. 113, § 27, do not authorize an action of replevin in the Court of Common Pleas in any case coming within the provisions of § 17; although the value exceeds twenty dollars.[7] Where a writ of replevin for cattle, brought originally in the Court of Common Pleas, alleged that

1 Per Putnam, J., 13 Pick. 386.
2 Field *v.* Jacobs, 12 Met. 118.
3 Ibid.
4 Bills *v.* Vose, 7 Fost. 212.
5 Ibid.
6 Pickard *v.* Howe, 12 Met. 198, overruling Bruce v. Holden, 21 Pick. 187; and affirming Wild *v.* Skinner, 23 ib. 251. See Kimball *v.* Adams, 3 N. H. 182; Brown *v.* Smith, 1 ib. 36; also, Mass. Gen. Sts.
7 Sackett *v.* Kellogg, 2 Cush. 88. See Gen. Sts.

the cattle were "now detained in the town pound;" and the defendant moved that the action be dismissed, on the ground that it was brought for the replevin of beasts distrained or impounded, in order to recover a penalty or forfeiture supposed to have been incurred for their going at large, or to obtain satisfaction for damages alleged to have been done by them, and consequently that, by the Rev. Sts. ch. 113, § 17, the action should have been commenced before a justice of the peace. Held, that it did not appear on the face of the writ, that the action was brought for any of the causes stated in § 17 of the same chapter. But if it appear *aliunde*, in the course of the trial, that the cause of action is within § 17, a motion may then be made, and the action dismissed, on the ground that the court has no jurisdiction.[1]

§ 16. In Connecticut, it is not essential to the regularity of a writ in replevin, that the bond should appear at length on the face of the writ, or disclose the fact, that the property belonged to the plaintiff, or had been impounded or distrained.[2]

§ 17. In Massachusetts, it is no ground for dismissing a writ of replevin, that two cows, included therein, are appraised, in the appraisers' certificate, at one sum.[3]

[1] Sackett *v.* Kellogg, 2 Cush. 88.

[2] Watson *v.* Watson, 9 Conn. 140.

[3] Mansir *v.* Crosby, 6 Gray, 334.

CHAPTER III.

DISTRESS FOR RENT.

§ 1. REPLEVIN is also the appropriate remedy in case of an unlawful distress for rent.[1] (*a*)

§ 2. No venue is necessary to a demise, in an avowry, for a distress, &c.[2]

§ 3. On the issue of "no rent in arrear," the title of the plaintiff does not come in question.[3]

§ 4. A defendant cannot make cognizance, as bailiff of his father, for rent in arrear due to his father, where the distress had been made in the name and in the right of the avowant, notwithstanding he had authority from his father to make the distress.[4]

§ 5. Where the defendant put in five cognizances, acknowledg-

[1] See Bloomer *v.* Jerkel, 8 Wend. 448.
[2] Davis *v.* Tyler, 18 Johns. 490.
[3] Williams *v.* Smith, 10 S. & R. 203.
[4] Swearinger *v.* Magruder, 4 Har. & M'Hen. 347.

(*a*) In New York, though, since 2 Rev. Sts. 529, § 41, an avowry that the goods were taken by way of distress for rent need not set forth the landlord's title in detail, nor name any person certain as the tenant; it must show all the essential facts giving the right to distrain. An avowry, that the goods were taken by way of distress for rent due from one W., who occupied as a tenant from a certain demise, &c., but not stating tenancy under the defendant or any other person from whom he derived title, is insufficient, inasmuch as it does not show that the defendant was landlord. Hill *v.* Stocking, 6 Hill, 277. See Christman *v.* Floyd, 9 Wend. 340; Burr *v.* Van Buskirk, 3 Cow. 263; Webber *v.* Shearman, 6 Hill, 20.

And though the plaintiff plead over, thus assuming that the relation of landlord and tenant is sufficiently set forth, and the defendant obtain a verdict and judgment; the defect in the avowry is fatal, on error. Hill *v.* Stocking, 6 Hill, 277.

An avowry, setting up distress on parcel of the demised premises, must show the facts essential to the landlord's right to distrain with as much certainty as an avowry relating to the whole. Ib.

The omission of the requisite averments cannot be aided by setting forth the distress-warrant and affidavit. Ib.

But it is not necessary to set forth the warrant and affidavit in the avowry; a general averment of the distress is sufficient. Ib.

In Virginia, it has been held, that by statute, replevin lies only in case of distress for rent. But such statute is not retrospective. Vaiden *v.* Bell, 3 Rand. 448.

In Connecticut, that it lies only in case of attachment and distress. Watson *v.* Watson, 9 Conn. 140.

ing the taking of goods for distress, three of them good and two bad, and a general judgment of *retorno habendo* was entered, on default of the plaintiff to plead; the judgment was reversed for defective pleading.[1]

§ 6. The defendant may avow, generally, for rent in arrear; but, if he state the lease specially, he must state it truly.[2] So the time at which the rent was payable, and the amount due, must be proved as laid.[3] So in New York, if the defendant set forth the name of the person claimed to be tenant, instead of availing himself of the statute in this particular, he will be bound to prove the allegation as laid.[4] So where three defendants avow for rent in arrear, and a fourth makes cognizance, proof of a demise by one does not support the issue.[5]

§ 7. If the plea to such an avowry be, that the tenancy of the person named had ceased, by assignment, &c., before the time for which the rent accrued, and issue be joined thereon; the plaintiff may prove the allegation, though, independent of the state of the pleadings, and upon the merits as disclosed by the evidence, the allegation appears to be immaterial.[6] So, as we have seen, the defendant may avow, generally, for rent, and adapt his proof to the avowry.[7] So, in replevin for goods distrained for rent, the defendant avowing the distress may recover a less sum than the avowry alleges to be due. The avowry need not state the exact amount of rent in arrear. The amount unpaid is not descriptive of the identity of the obligation out of which the right to a redelivery of the goods arises.[8]

§ 8. In replevin for taking the goods of the plaintiff in a house and close, the defendant made separate avowries as to the house and close, avowing the taking in each as for rent in arrear, in respect of each, to which avowries the plaintiff pleaded in bar, that the defendant took one joint distress upon the house and close for and in respect of the several arrears of rent. Held, the plea was bad.[9]

§ 9. Where a plaintiff in replevin, to an avowry for rent, pleads

[1] Pike *v.* Gandall, 9 Wend. 149.
[2] Taylor *v.* Moore, 3 Harring. 6.
[3] Waltman *v.* Allison, 10 Barr, 464.
[4] Hill *v.* Stocking, 6 Hill, 277.
[5] Ewing *v.* Vanarsdall, 1 S. & R. 370.
[6] Hill *v.* Stocking, 6 Hill, 277.
[7] King *v.* Lambden, 4 Har. 283.
[8] Barr *v.* Hughes, 44 Penn. 516. (Held not to be in conflict with the case of Waltman *v.* Allison, 10 Barr, 464, which "decides that only matters descriptive of the contract of demise must be proved as laid.")
[9] Phillips *v.* Whitsed, 6 Jur. (N. S.), 727 29 L. J., Q. B. 164.

a *tortious eviction* by the landlord; such plea is not sustained by proof, that the landlord entered by virtue of summary proceedings under the landlord and tenant act for non-payment of the rent. Although such entry be found by a special verdict, the landlord, under such verdict, is entitled to a judgment, *non obstante veredicto.*[1]

§ 10. A set-off of repairs cannot be pleaded to an avowry.[2] But such plea ought to be objected to by demurrer.[3]

§ 11. On a distress for rent in arrear, at a share rent, a witness, who examined the crop to form an opinion as to quality, may give that opinion in evidence.[4]

§ 12. A verdict in favor of the defendant, both on the plea of *non cepit* and an avowry for rent, is erroneous. If the avowry is sustained, the verdict on the issue of *non cepit* should be for the plaintiff.[5]

§ 13. On an avowry for rent in arrear, judgment is for the sum found due for rent, with costs, &c.[6]

§ 14. In Delaware, the value of a rent *in kind* may be found by the jury without appraisers.[7]

§ 15. In Mississippi, by statute, when property is distrained for rent, a claimant may replevy it, and, if he be cast in the suit, judgment shall be entered against him for double the amount of the rent; but, to authorize such judgment, the property must be replevied or delivered to the claimant.[8]

§ 16. In Virginia, the court will hear evidence after verdict, tending to show that the landlord distrained for more rent than was due, in order to avoid the entry of judgment for double the value of the rent, and confine it to the rent only.[9]

§ 17. Replevin lies by a tenant against his landlord, upon tender of the rent in arrear after levy of the distress, but before removal or impounding of the goods.[10]

§ 18. In case of rent and an avowry, the *amount* is the only question, and the damages are nominal.[11]

§ 19. To an avowry, a plaintiff pleaded a prior seizure under a

[1] McCarty v. Hudsons, 24 Wend. 291.
[2] Goslin v. Reddin, 3 Har. 9.
[3] Ibid.
[4] Townsend v. Bonwill, 5 Har. 474.
[5] Hill v. Stocking, 6 Hill, 277.
[6] Clark v. Adair, 3 Harring. 113; Caldwell v. Cleadon, ib. 420.
[7] Crawford v. Wright, 5 Har. 59.
[8] Pinchard v. Randell, 1 How. 508.
[9] Maxwell v. Light, 1 Call, 117.
[10] Hilson v. Blain, 2 Bai. 168.
[11] Peyton v. Robertson, 9 Wheat. 527.

writ of replevin issued in his favor against the tenant, and that the defendant took the goods before a reasonable time had elapsed for their removal; but not that any affidavit or bond was ever delivered to the officer by whom the writ was executed. Held bad. And, it seems, after the seizure of property on demised premises by a writ of replevin, it is to be deemed *in custodiâ legis*, and is not liable to distress for rent until a reasonable time for its removal has elapsed.[1]

§ 20. An avowry in replevin, that the goods were taken by way of distress for rent, need not expressly show that the distress was made by an officer, nor that the proper affidavit was annexed to the warrant.[2]

§ 21. In replevin for goods distrained for rent, against the officer serving the warrant, the defendant pleaded the warrant in justification, and the replication admitted the warrant, and did not deny that there was any rent in arrear and due when the warrant issued, but did deny that any was due on two certain days, neither of which was named in the warrant or plea of the defendant. On demurrer, the replication was held insufficient, and the defendant entitled to a return.[3]

[1] Milliken *v.* Seyle, 6 Hill, 623.

[2] Webber *v.* Shearman, 6 Hill, 20.

[3] Powell *v.* Triplett, 6 B. Mon. 420.

CHAPTER IV.

PROPERTY AND POSSESSION NECESSARY TO MAINTAIN REPLEVIN.

§ 1. It is the prevailing and almost universal rule, that the plaintiff in replevin must have a right to *immediate possession;* and also, that such right, as against a wrong-doer, without reference to property or actual possession, will be sufficient to maintain the action.[1] (*a*) Thus a mortgagee cannot replevy the property,

[1] Wespole *v.* Smith, 4 Blackf. 304; Ingraham *v.* Martin, 3 Shep. 373; Moorman *v.* Quick, 20 Ind. 167; Shaddon *v.* Knott, 2 Swan, 358; 46 Maine, 408; Prater *v.* Frazier, 6 Eng. 249; 7 Jones, 251; Noble *v.* Parkman, 24 Ind. 414. But see Pratt *v.* Epperly, 6 Pick. 42; Dunham *v.* Wyckoff, 3 Wend. 280; Chinn *v.* Russell, 2 Blackf. 172; Williams *v.* West, 2 Ohio (N. S.), 82; Warner *v.* Matthews, 18 Ill. 83; M'Coy *v.* Cadle, 4 Iowa, 557.

(*a*) Upon this ground, damages can only be given for interference with the possession. Therefore (in Maryland), in a suit on the bond for damages, the defendant cannot show title, since some title in the plaintiff has been found in the replevin suit; but he may show, in mitigation of damages, that the plaintiff's title was to a short possession only. Cumberland, &c. *v.* Tilghman, 13 Md. 74.

In Minnesota, in the action substituted for replevin, the plaintiff must allege such title as shows him entitled to the possession. Rev. Sts. p. 340, ch. 70, § 86–88, do not change this rule. Loomis *v.* Youle, 1 Min. 175.

Where, upon a plea of *non detinet,* the verdict was that the defendant "did unlawfully detain the goods," but was silent as to the ownership; the judgment only decided the right to retain the goods. Emmons *v.* Dowe, 2 Wis. 322.

In replevin, the question of *value* is not in issue. Thomas *v.* Spofford, 46 Maine, 408.

The rule stated in the text generally prevails in American law. The following are the slight modifications of it in some of the States: —

In New York, in replevin in the *cepit,* where the issue is upon the plaintiff's property he must prove a right to possession. Redman *v.* Hendricks, 1 Sandf. 32.

Where a chattel is tortiously taken from the actual or constructive possession of the owner, he may, at his election, bring trespass *de bon. aspor.* or replevin in the *cepit.* Ely *v.* Ehle, 3 Comst. 506.

The law requires a legal title or special property, with right of possession. Dodworth *v.* Jones, 4 Duer, 201; Hill *v.* Robinson, 16 Ark. 90.

The plaintiff must have the general or special property, and the right of possession. He must be the owner, or lawfully entitled to possession by virtue of special

where he has not the right of possession, till breach of condition.[1]

§ 2. A qualified possession sustains replevin.[2] So one who has a special property in a chattel may bring replevin against the seller of the chattel, for refusing to deliver it.[3]

§ 3. In replevin between the general owner of property and one having a special interest therein, the measure of damages in favor of the latter is the value of such interest.[4]

§ 4. By agreement between A and B, A was to furnish funds to purchase, in his name, a certain quantity of timber from different persons, to be selected in the woods, standing, by B, and to be cut, hewn, rafted, and delivered by him at T., for which he was to receive so much per cubic foot. Held, A had the general property in timber got out under the contract, and which B was transporting to T., but no right of possession. That, as between

[1] Curd *v.* Wunder, 5 Ohio (N. S.), 92. See, further, Bogard *v.* Jones, 9 Humph. 739; Smith *v.* Williamson, 1 Har. & J. 147; Bradley *v.* Michael, 1 Smith, 346; Collins *v.* Evans, 15 Pick. 63; Wheeler *v.* Train, 3 ib. 255; Baker *v.* Fales, 16 Mass. 147.

[2] Mead *v.* Kilday, 2 Watts, 110.

[3] Woods *v.* Nixon, Addis. 131.

[4] Rhoads *v.* Woods, 41 Barb. 471.

property. Rockwell *v.* Saunders, 19 Barb. 473.

And the owner is in constructive possession within this rule, although a bailee may have actual possession. Ely *v.* Ehle, 3 Comst. 506.

A declaration in replevin for taking and detaining goods must show that the plaintiff has either a general or special property in them. An allegation that he is *entitled to the possession* will not answer. Pattison *v.* Adams, 7 Hill, 126.

In Arkansas, it is not sufficient to prove that the plaintiff had a legal title, but he must also show that he was entitled to possession, and that the defendant wrongfully detained it. Beebe *v.* DeBaun, 3 Eng. 510.

Though it is not necessary that the plaintiff should once have had actual possession and bailed it, &c. Ib.

Where the plaintiff has the right of property, either general or special, and of immediate possession, of a chattel taken or detained by the defendant, the action of replevin in the *detinet* lies, as now regulated by statute. Cox *v.* Marrow, 14 Ark. 603; Wilson *v.* Royston, 2 Pike, 315.

In North Carolina, replevin will only lie in the case of an actual taking out of the possession of the plaintiff. Cummings *v.* M'Gill, 2 Murph. 357.

As against wrong-doers and trespassers, a paramount right of property is not necessary to support an action of replevin; but a naked possession, or a right of possession coupled with the beneficial interest, will do. Freshwater *v.* Nichols, 7 Jones, 251.

In Maine, either a general or special property will sustain an action of replevin. As between a school-district and a stranger, the possession of the records by the clerk is the possession of the district, and replevin may be maintained in the name of the corporation. School, &c. *v.* Lord, 44 Maine, 374.

In Missouri, replevin has been held to require general or special property; mere possession is insufficient. Broadwater *v.* Darne, 10 Mis. 277. But a later case decides, that, to maintain an action to recover specific personal property, the plaintiff must have the title or right of possession. Pilkington *v.* Trigg, 28 Mis. 95.

In South Carolina, the plaintiff must allege that the goods distrained were his own, or were taken from his possession. 8 Rich. 24.

In Indiana, a general or special property in goods, accompanied with possession, either actual or constructive, or a right to immediate possession, and unlawful taking or detention, is sufficient to support replevin. Walpole *v.* Smith, 4 Blackf. 304; Clark *v.* Heck, 17 Ind. 281.

In Connecticut, in replevin for goods attached, the plaintiff can recover only by proving himself to be the owner of them. Tomlinson *v.* Collins, 20 Conn. 364.

the parties, B had a special property and right of possession, liable to levy and sale on execution; and, in an action of replevin brought by C, an execution purchaser, against B, A's general property was not a good defence. That C was entitled to recover, having the right of possession as against B, and the right of property, united; but, as he had gained only a special property, he could only have a verdict finding the property in him, and an assessment of the value at the amount of B's special property therein, to wit, the agreed price per foot, deducting the cost of transportation to T. Also, that the case presented merely a question of law for the court.[1]

§ 5. The assignee of goods under attachment, having paid the claim of the first attaching creditor, may, upon giving the officer notice of such payment and of the assignment, and demanding possession of the goods, maintain replevin therefor against him, the delivery of the instrument being a sufficient delivery of the goods.[2] But a receiptor to an officer, or any other bailee for safe-keeping merely, has not sufficient interest to maintain replevin.[3]

§ 6. A plaintiff in replevin, as in other actions, must prevail on the strength of his own title; and, if he fails to show a title in himself, it is immaterial whether the defendant has or has not any title;[4] and the burden is upon him to prove his title, more especially if property in a stranger is pleaded, although not proved.[5] But, if he show a *primâ facie* right, he must recover as against all who do not prove better title.[6]

§ 7. In an action of replevin, it appeared that A, the former owner of the property, became an insolvent debtor, but his assignee had taken no possession and made no conveyance of the property. The plaintiff claimed under a conveyance from B prior to the insolvency. The action was brought against a sheriff who attached the property, after the insolvency, as belonging to A, in whose possession it remained. It was held, that, whether it was attachable or not, the plaintiff could not maintain the action, as he could derive title only from the assignee; and that he must, like plaintiffs in other actions, maintain his case on the strength

[1] Weaver *v.* Darby, 42 Barb. 411.

[2] Whipple *v.* Thayer, 16 Pick. 25.

[3] Warren *v.* Leland, 9 Mass. 265; Perley *v.* Foster, ib. 112; Waterman *v.* Robinson, 5 ib. 303. See Simpson *v.* McFarland, 18 Pick. 427.

[4] Johnson *v.* Neale, 6 Allen, 227.

[5] Simcoke *v.* Frederick, 1 Cart. 54.

[6] Ingersol *v.* Emmerson, 1 Cart. 76.

of his own title or claim, in the absence of which proof it is immaterial whether the defendant has or has not any title.[1]

§ 8. So replevin cannot be maintained, merely by evidence of the defendant's having gone into insolvency, and the failure of his assignee to appear and defend. The plaintiff is still bound to give affirmative proof of title. "Neither the assignment nor omission to interpose could oblige the defendant, without being heard, to suffer judgment against him in favor of those who prove no title, and from which a certificate would not protect him."[2]

§ 9. An officer, upon a writ against A, in favor of B, attached personal property. C served upon him and upon B a notice that a replevin suit would be brought, and the next day the writ of replevin was served upon the officer. After the notice, and before service of the replevin writ, the attachment suit was withdrawn, and the officer delivered the property to A. C applied for a mandamus, to compel the officer to deliver the property to the officer serving the writ of replevin; alleging that C was in possession of the property at the time it was attached, but not that he was the owner, nor that the writ of replevin alleged such ownership. The officer returned upon the writ of mandamus the withdrawal of the attachment suit, and the delivery of the property to A. To this C demurred. Held, 1. That the return would seem to be sufficient, since the object of the statute, providing for the action of replevin in such cases, was to give a claimant of the property an opportunity to try the question of title, and C could try this question in a suit against the original defendant as well as in the replevin suit. 2. But, whether the return was in itself sufficient or not, it was sufficient for the application, which was clearly demurrable in not alleging that the property sought to be replevied belonged to the plaintiff therein.[3] (It was doubted whether the application was not insufficient, in not also averring that the writ of replevin contained an allegation of property in the plaintiff.)

§ 10. The declaration stated the chattels to be the property of the plaintiff, and the plea to an avowry and cognizance, that the property and possession of the chattels were in the plaintiff. Held, no departure from the declaration, there being nothing in

[1] Johnson *v.* Neale, 6 Allen, 227.

[2] Hallett *v.* Fowler, 8 Allen, 93, per Metcalf, J. 94.

[3] Meriden, &c. *v.* Whedon, 31 Conn. 118.

the declaration inconsistent with the possession alleged in the plea.[1]

§ 11. In replevin for two oxen, the defendant pleaded that they were not the property of the plaintiff, and issue was joined thereon. The plaintiff had leased the oxen for three months, during which they were attached by the defendant, a deputy sheriff, as the property of the lessee. Held, the action could not be sustained, inasmuch as the plaintiff had not the right of possession; and, although the term had expired before judgment, a return was ordered, because the question in whom was the general property had not been tried.[2]

§ 12. A delivered to B cattle claimed by B as his own, upon receiving a receipt from him, conditioned to return them if B did not prove his title satisfactorily to A. Upon replevin brought for non-delivery, A not being satisfied with B's evidence, held, evidence of B's title was admissible.[3]

§ 13. By a bill of sale, eight family pictures were conveyed to A by his grandmother, subject to a life-interest in her. At her death, he took them to his father's house, and his father removed them to his daughter's house, when he went there to reside. Later, the father brought an action for these pictures against his daughter's husband, and made an affidavit that "he is owner" of the pictures. The father died pending this action, and A then began a similar action, in which this affidavit was objected to his title, but it was not shown that A ever read it. It was proved, however, that he signed an undertaking in that action as surety for his father, which recited, that the plaintiff therein "has made an affidavit that the defendants wrongfully detain certain personal property, &c., and the plaintiff claims the immediate delivery,' &c. The attorney who brought that action proved, that he advised that suit to be brought by A as owner, but that the father insisted on bringing it as bailee, and was advised that he could do so. Held, the finding of the court at special term, "that the plaintiff (A) is the owner of the eight several pictures mentioned," ought not to be disturbed. The expenditure of money on the pictures by the defendant, without objection by the plaintiff, the former not claiming, nor the latter disclaiming, their ownership, will not bar the plaintiff's recovery.[4]

[1] Judd *v.* Fox, 9 Cow. 259.
[2] Colins *v.* Evans, 15 Pick. 63.
[3] Dimond *v.* Downing, 2 Wis. 498.
[4] Hunt *v.* Moultrie, 1 Bosw. 531.

§ 14. Replevin will not lie for an article manufactured to order, until it is completed and delivered. Thus A accepted an order to build a boat for B, and proceeded to build one, which he repeatedly declared he was building for B, on the order; but, after it was finished, refused to deliver it. Held, B could not maintain replevin for the boat, his remedy being by an action on the contract.[1] So A contracted to build a house for B, and find the materials, for which he was to receive his pay as the work advanced. After the house was enclosed, he worked the house-plank, belonging to him, into columns for a piazza, and removed them, for convenience, to an adjoining house, where they were levied upon by virtue of an execution against A. Held, in replevin by B, he could not maintain the action, the materials being personal property, and not passing to B until delivery, or until affixed to the freehold.[2]

§ 15. A, residing abroad, having contracted with a manufacturer in Massachusetts for the building of certain machines, which were to be delivered to A's general agent here, by whom they were to be received and shipped, and paid for out of funds furnished him for the purpose; a part of the machinery was accordingly manufactured and delivered to the agent, and the whole thereupon paid for by him. Held, the agent, inasmuch as he was to pay the price only for A, and charge it to him, did not thereby acquire any such property in the articles not delivered, as would entitle him to maintain replevin therefor against the manufacturer.[3]

§ 16. A quantity of hides was delivered by A to B, for which B's note was taken, at their agreed value, payable in eight months. At the same time, a written agreement was made by B with A, that, in case of the non-payment of the note at maturity, the leather, which was to be manufactured from the hides, should be redelivered to A, to be sold by him, and the proceeds of the sale to be applied first to the payment of the note, and the surplus, if any, to be given to B. Held, the property in the hides was vested in B, and A could not maintain replevin for them against an attaching creditor of B.[4]

§ 17. A writing in these words, "We have this day sold to W.

1 Pettengill v. Merrill, 47 Maine, 109.

2 Johnson v. Hunt, 11 Wend. 137. See U. S. v. Kennan, Pet. C. 168.

3 Dixon v. Hancock, 4 Cush. 96.

4 Southwick v. Smith, 29 Maine, 228.

L. & Co., four hundred tons of pig metal at our landing or that will soon be delivered there," is not such evidence of delivery to the vendees, as will support an action of replevin by them against one who had obtained possession, before the arrival of their agent at the landing mentioned, under a valid contract with the vendor.[1]

§ 18. In replevin for a mare, alleged to have been stolen and sold by the plaintiff's son, it is error for the court to instruct the jury, that they might infer a ratification of the sale by the plaintiff, from his delay to sue for more than a reasonable time, to be judged of by them.[2]

§ 19. Where the master of a ship has received goods on board, under a contract to deliver them at A, and, being with the shipper in a port short of A, there refuses to proceed with the goods to A; the shipper may replevy the goods. If the owner of the ship again replevy them from the shipper, upon these facts being disclosed in a plea in abatement, such second writ shall abate. Otherwise, if the master and owners claim by distinct rights. In such second writ of replevin, it is improper to join the officer, who served the first writ, as a defendant, with the shipper.[3]

§ 20. In New York, in an action of replevin (or to recover possession of personal property), the plaintiff cannot recover, if the property belonged to a person deceased, and letters of administration have been issued, and the plaintiff has taken possession wrongfully.[4]

§ 21. Questions of title have arisen, as depending upon the possession of goods, obtained by the service of a writ of replevin itself, with the accompanying bond. Thus A, by a writ of replevin against B, obtained possession of B's property, and sold it to C; A's suit was abated by his death, and no judgment was rendered; and B afterwards demanded the property of C, and, on C's refusal to give it up, replevied it. Held, C acquired no title, and B might maintain replevin against him.[5] In this case, it was claimed that a plaintiff in replevin has the right to sell the property replevied. Mr. Justice Dewey remarks upon this proposition: "If it were limited to replevin in cases of wrongful distress for rent, or of cattle damage feasant, it might be more readily as-

[1] Winslow *v.* Leonard, 24 Penn. 14.
[2] Watkins *v.* White, 3 Scam. 549.
[3] Portland, &c. *v.* Stubbs, 6 Mass. 422.
[4] Rockwell *v.* Saunders, 19 Barb. 473.
[5] Lockwood *v.* Perry, 9 Met. 440.

sented to, as in such cases the property is held by the defendant in replevin for a particular purpose, and he does not claim to be the owner of it. And where the plaintiff, who in such case is the actual owner, has given the requisite security, by a bond, to pay such rent, or such damages, if the property is not returned, it may be all that is requisite to do perfect justice." The learned judge proceeds to comment upon the case of Gordon *v.* Jenney, 16 Mass. 469, in which the language of the court would seem to extend the same principle alike to all cases of replevin. "The case before the court was that of a plaintiff in replevin, who was the real owner. . . . . That had been already settled. . . . . In ordinary cases the purchaser buys subject to the question of the vendor's title; and we think none the less so because the vendor has acquired his possession under a writ of replevin issued upon his own representation, and which may be wholly unfounded in truth. . . . . The plaintiff in replevin has, by virtue of his writ, acquired the right of possession pending the action, and the real owner cannot lawfully disturb that right during the pendency of the action, nor institute an action against a third person who may become possessed of the goods. This is precisely the extent of the right." [1]

§ 22. It is held in Texas, that, in an action for damages for taking and carrying away property, the defendant may prove a title, though the property, when taken, was in possession of the plaintiff by replevin. But where A brought a suit against B for the recovery of slaves, and procured a writ of sequestration to be issued and the slaves seized; and B replevied the slaves; and A then forcibly took them out of the possession of B; whereupon B brought an action of trespass against A: held, this gave B the legal custody and possession of the slaves, for the purposes of the first suit, and the defendant had no right to disturb that possession; that it was not competent for A to prove, that he acted under the well-founded belief that B was about to place the property out of the reach of legal process, and to put it out of his power to comply with the condition of his bond; nor that B, before the first suit, had wrongfully taken the slaves out of A's possession, and attempted to remove them out of the State.[2]

§ 23. The alleged title or possession of the defendant is equally

[1] 9 Met. 444.

[2] Fowler *v.* Stonum, 6 Tex. 60.

essential to the maintaining of an action of replevin with that of the plaintiff. In order to maintain replevin in the *detinet*, the plaintiff must show that the defendant had the possession, either actual or constructive, by himself or his agent, at the time of the institution of the suit.[1] (*a*) Mere acts of ownership are insufficient.[2] In New York, before the Revised Statutes, the action of replevin was purely possessory, and could not be maintained against a party who had entirely divested himself of the goods claimed, except where a distrainor for rent proceeded fraudulently or in violation of the statute regulating distresses. And the remedy given by the Code, for the "claim and delivery of personal property," cannot be maintained, where the defendant has not, in fact or in law, the possession or control of the property claimed.[3]

§ 24. But it is held, that replevin may be maintained against one who has wrongfully taken the property, and for a time detained it, but before commencement of suit sold and delivered it to another.[4] And where the plaintiff fails to prosecute his suit with effect, the law presumes title in the defendant, and he has only to prove the amount of his damages in order to recover restitution.[5]

[1] Beebe *v.* De Baun, 3 Eng. 510; King *v.* Orser, 4 Duer, 431.

[2] Wallace *v.* Brown, 17 Ark. 449.

[3] Roberts *v.* Randall, 3 Sandf. 707; Brockway *v.* Burnap, 12 Barb. 347.

[4] Sayward *v.* Warren, 27 Maine, 453.

[5] Rickner *v.* Dixon, 2 Greene, 591.

(*a*) Proof of demand is not necessary in all cases; and conversion on the part of the defendant, or acts amounting to conversion, will dispense with proof of demand. Beebe *v.* De Baun, 3 Eng. 510.

CHAPTER V.

REPLEVIN FOR PROPERTY TAKEN BY LEGAL PROCESS.

§ 1. It is sometimes held, that goods taken under an execution, being *in custody of the law*, cannot be replevied by the defendant or a stranger; (*a*) though, after they are sold, they may be replevied by the true owner.[1] Replevin of goods taken on execution has been regarded as a *contempt*.[2] And late cases in this country recognize the rule, that, at common law, replevin cannot be maintained against an officer, who has the custody and possession of property under an attachment or a valid execution.[3] So it is held, that replevin will not lie by the owner of goods against an officer attaching them as the property of a third person, where the officer has never had actual possession, and no right to possession other than is founded upon the receipt for the goods given by the owner, in whose possession the goods are, in which there is no acknowledgment that the property is not in himself.[4] So

[1] Cromwell *v.* Owings, 7 Har. & J. 55; Reeside *v.* Fischer, 2 Har. & G. 320.

[2] Gilb. Replev. 161; Winnard *v.* Foster, 2 Lutw. 1191.

[3] Spring *v.* Bourland, 6 Eng. 658; McLeod *v.* Oates, 8 Ired. 387; Goodrich *v.* Fritz, 4 Pike, 525; Ilsley *v.* Stubbs, 5 Mass. 280; Smith *v.* Huntington, 3 N. H. 76.

[4] Lathrop *v.* Cook, 2 Shep. 414.

(*a*) The exemption of an officer, under § 5 of the Missouri act of March 3, 1855, from liability on account of levy of an execution, where a bond of indemnity has been given, as required by the act, extends to an action of replevin, brought against him. St. Louis, &c. *v.* Castello, 30 Mis. 124.

The owner of spirituous liquors, seized on a warrant lawfully issued under (Mass.) St. 1855, ch. 215, § 25, and legally served, cannot maintain replevin againstt he officer, for the liquors and the vessels containing them. Allen *v.* Staples, 6 Gray 491.

the defendant may avail himself of a delivery to him, pursuant to a writ of replevin issued out of a court of competent jurisdiction in another State, the litigants and the thing delivered being subject to the law of the place of delivery.[1] And this, on a plea of property and without special plea. Though, where a motion in arrest of judgment is made on the ground of process, the defendant, having neglected to demur to the declaration, cannot recover costs.[2] So a defendant in execution, whose property is levied on, cannot prosecute a writ of replevin, although the property may be exempted by law.[3] So it is held, that replevin does not lie against an officer who has received the amount of an execution after a levy.[4]

§ 2. The qualified rule is sometimes adopted, that an owner *in possession* of goods, which are taken on execution against a stranger, may replevy them.[5] But not where they are taken from the possession of the debtor.[6]

§ 3. But the distinction is made, and now generally prevails, — sometimes depending, however, upon express statute, — that although goods, taken by a sheriff on execution out of the possession of the defendant in the execution, being *in the custody of the law*, cannot be replevied; if an officer, having an execution against A, undertakes to execute it on goods in the possession of B, B may bring replevin for them.[7] So an officer is not protected in taking, under a writ of replevin, the property of a third person in no way a party to the replevin suit, although the goods seized are the specific chattels which the writ of replevin directs him to take.[8]

§ 4. Questions have often arisen in reference to the authority of an officer by virtue of the writ of replevin itself. It is held, that a writ of replevin does not justify the taking of property from one not in possession; and the owner, if in possession, may maintain an action against the officer. The court, in Ohio, remark: "While the rights of the defendant are sedulously

[1] Lowry *v.* Hall, 2 Watts & Serg. 129.

[2] Hathaway *v.* St. John, 20 Conn. 343.

[3] Reynolds *v.* Sallee, 2 B. Mon. 18; Saffell *v.* Wash, 4 ib. 92.

[4] Gardner *v.* Campbell, 15 Johns. 401.

[5] Judd *v.* Fox, 9 Conn. 259.

[6] Kellogg *v.* Churchill, 2 N. H. 412; Melcher *v.* Lamprey, 20 ib. 403.

[7] Thompson *v.* Bulton, 14 Johns. 84; 5 Mass. 280, Mass. Sts. 1789, ch. 26; Hanna *v.* Steinberger, 6 Blackf. 520; Clark *v.* Skinner, 20 Johns. 465; Chinn *v.* Russell, 2 Blackf. 172; Louisville, &c. *v.* Holborn, ib. 267; Philips *v.* Harriss, 3 J. J. Mar. 121; Caldwell *v.* Arnold, 8 Min. 265.

[8] Stimpson *v.* Reynolds, 14 Barb. 506.

guarded, by a bond required from the plaintiff, no guard or protection is afforded in the proceeding to the rights of third persons. . . . . Unlike (in) proceedings strictly *in rem*, as in admiralty and in chancery, where an officer is directed to take possession of specific property, that the rights of parties thereto may be ascertained, the property is not retained in the possession of the officer, but is delivered to the plaintiff, and no provision is made for third persons to intervene and assert their claims."[1] But replevin does not lie against an officer who replevies from one in possession.[2] In a very late case, it is remarked: "By the English law, if the defendant in replevin claim property in the goods, the officer cannot lawfully deliver them to the plaintiff until the question of property has been determined in his favor on a writ *de proprietate probanda*, sued out by him. But, by our law, the question of property is to be tried in the replevin suit."[3] (*a*)

§ 5. In New York, although, before the Code, the sheriff could not be made liable, as a trespasser, for taking the goods described in a writ of replevin from a third person, claiming to be the owner, yet, in the action which the Code has substituted for that of replevin, he can only take the property described in the affidavit of the plaintiff, when it is found in the possession of the defendant himself, or of his agent.[4]

§ 6. In the same State it is held, that the 17th section of the Replevin Act (2 Rev. Sts. 525) was enacted for the benefit of the sheriff, and not for that of the party. The indemnity therein mentioned is for his security, and what shall be the extent and form of it, is for him to determine. As soon as the inquisition is found by the jury, under that section, it becomes a question exclusively for the sheriff to decide to which party he will deliver the property; or, if he delivers it to the plaintiff, what indemnity he will require.[5]

§ 7. In Massachusetts, a creditor, at whose suit an attachment is made, of goods not the property of his debtor, is not liable in replevin, either alone, or jointly with the attaching officer.[6] But

[1] State, &c. *v.* Jennings, 14 Ohio St. 73. Per Gholson, J., 77.

[2] Willard *v.* Kimball, 10 Allen, 211.

[3] Per Metcalf, J., Willard *v.* Kimball, 10 Allen, 212.

[4] King *v.* Orser, 4 Duer, 431.

[5] Russell *v.* Gray, 11 Barb. 541.

[6] Richardson *v.* Reed, 4 Gray, 441.

(*a*) "There is a difference between a replevin and other process of law, with respect to the officers; for, in replevin, they are expressly commanded what to take, *in specie;* but, in writs of execution, the words are general, namely, to levy of the goods of the party, and therefore 'tis at their peril if they take another man's goods." Per Lord Holt, Hallett *v.* Byrt, Carth. 381.

it is held in Vermont, that the owner of property, attached in a suit against another, may maintain replevin therefor against the creditor and the officer jointly, when the former assisted in taking the property, and took it into his own possession after the attachment.[1] So in Indiana, replevin lies against an attaching creditor who assumes control, and directs as to the execution, of the writ.[2] So in New York, replevin lies against a party, jointly with the officer, who orders the levy of an execution upon the goods.[3] The court remark, that it is immaterial that the defendant never had the property in his possession. The order itself was a sufficient taking. A distinction is made between this case and that of Brockway *v.* Burnap, 12 Barb. 347, in which the defendant, who once had possession, had transferred the property and parted with the possession before suit brought. And the court further remark: "I do not think the Revised Statutes, or the Code of Procedure, have made any change in the law as to the nature of the possession in the defendant which is required to warrant an action for the delivery of personal property."[4] And in Connecticut, a writ of replevin for goods attached, in favor of a claimant who was not a party to the attachment, must be brought against the attaching creditor, and not against the officer. If the creditor resides in another State, the replevin may be served upon the goods, which will give jurisdiction to the court; and then the creditor may be made a party, in the same manner as though his property had been attached in this State.[5] So if the vendee of goods sold on condition procures them to be sold, on execution against him, to one who has knowledge of the condition; the original vendor may maintain replevin against the second purchaser, without a previous demand.[6] So replevin *in the cepit* lies against a judgment creditor, or the sheriff acting by his authority, in levying, by virtue of an execution, upon property which a vendor has a right to reclaim, because the conditions of the sale have not been complied with.[7]

§ 8. Substantially the same requisitions, as in other cases, of title in the plaintiff, are demanded in replevin against officers.

§ 9. Where property is left with a person who has advanced

[1] Esty *v.* Love, 32 Vt. 744.
[2] Firestone *v.* Mishler, 18 Ind. 439.
[3] Knapp *v.* Smith, 27 N. Y. (13 Smith) 277.
[4] Per Denio, C. J., 27 N. Y. 281.
[5] Bowen *v.* Hutchins, 18 Conn. 550.
[6] Blanchard *v.* Child, 7 Gray, 155.
[7] Acker *v.* Campbell, 23 Wend. 372.

money upon it, and which he is to keep in his own right until he shall be reimbursed, he may replevy it from an attaching creditor. And unless it is made to appear that the attaching party was really a creditor, he cannot complain that it was a design to protect the property for the debtor. The rights of the parties must depend upon the facts existing at the time the writ issued. The writ does not, of itself, show that the defendant in it was a debtor of the plaintiff. It only shows that the officer acted in behalf of an assumed creditor.[1]

§ 10. Where a firm, engaged in sawing lumber, contracted with the plaintiff to receive all pine saw-logs belonging to the plaintiff, and manufacture them into lumber, ship it, receive payment for it, and pay a certain percentage to the plaintiff per thousand feet, keeping the balance, for their services; and the contract provided that the logs should be the plaintiff's at all times, till he received his percentage as agreed; and the logs were attached in the hands and as the property of the firm: held, the plaintiff might maintain replevin, and had a right, as against the officer attaching, to immediate possession.[2]

§ 10 *a*. A owned corn, purchased for him by B, a warehouseman, who put it in a mixed mass with other corn, owned by different persons, who had stored it with B. B delivered the whole mixture to A, from whom it was wrongfully taken on execution by C. Held, A might maintain replevin against C.[3]

§ 11. By a custom among brewers and retailers of beer, as beer cannot be removed in warm weather without injury, the brewer in the spring delivers to the retailer such quantity of beer as he expects to retail in the ensuing season. The barrels belong to the brewer, and are to be returned to him when emptied. The retailer pays for all the beer that he sells in the course of the season, at the price at which it was originally furnished. If any of the beer becomes sour or stale, or is lost by casualty, the loss falls upon the brewer. If any remains unsold at the end of the season, the retailer has a right to return it, but the brewer has no right to take it without his consent. Payment is never made in advance. The profits of retailing belong to the retailer, and he bears all losses by bad debts. The brewer's price of beer never

[1] Currier *v.* Ford, 26 Ill. 488.
[2] Bassett *v.* Armstrong, 6 Mich. 397.
[3] Warner *v.* Cushman, 31 Ill. 283.

varies. Held, that beer so delivered was not liable to attachment as the property of the retailer. If the sale of the beer is stopped by the acts of the retailer, his right to retain ceases; and where the beer was attached as the property of the retailer, and the retailer assigned all his special property in it to the brewer, it was held that the brewer had such right of possession as would enable him to bring replevin against the attaching officer.[1]

§ 12. Personal property being attached in a suit by A against B, C served upon A and the officer a notice that he should bring replevin, and the next day a writ of replevin was served upon the officer. After notice, and before such service, the former suit was withdrawn and the property surrendered to B. B then applies for a mandamus to compel the attaching officer to deliver the property to the officer serving the replevin writ, alleging that C was in possession at the time of attachment, but not his ownership, or that the writ of replevin claimed such ownership. The officer returned upon the mandamus the withdrawal of the attachment suit, and the delivery to B. Upon demurrer by C, held, the return was apparently sufficient, since the purpose of the statute, providing for replevin in such cases, was, to give the claimant of property an opportunity to try his title, which could be done in a suit against B as well as in the replevin suit; but further, that the return was sufficient for the application, which was demurrable in not alleging title. Under the statute of Connecticut, the plaintiff in replevin must claim to be the owner.[2]

§ 13. Replevin lies at the suit of the owner of a chattel against an officer, who has taken it from his servant or agent while in his employ, by virtue of an execution against such servant or agent; the actual possession, in such case, being considered as remaining in the owner.[3]

§ 14. In Connecticut, the right of one person to replevy goods, attached in a suit against another, is given by the eighth section of the statute authorizing writs of replevin, as revised in 1821, and exists only in favor of the owner of the goods, who is required to make out a title thereto. It does not apply to one having a lien on goods, attached in a suit against the general owner.[4]

§ 15. The messenger of the commissioners of a bankrupt, hav-

[1] Meldrum *v.* Snow, 9 Pick. 441.

[2] Meriden, &c. *v.* Whedon, 31 Conn. 118, Conn. Rev. Sts. tit. 1, § 253.

[3] Clark *v.* Skinner, 20 Johns. 465.

[4] Brown *v.* Chickopee, &c. 12 Conn. 87.

ing delivered goods of the bankrupt to a stranger, taking his obligation to keep them safely and to redeliver them on demand; the bailee cannot maintain replevin against one who had taken them, not having property, either general or special.[1]

§ 16. Where a parol gift of slaves was made by a father to his daughter, who retained them two years and then exchanged them for others at the request of her father, still claiming them as her own; and, after they had been in the father's possession six years, they were sold under execution against him: held, an action of replevin did not lie by the daughter and the heirs of her husband.[2]

§ 17. In replevin against a sheriff, who sets up a right under civil process, and claims to have a return of the goods, the sheriff must show a good title *in omnibus*, and a foundation for the writ.[3] But, it seems, an officer sued in replevin may plead property in himself, and prove it by showing his special property under an attachment.[4]

§ 18. The distinction is taken, that, if an execution is levied on goods not of the defendant in execution, and the owner replevies; the officer, to defend the taking, must show a judgment and execution, and that the goods are the property of the defendant in execution. But if the defendant in execution be the plaintiff in replevin, it is sufficient to show judgment and execution.[5]

§ 19. Where the defendant in replevin was employed by a creditor to attach the goods, but the attachment proved ineffectual because the general property was in a third person; it was held, that the defendant might still justify under a lien of the attaching creditor, independent of the attachment, and as the servant of the creditor.[6]

§ 20. An officer, who defends in replevin, should set up that he took the property by execution.[7]

§ 21. In the cognizance of a constable in replevin, the statement of the amount of the *fi. fa.* from the justice in blank will not be fatal after issue and verdict.[8]

§ 22. An avowry of seizure upon execution must allege that the property belonged to the debtor and was liable to the execution.[9]

1 Waterman *v.* Robinson, 5 Mass. 303.
2 Scott *v.* Hughes, 9 B. Mon. 104.
3 Brown *v.* Bissett, 1 N. J. 46.
4 Quincy *v.* Hall, 1 Pick. 357.
5 Bruer *v.* Ogden, 6 Halst. 370.
6 Townsend *v.* Newell, 14 Pick. 332.
7 Wheeler *v.* McCorristen, 24 Ill. 42.
8 Herley *v.* Hume, 5 Monr. 181.
9 Dillon *v.* Wright, 4 J. J. Mar. 254.

§ 23. More especially, a plea of justification to an action of replevin against an officer, for seizing the property on execution, if the property was not in the possession of the defendant in execution when taken, must aver that it was his property.[1]

§ 24. The avowries admit the taking, and traverse property in the plaintiff. What precedes this traverse, to wit, the allegation of the delivery of the executions to the sheriff, the time when they were delivered, and when seizure was made, and that the goods were then the property of the judgment debtor, is matter of inducement merely, and not traversable.[2]

§ 25. If, in trespass for taking chattels, the defendant justifies as an officer under a writ of replevin; it is sufficient to allege in such plea, that the plaintiff in replevin gave bond, &c., before the chattels were delivered to him, though it is not alleged to have been done before the defendant took them.[3]

§ 26. In case of attachment, the officer can have a return only by showing property in himself or the debtor. It is not enough to rely upon a technical objection to a judgment for the plaintiff.[4]

§ 27. To justify under an attachment by his deputy, the sheriff must allege and prove his official authority to appoint a deputy, the court or magistrate that issued the writ, and annexation of the statutory affidavit.[5]

§ 27 *a*. It is held that a justification under a writ must allege that the writ was in full force, the money unpaid, and that the property was taken in pursuance of its authority.[6]

§ 28. Where all the proceedings upon a writ or plaint in replevin, subsequent to the issue of the process, are set aside by the court whence it issued; the plaintiff in such process cannot protect himself under it, in an action brought for the property delivered to him by virtue thereof.[7]

§ 29. Where personal property is taken in execution and claimed on a replevin by a third person, it cannot be taken from his possession, during the pendency of the replevin suit, by any writ or execution against the party as whose property it had been originally seized, unless he had acquired some new title to it, or

[1] Smith *v.* Winston, 10 Mis. 299.
[2] Boswell *v.* Green, 1 Dutch. 390.
[3] Cushman *v.* Churchill, 7 Mass. 97.
[4] Hall *v.* Gilmore, 40 Maine, 578. See Quincy *v.* Hall, 1 Pick. 357.
[5] M'Carty *v.* Gage, 3 Mis. 404.
[6] Dayton *v.* Fry, 29 Ill. 525.
[7] Smith *v.* Snyder, 15 Wend. 324.

unless the replevin suit was fraudulently instituted as a cover against creditors.[1]

§ 30. Replevin lies, where property of the plaintiff is taken on execution against a third person, peaceably restored to the plaintiff, and retaken by the sheriff.[2]

§ 31. A *fi. fa.* was issued in the county of O. against A, B, & C, under which the sheriff seized household furniture belonging to A, and certain property in the possession of B, but not enough to satisfy the *fi. fa.* The title to the last-mentioned property being disputed by D, he replevied it; and, after the return-day of the *fi. fa.*, the replevin being still pending, other property belonging to C was discovered, whereupon a second *fi. fa.* was issued to the same county, and C's property seized under it, the first *fi. fa.* not having been returned. Held, the second *fi. fa.* was irregularly issued. The officer may in such case return the seizure under the first *fi. fa.*, together with the fact of replevin, and, if the goods be afterwards restored, they may be disposed of in virtue of a *venditioni exponas*.[3]

§ 32. Replevin lies *in favor of* an attaching officer.[4] So one deputy sheriff may have replevin against another deputy of the same sheriff, for goods which he claims in virtue of a prior attachment made by him. "Although servants of the same master, they act independently of each other; and the one who first makes an attachment, acquires a special property."[5] But a constable, who has levied an execution on goods, after the execution and levy have been set aside, has not such a property in the goods as will sustain replevin against the creditor, to whom he had delivered the goods for safe-keeping.[6] And where goods are attached and replevied from the sheriff by a coroner; the creditor attaching cannot maintain an action against the coroner for taking insufficient pledges, or for other misfeasances in the service. Such action lies for the sheriff only, who has a special property in the goods, the general property being in abeyance.[7]

§ 33. It is held, that replevin lies by a receiptor against the execution defendant.[8] But not against a receiptor.[9]

§ 34. A purchaser of goods at a sheriff's sale may maintain

[1] Rhines *v.* Phelps, 3 Gilm. 455.
[2] Hall *v.* Tuttle, 2 Wend. 475.
[3] Ledyard *v.* Buckle, 5 Hill, 571.
[4] Fitch *v.* Dunn, 3 Blackf. 142.
[5] Gordon *v.* Jenney, 16 Mass. 465.
[6] Walpole *v.* Smith, 4 Blackf. 304.
[7] Ladd *v.* North, 2 Mass. 514.
[8] Miller *v.* Adsit, 16 Johns. 335.
[9] Chapman *v.* Andrews, 3 Wend. 240.

replevin for them, after demand and refusal.[1] On the other hand, an owner of property may bring replevin against one who purchased the property at a sale upon an execution against a third person.[2] The distinction is made, that such purchaser, who participates in the transaction only by purchasing, although he knows of the illegality of the sale, or that the goods did not belong to the defendant in the execution, is liable to the owner in replevin, but not in trespass.[3] But it is held, that goods irregularly attached by an officer are not in the custody of the plaintiff in the suit, and replevin does not lie against him.[4]

§ 35. In New York, a defendant in replevin, who puts in a claim of property, and agrees that his possession shall be considered the *possession of the sheriff*, until the claim be tried, is estopped from denying the sheriff's possession; and, on demand and refusal to deliver up the property, may be proceeded against in the action of replevin.[5]

§ 36. After levy and appraisement by an officer, he has such a special property as will maintain replevin, though the goods be left in the defendant's custody.[6] So, as against another officer attempting to levy on them; in which case no demand is necessary.[7]

§ 36 *a*. An officer need not produce in evidence the judgment, upon which the execution under which the levy was made was founded.[8]

§ 36 *b*. Where a marshal, by virtue of mesne process from the Circuit Court of the United States, attached certain railroad cars, which were afterwards taken out of his hands by the sheriff of the State Court, under a replevin writ brought by the mortgagees of the railroad company; it was held, that the sheriff had no right so to replevy the property.[9]

§ 37. Replevin will lie against an officer, who attaches property by leaving a copy in the town-clerk's office.[10] So where goods in the hands of a bailee are attached as his property and receipted for, replevin lies against the attaching officer by the general owner, although the goods remain in the possession of the bailee,

[1] Hazzard *v.* Burton, 4 Harring. 62.
[2] Dodd *v.* McCraw, 3 Eng. 83; Huber *v.* Sharck, 2 Browne, 160.
[3] Ward *v.* Taylor, 1 Penn. 238.
[4] Cogan *v.* Stoutenburgh, 7 Ham. (Part 2d), 133.
[5] Baker *v.* McDuffie, 23 Wend. 289.
[6] Polite *v.* Jefferson, 5 Harring. 388.
[7] Pugh *v.* Calloway, 10 Ohio (N. S.), 488.
[8] Ibid.
[9] Freeman *v.* Howe, 24 How. 450.
[10] Angell *v.* Keith, 24 Vt. 371.

the attachment not being dissolved.[1] But, to bring a case of replevin within § 2 of the Pennsylvania act of April 3, 1779, it must appear that the goods, when replevied, were in the possession, custody, or control of the sheriff.[2]

§ 38. Where goods have been taken by a sheriff, by a writ of replevin, they cannot be taken from him by another writ of replevin, at common law, nor by statute.[3] See chap. 1, § 17.

§ 39. Where property had been first replevied, and there was evidence that the plaintiffs in that suit had waived delivery to them under their writ, and it was then taken upon a subsequent writ of replevin; the court will not instruct the jury, that the plaintiff cannot recover, if they find that such subsequent writ issued while the property was in possession of the sheriff. But the objection may be made, unless there is evidence of such waiver, although the defendant subsequently may agree to waive the irregularity, and to ratify and confirm the proceedings of the sheriff.[4]

§ 40. Trespass cannot be maintained by the owner of goods against a sheriff, for taking them under a writ of replevin against another person having the goods in his possession. The law fully recognizes the owner's right, and, if he can without force obtain the property, will not hold him a wrong-doer for taking it; but it withholds from him an affirmative remedy by action against a ministerial officer; allowing him an action only against other persons concerned in, or who instigated, the taking.[5]

§ 41. Where attached goods are replevied from the officer, a judgment for the plaintiff in replevin is conclusive evidence of his title against the attaching creditor, and against one who has made a second attachment after notice of the replevin; though the latter erroneously supposed the former would defend the replevin suit.[6]

§ 42. Goods found in possession of A, an execution defendant, were levied on by the sheriff. B claimed the goods as his, and a jury, summoned to try the right of property, found that they belonged to A. Held, in replevin by B against the sheriff, that the finding of the jury was not conclusive against B.[7]

1 Small *v.* Hutchins, 1 App. 255.
2 Weed *v.* Hill, 2 Miles, 122.
3 Sanborn *v.* Leavitt, 43 N. H. 473.
4 Powell *v.* Bradlee, 9 Gill & Johns. 220.
5 Foster *v.* Pettibone, 20 Barb. 350.
6 Carlton *v.* Davis, 8 Allen, 94.
7 Chinn *v.* Russell, 2 Blackf. 172.

§ 43. If an officer voluntarily or collusively suffers property to be retained by the replevin plaintiff, after judgment in the officer's favor, it is an injury to the execution defendant. It is the duty of the officers to use ordinary diligence to procure a proper judgment on the replevin bond.[1]

§ 44. In replevin for a horse seized on a *fi. fa.*, irregularities in the proceedings before the justices cannot be taken advantage of.[2]

§ 45. In an action of replevin against a sheriff for the act of his deputy, it is sufficient for the plaintiff to show that the deputy was a deputy of the defendant, and that he acted *colore officii*, in order to make his declarations in relation to his official acts admissible in evidence against the sheriff.[3]

§ 45 *a*. Where replevin is brought for property taken in the hands of A, by a sheriff, which, two months afterwards, is restored to A; this is no answer to the action.[4]

§ 45 *b*. In case of replevin for a seizure on execution and sale; the plaintiff cannot prevail upon the ground that the property is exempt from execution.[5]

§ 46. Sect. 216 of the New York Code, requiring an affidavit of property to be served on the sheriff taking personal property, claimed by a person other than the defendant or his agent, applies only when the taking was in the proper discharge of his duty, not wrongful.[6]

§ 47. In Ohio, a party replevying property from a constable who has levied an execution upon it, upon the ground of a purchase prior to such levy, upon executing the undertaking required by law, acquires the right of possession and all the officer's interest by virtue of the levy, paramount to any title under a subsequent levy; although such purchase be found fraudulent and void against creditors. And an action of replevin lies against a purchaser under the subsequent levy.[7]

§ 48. In New York, in replevin, the judgment being for damages only in favor of the plaintiff, the sheriff is not liable for such damages by reason of the failure to justify sureties, who, on the arrest of the defendant in replevin, had given an undertaking for

1 Stewart *v.* Nunemaker, 2 Cart. 47.
2 Ranoul *v.* Griffie, 3 Md. 54.
3 Stewart *v.* Wells, 6 Barb. 79.
4 Caldwell *v.* Arnold, 8 Min. 265.
5 Howland *v.* Fuller, 8 Min. 50.
6 King *v.* Orser, 4 Duer, 431.
7 Crittenden *v.* Lingle, 14 Ohio St. 182.

delivery of the property, if adjudged, and for the payment of such sum as for any cause might be recovered against such defendant. To render him liable, there must be a judgment, under the execution upon which, the property might be sought and delivered.[1]

§ 49. In an action against an officer and his sureties on his official bond, for taking the property of A, under a writ of replevin against B; a verdict and judgment against the officer, in an action of trespass for such taking, are *primâ facie* evidence for the plaintiff, though the sureties had no notice of the former suit.[2] (*a*)

[1] Galarali *v.* Orser, 27 N. Y. (13 Smith), 277.

[2] State, &c. *v.* Jennings, 14 Ohio St. 73.

(*a*) The owner of goods, wrongfully levied upon by the marshal of the federal court, may sustain replevin against the marshal. Hanna *v.* Steinberger, 6 Blackf. 520.

Replevin may be maintained in a State court, against the marshal of the United States, by the owner of goods taken by such marshal by virtue of process issuing from a district court of the United States, in favor of the United States, and under the direction of the district attorney of the United States. Boner *v.* Ogden, 6 Halst. 370.

Upon the issue of *non cepit,* proof that the defendant took the goods as marshal is sufficient proof of the caption. De Wolf *v.* Harris, 4 Mason, 515.

It is held, that replevin does not lie for property seized for a sheriff's fee-bill. Morgan *v.* Craig, Hard. 101.

Property seized for a tax, under an act of Congress, and a warrant on its face, regular, cannot be replevied. The constitutionality of the act, or regularity of the proceedings, can be tried only in a proceeding for damages. O'Reilly *v.* Good, 42 Barb. 521.

"The constitutional relation of the State to the United States, and the most self-evident considerations of public policy," are held to forbid such proceeding. "Innumerable replevin suits might delay, if not wholly defeat, the collection of the national revenue." Per Sutherland, J., p. 523.

Replevin does not lie for goods seized for the water-tax of Philadelphia. Stiles *v.* Griffith, 3 Yeates, 82.

Nor for property taken on a warrant against the owner, issued by a magistrate having jurisdiction under a valid statute. Musgrave *v.* Hall, 40 Maine, 498.

Nor against a military officer authorized by the legislature to detain the goods. Gist *v.* Cole, 2 N. & McC. 456.

Nor for property seized for non-payment of a militia fine. Pott *v.* Oldwine, 7 Watts, 173.

CHAPTER VI.

PARTIES IN REPLEVIN.

§ 1. ONE joint tenant or tenant in common cannot maintain replevin against the other.[1] "Because they have each and equally the right of possession."[2] And, in New York, where one tenant in common brings replevin in the *detinet*, under the Revised Statutes, against the bailee of the other, and the property is taken and delivered to the plaintiff; the defendant is entitled to a verdict and judgment for the full value of the property, on waiving judgment for its return.[3] So where one tenant in common sells a right to cut timber on the land, the other cannot replevy it.[4] So it is held, that one of two joint owners of goods cannot maintain replevin to recover them of a stranger.[5] Nor for his undivided share.[6] Non-joinder of part-owners may be pleaded in bar or abatement,[7] or made a ground of motion in arrest of judgment.[8] And if it appear, from the plaintiff's own showing, that he is but part-owner, the court will abate the writ *ex officio*.[9]

§ 2. But the distinction is made, in a case of authority, that replevin will not lie by one joint owner; but the objection can only be taken by a plea in abatement, where he sues for the whole. If he sues for a moiety, the court will *ex officio* abate the writ.[10] And, in New York, one having a general or specific

[1] Russel *v.* Allen, 3 Seld. 173; Barnes *v.* Bartlett, 15 Pick. 71; Wills *v.* Noyes, 12 ib. 324; M'Eldery *v.* Flannagan, 1 Har. & Gill, 308; Noble *v.* Epperly, 6 Ind. 414.

[2] Per Shaw, C. J., 15 Pick. 75.

[3] Russel *v.* Allen, 3 Seld. 173.

[4] Alford *v.* Bradeen, 1 Neva. 228.

[5] M'Arther *v.* Lane, 3 Shep. 245; Low *v.* Martin, 18 Ill. 286.

[6] Ellis & Culver, 1 Har. 76; Pritchard *v.* Culver, 2 ib. 129.

[7] Cox *v.* Marrow, 14 Ark. 603.

[8] Pritchard *v.* Culver, 2 Har. 129.

[9] Hart *v.* Fitzgerald, 2 Mass. 509.

[10] D'Wolf *v.* Harris, 4 Mass. 515. See Talvande *v.* Cripps, 3 M'Cord, 147.

property in goods, either alone or in connection with others, can maintain replevin in the *detinet* against a stranger. Joint ownership with others is no bar to the action, either under the plea of *non detinet* or a special plea; although it would be proper matter for a plea in abatement. If the defendant connect himself with the title through any of the owners, he may avail himself of the rights thus acquired in bar of the action. But, as a stranger, he will not be permitted, by a technical defence, to defeat the claim of a person entitled to the possession as against him.[1]

§ 3. The general rule will not be applied as against a plaintiff in replevin, unless the case is strictly one of *joint* or *common* ownership. Thus, A being possessed of a quantity of coffee in bags, of which a certain part, contained in a number of bags, not distinguished by marks, nor in any manner separated from the rest, was the property of B; a creditor of A caused the whole to be attached as the property of A. B replevied from the sheriff the quantity owned by him; and, issue being joined on B's property, and a verdict found for him, he had judgment. The parties were not tenants in common. Though the bags of the plaintiff had no distinguishing marks, he might have taken the number and the quantity of coffee to which he was entitled by his own selection. If a return were to be ordered, the defendant would still be accountable to the plaintiff for the proceeds.[2] So A was to furnish wheat to stock a mill, and B, with money advanced by A, to purchase wheat and convert it into flour, and, after deducting the original cost of the wheat, and two and a half per cent. thereon, to receive the proceeds of the sale of the flour. If the wheat is levied on as the property of B, A may maintain replevin to recover it.[3] So where, in an action of replevin, there is proof tending to show that a part of the goods belong to a third person, the defendant is entitled to a verdict for the value of those goods.[4] But if A, a warehouseman, mix the goods of B, the plaintiff, with his own, so that they cannot be distinguished apart, but not wrongfully or without B's consent; B cannot maintain replevin for his goods against A, as they become joint owners of the whole.[5]

§ 4. A partner cannot maintain replevin against his copartner

1 Wright *v.* Bennett, 3 Barb. 451.
2 Gardner *v.* Dutch, 9 Mass. 427.
3 Johnson *v.* Miller, 16 Ohio, 431.
4 Morss *v.* Stone, 5 Barb. 516.
5 Low *v.* Martin, 18 Ill. 286.

for any of the partnership property. And where one partner has in his possession partnership property, which the other takes from him, and the former replevies; the defendant is entitled to judgment *pro retorno;* for, where one has been deprived of his property by an abuse of the process of the law, the law should restore it, and place the parties *in statu quo.*[1]

§ 5. In Kentucky, replevying a judgment against one obligor is a legal discharge, not only of the judgment for which it was executed, but of a separate judgment against another for the same debt.[2]

§ 6. In New York, an action for the penalty given by the statute, against an officer who makes a deliverance of property under a writ of replevin, before trying the validity of a claim of property interposed, must be brought in the names of all the claimants; and this, although one was a landlord and the other his bailiff in making a distress for rent, against whom a joint action of replevin was brought.[3] And the defendant need not plead *non-joinder* in abatement, but may avail himself of it at the trial.[4]

§ 7. If a constable deliver to the owner property taken under execution, thereby enabling him to impose on three persons having claims; they may replevy the property.[5]

§ 8. Where a sheriff takes partnership property in a suit against one of several partners and removes it to a place of safety; the others cannot bring replevin.[6]

§ 9. Replevin cannot be maintained, either at common law or under the Connecticut statute, by one joint owner of a personal chattel, against another joint owner, for a taking away of the joint property, by virtue of a writ of attachment against a third person.[7]

§ 10. Personal property owned in common being attached against A, one of the owners, and replevin brought in the name of all against the officer, and dismissed; the measure of damages in an action on the bond is the value of A's interest.[8]

§ 11. The seller of goods may bring a joint action to recover them, against the fraudulent purchaser, and his assignee for benefit of creditors, to whom the goods have been delivered, and who refuses to give them up on demand. It is said by the court, "the

1 Whitesides *v.* Collier, 7 Dana, 283.
2 Justices, &c. *v.* Lee, 1 Mon. 327.
3 Colton *v.* Mott, 15 Wend. 619.
4 Ibid.
5 Mulholm *v.* Cheney, Addis. 301.
6 Scrugham *v.* Carter, 12 Wend. 131.
7 Prentice *v.* Ladd, 12 Conn. 331.
8 Bartlett *v.* Kidder, 14 Gray, 449.

Code provides that any person may be made a defendant who has or claims an interest in the controversy adverse to the plaintiff, or who is a necessary party to a complete determination or settlement of the questions involved therein. Both these defendants claim an interest in the goods adverse to the plaintiffs; Pumer claiming that the purchase of the goods was free from fraud, and that they should be retained by his assignee, and disposed of for the benefit of creditors — Michael claiming the possession for the same purpose, and refusing to surrender on demand."[1]

§ 12. A judgment for the plaintiff in replevin, against one of two joint takers of goods, for a part of the goods taken, is a bar to a subsequent action against both to recover damages for the same trespass, if the other goods are not shown to have been concealed, or otherwise disposed of, so that they could not be replevied.[2]

§ 13. The owner of property, attached in a suit against another, may maintain replevin therefor against the attaching creditor and the officer jointly, when the former assisted in taking the property, and took it into his own possession after the attachment.[3]

§ 14. In replevin against two or more, one may be found guilty and the others not guilty.[4]

§ 15. The *death* of a party to the action of replevin has given rise to some questions.

§ 16. The suggestion, on record, of the death of the defendant, is held to abate the action, and it cannot be revived against the administrator.[5] And the distinction is taken in an early case in Massachusetts, that, "if the defendant in replevin die pending the suit, his executor or administrator cannot come in and defend, because the action is founded on a tort which does not survive. But if the plaintiff in replevin die, his executor or administrator may come in and prosecute, within the equity of the statutes of 4 Ed. III. ch. 7, & 31 Ed. III. ch. 11."[6] And in a subsequent case it was held, that the administrator of a deceased defendant in replevin could not be admitted on his motion to defend the suit. And further, the action being against a deputy sheriff for attaching property of the plaintiff in an action against a third person; that

1 Nichols *v.* Michael, 23 N. Y. (9 Smith), 264; per James, J., 269.

2 Bennett *v.* Hood, 1 All. 47.

3 Esty *v.* Love, 32 Vt. 744.

4 Carothers *v.* Van Hagan, 2 Greene (Iowa), 481.

5 Rector *v.* Chevalier, 1 Mis. 345.

6 Pitts *v.* Hale, 3 Mass. 321.

a statute, providing for the surviving of actions for the malfeasance of the sheriff or his deputies, did not apply to the case.[1]

§ 17. In New York, where a verdict was rendered for the defendant in replevin for a part of the property, and a new trial ordered, and the defendant died after such order and previous to the next circuit; the executors are not entitled to come in and ask that the suit be continued against them.[2]

§ 18. But, in South Carolina, co-heirs, or joint tenants, with a defendant in replevin, may come in and defend an action abated by his death.[3]

§ 19. Evidence, that a slave belonged to a person deceased, and that the plaintiff, who is his widow, administered jointly with another person who is still living; that there are several heirs, and has been no distribution of the estate; and that after the death of the intestate the plaintiff obtained possession of the negro, who has been called her own and been in her possession until a short time before suit commenced; clearly shows a want of title in the plaintiff to support replevin.[4]

§ 20. It is doubted whether an action of replevin in the *detinet* will lie against the *wife*, where the detention is in fact the joint act of both husband and wife.[5]

§ 21. It is held that replevin does not lie, by husband and wife, to recover chattels, the property of the wife before marriage.[6]

§ 22. In reference to the relation of *principal and agent* in connection with replevin, an auctioneer who, as the agent of the owner, sells and delivers goods on a condition which is not complied with, may maintain replevin therefor. He "has a possession, coupled with an interest, . . . not a bare custody, like a servant or shopman, but a special property, with a lien for the charges of sale, the commission, and the auction duty, which he is bound to pay. . . . The auctioneer might maintain trespass. He is liable to his employers for the goods, or for the price at which they were sold. . . . . He is also the 'party entitled to possession,' within the meaning of the Mass. Rev. Sts. ch. 113, § 27." [7]

§ 23. Replevin may be maintained in the name of a *parish* for the parish records.[8]

1 Mellen *v.* Baldwin, 4 Mass. 480.

2 Webber's Executors *v.* Underhill, 19 Wend. 447.

3 Talvande *v.* Cripps, 2 M'Cord, 164.

4 Robinson *v.* Calloway, 4 Pike, 94.

5 Huntington *v.* Gilmore, 14 Barb. 243.

6 Seibert *v.* McHenry, 6 Watts, 301.

7 Tyler *v.* Freeman, 3 Cush. 261; per Metcalf, J. 263.

8 First, &c., *v.* Stearns, 21 Pick. 148.

§ 24. Replevin is often founded upon an allegation of *fraud*, and brought by or against an alleged fraudulent seller or buyer. Thus, it may be brought in case of purchase by false representations, though upon credit.[1] And in an action commenced under § 206, &c., of the New York Code, for the claim and delivery of personal property, where the complaint is in the form of the old declaration in replevin in the *detinet*, and charges that the defendants have become possessed of, and wrongfully detain the goods and chattels, and the plaintiffs proceed upon the ground that the title to the goods was never changed, but remained in them, because purchased of the plaintiffs, and the delivery thereof procured, through the false representations of the vendees as to their solvency and credit; proof of the purchase of the goods by the agent of the defendants, by their direction, and that at the time the defendants were insolvent, is competent evidence on the question of fraud.[2] In such an action, it is not necessary that the complaint should aver a demand of the goods, or the insolvency of the defendants, or any of the facts going to establish the fraud. It is sufficient if it is in the form of the old declaration in replevin in the *detinet*, and charges that the defendants have become possessed of, and wrongfully hold, the goods and chattels.[3] And, to warrant a recovery against a purchaser from a fraudulent vendee, the actual *mala fides* of the defendant, that is, his positive knowledge or belief, is not necessary to be proved. It is sufficient to prove, that the circumstances known to him were such as ought reasonably to have excited his suspicions, and led him to inquire.[4]

§ 25. A chattel was attached, as A's, for a just demand, but by means of a set-off the defendant recovered a balance with costs. B, claiming under a sale from A, replevied the chattel from the officer, pending the suit. Held, the officer might avoid the sale as fraudulent; although, after the original judgment, B might have a right to the chattel as against him, he having no execution to levy upon it.[5]

§ 26. If tenants in common make separate conveyances to the same purchaser, one of which is fraudulent and void as against creditors; the purchaser cannot maintain replevin for such property against an officer attaching it as the property of the

[1] Hall *v.* Gilmore, 40 Maine, 578.

[2] Hunter *v.* The Hudson, &c., 20 Barb. 493.

[3] Ibid.

[4] Pringle *v.* Phillips, 5 Sandf. 157.

[5] Gates *v.* Gates, 15 Mass. 310.

vendors. "If either deed was void, the plaintiff would have a title to only an undivided share, for which replevin could not be sustained. . . . If either was the owner of an undivided share, . . . the taking by the officer was lawful."[1]

§ 27. Where A exchanged a horse, which he had stolen, with B, and afterwards sold B's horse to C for a valuable consideration, and without notice, on the part of B, of the theft; held, replevin did not lie by B against C.[2]

§ 28. If an owner sell chattels on condition of immediate payment, but waive the condition, and deliver them; he parts with the property, and cannot, in replevin for the chattels, avail himself of a fraud between the first and a second purchaser.[3] So a vendor cannot maintain replevin against a vendee, after delivering a quantity of flour on board a vessel, on a credit of sixty days, the defendant refusing to give his notes, having failed in the meantime, and having consigned the flour to a foreign house, who had advanced money on the consignment.[4]

§ 29. The defendant contracted to tan hides furnished him by a firm, and return the leather in reasonable time, at an agreed price for tanning and transportation, payable after delivery. He carted a quantity of finished leather from the tannery, by a different road to a different place from the usual place of shipment, to the merchants who had furnished the hides, and there stored them in a barn never before used for storage. Held, the evidence showed an intention to retain and sell the leather as the defendant's property; that he had no lien upon it, inasmuch as delivery was to precede payment; and that, in an action of replevin brought by the surviving member of the firm, an instruction to the jury, that there had been neither an unlawful taking nor detention, and the action did not lie, was erroneous.[5]

§ 30. Where goods are fraudulently sold by a carrier, and the purchaser takes them *without delivery*, it seems that replevin in the *cepit* will lie by the owner against the purchaser, although he bought the goods in good faith.[6]

§ 31. Mistake, as well as fraud, may be the ground of an action of replevin. Thus an inspector of tobacco, by mistake, delivered

[1] Kimball *v.* Thompson, 4 Cush. 441; per Wilde, J. 449.

[2] Brown *v.* Campsall, 6 Har. & J. 491.

[3] Mixer *v.* Cook, 31 Maine, 340.

[4] Clemson *v.* Davidson, 4 Binn. 405. See 5 ib. 392; Karthans *v.* Owings, 4 Har. & J. 263.

[5] Lee *v.* Gould, 47 Penn. 398.

[6] Ely *v.* Ehlie, 3 Comst. 506.

to the holder of certain notes other hogsheads of tobacco than those mentioned in such notes. The hogsheads corresponding with the notes were by A delivered over to B, his successor, and on B's advertising them for sale, under the Maryland act of 1802, ch. 27, they were demanded by A, and an action of replevin brought for them by him. Held, that he was not entitled to recover.[1]

§ 32. A mortgagee of personal property, in the absence of any agreement to the contrary, is entitled to immediate possession of the property, and may maintain replevin therefor before the time of credit has expired.[2] More especially, after default in payment of a chattel mortgage, the mortgagee's title becomes absolute at law, and he is entitled to immediate possession. Hence he may maintain replevin in the *cepit* against any one who tortiously takes the property from the mortgagor. So although after the default, the mortgagee filed a copy of the mortgage and a statement, pursuant to the New York act of April 29th, 1833; for that will not operate an extension of credit, or give the mortgagor any additional right of possession.[3]

§ 33. But where it was agreed, at the time of making a mortgage of a chattel, that the mortgagor should retain possession; the mortgagee cannot maintain replevin against one who takes the chattel.[4] In such case, the mortgagor has the right of possession, and a legal interest in the goods, capable of being seized upon a distress warrant or an execution.[5] And where the evidence conduced to prove, that the mortgagor held the possession by contract; instructions, that, if the plaintiff held a valid subsisting mortgage, &c., the law was for him, are erroneous, because they did not submit the question of possession to the jury.[6] But, in such cases, if at the time of trial the plaintiff have a right to possession, the defendant cannot have judgment for a return.[7]

§ 34. When a mortgagee has the right of immediate possession, no demand is necessary, in order to sustain replevin against a subsequent vendee of the mortgagor.[8]

§ 35. In an action of replevin, brought by the assignee of an insolvent debtor; the defendant, who claims under a mortgage

[1] Stevenson *v.* Ridgely, 3 Har. & J. 281.
[2] Ferguson *v.* Thomas, 26 Maine, 499.
[3] Fuller *v.* Acker, 1 Hill, 473.
[4] Pierce *v.* Stevens, 30 Maine, 184; Redman *v.* Hendricks, 1 Sandf. 32.
[5] Redman *v.* Hendricks, 1 Sandf. 32.
[6] M'Isaacs *v.* Hobbs, 8 Dana, 268.
[7] Ingraham *v.* Martin, 3 Shep. 373.
[8] Partridge *v.* Swasey, 46 Maine, 414.

from the debtor, by which the possession and control of the goods are secured to the mortgagor until after default, may show, by parol evidence, that the mortgagor has waived this right, and allowed him to take possession.[1]

§ 36. The service of legal process upon mortgaged property has often given occasion to the action of replevin in behalf of the mortgagee.

§ 37. In Massachusetts, independently of statute, the provisions of which must be strictly observed, personal property mortgaged cannot be taken on execution against the mortgagor; and replevin will lie by the mortgagee against a purchaser of the property at the sale on execution.[2]

§ 38. A, the owner of a vessel, resident in Nova Scotia, mortgaged her to B, also resident there, who had his mortgage duly recorded, under the laws of the province, at the custom-house, and a memorandum thereof indorsed on the register of the vessel, these acts, by the *lex loci*, making B the owner of the vessel, so far as was necessary to give him security for his debt. Held, he had thus acquired possession of the vessel, sufficiently to maintain replevin against an attaching creditor in Massachusetts.[3]

§ 39. Where an officer levies upon personal property mortgaged, which remains in possession of the mortgagor, the money not having become due, and replevin is brought against him for asserting his claim under such levy, and refusing to surrender the property after the mortgage money has become due; the plaintiff must declare for the *detention*, not for the *taking* of the property.[4]

§ 40. The Kentucky statute, subjecting the interests of mortgagors to execution, makes no reference to the state of the possession at the time of levy; and, as a levy on personal property implies that the officer takes possession of it, so, where an execution against the mortgagor is levied on the mortgaged property in possession of the mortgagee, the officer has a legal right to assume the possession and control of the property between the levy and sale, and the mortgagee cannot maintain replevin; and a failure of the officer to recognize the mortgage (because he did not know of it, or doubted its validity), it seems, would not

[1] Whitcher *v.* Shattuck, 3 Allen, 319.
[2] Lamb *v.* Johnson, 10 Cush. 126.
[3] Esson *v.* Tarbell, 9 Cush. 407.
[4] Randall *v.* Cook, 17 Wend. 53.

render the levy and seizure unlawful. If, in any case, where an execution against a mortgagor is levied on the property, it can be replevied by the mortgagee, it must be surrendered for the sale of the mortgagor's interest.[1]

§ 41. In replevin in the *detinet*, the finding was, that the plaintiff was a mortgagee and in possession; that the defendant as constable took and detained the chattel on an execution against the mortgagor; and that by law a mortgagee of a chattel in possession might maintain replevin in the *detinet* against a constable, who took and detained the mortgaged chattel for the mortgagor's debts. Held, the finding did not, even by necessary implication, show a right of possession in the plaintiff.[2] The finding further ordered an allowance of five per cent. on the value recovered by the plaintiff as indemnity for his expenses, and fixed the value at $105. Held, fatally defective, in that it did not assess damages for the taking; and that the judgment thereon could not stand.[3]

§ 42. A mortgagee of personalty, having the right to take possession whenever he deems the debt insecure, has an immediate right of possession, and may maintain replevin where the whole property has been sold on execution, instead of the mortgagor's interest.[4]

§ 43. Replevin will not lie for levying an execution against a mortgagor and mortgagee upon the mortgaged chattels by direction of the mortgagee.[5]

§ 44. In Ohio, personal property mortgaged may be attached as the mortgagor's, when in his possession. The levy and seizure creates a lien, which is not divested by the recovery of the property in replevin by the mortgagee. The attaching creditor may apply the surplus proceeds of a sale made by the mortgagee to his judgment, though after levy of the attachment, and before commencement of proceedings thus to subject the surplus, the mortgagor had assigned it to the mortgagee.[6]

§ 45. In the same State, if the lien of a mortgage exceeds the value of the property, the officer, against whom an action of replevin is brought for taking it upon process against the mortgagor, can recover only nominal damages.[7]

1 M'Isaacs *v.* Hobbs, 8 Dana, 268.
2 Bates *v.* Wilbur, 10 Wis. 415.
3 Ibid.
4 Frisbee *v.* Langworthy, 11 Wis. 375.
5 Talbot *v.* De Forest, 3 Iowa, 586.
6 Carty *v.* Fenstemaker, 14 Ohio St., 457.
7 Coe *v.* Peacock, 14 Ohio St., 187.

§ 46. To an action of replevin for detaining goods, the defendant may plead generally property in himself, and specially that the goods were delivered by the plaintiff to the defendant as a pledge, and retained until the plaintiff should pay, &c., which he had not done.[1] So A pledged goods to B, to secure his debt. A was indebted to C by note. By agreement between the three, A was to work for C, who was to apply his wages to the payment of B's debt. A worked for C until his wages exceeded the amount of his indebtedness to B. C then offered A his own note, and the balance of B's debt to A in cash, which A refused. C then paid A the amount of his wages in cash. Held, no satisfaction of the debt secured by the pledge, and therefore A could not maintain replevin for the goods, especially after receiving the full amount of his wages from C.[2]

§ 47. In replevin, under the Revised Statutes of Michigan, one having a lien or a special property, at the commencement of the suit, can recover only according to his special interest against the general owner; but against a stranger he may recover as though he were the general owner, the statute being intended to introduce in actions of replevin the rules governing in actions of trover.[3]

§ 48. It seems, the defendant in replevin cannot object that a third person had a lien, as against the plaintiff, upon the property attached.[4]

§ 49. Where the defendant, in replevin for manufactured articles, avows the detention of them on the ground of a mechanic's lien, the plaintiff may plead in bar an agreement by which the lien was waived.[5]

§ 50. Where a purchaser of horses, at a sale on execution, which were subject to a lien for keeping at a livery-stable, suffered them to come again into the custody of the stable-keeper, and afterwards took them away against the will of the latter, who claimed to detain them for his lien; it was held that replevin was the proper form of action for the stable-keeper in enforcing his lien.[6]

[1] Amos *v.* Sinnott, 4 Scam. 440.
[2] Ibid.
[3] Davidson *v.* Gunsolly, 1 Mann. 388.
[4] Wilson *v.* Nichols, 29 Maine, 566.
[5] Curtis *v.* Jones, 3 Denio, 590.
[6] Young *v.* Kimball, 23 Penn. 193.

CHAPTER VII.

WRIT, BOND, DECLARATION, PLEADINGS, EVIDENCE, ETC.

§ 1. WITH regard to the pleadings, practice, and forms of proceeding in replevin, we have already seen that they are for the most part peculiar to this action. In consequence of such peculiarity, the numerous statutory alterations in this country, with reference to mere matters of form, the purpose and effect of which is to simplify remedies and do away with long-established technicalities, have comparatively little application to the action of replevin. (*a*)

(*a*) There are, however, numerous points of form and practice in the action of replevin, which are variously regulated by the local usages and express legislation of different States.

Questions may frequently arise, in reference to the *bond*, which is generally required to accompany the writ of replevin. In Connecticut, if the plaintiff in an action of replevin be not an inhabitant, he must give bond for prosecution pursuant to the first section of the act regulating civil actions; otherwise the process is abatable. And this, notwithstanding the giving of a bond, pursuant to the 8th section of the statute authorizing writs of replevin, such bond not securing to the defendant his costs in replevin. Fleet *v.* Lockwood, 17 Conn. 233.

In Maine, the plaintiff in replevin is not a trespasser in taking the goods replevied, if he offers sureties satisfactory to the offi cer, although in fact insufficient. Harri man *v.* Wilkins, 2 App. 93.

In Kentucky, though no bond may have been executed, on suing out a writ of replevin, yet, if the writ be not executed, and the property not delivered to the plaintiff, it is error to quash the writ and render judgment for a return of the property. The writ is good as a citation, and the cause should progress. Greenwade *v.* Fisher, 5 B. Mon. 167.

Under a statute requiring "all original writs" to be indorsed, a writ of replevin must be indorsed. The fact that the replevin bond furnishes all the security derived from such indorsement cannot change the effect of an express statute. Nor does it make any difference that this statute is prior in time to the act providing for replevin. But if the defendant pleads the want of an indorser in abatement of the writ, without any suggestion entitling him to possession of the goods, and the writ is abated; he shall have judgment for his costs, but not for a return. Gould *v.* Barnard, 3 Mass. 199.

In Massachusetts, it is not necessary that it should appear, in an officer's return of a writ of replevin, either that the defend-

§ 2. The writ and declaration must contain a description of the goods,[1] which will enable the officer, with reasonable cer-

[1] Magee *v.* Siggerson, 4 Blackf. 70. See Story *v.* O'Dea, 23 Ind. 326.

ant was requested or had notice to appoint an appraiser of the property, or that the parties did not agree as to the value thereof. Wolcott *v.* Mead, 12 Met. 516.

Though it is the general duty of the officer to appoint three appraisers, yet he is justified or excused for omitting so to do, when the parties agree as to the value. If the parties do so agree, he should certify that fact in his return, when he for that reason omits to appoint appraisers. Ib.

In Massachusetts, a writ of replevin may be issued by the clerk of the courts in one county returnable in another. Judson *v.* Adams, 8 Cush. 556.

A constable has no authority, by Rev. Sts., ch. 15, to serve a writ of replevin, except where the sheriff or his deputy is a party, and the value of the property does not exceed seventy dollars. The statute provided, that constables might serve writs and executions in any personal action in which the damage is not laid higher than seventy dollars. By a subsequent section of the same chapter, "constables may also serve writs of replevin, in cases where the sheriff or his deputy shall be a party, and in which the value of the property to be replevied shall not exceed the sum of seventy dollars." The construction of the two provisions, taken together, is as above stated. "And this conclusion is confirmed by a reference to the subject-matter. In most personal actions, the matter ultimately claimed in the suit is a sum of money expressed in the *ad damnum*. The obvious purpose of the statute being to give constables a limited authority only to serve writs . . . this may be well measured in most personal actions by the *ad damnum*. But it is otherwise in replevin, where specific property, often of great value, may be the subject of judicial controversy, whilst the damages are merely incidental, and may be comparatively small." Conner *v.* Palmer, 13 Met. 302; per Shaw, C. J., ib. 303.

Under the Rev. Sts., ch. 113 (see Gen. Sts.), a writ of replevin may be delivered to an officer, and he may commence the service, but not deliver the property to the plaintiff, nor do anything more than is necessary to effect an appraisement, before taking a bond. Wolcott *v.* Mead, 12 Met. 516.

In New York, a plaintiff in replevin cannot regularly declare, until the writ be returned with the names of the sureties annexed. Wilson *v.* Williams, 18 Wend. 581.

A writ tested at one term, and returnable at the next term but one (an entire term intervening), is voidable. Cayward *v.* Doolittle, 6 Cow. 602.

In Wisconsin, an *alias* writ of replevin may be issued and directed to the sheriff of a county other than that in which suit is brought. Hiles *v.* McFarlane, 4 Chand. 189.

In Vermont, a writ of replevin of property attached cannot be served by a constable. Ralston *v.* Strong, Brayt. 216; ib. 1 Chip. 287.

In Connecticut, a writ to replevy goods, taken by attachment, is not an adversary suit, but a mandatory precept, and ought to be directed to the officer who served the attachment. Denison *v.* Raymond, Kirby, 274.

In Arkansas, if a writ of replevin is improperly executed, the clerk can issue an *alias* without any order of court. The return must show execution by reading, or delivering a copy, or leaving a copy at the defendant's usual place of abode, with some white person of his family over fifteen years of age. It must also set forth with certainty the contents of the notice required to be delivered to, or left for him, and state that it was signed by himself. A defect in the return is not ground for dismissing the suit. Nor is a refusal of the plaintiff to amend. Pool *v.* Loomis, 5 Pike, 110.

In Illinois, where part of the property claimed cannot be found, and there is personal service, the plaintiff may add a count in trover. Dart *v.* Horn, 20 Ill. 212.

The failure of a sheriff to return the value of property replevied, as required by the third section of the Kentucky act of 1830, is no cause for quashing the writ. Fryer *v.* Fryer, 6 Dana, 54.

In Maine, a writ of replevin returnable before a justice of the peace, like other justice writs, is to be "duly served, not less than seven, nor more than sixty days before the day therein appointed for trial." Lord *v.* Poor, 10 Shep. 569.

In Indiana, a writ of replevin need not show that the statutory affidavit has been made by the plaintiff. Magee *v.* Siggerson, 4 Blackf. 70.

If, in an action before a justice of the peace, the affidavit filed be such as the statute requires, no other statement of the demand is necessary. Andre *v.* Johnson, 6 Blackf. 188.

In Michigan, the affidavit, required in actions of replevin to be annexed to the writ before it can be executed, must contain the statement "that the property was

tainty, to distinguish them from other property of like nature. Thus "a quantity of corn (consisting of about 200 bushels), and a quantity of rye (consisting of about 100 bushels)," is not a sufficient description.[1] So, although "fifteen hundred pounds of seed cotton" is sufficiently descriptive of the article and of the quantity; as the officer was required to take it into his possession, it was doubted whether some further identification, of the particular cotton sought to be recovered, should not have been made, as, that it was at a certain place, in a pen, house, or pile.[2]

§ 3. It is held that a defective description must be taken advantage of by special demurrer, as it will be sufficient after verdict, avowry, or plea of property.[3] But, unless the writ specify the goods, it may be quashed, even after an appearance.[4]

§ 4. The declaration should not include any property not taken under the writ.[5]

§ 5. On a writ of replevin for *about four hundred tons of bog ore*, the sheriff is not authorized to deliver to the plaintiff seven hundred and twenty tons. It seems, he would have been justifiable in refusing to execute such a writ. Where, however, he did execute it, and delivered to the plaintiff seven hundred and twenty tons of ore, and the defendants obtained a judgment of return, and executed a writ of inquiry to assess the value of the property and damages of detention; held, it was competent for the plaintiff to show, in mitigation, that shortly after the delivery of the property to him the defendants repossessed themselves of the greater part thereof.[6]

§ 5 *a*. In a case of replevin for a certain number of barrels of mackerel, the writ was served, with the assent of the defendant, by taking, in part, two half barrels as equivalent to one barrel. Held, he could not claim a return, on the ground that property was taken which was not described in the writ.[7] (*a*)

[1] Stevens *v.* Osman, 1 Mann. 92.
[2] Hill *v.* Robinson, 16 Ark. 90.
[3] Stevens *v.* Osman, 1 Mann. 92.
[4] Snedeker *v.* Quick, 6 Halst. 179.
[5] Sanderson *v.* Marks, 1 Har. & Gill, 252.
[6] DeWitt *v.* Morris, 13 Wend. 496.
[7] Gardner *v.* Lane, 9 Allen, 492.

not taken for any assessment levied by virtue of any law in this State;" also, that it was not seized under any execution against the goods and chattels of the plaintiff liable to execution. These averments are made necessary by the statute, without regard to the nature of the property replevied. Phenix *v.* Clark, 2 Mich. 327.

(*a*) In New York, a summons in replevin need not specify the property; and such specification may be rejected as surplusage. Finchout *v.* Crain, 4 Hill, 537.

Where, in replevin, several articles of property were described in the writ, but, in consequence of directions given by the plaintiff, a part of them only was seized by

§ 6. A declaration in replevin for taking and detaining goods must show either a general or special property. An allegation of title to the possession is not sufficient.[1] Nor a statement of *the evidence of title* instead of title itself,[2] by direct and issuable averment.[3] Nor that the goods were taken by the defendant out of the plaintiff's possession.[4] Nor (in New York) that the plaintiff is entitled to the possession of the goods, and they are the property of him, the plaintiff, by virtue of attachments duly issued, by a justice of the peace, and delivered to the plaintiff, as a constable, to be executed.[5] So a declaration in replevin by husband and wife should show especially the wife's interest in the goods.[6] But where a declaration alleges that the "plaintiffs were the owners" of the goods in suit, "and entitled to the possession thereof;" the last clause may be disregarded as surplusage, the allegation of ownership being equivalent to an assertion of property.[7]

[1] Pattison *v.* Adams, 7 Hill, 126. See Prosser *v.* Woodward, 21 Wend. 205.

[2] Bond *v.* Mitchell, 3 Barb. 304.

[3] Vandenburgh *v.* Van Valkenburgh, 8 Barb. 217.

[4] Bond *v.* Mitchell, 3 Barb. 304.

[5] Vandenburgh *v.* Van Valkenburgh, 8 Barb. 217.

[6] Gentry *v.* Borgis, 6 Blackf. 261.

[7] Pattison *v.* Adams, Hill & Den. 426.

the officer; held, the plaintiff might nevertheless include the whole in his declaration, and this though the summons served described the articles seized without mentioning the residue. Finehout *v.* Crain, 4 Hill, 537.

It seems, a sheriff is not liable in trespass for replevying the property mentioned in the writ, though it belong to a third person, and be found in his possession. Otherwise with the party who sued out the writ. Shipman *v.* Clark, 4 Denio, 446.

In Indiana and Alabama, in replevin in the *detinuit*, which is now the usual form, the declaration need not state the value of the goods. Britton *v.* Morss, 6 Blackf. 469; Haynes *v.* Crutchfield, 7 Ala. 189. See Wilcoxon *v.* Annesley, 23 Ind. 285.

In Indiana, if, in an action of replevin before a justice of the peace, the statement of demand filed before the writ issued state the value of the property, the omission of the averment of such value in the affidavit is not material. Mooney *v.* Myers, 5 Blackf. 331.

In New York, where the complaint alleges the value of the chattel as "about one hundred and thirty dollars," which allegation is not controverted by the answer, the defendant may show the true value. Woodruff *v.* Cook, 25 Barb. 505.

In Massachusetts, in a writ of replevin directed to a deputy sheriff, it is not necessary to state the value of the goods. This conclusion is arrived at by Mr. Justice Gray, after an elaborate citation of the early Massachusetts statutes, and the decisions by which they have been construed. Pomeroy *v.* Trimper, 8 Allen, 399. See Davenport *v.* Burke, 9 ib. 116.

"In a case in the Year Books, a man brought replevin of a heifer (*juvenca*), and was afterwards nonsuit, and sued out his writ of second deliverance of a cow (*vacca*); to which the defendant's counsel objected on the ground of variance; but Fitzherbert, J., said: "The writ is good; for it may be that it was a heifer at the time of suing out the replevin, and that it is now a cow." Year Book, 26 H. 8, p. 6, pl. 27; cited by Gray, J., in Pomeroy *v.* Trimper, 8 Allen, 404.

In New York, the declaration must state a place certain, within the village or town; but the omission may be cured by the defendant's pleading over. Gardner *v.* Humphrey, 10 Johns. 53.

In Pennsylvania, in replevin for articles not distrained, it is sufficient if the taking be laid in the county. Muck *v.* Folkroad, 1 Browne, 60.

In Maryland, an omission to allege damage in the declaration is fatal. Faget *v.* Brayton, 2 Har. & J. 350.

After trial in replevin and verdict for the defendant, the plaintiff cannot avail himself of any uncertainty in his declaration. Wilson *v.* Gray, 8 Watts, 25.

§ 7. Where two issues are presented by a declaration, one claiming property, and the other that the defendant detained the goods, a general verdict in favor of the plaintiff will be set aside.[1]

§ 8. On a bill in equity, under Mass. Rev. Sts. ch. 81, § 7, to obtain possession of a horse, secreted from the plaintiff so that it cannot be replevied, an allegation that the plaintiff was the owner of the horse and had the right of possession is sufficient, without setting forth the particulars of his title; especially when the plaintiff seeks no discovery and waives an answer under oath. The court make a distinction between this case and that of Clap *v.* Shepard, 23 Pick. 228, 2 Met. 127; the bill in that case disclosing the fact, that the note sought to be restored to the plaintiff was a note payable to a third person, and therefore it being proper that further facts should be stated, which would show a transfer to the plaintiff.[2]

§ 9. With regard to the pleadings in replevin, subsequent to the declaration, there is no action in which what are termed *dilatory* motions and pleas are of more frequent occurrence.

§ 10. In Kentucky, the want of a sufficient bond in replevin may, it seems, be pleaded in abatement; it is no cause for dismissing the suit upon motion. The court should permit the plaintiff to give a sufficient bond, or order restitution of the property.[3]

§ 11. In Illinois, it is not cause for dismissing an action of replevin, that no declaration was filed at the first term; the cause in such case should be continued at the plaintiff's cost.[4]

§ 12. In Massachusetts, a motion to dismiss an action of replevin, on the ground that the writ was served by a constable, or that there was no appraisal of the goods, must be made at the first term.[5]

§ 13. In the same State, it is no ground of dismissal that the bond has one surety only, unless the fact is distinctly specified, at the first term, as a cause for dismissal. The action will not be dismissed, for that cause, upon a motion which merely states, as a reason for dismissing it, that the officer made his service, or commenced his service, before any bond was given, as the law requires.[6]

[1] Donaldson *v.* Johnson, 2 Chand. 160.

[2] Strickland *v.* Fizgerald, 7 Cush. 530–532.

[3] Bloomer *v.* Craige, 6 Dana, 310.

[4] Amos *v.* Sinnott, 4 Scam. 440.

[5] Jaques *v.* Sanderson, 8 Cush. 271

[6] Wolcott *v.* Mead, 12 Met. 516.

§ 14. In Massachusetts, where a writ of replevin was framed according to the form prescribed by the repealed statute of 1789, ch. 26, and the officer proceeded in the service, according to that statute, taking and returning a bond from the plaintiff to the defendant with one surety only, and in a certain sum, without causing an appraisement, &c., as directed by Rev. Stats. ch. 113; held, a motion to dismiss the action could not be received after the return term, at which the defendant appeared, and the action should proceed to trial, as the bond taken and returned was valid by the common law, and the court had jurisdiction of the parties and of the subject-matter.[1]

§ 15. It is no ground for dismissing a writ of replevin, that an animal described in the writ as a heifer is termed a cow in the certificate of appraisement; that the plaintiff has caused the officer intrusted with the writ to bring an action against the defendant and another officer, for taking the property from him before its delivery to the plaintiff; or that the plaintiff, as executor, has brought a suit against the defendant and the latter officer for conversion of the property, unless such conversion is shown to be the same for which the replevin was brought.[2]

§ 16. The pleadings in replevin are termed *avowry* and *cognizance*. "An avowry is where the defendant, in an action of replevin, avows the taking of the distress in his own right, or in right of his wife, and sets forth the cause of it, as for arrears of rent, damage done, or the like."[3] Cognizance is "where the defendant (not being entitled to the distress or goods) acknowledges the taking, and insists that such taking was legal, not because he himself had a right to distrain on his own account, but because he made the distress by the command of another, who had a right to distrain."[4] On the same subject, it is further remarked as follows: "The plaintiff and defendant are considered as actors, the defendant in respect of his having made the distress (being a claim of right, and the avowry in the nature of a declaration), and the plaintiff in respect of his action."[5] "An avowry partakes of the nature of a declaration. It is the assertion of a claim for the return of the goods replevied."[6] "There

1 Simonds *v.* Parker, 1 Met. 544.

2 Pomeroy *v.* Trimper, 8 Allen, 398.

3 Bouv. Law Dict.

4 Ibid.

5 3 Steph. N. P. 2482; 1 Saun. 347, b, e.

6 Per Strong, J., Barr *v.* Hughes, 44 Penn. 517.

is a difference between a justification to an action of trespass, and an avowry or cognizance. In trespass, it is sufficient for the defendant to allege in his plea matter to excuse the trespass; but, in replevin, the avowant, or person making cognizance, is in the nature of a plaintiff, for he is to have a return; and, therefore, the avowry or cognizance, which is in the nature of a declaration, must show a good title *in omnibus*, and contain sufficient matter to entitle him to a return."[1]

§ 17. "By the common law, replevin lies only for the wrongful taking of chattels, and the general issue is *non cepit*,(*a*) which admits that the property . . . . is in the plaintiff, and denies only the taking. Of course, property in the defendant cannot be given in evidence, under this issue."[2] (*b*)

§ 18. The most frequent defence, in replevin, is a denial of

[1] Potter *v.* North, 1 Wms. Saun. 347 b, n. 3. See Bloomer *v.* Jubel, 8 Wend. 448; Southall *v.* Garner, 2 Leigh, 372.

[2] Per Metcalf, J., Miller *v.* Sleeper, 4 Cush. 370; Eaves *v.* King, 1 Har. 141; Vickery *v.* Sherburne, 2 App. 34; Wilson *v.* Royston, 2 Pike, 315; Trotter *v.* Taylor, 5 Blackf. 431; Galusha *v.* Butterfield, 2 Scam. 227; Harper *v.* Baker, 3 Mon. 421; Ely *v.* Ehlie, 3 Comst. 508, 1 Mass. 153; Rowland *v.* Mann, 6 Ired. 38; Carroll *v.* Harris, 19 Ark. 237.

(*a*) In replevin for the unlawful detainer of goods, *non cepit* is not a good plea, but presents an immaterial issue, and is bad on demurrer. The general issue in such a case is *non detinet*. Amos *v.* Sinnot, 4 Scam. 440; Walpole *v.* Smith, 4 Blackf. 304.

(*b*) It was early held, that replevin is not within the Mass. statute of 1783, ch. 42, § 7, which authorizes defendants, in *all civil actions* triable before a justice of the peace, with certain exceptions, to give a special justification or excuse in evidence under the general issue; but the pleadings, verdict, and judgment must pursue the rules of the common law. Mr. Chief Justice Parsons remarks: "Replevin is not a civil action, within a reasonable construction of this section. Cases within the section must be those where a verdict, finding the general issue, and a judgment on the verdict, will do justice. Now, in replevin, if the defendant has a legal justification or excuse for taking the chattels, his defence is directly repugnant to a denial of the taking, for he admits the caption complained of, and claims a return, with his damages. But, on the plea of *non cepit*, he cannot have a return, nor damages, if the issue joined on that plea be found for him. Such, therefore, is the legal effect of this plea, that, if the defendant has a good justification, he cannot have justice, if he plead the general issue; and in this action, where the defendant claimed damages for the injury done him by the plaintiff's cattle, had the verdict found the issue in favor of the defendant, no damages could have been assessed for him." Holmes *v.* Wood, 6 Mass. 13.

But the defendant in an action of replevin, since the Rev. Stats., ch. 113, § 28, directing that the general issue in replevin shall be joined on the plea of not guilty, and the stat. 1836, ch. 273, § 1, by which special pleas in bar are prohibited, may, under the general issue of not guilty, prove that the property of the goods alleged to be taken is in himself. Miller *v.* Sleeper, 4 Cush. 369; Scudder *v.* Worster, 11 ib. 573.

In Indiana, the defendant in an action of replevin commenced before a justice of the peace, and taken by appeal to the circuit court, may, by the statute of Indiana, prove property in himself or a stranger without pleading it. Lewis *v.* Masters, 6 Blackf. 243.

In Missouri, under the general issue, the defendant may prove that the plaintiff is not entitled to the property, and that the deed under which the property is claimed is void. Gibson *v.* Mozier, 9 Mis. 256.

The general issue — not guilty — in replevin, under Rev. Stat. of Michigan, as amended by the act of 1839, puts in issue every fact stated in the declaration necessary to sustain the action, and not the de-

the plaintiff's ownership of the goods replevied. This is often accompanied with a claim of title in the defendant himself, which may be sustained by any legal title.[1] (*a*) But, if the declaration allege title in the plaintiff, and the defendant plead any matter showing a special title or property in himself or a third person, or joint title either of himself or the plaintiff; he must still traverse the plaintiff's title. The issue must be joined on the latter, the former being mere inducement; and the defendant's special right or property will, as evidence, sustain him in his traverse,[2] (*b*) and entitle him to a return.[3] The *onus probandi* is upon the plaintiff to show an exclusive property, giving the right of possession.[4] (*c*)

[1] O'Connor *v.* Union, &c., 31 Ill. 230.

[2] Pringle *v.* Phillips, 1 Sandf. 292, 1 Gilm. 365; 3 Harr. 339; Phillips *v.* Townsend, 4 Mis. 101; Rogers *v.* Arnold, 12 Wend. 30.

[3] Ingraham *v.* Hammond, 1 Hill, 353.

[4] Anderson *v.* Talcott, 1 Gilm. 365; Chambers *v.* Hunt, 3 Harr. 339; M'Ilvaine *v.* Holland, 5 Harr. 226; Simcoke *v.* Frederick, 1 Smith, 64; Cullum *v.* Bevans, 6 Harr. & J. 469. But see Amos *v.* Sinnott, 4 Scam. 440.

tention only. Loomis *v.* Foster, 1 Mann. 165.

In Maine, a plea of the general issue, accompanied by a brief statement denying property in the plaintiff, does not admit the plaintiff's property, but leaves him to prove it. Dillingham *v.* Smith, 30 Maine, 370.

In Wisconsin, the plea of "not guilty" puts in issue the right of property or possession. Heeron *v.* Beckwith, 1 Wis. 17.

And the jury must find that issue for the plaintiff, in order to warrant a judgment of return or delivery. Ib.

This plea, in replevin in the *cepit* and *detinet*, puts in issue both the right of possession and the wrongful taking. Ford *v.* Ford, 3 Wis. 399.

In New York, an officer may give special matter in evidence, without notice, under the general issue. Coon *v.* Congden, 12 Wend. 496.

But, in general, property in the defendant cannot be shown without notice. Smith *v.* Snyder, 15 Wend. 324.

Under the plea of *cepit in alio loco*, the burden of proof is upon the plaintiff, as upon the general plea of *non cepit.* Williams *v.* Welch, 5 Wend. 290.

In Illinois, the plea of *non detinet* admits the right of property to be in the plaintiff, and only puts in issue the detention. Ingalls *v.* Bulkley, 15 Ill. 224.

In Ohio, under this plea, all the defences allowable under it and under a plea of property in the defendants are admissible. Coverlee *v.* Warner, 19 Ohio, 29.

In an action of replevin in the *cepit*, not following the Arkansas statute of replevin, where the defendant pleads *non cepit*, the plaintiff is bound to prove the wrongful taking. Town *v.* Farrel, 1 Eng. 260.

(*a*) In Massachusetts, an answer that the defendant was and is the owner of the property replevied, and denying the plaintiff's right to maintain the action, puts in issue the plaintiff's title. Chase *v.* Allen, 5 Allen, 599.

(*b*) A plea, however defective in this particular, may be cured by the plaintiff's replication of right of property. 1 Gilm. 365.

Notwithstanding the rule stated in the text, a plea that the goods and chattels in the declaration mentioned were not the property of the plaintiff, without showing whose they were, is bad. It should aver that they were the property of the defendant, or of some third person, naming him, and not the property of the plaintiff. Anstice *v.* Howes, 3 Denio, 244.

(*c*) Under a plea of *non cepit*, with brief statement that "the property was the property of the defendant and not the property of the plaintiff," the burden is on the plaintiff, under the statute of Maine, to prove property in himself. Otherwise, it seems, if the brief statement merely alleges property in the defendant. Cooper *v.* Bakeman, 32 Maine, 192; Green *v.* Dingley, 11 Shepl. 131.

§ 19. A plea that the goods taken were the property of a third person, naming him, and denying property in the plaintiff, is not an avowry, but at most a plea of property in a third person. The office of an avowry is not to deny property in the plaintiff, but to set up some right in the defendant to take the property without regard to the ownership.[1]

§ 20. A plea, or brief statement, filed by the defendant, alleging that the defendant was not in possession of the property, at the time the same was replevied, nor claimed to own it at that time, is bad in substance.[2]

§ 20 *a*. A plea of property in a stranger or in the defendant denies the plaintiff's property, and gives the plaintiff a right to begin.[3]

§ 21. An avowry must set forth the title and estate of the defendant. An omission to do so is not cured by the plaintiff's pleading over, and a verdict upon the issue.[4]

§ 22. Upon plea of property, a mere naked possessory right, without any title to a right of possession at the time of suing out the writ, is not sufficient. On such issue the plaintiff can never have judgment, unless the jury find the property to be in him as alleged in his declaration and maintained in his replication. It is not sufficient, that the inducement to the defendant's plea is not proved true.[5]

§ 23. A plea, that the goods had been distrained for taxes, is good either in abatement or in bar.[6] But a plea justifying under a writ is demurrable, unless it aver that the writ was in full force, the money unpaid, and the property taken in pursuance of its authority.[7]

§ 24. In Delaware, the short plea of *property in defendant* can be understood only as a claim of the entire property in the thing. It is to be construed as if drawn out in form. Even where, under an agreement, parties were changed, and the case went to trial on a plea of property; the court would not look beyond the legal meaning of the plea, into any supposed intention of the parties, to try the case on a general claim of property, not covered by the plea, nor allow an amendment of the plea after the jury was

[1] Simcoke *v.* Frederick, 1 Smith, 64.

[2] Sayward *v.* Warren, 27 Maine, 453.

[3] Gentry *v.* Borgis, 6 Blackf. 261.

[4] Harrison *v.* M'Intosh, 1 Johns. 380; Hopkins *v.* Hopkins, 10 ib. 369; Bain *v.* Clark, ib. 424.

[5] Chambers *v.* Hunt, 3 Harr. 239.

[6] Deshler *v.* Dodge, 16 How. 622.

[7] Dayton *v.* Fry, 2 ib. 525.

sworn. The court will, on motion, allow any short pleading to be drawn out.[1]

§ 25. As has been already suggested, a plea that the property of the goods is in a stranger, not in the plaintiff, is a good plea in bar or abatement, and justifies a return without an avowry,[2] (*a*) and without connecting the defendant with the title.[3] So a clause in a plea, averring that the property is in the succession of A, without naming the persons in succession, is good on demurrer, it being inducement to a traverse of the plaintiff's title.[4]

§ 26. It has been sometimes held, that a statute authorizing double pleading does not apply to replevin.[5] In Virginia it has been held, that the defendant cannot plead several pleas. But the error is cured by the statute of *jeofails*.[6] But, in general, several pleas are now allowed.[7] Thus a defendant may plead *non cepit* and property in himself or a stranger, and will not be compelled to elect by which plea he will abide.[8] Where both *non cepit* and property are pleaded, a verdict upon the former plea only will be set aside.[9]

§ 27. So, in Maryland, by usage, the defendant may plead *non cepit*, property in himself, and property in a stranger; and the plaintiff may join issue on the first, and traverse the second and third by affirming property in himself; on which traverses issues may be joined.[10] So, in Illinois, property may be pleaded generally, and also by a plea setting out the title, specially.[11]

§ 27 *a*. The forms of pleading in case of *seizure under legal process* require special notice. (See Chap. V.)

§ 28. A party justifying under an execution must show the judgment, execution, and levy.[12] And a plea, relying on the defendant's seizure of the goods as a constable, under an execution against a third person, should aver the property to be in such third person.[13] (*b*)

1 McIlvaine *v.* Holland, 5 Har. 10.

2 Harrison *v.* M'Intosh, 1 Johns. 380; Edwards *v.* McCurdy, 13 Ill. 496; Martin *v.* Ray, 1 Blackf. 291. See People *v.* New York, &c., 2 Wend. 644; Wright *v.* Williams, ib. 632.

3 Loomis *v.* Youla, 1 Min. 176.

4 Anderson *v.* Dunn, 19 Ark. 650.

5 People *v.* Supervisors, &c., 6 Wend. 505.

6 Vaiden *v.* Bell, 3 Rand. 448.

7 Martin *v.* Ray, 1 Blackf. 291.

8 Shuter *v.* Page, 11 Johns. 196; Dickson *v.* Mathers, 1 Hemp. 65; Simpson *v.* M'Farland, 18 Pick. 427.

9 Sprague *v.* Kneeland, 12 Wend. 161; Boynton *v.* Page, 13 ib. 425.

10 Smith *v.* Morgan, 8 Gill, 133.

11 O'Connor *v.* Union, &c., 31 Ill. 230.

12 Truitt *v.* Revill, 4 Harring. 71.

13 Gentry *v.* Borgis, 6 Blackf. 261.

(*a*) In Michigan, the defence, that the property belonged to a third party, and was taken by legal proceedings against him in replevin, is admissible under the general issue, without notice. Snook *v.* Davis 6 Mich. 156.

(*b*) In Ohio, under the plea of *non detinet*, the defendant may show that he held the goods as a constable, by virtue of certain executions, without special plea or notice. Oaks *v.* Wyatt, 10 Ohio, 344.

§ 29. Where the first plea was of property in one A; the second, that the defendant took the goods as constable by virtue of an execution against A, and that the goods belonged to A: held, the second plea might be rejected, on motion of the plaintiff, it being substantially the same with the first.[1] But where a sheriff pleaded, that he had taken the property under an attachment which was in force at the time of the taking, and that the property belonged to the defendant in the process, and also, as a distinct plea, that the property belonged to the defendant in the process; held, both pleas were good.[2]

§ 30. The defendant avowed, that he took the goods by virtue of a writ of attachment, delivered to him as sheriff, &c. The plaintiff replied, that he was not sheriff on the day of the issuing of the attachment, and at the time of the levy. Held, the plea was bad, in attempting to put in issue the fact, whether the defendant was sheriff on the day of the issuing of the attachment, which was wholly immaterial.[3]

§ 31. The defendant avowed the taking, &c., by virtue of an attachment against certain non-resident debtors; averred that said goods were the goods of said debtor, and not of the plaintiff; and prayed a return. The plaintiff, by his plea, denied the introductory part of the avowry, such as the writ, the proceedings of the sheriff, the levy, &c. Held, the plea was bad; the denial of property in the plaintiff being the material allegation in the avowry.[4]

§ 32. Where, in trespass, the defendant justifies as an officer under a writ of replevin, it is sufficient to allege in such plea, that the plaintiff in replevin gave bond, &c., before the chattels were delivered to him.[5] The plea must allege that a bond was given pursuant to the statute; and that the goods were not detained upon mesne process, &c., against the plaintiff in replevin.[6]

§ 33. The defendant justified the taking, as a distress for rent in arrear, in the form of a *plea in bar;* concluding with a prayer of judgment and for a return, the plea differing from a *cognizance* only in the commencement. The plaintiff treated the plea as a cognizance, and put in three pleas in answer thereto. The defendant moved to strike out the pleas of the plaintiff, on the

[1] Mann *v.* Perkins, 4 Blackf. 271.
[2] Scott *v.* Hughes, 9 B. Monr. 104.
[3] James *v.* Dunlap, 2 Scam. 481.
[4] Brown *v.* Bissett, 1 N. J. 267.
[5] Cushman *v.* Churchill, 7 Mass. 97.
[6] Moors *v.* Parker et al. 3 Mass. 310.

ground that but one answer could be put in to such plea, and that by way of *replication.* The motion was denied, because the defendant had committed the first fault. It was doubted, whether a justification thus pleaded would be bad on demurrer.[1]

§ 34. The subsequent recovery for rent due will not prejudice the defence of an avowant in replevin, if rent was due at the time of the distress made.[2]

§ 35. In replevin for a horse (in Indiana), it is a good plea that the defendant took him up as an estray, &c., at his residence, &c., and advertised him, &c., and that the plaintiff brought this action before ten days had expired, &c.[3]

§ 35 *a.* A plea of property is sustained by proof of purchase at a valid execution sale.[4]

§ 35 *b.* Where an insolvent debtor sells goods, the messenger may set up the title of the purchaser, after a demand, against an action of replevin brought by another purchaser from the insolvent.[5]

§ 36. The general replication *de injuria,* &c., to an avowry, is bad on special demurrer.[6]

§ 37. In Ohio, the law allows a double replication.[7]

§ 38. To a plea of property in a stranger; that the defendant entered the plaintiff's house at night and took the goods, is not a good answer.[8]

§ 39. The replication must state the time of a plaint relied upon with precision.[9]

§ 40. It is a good replication, that the defendant abused a distress, and thereby became a trespasser *ab initio.*[10]

§ 41. A plea of property avoids the injustice of the taking, and the replication must set forth such facts as will give the right of dominion and control even against the legal title.[11]

§ 42. On a plea of property in A and B, a replication that A and the plaintiff are the same is bad.[12]

§ 43. Where the defendant pleads *non detinet* and property, the want of a replication to the latter plea is not ground to reverse the judgment.[13]

1 McPherson *v.* Melhinch, 20 Wend. 671.
2 Lander *v.* Ware, 1 Strobh. 15.
3 Barnes *v.* Tannehill, 7 Blackf. 604.
4 O'Connor *v.* Union, &c. 31 Ill. 230.
5 Ropes *v.* Lane, 9 Allen, 502.
6 Hopkins *v.* Hopkins, 10 Johns. 369.
7 Cotter *v.* Doty, 5 Ham. 393.
8 Harrison *v.* M'Intosh, 1 Johns. 380.
9 Lisher *v.* Peirson, 2 Wend. 345.
10 Hopkins *v.* Hopkins, 10 Johns. 369.
11 Dixon *v.* Thacher, 14 Ark. 141.
12 Phillips *v.* Townsend, 4 Mis. 101.
13 Ferrell *v.* Humphrey, 12 Ohio, 112.

§ 44. Where the defendant avows the taking, under a vote of the town to raise money to be expended upon a highway, a replication, that the highway was never legally laid out, is sufficient.[1]

§ 45. One joint-owner of a sloop brought replevin against his co-owner. The defendant pleaded property in himself, and negatived the plaintiff's allegation of property, and the plaintiff replied, denying the defendant's claim of property, and affirming his own. Held, the plaintiff was bound to show that he was the owner, and entitled to exclusive possession; and, as the jury found that the parties were joint-owners, the defendant was entitled to a verdict.[2]

§ 46. Where property in the defendant was pleaded, and the plaintiff replied that the property was not in the defendant but in the plaintiff; held, the burden of proof was on the plaintiff, to show an exclusive right of possession; that the defendant, having traversed the title of the plaintiff, was not bound to prove the affirmative part or inducement of his plea, but might rebut the proof offered by the plaintiff; and might show that he and the plaintiff were joint-owners, in order to rebut the exclusive possession of the plaintiff.[3]

§ 47. Where a defendant in replevin pleads property in a third person, traversing the plaintiff's right; a replication, traversing the former right, and setting up a general property in another, and a special property in the plaintiff, is bad; 1, for not taking issue upon the traverse; 2, for traversing matter of inducement; 3, if such matter could be replied, for alleging the evidence of title, instead of the legal effect of the evidence. The plaintiff should have accepted the issue tendered, reaffirmed his title, and concluded to the country.[4]

§ 48. Plea of property in two of the plaintiffs and A. Replication, that the goods had been possessed jointly by the plaintiffs and A; that they had been put into a company composed of the plaintiffs and A, and converted into stock represented by scrip transferable by assignment; and that A transferred and assigned all his stock to the plaintiffs, or some of them, and the goods in suit are part of the goods so transferred and assigned. Held, this replication was bad in substance as well as form.[5]

§ 49. Plea of property in A, and that the defendant was entitled

[1] Stoddard *v.* Gilman, 22 Vt. 568.
[2] Chambers *v.* Hunt, 2 N. J. 552.
[3] Hunt *v.* Chambers, 1 N. J. 620.
[4] Prosser *v.* Woodward, 21 Wend. 205.
[5] Pattison *v.* Adams, Hill & Den. 426.

to possession, with a direct denial of the ownership of the plaintiffs. Replication, a sale of the right and title of A to the plaintiffs, and that the plaintiffs, at the time when, &c., were owners, and entitled to possession. Rejoinder, that the plaintiffs were not owners nor entitled to possession. Held, on demurrer, a material issue was raised by the rejoinder; that the plea alleged a superfluous fact (the right of possession in the defendant), and the replication was defective, in not showing the time of the alleged sale; but both these statements might be disregarded in view of the issue substantially raised.[1]

§ 50. Where the plaintiffs sued out a writ, in the (Michigan) Circuit Court, for detention of property in Hampton, in Saginaw county, and the defendants, taking issue on this in their notice, justified the detention in that county; held, the plaintiffs were not estopped from proving, that the property was taken under attachment at Hampton in Bay county.[2]

§ 51. A writ of replevin may be *amended* by adding to the description of the property sued for the words "of the value of twenty-five dollars."[3] So a writ of replevin, in an action pending in one county, which alleges the taking of the goods to have been in another, may be amended by alleging the taking to have been in the former, it being obviously a clerical error, and it being apparent that the real grievance complained of is a taking in the former.[4] So an officer, directed by a writ of replevin to replevy certain goods, provided the plaintiff should give a bond to the defendant, "with sufficient *surety* or sureties, in the sum of dollars, being twice the value of the said goods," took a bond, with two sureties, and served the writ. Held, under a statute allowing amendments in form or substance "of any process," the plaintiff might amend his writ by striking out the words "surety or," and the service was valid.[5]

§ 52. With regard to the *evidence* in the action of replevin, it is held, that, in general, a demand is not necessary to sustain replevin for an unlawful detainer.[6] As, upon plea of property,[7] or in an action against the purchaser from a bailee;[8] or a *bonâ fide* purchaser from a wrong-doer.[9] But, on the other hand, the rule

[1] Pattison *v.* Adams, Hill & Den. 426.

[2] Craig *v.* Grant, 6 Mich. 447.

[3] Jaques *v.* Sanderson, 8 Cush. 271. See Wheaton *v.* Catterlin, 23 Ind. 85.

[4] Judson *v.* Adams, 8 Cush. 556.

[5] Poyen *v.* McNeill, 10 Met. 291.

[6] Lewis *v.* Masters, 8 Blackf. 244.

[7] Seaver *v.* Dingley, 4 Greenl. 306.

[8] Galvin *v.* Bacon, 2 Fairf. 28.

[9] Conner *v.* Comstock, 17 Ind. 90.

is laid down, that, in replevin in the *detinet* alone, the same proof is required, as in trover and conversion.[1] That the owner of goods cannot maintain replevin against one lawfully in possession, without a previous demand and refusal, or acts amounting to a conversion; (*a*) which acts may consist in a repudiation of the right of the owner, or the exercise of a dominion inconsistent therewith. Thus A mortgaged oxen to B, to secure a note. After the note was due, B requested payment. A did not pay, but took the oxen into the woods for lumbering. B, without demand, brought replevin. Held, the action could not be maintained.[2]

§ 53. In replevin in the *detinet*, if necessary to prove a demand and refusal, the demand must be made either by the plaintiff or an authorized agent, showing such evidence of authority as would satisfy a prudent man. The question of authority is for the jury.[3]

§ 54. But, notwithstanding lawful possession, the owner may bring replevin without demand, if the possessor has exercised acts of ownership inconsistent with the plaintiff's title; as by attempting to sell, &c.[4] And it is held, that a demand is not often necessary in case of unlawful detainer. It may be necessary where the defendant has the goods by leave and license. But not where, without such demand, there is a wrongful possession; as where they were obtained by force, fraud, or otherwise, without the owner's consent.[5] (*b*)

[1] Ingalls *v.* Bulkley, 13 Ill. 315.
[2] Newman *v.* Jenne, 47 Maine, 520.
[3] Ingalls *v.* Bulkley, 13 Ill. 315.
[4] Prater *v.* Frazier, 6 Eng. 249.
[5] Lewis *v.* Masters, 8 Blackf. 244; acc. M'Neill *v.* Arnold, 17 Ark. 154.

(*a*) In Arkansas, the plaintiff, in replevin for detaining property, must adopt the statutory form of declaring, and allege a receipt of the property by the defendant from the plaintiff, or some other person, to be delivered to the plaintiff, and a refusal to redeliver after a special request or demand. Pirani *v.* Barden, 5 Pike, 81.

(*b*) In New York, where the action is in the *detinet*, a previous demand is not necessary; nor except as against an innocent holder. To charge the defendant with notice, it is necessary only to prove that the circumstances and facts known were such as ought to have led him to inquiry. Pringle *v.* Phillips, 5 Sandf. 157.

So in replevin in the *detinet* no demand is necessary, where the taking was unlawful. Stillman *v.* Squire, 1 Denio, 327.

Which may be proved in this form of action. Pringle *v.* Phillips, 5 Sandf. 157; 6 Hill, 613.

A, having wrongfully taken a note belonging to B from his possession, afterwards delivered it to C, an attorney at law, and B then brought replevin in the *detinet* against C, without demand. Held, B was entitled to recover, unless C held the note *bonâ fide* and for a lawful purpose, *e. g.* to collect; and the *onus* of proving this lay upon him. A receipt signed by C, and dated at or about the time of the delivery of the note to him, acknowledging that it was left by A for collection, is not *per se* evidence of the fact. Pierce *v.* Van Dyke, 6 Hill, 613.

In Mississippi no demand is essential to an action of replevin, by statute; but if, after suit brought, the defendant, whose original possession was lawful, tenders the

§ 55. The necessity of a demand is often brought in question in connection with the taking of goods by virtue of a writ or execution. (See Chap. V.)

§ 56. No demand is necessary, to sustain replevin against a constable who levies on goods in possession of the debtor.[1] Nor against a sheriff, to recover property illegally seized on execution.[2] So where goods, obtained by fraudulent purchase, are seized under a warrant of insolvency, as the property of the buyer; the seller may maintain replevin therefor against the messenger, without demand. In cases of a writ of attachment and a warrant, alike, "the taking, in order to be rightful, must be confined to the property of the party against whom the precept is issued; and the rights of third persons whom such party has deceived and defrauded cannot be impaired." [3]

§ 57. Goods of a company were attached, and A and B gave a receipt therefor to the officer; the company then conveyed all its personal property to A, B, C, D, E, and others, to be held by them as their security and indemnity against all existing and future liabilities, as indorsers, sureties, receiptors, or promisors for said company. The property was delivered to A and B for themselves and the others, with an understanding that the company should proceed in its business, and that, as the property should be wrought up and changed and new property acquired, the same should go into B's possession. The company proceeded as it had done before; D and E and others became sureties for some of the goods purchased for the company; and all the company's property, subsequently acquired, went into B's possession. A and B paid the judgment in the suit. C attached the property in B's possession, to secure a sum which he had paid for the company, and A and B replevied it. Held, that, if the conveyance to A and others was valid, yet A and B could not maintain replevin without a demand on the officer or creditor, and stating an account of the sum due to them pursuant to the (Mass.) Rev. Sts. ch. 90, §§ 78, 79.[4]

§ 58. The issuing of a writ of replevin to the sheriff is the commencement of the suit, and demand, if necessary, must

1 Bancroft *v.* Blizzard, 13 Ohio, 30.

2 Ledley *v.* Hays, 1 Cal. 160.

3 Bussing *v.* Rice, 2 Cush. 48; per Metcalf, J., 49.

4 Buck *v.* Ingersoll, 11 Met. 226.

property to the plaintiff, and delivers it with a proper plea; the action will be discharged. Deering *v.* Ford, 13 S. & M. 269.

be made before that time.[1] But where a writ of replevin is delivered to an officer, and he is directed before serving it to demand the goods, which he does on the same day it is made; the writ and service thereof are good. The court remark: "If the defendant had delivered the goods upon the demand, there would have been no necessity to serve the writ. It may be considered as purchased at any moment of the day of its date, which will most accord with the truth and justice of the case." [2]

§ 59. Where one claiming bales of cotton on board a ship, for which bills of lading have been signed, demands the bills of lading, it is a sufficient demand of the cotton.[3]

§ 60. A defendant in replevin, who succeeds at the trial, under the plea of *non detinet*, on the sole ground that the property should have been demanded before suit brought, is not entitled to judgment for a return, or for the value of the property.[4]

§ 61. Where *non cepit* only is pleaded, the right of property is not put in issue; it is only necessary that the plaintiff should prove that the defendant was in possession, at the place named, when the suit was commenced; though without such proof the action cannot be maintained.[5] But where property is set up in the answer, the burden of proof is on the plaintiff.[6]

§ 62. Evidence of forcible taking may be given, though the issue be formed exclusively on a plea of property.[7]

§ 63. The plaintiff, in proving property, may use an execution in which he is defendant, and under which the property was delivered to him on a forthcoming bond, without producing the judgment.[8]

§ 64. In replevin for negroes, the plaintiff introduced an agreement, under which he claimed title, derived from A, having first shown title in A. The defendant objected, that the plaintiff had not shown the identity of the negroes. Held, the evidence was admissible, although the identity was to be afterwards shown.[9]

§ 65. In replevin for a horse, the plaintiff may prove that the defendant gave a general order to his servants, before the commencement of the suit, not to deliver the horse to the plaintiff, as tending to prove an unlawful detention.[10]

1 Underwood *v.* Tatham, 1 Cart. 226.
2 Badger *v.* Phinney, 15 Mass. 359; per Putnam, J., 364.
3 Zachrisson *v.* Ahman, 2 Sandf. 68.
4 Pierce *v.* Van Dyke, 6 Hill, 613.
5 Sawyer *v.* Huff, 25 Maine, 464.
6 Turner *v.* Cool, 23 Ind. 57.
7 Moore *v.* Shenk, 3 Barr, 13.
8 Lynch *v.* Welsh, ib. 294.
9 Brooke *v.* Berry, 1 Gill, 153.
10 Johnson *v.* Howe, 2 Gilm. 342.

§ 66. In replevin for six cases of prints, containing a specified number of pieces, and a property bond given, reciting the tenor of the writ, the return was "replevied, summoned, and claim, property bond given." Held, evidence was not admissible to show that a less number of pieces was replevied.[1]

§ 67. In an action of replevin of goods attached by the defendant as an officer, on a writ against a stranger, such stranger is an incompetent witness, by reason of interest, to prove that the property was in himself.[2]

§ 68. Goods sold were attached as the property of the vendor, and replevied from the officer by the vendee, and the subscribing witness to the bill of sale became a surety on the replevin bond. For this reason, at the trial of the action of replevin, the officer objected to the introduction of such witness to prove the execution of the bill of sale, and the vendee thereupon offered to procure a new surety, but the officer would not consent. Held, the execution of the bill of sale might be proved by other evidence; and the vendee was not bound to procure the vendor as a witness for this purpose.[3]

§ 69. Where several actions of replevin are tried together before the same jury, by order of the judge, a surety in one of the bonds is a competent witness in the cases in which he is not interested, though the party offering him does not substitute a new surety in his place.[4]

§ 70. In replevin, the defendant justified as a deputy sheriff, alleging the property in the chattels to be in A. B. and C. D., and that he had attached a moiety as the property of C. D. The issue being on the property of the plaintiff, C. D. is a competent witness to prove the property in himself and A. B.[5]

§ 71. In reference to the form of the *verdict*, where there is an allegation of ownership, a general finding for the plaintiff settles this point in his favor.[6] So a verdict, "the jury find for the plaintiff and against the defendant," is sufficient in substance.[7] So, in Indiana, in a suit to recover personal property, where one defendant claims title and the other disclaims title and possession; a finding, "that the possession of the property mentioned in

[1] Knowles *v.* Lord, 4 Whart. 500.
[2] Pratt *v.* Stephenson, 16 Pick. 325.
[3] Haynes *v.* Rutter, 24 Pick. 242.
[4] Kimball *v.* Thompson, 4 Cush. 441.
[5] Page *v.* Weeks, 13 Mass. 199.
[6] Rowan *v.* Teague, 24 Ind. 304.
[7] Coil Waples, 1 Min. 134.

the complaint be given to the plaintiff," is equivalent to finding the property in the plaintiff, and that he is entitled to the possession.[1] So a verdict "for the defendants" settles the unlawful taking, that the defendant is entitled to possession, and a breach of the bond to prosecute the action with effect.[2] And it is held, that, if the answer admits a taking and detention, the verdict need not find it.[3] So in a suit for unlawful taking and detainer, and an answer of property in the defendant, property in one A, and a denial; a verdict "for the plaintiff; find the property in the horse to be in him, and that he is entitled to the possession," &c.; also finding the value; was held sufficient.[4]

§ 72. Where the defendant pleads property in himself and others, representatives of A, property in B, and also property in himself alone, and issues are joined; a verdict on the first plea alone, disregarding the other, is sufficient.[5] So where the defendant pleaded, 1st, *non cepit;* 2d, an avowry, averring the goods taken to be his property; to which the plaintiff replied, and took issue, &c.; and the jury found a general verdict for the plaintiff on the issue of *non cepit*, without any finding as to the other issue: judgment was given according to the verdict.[6] So the defendant pleaded, first, that the property was in himself and not in the plaintiff, and, secondly, that the property was in one W, and was taken by the defendant, a deputy sheriff, as his property, and traversed that the property was in the plaintiff. The latter replied that the property was in himself, and tendered an issue, which was joined. Held, upon these pleadings, the jury might find that a part of the property belonged to the plaintiff, and assess damages for its detention, and that the residue of the property did not belong to the plaintiff, and assess damages for the defendant. In such a case, the verdict is considered as returned upon an issue joined, because effect is given to it in the same manner as though the declaration had contained two counts for the respective articles, or the defendant had avowed for each respectively.[7]

§ 73. Where a verdict for the plaintiff does not assess the damages, nor the value of the property, the court may amend the verdict so far as to give nominal damages. The value need not be

1 Robertson *v.* Caldwell, 9 Ind. 514.
2 Wheat *v.* Catterlin, 23 Ind. 85.
3 Wilcoxon *v.* Annesley, 23 Ind. 285.
4 Clark *v.* Heck, 17 Ind. 281.
5 Ramsey *v.* Waters, 1 Mis. 406.
6 Thompson *v.* Button, 14 Johns. 84.
7 Williams *v.* Beede, 15 N. H. 483.

assessed at common law or under the statute of Minnesota, as the verdict does not require a return.[1]

§ 74. A verdict and judgment in replevin are conclusive only as between the parties and their privies.[2] Thus, although the defendant is at liberty to plead property in a third person, such third person is not bound by the verdict, unless he is in some way connected with the defendant.[3] And, between the parties, a verdict of *non cepit*, and judgment for return, are not conclusive upon the question of property. They only show, that for some cause the defendant is entitled to possession.[4]

§ 75. The subject of *damages* in replevin, awarded either by verdict or judgment, is very generally regulated by express statute. Independently of statute, inasmuch as the plaintiff is put in possession of the property by service of the writ, he of course cannot recover the value of it by way of damages. On the other hand, the defendant, as will be hereafter explained, if he prevail, has judgment for a return of the property, and therefore recovers damages merely for its seizure by the writ and subsequent detention. It is, however, sometimes stated, in general terms, that the plaintiff is entitled to damages for the caption and detention only; but the defendant to the value of the property.[5] (*a*)

[1] 1 Min. 134.
[2] Edwards *v.* McCurdy, 13 Ill. 496.
[3] Ibid.
[4] Moulton *v.* Smith, 32 Maine, 406.
[5] Messer *v.* Bailey, 11 Fost. 9.

(*a*) Upon this ground it was held, that defendants in replevin cannot stay execution by giving bond to review. The argument urged against it was, that in replevin damages were always a subject of minor consideration, and the goods were the main object of the suit; and the case was likened to that of real actions, where a review bond is never taken to stay execution for the costs. Luckfast *v.* Kane, 7 Mass. 500.

In Pennsylvania, upon plea of property, verdict for the plaintiff will be for the value and damages for detention. Warner *v.* Aughenbaugh, 15 S. & R. 9; McDonald *v.* Scaife, 11 Penn. 381.

In New York, in replevin by a party having a lien, the plaintiff, as in other actions of replevin, is entitled to a return, or, if a return cannot be had, to the value. Dows *v.* Rush, 28 Barb. 157.

In Ohio, in suits for specific property and damages for the detention, the statute provides that, if the plaintiff does not give a bond, the sheriff shall return the property to the defendant, and that the plaintiff shall then be entitled to such damages as are proper. Under this act, the plaintiff may have damages for the value, without amendment, upon his original petition, which asks only damages for the detention. Pugh *v.* Calloway, 10 Ohio (N. S.), 488.

In Missouri, in actions for the recovery of specific property, the plaintiff, at his option, may take the property or its value; and, if slaves be the subject of the suit, and after its commencement they die in the defendant's possession, without fault or negligence on his part, he will not be liable therefor; but, if the death be occasioned by his fault, or the slaves be sold by him to another, the rule may be different. Pope *v.* Jenkins, 30 Mis. 528.

In Mississippi, after the jury have rendered a verdict for the plaintiff, and assessed the entire value of the property, and have been discharged; it is improper and erroneous to recall them on the next day, for the purpose of assessing the value of

§ 76. Independently of statutory regulation, "damages must be assessed (for the defendant) according to the magnitude of the injury, agreeably to the rule of the common law." [1] (*a*)

[1] Per Parsons, C. J., Bruce *v.* Learned, 4 Mass. 616.

the separate articles replevied. Dearing *v.* Ford, 13 S. & M. 269.

The value of each distinct article must be assessed in the verdict; a verdict, valid in other respects, may be remanded to the inferior court, with order to award a writ of inquiry, to ascertain such separate values. Duane *v.* Hilzheim, 13 S. & M. 336.

In Delaware, in replevin in the *detinuit*, the plaintiff can recover damages for the detention only until replevin, though he should prove the property to be still in the defendant's possession. Truitt *v.* Revill, 4 Harr. 71.

In Illinois, the plaintiff may recover the value of the use of the property while it is detained. But not for the natural depreciation in value of a horse while in the possession of the defendant. But the defendant is bound to take reasonable care of the property, and is liable for any default in performing that duty. Odell *v.* Hole, 25 Ill. 204.

In an action of replevin before a justice of the peace, the jury rendered a verdict for the plaintiff for six cents damages for the detention, and found the value of the property to be fifteen dollars. The justice rendered judgment for delivery to the plaintiff, and for six cents damages with costs. Held, the value of the property as found by the jury constituted a part of the recovery, as if the plaintiff had taken judgment for the value instead of a return; and, the whole recovery having been for more than fifteen dollars, an appeal would lie to the Circuit Court. Inman *v.* Gower, 3 Chand. 162.

Where the property has been replevied, and delivered to the plaintiff, he cannot elect to take judgment for the value. Rockwell *v.* Saunders, 19 Barb. 473.

In replevin against a sheriff for flour taken by him on execution, on his electing to take judgment for its value, he will be limited to the value at the commencement of the suit, with interest from that time; although it appear that flour, between that period and the trial, was worth about double its then market price. He cannot add, as damages, the difference between the value at the replevin and the highest subsequent market value up to the time of the trial. Suydam *v.* Jenkins, 3 Sandf. 614.

(*a*) In Massachusetts, it was held, under an early statute, that, if the plaintiff be nonsuited, the defendant shall recover six per cent. damages on the penal sum of the bond, as well where the taking was on mesne process as on execution. The court remark: "If the plaintiff attaching fails to support his action, the officer is then accountable to the defendant in that action whose goods he had attached, . . . and is to pay over to him the six per cent. damages recovered and redeliver to him the goods. In the other case (that of an execution), the officer (as the case may be) is accountable to both the creditor and debtor; to the creditor, to the amount of his judgment, and to the debtor, for what may remain in his (the officer's) hands, after satisfying the creditor. The officer is merely a trustee, and, after indemnifying himself, is accountable over. The plaintiff in replevin, who fails to support his action, and is therefore proved to be a wrong-doer, has nothing to do with the merits of the claim of the attaching creditor. And the damage to the real owner of the goods is precisely the same in cases of attachment as in those of taking on execution." Pike *v.* Huckins, 1 Mass. 421.

Where goods not held under legal process are replevied, and the plaintiff becomes nonsuit, and a return is awarded, the defendant recovers for damages interest at six per cent. on the value of the goods, from service of the writ to the entry of judgment, although the statute would seem to provide that measure of damages only in the two cases where the action is not entered, and where an issue is tried. Wood *v.* Braynard, 9 Pick. 322.

In a subsequent case it was decided, that the statute of replevins (1789, ch. 26) had prescribed six per cent. on the bond as the measure of damages, when the plaintiff shall fail to prosecute his suit, and when goods taken in execution are unlawfully replevied; in all other cases his damages are left to be assessed according to the magnitude of the injury. The court remarked: "It may be within the equity of this last case (that of an execution) if the plaintiff shall have unlawfully replevied goods duly attached, . . . if execution has been thereby delayed." Bruce *v.* Learned, 4 Mass. 614; per Parsons, C. J., ib. 616.

After a debtor's goods were seized on a writ of attachment, and also on an execution, he was discharged under the United

§ 77. The jury may find one part of the property to belong to the plaintiff, and the other part to the defendant.[1] And where issue

[1] O'Keefe *v.* Kellogg, 15 Ill. 347; Philips *v.* Harriss, 3 J. J. Mar. 121.

States bankrupt law of 1841. The goods were replevied, and the defendant in replevin obtained judgment for a return, and brought a suit on the bond. Held, he was entitled to recover, as damages, the full value of the goods, unless shown to be unnecessary to satisfy the execution. Parker *v.* Simonds, 8 Met. 205.

In another case, turning upon the validity and effect of a sale, it was held, that the defendant was entitled to recover as damages the value of the property replevied, with interest from the service of the writ of replevin to the rendition of judgment, no special damage being shown; and that the valuation of the oil in the writ was *primâ facie* evidence of the true value. The court remark: "The case is not within the letter nor the equity of the statute which gives a per cent. on the penalty of the bond, and requires that such penalty be given for double the value of the goods; that applies to cases where the process of law has been delayed by the replevin." Barnes *v.* Bartlett, 15 Pick. 71; per Shaw, C. J., 78.

In New Hampshire, the defendant pleaded property in B, that B was indebted to A, and that he attached the property. The plaintiff replied, 1, property in himself; 2, that B was not indebted to A; 3, that the defendant did not attach the property on a writ in favor of A against B, and issues were joined. Held, 1, the only material issue was upon the plaintiff's property; 2, that the allegations, that the goods were the property of B, that B owed A, and that the defendant attached the goods on A's writ, were merely inducement, and not traversable; and that the issues joined on those matters were immaterial; 3, that on these pleadings, if the issues were found in his favor, the defendant was at common law entitled to judgment for a return, without an avowry or conusance, or any suggestion of that nature; 4, that in this state he was entitled to a judgment for damages instead of a return; and, 5, that those damages were not necessarily limited to the value of the property and interest. Dickinson *v.* Lovell, 35 N. H. 9.

In Maine, in case of replevin of goods taken by a collector of taxes, if judgment is rendered for the defendant in replevin, he is entitled to six per cent. damages on the replevin bond. Dore *v.* Hight, 3 Shep. 20.

Where the value is stated in the writ, the plaintiff cannot except that the jury should have found the value, if he did not request instructions to that effect. Heald *v.* Cushman, 30 Maine, 461.

In an action of replevin, submitted on questions of law, without any stipulation as to the allowance of damages, the court, at another term, after judgment of nonsuit and return, has no power to assess the defendant's damages, or send the question to a jury. Dillingham *v.* Smith, 32 Maine, 182.

In New York, in an early case, it was held, that, where the defendant makes avowry, justification, or cognizance, if found for him, or if the plaintiff be nonsuited, or otherwise barred, the defendant is entitled to damages under the act, sess. 36, c. 96, § 4 (1 N. R. L. 344), and the decrease in value from the time of the replevin, and interest on their entire value, are a proper measure of damages. Rowley *v.* Gibbs, 14 Johns. 385.

An inquisition, assessing the damages of a defendant after discontinuance of the suit, will not be set aside, because the damages are excessive, where the proceeding by the plaintiff is vexatious, if the rules of law have been observed by the jury. And a jury, in such case, may give smart money. Cable *v.* Dakin, 20 Wend. 172.

When, in an action to recover possession, the property has been delivered to the plaintiff, and the defendant claims a return, he is not entitled to judgment for the value or the return, as he shall elect; but the jury should be instructed to find for the defendant generally, and to assess the value of the property, together with the damages for the taking and withholding thereof. It is the right of the plaintiff to have such damages assessed, and judgment should be accordingly. He also has the right to return the property instead of paying its value, which can only be required of him in case a return cannot be had. If the defendant will waive the damages for taking and withholding, judgment may be entered for him for a return of the property if a return can be had; and, if not, then that the defendant recover the value as assessed by the jury. Glann *v.* Younglove, 27 Barb. 480.

When the defendant who recovers in replevin elects to take judgment for the value of the goods, he is en-

is joined upon the plaintiff's property, and the jury find the property of part in the plaintiff and of part not; each party is entitled

titled to damages equally as if he had elected to have a return. The value is that at the time of the replevin, not at the time when he makes his election. If such value be an insufficient redress, the deficiency may be made good in the estimate of damages. The measure of damages is the same as in trover. Suydam *v.* Jenkins, 3 Sandf. 614.

A judgment for the value of the property only, with damages and costs, though it is not in the alternative form prescribed by Code, § 277, is not void, but is valid until reversed or amended. Gallarati *v.* Orser, 4 Bosw. 94.

In Pennsylvania, the jury are not confined, in assessing damages, to interest on the value of the property, but may give more, if necessary to compensate the defendant. McCabe *v.* Morehead, 1 W. & S. 513.

The defendant, on a plea of property, is not entitled to specific damages for an interruption of business. Ib.

Where goods are delivered to the plaintiff on a claim of property, and the plea of property is found for the defendant; the damages for detention consist of the interest on the value of the goods when taken, from the time of the taking until judgment. But if the writ was sued out fraudulently, and without color of right, the jury may give exemplary damages, as in case of a wanton and malicious trespass. Ib.

A plaintiff in replevin recovered judgment against the defendant, who had retained the goods and given bond, and issued his execution; whereupon it was agreed that the goods should be appraised and taken by the plaintiff at the appraisement. The valuation was not thus made, and the goods were sold by the sheriff for an amount much below that of an appraisal by persons selected by the defendant alone, who then applied to the court for an issue, that he might have credit for the difference on the replevin judgment. On trial of an issue awarded, to ascertain what *credit* he was entitled to, if any; held, it was incompetent for the defendant to offer evidence of the value as estimated by his own appraisers, or proved by the witnesses in the replevin suit, or the prices obtained by the officer, this evidence not showing any *credit* upon the judgment, but only a claim for damages for breach of agreement; not a subject of set-off, but only of an action for damages. Kennedy *v.* Kennedy, 41 Penn. 185. The court remarked, "Such unsuccessful attempts to control the final process of the court, and to pay a judgment by damages for breach of an alleged contract, uncertain in its character, and in one respect practically impossible, should be frowned upon by the courts. Their tendency is to foster litigation, and to make it interminable." Per Read, J., ib. 187.

In Delaware, judgment on a discontinuance in replevin is for costs only, and not for a return. McIlvaine *v.* Holland, 5 Harring. 226.

In Michigan, where in the court below there was no evidence submitted as to the value of the property, and the court awarded more than nominal damages; the judgment was held erroneous. Phenix *v.* Clark, 2 Mich. 327.

Under the Michigan statutes on replevin (Rev. Sts. 523), the circuit court has no power, in an action brought before it from a justices' court, to impanel a jury to assess the value of the property. The statute (Rev. Sts. 525, § 61) applies only to actions originally brought in that court. People *v.* Judges, &c. 1 Doug. 302.

The court, however, have power, it seems, under § 170 and § 135 of the justices' act of 1841 (Laws 1841, p. 81) to award a restitution. Ib.

But the motion is too late if made at a term subsequent to the one in which the judgment brought from the justices' court was reversed, the parties then being out of court. Ib.

In Illinois, where there is a judgment of *retorno*, the value of the use of the property during detention is the true measure of damages, not speculative or expected profits or smart money. Damages may be assessed by the court, or a jury may be called. Butler *v.* Mehrling, 15 Ill. 488.

The statute of Illinois concerning practice has no reference to the assessment of damages in the action of replevin, but applies to a suit on the bond. Campbell *v.* Head, 13 Ill. 122.

In Missouri, on a nonsuit, the defendant is entitled to the same judgment and damages as if he had recovered a verdict. Smith *v.* Winston, 10 Mis. 299.

If the plaintiff fails to prosecute his suit with effect, the assessment of damages is imperative, and may be made by the court if neither party objects. Reed *v.* Wilson, 13 Mis. 28.

Where a slave has been detained by virtue of a writ of replevin, a judgment for his value, in damages, for the defendant,

to damages and costs.[1] Where the verdict is for both parties; for one, damages and costs, as to that portion upon which he main-

[1] Powell *v.* Hinsdale, 5 Mass. 343.

would be erroneous. Lawrence *v.* Lawrence, 24 Mis. 269.

A verdict for the defendant in an action for possession, where the plaintiff receives the property and gives bond, should regularly assess both the value and the damages. Hohenthal *v.* Watson, 28 Mis. 360.

A defendant having only a special interest recovers the full value of the property. Fallon *v.* Manning, 35 Mis. 27.

In Minnesota, in an action for the return of property, the respondent cannot take more damages for the detention than he claims by his answer; if he desires judgment for the value of the goods, in addition to damages, in case the goods are not returned, he should have the jury assess the value. Eaton *v.* Caldwell, 3 Min. 134.

The respondent claimed fifty dollars damages; the jury found for the respondent with seventy-five dollars damages. Held, that the verdict would authorize a judgment for a return and fifty dollars, if he remitted the excess; but that it would not authorize a judgment for a return, or seventy-five dollars, as the value of the goods. Ib.

In Indiana, the defendant has the right, under Rev. Sts. 1843, § 182, p. 702, to show title, and to have judgment in his favor, and damages assessed for the detention, by writ of inquiry. Mikesill *v.* Chaney, 6 Ind. 52.

Where a plaintiff, after closing his evidence, suffers a nonsuit, the refusal of such judgment by the court, and the entry of a judgment in favor of the defendant for costs only, is error. Ib.

If the jury return a general verdict for the defendant, they may be remanded by the court, with instructions to find the value of the property, and the damages for its detention. Noble *v.* Epperly, 6 Ind. 468.

The damages in such case must depend on the nature of the defendant's interest, whether that of a bailee or absolute owner, the time he has been deprived of it, the character of the property, &c. Ib.

In Tennessee, where A sued B in replevin, under the Tennessee act of 1846, ch. 65, for several slaves, and a verdict and judgment were rendered for their aggregate value; held erroneous; that, if all the property replevied was alike in its character, and not possessed of a distinct separate quality, and was so described in the proceedings, then a general assessment of value ought to be made; but if the articles were distinct and separate, having no identity of character, then the value of each should be assessed. And this, in order that the party should have his right to deliver what he could, and to pay for that which he could not. Pickett *v.* Bridges, 10 Humph. 171.

The Tennessee act of 1846, ch. 65, passed to regulate the proceedings in replevin, directs that in case the plaintiff, who has seized the property by his writ, and taken it out of the possession of the defendant, shall enter a *nolle prosequi*, or otherwise fail in his suit without returning the property, the defendant may have a jury impanelled to inquire of the value and damages for the detention. The value and damages must be assessed separately, that the plaintiff may know what damages he is to pay, if he returns the property. Nashville, &c. *v.* Alexander, 10 Humph. 378.

In replevin, under the Mississippi statute of 1842, by the owner of a life-estate against one who had taken possession at the instance of the remainder-man, a verdict for the plaintiff for the full value of the property or its restoration to him, with damages for detention, is erroneous; the verdict should have been for the value of the plaintiff's interest. Lloyd *v.* Goodwin, 12 S. & M. 223.

Objection to excess of damages is not sustainable as to the action of replevin, under the statute (Hutch. Code, 818). White *v.* Graves, 24 Miss. 166.

In South Carolina, the plaintiff may recover vindictive damages as in trespass. But if such damages are claimed, or tortious proceedings are charged, the matter must be pleaded specially. Lander *v.* Ware, 1 Strobh. 15.

In North Carolina, where replevin is brought to recover possession of a slave, in which an estate for the life of another is claimed, and the tenant for life dies pending the action, the plaintiff is only entitled to recover the value of the life-estate, and damages for the detention. Barham *v.* Massey, 5 Ired. 152.

By chapter 191, Revised Statutes of North Carolina, where the plaintiff in replevin is nonsuited, the defendant can have judgment for the thing replevied and costs, but

tained his replevin; and for the other, for the return of the property improperly taken by the writ, damages for its detention, and costs: the judgment must follow the verdict, and the costs must be apportioned according to equity.[1]

§ 78. Replevin for a horse. Pleas, 1st, that the defendant had not taken or detained the property; 2d, property in a stranger; 3d, property in the defendant. The plaintiff joined issue on the first plea, and replied to the second and third, property in himself. Verdict: "We find the property to be in the plaintiff," but not that the horse had been taken or detained by the defendant. Judgment against the defendant for costs. Held, erroneous.[2]

§ 79. Where, besides *non cepit*, the defendant pleads property in a third person, and prays a return, the jury must pass upon all the issues; and where in such case it appeared from the *record* brought up by a writ of error, that the jury had passed only upon the plea of *non cepit*, finding a verdict for the plaintiff, the judgment was reversed, although, from the bill of exceptions attached to the record, it appeared that all the issues were found for the plaintiff.[3]

§ 80. A judgment for the plaintiff, where the defendant has elected to give bond and retain possession, should be entered against both principal and surety.[4]

§ 81. In an action of replevin, under the Mississippi statute of 1842, a judgment in favor of the plaintiff for so much money is erroneous; it should be in the alternative; for the property, if to be had; if not, then for its value.[5]

§ 82. Where there are several avowries, all presenting substantially the same defence, upon some of which issues of law are joined, and upon others issues of fact, and the defendant succeeds upon the issues of law, and the judgment is rendered upon the whole record in his favor, leaving the issues of fact undisposed of; the judgment will not, for such omission, be reversed, where it is manifest that, if they had been tried and found for the plaintiff, the court would have given judgment for the defendant, *non obstante veredicto*.[6]

[1] Poor *v.* Woodburn, 25 Vt. 234.
[2] Huff *v.* Gilbert, 4 Blackf. 19.
[3] Boynton *v.* Page, 18 Wend. 425.
[4] Huff *v.* Gilbert, 4 Blackf. 19.
[5] Anderson *v.* Tysen, 6 Sm. & M. 244.
[6] Jack *v.* Martin, 14 Wend. 507.

not for damages, to be assessed by a jury. At common law, the judgment was for the return. Pannell *v.* Hampton, 10 Ired. 463. As to the practice in Kentucky, see Yantes *v.* Burditt, 2 Dana, 254.

§ 83. Where the defendants recover a judgment for the value, and collect it, by operation of law the title passes to the plaintiff; and, in trespass brought by him against the defendants for taking and carrying away the property, the defendants will be estopped from disputing his title. After having recovered the property, or its value, on the ground that the sheriff has delivered it to the plaintiff, the defendants in replevin cannot defeat an action of trespass brought against them by the latter, for taking and carrying away the property, by impeaching the return upon which they have so recovered.[1]

§ 84. The most striking peculiarities connected with the action of replevin, are the judgment in favor of the defendant, if he prevail in the suit, for a *return* of the property replevied, (*a*) and the various and successive processes of execution for enforcing such judgment. The ancient course of proceeding upon these points, founded upon St. Westminster 2d (13 Edw. I.), ch. 2, and Sts. 7 Hen. VIII., ch. 4, § 3, and 21 Hen. VIII., ch. 19, § 3, which, though for the most part practically obsolete, either by express statute or local usage, may still be regarded as part of the law of the land, is thus described by a writer of high authority: "The defendant accordingly sued out upon the judgment a *retorno habendo*, and an inquiry of damages, generally in the same writ, or sometimes in separate writs, and upon the return thereof by the sheriff, final judgment was entered up for the defendant to recover as well the damages and costs assessed by the jury, as the costs of increase assessed by the court; and the defendant might enforce the payment of them by a *capias ad satisfaciendum* or *fieri facias*. This was the regular form of the judgment; but it sometimes happened that the plaintiff, after the cattle, &c., were delivered to him by virtue of the replevin, secreted, or otherwise disposed of them, so that the sheriff could not restore them to the defendant according to the exigence of the writ. In that case, the sheriff returned an *averia elongata*, that the cattle, &c., were *eloigned*, as it is called, that is, were conveyed to places unknown to him, so that it was not in his power to obey the writ. Upon this return, it was usual to award another writ to the sheriff, directing him to take

[1] Russell *v.* Gray, 11 Barb. 541.

(*a*) In replevin for several articles, if, on an issue as to the plaintiff's property, he prove himself entitled to a part, the defendant has a right to a return of the others, and to damages for the taking of them. Wright *v.* Matthews, 2 Blackf. 187.

other cattle of the plaintiff, &c., of equal value with those eloigned, and deliver them to the defendant, to be by him detained irreplevisable, until such time as the cattle first taken should be forthcoming; this was called a *capias in withernam*. If the plaintiff had no cattle, &c., which could be so taken, the sheriff returned *nihil* to that writ, and the defendant thereupon sued out a *scire facias* against the pledges, who had undertaken to the sheriff, in pursuance of the statute Westminster 2d, that the cattle, &c., should be returned to the defendant, to show cause why their cattle, &c., to the value of the cattle, &c., eloigned, should not be delivered to the defendant. And if no cause was shown, a writ issued to take their cattle, &c.; but if they had none, the sheriff returned *nihil* also to that writ, and then a *scire facias* was awarded against the sheriff himself, that he render to the defendant as many cattle. But these proceedings did not at all prevent the defendant from recovering his damages and costs under the statutes of Hen. VIII. However, a less circuitous practice has been adopted in modern times. For now, upon the return of an *elongata* to the writ of *retorno habendo*, it is no longer necessary to sue out a *capias in withernam* against the plaintiff, or a *scire facias* against the pledges or sheriff, but the defendant, in case the sheriff has taken no pledges at all, or such as are insufficient, may bring an action upon the case against him."[1] (*a*)

§ 85. Upon the plea of *non cepit* or *non detinet*, no judgment *de retorno habendo* can be rendered. To authorize such judgment, the defendant must become *actor*, and assert property in himself.[2] The plea of *non cepit* only puts in issue the taking.[3]

§ 86. And where a defendant pleaded *non cepit*, and also avowed and justified, and issues were taken on both pleas, and a verdict given for the defendant, with judgment for restitution; held, as he was clearly not entitled to that judgment upon the

[1] Mounson *v.* Redshaw, 1 Wms. Saun. 195, n. 3. See Gibbs *v.* Bull, 18 Johns. 435.

[2] Bonner *v.* Coleman, 3 B. Mon. 464; People *v.* Niagara, 4 Wend. 217; Johnson *v.* Howe, 2 Gilm. 342. See Price *v.* Van Dyke, 6 Hill, 613; Montgomery *v.* Black, 4 Har. & McH. 391.

[3] Vose *v.* Hart, 12 Ill. 378.

(*a*) A writ of replevin is made returnable by statute in South Carolina, and, if a sheriff makes return of *elongata*, a *withernam* may issue. The court will not decide on motion on the claim of a third person, not a privy, to property taken by a *withernam*. M'Colgan *v.* Huston, 2 N. & M. 444.

No evidence will be admitted, in Pennsylvania, to contradict the sheriff's return of *elongatur*, after judgment *de retorno habendo* in replevin. Phillips *v.* Hyde, 1 Dall. 439.

plea of *non cepit*, and as there was nothing in the record to show that the trial was confined to the other issue, or that the verdict was found on that alone, judgment must be reversed.[1] But, in Maine, if a verdict of *non cepit* is rendered on a plea of *non cepit* filed with a brief statement, the defendant is entitled to a return.[2] So, in Massachusetts, the general issue pleaded, with notice, pursuant to St. 1836, ch. 273, of the matter intended to be given in evidence, is equivalent to an avowry, or plea of property in another, at common law, with a suggestion for a return; and judgment for a return may be awarded, if the defendant prevails.[3] So, in Wisconsin, by statute, a defendant is entitled, under the plea of *non detinet*, to a return of the property and damages.[4] And, in New York, *it seems*, a defendant, on a plea of *non detinet*, will be entitled to a return, where the jury find that the plaintiff has no property in the goods.[5]

§ 87. With the exception already stated in regard to the plea of *non cepit* or *non detinet*, the precise manner in which the defendant prevails in the suit seems to be immaterial, as affecting his right to a return of the property. (*a*) It is held, generally, that, if the writ be returned "executed," and the defendant succeeds in the action, a judgment *de retorno* is proper.[6] Thus the plaintiff is liable for a return, though, by order of court, the proceedings subsequent to the writ are set aside.[7] So, where a plaintiff discontinues his suit, the necessary result must be a liability for the property and damages for detention; and the defendant may elect to have a return and his damages.[8] So, after dismissal of an action of replevin for want of a sufficient bond, a judge of the (Mass.) Superior Court has jurisdiction to order judgment for a return, although no answer has been filed; and such order should be passed, upon a motion made at the same term when the action is dismissed, with an averment and offer of proof that the defendant has a special property in the goods.[9] So, where the plaintiff enters a *nol. pros.* upon *cognizance* and claim of property, there must be judgment for return, unless the judgment

1 Gaines *v.* Tibbs, 6 Dana, 143.
2 Moulton *v.* Bird, 31 Maine, 296.
3 Hoffman *v.* Noble, 6 Met. 68.
4 Saunderson *v.* Lace, 1 Chand. 231.
5 McKnight *v.* Dunlop, 4 Barb. 36.
6 Stephens *v.* Frazier, 12 B. Mon. 250.
7 Smith *v.* Snyder, 15 Wend. 324.
8 Saunderson *v.* Lace, 1 Chand. 231.
9 Lowe *v.* Brigham, 3 Allen, 429.

(*a*) It is held, that the answer need not claim a return. Conner *v.* Comstock, 17 Ind. 90; Matlock *v.* Straughn, 21 ib 128.

shows the defendant is not entitled to it. And denial of the plaintiff, by his replication, that the defendant had a right to the property, does not affect his right to judgment for it.[1] So, where a demurrer is overruled, to a plea which is good, alleging property in a stranger, and the jury find damages for the detention, judgment *de retorno habendo* and for the damages assessed is proper.[2] So judgment *de retorno habendo* is proper, where the defendant pleads property in a stranger, and the issue is found for him.[3] And an avowry, or suggestion in the nature of an avowry, by the defendant, is not necessary to authorize a judgment of return, where the writ is abated or set aside on account of an irregularity or defect in the replevin process.[4] So if a debtor, whose goods are attached and replevied, takes advantage of the insolvent law, and the defendant in replevin obtains a verdict; he will still be entitled to judgment for a return, and will thereupon be bound to deliver over the property to the assignee for the benefit of creditors.[5] So there shall be a return, though the defendant has gone into insolvency pending the action, unless the assignee becomes a party.[6] So, after a verdict for the defendant in replevin against an attaching officer, in which the question of property in the plaintiff was tried, and a verdict found against him; judgment for a return will be ordered, although since the verdict the attachment has been dissolved.[7] So, where a writ of replevin for goods, attached as the property of another person, is abated for want of the requisite bond, a judgment for return to the officer is correct.[8] And to authorize a judgment *de retorno habendo* in favor of the sheriff, it is sufficient that he allege the taking by *fi. fa.* against the plaintiff, and that the property belonged to the defendant, subject to the writ, and that the jury so found.[9] So, in replevin against two defendants, A and B, A avowed and justified, under an execution levied by him as deputy sheriff; B made cognizance as plaintiff in the same execution. A having died before the trial, B filed a new avowry, justifying the taking by himself alone, as both had justified before, on which the plaintiff took issue, and judgment was given for B, awarding restitution. Held, the judgment was correct.[10]

1 Kerley *v.* Hume, 3 Mon. 181.
2 Tuley *v.* Mauzey, 4 B. Mon. 5.
3 Ibid.
4 Fleet *v.* Lockwood, 17 Conn. 233.
5 Kimball *v.* Thompson, 4 Cush. 441.
6 Hallett *v.* Fowler, 10 Allen, 36.
7 Dawson *v.* Wetherbee, 2 Allen, 461.
8 Fleet *v.* Lockwood, 17 Conn. 233.
9 Stephens *v.* Frazier, 2 B. Mon. 250.
10 Gaines *v.* Tibbs, 6 Dana, 143.

§ 88. But the general rule above stated is subject to many qualifications and exceptions. In New Hampshire, it has been held that a judgment for the defendant must be for the value of the chattels in damages, and not for a return.[1] So, if the action is defeated solely by reason of its being prematurely brought, judgment for a return will not be ordered.[2] So an officer, against whom replevin is brought, has no right to a judgment for the return of property, which he has no right to sell.[3] And where the return upon the writ shows a restoration of the property, a judgment for return is erroneous, notwithstanding a *remittitur* of the damages.[4] So where chattels, mortgaged by the defendant to the plaintiff, but without a proper record, were attached as the defendant's; in replevin, held, the plaintiff was not entitled to judgment, because there was no wrongful taking or detention by the defendant, but the defendant was not entitled to a return, because as against him the plaintiff had a right to the chattels, although the mortgage was not recorded, and the defendant was not accountable for them to the officer or the creditor.[5] So, in Indiana, there shall be no return, unless it be proved that the property was delivered to the plaintiff, or unless the value is assessed.[6]

§ 89. An action of tort against an officer, for taking property from the plaintiff by a writ of replevin, in which the bond was defective, is not defeated, by proof that the plaintiff in replevin became nonsuit, and the present plaintiff had judgment therein for damages and a return, if that judgment remains unsatified, and the goods have not been returned.[7]

§ 90. If an action of replevin is dismissed for informality in the bond, and judgment given for a return, and the plaintiff returns the property to the place from whence he first took it; he may afterwards bring another action of replevin against the same defendant, although the defendant has not taken out a writ of return, nor actually received the property, under the judgment in the first action.[8]

§ 91. Wherever the defendant in a replevin suit, under the pleadings, may try the title, and, in case he succeeds, have a return, he is bound to try the title, and take judgment for a

[1] Bell *v.* Bartlett, 7 N. H. 178.
[2] Martin *v.* Bayley, 1 Allen, 381.
[3] Saffell *v.* Wash, 4 B. Mon. 92.
[4] Harrod *v.* Hill, 2 Dana, 165.
[5] Simpson *v.* McFarland, 18 Pick. 427.
[6] Conner *v.* Comstock, 17 Ind. 90.
[7] Dearborn *v.* Kelley, 3 Allen, 426.
[8] Walbridge *v.* Shaw, 7 Cush. 560.

return, or the value, and he cannot forego such remedy, and seek redress in a cross suit.[1]

§ 92. Where the plaintiff became nonsuit, and a judgment was rendered for a return and restitution; if the clerk, in issuing the writ of restitution, inserted therein *the value* of the property as named in the replevin writ, this being unauthorized by the judgment, and a mere ministerial act, will be regarded as a nullity.[2]

§ 93. After judgment for the defendant in an action of replevin, in which the title was tried, it is too late for the plaintiff, in order to prevent the entry of judgment for a return, to allege and prove facts which were known to him at the trial on the merits, for the purpose of defeating the defendant's title.[3]

§ 94. The right of property acquired by the plaintiff in replevin, by the delivery to him of the chattel by virtue of the writ, is a temporary right of possession, which terminates upon the abatement or discontinuance of the suit, or by a judgment in favor of the defendant, although a return be not adjudged. Therefore, where one sued in replevin in the *detinet* pleads only *non-detinet*, and has a verdict in his favor and a judgment for costs, but not for a return; and afterwards demands the property: he may maintain trover for it, though he might have so pleaded in the first suit, as to have entitled himself to a return, or the value of the property in damages.[4]

§ 95. It is an irregularity for the court to order a writ of return and restitution before final judgment; it should be made a part of the final judgment.[5] But a judgment for a return, not technically conformed to statute, but substantially correct, will be affirmed.[6] (*a*)

[1] McKnight *v.* Dunlop, 4 Barb. 36.
[2] Thomas *v.* Spofford, 46 Maine, 408.
[3] McNeal *v.* Leonard, 3 Allen, 268.
[4] Yates *v.* Fassett, 5 Denio, 21.
[5] Branch *v.* Branch, 5 Florida, 447.
[6] McArthur *v.* Hogan, 1 Hemp. 286.

(*a*) In Indiana, in replevin, the plea was property in the defendant. Verdict for the defendant, assessing his damages at $40.75. Judgment, that the defendant have a return and recover the damages assessed with costs. Held, the assessment of damages was surplusage, that the part of the judgment founded upon it was erroneous, and the residue of the judgment was right. Wolf *v.* Blue, 5 Blackf. 153.

As already suggested, the statutory law has modified the rules relating to return, as well as most other points in the action of replevin.

In New York, where a plaintiff in replevin submits to a nonsuit, and the defendant, entitled to a judgment *de retorno*, elects to take judgment for the value, he may have such value assessed by the jury impanelled in the cause, and need not issue a *writ of inquiry* for that purpose. Van Alstyne *v.* Kittle, 18 Wend. 524.

Where the defendant, in replevin of goods distrained, obtains a nonsuit or a verdict, after issue joined, so that he would be entitled to judgment for a return; he cannot take the alternative judgment for its value, and have such value determined on a writ of inquiry. His only course to obtain a judgment, in the nature of damages for its value, is to procure a valuation from the jury impanelled at the trial. And, if the distress were for rent, the jury must also find the amount in arrear, and the judgment will be limited to such amount. The same rule applies, where the plaintiff is nonsuited at the trial on his opening proof, and the defendant gives no evidence; if the defendant has in fact put in avowries claiming the property under distress for rent, or if it otherwise appear that the property was distrained for rent. The statute of replevin excepts cases, where the goods replevied were distrained, from the general provision for ascertaining their value by a writ of inquiry, after a nonsuit or discontinuance. Redman *v.* Henricks, 1 Sandf. 32.

Where, in an action for the recovery of personal property, the property is delivered to the plaintiff, and he fails in the action; the defendant cannot now have a judgment for return, or for the value, at his election. But he must, under § 277 of the Code, take a judgment in the alternative, for the return, or for the value thereof as assessed, in case a return cannot be had. Seaman *v.* Luce, 23 Barb. 240. And a later case decides, that the defendant in an action for the recovery of personal property can take judgment for the value only as an alternative judgment. The judgment must be either for the return of the property or its value. Dwight *v.* Enos, 5 Seld. 470.

Where the plaintiffs have only a special property, and judgment has been entered for the amount of their interest; it may be amended, by changing it into a judgment for the goods, or for their value, assessed at this amount. Fitzhugh *v.* Wiman, 5 Seld. 559.

In Delaware, judgment for the defendant on a plea of property is *pro retorno habendo;* but, if he cannot have a return, he may have judgment for damages to the value of the goods, &c. Clerk *v.* Adair, 3 Harring. 113.

In Arkansas, if the goods are not taken and delivered to the plaintiff, a judgment for the plaintiff should be not only for costs and damages, but also, as the statute provides, in the alternative, that the goods and chattels shall be replevied and delivered to him, or that he recover their assessed value. Rowark *v.* Lee, 14 Ark. 425.

In Wisconsin, judgment may be in the alternative for a return, or, in default thereof, the assessed value. Heeron *v.* Beckwith, 1 Wis. 17.

In Missouri, where, under Practice Act, art. 7, the plaintiff upon giving bonds obtains possession of the property, and fails to prosecute his action with effect, and the defendant, as against the plaintiff, has only a lien; the judgment in favor of the defendant should be only for the value of his interest, or for a return, until such value should be paid, at the defendant's election. But if the plaintiff has no interest, the judgment should be for the defendant for the full value of the property, and he will be answerable over to the owner for the balance due to him. Dilworth *v.* McKelvey, 30 Mis. 149.

In Massachusetts, in case of judgment for a return, the plaintiff is bound by the bond prescribed by the Rev. Sts. ch. 113, as well as that prescribed by Sts. 1789, ch. 26, to restore the goods in like good order and condition as when taken. Parker *v.* Simonds, 8 Met. 205.

In Pennsylvania, if the plaintiff recovers the whole value in damages; the dedefendant has judgment *de retorno habendo,* and a condition in a bond given by him, to return the property to the plaintiff if it should be so adjudged, is simply void. Moore *v.* Shenk, 3 Barr, 13.

A late case in Vermont settles some points in relation to return, as well as other collateral questions. Where an action of replevin is dismissed on motion, upon the ground that it was not brought in the county where the property was detained, though brought in the county where one of the parties resided; the court still has jurisdiction and is bound to render judgment for a return, without proof of any right to such return, or any formal plea or avowry; and the plaintiff cannot set up title as ground for contesting such judgment. But he is not debarred from disputing the defendant's title in another action. After dismissal of the action for ground not affecting the merits; the defendant cannot claim an award of damages for the taking, detainer, or misuse of the property. Collamer *v.* Page, 35 Vt. 387.

The defendant in this case claimed damages for the wool taken from the sheep which were the subject of the action. Mr. Chief Justice Poland remarks: "There would not seem to me any good reason why the defendants might not have their remedy on the bond for not returning the wool, which was a part of the sheep, when replevied. However this may be, if the defendants were legally entitled to hold the sheep and the wool, no doubt is expressed by their counsel that they can maintain some action to recover it, and although it is said that they might fail to get satisfaction, by reason of the want of ability in the plaintiff to respond to the judgment, we think they should rather incur that risk, than that they should have a final judgment for it, while the question of ownership is unsettled." Ib. 397.

"The judgment for the return is a mere

incident of the principal judgment, which makes a determination of the cause. When that is upon trial, and upon the merits, so as to be conclusive, then the judgment for a return is of the same character. If the judgment for the defendant is merely in abatement, or of that character, it is only an end of that particular action, and no bar to the commencement of another for the same cause, and if such judgment be followed by a judgment for a return, it is of the same character." Per Poland, C. J., 395.

In this case, Mr. Chief Justice Poland goes into an elaborate review of the authorities on the subject of return. The word *nonsuit*, used in the statute, was held to be used in a liberal sense, and to include the termination of the suit in the manner above stated.

CHAPTER VIII.

REPLEVIN BONDS.

§ 1. As we have already, in other connections, explained, a bond for the restoration of the property replevied, if the defendant shall prevail in the suit, is, unless otherwise provided by statute, an indispensable accompaniment to the writ of replevin. (*a*) The right to prosecute an action of replevin, and to take possession of goods upon a mere claim of title, before trial, is said to be purely a statutory right, and is only to be exercised upon a compliance with the terms of the statute.[1] Thus, in New York, it was held that a replevin bond must be executed and delivered to the sheriff, or the proceedings will be irregular; it is no longer optional with the sheriff to dispense with a bond.[2] And in justifying the taking of property by a sheriff, under a writ of replevin, it must be averred that a bond for a return of the property was delivered with the writ to the officer.[3] The officer may hold the property a reasonable time for the plaintiff to prepare the bond. But if he neglects or refuses to do it, the officer should restore the property. And where the

[1] Bennett *v.* Allen, 30 Vt. 684.

[2] Wilson *v.* Williams, 18 Wend. 581; Pironi *v.* Borden, 5 Pike, 81; Pool *v.* Loomis, ib. 110; Baldwin *v.* Whittier, 4 Shep. 33.

[3] Morris *v.* Van Voast, 19 Wend. 283; Smith *v.* McFall, 18 ib. 521. See Buel *v.* Davenport, 1 Root, 261; Webster *v.* Price, ib. 56; Smith *v.* Travol, ib. 165.

(*a*) In Delaware, in cases of distress for rent, the condition of the replevin bond is to prosecute the suit and satisfy the judgment; in other cases, it is to prosecute the suit and make return, if return be awarded. Clark *v.* Adair, 3 Harring. 113.

As to the general nature and effect of a replevin bond, more particularly upon the point of its being a *substitute for the goods* replevied, see the remarks of Mr. Justice Wilde, in the case of Badlam *v.* Tucker, 1 Pick. 284. That it is no substitute, see Lovett *v.* Burkhardt, 44 Penn. 173.

In Ohio, on the other hand, "the bond takes the place of the property to the extent of the interest of the defendant in replevin." Per Wilder, J., Crittenden *v.* Lingle, 14 Ohio St. 185; Smith *v.* M'Gregor, 10 ib. 461.

The obligation of a replevin bond is held to be like that of other bonds. Morehouse *v.* Bowen, 9 Min. 314.

officer continued to hold the property, the writ was quashed, and judgment rendered of discontinuance and return, and for damages.[1]

§ 2. But a writ of replevin will not be quashed for insufficiency of the bond, after a trial on the merits.[2] And it is sometimes held, that the omission to give bond and security, before the issuing of the writ, does not invalidate the writ, but only subjects the sheriff to an action by the defendant.[3] Also, that the statutory bond may be waived by agreement.[4]

§ 3. Questions have often arisen as to the precise form of the bond; and whether, if not exactly conformable to statutory requirement, it can be held valid at common law. (*a*) It is held that a statutory bond, in part conformable to the act, is good for that part;[5] and that statutory bonds of replevin will, in general, be sustained as voluntary bonds good at common law, unless the statute has expressly declared them void, or they have been obtained by fraud, or by coercion or oppression *colore officii*.[6] Thus, in Massachusetts, the condition of a replevin bond, to prosecute the action at the *county court* next to be holden at, &c., rightly describing the next term of the Court of Common Pleas, was held good.[7] The court remarked, that, if invalid under the statute, it would be good at common law. So a replevin bond, executed by the surety before service, but not by the principal until after the return of the writ and entry of the action, is good against both. Although the defendant in replevin might by plea in abatement or motion have avoided the process; yet the plaintiff in replevin, having suffered his name to be used to take property which did not belong to him, permitted the action to proceed to trial, and claimed the property until judgment was rendered against him, is estopped to say that the bond was made on a day different from its date.[8] So, under Rev. Sts. of Maine, ch. 130, in order that the bond should be a statute bond, it is not necessary that the plaintiff in replevin should sign it, or that it should appear on the bond to be given in his behalf.[9] So a replevin bond was held

[1] Morris *v.* Baker, 5 Wis. 389.
[2] Johnson *v.* Richards, 2 Fairf. 49.
[3] Vaiden *v.* Bell, 3 Rand. 448.
[4] Rabb *v.* Kilgore, 1 N. & M'C. 331.
[5] Lambden *v.* Conoway, 5 Harring. 1.
[6] Branch *v.* Branch, 6 Fla. 314; Morse *v.* Hodsdon, 5 Mass. 314; Claggett *v.* Richards, 45 N. H. 360.
[7] Arnold *v.* Allen, 8 Mass. 147.
[8] Cady *v.* Eggleston, 11 Mass. 282.
[9] Howe *v.* Handley, 28 Maine, 241.

(*a*) See Cook *v.* Bank, &c., 5 J. J. Mar. 163; Clarke *v.* Bell, 2 Litt. 164; Meaux *v.* Rutgers, Ky. Dec. 341; Whittemore *v.* Jones, 5 N. H. 362; Glassford *v.* Hackett, 3 Call, 193.

valid, where A sued B and C for property of B in possession of C, and the bond was made to B and C; the suit being dismissed, and judgment rendered against A in favor of the defendants for costs, and a return to B.[1] So, if a bond recite that it is executed upon institution of the suit; a surety is estopped to dispute its validity, upon the ground that he executed it by order of court to renew the sureties, made as a condition of postponement, and without the knowledge of other obligors, judgment being recovered against him, but in favor of the original sureties.[2] So the (Connecticut) statute (Rev. Stat. tit. 1, § 265), which provides a form to be used in taking replevin bonds, was not intended to prescribe the exact form of the bond, and the form there given need not be followed strictly.[3] So where the condition of the bond was, to prosecute to effect before A B, *justice of the peace*, and the justice had not final jurisdiction; held, the bond was not void, as not complying with the statute, which requires a bond to prosecute to effect generally.[4] So a bond in replevin for a slave, in Kentucky, stipulated, that the plaintiffs should well and truly prosecute their writ, pay all damages which might ensue to the defendant, and be adjudged against them, "and also perform any judgment of the court." Held sufficient, without stipulating specifically for paying hire and returning the slave, in event of the failure by the plaintiffs to establish their right.[5] So, in Delaware, a bond to indemnify the sheriff, instead of "to prosecute the suit," is good.[6] So an undertaking given by the defendant, in an action for the possession of personal property, under § 221 of the New York Code, to procure a return of the property to himself, may be made to the plaintiff instead of the sheriff.[7] So, under the statute of Florida (Thompson's Dig. 388), it is not necessary that a replevin bond should contain a description of the property; this must be in the affidavit. Under the same statute, requiring that the bond must be for any amount, at least double the value of the property; this value must be ascertained before the declaration has been filed, and the plaintiff cannot be allowed, by putting a higher value on it in his declaration, to invalidate his own bond. So where a bond, approved by "R. B., clerk, and an affidavit, sworn before "R. B., clerk of the circuit court for Marion county," appeared to have been executed

[1] Story *v.* O'Dea, 23 Ind. 326.

[2] Decker *v.* Judson, 16 N. Y. (2 Smith), 439.

[3] Kersse *v.* Waterhouse, 30 Conn. 129.

[4] Ibid.

[5] Cooper *v.* Brown, 7 Dana, 333.

[6] Lambden *v.* Conaway, 5 Harring. 1.

[7] Slack *v.* Heath, 4 E. D. Smith, 95.

on the day the writ issued, in the teste of which the clerk described himself as R. B., clerk of the Circuit Court for Marion county, and filed in the office of the clerk of that court on the same day, and there was no other action of replevin pending between the parties; held, the word "clerk" in the bond was a sufficient designation, it not being denied that he was such clerk.[1] So a bond is sufficient, although bearing date the day after service of the writ, executed by only two of the plaintiffs, and conditioned for a return in like good order *as when replevied* instead of *as when taken*.[2] So, if there is a sufficient correspondence between the judgment, execution, and bond to connect them, no motion to quash can be sustained for a variance.[3] So it is no objection to a replevin bond, that, in reciting the judgment on which it is predicated, it omits a credit entered on the judgment.[4] So, although a plaintiff in Kentucky may quash a replevin bond, if all the defendants in the execution have not united in it, the obligors cannot complain on this ground.[5]

§ 4. But a replevin bond, made to the replevying officer, instead of the defendant in replevin, is held void. It is given to one who had no lawful authority to take it, and the purpose and effect of it were to aid and abet him in a trespass. It does not belong to that class of instruments, which, though deviating from the form prescribed, are held good at common law, where the parties are right, and the bond itself substantially correct.[6]

§ 5. In Delaware, — and this is doubtless the general rule, — the bond should be taken in an amount sufficient to secure the return of the goods attached, or an equivalent value.[7] But it is no sufficient ground to quash a writ of replevin, that the officer has taken bond for a larger sum than the writ directed.[8]

§ 6. In Massachusetts, no action lies on a bond, the penalty of which is "double the value of the property hereinafter mentioned to be replevied," to be fixed by appraisers, without stating the value; especially if never appraised, and afterwards agreed between the parties.[9] So (as also in Vermont), if the bond does not contain a penalty in a definite sum, but merely states it as "double the value of the goods, or the property hereinafter named to be

[1] Branch *v.* Branch, 6 Fla. 314.
[2] Chandler *v.* Smith, 14 Mass. 313.
[3] 4 Monr. 132.
[4] Doe *v.* Cunningham, 6 Blackf. 430.
[5] Stevens *v.* Wallace, 5 Monr. 404.
[6] Purple *v.* Purple, 5 Pick. 226.
[7] Plunkett *v.* Moore, 4 Har. 379.
[8] Clapp *v.* Guild, 8 Mass. 153.
[9] Case *v.* Pettee, 5 Gray, 27.

replevied;" the action will be dismissed, upon a motion made at the proper stage of the case.[1]

§ 7. In South Carolina, the assignee of a replevin bond may sue upon it in his own name.[2] In Delaware, the assignment of a replevin bond, authorized by § 2656 of the Code, relates to bonds taken in cases of *distress for rent.* It does not extend to replevin bonds generally. Suit cannot, therefore, be brought in such case by the assignee. But this matter is amendable under ch. 112 of the Code.[3] In New York, a replevin bond, duly executed by the coroner, may be assigned by him, pursuant to 2 R. S. 533, § 64; and the assignee may sue thereon in his own name.[4] In California, under Stat. 1850, ch. 121, § 2, a replevin bond may be assigned by the sheriff to the creditor.[5]

§ 8. In Vermont, an officer, who serves a replevin writ in behalf of a defendant, to recover possession of property attached, is bound to take sureties on the bond who are at the time *actually* responsible for its amount. It is not enough that they are in good credit and *apparently* responsible. But, on the other hand, he is not liable, if, being actually responsible when taken, they cease to be so before the bond is put in suit. The fact, that the attorney of the plaintiff in the original suit acts also as the attorney for the defendant in making the replevin writ, and draws up and consents to the bond, does not necessarily discharge the officer from such liability, unless the officer were aware of this fact, nor unless such attorney either act in behalf of the plaintiff in consenting to the bond, or give the officer good reason to believe that he consents to it in his behalf.[6]

§ 9. Although a statute requires two sureties, the party for whose benefit the bond is taken may waive the objection that there is only one. And if he does, the obligors are bound. Such bond is not within the statute declaring void certain bonds, agreements, &c., taken by sheriffs and other officers *colore officii.*[7]

§ 10. Where there is but one surety, the defendant may move to set aside the proceedings, and is not bound to except. The plaintiff, however, on payment of costs, will be allowed to amend, by filing a new bond, with sureties, and the sureties justifying.[8]

[1] Clark *v.* Connecticut, &c. 6 Gray, 363; Bennett *v.* Allen, 30 Vt. 684.

[2] City Council *v.* Price, 1 M'Cord, 299.

[3] Waples *v.* McIlvaine, 5 Har. 381.

[4] Acker *v.* Finn, 5 Hill, 293.

[5] Wingate *v.* Brooks, 3 Cal. 112.

[6] Bank, &c. *v.* Rutland, 33 Vt. 414.

[7] Shaw *v.* Tobias, 3 Comst. 188.

[8] Whaling *v.* Shales, 20 Wend. 673.

§ 11. Where one surety was sufficient when the bond was executed, and the other not, and the former is not proved to have become insufficient since; the officer is not liable.[1]

§ 12. It is no ground for dismissing an action of replevin, that, in the bond, the sureties are described as partners, and sign and seal in their partnership names. A motion to dismiss is founded upon errors apparent on the face of the bond. The bond is to be construed in connection with the return of the officer, that it was duly executed. Any question, in relation to the bond, should be raised by plea in abatement.[2]

§ 13. It is held, in New York, that, in a suit upon a replevin bond, the plaintiff must prove the return of an execution unsatisfied in whole or in part, though the plea of *non est factum* alone be interposed.[3] But a late case in Rhode Island decides, that a defendant in replevin may bring an action upon the bond immediately upon recovering judgment in the suit, without reference to the issue, return, or return-day of the execution. The recovery of damages and costs, for the payment of which the bond provides, "refers to the *judgment*, and not to the *execution*, which is the means only of enforcing it. It is because these means may fail, that the statute requires, in addition, a bond with sureties. The liability of the plaintiffs in replevin was immediately consequent upon the judgment against them, enforceable at any moment, under the execution. By the terms of the bond sued, their liability and that of their sureties was precisely the same, the bond giving an additional remedy and further security for it; and neither can set up any defence, except performance of the conditions. The peculiar rights and obligations of bail can shed no light upon the liabilities of either the principals or sureties of a replevin bond."[4]

§ 14. The sureties are not discharged by delay in the prosecution of the suit without their knowledge, although assented to by the defendant, unless it be unreasonable and improper. Where the delay is unreasonable and improper, and is by consent of the defendant in the suit, he cannot have an action on the bond for want of prosecution merely. But mere delay, however long, and although assented to by the defendant without any special reason,

[1] Lord *v.* Bicknell, 35 Maine, 53.

[2] Judson *v.* Adams, 8 Cush. 556.

[3] Cowdin *v.* Stanton, 12 Wend. 120.

[4] Potter *v.* James, 7 R. I. 312; per Ames, C. J. 316, 317.

is no defence in favor of the sureties, where the breach complained of is the non-payment of the sum of money recovered by the defendant in the replevin suit.[1]

§ 15. In California, the proper judgment in replevin is, that the party re-deliver, or pay the value as found by the jury, with damages and costs. The surety is responsible, only on failure of the plaintiff to respond to the judgment, and therefore, in an action on the bond, non-performance of both alternatives of the judgment must be averred.[2]

§ 16. In Missouri, as against sureties, § 9 of art. 8 of act of 1849 provides the exclusive statutory remedy. The obligation of sureties under § 8 of the Practice Act of 1849 cannot be extended to the payment of double damages for detention.[3] In Kentucky, the liability of a defendant, upon a bond executed to the plaintiff, according to the provisions of the Civil Code, § 215, "to perform the judgment of the court in the action," extends only to such judgment as the court may render on the claim for possession of the property sued for.[4]

§ 17. The measure and amount of damages, to be recovered upon a replevin bond, are almost universally regulated in the different States by express statutes; which are by no means uniform, even in reference to the same facts, and the provisions of which vary with the varying circumstances of replevin suits.[5]

§ 18. If, in a judgment for a return, there is no assessment of damages for detention, and if upon the restitution writ no return was obtained; such damage may be assessed and allowed in an action upon the bond, and will be computed from the original taking.[6]

§ 19. The plaintiff in replevin cannot, by discontinuance or nonsuit, prevent a judgment against him for damages or for the return of the property. A voluntary nonsuit is, however, a breach of the condition in the bond to prosecute with effect, and on such breach the obligee may recover full damages within the penalty, without first obtaining a judgment for return or for damages.[7] But if the suit was dismissed by the plaintiff for defect in the affidavit, and the title is shown to be in a third

[1] Daniells *v.* Patterson, 3 Comst. 47. See Clary *v.* Rolland, 24 Cal. 147.

[2] Nickerson *v.* Chatterton, 7 Cal. 568.

[3] Collins *v.* Hough, 26 Mis. 149.

[4] McKee *v.* Pope, 18 B. Mon. 548.

[5] See Mattoon *v.* Pearce 12 Mass. 406.

[6] Smith *v.* Dillingham, 33 Maine, 384.

[7] Berghoff *v.* Heckwolf, 26 Mis. 511.

person, only nominal damages are recovered.[1] And though it is no defence to an action on the bond, that the defendant in replevin forcibly took the property from the plaintiff; it might, perhaps, bar a recovery of the value of the property.[2]

§ 20. In case of nonsuit, damages for failure to return, though not for the original taking and detention, may be assessed in an action on the bond.[3]

§ 21. In Illinois, the defendant may, under the act of March 1, 1847, "concerning practice" (Laws, 1847, 62), plead specially, that the plaintiff ought not to recover more than nominal damages, for that the merits of the case were not tried; and also the defendant's title.[4]

§ 22. Where the value of the property is within the jurisdiction, the court may render judgment on the bond for more than the sum to which the jurisdiction is limited.[5]

§ 23. In Massachusetts, goods attached were replevied, and the plaintiff in replevin became nonsuit, and in the mean time judgment was recovered and execution issued and returned unsatisfied in the original action. In an action upon the bond, held, that, in assessing damages, interest should be cast on the valuation of the property in the writ of replevin at the rate of six per cent. from the time when the property was replevied until the issuing of the execution in the original action, and at the rate of twelve per cent. thereafter until the entering up judgment in the action upon the bond.[6]

§ 24. Where the goods when attached were subject to duties, which the plaintiff in replevin paid; held, such interest should be cast only upon the difference between the amount so paid and the valuation in the writ of replevin.[7]

§ 25. In debt on a replevin bond, the plaintiff is entitled to recover the value of the goods replevied, with the damages and costs from the date of the judgment in replevin to the time of rendering judgment on the bond.[8]

§ 26. A plaintiff, in replevin of furniture, horses, &c., sold part thereof, and so used other parts as to lessen their value. The defendant obtained judgment for a return, and twelve per cent.

[1] Stockwell *v.* Byrne, 22 Ind. 6.

[2] Story *v.* O'Dea, 23 Ind. 326.

[3] Ginaca *v.* Atwood, 8 Cal. 446.

[4] Chinn *v.* McCoy, 19 Ill. 604.

[5] Berghoff *v.* Heckwolf, 26 Mis. 511.

[6] Huggeford *v.* Ford, 11 Pick. 223. See Wood *v.* Braynard, 9 ib. 322; Mass. Gen. Sts.

[7] Ibid.

[8] Arnold *v.* Baily et al. 8 Mass. 145.

damages and costs, which were paid. Twelve months after such judgment, the defendant sued out a writ of return, upon which the officer returned that he could not find the property. The defendant then brought his action on the bond. Held, he was entitled to recover the value of the property, as set out in the bond, with six per cent. damages from the time of the judgment for a return.[1]

§ 27. Where the plaintiff in replevin had become nonsuit, the defendant cannot show property in the plaintiff in replevin in reduction of damages.[2]

§ 28. The finding of the jury as to the value of the property will not be evidence of its value against the plaintiff, or his sureties on the bond, except in such actions of replevin as are authorized by statute.[3]

§ 29. In Maine, the damages recovered by an officer, in a replevin suit brought against him, in which the property attached is replevied, being recovered in trust, are not conclusive upon the parties in a suit upon the replevin bond.[4] And, in a suit upon a replevin bond, the plaintiff is not estopped from showing, that the actual value of the property exceeded the sum inserted by the defendant in his writ and bond, if the plaintiff did not assent to this estimate; and the plaintiff is also entitled to damages for detention.[5]

§ 30. If a horse attached and replevied dies pending the suit, without any one's fault, the plaintiff in replevin is discharged from his liability upon the bond for a return.[6]

§ 31. An absolute release "of all demands whatever," executed by the plaintiff to the principal obligor of a replevin bond on which the suit was brought, is a discharge of the bond.[7]

§ 32. A surety in a replevin bond, conditioned that his principal "shall abide the judgment of the court," is discharged by an amicable submission of all matters in dispute to arbitrators, not under rule, on whose award no judgment of court was or could be entered.[8]

§ 33. A replevin bond is discharged by the rendition and discharge of a judgment in the replevin suit, on a verdict for the defendant that "defendant recover his costs." [9]

[1] Parker v. Simonds, 8 Met. 205.
[2] Smallwood v. Norton, 2 App. 83.
[3] Gordon v. Williamson, 1 Spencer, 77.
[4] Howe v. Handley, 28 Maine, 241.
[5] Thomas v. Spofford, 46 Maine, 408.
[6] Melvin v. Winslow, 1 Fairf. 397. See Carpenter v. Stevens, 12 Wend. 589.
[7] Thomas v. Wilson, 6 Blackf. 203.
[8] Eldred v. Bennett, 33 Penn. 183.
[9] Chambers v. Waters, 7 Cal. 390.

§ 34. When the condition of a bond is broken by a failure to deliver up the property on demand, after judgment for a return, a discharge in insolvency of a surety on the bond, from all debts due at a time previous to such demand, though subsequent to the commencement of the action of replevin, is no bar to an action against him on the bond.[1]

§ 35. To an action against a surety in a replevin bond, it is no answer that the principal has since become bankrupt and obtained a discharge; and that the property in the chattels having, by force of the commission of bankruptcy, vested in the commissioners, it had become, by the act of law, impossible to fulfil the condition of the bond. The court remark: "The discharge of the bankrupt does not . . . release or discharge his partner, or any person bound with him for the same debt. . . . The impossibility of retaining the goods . . . is not the act of law, independent of the bankrupt's default. It is from his becoming a bankrupt that the title of the commissioners to his goods is derived. . . . By the operation of the bankrupt law this attachment, or the effect of it, for the benefit of the creditor of the bankrupt, is perhaps avoided. This event may be important to be considered in determining in chancery what damages are to be awarded."[2]

§ 36. Where goods were replevied from an attaching officer, and it appeared that the plaintiff in replevin was a wrong-doer, without title to any part of the goods; in an action upon the bond, the defendant cannot show in defence the invalidity of the attachments, nor claim that the officer, after paying off the attachments, was accountable for the residue of the property attached to him. Nor could a mere release to the officer by the debtor of all claim to the goods inure to the benefit of the defendant.[3]

§ 37. In debt upon a replevin bond against the surety, the defendant cannot plead that the goods were the proper goods of the plaintiff in replevin; and were attached and held as such by the defendant in replevin, who was a deputy-sheriff, upon mesne process against the plaintiff in replevin. The principal cannot be admitted to say, in his own defence, that he sued his writ against law, and the surety is responsible to the same extent.[4]

§ 37 *a*. After final trial and judgment for a return, in a suit

[1] Sleeper *v.* Miller, 7 Cush. 594, n.

[2] Flagg *v.* Tyler, 6 Mass. 33, per Sewall, J. 35.

[3] Farnham *v.* Moore, 8 Shep. 508.

[4] Flagg *v.* Tyler, 3 Mass. 303.

on the bond, the defendant cannot avoid a judgment for the value by showing title in a stranger.[1]

§ 38. The plaintiff may recover damages for detention, although not assessed in the judgment in the replevin suit.[2]

§ 39. Where, in replevin before a justice of the peace, a defendant goes to trial without objection to the bond, a defect in the bond, in not being for double the value of the property, is waived.[3]

§ 40. Where the right of property has been tried, it cannot be retried in a suit on the bond.[4] That the defendant had commenced his action before a tribunal incompetent to try the matter in dispute, is no defence; and the plea, that the title to the property was in him, is bad.[5]

§ 41. In New York, it is no defence to an action against sureties in a replevin bond, that they were excepted to, and failed to justify. It is doubted whether the complete substitution of new bail, as a consequence of the exception, would constitute a defence.[6]

§ 42. In California, it must be alleged that the property was restored to the plaintiff in replevin.[7]

§ 43. In an action upon a statutory security, as a replevin bond, the declaration need not aver in terms that the bond was taken in pursuance of the statute. It is enough if the instrument, as set forth, is in accordance with the statute.[8]

§ 44. When the action is on a bond executed to a *coroner*, the declaration need not state that the writ of replevin was directed to the coroner. That fact will be presumed from the giving of the bond to him, the commencement of the suit in replevin, and the taking of the property under the writ.[9]

§ 45. In debt on a replevin bond, the defendants pleaded performance generally; the plaintiff replied, that he had judgment for a return, and that no return had been made. The defendants rejoined, that the plaintiff in replevin reviewed the action; that the present plaintiff had judgment and execution, on which the chattel replevied was seized and sold. The rejoinder was adjudged bad, as being a departure from the plea in bar.[10]

[1] Smith *v.* Lisher, 23 Ind. 500.
[2] Thomas *v.* Spofford, 46 Maine, 408.
[3] Spencer *v.* Dickerson, 15 Ind. 368.
[4] Denny *v.* Reynolds, 24 ib. 248.
[5] McDermott *v.* Isbell, 4 Cal. 113.
[6] Van Duyne *v.* Coope, 1 Hill, 557.
[7] Nickerson *v.* Chatterton, 7 Cal. 568.
[8] Shaw *v.* Tobias, 3 Comst. 188.
[9] Ibid.
[10] Larned *v.* Bruce, 6 Mass. 57.

§ 45 *a*. In an action on the bond, upon a denial, the plaintiff must offer the bond in evidence.[1]

§ 46. Questions have often arisen as to the construction of replevin bonds; more especially with reference to the prosecution of the former suit and the rendering of judgment therein. (*a*)

§ 47. To a replevin bond the defendant pleads in bar, that he duly entered his action at the Court of Common Pleas, and prosecuted it with effect; that, upon a judgment there, an appeal was interposed by the plaintiff in replevin; that the creditor, at whose suit the chattels had been attached, had received full satisfaction for his damages and costs; and that the officer, plaintiff in the action on the bond, had been indemnified and kept harmless, &c. Held, on demurrer, the plea was good. The court remark: "The original creditor was satisfied, and therefore he can have no claim on the plaintiff on account of the attachment. The plaintiff was to be saved harmless; and the plea in bar avers that he has been so. If the cattle have not been returned, still the plaintiff should not have commenced his action until he was in some way damnified."[2] So A, in a suit against B, attached an undivided proportion of a vessel and cargo, and recovered final judgment. C, by a suit in the form of an action of trespass, replevied the property as his own, and gave a statute bond. On the trial of the replevin, on the plea of not guilty, it appeared that A, at the time of the attachment, was a joint owner with C of the property attached, which was known to C, and judgment was accordingly rendered against C. B had no interest in the property, but C owned the proportion attached as his. C did not return the property replevied, or pay the debt and costs which A had recovered against B. In an action by A against C, on the replevin bond, held, C was not liable, the judgment against C in the replevin suit not showing a failure to prosecute his action to effect, and to make his plea good, within the meaning of the statute, or the bond.[3]

§ 48. But it is no good bar to an action of debt on a replevin bond, that the plaintiff recovered judgment for a return, damages, and costs, and that the defendant delivered part of the goods and

[1] Smith *v*. Fisher, 23 Ind. 500.
[2] Arnold *v*. Allen, 8 Mass. 147, 150.
[3] Ladd *v*. Prentice, 14 Conn. 109.

(*a*) See, as to the effect of the words "prosecute with effect," Tummons *v*. Ogle, 37 Eng. L. & Eq. 15.

tendered the remainder, which were not received; and as to the residue, and damages and costs, acknowledging a good cause of action. The relief of the defendant, in such case, is in equity, not by a defence to the action.[1] Nor that the defendant has always been ready to return the goods and pay the damages and costs, but the plaintiff never demanded them nor delivered his writ of *retorno habendo* to an officer to be executed; for want of an allegation that the defendant prosecuted his action to final judgment.[2]

§ 49. So to an action on a replevin bond, the condition of which was, that the plaintiff in replevin should prosecute his writ to final judgment, pay such damages and costs as shall be adjudged against him, and return the cattle; it is a bad plea, that there has been no final judgment that he should return the cattle, or that he should pay damages or costs.[3] So where a replevin bond is conditioned to prosecute the suit without delay, and to return the goods if a return should be awarded; it is a breach of the condition, if the plaintiff in replevin do not succeed, though there be no award of a return.[4] So a replevin bond, the condition of which is, that the plaintiff shall prosecute his suit to effect or return the goods, is broken by the withdrawal of the writ of replevin from the hands of the officer by the plaintiff before the return day, and the discontinuance of the suit. Although the defendant in a replevin suit is an actor therein as well as the plaintiff, yet he is not such until after avowry, and it is no part of his duty to see that the writ is returned.[5] The court remark, on the general subject, that there are many cases where a replevin bond becomes, by subsequent events, *functus officio* and inoperative, and where the liability of the obligor terminates, although the condition has not been fulfilled. These events may be classified as follows: First, such as terminate the suit of the attaching creditor adversely to him, and thus put an end to his lien; second, a termination of such suit and lien by the death of the defendant therein, which dissolves the attachment; third, events like the death of a party in the replevin suit, which determine that suit, and render the performance of the condition impossible by the act of God; fourth, where the defendant in replevin, by his laches or

[1] Sevey *v.* Blacklin, 2 Mass. 541.
[2] Ibid.
[3] Lindsay *v.* Blood, 2 Mass. 518.
[4] Brown *v.* Parker, 5 Blackf. 291.
[5] Persse *v.* Waterhouse, 30 Conn. 139.

misconduct, loses or waives his rights under the attachment, or renounces his right to a return by failing to make avowry and pleading the general issue, or otherwise loses his rights in the particular case by his own neglect. But where the defendant in replevin is prevented from avowing his right and obtaining a judgment thereupon by the act or fault of the plaintiff, as where the latter takes out a defective writ, and the suit is abated, or he becomes nonsuit, or discontinues or withdraws the action; the defendant may have a judgment of return, if the position of the case in court will permit it, or may have his remedy on the replevin bond; for, in all such cases, there is a failure to prosecute. So the alternative condition of the bond was, to return the goods to the attaching officer, or to the officer having the execution in the original suit. Held, a demand upon the debtor, by the officer, on the execution in that suit, was not necessary, before the attaching creditor could become entitled to a return; also, that no demand upon the bond, either for the penalty or for the amount of the judgment in the attachment suit, was necessary, before bringing suit on the bond.[1]

§ 49 *a*. In Tennessee, under the act of 1831, ch. 25, if several executions are levied on the same property, the obligors in a bond executed to the plaintiffs in one of them, conditioned to deliver the whole property, will be bound to deliver only so much of it, as the obligees would necessarily have been entitled to, had the property been distributed *pro rata* among all the creditors.[2]

§ 50. In Delaware, an action on a replevin bond does not abate by death.[3]

§ 51. Where the original debtor died after property was attached and replevied, but before judgment was rendered in the suit; held, in an action on the bond, the attachment was dissolved, and the creditor could not recover.[4] So, though the replevin suit had been withdrawn, and judgment thereupon in fact rendered for the return of the property.[5]

§ 52. A condition in a replevin bond, that the obligor should prosecute his action of replevin to final judgment, is saved by his prosecuting it until the writ is abated by the death of the defendant.[6] The court favor the opinion, that this was a prosecution to

[1] Persse *v.* Waterhouse, 30 Conn. 139.
[2] Kercheval *v.* Harley, 1 Meigs, 412.
[3] Waples *v.* McIlvaine, 5 Har. 381.
[4] Green *v.* Baker, 14 Conn. 432.
[5] Ibid.
[6] Badlam *v.* Tucker, et. al. 1 Pick. 284.

final judgment, and a fulfiment, in terms, of the condition. But, without deciding this point, they hold, that the performance was excused by the defendant's death. Mr. Justice Wilde remarks: "It has been argued, that the replevin bond was substituted for the property, and that therefore there was a vested right in the obligee. But how was there a vested right? . . . In replevin both parties are actors, and the possession of the goods by the defendant in replevin furnishes no legal presumption of property in him. . . . Before we can hold the defendants liable, . . . we must be satisfied that the present plaintiff had, at the time of the commencement of the replevin suit, the right of possession; and this right cannot be determined in the present action. The liabilities of the sureties on a replevin bond are similar, or nearly so, to the liabilities of bail. The security in the one case is no more a substitute for the goods, than that in the other is a substitute for the person. A replevin bond is an executory contract. . . . There is no vested right in the obligee, not even the right of an action, until there is some breach of the condition."

§ 53. It is a good bar to an action on a replevin bond, that the plaintiff in replevin entered his action, that the Court of Common Pleas gave judgment against him, from which he appealed, and before the sitting of the court appealed to he died.[1] Mr. Chief Justice Parker says: "Although by law the cause of action survived, it was not a duty of the administrator . . . to enter and prosecute the action at the Supreme Judicial Court, until summoned thereto by the defendant. . . . The action could only be restored by the act of the executor or administrator, if he voluntarily came in, or of the defendant, if upon suggestion of the death, he had moved for a citation. If the facts would have admitted of it, the present plaintiff . . . should have replied a judgment recovered, after notice to the administrator; and if no administration had been granted, . . . he should have applied . . . for letters, . . . to some one who could have answered to the suit."

§ 53 *a*. The bond does not extend to a judgment on a review.[2]

[1] Jenney *v*. Jenney, 24 Mass. 231, 232.

[2] Bell *v*. Bartlett, 7 N. H. 178.

BOOK II.

DISSEISIN, EJECTMENT, REAL ACTION.

§ 1. In the United States, the possession of real property, wrongfully withheld from the owner, is recovered, specifically, by an action indiscriminately termed *ejectment*, *writ of entry*, and *real action*. Under one or the other of these names, the remedy is almost universally provided and regulated by express statutes, (*a*) which have for the most part superseded the common-law actions

(*a*) In reference to the statutory provisions of this nature, it is held, in New York, that all the general provisions in the Revised Statutes relating to real estate, where no specific inconsistent provision is made in the Code on the same subject, remain in full force, and are to be applied and adapted to the actions under the Code. St. John *v.* Pierce, 22 Barb. 362.

Sect. 31 of the Ejectment Act (2 Rev. Sts. 308) is one of those general provisions which the court is bound to apply to actions under the Code (§ 455), and, by reasonable interpretation, it applies to all cases where the title, upon which the plaintiff seeks to recover possession, has from any cause ceased to exist before the trial; and the defendant may avail himself of its provisions, without filing a supplemental answer. Lang *v.* Wilbraham, 2 Duer, 171.

In Illinois, if a party in ejectment allows the year to elapse without having the judgment vacated in the Circuit Court, he must

of the same nature. (*b*) The plan of the present work does not admit that technical treatment of the subject, which would be

take the risk of getting it reversed in the Supreme Court, and, if he fails there, the judgment becomes conclusive, and he has no remedy. The statute gives the Circuit Court power to vacate the judgment within the year, where an appeal is taken, or a writ of error is prosecuted. Gibson *v.* Manly, 15 Ill. 140.

(*b*) The following view is given, by Blackstone, of the obsolete remedies referred to in the text. That portion relating to the fictitious action of ejectment, with its so-called *ingenious* contrivances, for reaching what might be thought so simple and accessible a point as justice between man and man, must pass for one of the quaintest curiosities of historical jurisprudence : "*Real* actions (or, as they are called in the Mirror, *feodal* actions), which concern real property only, are such whereby the plaintiff, here called the demandant, claims title to have any lands or tenements, rents, commons, or other hereditaments, in fee-simple, fee-tail, or for term of life. By these actions formerly all disputes concerning real estates were decided ; but they are now pretty generally laid aside in practice, upon account of the great nicety required in their management, and the inconvenient length of their process ; a much more expeditious method of trying titles being since introduced, by other actions personal and mixed."

Note to the above. — "Real actions, with the exception of three — dower, right of dower, and *quare impedit* — were entirely abolished by Stat. 3 & 4 W. 4, c. 27, § 36. All mixed actions, with one exception, — the action of ejectment, — were abolished by the same statute. The action of ejectment thus preserved has now, by the Common-Law Procedure Act, 1852, been also swept away, and a new procedure or action of ejectment substituted in its place. Stewart." 3 Sharsw. Bl. Comm. 118.

A writ of entry "is that which disproves the title of the tenant or possessor, by showing the unlawful means by which he entered or continues possession. The writ is directed to the sheriff, requiring him to command the tenant of the land that he render (in Latin, *præcipe quod reddat*) to the demandant the land in question, which he claims to be his right and inheritance ; and into which, as he saith, the said tenant had not entry but by (or after) a disseisin, intrusion, or the like, made to the said demandant, within the time limited by law for such actions ; or that upon refusal he do appear in court, on such a day, to show wherefore he hath not done it. This is the original process, the *præcipe* upon which all the rest of the suit is grounded : wherein it appears that the tenant is required, either to deliver seisin of the lands, or to show cause why he will not. This cause may be either a denial of the fact of having entered by or under such means as are suggested, or a justification of his entry by reason of title in himself or in those under whom he makes claim : whereupon the possession of the land is awarded to him who produces the clearest right to possess it." 3 Sharsw. Bl. Comm. 179. "The remedy by writ of entry was abolished by 3 & 4 W. 4, ch. 27, § 36. Stewart." Ib. 183, n.

"The remedy by ejectment is in its original an action brought by one who hath a lease for years, to repair the injury done him by dispossession. In order, therefore, to convert it into a method of trying titles to the freehold, it is first necessary that the claimant do take possession of the lands, to empower him to constitute a lessee for years, that may be capable of receiving this injury of dispossession. For it would be an offence, called in our law *maintenance* . . . to convey a title to another, when the grantor is not in possesion ; and, indeed, it was doubted at first, whether this occasional possession, taken merely for the purpose of conveying the title, excused the lessor from the legal guilt of maintenance. When, therefore, a person, who hath right of entry into lands, determines to acquire that possession, which is wrongfully withheld by the present tenant, he makes (as by law he may) a formal entry ; . . . and being so in the possession of the soil, he there, upon the land, seals and delivers a lease for years to some third person or lessee; and having thus given him entry, leaves him in possession. This lessee is to stay upon the land, till the prior tenant . . . enters thereon afresh and ousts him, or till some other person (either by accident or by agreement beforehand) comes upon the land and turns him out or ejects him. For this injury the lessee is entitled to his action of ejectment against the tenant, or this *casual ejector* . . . to recover back his term and damages. But where this action is brought against such a casual ejector, . . . the court will not suffer the tenant to lose his possession without any opportunity to defend it. Wherefore, . . . no plaintiff shall proceed in ejectment to recover land against a casual ejector, without notice given to the tenant in possession (if any there be) and making him a defendant if he pleases. And . . . the

expected in a treatise specially devoted to its consideration. All that is here attempted, is such a practical and summary view, as

plaintiff must . . . make out four points; namely, *title, lease, entry, and ouster.* First, . . . a good title in his lessor, which brings the matter of right entirely before the court; then, that the lessor being seised or possessed by virtue of such title, did make him the *lease;* thirdly, that he . . . did *enter* . . . in consequence of such lease; and then, lastly, that the defendant *ousted* or ejected him. Whereupon he shall have judgment to recover his term and damages; and shall, in consequence, have a *writ of possession.* . . . But a new and more easy method, . . . where there is any actual tenant, . . . was invented, . . . by the Lord Chief Justice Rolle. This depends upon a string of legal fictions; no actual lease is made, no actual entry by the plaintiff, no actual ouster by the defendant; but all are merely ideal, for the sole purpose of trying the title. . . . A lease, . . . is stated to have been made, by him who claims title, . . . to the plaintiff, . . . which plaintiff ought to be some real person. . . . It is also stated, that Smith, the lessee, entered, and that the defendant, William Stiles, who is called the *casual ejector*, ousted him; for which ouster he brings this action. . . . Stiles . . . sends a written notice to the tenant . . . as George Sanders, informing him of the action; in that assuring him that he, Stiles, has no title, and shall make no defence. If the tenant does not, within a limited time, apply to the court to be admitted as a defendant, he is supposed to have no right; and, upon judgment being had against Stiles, Sanders will be turned out of possession by the sheriff. But if the tenant applies to be made a defendant, it is allowed him upon this condition, that he enter into a rule of the court to confess the *lease, entry,* and *ouster.* The trial will now stand upon the merits of the *title* only." 3 Sharsw. Bl. Comm. 199.

"New proceedings for the recovery of land have been created by the Common Law Procedure Act, 1852, and the former action of ejectment has given place altogether to this new procedure. Many of the United States had long preceded England in this valuable reform; but several still continue to employ the ancient form; and in the circuit courts of the United States, in those States in which it was in use when those courts were established, it is still employed." Ib. 205. Notes of Stewart & Sharswood.

It is held in New Hampshire, that a writ of entry *sur disseisin* is a proper and recognized form of action. Potter *v.* Baker, 19 N. H. 166.

In reference to the technical action of ejectment, it is held to be merely a possessory action, and confined to cases where the claimant has a possessory title; that is to say, a right of entry upon the lands. To support it, four things are necessary, namely, title, lease, entry, and ouster. Payne *v.* Treadwell, 5 Cal. 310. See Connor *v.* Peugh, 18 How. 394; Grande *v.* Foy, 1 Hemp. 105; Seabury *v.* Stewart, 22 Ala. 207; Rawls *v.* Doe, 23 ib. 240; Hancock *v.* Aiken, 4 Zabr. 544.

The fictions in an action of ejectment, being necessary to this form of action, will not be allowed to prejudice the parties. Warner *v.* Hardy, 6 Md. 525.

A applied to the orphans' court for partition, and B resisted, on the ground that the land belonged to him by a parol gift. The court ordered an amicable ejectment to try the right, which resulted in a verdict in favor of B. Held, this was only a feigned issue, to inform the conscience of the court, and of no conclusive effect. Wible *v.* Wible, 1 Grant, 406.

A recovery in ejectment is only for the unexpired portion of the term laid in the demise. Kennedy *v.* Reynolds, 27 Ala. 364.

The power to lease passes by implication the power to defend or recover the possession as by ejectment. Windham *v.* Chisholm, 35 Miss. 531.

In general, to prevent surprise, possession of the defendant must be proved, notwithstanding confession of "lease, entry, and ouster," in the common rule. But it is otherwise where one is served with a copy of the declaration, after leaving the premises, enters into the common rule, and contests the title deeds, without questioning the identity of the land. Atwell *v.* McLure, 4 Jones, 371.

Ejectment does not lie upon a demise from one deceased at the date of such demise. Goodtitle *v.* Roe, 20 Geo. 135.

Nor from one having no title at the commencement of suit; nor from an administrator appointed by a court without jurisdiction. Ib.

The lessor of the plaintiff must have the legal title, at the time of the demise laid, and at the time of the action brought. The doctrine of *relation* has never been extended further, than that a legal title, when acquired, shall relate back to the period when the right accrued to the prop-

may be derived from the decided cases in the several States, more especially those of the most recent date. Some of them doubtless turn upon express statutory provisions; but the attempt is made to cite, for the most part, those only which are of universal, and not mere local, applicability. It will be seen, that the *wrong* of *ouster* or *disseisin*, and the *remedy* of ejectment, are, for the reasons heretofore stated, considered together, as inseparable parts of one and the same general topic.

§ 2. Entry upon land is of course an important point in connection with suits relating to the title.

§ 3. Ejectment may be maintained without actual entry.[1]

§ 4. An entry, for the purpose and with an offer to sell, made

[1] Cornelius *v.* Ivins, 2 Dutch. 376.

erty, so as to defeat subsequent claimants or incumbrancers, holding adversely to the right. Laurissini *v.* Doe, 25 Miss. 177.

In addition to the remedies for recovery of real property above described, is *the writ of right;* which, however, if not expressly abolished, is of such rare occurrence as to require only a very brief notice. In case the right of possession be barred by a recovery upon the merits in a possessory action, or, lastly, by the Statute of Limitations, a claimant in fee-simple may have a *mere writ of right*. . . . This writ lies *concurrently* with all other real actions, in which an estate of fee-simple may be recovered; and it also lies *after* them, being, as it were, an appeal to the mere right, when judgment hath been had as to the possession, in an inferior possessory action. . . . In case the right of possession be lost by length of time, or by judgment against the true owner in one of these inferior suits, . . . this is then the only remedy, . . . and it is of so forcible a nature, that it overcomes all obstacles, and clears all objections that may have arisen to cloud and obscure the title. And, after issue once joined in a writ of right, the judgment is absolutely final; so that a recovery had in this action may be pleaded in bar of any other claim or demand." 3 Sharsw. Bl. Comm. 192.

A writ of right at common law would lie only to recover a fee-simple estate, and in favor of him who had the fee-simple title. A count which does not allege a seisin in fee-simple, either in the demandant or in the ancestor through whom he claims, is defective as a count in a writ of right, although it alleges the disseisin of the demandant's ancestor. But it is sufficient, and must be considered, as a count in a writ of entry *sur disseisin*, especially after verdict, the gist of that action being wrongful disseisin without regard to the mere right of property. Lyon *v.* Mottuse, 19 Ala. 463.

The writ of right, which existed as a remedial process in the State of Massachusetts at the time of the passage of the Judiciary Act, still exists as a process in the courts of the United States in Massachusetts, though it has been abolished in the state courts by an act of the Legislature. The time in which it may be brought, however, is still fixed by the statutes of Massachusetts, limiting the time within which such a remedy may be prosecuted in its own courts. Homer *v.* Brown, 16 How. 354.

Where a demandant in a writ of right claims only part of a tract claimed by the tenant; the tenant, to protect himself under the Virginia statute, must prove continued adverse possession of some part of the land in controversy. Koiner *v.* Rankin, 11 Gratt. 420.

In a writ of right, the failure to file a plea is an error not cured by a verdict in favor of the tenant. Rowans *v.* Givens, 10 Gratt. 250.

In a writ of right, a verdict and judgment, in a case of forcible entry and detainer, brought by the tenants against the demandants for the same land, is admissible as an admission by the tenant that the demandant was in possession, when, or within three years before, the proceedings were commenced. Breathed *v.* Smith, 1 P. &. H. (Va.) 301.

by one having a deed, under which he claims, gives seisin and title as against all persons not showing an elder and a better one, although no lines were marked, nor other traces or monuments of the entry left.[1]

§ 5. A entered, in 1836, under a deed, and in 1847 conveyed with warranty to B and C, who in 1851 conveyed to the defendants, who entered. The court will not presume an abandonment of the seisin so acquired by A, in favor of a party who had made improvements upon the lot, claiming it under a deed and residing upon it for twelve years, and whose possession was later than that of A.[2]

§ 6. A party entering upon land under color of title is presumed to enter and occupy according to his title.[3]

§ 7. The motive or mode of entry is held not to affect its legal validity. Thus ejectment cannot be maintained against one with a right of entry, who enters by force or fraud.[4] Nor can the plaintiff show entry of the defendant by collusion with one not having the right of entry.[5]

§ 8. Ejectment is maintained, by a right of possession in the plaintiff, and actual possession in the defendant.[6] It is not necessary that a plaintiff should show a good title against all the world, but only against the defendant;[7] as where the defendant is a trespasser,[8] or an *intruder*, whether the plaintiff holds the legal title absolutely or only in trust. So an attorney, taking a deed in his own name, may recover against any one but his client or those claiming under him.[9]

§ 9. In reference to a derivative title, it is held, that want of actual seisin in a person through whom the plaintiff claims is not a ground of nonsuit, if he had a seisin by deed; but it may be, if there was a descent cast.[10]

§ 10. It is the general rule, that ejectment will lie, and can only be maintained, by an *owner*.[11] (*a*) By one in whom the legal title

1 Jones *v.* Merrimack, &c. 11 Fost. 381.

2 Ibid.

3 Tappan *v.* Tappan, 11 Fost. 41.

4 Depuy *v.* Williams, 26 Cal. 313.

5 Ibid.

6 Owen *v.* Fowler, 24 Cal. 194; Owen *v.* Morton, ib. 379.

7 Garrett *v.* Lyle, 27 Ala. 586.

8 Turner *v.* Aldridge, ib. 229; Coucy *v.* Cummings, 12 La. An. 748.

9 Lair *v.* Hunsicker, 28 Penn. 115.

10 McGregor *v.* Comstock, 16 Barb. 427.

11 Lamar *v.* Raysor, 7 Rich. 509.

(*a*) It is foreign from the purpose of the present work, to consider the acquisition of title by lapse of time, prescription, or a statute of limitations. The whole subject

is vested, or his legal representative.[1] And the plaintiff is bound to show title in himself at the commencement of the action.[2] Or, according to the general rule, he must show *a possessory right.*[3] And he may show a vested legal title, no matter how, if fairly acquired, or through whom it may have been derived.[4]

§ 11. The same rule is sometimes expressed in the form, that the plaintiff must show *the best* title.[5] He must recover on the strength of his own title, and cannot, in general, rely upon the weakness of the defendant's.[6] Until the plaintiff shows a legal and possessory title, the defendant need not show title in himself or a third person.[7] (*a*)

§ 12. A plaintiff may claim both upon the ground of title, and of possession as against a trespasser; and, failing in the former, may then rely upon the latter.[8] So, if he fails to establish his right to recover by one title, he may resort to another, and is not obliged to make any election between them.[9]

§ 13. In case of conflicting titles, it is a correct instruction to the jury to find for the party having the best title.[10]

§ 14. In the not uncommon case where both parties claim title from the same person, the plaintiff is not bound to establish the

[1] Caze *v.* Robertson, 14 La. An. 232; 33 Miss. 46; 12 Geo. 166; 19 Ark. 201.

[2] Layman *v.* Whiting, 20 Barb. 559.

[3] Batterton *v.* Yoakum, 17 Ill. 288; Williams *v.* Hartshorn, 30 Ala. 211; Heffner *v.* Betz, 32 Penn. 376; 12 Geo. 166; 19 Ark. 201.

[4] New York, &c. *v.* Hicks, 5 McLean, 111.

[5] Seabury *v.* Field, 1 McAllis. 1.

[6] Woodworth *v.* Fulton, 1 Cal. 295; Webster *v.* Hill, 38 Maine, 78; Bruce *v.* Mitchell, 39 ib. 390.

[7] Hammond *v.* Inloes, 4 Md. 138.

[8] Davison *v.* Gent, 38 Eng. L. & Eq. 469.

[9] St. Louis, &c. *v.* Risley, 28 Mis. 415.

[10] Busenius *v.* Coffee, 14 Cal. 91.

is variously regulated by the statutes of the several States. In reference to the operation of a statute, it is held, in New York, that, where one had a right of entry on lands in the possession of another, when the Revised Statutes took effect, such adverse possession must have continued twenty-five years to raise the presumption of a grant. Poor *v.* Horton, 15 Barb. 485.

In Kentucky, twenty years' possession is necessary in case of a void deed. Breeding *v.* Taylor, 13 B. Mon. 477.

In Illinois, twenty years' possession is required, where the occupation commenced by disseisin. Turney *v.* Chamberlain, 15 Ill. 271. See State *v.* Trustees, &c. 5 Ind. 77.

In Missouri, an adverse possession for twenty years confers an absolute title against every one not excepted by statute. Blair *v.* Smith, 16 Mis. 273.

In Pennsylvania, if a plaintiff claims title by twenty-one years' adverse possession, he must prove every element necessary to constitute a title under the Statute of Limitations; otherwise, it is the duty of the court to instruct the jury, that there is not sufficient evidence to entitle him to recover. De Haven *v.* Landell, 31 Penn. 120.

Where it is declared by statute that no action shall be brought for land unless the demandant was seised within twenty-five years, an averment of seisin within sixty years is bad. Bockee *v.* Crosby, 2 Paine, C. C. 432.

(*a*) In an action under the Mississippi Pleading Act of 1850, to recover possession of land, the plaintiff must show a complete title, or that the defendant had acknowledged his title. Cunningham *v.* Dean, 33 Miss. 46.

absolute title of that person, but proof of prior possession in him and the plaintiff is sufficient.[1] It is not necessary for either to show title beyond the person in question.[2] But though both parties claim under A, the defendant may show that, before conveying to the plaintiff, A conveyed to him, and he to B, without notice, and for consideration.[3]

§ 15. It is a necessary result of what has been already stated, that the defendant may set up title in a third person.[4] Even an outstanding life-estate.[5] And where the only question was, whether there was an outstanding title superior to that of the plaintiff, it was held not to be material for the jury to consider whether the defendant's title connected with it or not.[6] So the tenant may show, that, as to a part of the premises, the demandant's grantor had no title, and so far defeat the recovery, though he himself sets up no title.[7] And it is held, that the defendant may show a presumption of title in a third person by slight circumstances.[8] Or possession under color of title; except where the plaintiff is entitled to possession without a naked legal title, as in some cases of trust.[9] But an *inchoate* title is no bar against a legal title.[10] And an outstanding title in a third person must be one enforceable by action; a present, subsisting and operative title.[11] It must exist at the commencement of suit.[12] And, as we have seen, title in a third person is no defence to an action by one in possession against a trespasser.[13] So a defendant in ejectment cannot set up an outstanding *mortgage* of the plaintiff to a stranger, either to show that the plaintiff has no legal title, or to show that his actual title is different from that alleged.[14]

§ 16. It is the general rule, that an *equitable* estate will not sustain a writ of entry.[15] Thus a *cestui que trust* cannot recover against a trustee, unless the circumstances raise the presumption of a surrender.[16] See § 46.

[1] Turner *v.* Reynolds, 23 Penn. 199; Holbrook *v.* Brenner, 31 Ill. 501; Gantt *v.* Cowan, 27 Ala. 582; Miller *v.* Surls, 19 Geo. 331; Hughes *v.* Wilkinson, 28 Miss. 600.

[2] Wood *v.* McGuire, 17 Geo. 303.

[3] Newlin *v.* Osborne, 2 Jones, 163.

[4] Rupert *v.* Mark, 15 Ill. 540; Sutton *v.* M'Leod, 29 Geo. 589; Atkins *v.* Lewis, 14 Gratt. 30.

[5] Batterton *v.* Yoakum, 17 Ill. 288.

[6] Clegg *v.* Fields, 7 Jones, 37.

[7] Bruce *v.* Mitchell, 39 Maine, 390.

[8] Townsend *v.* Downer, 32 Vt. 183.

[9] Fowler *v.* Whiteman, 2 Ohio, N. S. 270.

[10] Mezes *v.* Greer, 1 McAll. C. C. 401.

[11] M'Donald *v.* Schneider, 27 Mis. 405.

[12] Norcum *v.* D'Œnch, 17 Mis. 98.

[13] Bequette *v.* Caulfield, 4 Cal. 278.

[14] Burr *v.* Spencer, 26 Conn. 159.

[15] Chapin *v.* Universalist, &c. 8 Gray, 580; Smith *v.* M'Cann, 24 How. 398; Emeric *v.* Penniman, 26 Cal. 122; Thompson *v.* Lyon, 33 Mis. 219. See Baptist, &c. *v.* Turner, 6 M'L. 43; Gloninger *v.* Hazard, 42 Penn. 389.

[16] Brown *v.* Combs, 5 Dutch. 36.

§ 17. This rule, however, has been extensively changed in the United States, generally by the express terms or natural construction of the statutory law. (*a*) Thus, under the practice in California, possession, with an equitable title, is as good as a legal title.[1] And the same practice is adopted in Pennsylvania,[2] where ejectment on an equitable title is in substance a bill for specific performance, and is therefore governed by general principles of equity.[3]

§ 18. It is also the general rule, that an equitable title constitutes no *defence* to the action of ejectment.[4] See § 46.

§ 19. And the rule has been applied, even where the general terms "title or interest" are used in a statute. The title must be *legal*.[5] Thus it is no defence to a writ of entry, that the demandant holds, subject to a resulting trust in favor of the tenant.[6] So one holding a naked legal title cannot set up, in defence to an action by one in possession, and claiming an equitable title, a countervailing equity in a third person, who is also a party defendant, and is defaulted.[7] So a defendant with a legal title is not bound to show in the first instance a good equitable title; it is for the plaintiff to show a superior equitable title in himself.[8] More especially a defendant in ejectment cannot, on trial, rely on an equitable defence not stated in his answer, which sets up a legal defence.[9] And two inconsistent equitable defences cannot be brought forward for the court to choose between them.[10]

§ 20. This rule, however, as in case of the plaintiff, has been changed in many of the States. Thus, in New York, under the amended code, the defendant may set up an equitable title in himself or another, and a claim for the conveyance of the legal estate.[11] Though, in order to defeat the action, he must become an *actor*, and claim affirmative relief; and his answer must contain all the elements of a bill for specific performance.[12] An equitable right to possession, in a defendant in ejectment, as

[1] Morrison *v.* Wilson, 13 Cal. 494.
[2] Meyers *v.* Hill, 46 Penn. 9.
[3] Deitzler *v.* Mishler, 37 Penn. 82.
[4] Stinebaugh *v.* Wisdom, 13 B. Mon. 467; Page *v.* Cole, 6 Clarke, 153; Wales *v.* Bogue, 31 Ill. 465.
[5] Langford *v.* Love, 3 Sneed, 308.
[6] Crane *v.* Crane, 4 Gray, 323.
[7] McKenzie *v.* Perrill, 15 Ohio St. 162.
[8] Barnes *v.* Jamison, 24 Tex. 362.
[9] Kennedy *v.* Daniels, 20 Mis. 104.
[10] Cox *v.* Cox, 26 Penn. 375.
[11] Safford *v.* Hynds, 39 Barb. 625; 15 Barb. 365.
[12] Dewey *v.* Hoag, 15 Barb. 365.

(*a*) See Neave *v.* Avery, 30 Eng. L. & Eq. 471.

against the plaintiff, entitles him to judgment.[1] So an equitable mortgage, after condition broken, is a good defence, under the Code, to ejectment by an execution-purchaser, claiming that the mortgagor had conveyed fraudulently. If such purchaser desires the possession, he must file his bill to redeem.[2] So, under the statute allowing equitable defences to an ejectment, the defendant may explain a sheriff's deed, by showing by parol that a part of the land it appears to convey was expressly excepted at the sale; and may have the deed treated as reformed.[3] So, in Wisconsin, a defendant may show a mistake in the description of his deed.[4] So, under the Missouri practice act of 1849, an equitable defence may be set up.[5] So, in Kentucky, in an action to recover possession of land, a defendant may set up and rely upon any equitable or legal defences, and either party may move to transfer an equitable issue, presented by the pleadings, to the equity docket; but, if no such motion be made, the issue must be disposed of by the court, before judgment can be rendered for the plaintiff.[6]

§ 21. An equitable defence in the answer presents a question for the *court* to decide.[7] In case of equitable defence, the answer must have the requisites of a bill in equity. The title must be such as the decree may make a legal one, available as an estoppel.[8]

§ 22. The question of equitable title in plaintiff or defendant has often arisen, in case of a *purchase* of the land, not accompanied or followed by an actual, executed conveyance. Upon this point it is held, that the defendant, in a writ of entry, cannot defend against the legal title of the plaintiff, by proving that he entered under a written agreement with the plaintiff for the purchase of the demanded premises, and since the entry had paid the stipulated price, and was entitled, by performance of the agreement, to a conveyance of the legal estate.[9] So a sheriff's vendee cannot, where the execution-defendant is the father who has paid the purchase-money and taken the title in his son's name, maintain ejectment against the son.[10] So a bond for title, the sale being under a mortgage, cannot defeat ejectment by the vendor,

[1] Thurman v. Anderson, 30 Barb. 621.
[2] Chase v. Peck, 21 N. Y. 581.
[3] Bartlett v. Judd, 21 N. Y. 200.
[4] Prentiss v. Brewer, 17 Wis. 635.
[5] Hayden v. Stewart, 27 Miss. 286.
[6] Petty v. Malier, 15 B. Mon. 591.
[7] Downer v. Smith, 24 Cal. 124.
[8] Blun v. Robertson, 24 Cal. 146; Downer v. Smith, ib. 124.
[9] Ela v. Pennock, 38 N. H. 154; Moody v. Farr, 33 Miss. 192.
[10] You v. Flinn, 34 Ala. 409.

brought either against the obligee in the bond or a purchaser of his rights; even although the purchase-money has been paid to the vendor.[1]

§ 23. A different doctrine, however, is now adopted in many States, either by direct statutory provision, or by way of natural and necessary inference from statutes or usages relating to law and equity. Thus it is held that a parol sale, delivery of possession, and payment of the whole or even most of the price, are a defence to an ejectment.[2] And a vendee once fairly in possession of land under articles of purchase, but illegally ousted, may recover in an action of ejectment, without bringing into court the balance of purchase-money due.[3] So a verbal contract partly performed, as where the party has entered and in good faith made valuable improvements, may be set up as a defence to ejectment by the vendor. And if the answer set out the contract as verbal, but also set out the facts of part-performance, it is not demurrable.[4] So ejectment cannot be maintained by one who has sold the land by bond, taken a note for the price, and transferred the note.[5] And a purchaser, having tendered the balance due, and demanded a deed, may, upon the trial of an ejectment suit against him, pay the money into court, without interest after the tender.[6] (*a*)

§ 24. Even, however, where this more liberal practice is adopted, it is subjected to equitable conditions and restrictions in favor of the legal owner. Thus it is not by legal right, but by equitable defence, that one holding under another by title-bond can resist ejectment; and generally he must do that by showing full performance, or readiness to perform, and, if he has failed to perform, it is incumbent upon him to show a waiver of his default, or an equitable excuse for it, and to make reparation, in some way or other, by compensation or damages.[7] So a party, who has an

[1] Collins *v.* Robinson, 33 Ala. 91.

[2] Young *v.* Montgomery, 28 Mis. 604; Traphagen *v.* Traphagen, 40 Barb. 537; Patterson *v.* Wilson, 19 Penn. 380; Tibeau *v.* Tibeau, 19 Mis. 78.

[3] D'Arras *v.* Keyser, 26 Penn. 249.

[4] Arguello *v.* Edinger, 10 Cal. 150.

[5] Tompkins *v.* Williams, 19 Geo. 572.

[6] Thompson *v.* McKinley, 47 Penn. 353.

[7] Hill *v.* Still, 19 Tex. 76.

(*a*) But where the defendants alleged a parol gift of land by the plaintiff's ancestor to their own; it was held an error to instruct the jury that, if such contract was proved, they might find for the plaintiff, upon condition that he should pay to the defendants, within a reasonable time, one-tenth of the value of the improvements made by their ancestor. Such an assessment of damages, in an action of ejectment, is not only novel, but impracticable and dangerous. Gill *v.* Gill, 37 Penn. 312.

equity resulting from the payment of a part of the purchase-money, cannot recover in ejectment, without a tender of the balance of the unpaid purchase-money; at most, he can only have a conditional verdict.[1]

§ 25. Ejectment is sometimes provided as the appropriate remedy, in case of purchase, to enforce payment of the price;[2] or to compel specific performance.[3] And this without previous notice.[4]

§ 26. The *condition* annexed to a recovery, in an ejectment for purchase-money, is, that, upon performance of the condition, the recovery shall be released, and not the title to the land.[5] In an ejectment to enforce payment of an instalment, where a conditional recovery is had, and the money paid in accordance with the finding; the title still remains in the plaintiff, as a security for the payment of the unpaid instalment.[6]

§ 27. Where the plaintiff brought ejectment on his legal title, and the defendant set up a contract for the purchase of the land, and tendered the balance unpaid of the purchase-money; held, the plaintiff was entitled to judgment for nominal damages and costs.[7]

§ 28. A sold land to B for $1,500, a deed to be given when the whole purchase-money should be paid. B went into possession; but neglecting to pay the whole purchase-money when due, A brought ejectment. B confessed judgment, to be released on payment of the balance due, which was $322.04, on or before a certain day. The sum was not paid on the day, but was tendered a few weeks afterwards. Held, A was entitled to his writ of possession.[8]

§ 29. In ejectment to enforce specific performance of a sale, an award of judgment, to be released on payment of a certain sum, is not an ordinary judgment at law, but contains also the substance of a decree in equity. As the law of Pennsylvania stood in 1839, it was conclusive of the rights of the parties. Subsequent legislation has had no retrospective operation to divest rights thus vested.[9]

§ 30. The plaintiff took out a writ of *hab. fac. poss.* on such judgment, which was returned executed, the tenant in possession having agreed to hold under the the plaintiff, and having taken a

[1] Chadwick *v.* Felt, 35 Penn. 305.

[2] Hamm *v.* Beaver, 31 Penn. 58; Laner *v.* Lee, 42 ib. 165; Taylor *v.* Abbott, 41 ib. 352; Hill *v.* Oliphant, ib. 364.

[3] Corson *v.* Muloany, 49 Penn. 88.

[4] Dean *v.* Comstock, 32 Ill. 173.

[5] Hamm *v.* Beaver, 1 Grant, 448.

[6] Ibid.

[7] Cadwallader *v.* Berkheiser, 32 Penn. 43.

[8] Chew *v.* Phillippi, 32 Penn. 205.

[9] Coughanour *v.* Bloodgood, 27 Penn. 285.

lease from him. Held, that, when the writ was set aside by the court as improvidently granted, the tenant was thereby restored to his condition of subordination to his former landlord without a writ of restitution.[1]

§ 31. An ejectment by *cestui que trust* to compel a trustee to execute a conveyance, on payment of the purchase-money by the plaintiff, is in the nature of a bill in equity, involving an account of the rents and profits, and no subsequent action of covenant for them can be entertained.[2]

§ 32. In ejectment to enforce payment of unpaid purchase-money, the plaintiff recovered a judgment, to be released on payment of a stipulated sum on or before a day certain, when a good and sufficient deed was to be delivered to the defendant. Before the appointed day, the defendant obtained an award of arbitrators against the plaintiff in a personal action, which award was a lien in favor of the defendant on the plaintiff's interest in the land. The arrears of purchase-money were not paid at the appointed day. The plaintiff filed a deed, caused it to be tendered to the defendant, sued out a writ of possession, and obtained possession of the land. Held, that, by the failure of the defendant to pay, the plaintiff's title became absolute; that the award was no excuse, though, had the defendant paid the sum due into court, he would have extinguished the plaintiff's lien.[3]

§ 33. As has been often suggested, in the action of ejectment, one party or both generally rely upon *documentary* evidence of title. Of course it is no part of the plan of the present work, to consider the nature, form, and effect of transfers of real estate, which is of itself a most important and copious subject. The topic is here considered, only under the precise limitation above referred to. (*a*)

[1] Coughanour *v.* Bloodgood, 27 Penn. 285.

[2] Cox *v.* Henry, 32 Penn. 18.

[3] Waters *v.* Waters, 32 Penn. 307.

(*a*) Ejectment may be maintained upon *a former judgment* for the land. Stevens *v.* Hughes, 31 Penn. 381; Peterman *v.* Huling, ib. 432.

Or upon a *tax* title. Townsend *v.* Downer, 32 Vt. 183.

And, on the other hand, a writ of entry will lie by the former owner of land sold for non-payment of taxes, if he have tendered the proper sum to the purchaser within two years, under Massachusetts Rev. Sts. ch. 8, § 32, although he might also have a bill in equity to compel a reconveyance, under St. 1849, ch. 213. Rand *v.* Robinson, 11 Cush. 289.

A party may rely upon a *public grant or patent*. See Gratz *v.* Beates, 45 Penn. 495; Franklin, &c. *v.* Hall, 16 B. Mon. 472; Schoenberger *v.* Baker, 22 Penn. 398; Manny *v.* Smith, 10 Wis. 509.

Title to lands from the State draws the seisin or actual legal possession to it; so that a party is, by force of his title, in possession, until an ouster or disseisin by some

§ 35. The most frequent claim of title is by *deed of conveyance.* (*a*) An ordinary quitclaim deed will maintain ejectment,

one entering with an adverse claim. Hoye *v.* Swan, 5 Md. 237.

Ejectment may be brought for lands under water, granted by the State, for a certain specific use which requires actual occupation. Champlain, &c. Co. *v.* Valentine, 19 Barb. 484.

Where the plaintiff relies on a prior possession of public lands, the defendant cannot show an anterior possession in a stranger. Piercy *v.* Sabin, 10 Cal. 22.

Under the Miss. statute of 1822 (Hutch. Dig. 858), a certificate issued in pursuance of an act of Congress, by any legally authorized officer, for the purchase or entry of lands belonging to the United States, is sufficient evidence of title to support an action of ejectment. But only when regularly issued and remaining in full force and uncancelled. Davis *v.* Freeland, 32 Miss. 645.

In California, a mere survey and marking boundaries is not possession sufficient to maintain ejectment, unless made so by complying with the statute of April 20, 1852. Bird *v.* Denison, 7 Cal. 297.

If one be in possession of lands, with known and visible boundaries, and, before possession has continued long enough to raise the presumption of a grant, another procures a patent for such lands, or a part thereof; from that time the time of presumption ceases to run. Brown *v.* Potter, Bush. 461.

Where two grants lap, so that both cover in part the same land, the possession of the *lappage* is in law to him who has the better title, unless there be, by the party claiming under the other, an actual possession, or *possessio pedis*, thereon. Ib.

If two grants lap, and one only of the claimants be seated on the lapped part, the possession of the whole interference is in him; possession of a part of the land included in both deeds being possession of the whole. McCormick *v.* Munroe, 3 Jones, 332.

If a patent was obtained under such circumstances as would make the grantee in it a trustee; such circumstances must be set up in the answer to an action for possession, with the same particularity that would be necessary in a bill of chancery. Carman *v.* Johnson, 20 Mis. 108.

A person claiming title to a lot in San Francisco, under an alcalde's grant, made in 1847, cannot maintain a possessory action, or an action of ejectment, against one in the actual possession, when it only appears that the alcalde's grantee went upon the lot in 1848, drove some stakes, and cleared away some brush for the purpose of erecting a dwelling-house. Woodworth *v.* Fulton, 1 Cal. 295.

It is held in the United States court, that the plaintiff in ejectment must, in all cases, prove a legal title at the time of the demise laid in the declaration, and not a mere equitable estate; and the practice, in some States, of permitting ejectment to be maintained upon warrants for land, and upon titles not complete or legal in their character, can in nowise affect the jurisdiction of courts of the United States. Thus the holder of a new Madrid certificate, upon which no patent had issued, cannot recover in ejectment, the legal title being in the general government. Fenn *v.* Holme, 21 How. 481.

Where the plaintiffs in an action of ejectment offered, in support of their title, two patents of tracts of land, called "Black Walnut Thicket," and "Content," and also a deed of two tracts of the same names (the metes and bounds describing the tracts in the deed not being identical with those of either patent), and proved possession by their ancestor of the land described in the deed, there being no evidence of any adverse claim; the jury were warranted in finding that the land described in the deed was the same as that granted by the patents. Carroll *v.* Carroll, 16 How. 275.

In reference to the obsolete assurance of *fine*, a recent case in New York decides, that a fine has no validity, unless the parties have some interest in the land. The person who levies it must have a freehold by right or by disseisin; and the disseisin need not be by violence; but where, from the circumstances of the case, there can be no violence, the law will infer a disseisin from such other acts, as show that the possession is adverse and hostile to that of the true owner. M'Gregor *v.* Comstock, 16 Barb. 427.

A party may claim under *an ancient vote of proprietors.* Gloucester *v.* Gaffney, 8 Allen, 11.

In general, the plaintiff must show title from the State, or possession of himself or the person under whom he claims. Graves *v.* Amoskeag, &c., 44 N. H. 462.

(*a*) A deed may be *conditional,* as well as absolute. A grantee, who has performed for a time an agreement to support the grantor, and who is ready to continue such performance, may maintain ejectment against the grantor. Spalding *v.* Hallenbeck 30 Barb. 292.

if the grantor could have done so.[1] So where a person, having a quitclaim deed from one who held by deed of warranty, made entry, and then conveyed to the demandant; held, the latter had such seisin as would maintain a writ of entry against a wrong-doer.[2] And one who enters under a deed with warranty, purporting to convey the fee, is presumed to enter claiming according to such title, and may maintain a writ of entry, though his predecessors had an estate less than a freehold.[3] A deed gives *color of title*.[4] It is held to be admissible in evidence, though not recorded. Notice, which is equivalent to recording, may be subsequently proved.[5]

§ 36. If a grantee in an absolute deed leave his grantor in possession, the latter becomes his *quasi* tenant, and may be joined in an action of ejectment against him.[6]

§ 37. But a recorded deed does not disseise the owner, unless the grantor occupy some part of the premises.[7] So, in ejectment, a deed from one, who is not shown to have had any interest in the land, is inadmissible in evidence.[8] And a mere entry upon land, under a deed defectively executed, not followed by any acts

[1] Sullivan *v.* Davis, 4 Cal. 291; Downer *v.* Smith, 24 ib. 123.
[2] Edmunds *v.* Griffin, 41 N. H. 529.
[3] Melcher *v.* Flanders, 40 N. H. 139.
[4] Dickenson *v.* Breeden, 30 Ill. 279.
[5] Ross *v.* Hole, 27 Ill. 104. See Hill *v.* Kricke, 11 Wis. 442.
[6] Patch *v.* Keeler, 1 Williams, 252.
[7] Putnam, &c. *v.* Fisher, 38 Maine, 324.
[8] Shrack *v.* Zubler, 34 Penn. 38.

Questions also arise, in connection with deeds of mortgage. See Koons *v.* Steele, 19 Penn. 203.

A purchaser under the foreclosure of a mortgage, made by the party disseised, has, and can assert, precisely his rights. Clute *v.* Voris, 31 Barb. 511.

A conditional judgment in a writ of entry on a mortgage, followed by fifty years' quiet and peaceable possession by the mortgagee, is sufficient evidence of an absolute title, without proof that possession was ever delivered to him under such judgment by legal process. Creighton *v.* Proctor, 12 Cush. 433.

In ejectment to try title, where a mortgage has been paid under a mistake, the defendants, whose only equity grows out of this mistake, cannot have a conditional verdict found for the plaintiffs, requiring them to pay the mortgage before they can gain possession. The verdict should be for the plaintiffs, unconditionally. If the mistake had never been made, the mortgage would be no protection to the defendants. Peters *v.* Florence, 38 Penn. 194.

An old mortgage, without possession, is no defence in ejectment. Moreau *v.* Detchemendy, 18 Mis. 522.

A mortgage is a good defence without disclaimer of an absolute title. Hoxie *v.* Finney, 11 Gray, 511. See Sheridan *v.* Welch, 8 Allen, 166.

A writ of entry will not lie in favor of a second mortgagee against a tenant of a prior mortgagee, who has taken possession for condition broken. Batcheller *v.* Pratt, 10 Cush. 185.

A demandant is not precluded from maintaining his writ, by having mortgaged the land pending the action. Woodman *v.* Smith, 37 Maine, 21.

A title acquired by the tenant, without the concurrence of the demandant, after the commencement of a real action, although pleaded at the first term after it is acquired, will not bar the defendant,—especially when it is merely a title under a mortgage,—even if the tenant has given the demandant notice that he is in possession for the purpose of foreclosure. Curtis *v.* Francis, 9 Cush. 427.

of ownership or continued possession, will not sustain a writ of entry.[1]

§ 38. When one enters upon land, under a deed giving definite and certain boundaries, the possession of any part is a possession of the whole, though the deed be not recorded.[2] (*a*) But such possession may be disproved.[3]

§ 38 *a*. A conveyed to B a tract of land, excepting therefrom the land within its boundaries, which was included in the highway. Held, A could maintain ejectment against B, for an encroachment on the land excepted.[4] And a party cannot recover under a deed which does not include within its description the property claimed, although the party under whom he claims, holding by a deed with a similar description, may have acquired title by adverse possession or otherwise.[5]

§ 39. Where the defendants show no title, and the plaintiff is in possession, they cannot rely on the invalidity of his documentary title.[6] But if the demandant offer no evidence of title beyond possession, the defendants may show that the conveyances under which he claimed did not include the land in dispute, and that the entry made by his grantor was not under claim of title.[7]

§ 40. A plaintiff, who had no title at the time of bringing suit, cannot recover on the strength of a deed of confirmation made to him before the trial.[8] But a deed of land from A to B, in 1822, the consideration money being paid, the grant for which was not issued until 1831, vests a title sufficient to support ejectment, as against a subsequent sheriff's deed.[9] And if the party has a deed from A, and also one from B, who claimed under A, it is immaterial whether the deed from A to B be good or bad.[10]

§ 41. Ejectment does not lie upon a grant by one disseised;[11] nor without proof of title, or claim of title and possession, in the grantor. But possession under color of title for eight or ten years is sufficient.[12]

[1] Nichols *v.* Todd, 2 Gray, 568.

[2] Spaulding *v.* Warren, 25 Vt. 316. See Baird *v.* Bell, 1 Duv. (Ky.), 384.

[3] Gardner *v.* Gooch, 48 Maine, 487.

[4] Etz *v.* Daily, 20 Barb. 32.

[5] Menkins *v.* Blumenthal, 19 Mis. 496.

[6] Boyreau *v.* Campbell, 1 McAll. C. C. (Cal.), 119.

[7] Edmunds *v.* Griffin, 41 N. H. 529.

[8] Shrack *v.* Zubler, 34 Penn. 38.

[9] Hand *v.* McKinney, 25 Geo. 648.

[10] Prescott *v.* Jones, 29 Geo. 58.

[11] Mosher *v.* Yost, 33 Barb. 277.

[12] Dominy *v.* Miller, ib. 386.

(*a*) Where, under a deed, one makes the first entry, and part of the land is unenclosed, he has a better title than one claiming by subsequent entry on the unenclosed part, with mere color of title. Hicks *v.* Coleman, 25 Cal. 130.

§ 42. The defendant in ejectment, as well as the plaintiff, may claim under a deed and conformable possession.[1] A legal subsisting title, outstanding in another, defeats the plaintiff. As, for example, a deed to an illegitimate son of the father of the plaintiff, delivered by putting it on record for his benefit, although the minor die before coming of age.[2] And, on the other hand, the plaintiff may offer in evidence a deed to the defendant, to explain the latter's possession.[3] Or prove that the defendant, at the time he executed a deed relied on by the plaintiff, stated that the land conveyed was the same as that on which the defendant lived, there being no variance between the deed and the declaration in the writ.[4]

§ 43. Where the defendant is proved to be in possession, and the plaintiff produces registered deeds showing an apparent chain of title from the lessor's ancestor to the defendant; it is *primâ facie* evidence that the defendant is in possession, claiming under such title.[5]

§ 44. Where a person made a deed to A of a life-estate in unoccupied land, and A conveyed to B in fee; held, B was not precluded, by the rule of practice in ejectment, from denying the title of A, except as to the life-estate; and that the heirs of A could only recover by showing, either that their ancestor had a deed purporting to convey a fee, or that he was in possession, claiming a fee.[6]

§ 45. Fraud may be set up for the first time, in an action of ejectment, to impeach a deed.[7]

§ 46. Questions often arise, relating to adverse title, and the right of recovery in ejectment, where the parties stand in the relation of vendor and purchaser. See §§ 16, 18.

§ 47. The distinction is made, that one in possession under an executory contract may hold adversely as against strangers. But his possession is not adverse to the vendor, until after performance.[8] Thus a vendee entering into possession, under a contract of purchase, with an unconditional bond for title to be given at a stipulated time, does not hold adversely to the vendor until the purchase-money is paid.[9]

[1] Schuyler *v.* Marsh, 37 Barb. 350; Holbrook *v.* Brenner, 31 Ill. 501.
[2] Masterson *v.* Cheek, 23 Ill. 72.
[3] McMinn *v.* Mayes, 4 Cal. 209.
[4] Wilkerson *v.* Moulder, 15 Mis. 609.
[5] Register *v.* Rowell, 3 Jones, 312.
[6] Worsley *v.* Johnson, 5 Jones, 72.
[7] Reynolds *v.* Vilas, 8 Wis. 471 (under the Code). See Judd *v.* Gibbs, 3 Gray, 539.
[8] Vrooman *v.* Shepherd, 14 Barb. 441; McClanahan *v.* Barrow, 27 Miss. 664; Secrest *v.* M'Kenna, 6 Rich, Eq. 72.
[9] Stamper *v.* Griffin, 12 Geo. 450.

§ 48. Where the plaintiff was in possession several years, claiming title, and the defendant went into possession under a contract, whereby he agreed to purchase the improvements of the plaintiff and his title, as soon as it should be settled, should it prove to be good, the contract reciting that the title was then in dispute; held, abundant evidence of title in the plaintiff to sustain an action of ejectment against the defendant, aside from the rights of the defendant under the contract.[1]

§ 49. An *execution*, as well as a voluntary conveyance, may be the foundation of adverse title.[2] Thus, in ejectment brought by the execution defendant, to recover land levied on and sold by the sheriff, against the purchaser at the sheriff's sale; such purchaser need only show, *primâ facie*, a judgment, execution, sale, and sheriff's deed.[3] (*a*)

§ 50. This form of title often involves questions relating to an alleged fraudulent conveyance.

§ 51. In Massachusetts, a writ of entry lies, under Stat. 1844, ch. 107, § 4, to recover possession of real estate taken on execution against a debtor, who has purchased it, and caused it to be conveyed to a third person, in order to secure it from his creditors, only when the estate has been set off by appraisement to the judgment creditor; and not when the estate, being an equity of redeeming land mortgaged, has been sold on execution.[4]

§ 51 *a*. Land belonging to A was attached at the suit of Hollis B., which name was used, by mistake, for Horace B. While under attachment, A conveyed the land to C. In the suit, judgment and execution were recovered, and the land duly levied upon. Held, C could not recover the land, whether evidence was or was not admissible to show the mistake.[5]

§ 52. Under the law of Maryland, where the distinction between law and equity is accurately preserved, a plaintiff, who has both sold and bought the land in question on execution, cannot, in a subsequent ejectment, introduce parol evidence that the de-

1 Spencer *v.* Tobey, 22 Barb. 260.
2 See Spaulding *v.* Goodspead, 39 Maine, 564; Wilson *v.* Palmer, 18 Tex. 592; Hill *v.* Oliphant, 41 Penn. 364; Gautt *v.* Cowan, 27 Ala. 582; Bank, &c. *v.* Eastman, 44 N. H. 431; Blain *v.* Coppedge, 16 Mis. 495.
3 Mercer *v.* Doe, 6 Ind. 80.
4 Foster *v.* Durant, 2 Gray, 538.
5 Emerson *v.* Collamore, 33 Maine, 581.

(*a*) In England, the writ of *elegit*, with the inquisition and return thereupon, is conclusive proof of title prior to the return, as against the judgment debtor. Martin *v.* Smith, 3 H. & N. 959.

fendant's title, which, upon the face of his deed, was held in trust for his wife and children, was so held in fraud of creditors.[1]

§ 52 *a*. An officer's deed, under an execution against a third party, is not admissible in favor of a defendant in ejectment, without proof that he thereby acquired some title.[2]

§ 53. Where a purchaser at sheriff's sale was guilty of actual fraud in making the purchase, the tenant in ejectment, claiming under him, is not entitled to a return of the purchase-money, either before suit or by a conditional judgment, from the assignee of the insolvent seeking to vacate the sale.[3]

§ 53 *a*. In Maine, the proceedings should be by bill in equity, and not by writ of entry, for the recovery of land by one, who claims title under a levy against a debtor having only an equitable interest.[4]

§ 54. As has been already explained, the object of the action of ejectment is to recover *possession* of the land in question. Possession, or the right of possession, therefore, on the part of the respective parties to the action, becomes a most material inquiry.[5] (*a*) When an ejectment is brought against a party in possession, by one who has never had actual possession, and none is shown in his grantor at the date of the grant; the claimant must go back and show that some one, under whom he claims, had at one time possession and title, or at least the latter, and that he has succeeded absolutely to all such right.[6] On the other hand, the demandant who shows a possession of himself or those under whom he claims, prior in time, is entitled to recover against a tenant, who shows no title, but merely possession at the time of suit brought; although such demandant may be a wrong-doer as to the real owner.[7] So a party in quiet possession cannot

1 Smith *v.* McCann, 24 How. 398.

2 McGarrity *v.* Byington, 12 Cal. 426.

3 McCaskey *v.* Graff, 23 Penn. 321.

4 Eastman *v.* Fletcher, 45 Maine, 302.

5 See Sheik *v.* M'Elroy, 20 Penn. 25.

6 Bartow *v.* Draper, 5 Duer, 130.

7 Hubbard *v.* Little, 9 Cush. 475; Nagle *v.* Macy, 9 Cal. 426. See Bird *v.* Lisbros, ib. 1; Perkins *v.* Blood, 36 Verm. 273; Schultz *v.* Arnot, 33 Mis. 172.

(*a*) A person in possession is presumed to have acquired the title which the people, in their capacity of sovereign, once held. But when the people are plaintiffs, *it seems*, the presumption in the defendant's favor is shifted to the other side, on showing that the possession has been vacant at any time within forty years. People *v.* Trinity Church, 22 N. Y. (8 Smith), 44.

In Louisiana, to sustain a possessory action, it is incumbent upon the plaintiff to prove that he had real and actual possession at the instant when the disturbance occurred, and that he has suffered a real disturbance, either in fact or in law, within a year before the suit was brought. Millard *v.* Richard, 13 La. An. 572.

An action of *jactitation* cannot be maintained by a party not in possession. Arrowsmith *v.* Durell, 14 La. An. 849.

In California, in an action of ejectment to settle title, the plaintiff must have possession. Lyle *v.* Rollins, 25 Cal. 437.

be legally dispossessed by force, although he cannot show a perfect title.[1] And the person owning the title to land is constructively in possession, until some adverse claimant goes into the occupancy, with intent to claim the fee, as against the true owner; manifested by declarations or by acts of ownership, which are open, notorious, and visible.[2] But ejectment cannot be maintained for land of which the plaintiff is himself in possession.[3]

§ 55. Substantially the same proposition is stated in the terms, that possession will sustain an action against an intruder;[4] that possession gives a *primâ facie* title;[5] that possession *with color of title* is sufficient, unless a better title is shown in defence.[6] So it is held, that mere possession is sufficient, though a title in fee is alleged.[7] So a person evicted from possession can, without showing any title in himself, maintain an action against the grantee of his disseisor, who is also without title.[8] So a defendant without valid title cannot put the plaintiff, who was in possession until dispossessed by the defendant, with a claim of right, to proof that he has not conveyed away his title.[9] In ejectment, a prior occupancy is a sufficient title against a wrong-doer; though the evidence must show a continuous possession, or at least that it was not abandoned, in order to entitle the plaintiff to recover merely by virtue of such possession.[10]

§ 56. Possession, to justify a claim of title in ejectment, must be *adverse*. The subject of adverse possession, therefore, lies at the foundation of the particular remedy which we are now considering. Adverse possession is equivalent to, or commences with, *disseisin* or *ouster*. "An ouster is a wrongful dispossession or exclusion of a party from real property, who is entitled to the possession." [11] (*a*) Like other wrongful acts, it is held that ouster may be committed by an *agent*.[12]

§ 57. It is the general rule, though in many States altered by statute, that land cannot be conveyed which is at the time (and

[1] Ladd *v.* Stevenson, 1 Cal. 18.
[2] Morrison *v.* Hays, 19 Geo. 294.
[3] Kribbs *v.* Downing, 25 Penn. 399.
[4] Shumway *v.* Phillips, 22 Penn. 151.
[5] Hutchinson *v.* Perley, 4 Cal. 33; Hicks *v.* Davis, ib. 67; Plume *v.* Seward, ib. 94.
[6] Winans *v.* Christy, 4 Cal. 70.
[7] Ibid.
[8] Clute *v.* Voris, 31 Barb. 511.
[9] Russell *v.* Brooks, 1 Williams, 640.
[10] Wilson *v.* Palmer, 18 Tex. 592.
[11] Per Butler, J., Newell *v.* Woodruff 30 Conn. 497.
[12] Munson *v.* Munson, ib. 425.

(*a*) In Vermont, an entry upon land by a stranger, under claim of right, is an actual eviction of the owner, of which he is bound to take notice, at the peril of losing his estate, after fifteen years. Whitney *v.* French, 25 Vt. 663.

continues to be), in the actual adverse possession of another.[1] But the mere purchase of an outstanding invalid claim does not make an adverse possession less hostile to the true title, nor devest a title already complete under the Statute of Limitations.[2]

§ 58. An entry, to constitute an ouster, and give possession, must be with claim of title; but such claim need not be under a deed or other writing. If under a deed, the possession may extend further than the precise boundaries described in it.[3] A hostile invasion of another's rights is one of the elements of title by adverse possession; if there be consent on the part of the owner, the entry for the purpose of doing the act is not tortious. The possession must be actual, adverse, exclusive, and continuous, and under claim of title, to authorize the presumption of a deed; and these facts are questions for the jury.[4]

§ 59. There are various exceptions to the rule of title by adverse possession. Thus, upon a universally recognized ground of public policy, there can be no adverse possession against the commonwealth.[5] So, whether a possession is adverse, depends upon the intention with which it was taken and held. If taken in subordination to the title of another, it cannot be changed into an adverse possession by the party himself, except by a disclaimer, and an assertion of an adverse title, with notice thereof to the party under whom he entered. Thus an open, exclusive, and uninterrupted possession of land for more than twenty years, taken, held, and claimed under a parol gift from the plaintiff for a life not yet terminated, is not such an adverse possession as will bar an action. Such entry and claim are a recognition of the continued existence of a subsisting title in the legal owner, and an admission of holding in subordination thereto.[6] So where a party has taken possession by a lawful title, and holds over after his right has expired, this possession is not adverse to the reversioner.[7] (*a*) So where a grantor enters and occupies for non-payment of ground-rent, under and by virtue of the deed; such entry and occupation

[1] Kincheloe *v.* Tracewells, 11 Gratt. 587.

[2] Owens *v.* Myers, 20 Penn. 134.

[3] Kincheloe *v.* Tracewells, 11 Gratt. 587.

[4] Armstrong *v.* Risteau, 5 Md. 256.

[5] Koiner *v.* Rankin, 11 Gratt. 420.

[6] Clark *v.* McClure, 10 ib. 305.

[7] Day *v.* Cochran, 24 Miss. 261.

(*a*) Before 1829, a deed was made, conferring a life-estate in land upon A and his wife; and about this time A conveyed in fee to B. The wife survived A, and died in 1849. Held, the possession of B did not become adverse to those having the remainder, until after the death of A's wife. Todd *v.* Zachary, 1 Busb. Eq. 286.

do not constitute an adverse possession, as against the grantee or those claiming under him; nor will the declaration of the grantor, made to a stranger, after he had been in possession seventeen years, that in four years more he should have title by lapse of time, affect the nature of the previous occupancy, even if it should that of the future.[1]

§ 60. In reference to the general nature of the possession which may be claimed as adverse, it is held that there must be an actual *bonâ fide* occupation or *possessio pedis*, a subjection to the will and control of the possessor; not mere assertion of title, and casual acts of ownership, such as recording deeds, paying taxes, etc. But occupation of a part of the land marked by distinct boundaries is sufficient. Neither cultivation nor any particular kind of enclosure is necessary, if the land is subjected to the party's use in the manner indicated.[2] Or, as is elsewhere held, actual possession, or a civil or legal possession, preceded by a natural possession in the plaintiff or his *authors*, is necessary to sustain the possessory action.[3]

§ 61. Possession, however short, will maintain an action, unless the defendant explain it, or show a prior possession or title in himself or a third person.[4] Where the evidence shows possession by the same party at two periods, the presumption is, that it was the same in the interval.[5] So, on the other hand, uncontradicted proof, that the defendant commenced building a brick house on the premises in 1848, and that he and his family had resided in it since 1849 or 1850, the trial taking place in 1858, is sufficient evidence of possession at the time the suit was brought, which was in September, 1856.[6]

§ 62. As we have already suggested, the question of adverse possession is for the jury.[7] Thus, in reference to the possession of the defendant.[8] So a question of *mixed* possession is for the jury.[9] So it is open to a jury to infer, from proof that the defendant in ejectment was living on a portion of a lot of land, that he claimed the whole of it.[10] So the question of a change in the nature of a party's possession. Thus the defendant in ejectment took one to a

[1] McCracken *v.* Roberts, 19 Penn. 390. See Corning *v.* Troy, &c., 39 Barb. 311.

[2] Plume *v.* Seward, 4 Cal. 94.

[3] Searles *v.* Costillo, 12 La. An. 203.

[4] Potter *v.* Knowles, 5 Cal. 87.

[5] People *v.* Trinity Church, 22 N. Y. (8 Smith), 44.

[6] Goodhue *v.* Baker, 22 Ill. 262.

[7] Gage *v.* Smith, 27 Conn. 70.

[8] Scisson *v.* M'Lane, 12 Geo. 166.

[9] O'Hara *v.* Richardson, 46 Penn. 385.

[10] Fitzgerald *v.* Williams, 24 Geo. 343.

cabin, which was the only building on the place, let him the land for a year, then nailed up the cabin, and both retired, the tenant being charged not to divulge the transaction. Held, if this was colorable merely, it was no change of any previous possession, and the question, whether it was or not, should be left to the jury.[1]

§ 63. Adverse possession being thus for the most part a question of fact, depending on act and intent, much latitude is usually allowed in the introduction of evidence which bears upon these points. Thus the plaintiff may show his claim of title to explain his possession.[2] So a defendant may prove his own act of taking possession, to show its character and extent, as well as his purpose in doing so, as that was at the time manifest, from his own concurrent declarations.[3] But, under some circumstances, parol evidence is held inadmissible as to adverse possession.[4]

§ 64. It has already appeared, that the possession necessary to give seisin, and establish the requisite title in ejectment, may be *constructive* or *implied*, as well as actual. And this principle is affirmed in many of the States by express statutes, which attempt to define, usually in conformity with previous judicial decisions, what precise acts shall constitute constructive possession.[5]

§ 65. Much strictness is sometimes adopted upon this subject.[6] Prior possession is held insufficient, without compliance with the statute concerning possessory actions, or proof of actual *bonâ fide* occupation. Mere entry, without color of title, accompanied by a survey and marking of boundaries, is insufficient.[7]

§ 66. So, to maintain an action upon the ground of adverse possession *by the defendant;* he must have actual adverse and exclusive possession.[8] Thus an action may be maintained, by the owner of land subject to a highway, against a railroad company who appropriate the land for their own purposes.[9] But an action does not lie against a city, for land used as a public street, notwithstanding the grading, paving, and cleaning of the street by the city; these acts involving no possession or claim of title.[10] So

1 Oliver *v.* Williams, 25 Geo. 217.

2 Piercy *v.* Sabin, 10 Cal. 22.

3 Hood *v.* Hood, 2 Grant. 229.

4 Pasley *v.* English, 10 Gratt. 236.

5 Royall *v.* Lisle, 15 Geo. 545; O'Hara *v.* Richardson, 46 Penn. 385; Hollingshead *v.* Naumair, 45 Penn. 141; People *v.* Batchelder, 27 Cal. 72; Doolittle *v.* Tice, 41 Barb. 181; Gardner *v.* Gooch, 48 Maine, 487.

6 See Royall *v.* Lisle, 15 Geo. 545; Wood *v.* M'Guire, 15 Geo. 202; Sheik *v.* M'Elroy, 20 Penn. 25.

7 Murphy *v.* Wallingford, 6 Cal. 648.

8 Schuyler *v.* Marsh, 37 Barb. 350; Girard *v.* New Orleans, 13 La. An. 295; Eaton *v.* Jacobs, 49 Maine, 559.

9 Lozier *v.* N. Y. &c., 42 Barb. 465.

10 Comerhoven *v.* Brooklyn, 38 Barb. 9.

where the ancestor of the demandant was disseised, and neither the demandant nor his ancestor entered or demanded possession afterwards, nor did any other similar act to assert his title, while the defendants, who were not the original disseisors, were on the land; they cannot be charged as disseisors and tenants of the freehold, at the election of the demandant, and are not liable as such, if they neither have nor claim any freehold interest in the demanded premises.[1] So an admission of the plaintiff's title is not sufficient ground for a judgment against the defendant.[2] And, in general, as we have seen, intention is necessary to disseisin.[3]

§ 67. The class of cases, in which the question of constructive possession has chiefly arisen, are those relating to lands not built upon, and partially wild and unimproved; turning more particularly upon the point, whether and to what extent the enclosure, cultivation, &c., of a part will give title to the whole. It is held, that, while lands remain in a state of nature, there cannot be adversary possession against an elder title, except by such acts of ownership as change their condition.[4] So proof, that no person but the demandant had occupied the land for thirty years, and that he had cut wood upon it, and had always fenced portions of it, does not sufficiently show an open, exclusive, and adverse possession.[5] Nor the occasional occupation of a station in water for one or two months every year, during the fishing season.[6] Nor cutting grass nearly every year on flats covered a part of the time by the tide.[7] Nor cutting timber for fences, by one tenant in common, at intervals, for over twenty years, in a cedar swamp, surrounded by cultivated lands.[8] Nor an insufficient fence enclosing a part of the land.[9] Nor the mere throwing of manure on another's land.[10] Nor cutting of trees on land, susceptible of other uses and enjoyment, and feeding hogs on it, under color of title, for seven years.[11] And, in general, where a tenant in possession exercises the ordinary rights of an owner, but acknowledges, during the whole period of his occupation, that the demandant or his ancestor owns the premises; such acknowledgments qualify and explain his

[1] Tappan *v.* Tappan, 36 N. H. 98.
[2] Girard *v.* New Orleans, 13 La. An. 295.
[3] Riley *v.* Griffin, 16 Geo. 141.
[4] Koiner *v.* Rankin, 11 Gratt. 420.
[5] Frye *v.* Gragg, 35 Maine, 29.
[6] McCullough *v.* Wall, 4 Rich. 68.
[7] Commonwealth *v.* Roxbury, 9 Gray, 451. See Hammond *v.* Inloes, 4 Md. 138.
[8] Ewer *v.* Lowell, 9 Gray, 276.
[9] Baldwin *v.* Simpson, 12 Cal. 560.
[10] Shroder *v.* Breneman, 21 Penn. 225.
[11] Loftin *v.* Cobb, 1 Jones, 406.

acts, and, if there is no evidence to the contrary, the demandant is entitled to a verdict.[1] (*a*) So where the defendant claimed adversely to a line not discernible; held, the claim could not be sustained, though he had for over twenty years enclosed the land in dispute, with his other lands, by a fence which embraced other land of the plaintiff, beyond the line to which he claimed.[2] And it is held, in the new State of Nevada, that the right to bring ejectment, on the ground of possession, for public land, depends on the elements of *character*, *locality*, and *purpose*. The possession must be *bonâ fide*, not a mere *staking off*.[3]

§ 68. But where an owner of land conveyed it, reserving a stream running over the land, but for nearly thirty years neglects to take possession thereof, and others divert the stream, and have the open, notorious, and exclusive use and enjoyment during that time; such adverse enjoyment is sufficient to support a title.[4] So A built a mill a mile from B's pond, and entered upon a dam and flume, previously built by C at the outlet of the pond to supply his mill, which formerly stood near the site of A's mill; and used it eighteen years. The mill chiefly depended on the water thus obtained. Held, A's possession was adverse; that there was a presumption of notice, though the lands about the pond were wild lands.[5] So actual possession or cultivation of part of a tract of land, use of the unenclosed portions as woodland, and payment of taxes on the whole for twenty-one years, are circumstances which constitute title to the whole. The distinction is made, that payment of taxes on unseated land is an *indicium* of ownership, and, in connection with actual possession and cultivation, strong evidence of title. But, without possession or cultivation of part of the tract, entries from time to time to take wood are mere trespasses, and confer no right, even when accompanied by payment of taxes.[6] So A, the owner of three adjoining

[1] Cilley *v.* Bartlett, 19 N. H. 312.
[2] Wood *v.* Willard, 37 Verm. 377.
[3] Sankey *v.* Noyes, 1 Neva. 68.
[4] Hoyt *v.* Carter, 16 Barb. 212.
[5] Perrin *v.* Garfield, 37 Verm. 304.
[6] Murphy *v.* Springer, 1 Grant, 73.

(*a*) By the Mexican law, as well as the common law, the possession of one having neither title nor color of title does not extend beyond the bounds of his actual occupation; and the fact, that his cattle and horses have roamed and grazed upon a particular tract of land, does not of itself make out an actual possession in him. Actual possession of a small portion of a large tract of land, with a claim of title to the whole, will not, under the law of Mexico, entitle the party to maintain a possessory action, when it appears, on the face of the papers under which he claims, that his title is void. Sunol *v.* Hepburn, 1 Cal. 254.

surveys, containing in all about two hundred acres, resided on the middle survey, and improved it, and exercised notorious acts of ownership — such as cutting firewood, saw-logs, and other timber — over the other surveys, for twenty-one years, using the whole as one farm. Most of the land was covered by a warrant and survey for four hundred acres, older than A's surveys of the woodland lots, but there had been no improvement or occupancy by the warrantee, nor were any taxes assessed to or paid by him, for more than twenty-one years, but A had paid them. Held, A had acquired a title to all three tracts, as against the warrant and survey; and a purchaser from him could not set up title under such warrant, in an action against him for the purchase-money.[1] So where one has had continued possession for more than twenty years, exercising acts of ownership, as by clearing, &c.; he will be presumed to have had a conveyance, so as to enable him to maintain ejectment against a stranger who enters, though the former has not had *possessio pedis* of the particular part of the tract occupied by the latter.[2] So residence, though necessary to constitute a settlement, is not necessary to adverse possession. The latter may be by cultivation and enclosure, by cultivation without enclosure, or by enclosure without cultivation; and, in every case, without regard to the design of the occupant, further than that it be to resist an entry by any one else. But when adverse possession is claimed by enclosure, it is requisite for the occupant to keep up the fences or building, and prevent the place from being turned into common. An intention to resume a suspended intrusion, of which the legal owner of the title may know nothing, falls short of the requirement of the statute. It is not what the outgoing occupant intended, but what he did, which determines the question of abandonment of possession.[3]

§ 69. As appears from what has been said, the doctrine of constructive possession most frequently comes in question, in connection with the claim of title to the *whole* of certain premises, of which the claimant actually occupies or improves only a *part*.[4] Upon this subject, it is a familiar distinction, though not of universal application, that part possession of land claimed under, and included within, the terms of a deed or other writing, gives title to

[1] Baker *v.* Findley, 20 Penn. 163.
[2] Smith *v.* Bryan, Busb. 180.
[3] Stephens *v.* Leach, 19 Penn. 262.
[4] See Evans *v.* Corley, 4 Rich. 315; Brown *v.* Roberts, 1 Neva. 402; Barnhart *v.* Petit, 22 Penn. 135.

the whole, being *under color* of title; while a title resting on possession alone is confined within the limits of actual occupancy.[1] Thus entry and possession for twenty years of the improved portion of land, under a conveyance in fee of the whole, is possession of the whole, if there is no adverse possession.[2]

§ 70. But while a party entering, and claiming title *bonâ fide*, acquires in law actual possession to the extent of the boundaries contained in his title, whether valid or not; the possession of a wrong-doer does not extend beyond actual enclosure.[3] And there cannot be adverse possession, without an actual possession of the *locus in quo*, or of some part of a legal subdivision of which it formed a part.[4] So the constructive possession of one claiming under adverse possession will not be extended beyond the tract or tracts, of usual and ordinary dimensions, actually marked out, and severally entered upon and possessed, by the claimant.[5] And possession of two tracts, adjacent to the one in controversy, for seven years, with color of title, though all conveyed in one deed, by separate and distinct descriptions, is not a possession of the land in question, and will not amount to a bar under the Statute of Limitations.[6] So the fact, that a party had cattle on the land, or was there for short periods himself, or that he claimed within given limits, is, in the absence of any enclosure or visible signs of the extent of his claim, insufficient to show possession of any particular tract, when others were also in possession.[7]

§ 71. As has been already stated, possession is but *primâ facie* evidence of title.[8] Thus the possession of the defendant is a good defence, until a better title is shown.[9] But where the line contended for by the defendant is clearly shown to be erroneous; no acquiescence by the plaintiff, short of twenty years, will bar a recovery according to the true line, unless there be an *estoppel in pais*.[10] If the plaintiff relies upon possession, the defendant may set up a *bonâ fide* possession of his own, and title for a third person, or the transfer, by the plaintiff, of a bond for title to a third person. Though it is otherwise, where the defendant is a mere trespasser.[11] In other words, where nothing but possession is

[1] Royall *v.* Lisle, 15 Geo. 545; Swift *v.* Gage, 26 Verm. 224; Turney *v.* Chamberlain, 15 Ill. 271.

[2] Fairman *v.* Beal, 14 Ill. 244.

[3] Hoye *v.* Swan, 5 Md. 237.

[4] Shipman *v.* Baxter, 21 Ala. 456.

[5] Hole *v.* Rittenhouse, 19 Penn. 305.

[6] Loftin *v.* Cobb, 1 Jones, 406.

[7] Wilson *v.* Corbier, 13 Cal. 166.

[8] See Tucker *v.* Phillips, 2 Met. Ky. 416.

[9] Hipp *v.* Forester, 7 Jones, 599.

[10] Emerick *v.* Kohler, 29 Barb. 165.

[11] Jones *v.* Scoggins, 11 Geo. 119.

shown by either party, priority of possession sustains the action. But the presumption of title may be rebutted by proof of title in a third person.[1] As between two possessions, the first will prevail.[2]

§ 72. In an action for a portion of a tract of land, both parties relying on possession, and the defendant proving a prior possession by actual enclosure of the whole tract; the defendant's possession may be valid, though not in conformity with the preemption laws of the United States, or the possessory laws of the State.[3]

§ 73. Actual enclosure, in cases of mixed possession, is necessary to defeat the title of the real owner. It makes no difference between him and the wrong-doer, whether he is in actual possession of any part of the land or not; for, in either case, the title by possession holds only to the extent of actual enclosure.[4]

§ 74. In reference to the possession of *the defendant*, the plaintiff may recover upon his prior possession, against one in possession without claim of title, if only abandoned *animo revertendi*.[5] And the law is the same as against a wrong-doer, claiming title by possession alone, whether the real owner be in actual possession of any of the land or not.[6] But, as has been already suggested, ejectment lies only against one who has or has had possession,[7] (*a*) or received the rents and profits, since the plaintiff ac-

[1] Brewster *v.* Striker, 1 E. D. Smith, 321.
[2] Potter *v.* Knowles, 5 Cal. 87.
[3] Bradshaw *v.* Treat, 6 Cal. 172.
[4] Armstrong *v.* Risteau, 5 Md. 256.
[5] Jones *v.* Nunn, 12 Geo. 469.
[6] Hoye *v.* Swan, 5 Md. 237.
[7] Klink *v.* Cohen, 13 Cal. 623; 13 Barb. 526; Scisson *v.* M'Lanes, 12 Geo. 166; Daniel *v.* Le Fevre, 19 Ark. 201; Cochran *v.* Whitesides, 34 Misso. 417.

(*a*) The point referred to in the text sometimes turns upon *the nature of the property*, out of the claim for which the controversy arises. Whether plaintiff or defendant may rely upon a mere *easement*, is a question not very definitely settled. See Tracy *v.* Atherton, 36 Verm. 503.

It is held, that, where the plaintiff has the right of mining on the land, he can maintain ejectment for the land against an intruder. Turner *v.* Reynolds, 23 Penn. 199.

If A's building inclines from the perpendicular over B's land, B may have ejectment for the land over which it impends. Sherry *v.* Frecking, 4 Duer, 452.

The owner of the fee may maintain ejectment against one, who has exclusively appropriated a part of a public street or highway. Brown *v.* Galley, Hill & Denio, 308.

Or to establish his title against the owner of a perpetual right to use it for a passage-way. Morgan *v.* Moore, 3 Gray, 319.

Or against an individual who appropriates to his own use a portion of the highway. Wright *v.* Carter, 3 Dutch. 76.

In an action of ejectment (in California), evidence is inadmissible to show that the fee of the land is in the government of the United States, or that the title is in a third party. Winans *v.* Christy, 4 Cal. 70.

But, on the other hand, ejectment is held not to lie to try title to a road or way. Wood *v.* Truckee, 24 Cal. 487.

quired a title.[1] In order to render the possession of a defendant adverse, he must have entered in good faith, believing he had a title; his possession must be under color and claim of title.[2]

§ 75. A party may claim by the adverse possession not only of himself, but of others to whose title he succeeds. And a continuous successive occupation may be relied upon under deeds, although the land have been omitted by mistake.[3] But where different persons enter upon land in succession, without title, the last possessor cannot add the possession of his predecessors to his own, so as to make out continuity of possession, sufficient to bar the entry of the owner. The possession of one cannot be the possession of the other. So possession of a part of the land, by a party entitled to the whole, is possession of the whole, and he cannot be barred by adding together the different possessions and acts of the defendant, at long intervals, so as to make out twenty years.[4] And where one has such possession as is insufficient to give an adverse title, and another succeeds him, holding the land in the same manner; the imperfect possession of the former, when

[1] Van Horne *v.* Everson, 13 Barb. 526.
[2] Moore *v.* Worley, 24 Ind. 81.
[3] Smith *v.* Chapin, 31 Conn. 530.
[4] Armstrong *v.* Risteau, 5 Md. 256.

Or, in general, against one claiming merely an easement. Child *v.* Chappell, 5 Seld. 246.

As in the case of the projection of eaves or gutters. Aikin *v.* Benedict, 39 Barb. 400.

Or flowage. Wilklow *v.* Lane, 37 Barb. 244.

The easement of drainage is held no defence. Commonwealth *v.* Roxbury, 9 Gray, 451.

A question of a different character, in reference to *the nature of the property*, arose in a late case in New York. It was there held, that, upon the destruction of buildings, of which demised premises are a part, the right of entry is gone, because the interest of the lessee is not tangible or visible, and the delivery of possession by the sheriff, upon a writ of *habere facias*, would be impossible. The true test of the action of ejectment seems to be, that the thing claimed should be a corporeal hereditament, that a right of entry should exist at the commencement of the action, and that the interest be visible and tangible, so that the sheriff may deliver possession. Lease of a room on the first floor and southwardly end of a building in Brooklyn, being eighty feet on one street, and fifty on another, with the cellar, and also a lot in the rear, of like dimensions. The lessor covenanted to make all the necessary repairs, and reserved the right to reënter at all times for that purpose. The lessee used the premises as a stable. The building having become dangerous, the lessor was compelled, by the competent authority, to repair it; and, in so doing, took down and rebuilt the front and rear walls upon the same foundation. The size of the building was not altered, but its interior arrangements were, and kitchens were finished off in the basement. Ejectment having been brought by the lessee, held, the demised premises could be identified; that they remained substantially the same, and what was done by the lessor must be regarded as done in execution and performance of the covenants. Also, that the lessee took an interest in the land in the rear, of which he could not be divested, against his will, by anything done to the building itself; and had a right to recover to that extent. Rowan *v.* Kelsey, 18 Barb. 484.

united to that of the latter, cannot make it adverse, continuous, and exclusive, as against the real owner.[1]

§ 76. In determining whether a possession has been adverse, the point of *notice* often becomes material. (*a*) Thus, in an action of ejectment, it was proved that the plaintiff and defendant, who were adjoining proprietors of land, each claiming to own the premises in controversy, had each occasionally occupied beyond his own line, and that the defendant had given the plaintiff a written notice not to trespass upon his land, claiming, in it, to own all the land north of a certain line mentioned therein. The plaintiff claimed to have proved an ouster by the defendant, and the court submitted such notice, in connection with evidence of the acts of the parties, to the jury, instructing them that an ouster was not constituted by mere words, but that the notice might serve to give a construction to such acts as the defendant had committed upon the land beyond his line, and directing them to find whether said notice, in connection with the acts proved, was, or was not, sufficient evidence of such ouster. Held, such course was correct.[2]

§ 77. Where the defendant acquires and holds possession under the plaintiff, and, on suit brought after the expiration of six years, attempts to defeat the action by showing adverse possession; the character of that possession must be brought home to the knowledge of the plaintiff, and the jury are not bound to infer such knowledge from the fact that the defendant claimed the property publicly and notoriously under an adverse title.[3] A note given for rent, reciting that the maker was the tenant of the payee, and had been for ten years, is evidence to qualify and explain the then possession, but it cannot run back and prove a tenancy for any length of time.[4] So the admission of a certain party, in an action of ejectment, to defend as landlord, is no evidence that he who first sued held as his tenant.[5] And, under Mass. Rev. Sts. ch. 101, § 7, a writ of entry may be maintained against a tenant at will, who refuses to surrender the premises on demand.[6]

§ 78. There are some cases, where one party is *estopped* or pre-

[1] Hoye *v.* Swan, 5 Md. 237.
[2] Dikeman *v.* Taylor, 24 Conn. 219.
[3] Benje *v.* Creagh, 21 Ala. 151.
[4] McKay *v.* Glover, 7 Jones, 41.
[5] Curry *v.* Raymond, 28 Penn. 144.
[6] Dolby *v.* Miller, 2 Gray, 135.

(*a*) It is sometimes held, that, to maintain ejectment, notice is not necessary, unless the defendant was a tenant of the plaintiff. Eaton *v.* George, 3 Jones, 385.

cluded, by his peculiar relation to the other, from setting up an adverse title against the latter.[1] Thus the mere holding over of a tenant, after his term has expired, is not adverse to the landlord; more especially in case of tenancy at will, without notice to quit.[2] The holding is a tenancy by sufferance.[3] So where the defendant in ejectment sets up an adverse possession, for a period sufficient to bar the plaintiff's right of action; such defence is inconsistent with a tenancy at will, and he cannot therefore claim that he was entitled to notice to quit before the suit was brought.[4] So in an action of ejectment, where the defendants acquired possession from the tenant of the plaintiff, with a full knowledge of the tenancy, they cannot deny the plaintiff's title.[5] So a defendant in ejectment, who became possessed under a contract to purchase, which has been rescinded and the purchase-money refunded, cannot object to his vendor's want of title, nor set up an outstanding one.[6] So a defendant in ejectment cannot show title out of the plaintiff, and in a third person, where the plaintiff claims by a general warranty deed from the defendant.[7] So if C, the highest bidder at an auction, is acting as agent for A, but, when the payment is to be made, A, B, and C agree that the deed shall be made to B, instead of A, and B pays for the same; A cannot deny B's title in a subsequent action against him for the premises.[8] So a sale cannot be questioned by a *cestui que trust*, after receiving the proceeds of land sold by the trustee.[9] But where plaintiffs and defendant claim under the same lessor; a deed from the defendant, conveying the premises to one of the plaintiffs, in trust for the payment of a debt to a third person, does not operate as an estoppel against the plaintiff's recovery.[10] So it is sometimes held, that a vendee may deny his vendor's title, and claim adversely.[11] So the plaintiff was in possession, claiming under a tax-sale. A afterwards entered, claiming to have paid the tax, and to have a receipt therefor. They then agreed, that A should remain in possession through the season, and, if he did not produce the receipt, should quit, which he did in the fall without producing the receipt.

[1] See Potter *v.* Baker, 19 N. H. 166; Worsley *v.* Johnson, 5 Jones, 72; Taylor *v.* Abbott, 41 Penn. 352.

[2] Volkenburgh *v.* Rahway, &c. 3 Zabr. 580; Floyd *v.* Mintsey, 7 Rich. 181.

[3] Creigh *v.* Henson, 10 Gratt. 234.

[4] Williams *v.* Cash, 27 Geo. 507.

[5] Anderson *v.* Parker, 6 Cal. 197.

[6] Walker *v.* Williams, 30 Miss. 165.

[7] Mathews *v.* Lecompte, 24 Mis. 545.

[8] Baggott *v.* Fleming, 10 Cush. 451.

[9] Johnson *v.* Bennett, 39 Barb. 237.

[10] Seabury *v.* Stewart, 22 Ala. 207.

[11] Cutter *v.* Waddingham, 33 Mis. 269.

Held, A's possession was not under the plaintiff, but an interruption of the plaintiff's possession.[1] (a)

§ 79. An adverse title may be lost by voluntary *abandonment.* Where one holding adversely abandons or quitclaims the premises, before his adverse possession gives him a title, he is concluded to the same extent as if he had been evicted by process of law.[2] But the act must indicate an intent to abandon. Thus removal of a fence, to replace it by a better one, is no abandonment. And an entry, with notice, during such removal, is not valid, as upon unenclosed land.[3]

§ 80. Where the plaintiff relies on his grantor's possession; the defendant, in possession, may show an abandonment by the grantor prior to his grant.[4]

§ 81. Abandonment is sometimes relied upon as a defence. Thus no action lies against a party who has abandoned the land, whether accepted or not. As where a mechanic, having possession of a school-house for repairs, offered the key to a trustee.[5] But prior possession, voluntarily abandoned without purpose of return, is no defence to an action founded on possession.[6]

§ 82. Where two parties both claim by possession, and the prior occupant surrenders to the other, his title is held to be lost.[7] But a verbal surrender, after title acquired by adverse possession, is invalid.[8]

§ 83. Somewhat in analogy with the general doctrine of abandonment, evidence is admissible, that since the commencement of suit the plaintiff has conveyed the land to the defendant; and constitutes a good defence.[9] So, if the plaintiff convey all his

[1] 37 Vt. 219.

[2] Poor *v.* Horton, 15 Barb. 485. See Wood *v.* M'Guire, 21 Geo. 576; Grant *v.* Allison, 43 Penn. 427; Altemose *v.* Hufsmith, 45 Penn. 121; Tayon *v.* Ladew, 33 Mis. 205.

[3] Sweetland *v.* Hill, 9 Cal. 556.

[4] Bird *v.* Lisbros, 9 Cal. 1.

[5] Allen *v.* Dunlap, 42 Barb. 585.

[6] Bequette *v.* Caulfield, 4 Cal. 278.

[7] Austin *v.* Bailey, 37 Verm. 219.

[8] Ibid.

[9] Torrance *v.* Betsey, 30 Miss. 129. See Putnam, &c. *v.* Fisher, 38 Maine, 324.

(*a*) In 1830, A enclosed about six acres of waste land, and built a cottage thereon, and was allowed to remain in possession without acknowledgment or payment of rent till 1845, when the owner served him with a declaration and notice in ejectment; whereupon A consented to give up four acres, on being allowed to retain the cottage and the other two acres till his death. A died in 1861. Held, the proceedings in 1845 amounted to an actual entry, terminated the original tenancy at will, and created a new one; and the period of limitation began at that time. Locke *v.* Matthews, 13 Com. B. N. S. (106 Eng. C. L.) 753.

It is held, that, in case of a right, by adverse use, a license for further use does not defeat the title, but is evidence that the former use was by permission. Perrin *v.* Garfield, 37 Verm. 304.

interest in the demanded premises to a third person, after action brought, the defendant may, by proper plea, avail himself of this fact, against the plaintiff's right further to maintain the suit.[1]

§ 84. In reference to the *parties* to the action of ejectment, involving the rights acquired by adverse possession; it is the general rule, founded on obvious grounds of public policy, that no title can be gained by adverse possession against *the State*.[2] (*a*)

§ 85. A plaintiff who has no title cannot recover, though he sue for the use of another who has the title.[3] But a purchaser has sometimes a right to use the name of his bargainor in ejectment.[4] And although a deed is void, if made by one disseised, it is held that the grantee may recover the land in the grantor's name.[5] (*b*)

§ 86. An insolvent debtor, who has commenced a real action before his insolvency, and afterwards purchased the land from his assignee, and taken a deed thereof, may prosecute to final judgment in his own name, if no plea in abatement has been filed.[6]

§ 87. Succeeding trustees may be substituted in ejectment for those by whom the suit was brought, and the omission of one or more may be supplied by adding them at any time before trial.[7]

§ 88. Proof of title in the demandant's ancestors is sufficient to sustain a verdict in his favor in a writ of entry, if there has been no subsequent adverse possession.[8] And if the ancestor die

[1] Rowell *v.* Hayden, 40 Maine, 582.
[2] Cary *v.* Whitney, 48 Maine, 516.
[3] Brooking *v.* Dearmond, 27 Geo. 58.
[4] Hassell *v.* Walker, 5 Jones, 270.
[5] Thompson *v.* Richards, 19 Geo. 594.
[6] Gerish *v.* Gary, 1 Allen, 213.
[7] Dillon *v.* Dougherty, 2 Grant, 99.
[8] Osgood *v.* Coates, 1 Allen, 77.

(*a*) But, in New York, where a tenant is in possession, the fair presumption is, that the possession is legal, and, until the plaintiffs show that they have had some right to the possession within forty years, the tenant shall have the benefit of that presumption, and shall not be dispossessed. Thus where, in an action by the people to recover real estate, the answer averred, that no title accrued to the people within forty years, and that the defendants acquired title in 1786, and had had possession ever since; held, the plaintiffs must show title in themselves, or a vacant possession; that they could not maintain their action on the ground that they are presumptive owners of all land until title in another is shown, and that in ejectment the people need not therefore show title in the first instance. People *v.* Trinity Church, 30 Barb. 537.

(*b*) See, as to the practice in England, by which a third party is allowed to defend; Thompson *v.* Tomkinson, 33 Eng. L. & Eq. 487; Croft *v.* Lumley, 29 Ib. 78; Whitworth *v.* Humphries, 5 H. & N. 185.

in adverse possession, and the heirs remain in possession, this is *primâ facie* sufficient to entitle them to recover.[1] So occupation under a disseisor is presumed to continue under his heirs.[2] But heirs of a patentee of land, forfeited for non-payment of taxes, and never redeemed, have no title, on which they can maintain ejectment.[3]

§ 89. A statement in ejectment, that upon the death of A. B. the title to the premises descended to C., as sole heir at law, is a substantial allegation that C. is the sole heir at law of A. B.[4]

§ 90. An action of ejectment was commenced in 1821, in the name of W. C. In 1844, the defendant pleaded the death of the plaintiff before impetration of the writ. In 1845, the death of the plaintiff was suggested, and "W. C., executor," substituted. It appeared, that W. C. had title in 1817; that in that year he died, and his will was proved, whereby he devised to his son, of the same name. Held, upon the record, the suit must be presumed to have been commenced in the name of the first W. C.; and the plea of his death before impetration of the writ was good.[5]

§ 91. In ejectment, the death of the original plaintiff was suggested, and the heirs substituted, except one; but the jury brought in a verdict in favor of all the parties having title. Held, such omission was amendable, and, though an amendment by the jury was an irregularity, it was not such as would entitle the appellant to a reversal of judgment.[6]

§ 92. If the lessor of the plaintiff in ejectment be dead at the time of trial, no recovery can be had on his demise; if alive at the commencement of suit and dead before trial, costs only can be recovered; if dead at the commencement of suit, no recovery can be had at all.[7]

§ 93. Where the plaintiff dies after issue joined; there being no voluntary appearance on the part of the defendant, and no *scire facias* served on him, according to §§ 16, 18, art. 5 (Missouri), Rev. Code, 1845, there can be no revival of the suit in the name of devisees.[8]

[1] Hanna *v.* Renfro, 32 Miss. 125.
[2] Currier *v.* Gale, 9 Allen, 522. See Peele *v.* Chever, 8 Allen, 89.
[3] Usher *v.* Pride, 15 Gratt. 190.
[4] St. John *v.* Northrup, 23 Barb. 25.
[5] Morford *v.* Cook, 24 Penn. 92.
[6] Lynch *v.* Cox, 23 Penn. 265.
[7] Watson *v.* Tindall, 24 Geo. 494; Jones *v.* Tarver, 19 ib. 279; Doe *v.* Lewis, 29 ib. 45.
[8] Fine *v.* Gray, 19 Mis. 33.

§ 94. A testator devised land, subject to a right, which he gave to a trustee, to sell and convey any of the same at his discretion, for the payment of certain legacies and debts. The devisee brought a writ of entry to recover the land against one having no title. Held, a sale and conveyance, duly made by the trustee to the tenant, pending this action, was no bar to the demandant's recovery.[1]

§ 95. A died in possession of land, the title to which was in dispute between himself and B, and devised his interest to his widow, whom, with another person, he appointed as executor. Afterwards, with the consent of the Probate Court, the executors and B compromised their claims, and divided the lot between them, giving mutual releases, the release to the widow being to her in her own name, without any mention of her husband or of his estate. Subsequently the executors, by license of court, for payment of debts, sold to C, and the widow, as executrix, conveyed to him all the right and interest which A had in the premises at the time of his death. After A's death, the widow remained in possession up to the time of the sale to C. In ejectment by the widow, claiming under her deed from B; held, the widow could not defeat the estate provided for the payment of debts by annexing her possession as devisee to the title acquired from B; that the sale by the executors transferred to C the possession held by her under the will as devisee; and that he, in defending against the suit brought by the widow, might connect his possession after the sale with the previous possession of the widow and of A before his death.[2]

§ 96. It is held that ejectment may be maintained by an executor, empowered by will to sell real estate.[3]

§ 97. In ejectment by an administrator, where no seisin accrued to the ancestors, and the disseisin arose after the death of the intestate, and, in contemplation of law, since the appointment of the administrator; proof of the appointment becomes part of his title to recover, and must be made.[4]

§ 98. Where the actual occupant, upon whom service was made in accordance with the law of Illinois, and who was the defendant in ejectment in the court below, died after judgment; and his

[1] Tainter *v.* Hemenway, 7 Cush. 573.
[2] Shaw *v.* Nicholay, 30 Mis. 99.
[3] Chew's, &c. *v.* Chew, 28 Penn. 17.
[4] Austin *v.* Downer, 25 Verm. 558.

attorney and landlord, who had conducted the suit in the name and with the consent of the deceased, sued out a writ of error in the name of the heirs, and gave a bond for the prosecution of the writ and for costs: it appearing that the attorney of the deceased was a *bonâ fide* claimant of the land, and prosecuting the writ of error in good faith, a motion to dismiss the writ was denied, although the heirs authorized the motion.[1]

§ 99. If an action of ejectment be brought upon the joint and several demise of two, and one die before trial and judgment, and the action be not revived in favor of his heirs; the suit must be considered as discontinued or abated as to the demise of such lessor, the validity of whose title will not be affected by a final judgment against the plaintiff.[2] (*a*)

§ 100. Grantees, and all who enter upon the land, pending the action of ejectment, are subject to be removed by the final process.[3] And it is not necessary to make any other party than the occupant a defendant; a judgment against him binds all persons who are in privity.[4] (*b*) One claiming an interest, but not in possession, is not a necessary party.[5] But where land is owned by A, B, and C, and A's share is levied on by D, under a judgment against A; neither B and C nor their grantees can be dispossessed by the execution.[6]

[1] Kellogg *v.* Forsyth, 24 How. 186.
[2] Pintard *v.* Griffing, 32 Miss. 133.
[3] Watson *v.* Dowling, 26 Cal. 125; Wallen *v.* Huff, 3 Sneed, 82.
[4] Hanson *v.* Armstrong, 22 Ill. 442.
[5] Van Buren *v.* Cockburn, 14 Barb. 118.
[6] Wattson *v.* Dowling, 26 Cal. 125.

(*a*) Questions may arise, in connection with the death of a party interested, with reference to the defence as well as the maintaining of the action. In Texas, in an action by a stranger for the recovery of land against an administrator, proof of title in his intestate is a good defence, though the administration be void. Victory *v.* Stroud, 15 Tex. 373.

In Iowa, in an action of right commenced against the ancestor, and to which the heirs are made parties after his death, they are not liable for the rents and profits while he was in possession; but only liable for such time as they are shown to have been in possession. In such a case, if the plaintiff seeks to recover damages from the ancestor, his administrator should be made a party with the heirs, or a separate action should be instituted against him. Cavender *v.* Smith, 8 Clarke, 360.

In England, in ejectment for a vacant possession, it is sufficient to direct the writ to the assignees and personal representatives of A. B., deceased, the last occupier. Harrington *v.* Bytham, 28 Eng. L. & Eq. 443.

In Pennsylvania, in ejectment, where the plaintiffs claimed title by sale on a judgment against an administrator, to which the heirs were not parties; held, the record of the judgment and proceedings was admissible in evidence; and the title of the deceased was conveyed by such sale, as against strangers to the suit. Riland *v.* Eckert, 23 Penn. 215.

(*b*) The rule of the New York Rev. Sts., that only the tenants in actual occupation can be made defendants in ejectment, has not been altered by the Code. People *v.* Mayor, 28 Barb. 240.

The plaintiff cannot dismiss the action, as against one whom the defendant has made a co-defendant. Hayden *v.* Stewart, 27 Mis. 286.

§ 101. If a female defendant marries, pending the case, the plaintiff is not bound to make the husband a party, unless he applies to be made such.[1]

§ 102. Ejectment cannot be maintained against minors, upon the possession of their guardian.[2]

§ 102 *a. Joint* ownership, or ownership *in common*, gives rise to numerous questions.[3]

§ 103. A person with an undivided interest in land may bring an action of right, and recover a verdict and judgment. But not for the fee-simple of the entire estate, nor the possession thereof, but merely for the interest proved, although declaring for the entire fee. And the possession is a necessary result of the verdict and judgment, and must be held subject to the rights of his co-tenant.[4]

§ 104. In a writ of entry, brought by one tenant in common against a stranger, for his undivided share of the land, it is no objection to a recovery, under the general issue, that, after suit brought, he procured his undivided share to be set off to him in severalty by proceedings for partition. But the verdict and judgment must still be for the undivided interest.[5]

§ 105. To sustain ejectment by several plaintiffs, all must show a legal title, and the right to immediate possession, not only at the commencement of the suit, but also at the time of the trial and judgment.[6]

§ 106. In Georgia, a recovery may be had in ejectment by a surviving joint lessor, to the extent of a moiety of the land and of the mesne profits.[7]

§ 107. Where a trial in ejectment is had before counsel are apprised of the death of one of the joint lessors, a suggestion of the death may be made after verdict, and entered *nunc pro tunc*, vacating the judgment as to the deceased.[8]

§ 108. A conveyance by one of several plaintiffs, pending a cause, of his interest in the land in suit, will not abate the action as to him, but it may be continued at least for mesne profits up to the time of his parting with his title.[9]

§ 109. Where the plaintiff claims the entire premises from a stranger to his title, he may recover an undivided interest, and

[1] Evans *v.* Greene, 21 Mis. 170.

[2] Spitts *v.* Wells, 18 Mis. 468.

[3] See Tucker *v.* Phillips, 2 Met. Ky. 416; Fosgate *v.* Herk. &c. 2 Kern. 580.

[4] Hughes *v.* Holliday, 3 Iowa, 30.

[5] Hall *v.* Dodge, 38 N. H. 346.

[6] Cheney *v.* Cheney, 26 Verm. 606.

[7] Bryan *v.* Averett, 21 Geo. 401.

[8] Ibid.

[9] Wood *v.* McGuire, 21 Geo. 576.

will hold in common with the defendant.[1] If a sufficient title in one lessor is shown, the non-production of proof of title in other lessors will not authorize the court to order their demises stricken from the declaration. Otherwise, if demises were shown to have been laid, from persons with good title, to support a fraudulent one, and without authority from the lessors.[2]

§ 110. A tenant in common may maintain ejectment alone, though also a surviving partner.[3] (*a*)

§ 111. In an action by A and B, who prove a joint title, under the plea of *nul disseisin*, the tenant may prove a conveyance from A to B prior to the date of the writ.[4] So a declaration in ejectment, containing only a count, upon the joint demise of two persons, of whom only one had title, cannot be sustained.[5]

§ 112. Husband and wife must join in ejectment for her land.[6]

§ 113. The question of joint title also arises in relation to the defendants.[7]

§ 114. In a writ of entry, upon an issue of alleged joint tenancy of the defendants, it is sufficient for the demandant to show, that he owns and is entitled to possession of the premises, and that the tenants are in joint possession, claiming the property. He is not bound to go into the title of the tenants. Where such issue was made, an instruction to the jury, that they should return a verdict for the tenants, unless they should find that they were in possession, claiming under a common title, or by an agreement among them that the occupation should be by them in common for their joint benefit, for the lifetime of any one, was held erroneous.[8]

§ 115. One who claims title to land may bring one suit against all the tenants in possession, although they may severally possess distinct portions of it; and they may protect themselves from a joint judgment for damages, by showing the character and extent

[1] Gray *v.* Givens, 26 Mis. 291.
[2] Martin *v.* Anderson, 21 Geo. 301.
[3] Robinson *v.* Roberts, 31 Conn. 145.
[4] Patten *v.* Adams, 8 Allen, 204.
[5] Elliott *v.* Newbold, 6 Jones, 9; Bryan *v.* Manning, ib. 334.
[6] Allie *v.* Schmitz, 17 Wis. 169.
[7] See Hollingshead *v.* Nauman, 45 Penn. 141; Dillaye *v.* Wilson, 43 Barb. 261; Fosgate *v.* Herk. &c. 2 Kern. 580; Ellis *v.* Jeans, 26 Cal. 275.
[8] Tappan *v.* Tappan, 11 Fost. 41.

(*a*) Under § 169, Sched. (A.) No. 13, and § 180, of the Common Law Procedure Act, 1852 (15 & 16 Vict. c. 76), two tenants in common may join in ejectment, stating that they, or some or one of them, claim to be entitled; and the whole of the property to which they are entitled in common may be recovered on such writ. Elliss *v.* Elliss, 1 Ell., B. & E. 81.

of their possession.[1] But where defendants in ejectment claim different parcels of land under distinct titles, and do not sustain the relation of landlord and tenant; a joint action cannot be maintained against them for the premises and mesne profits.[2]

§ 116. Where a complaint alleges, that the defendants entered on certain land, and unlawfully withheld the possession from the plaintiffs, and all the proof against one defendant is, that he is the landlord of the other defendant, who has actually entered; ejectment will not lie against him.[3]

§ 117. That one co-defendant had surrendered possession to the other, authorizes a finding of possession by one and not by the other, and judgment thereupon against the former only. But such judgment is not conclusive that the latter had no right to the possession.[4]

§ 118. Where the defendants plead severally the general issue, the court may order a general verdict against all those who have not shown that they were in possession of separate parcels.[5]

§ 119. Where one claiming title to land, in the possession of two or more, brings a joint action against all; if the possession is several, they may sever in defence, and disclaim as to the residue.[6]

§ 120. In ejectment against several, proof by the plaintiff of what portion was occupied by one is admissible.[7]

§ 121. Where several defendants are sued in ejectment, and one of them shows color of title, and seven years' possession, distinct from the possession of the others; the defence of the one cannot avail the others.[8]

§ 122. A general verdict will bind all the defendants in ejectment, unless they answer separately, or demand separate verdicts.[9]

§ 123. A and two others were tenants in common. B entered under color of title, and held possession several years, but, before the statutory period was completed, A and his cotenants made partition, and to A was assigned a part over which B's color of title extended, but of which he had no actual possession. B con-

[1] Rowland *v.* Ladiga, 21 Ala. 9.
[2] Wood *v.* M'Guire, 17 Geo. 303.
[3] Champlain, &c. *v.* Valentine, 19 Barb. 484.
[4] Burke *v.* Table, &c. 12 Cal. 403.
[5] Greer *v.* Mezes, 24 How. 268.
[6] Wilson *v.* Guthrie, 2 Grant, 111.
[7] Ellis *v.* Janes, 10 Cal. 456.
[8] McKay *v.* Glover, 7 Jones, 41.
[9] Ellis *v.* Jeans, 7 Cal. 409.

tinued in possession after the partition, as before, until the statutory period was complete. Held, B had not, as against A, acquired a title by possession to the part allotted to A.[1]

§ 124. The questions of adverse title, and the right to maintain ejectment, often arise between tenants in common themselves. Occupancy by one tenant in common, accompanied with a total denial of the other's title, is a disseisin.[2] And this without demand of possession.[3] So where a boiler, engine, and stack were erected on land of the plaintiff at the joint expense of himself and the defendant, under an agreement to use them as a common source of power, without limitation as to time; held, the interests were in the nature of real estate, and for exclusion therefrom the action of ejectment might be maintained.[4]

§ 125. But, in general, the doctrine of *possessio fratris* applies to the several occupancy of one tenant in common, and ejectment does not lie.[5] So where there is a negotiation between them concerning the property.[6] Thus an agreement was made by A and B to purchase land and jointly erect a house. A paid for the land and took a deed to himself, and B built the house, finishing a part to suit A, and a part himself. B with his family moved into the house, and boarded A, each occupying a distinct portion of the house, with no agreement that B should pay rent or occupy as tenant, but his occupation being under claim of title, and without express objection from A. Held, no disseisin of A.[7]

§ 126. The statutory changes in actions for the recovery of real property have done away with most of the numerous technicalities in *pleading*.

§ 127. The declaration in ejectment must describe the premises with such substantial accuracy, that they can be identified by application of the evidence to the description.[8] (*a*)

1 Hill *v.* Saunders, 6 Rich. 62.

2 Peterson *v.* Laik, 24 Mis. 541; Larman *v.* Huey, 13 B. Mon. 436; Van Valkenburg, *v.* Huff, 1 Neva. 142; Mallett *v.* Uncle, &c. ib. 188; Carpentier *v.* Webster, 27 Cal. 548.

3 Harrison *v.* Taylor, 33 Mis. 211.

4 Hill *v.* Hill, 23 Penn. 521.

5 Stevenson *v.* Huddleson, 13 B. Mon. 299; Tulloch *v.* Worrall, 49 Penn. 133.

6 Newell *v.* Woodruff, 30 Conn. 492.

7 Winter *v.* Stevens, 9 Allen, 526.

8 Munson *v.* Munson, 30 Conn. 425; Riley *v.* Smith, 9 Allen, 370. See Wyman *v.* Brown, 50 Maine, 139.

(*a*) In California, a complaint, that the plaintiff was in possession, and lawfully entitled to the possession, at the time he was evicted by the defendant, is a declaration in ejectment. Ramirez *v.* Murray, 4 Cal. 293.

The plaintiff need not aver title; an averment of prior possession and an ouster

§ 128. Where the description of the premises in the consent rule is "about five chains and twenty-five links in depth," and in fact the lot is a few links deeper, the description entitles the plaintiff to recover the premises as described in his deed.[1] But ejectment cannot be maintained for an undesignated part of a lot.[2] And the description in the declaration will not be aided by reference to any other instrument.[3] So where the writ was indescriptive except by adjoiners, and the verdict was general for the land described in the writ; the judgment was reversed, on the ground that the finding was too vague to sustain it.[4] So a declaration, after describing the tract owned by the plaintiff, and giving its boundaries, alleged that the defendant unlawfully withheld possession "of two hundred acres in and adjacent to the waters of Hughes' and Bunnell's runs; it being a portion of the above-mentioned tract of eleven hundred acres of land." Held defective for uncertainty; and the verdict, following the declaration, was set aside.[5]

§ 129. The declaration must allege a seisin of the fee or freehold (or for years), according to the facts.[6] (*a*) An undivided interest cannot be recovered, where the declaration claims title to the whole.[7] But a declaration, demanding the whole of a tract in fee-simple, may be amended, so as to demand a life-estate in an

[1] White *v.* Woodruff, 4 Zabr. 753.
[2] Miller *v.* Smith, 33 Penn. 386.
[3] Flagg *v.* Bean, 5 Fost. 49.
[4] Hunt *v.* McFarland, 38 Penn. 69.
[5] Hitchcox *v.* Rawson, 14 Gratt. 526.
[6] Flagg *v.* Bean, 5 Fost. 49. See 34 Maine, 566.
[7] Rupert *v.* Mark, 15 Ill. 540; Petty *v.* Malier, 14 B. Mon. 246; Murphy *v.* Orr, 32 Ill. 489.

is sufficient, for prior possession is evidence of title, and cannot be made to yield to mere color of title. Norris *v.* Russell, 5 Cal. 249.

But the declaration must allege title or at least actual possession, not merely occasional use, by the plaintiff, and a continued adverse holding by the defendant. Steinback *v.* Fitzpatrick, 12 Cal. 295.

And the demandant must allege, and, if traversed, prove, a seisin, either in himself or his ancestors, through whom he claims; and, also, in general, that he was seised by taking the esplees or profits. Payne *v.* Treadwell, 5 Cal. 310.

The complaint need not allege ownership at the commencement of the action. An allegation of previous title and an ouster is sufficient. Salmon *v.* Symonds, 24 Cal. 266.

The latest cases in California decide that no particular form is necessary in the complaint. Caperton *v.* Schmidt, 26 Cal. 490.

But that it must not state *evidence*. Depuy *v.* Williams, 26 Cal. 313.

In Wisconsin, an allegation of possession is unnecessary. Herrick *v.* Graves, 16 Wis. 157.

In Minnesota, a right of possession is alleged. Armstrong *v.* Hinds, 8 Min. 254.

In an information, under Mass. Rev. Sts. ch. 108, to recover lands below low-water mark, and more than a hundred rods below high-water mark, an allegation that the Commonwealth is owner in fee of all said channels, lands, and flats, is sufficient. Carr *v.* Roxbury, 9 Gray, 451.

(*a*) And a verdict must be equally specific, and follow the statute. Rawlings *v.* Bailey, 15 Ill. 178.

undivided part only.[1] And if the plaintiff shows title to any part of the land contained in the demise, which is in the defendant's possession, the jury may render a general verdict; or they may, under the direction of the court, find specially, so as to enable the parties to run their lines.[2] (*a*)

§ 130. To enable a plaintiff to recover on prior possession, he must allege and prove an actual ouster, notwithstanding a default through the mistake or inadvertence of counsel.[3] Thus a declaration, "that the plaintiffs have lawful title as owners in fee-simple of the premises, and that the defendant is in possession, and unlawfully withholds the same," is insufficient. Although a statute have dispensed with the old form of pleading, and the allegation of a fictitious demise; still facts must be pleaded, sufficient to show the plaintiff's right to recover, and not mere conclusions of law.[4]

§ 131. In New York, the complaint, in an action to recover possession of real estate, stated, that the legal title was in the plaintiff as owner in fee, and that the defendant was in possession, and unlawfully withheld possession from the plaintiff, and that the plaintiff demands that the defendant may be adjudged to render up possession to the plaintiff, and pay damages for the detention. Held, a sufficient declaration under the Code.[5] So a complaint, that, on a day named, one A was in possession and seised in his own right in fee, and died so seised; that the complainants are his only heirs at law, and as such entitled to possession; and that the defendant unlawfully holds the premises, claims title, and refuses to give them up, though requested.[6]

§ 132. A plea of the general issue admits the defendant's possession.[7] The title only comes in question.[8]

[1] Howe *v.* Wildes, 34 Maine, 566.
[2] Kay *v.* Glover, 7 Jones, 41.
[3] Watson *v.* Zimmerman, 6 Cal. 46.
[4] Payne *v.* Treadwell, 5 Cal. 310.
[5] Walter *v.* Lockwood, 23 Barb. 228.
[6] Garner *v.* Manhattan, &c. 6 Duer, 539. See Bockee *v.* Crosby, 2 Paine, 432; Fraser *v.* Weller, 6 M'L. 11.
[7] Graves *v.* Amoskeag, &c., 44 N. H. 462; Burridge *v.* Fogg, 8 Cush. 183; King *v.* Kent, 29 Ala. 542; 43 Maine, 280.
[8] Wyman *v.* Brown, 50 Maine, 139; Blake *v.* Dennett, 49 ib. 102.

(*a*) Colorable title in the plaintiff's grantor to the whole tract being shown, evidence of his possession and occupancy by mining on any portion of it is admissible. Turner *v.* Reynolds, 23 Penn. 199.

As to possession of a part, and ejectment for the whole, see Hipp *v.* Forester, 7 Jones, 599.

Where the plaintiff claimed three undivided fourth parts of certain tracts, a judgment that he do recover his term aforesaid in said tracts of land is correct. Carroll *v.* Carroll, 16 How. 275.

§ 133. A denial that the defendant unlawfully possessed is no denial, and consequently is an admission, of the material allegation that he was in possession.[1] So where a verified complaint charged an unlawful and wrongful entry and dispossession, and the answer denied that the defendant wrongfully and unlawfully entered and dispossessed; held, not the positive and unequivocal denial of the entry and ouster required by a verified complaint (Cal. Pr. Act, § 65), and therefore an admission thereof, and a denial of the wrongfulness only.[2] So a complaint alleged, that the plaintiff was lawfully seised and possessed on a certain day, and afterwards the defendant entered the tract and ousted him. Held, an answer, not guilty of the supposed trespasses and ejectment, raised no issue. And where the complaint alleges possession on a certain day, an answer that the party is not in possession on a subsequent day is a confession.[3]

§ 134. The want of a *similiter* is cured by a verdict, or the defendant may add it, if he chooses, as a matter of form. The plea of not guilty is the issue.[4]

§ 135. An answer, in an action to recover possession, which denies that the defendant is in possession, or that there has been any demand of the possession by the plaintiff, or any unlawful withholding thereof, does not put in issue the title of the plaintiff, or raise the question of adverse possession. If the defendant designs to question the validity of the deed, under which the plaintiff claims, to pass the title to the lands while a stranger was in possession, claiming title; he should so frame his answer, and set up a title in himself, or title out of the plaintiff.[5]

§ 136. If the demandant have title and a right of entry, his allegation that he was himself seised will be maintained in law, upon the supposition that he has entered and become seised according to his title, though he may never have had actual seisin. In such case, upon the plea of the general issue, the defendant will be held a disseisor, though he may not have actually disseised the demandant, upon a like supposition that the demandant has entered and been expelled by the defendant. Under the (New Hampshire) Statute of Limitations, whoever has a right of action has also a right of entry; and upon plea of the

[1] Burke *v.* Table, &c. 12 Cal. 403.
[2] Busenius *v.* Coffee, 14 Cal. 91.
[3] Schenck *v.* Evoy, 24 Cal. 113.
[4] Walker *v.* Armour, 22 Ill. 658.
[5] Ford *v.* Sampson, 30 Barb. 183.

general issue the only question is one of title. This local practice is confined in its operation to a simplification of the remedy by writ of entry, and does not affect the substantial rights and liabilities of the parties; and whether defendants in that suit are liable as tenants of the freehold, or as sole or joint tenants, when the question is raised by appropriate pleas, is determined by the rules of the common law.[1]

§ 137. As a plea of the general issue admits the disseisin, the tenant cannot, under this plea, introduce proof, that a third person has a present title superior to that of the demandant,[2] or that he was a tenant of the plaintiff.[3]

§ 137 *a*. A common plea in ejectment is *disclaimer* or *non-tenure*.[4] (*a*) The general issue admits the tenant to be in possession of all the land not specially disclaimed. A disclaimer as to part only leaves the tenant guilty of disseisin.[5] In Pennsylvania, when the plaintiff files a description of the land, the defendant is bound to file, with his plea, a description of the part as to which he defends; otherwise, the plea of the general issue applies to the whole land claimed; and the defendant cannot allege, as error, that the judgment included more than was in dispute.[6] And where the tenant, without entering a disclaimer of title to

[1] Tappan *v.* Tappan, 36 N. H. 98.

[2] Warren *v.* Miller, 38 Maine, 108; Melcher *v.* Flanders, 40 N. H. 139.

[3] Williams *v.* Noiseaux, 43 N. H. 388; Melcher *v.* Flanders, 40 ib. 139.

[4] See Tripner *v.* Abrahams, 47 Penn. 220.

[5] Perkins *v.* Raitt, 43 Maine, 280.

[6] Hill *v.* Hill, 43 Penn. 521.

(*a*) Disclaimer is abolished in California. Ellis *v.* Jeans, 26 Cal. 275.

In New Hampshire, a plea of non-tenure or disclaimer is in the nature of a plea in abatement. Tappan *v.* Tappan, 11 Fost. 41.

It is in the discretion of the court to allow such a plea to be filed at the fourth term after the entry of the action. Ib.

Non-tenure, general or special, is a good plea in abatement to a writ of entry brought to foreclose a mortgage. Stark *v.* Brown, 40 N. H. 345.

But if there be no disclaimer, the plaintiff may always reply, maintaining his writ; and if on trial it appear that the defendant is in possession under a title subject to that of the plaintiff, the plaintiff will be entitled to judgment. Ib.

Hence a defendant in possession can only successfully plead non-tenure special. Ib.

In Maine, non-tenure, being a plea in abatement, must be filed within the time prescribed by the rules of the court. Newbegin *v.* Langley, 39 Maine, 200.

Non-tenure must, by Stat. 1846, ch. 221, be pleaded within the time required for filing pleas in abatement; and a brief statement of non-tenure is within the rule. Young *v.* Tarbell, 37 Maine, 509; Eldridge *v.* Preble, 34 Maine, 148.

In Massachusetts, it is irregular to plead the general issue as to one moiety of the demanded premises, and a disclaimer as to the other. The general issue should be pleaded as to the whole demand, and a disclaimer as to part filed by way of a specification of defence. But if no objection is raised by the demandant, and the latter proves a deed from the tenant to himself of one half of the premises claimed, this is not evidence of title in him to the whole. Fisk *v.* Fisk, 12 Cush. 150.

In the same State, under the general issue, the tenant cannot specify and rely upon a claim of title in himself, and also upon the defence of non-tenure. Creighton *v.* Proctor, 12 Cush. 433.

any part of the land, proves that he is in possession, claiming title to only a part of it, a verdict may be rendered for all the land claimed.[1] When there is a disclaimer as to part, and the general issue as to the residue, and the jury return a verdict for the whole in favor of the demandant; he may have judgment for the parcel intended to be found, if the materials for a sufficient description exist, upon entering a remittitur as to the residue.[2]

§ 138. A plea, that the *locus* is in the actual adverse possession of A, under a claim of title, and that the defendant has license from him, is bad on demurrer; if only intended to deny the plaintiff's possession, it is bad as only amounting to the general issue already pleaded; if intended as a plea of license under the true owner, it is bad as denying the plaintiff's possession, and as not alleging title in A.[3]

§ 138 *a*. A disclaimer of title and possession does not authorize a judgment by confession, for which possession is necessary. The judgment should be in such case for a nonsuit.[4] (*a*)

§ 139. An answer, purporting to go to the whole case, setting up title to half the land sued for, is bad.[5]

§ 140. The answer must not state *evidence*.[6]

§ 141. Where a second ejectment is brought, pending the first, on a new title; the answer must negative such title.[7]

§ 142. Questions of pleading arise in case of *joint* parties.[8] Thus suit was brought for three lots, A, B, and C. Plea, the general issue, with a specification of title to lot A. The demandant proved the conveyance of the three lots to himself, and showed a title in his grantor to A and B, but none to C. Held, he might recover lot C, the defendant showing no title.[9]

§ 143. In reference to the *evidence* in an action of ejectment;

[1] Carrington *v.* Goddin, 13 Gratt. 587.
[2] Odlin *v.* Gove, 41 N. H. 465.
[3] Alexander *v.* Eastland, 37 Miss. 554.
[4] Noe *v.* Card, 14 Cal. 576.
[5] Slaughter *v.* Detiney, 10 Ind. 103.
[6] Moore *v.* Murdock, 26 Cal. 524.
[7] Vance *v.* Olinger, 27 Cal. 358.
[8] See Wyman *v.* Brown, 50 Maine, 139.
[9] Mara *v.* Pierce, 9 Gray, 306.

(*a*) By statute, the rules stated in the text are extensively changed, all pleadings except the general issue being abolished. See Vail *v.* Halton, 14 Ind. 344; 15 Ill. 236.

As to the question of jurisdiction, see Roberts *v.* Pillow, 1 Hemp. 624.

With reference to statutory defences; in Mississippi, under Stat. 1850, the defendant may set out the facts by special plea and then rely on the statute, instead of showing them under the general issue. Tegarden *v.* Carpenter, 36 Miss. 404.

In the same State, when seisin is denied, the demandant is bound to prove it within the prescribed time, and the defendant is not required to plead the Statute of Limitations. Ellis *v.* Murray, 28 Miss. 129.

it sufficiently appears, from what has been already stated, that the *burden of proof* is on the plaintiff to prove title.[1]

§ 144. Proof of two deeds from the tenant to the demandant, each of an undivided half of premises, the whole of which is demanded, although made at different times, does not shift the burden of proof upon the tenant to show that the two deeds do not refer to different portions; but the burden is still on the demandant to prove a title to the whole. And parol evidence is competent for the tenant, that the second deed was by agreement merely a substitute for the first, on account of some real or supposed defect therein.[2]

§ 145. Evidence of general reputation, and the individual opinions of witnesses, are inadmissible to show that the plaintiff's ancestor, who lived on the land, was considered as the owner.[3] Evidence may be offered of circumstances in connection with long and peaceable possession, to raise the presumption of a grant.[4]

§ 146. Upon a question of disputed boundary, respecting which a survey and plats have been made, it is not competent to ask a witness the position of an object, which it does not appear from the plats and explanations he had pointed out to the surveyor.[5]

§ 147. Where ejectment is brought to enforce specific performance, parol evidence is admissible, and the question is for the jury.[6]

§ 148. A bond given to indemnify against defects in the title, on the sale of land, is not admissible in evidence against the grantee, on an ejectment brought by a third party.[7]

§ 149. A plaintiff in ejectment may withdraw from the consideration of the jury a record of sale by a guardian, and a deed which was so defective as not to vest title.[8]

§ 150. On the trial of a second ejectment, between the same real parties, the record of the former action is admissible in evidence, though the fictitious parties be different, and also the term sued for.[9]

§ 151. Ejectment or a real action is brought, primarily, to recover the land alone. By a very general statutory practice,

[1] Boylan *v.* Meeker, 4 Dutch. 274. See Funk *v.* Kincaid, 5 Md. 404.
[2] Fisk *v.* Fisk, 12 Cush. 159.
[3] Taliaferro *v.* Peyer, 12 Gratt. 277.
[4] Townsend *v.* Downer, 32 Vt. 183.
[5] Carroll *v.* Granite, &c. 11 Md. 399.
[6] Moore *v.* Small, 19 Penn. 461.
[7] Washabaugh *v.* Entriken, 34 Penn. 74.
[8] Chapin *v.* Curteninus, 15 Ill. 427.
[9] Dean *v.* Dazey, 5 Harring. 440.

however, *damages* may now be recovered, in connection with the property itself, which is the principal object of the suit.[1] (*a*)

§ 152. Independently of statute, the remedy for *mesne profits* is an action of trespass, subsequent to the recovery in ejectment. (*b*)

[1] Garner *v.* Jones, 34 Miss. 505. See Moss *v.* Shear, 25 Cal. 44.

(*a*) In an action of right, in Iowa, a plaintiff, who has both title and right of possession, can also recover for use and occupation. Dunn *v.* Starkweather, 6 Clarke, 466.

So, under the Practice Act of California, it is competent for the plaintiff to recover real property, with damages for withholding it, and the rents and profits, all in the same action, and as one cause of action. Sullivan *v.* Davis, 4 Cal. 291.

Where judgment was rendered for the land, and for large several damages against the defendants; the plaintiff was allowed to release the damages, which should have been joint, if given at all, and to retain the judgment for the land. Curtis *v.* Herrick, 14 Cal. 117.

But the plaintiff in ejectment recovers mesne profits only from the accrual of his right of possession. Thus an execution purchaser, only from the date of the sheriff's deed, not of the sale. Clark *v.* Boyreau, 14 Cal. 634.

And if the plaintiff is in possession of part of the land, he cannot recover damages for all. Ellis *v.* Jeans, 26 Cal. 275.

So, in Kentucky, the plaintiff may unite in his petition claims for the recovery of specific real property, and the rents, profits, and damages for withholding the same. Walker *v.* Mitchell, 18 B. Mon. 541.

So, in New York, the inquisition, after an action of ejectment, to recover damages for use and occupation, is a substitute for the action of trespass for mesne profits. The fact, that the defendant occupies under a joint lease with another party, is no ground for reduction of damages. But damages cannot be assessed for any time during which the defendant was not in possession, either in fact or in judgment of law. Ryers *v.* Wheeler, Hill & Denio, 389.

Under the Code, mesne profits are recovered by action, not by suggestion, after recovery in ejectment. Holmes *v.* Davis, 19 N. Y. (5 Smith) 488.

In Massachusetts, by the Rev. Sts. ch. 101, §§ 15, 24 (see Gen. Sts.), an application for the assessment of rents and profits upon a writ of entry cannot be made after verdict for the demandant on the title, unless an order is passed by the court, before such verdict is recorded, postponing the assessment. Judd *v.* Gibbs, 8 Gray, 435.

In the same State, the recovery of rents, &c., is limited to six years. Curtis *v.* Francis, 9 Cush. 427.

When issue is taken on disclaimer, the demandant, if he recover, is entitled to the mesne profits. Richards *v.* Randall, 4 Gray, 53.

In Maine (and probably elsewhere), to entitle the demandant to recover for mesne profits, in a writ of entry, under Rev. Sts. 145, he must set forth his claim for them in his writ. Though specially declared for, they are recoverable only to the date of the writ. Such as accrue before cannot be recovered in any future action. Such as accrue after, and prior to the time of possession taken, may be recovered in an action of trespass. Larrabee *v.* Lumbert, 36 Maine, 440.

In Minnesota, the plaintiff recovers damages. Armstrong *v.* Hines, 8 Min. 254.

So, in Missouri, the annual value, though the parties hold in common. Cutter *v.* Waddingham, 33 Mis. 269.

(*b*) In Mississippi, and probably elsewhere, a judgment for the plaintiff, in an action for possession, is conclusive evidence in an action for mesne profits, to show that the title was in the plaintiff from the time he brought his ejectment. And as his right to mesne profits depends upon his title, not upon his possession, at the time of suit, he can recover upon such proof, though he has never actually been put in possession under his judgment in ejectment. Brewer *v.* Beckwith, 35 Miss. 467.

But, in Pennsylvania, one who has recovered in ejectment, but not entered into possession, cannot sustain trespass for the mesne profits. Caldwell *v.* Walters, 22 Penn. 378.

So, in North Carolina, although the defendant has left the premises. Carson *v.* Smith, 1 Jones, 106.

After recovery in ejectment, an action for mesne profits may be brought in the name either of the nominal plaintiff, or of

§ 153. If one puts a party in possession, having no right to do so, and afterwards leases to others; he is liable, with his lessees, for mesne profits.[1]

§ 154. Mesne profits must be limited by the annual rent, or some other definite standard. It is error to charge, that the jury may give such extra damages as they may think the particular circumstances of the case demand.[2]

§ 155. The statute law very generally provides for an allowance to the defendant, in the nature of set-off, on account of any permanent improvements, or those having the character of fixtures, which he may have made upon the land recovered.[3] The qualification is usually expressed or implied, that the improvements were made in good faith, under color of title.[4] Or by a *bonâ fide* possessor, who supposes himself to be the true owner of the land, and is ignorant that his title is contested by any person claiming a better right.[5] (*a*)

§ 156. With reference to the *verdict* in an action of ejectment, it must be *certain*, and, if it be for part only of the land described in the declaration, the part should be described by metes and bounds, (*b*) or by reference to natural or artificial objects, or to the lines of other tracts.[6] (*c*)

[1] Storch *v.* Carr, 28 Penn. 135.

[2] Hanna *v.* Phillips, 1 Grant, 253.

[3] M'Minn *v.* Mayes, 4 Cal. 209; 14 Cal. 465.

[4] Welch *v.* Sullivan, 8 Cal. 511.

[5] Houston *v.* Sneed, 15 Tex. 307. See Rector *v.* Gaines, 19 Ark. 70; Butler *v.* Same, ib. 95; Dothage *v.* Stuart, 35 Mis. 251.

[6] Loard *v.* Philips, 4 Sneed, 566; 5 ib. 689.

his lessor, but not of both. Den *v.* Lunsford, Busb. 401.

As to the time for which mesne profits may be recovered, see Lynch *v.* Cox, 23 Penn. 265; Hill *v.* Meyers, 46 Penn. 15.

(*a*) Where, in an action of ejectment, the jury assessed the amount of the rents and profits due to the plaintiff's lessor, and also the value of the improvements made by the defendant, which sum exceeded the former; held, the judgment should have been for the defendant for such excess, and the *hab. fac. poss.* stayed until it was paid. Abbey *v.* Merrick, 27 Miss. 320.

In Pennsylvania, ejectment, in the nature of a bill in equity, does not lie to compel payment for improvements made during possession under a condemned title. The claim for improvements should have been interposed in the action of ejectment, and enforced by a conditional verdict. Paull *v.* Eldred, 29 Penn. 415.

In ejectment, the tenant cannot be allowed to prove that he has made valuable improvements since the termination of a former unsuccessful action between the same parties for the same premises. Wilkinson *v.* Pearson, 23 Penn. 117.

In California, where no proof is introduced to show damages, it is held no error to allow the defendant to prove the value of improvements. Ford *v.* Holton, 5 Cal. 319.

But, in a later case, it is decided that the value of improvements can only be allowed by way of set-off against damages for use and occupation, and therefore cannot exceed them. Yount *v.* Howell, 14 Cal. 465.

(*b*) And there should be a delay of the cause, if necessary, for that purpose. Brogan *v.* Savage, 5 Sneed, 689.

A conditional verdict must fix the time for payment of the money. Thompson *v.* M'Kinley, 47 Penn. 353.

(*c*) Under ch. 152 of Tennessee St.

§ 157. A verdict, sufficiently certain, either in itself, or by reference to something of a permanent and public nature, to enable the court to give judgment, and the sheriff to deliver possession, will be sustained. But a verdict, uncertain in itself, is not helped by reference to a line proved by witnesses on the trial; or a line, the starting-point of which is not fixed with reasonable certainty. "The middle of a stone-wall" is too indefinite a starting-point for the boundary of a town lot, as fixed by verdict.[1] But if the plaintiff demands the whole of a piece of land, the verdict may be for an undivided part.[2] And a verdict, which finds that the plaintiff is the owner of the land, is sufficiently explicit as to title.[3] So a verdict which finds the defendant guilty, and the estate established in the plaintiff to be an estate in fee, is responsive to the issue, and is sufficient.[4] So, on a plea of the general issue, with a specification of defence, claiming title to part of the demanded premises, and disclaiming as to the residue; a verdict, that "the tenant did not extend his building over land of the demandant," is a good finding in favor of the tenant as to the part claimed by him, since the (Mass.) St. of 1836, ch. 273, abolishing special pleading.[5] So the verdict set out the wills of a grandfather and father, and, if a son took under the father's will, for the plaintiff; if under the grandfather's, for the defendant. Held, the verdict was sufficiently certain, and submitted to the court merely the construction of the wills.[6] So a verdict may refer to monuments, recorded deeds, or diagrams, warrants of survey, or identified agreements.[7]

§ 158. The judgment in ejectment must follow the complaint, and the execution the judgment.[8]

§ 159. With regard to the effect of a judgment, although not conclusive, yet, if title was really suggested and decided, and possession under the title given, there can be no better evidence of title in the court of chancery.[9] (*a*)

[1] Hagey *v.* Detweiler, 35 Penn. 409.
[2] Callis *v.* Kemp, 11 Gratt. 78.
[3] Hadlock v. Hadlock, 22 Ill. 384.
[4] Goodhue *v.* Baker, 22 Ill. 262.
[5] Johnson *v.* Rayner, 6 Gray, 107.
[6] Callis *v.* Kemp, 11 Gratt. 78.
[7] Miller *v.* Casselberry, 47 Penn. 376.
[8] Orton *v.* Noonan, 18 Wis. 447. See Taylor *v.* Abbott, 41 Penn. 352; Minkhart *v.* Hankler, 19 Ill. 47.
[9] Obert *v.* Obert, 2 Stockt. 98.

1852, a verdict for the plaintiff, which does not specify the plaintiff's estate, is a nullity. Van Fossen *v.* Pearson, 4 Sneed, 362.

(*a*) The (Pennsylvania) act of April 21, 1846, restores the rule making one judgment in ejectment conclusive, only in cases "wherein time becomes of the essence in the finding of the jury, or in a judgment by confession, by fixing a time for such payment" of purchase-money. Lykens *v.* Tower, 27 Penn. 462.

§ 160. A deed, conveying land to the county, upon a conditional limitation, for a court-house, contained a covenant that, should the building erected cease to be occupied as a court-house, the county might remove it within a reasonable time. Held, in a writ of entry, that this right in the tenant was no objection to a general judgment for the demandant; and a motion for a qualified judgment, reserving the right, was denied.[1]

§ 160 *a*. In Louisiana, when the defendant in a petitory action is evicted from land upon which he has for several years paid the taxes, the writ of possession should be suspended until the taxes are refunded to the defendant, as *negotiorum gestor* of the plaintiff.[2]

§ 160 *b*. Where two ejectments had been brought for parts of the same land, in one of which a verdict and judgment were given for the undivided moiety of a lot, and in the other for the entire tract; held, they were conclusive as to the moiety only, and a third action would lie for the remainder of the land.[3]

§ 161. Where a former judgment is set up, parol evidence is admissible as to identity.[4] (*a*)

[1] Wood *v.* Cheshire, 32 N. H. 421.
[2] Weber *v.* Coussy, 12 La. An. 534.
[3] Kinter *v.* Jenks, 43 Penn. 445.
[4] Meyers *v.* Hill, 46 Penn. 9.

(*a*) In some States, an erroneous judgment in ejectment is corrected by the summary process of *restitution*. Thus, in Pennsylvania, where a defendant has been deprived of the possession of his premises under an execution on an erroneous judgment, he is entitled, upon reversal, to be restored to the possession without further action, and also to the crops, either by judgment of restitution or by an action on the case. Breading *v.* Blocher, 29 Penn. 347.

In Mississippi, after judgment, by which the plaintiff takes under the *habere facias* more than he is entitled to recover, the defendant cannot have restitution by motion in the court issuing the writ, if the premises are specifically described in the judgment. Natchez *v.* Vandervelde, 31 Miss. 706.

In ejectment against a husband, the wife cannot prevent execution of the *hab. fac.* by setting up a title to the land. In such case, the court having awarded a writ of restitution, held, it was irregular; but it was not set aside, the plaintiff being left to his action against both husband and wife, more especially as judgment was improperly entered upon the pleading. Johnson *v.* Fullerton, 44 Penn. 466.

In Massachusetts, in an action for land, in which the defendant, a married woman, has a homestead, a qualified judgment for possession may be given, subject to this right. Castle *v.* Palmer, 6 Allen, 401.

Some points of *practice*, often of a local nature, connected with the subject of this chapter, demand a brief notice. See Short *v.* Coulee, 28 Ill. 219.

A *receiver* is sometimes applied for in the action of ejectment. But where the plaintiffs in an action for a mill, but with a doubtful right, applied for a receiver, on the ground that they believed that the possessor was insolvent, and that the property could not be left in his possession without injury to them; a receiver was refused. Cofer *v.* Echerson, 6 Clarke (Iowa), 502.

A statute, requiring security for costs and damages to be filed by a tenant holding over, before he can be admitted to plead in ejectment, applies in favor of a party who purchased the land during the lease. Shannonhouse *v.* Bagley, 3 Jones, 295.

The affidavit, required by statute to be made by the lessor of the plaintiff to compel such security for damages, need not state the length of the term, or whether it was for years, or from year to year. Ib. See Farnsworth *v.* Agnew, 27 Ill. 42.

The acts of assembly, in Pennsylvania, allowing writs of *estrepement* in ejectment, are only declaratory of the common-law authority of the courts, and were passed because this power was not exercised as fully as it should have been. Berne *v.* Boyle, 37 Penn. 260.

The writ of estrepement may be dissolved by the court, on hearing, with or without security. If security be ordered, a bond to the plaintiff is a proper form of giving it. Ib.

In California, the court can restrain *waste* pending the action. Natoma, &c. *v.* Clarkin, 14 Cal. 544.

But, for that purpose, the plaintiff should add to the ordinary complaint a distinct paragraph, stating the grounds on which the special relief is asked, and praying for it. Ib.; Atwell *v.* McLure, 4 Jones, 371.

In England, where a writ in ejectment has not been addressed to, but has been served on, the tenant in possession, it is questionable whether the tenant can apply to set the writ aside as irregular. But if, instead of so applying, he applies for particulars or for other information, and allows ten days to elapse, he will be deemed to have waived the irregularity, supposing it to be such, and his application should then be, not to set aside the writ, but to be allowed to appear and defend. Thompson *v.* Slade, 37 Eng. L. & Eq. 582.

Where a landlord or lessor proceeds by ejectment, under the 15 & 16 Vict. ch. 76, for the recovery of a dwelling-house and other premises demised by one lease; if the dwelling-house is unoccupied, and the rest of the premises are in the occupation of a tenant, service of the writ of ejectment may be effected by personally serving the tenant with a copy, and affixing another on the front-door of the dwelling-house. Clinton *v.* Wales, 38 Eng. L. & Eq. 442.

The commencement of an action of ejectment is the service of the declaration. Thompson *v.* Red, 2 Jones, 412.

In Illinois, a motion for a new trial in ejectment, upon common-law grounds, may be granted; but, if applied for under the statute, the conditions required must be complied with. Goodhue *v.* Baker, 22 Ill. 262. See Singer *v.* Bett, 8 Ohio, (N. S.) 291.

BOOK III.

PLEADING.

CHAPTER I.

GENERAL RULES OF PLEADING.

§ 1. THE general principles of pleading are not materially different in actions of tort and of contract. (*a*) The following definition, therefore, though general in its terms, forms a proper introduction to the present division of this work.

§ 2. " Pleading is the statement in a logical and *legal form*, of the *facts*, which constitutes the plaintiff's cause of action, or the defendant's ground of defence; it is the formal mode of alleging that on the record, which would be the support or the defence of the party in evidence. . . . The observations of Lord Chief Justice De Grey, on the structure of an indictment, are very forcible, and equally applicable to the pleadings in civil actions: 'The charge must contain such a description of the injury or crime, that the defendant may know what injury or crime it is which he is called upon to answer, that the jury may appear to be warranted in their conclusion of " guilty " or " not guilty " upon the

(*a*) The consideration, that the present work, like the one to which it is designed as a supplement, relates exclusively to *torts*, will furnish a sufficient reason for not treating the important and copious subject of pleading in the exhaustive mode which is adopted by works relating to that branch of the law alone. The *illustrations* are exclusively cases of tort.

premises delivered to them, and that the court may see such a definite injury or crime, that they may apply the remedy or the punishment which the law prescribes.' "[1] (*a*)

§ 2 *a*. The pleadings in actions for torts, as in other actions, have become a subject of comparatively less importance, in consequence of the numerous statutory provisions in the several States, having for their object to do away with many technical formalities, with which they have heretofore been incumbered. (*b*) Still, however, it will be found, on examining the recent American reports, that the changes in question have not prevented the constant occurrence of questions relating to the sufficiency of the declaration and subsequent pleadings; often requiring, for their solution, by way of analogy, though not of absolute requirement, the application of those ancient rules which it has been attempted to abrogate. (*c*)

[1] 1 Chit. Pl. 217.

(*a*) "The established principles of pleading, which compose what is called its science, are rational, concise, harmonious, and admirably adapted to the investigation of truth." Chancellor Kent, Bayard *v*. Malcolm, 1 Johns. 471.

A brief but very just and well-expressed encomium upon "the science of pleading" is found in "the Reports" of Mr. Wallace, in his notice of *Saunders;* whose reports it is stated that Mr. Webster translated from the Latin, and thus, in his own words, made himself "familiarly and accurately acquainted with the language of pleading."

(*b*) "One of the main purposes of the Practice Act was to dispense with all useless and immaterial averments, which, under the old rules of pleading, were deemed essential." Per Bigelow, J., Knapp *v*. Slocomb, 9 Gray, 74.

(*c*) The following decisions in different States sufficiently indicate the nature and purposes of these statutory changes.

It is held, in California, that only the forms of pleading are abolished; the substantial allegations remain the same. Miller *v*. Van Tassel, 24 Cal. 463.

Though by the Mississippi act of 1850, abolishing the forms of pleading, no complete and well-defined system of pleading was established; yet it is not probable that any substantial remedy for wrong was intended to be taken away, but that only the form of asserting it was intended to be altered. Cooper *v*. Benson, 28 Miss. 766.

When a statute, prescribing a form of declaration, dispenses with an averment which would otherwise be indispensable; the statute, by dispensing with the averment, stands itself in the place of such averment. Shinloub *v*. Ammerman, 7 Ind. 347.

The Kentucky code of practice has abolished the preëxisting forms of action and of pleading. It provides that the petition, the only process by which a suit can be instituted, must contain a statement of facts constituting the plaintiff's cause of action, in ordinary and concise language, without repetition; with a very few additional rules respecting the mode or manner of alleging the facts relied on. It makes no change in the law which determines what facts constitute a cause of action. This is determined by the general rules or principles of law respecting rights and wrongs, and by a long course of adjudications and practice. It does not authorize a recovery on a statement of facts which did not before constitute a cause of action in some form. It requires that where the action is founded on a writing, such writing shall be filed as a part of the petition, which implies that it shall also be referred to therein, and does not dispense with the necessity of stating so much of the contract as shows that the plaintiff, by reason of the alleged acts or omissions, on his part, and of those on the part of the defendant, is entitled to an action and to relief. Hill *v*. Barrett, 14 B. Mon. 83.

See, also, Trustees, &c. *v*. Rowell, 49 Maine, 330; Fry *v*. Bennett, 5 Sandf. 54; Hartman *v*. Keystone, &c. 21 Penn. 466; Boyce *v*. Brown, 7 Barb. 80.

§ 3. A declaration or plea must allege *issuable* facts, not those facts and circumstances which merely go to establish other essential facts;[1] nor the *evidence* of facts;[2] nor the legal result of facts, or arguments and inferences.[3] Thus, to a suit to recover possession of personal property, an answer, that the defendant is entitled to the possession, is bad; it should set out the grounds of his right.[4] And a plaintiff is not at liberty to make out his case, by giving in evidence facts which he has not stated in his complaint.[5]

§ 4. It is the general rule, that, where a right exists only *by statute*, all the facts necessary under the statute must be set out.[6] In an action for breach of duty imposed by statute, it is necessary to allege the facts upon which the duty arises; and a general allegation of duty is insufficient.[7] (*a*) So where the defence to a

[1] Knowles *v.* Gee, 8 Barb. 300.

[2] Stone *v.* De Puga, 4 Sandf. 681. Bomberger *v.* Turner, 13 Ohio St. 263; Corwin *v.* Corwin, 9 Barb. 219; ib. 158.

[3] Boyce *v.* Brown, 7 Barb. 80; Howard *v.* Tiffany, 3 Sandf. 695.

[4] McTaggart *v.* Rose, 14 Ind. 230.

[5] Bristol *v.* Rensselaer, &c. 9 Barb. 158.

[6] Gillis *v.* Black, 6 Clarke, (Iowa) 439; Henniker *v.* Contokook, &c. 9 Fost. 146; Smith *v.* Woodman, 8 ib. 520.

[7] Metcalf *v.* Hetherington, 32 Eng. L. & Eq. 599.

(*a*) The case here referred to (32 Eng. L. & Eq. 599,) contains an elaborate statement of the law, and review of other cases, relating to the *averment of facts* as one of the requirements in pleading. The court remark: "The count is clearly bad for not stating the facts that they had funds which they were bound, at least *primâ facie*, so to apply. The words 'negligently and improperly, and contrary to their duty,' . . . cannot put the plaintiff's case in a more favorable position than if the count had stated that it was . . . the duty of the trustees to have prevented coals and rubbish accumulating in the harbor . . . As that duty was not imposed by the statute, except in the event of their having funds which they were bound so to apply, the rules of special pleading require that the fact should be stated. . . . An averment . . . that it was the defendant's duty to do certain things, being mere matter of law, will not supply the want of these allegations of matter of fact, from which the court would infer the law to be as stated; such allegation (of duty) is useless where the declaration is insufficient, and superfluous where it is sufficient." In reference to the cases which have departed from this rule, the learned judge adds: "these are all cases of a compendious statement of a right where the plaintiff's action is founded on the possession of that right, and is for the violation of it, and possession of that right is *primâ facie* sufficient; or they are compendious statements of a duty arising from prescription or custom. . . . Thus it is sufficient for the plaintiff to declare, on his possession of a right of way or a right of common or other easement, by describing them and claiming them by reason of his possession of land. . . . It is unnecessary . . . to describe whether it arises from grant or prescription. . . . There is another class of cases in which an obligation is cast on the defendant, as to repair a way to a close of the plaintiff over the defendant's land, to repair fences against the plaintiff's land, or to repair a wall adjoining the plaintiff's house. In those cases, it is enough to state, in a general way, the defendant's obligation by reason of the possession of his land or wall, or an equivalent averment." Per Parke, B., 32 Eng. L. & Eq. 606. See Brown *v.* Mallett, 5 Com. B. 599; Chadwick *v.* Trower, 6 Bing. N. 1; Priestly *v.* Fowler, 3 M. & W. 1; Seymour *v.* Maddox, 19 Law J. Rep. (N. S.) Qu. B. 525; 2 Wms. Saun. 113 a. b.; The Queen *v.* Bucknall, 2 Ld. Ray. 804.

In another recent case, the subject of pleading in actions founded upon statute is thus spoken of: "It has always been customary, and was formerly deemed necessary, in an action founded upon a statute, to invoke it specially, in the declaration. It is well settled, however, that the courts are bound to take notice of public statutes without their being specified in

note is, that it was made in consideration of money lent to be wagered upon the result of an election; the answer must allege, conformably to the statutory provision, that the money was lent at the time of such wager.[1]

§ 5. This rule, however, is not always rigidly enforced. Thus, in an action against a bank for the statutory penalty for delaying payment of its bills, a demurrer to the declaration will not be sustained, because copies of the bills are not set forth; the statute merely providing, that writings or their "legal effect" shall be set forth, and the demurrer not objecting except as above stated.[2] So in an action upon Mass. Rev. Sts. ch. 58, § 13, to recover double damages for an injury by a dog, judgment will not be arrested, because the declaration does not set forth that the acts were done *contra formam statuti;* the act being remedial, not penal.[3] So a declaration alleged, that the defendants erected a bridge across a canal, part of the bed of which belonged to the plaintiff, and also certain walls adjoining, and caused the bridge and walls to be so constructed as to project over parts of the said land of the plaintiff. Plea, that the several acts, &c., complained of were lawfully done by the defendants under and by virtue of powers given to them by a certain act of parliament (setting out the year and title). Held good, without alleging the particular facts upon which the defendants relied as bringing them within the statute.[4] And, in pleading, the language of the statute itself is held sufficient.[5]

§ 6. A count in debt, for the penalty provided by statute for cutting trees, may be joined with debt for the value of the trees carried away. But trespass cannot be joined with debt for the penalty.[6]

[1] Ensley *v.* Patterson, 19 Ind. 95.
[2] Suffolk, &c. *v.* Lowell, &c., 8 Allen, 355.
[3] Mitchell *v.* Clapp, 12 Cush. 278. See Com. *v.* Thompson, 2 Allen, 507.
[4] Beaver *v.* Manchester, 8 Ell. & B. 44.
[5] Jarvis *v.* Hamilton, 16 Wis. 574.
[6] Elder *v.* Hilzheim, 35 Miss. 231.

the pleading; and that it is only necessary to state facts which bring the case within the act. . . . The Code abolishes the pre-existing forms of pleading (§ 140), and, so far as relates to the complaint, requires only a plain and concise statement of the facts constituting a cause of action. The existence of a legal principle, whether of common law or founded upon a statute, cannot be deemed one of the essential facts which it is necessary to state. It was formerly held, too, that, in an action founded upon a recent statute, it was necessary to aver that the cause arose after the passage of the act. It seems to me that all that can be requisite . . . is to state . . . a time subsequent to the adoption of the statutory provision. . . . If it should appear . . . that the transaction occurred at too early a date, that would be a ground for a nonsuit." Per S. B. Strong, J., Brown *v.* Harmon, 21 Barb. 510.

§ 6 *a*. A plea, justifying flowage under an act which authorized the erection of a dam, must allege that compensation was made under the act.[1]

§ 7. In reference to statutory liabilities, the distinction is well established, that, where any qualification or exception is stated in the enacting clause, a declaration or plea, founded on it, must allege the facts necessary to bring the case within the qualification, or to exclude it from the exception.[2] But an exception in a subsequent clause is matter of defence, and the other party must show it to exempt himself from the penalty.[3] (*a*) Thus the

[1] Thien *v*. Voegtlander, 3 Wis. 461.

[2] Clough *v*. Shepherd, 11 Fost. 490; 20 Ill. 390.

[3] Chicago, &c. *v*. Carter, 20 Ill. 390.

(*a*) It is necessary, under the New York code of practice, that a complaint, founded wholly upon a statute, should contain a positive allegation of all the acts, and also of the qualifications, if any, prescribed by the statute; and when the action is upon a statute, granting a remedy in damages unknown to the common law, for death caused by wrongful act, neglect, or default, a merely inferential charge of negligence on the part of defendants is not sufficient. It is not necessary that the complaint should allude directly to the statute, but it must state a time subsequent to the enactment of, and all the facts which are requisite to bring the case within, the statute. Brown *v*. Harmon, 21 Barb. 508.

Somewhat analogous to a statute, is a *custom*, variant from the common-law rule. But with reference to a *general* custom it is laid down, that, in an action against a common carrier or innkeeper, for the loss of goods, &c., which is a liability founded on the common law or custom of the realm; it is not only unnecessary, but improper, to recite such custom, because it tends to confound the distinction between special customs, which ought to be pleaded, and the general customs of the realm, of which the courts are bound to take notice, without pleading. 1 Chit. Pl. 220.

Questions of pleading, in connection with express statutes, have often arisen, in actions against railroad corporations, or other parties, for causing the death of human beings, or injury done to animals upon their roads.

A declaration in case alleged, that a railroad engine, by the negligence of the servants of the defendants in managing the same, was run upon the intestate, *whereby he was killed*. Held, a sufficient allegation of the injury. The decision rests upon the grounds, that the statutory law has changed the common-law rule, by which an action cannot be maintained for an act causing death; and that the declaration did not imply the party's instantaneous death, although, even in that case, under the language of the statute, differing from that in Massachusetts, the action would lie. Murphy *v*. New York, &c. 30 Conn. 184.

In an action under the 9 & 10 Vict. ch. 93, by the personal representative of one who had been accidentally killed by the instrumentality of the defendant, the declaration alleged that the defendant's horse, while being driven and trained by him, in a public place or thoroughfare in the city of Dublin, to the annoyance of great numbers of passengers, and, among others, of the deceased, contrary to the provisions of the Dublin Police Act (5 Vict. sess. 2, ch. 24, § 14), ran against and injured the deceased, whereby she shortly afterwards died. No negligence was alleged, or that the death was the necessary result of the illegal act of the defendant. Held, bad. Roe *v*. Lalonette, 9 Ir. Com. Law Rep. 9; C. P.

In an action against a railroad corporation under the Illinois statute, "for causing death by wrongful act, neglect, or default," a declaration, which does not aver that the railroad was used in the state and county in which the action was brought, would be defective on demurrer, but is good after verdict. C. & R. &c. *v*. Morris, 6 Ill. 400.

Before recovery, under this statute, it must be averred and proved, that the deceased left a widow or next of kin, to whom the damages can be distributed. There may be persons isolated or unknown,

owner of animals killed or injured by a railroad, in order to recover against the company, must, by proper averments in his declaration, not only show that the company were required to fence their track, and had failed to do so, but must negative the various exceptions in the enacting clause of the statute, and aver that the animals were not injured at a point on the road within these exceptions; and also that the road had been opened for use six months before the occurrence of the accident.[1]

§ 8. It is a well-settled principle, that an action can be maintained only for damages naturally, immediately, or directly resulting from the act or neglect complained of. (See Hilliard on Torts, Chap. III.) And to this rule the pleadings are required to conform. Thus a declaration alleged, that the plaintiff, defendant, and C had entered into a joint speculation in railway shares; that C had advanced £6000; £2000 on his own behalf, £2000 as a loan to the plaintiff, and £2000 on behalf of the defendant; that C was desirous of retiring from the adventure, and the defendant offered to take upon himself the whole of the adventure and debt of £6000, provided the plaintiff would abandon his share to the defendant, and C would accept the defendant as his debtor in the place of the plaintiff for the £2000; that the plaintiff did thus abandon his share, and the defendant agreed to take upon himself the whole and become debtor to C for the whole £6000, and C, on the faith and in the belief that such an arrangement was made, consented to accept the defendant as such debtor in the place of the plaintiff. Nevertheless, the defendant, knowing that he alone was capable of proving that the plaintiff had assented to the said arrangement, fraudulently, falsely, and maliciously, and before the Evidence Act, 14 and 15 Vict. ch. 99, and in order to induce C to believe that the adventure had never been put an end to, and to induce C to sue the plaintiff for the £2000, and to deter the plaintiff from calling the defendant as a witness, and to destroy his credit as a witness, if so called, wrote and sent to C a letter, purporting to be addressed to the plaintiff, but directed to C, wherein he fraudulently and

[1] Galena, &c. *v.* Sumner, 24 Ill. 631; Ohio, &c. *v.* Brown, 23 Ill. 94.

who do not and would not afford any support to their relatives; in the case of the death of such, there would not be any next of kin sustaining a pecuniary loss. The damage is exclusively for a pecuniary loss, not as a *solace*. Ib.

falsely pretended to expostulate with the plaintiff, and asserted that the plaintiff had positively refused to concur in the said arrangement. By means whereof C was induced to, and did believe, that the plaintiff had never agreed to retire from the said adventure, and, acting on such belief, C brought an action against the plaintiff to recover the £2,000; that the said action was referred to an arbitrator, upon the terms that neither the plaintiff nor the defendant should be examined; and C recovered against the plaintiff £2,486, which he was compelled to pay. Held, the declaration disclosed no cause of action, since it did not appear that the damage to the plaintiff was a natural result of the wrongful act of the defendant.[1]

§ 8 *a*. Conformably with the rule, that a party himself in fault cannot recover of another though also in fault; (*a*) it is held, that, in an action for injury to the person by negligence, the complaint must allege or show by facts that the plaintiff was not in fault.[2] So a declaration in case stated that the defendant, knowing that a certain house was in such a ruinous and dangerous state as to be dangerous to enter, occupy, or dwell in, and knowing that the state of the house was unknown to the plaintiff, by agreement in writing demised the said house to the plaintiff, and the plaintiff agreed to take the same at a certain rent, the plaintiff having previously proposed to take the house for the purpose of immediately occupying and dwelling in the same; that the plaintiff commenced dwelling in the house without notice of its state, and so continued to the knowledge of the defendant; and that the defendant neglected his duty in not giving the plaintiff notice that the house was in the said state before entering into the said agreement, and before the plaintiff commenced occupying; and that, shortly after the plaintiff commencing occupying, the house fell down; alleging special damage. Held (on demurrer to the plea), that this declaration was bad, there being nothing to show that the plaintiff was not to put the house into repair before he commenced occupying, and it not being alleged that he was induced by his belief of the soundness of the house to enter into the agreement, or that any misrepresentation was made by the defendant to the

1 Collins *v.* Cave, 4 Hurl. & Nor. 225.

2 Evansville, &c. *v.* Dexter, 24 Ind. 411. See Wright *v.* Indianapolis, &c., 18 Ind 168.

(*a*) See Hilliard on Torts, ch. 4.

plaintiff as to the condition of the house.[1] So, in case of death occurring upon a railroad, it is held not sufficient to allege that the plaintiff "was at the time lawfully on the track."[2] A declaration in case against a corporation, for injuries sustained, should allege that the defendant was guilty of negligence, and that the plaintiff exercised proper care; and the proof should support the allegations.[3] But, in Illinois, a declaration against a railroad, for killing cattle, need not negative the possibility that the animals may have been killed at a farm-crossing. If the road is not properly fenced at such crossing, the company will be liable; and if it were properly fenced, that is a matter of defence.[4] And, in the analogous case of *concurrent* causes of damage, a petition alleged the flooding of a cellar by obstructing the street, and the answer was a denial. Evidence was offered, without objection, that the flooding was caused by the defendant's wrongful opening of the sidewalk, making a channel, through which the water was forced into the cellar by obstructions which others placed in the street. Held, under the provision of a statute, that a material variance must be one which actually misled the party to his prejudice; the court might give judgment upon this evidence for the plaintiff; the injury being caused by the concurrent acts of the opening and obstructing, and the former being a proximate cause.[5]

§ 8 *b*. A late case in Massachusetts adopts a rule of pleading, in reference to the defence depending upon the fault of the plaintiff, as favorable, perhaps, to the defendant as any one to be found in the books.

§ 8 *c*. In an action against a town, for injury sustained by reason of a defective road, the defendants may rely upon the fact, that the accident occurred on the Lord's day, without alleging it is in the answer.[6] With regard to the allegations in the declaration and plea, respectively, the court remark as follows: "The case is at issue solely on a denial of the averments in the declaration. Of these, the only one which can be said to include the fact that the plaintiff was lawfully on the highway at the time of the accident is, that he was travelling thereon, 'using due care.' The

[1] Keates *v*. Cadogan, 2 Eng. L. & Eq. 318.

[2] The Indianapolis, &c. *v*. Keely, 23 Ind. 133.

[3] C. B. & Q. R. R. Co. *v*. Hazzard, 6 Ill. 373.

[4] Great Western, &c. *v*. Helm, 27 Ill. 198.

[5] Hoffman *v*. Gordon, 15 Ohio St. 211.

[6] Jones *v*. Andover, 10 Allen, 18. See Hulet *v*. Stratton, 5 Cush. 539.

term 'due care,' where the gist of the action is the negligence of the defendant, implies that he has been guilty of no violation of law in relation to the subject-matter. The averment in the declaration of the use of due care, and the denial of it in the answer, put in issue the legality of the conduct of the party. If the plaintiff had not been engaged in the doing of an unlawful act, the accident would not have happened, and the negligence of the defendants would not have contributed to produce an injury to the plaintiff. . . . . We have assumed that the allegation of the use of due care by the plaintiff comprehends the fact that the plaintiff was then lawfully on the highway. Such, we think, is the reasonable construction of the form of declaration prescribed in the forms annexed to the Practice Act, Gen. Sts. ch. 129; otherwise, it would seem that a material fact, which it was the duty of the plaintiff to prove, was not included in the statute form of pleading. But, if it were not so, it would not change the result. If it is not necessary to aver the fact in the declaration, it certainly cannot be required of the defendant to deny its existence, or make any averment respecting it.[1]

§ 9. In order to sustain an action, the declaration and evidence must conform. It is held, that there is no rule which has been so stringently enforced, as the rule that the *allegata* must be broad enough to let in the proof, and that no evidence, not supported by the *allegata*, can sustain a verdict.[2] And, in a late case, it is remarked: "Although the language of pleadings under the Ohio Code will be construed according to its ordinary and popular meaning, that meaning must conform substantially to the proof on the trial."[3]

§ 10. Thus, although pleadings are to be liberally construed under that Code, an allegation, that the defendant obstructed the road by erecting a stone fence across it, cannot admit proof that he erected a stone fence fifteen rods away from the road, whereby water flowed upon the road and obstructed it.[4] So, under a declaration for damages to property, by the wrongful and improper grading of a certain avenue, the plaintiff cannot claim compensation for loss by the grading and paving of other streets.[5]

1 Per Bigelow, C. J., 10 Allen, 20.
2 Denison *v.* League, 16 Tex. 399.
3 Per Swan, C. J., Hill *v.* The Supervisor, &c., 10 Ohio St. 621.
4 Ibid.
5 Ortwine *v.* Baltimore, 16 Md. 387.

So, if the declaration alleges injuries done by the defendant's children and servants, the plaintiff cannot prove injuries done by himself in person; and threats are therefore inadmissible in evidence.[1] So evidence of an injury caused by the unmanageableness of the defendant's horses, or his want of skill in managing them, does not sustain an action for wilful injury.[2] So, under a declaration for doing work badly, a recovery cannot be had for the not doing of it at all.[3] So evidence that the plaintiff bought an article of one A, who obtained it from the defendants, does not sustain a declaration, that the plaintiff, through his agent, procured the defendants to furnish and deliver him a certain article, but they negligently furnished a different one.[4] So an allegation of a right to a public alley is not sustained by proof of a private alley-way.[5] So an allegation, that the plaintiff was possessed of mines, lands, and premises, and of right ought to have had and enjoyed, and still of right ought to have and enjoy, the water of a stream which had been used to flow alongside the said lands and premises, is not supported by proof, that the plaintiff was a lessee of mines under land adjoining the stream, with a grant from the surface owner of the use of the water for colliery purposes.[6] So a complaint alleged, that a registrar in chancery, whose sureties were sought to be charged for his default, sold certain property, under an order of a chancellor, and collected the greater portion of the proceeds; that his report of the sale, showing these facts, was confirmed by the chancellor, and he was ordered to loan out "the money in his hands;" that he afterwards collected and retained, "as such registrar," the balance of the proceeds of sale; and that he subsequently collected the money loaned out, and failed to pay over or account for it. The proof was, that he failed to pay over or account for the balance of the proceeds of sale collected by him, after he had been ordered to loan out the funds in his hands. Held, the variance was fatal.[7] So a declaration, that a party was "violently thrown from a wagon upon the ground by reason of a defect in the highway," is not supported by proof, that he voluntarily leaped from the wagon to avoid coming in contact with such defect; though such objection ought ordinarily to

[1] Smith *v.* Causey, 28 Ala. 655.

[2] Baird *v.* Dunning, 11 Wis. 68.

[3] Times, &c. *v.* Hawke, 5 Hurl. & Nor. 935.

[4] Davidson *v.* Nichols, 8 Allen, 75.

[5] Satchell *v.* Doram, 4 Ohio (N. S.) 542.

[6] Insole *v.* James, 37 Eng. L. & Eq. 523.

[7] Dill *v.* Rather, 30 Ala. 57.

be taken before the case is submitted to the jury.[1] (*a*) So if, to a plea of justification under a rate-bill and warrant, the plaintiff reply *de injuria*, &c., and no objection is taken to the replication; the defendant must prove every material allegation in his plea.[2] So, in a suit against a justice of the peace in Pennsylvania, for the penalty for taking illegal fees, the previous notice to the defendant, prescribed by law, stated the penalty to have been incurred under "the twenty-sixth section of the act of 1814, which said section is reënacted by the act of 1821;" but the declaration was upon the act of 1814. Held, a fatal variance, the allegation being not surplusage, but a substantial averment that the party intended to proceed on that act.[3]

§ 10 *a*. Upon the subject of variance, however, the following distinction is well established: "Where a party takes upon himself to state in any pleading a substantive averment, or to allege a precise estate, which he is not bound to do, if they are material . . . he gives the other side an advantage of traversing them. As . . . if in an action on the case against the sheriff, for levying under an execution against the tenant, without paying the landlord a year's rent, if the plaintiff, though unnecessarily, profess to set out the terms of the tenancy . . . and misdescribe them, the variance will be fatal. . . . If, however, the matter . . . be wholly foreign and impertinent . . . so that no allegation on the subject was necessary, it will be rejected as surplusage, and it need not be proved . . . except where, by the unnecessary allegation, the plaintiff shows that he has no cause of action."[4] Conformably with these rules, superfluous allegations in a declaration may be rejected, and treated as if they had not been there.[5] If the whole of an averment may be stricken out without destroying the plaintiff's right of action, it is not necessary to prove it.[6] Immaterial averments, which must be proved when alleged, are those which enter into the foundation of the action, as an averment of a particular estate, when occupancy merely would

1 Lund *v.* Tyngsboro, 11 Cush. 563.
2 Downer *v.* Woodbury, 19 Verm. 329.
3 Apple *v.* Rambo, 13 Penn. 9.
4 1 Chit. Pl. 232.
5 Hoyt *v.* Seeley, 18 Conn. 353.
6 Maxwell *v.* Maxwell, 31 Maine, 184.

(*a*) If such case is tried and submitted to the jury entirely upon the hypothesis that the plaintiff was so thrown to the ground, and afterwards, in answer to an inquiry by the jury, the judge instructs them, that the action can be maintained if the plaintiff voluntarily jumped to the ground through imminent peril; a verdict against the defendants will be set aside. 11 Cush. 563.

support the action. Impertinent matter is that which has no necessary connection with the cause of action, and may be stricken out on motion.[1]

§ 10 *b*. A strong illustration of these rules is found in a late case in Massachusetts, which decides that, in an action on a policy of insurance, the defendants may prove a *false*, though not *fraudulent*, representation as to value, though alleged in the answer to be both false and fraudulent; it being immaterial, for the purposes of the action, whether or not the representation was designedly erroneous, and made in order to gain an undue advantage.[2]

§ 11. And the rule as to variance is not enforced in other respects with unreasonable strictness. (*a*) As remarked by an approved writer, "it does not generally apply to allegations of number, magnitude, quantity, value, time, (*b*) sums of money, and the like, provided the proof in regard to these is sufficient to

[1] Grubb *v*. Mahoning, &c. 14 Penn. 302.

[2] Lewis *v*. Eagle, &c. 10 Gray, 508.

(*a*) In New York, provisions in the Code of Procedure have changed the rule as to a variance between pleadings and proofs, and they apply to cases wherein usury is alleged and sought to be established. Catlin *v*. Gunter, 1 Kernan, 368.

(*b*) A declaration against a master, for negligence of his servant, alleged, by way of inducement, "that the defendants were possessed of a cart and horse, which was being driven by their servant," without stating, "at the time of the grievance" complained of. Held, an immaterial allegation, and not traversable. Mitchell *v*. Crasweller, 16 Eng. L. & Eq. 448.

In an action for an injury suffered against a railroad company, it is not a fatal variance, that the injury is proved to have been sustained on a day different from that alleged. Augusta, &c. *v*. McElmurry, 24 Geo. 75.

With reference to time, however, although time stated in a pleading is often not material, that is, it may be departed from in evidence; the rule is still applied, that all allegations are evidence against the party making them, as his admissions. All presumptions of law in favor of a party must be consistent with his allegations, and none will be indulged for his benefit in opposition to them. Andrews *v*. Chadbourne, 19 Barb. 147.

Inasmuch as time laid under a *videlicit* is not required to be proved as alleged; when the time of killing an estray is thus laid, although the time specified is within twelve months after the alleged straying, it is not a sufficient averment that it was within the twelve months. Simpson *v*. Talbot, 25 Ala. 469.

The immateriality of time in pleading may appear in other aspects than that of variance. Administrators brought an action to recover damages for an injury done to their intestate, which resulted in his death. The complaint averred, that on or about the 18th day of December, 1849, at M., the defendant assaulted the deceased, &c., by means of which he died on the 25th day of December, 1849. The defendant denied that on or about the 18th day of December, 1849, at M., or at any other place, he wrongfully made an assault, &c., or that "on or about the 25th day of December, 1849, the said deceased died of injuries inflicted by defendant." Held, that, time and place being immaterial, this was a clear case of negative pregnant, and, as the pleadings stood, no evidence could be given that the injury was caused by another person. The court remark: "There were two ways in which the defendant might have . . . put in issue the fact of his doing the act. He might have negatived any other assault on a different day . . . or he might have denied the assault *in modo et forma*, which does not put time in issue." Baker *v*. Bailey, 16 Barb. 54–56.

substantiate the claim set up; except in those cases where they operate by way of limitation, or description of other matters, in themselves essential."[1] (a) And the statutory law has undoubtedly, in some degree, relaxed the rule, where it would be otherwise applicable. So, in general, an allegation which is merely *descriptio personæ* is surplusage and need not be proved.[2] So where a suit is brought to recover property in the possession of the defendant, it is immaterial whether the possession was obtained in the manner described in the petition or not.[3] So where the plaintiff, in an action on the case for false warranty of a horse, described the horse as "a certain sorrel horse belonging to the defendant," and the proof was, that the horse was owned by the defendant and another; held, the allegation regarding the title of the horse was not descriptive of the cause of action, but was mere surplusage, and consequently there was no variance. The court remarked, that this allegation was as much surplusage as would be an allegation of the age, size, or pedigree of the horse. That the defendant sold the horse, took the pay for it, and impliedly warranted the title, was enough to satisfy the material allegations of the declaration.[4] So in case, for deceit, by a warranty that a horse was well and sound, a breach was alleged, that he was not well and sound, but that he was infected with glanders, and otherwise unsound and diseased. Held, the allegation as to the glanders might be struck out as surplusage, there being a sufficient breach without it, and it need not, therefore, be proved.[5] So in all actions for injuries, *ex delicto*, to the person or to personal property, the *venue* is in general transitory, and may be laid in any county, though committed out of the jurisdiction of the court or out of the state.[6] And, "in the averment of damages, it is not necessary to be exact."[7] Hence, in an action by a seller against a buyer, for fraudulent representation and comment as to the value of the property, it is not a fatal variance, that the price paid was more than that alleged.[8] So evidence that a

[1] 1 Greenl. Ev. 133, § 63.
[2] Agee *v.* Williams, 27 Ala. 644.
[3] Oliver *v.* Chapman, 15 Tex. 400.
[4] Starr *v.* Anderson, 19 Conn. 338.
[5] Fisk *v.* Hicks, 11 Fost. 535.
[6] Northern, &c. *v.* Scholl, 16 Md. 331.
[7] Per Aldis, J., Mallory *v.* Leach, 35 Verm. 165.
[8] Ibid. 156.

(a) The same writer further remarks: "But the party may now, in almost every case, *avoid the consequences of a variance by amendment*." This power "has been given by statutes to the courts of most of the United States." 1 Greenl. Ev. 145, § 73.

party, by making a dam higher or tighter, caused the water to flow the plaintiff's land to a greater height, is admissible in an action on the case for maintaining and keeping up a dam.[1] So, in Missouri, where the plaintiff sued for negligence in the construction of a sewer, and alleged that, at the time of the accident, "the sewer gave way;" and the proof was, that the sewer had given way previous to the accident: held, no such variance, under the new practice, as to occasion a nonsuit.[2] So, in New York, under the Code, in an action against common carriers for non-delivery of goods, the complaint may allege that the goods were delivered to them at their principal office in one street, though the proof is of a delivery to their agent at an office of the defendants in another street.[3] So, in an action against a railroad for negligently killing the plaintiff's horses, the declaration may allege that the horses had escaped from his close into the close of divers other persons between his land and the railroad, though the proof is of but one intermediate close.[4] So in trespass *qu. claus.*, and a justification as a "public highway," any public way, however named, by land or water, may be proved.[5] So, under a declaration setting forth an obstruction of a way appurtenant to a close, damages may be recovered, if the way is appurtenant to any part of the close.[6] So the want of a safeguard against a danger near a highway may be alleged as a defect in the road.[7] So a declaration in a real action against a married woman, that she disseised the plaintiff, is consistent with evidence of fraudulent conveyances to her to her sole and separate use; such conveyances being void against the plaintiff, though valid between the parties.[8] And more especially a court above will disregard an unimportant variance as ground of error. As where, under a count for negligence in not collecting a note, the case had been tried on the merits without objection, and the recovery was on the ground of neglect to inform the depositor of the non-payment, and to return him the note.[9]

§ 11 *a.* It may be added, in connection with the subject of variance, that *truth* is generally enumerated as one of the elements of

[1] Curtice *v.* Tompson, 19 N. H. 471.
[2] Reeves *v.* Larkin, 19 Mis. 192.
[3] Newstadt *v.* Adams, 5 Duer, 43.
[4] Underhill *v.* New York, &c. 21 Barb. 489.
[5] Heyward *v.* Chisolm, 11 Rich. 253.
[6] Pettingill *v.* Porter, 3 Allen, 349.
[7] Willey *v.* Portsmouth, 35 N. H. 303.
[8] Blake *v.* Sawin, 10 Allen, 340.
[9] Wingate *v.* Mechanics', &c., 10 Barr, 104.

good pleading. With reference, however, to this particular point, as well as others, the general rule is often departed from. Although truth is one of the elements of a good plea, there are some instances where fiction is allowable. As, in the action of ejectment, a demise to the nominal plaintiff. Or, in trover, that the defendant found the goods. So it is allowable to exceed the truth, in pleading, with reference to number, quantity, and value.[1]

§ 11 *b*. Somewhat analogous to the rule, as to variance between the pleadings and the evidence, is that requiring consistency of successive pleadings with each other. Upon this subject it is said: "A *departure* in pleading is said to be when a party quits or departs from the case or defence which he has first made, and has recourse to another, and may occur in a replication, rejoinder, or other subsequent pleading; it is when his replication or rejoinder contains matter not pursuant to the declaration or plea, and which does not support and fortify it. A departure in pleading is not allowed, because the record would, by such means, be spun into endless prolixity; for, if it were permitted, he who has departed from and relinquished his first plea, might, in every different stage of the cause, resort to a second, third, or even further defence, and thereby pleading would become infinite."[2] And, in a late case, it is said: "The practice does not allow suit to be brought on one cause of action, and, when a complete bar is presented, to set up and rely upon another for recovery."[3]

§ 11 *c*. As we have seen, the defect of departure applies alike to the pleading following the *plea*, so called; and to the declaration, as compared with the replication. The example given by Lord Coke is of this latter description. If the declaration be founded on the common law, the plaintiff, in his replication, cannot maintain it by a special custom.[4] And, in a late case, the rule was distinctly applied, that, where suit is brought on one cause of action, to which a complete bar is presented, the plaintiff cannot, by his replication, set up and rely upon another.[5] (*a*)

[1] 1 Chit. Pl. 229.

[2] Ibid. 634; 2 Saun. 84 *a*, n. 1. See Gerrish *v*. Johnson, 1 Jones, 335; M'Connel *v*. Kibbe, 29 Ill. 483; Thompson *v*. Fellows, 1 Fost. 425.

[3] Per Walker, J., 29 Ill. 486.

[4] Co. Lit. 304 *a*.

[5] McConnel *v*. Kibbe, 29 Ill. 483.

(*a*) This case furnishes a very rigid application of the rule as to *departure*. The declaration alleged, that the defendant cut away and removed a portion of the parti-

As where, in an action for a nuisance, to which the statute of limitations was pleaded, the plaintiff replied, that the injury resulted from a continuance of the nuisance, and within five years.

§ 12. *Directness* and *certainty* are required in pleading. By certainty "is signified a clear and distinct statement of the facts, which constitute the cause of action or ground of defence, so that they may be understood, by the party who is to answer them, by the jury who are to ascertain the truth of the allegations, and by the court, who are to give judgment."[1] It must be assumed that the pleader has stated his claim as strongly as he can safely. Thus, in pleading a right of way, it is necessary to state that the privilege of passing extends to servants, or the justification will not extend to them. "The court cannot say that a right of way of course extends to servants. It may be, either by grant or prescription, the personal right of the owner and his tenants, and servants may have been expressly excluded."[2] So, in two actions against a city corporation, each petition charged, directly, that the money sued for was paid by the plaintiff, as taxes, based upon an illegal assessment of his surplus made by the city, and in ignorance of his rights, or of the fact that such assessment was illegal, but that he believed at the time that it was legal and collectable. The answer to one petition was to the effect, that the plaintiff was apprised of the existence of the law and the facts in relation to said assessment; and with such knowledge went forward and voluntarily paid the tax, and in the year 1856 went to the assessor and required him to assess his surplus for that year. The answer to the other petition alleged, that the plaintiff assented to the assessment, and, with a full knowledge of "the law and facts" in relation to said tax, voluntarily and of his own accord paid the taxes, if at all, to the city. Held, the answers were equivocal

[1] Chit. Pl. 236.

[2] Bartlett *v.* Prescott, 41 N. H. 493; per Bell, J., ib. 500.

tion-wall, &c., whereby the plaintiff's part of the tenement was injured. Also, that the change made in the wall occurred in three successive years, and at divers times since, till suit commenced; and that the wall had been and continued to be injured permanently. "The gravamen of the suit was the creation, and not the continuance, of the nuisance."

To authorize the court to reject a declaration, for variance from the cause of action indorsed on the writ, there must be a total departure from the latter. Tenison *v.* Martin, 13 Ala. 21.

Where a *capias* was in case, for money received by the defendant in a fiduciary capacity, and the declaration, for a breach of duty as an auctioneer, in omitting to pay over money, &c., with a count in trover; held, not such a variance as to warrant setting aside the declaration, on motion. Haviland *v.* Tuttle, 1 Sandf. 668.

and evasive, and insufficient upon demurrer.[1] So a warrant against a railroad "for the non-payment of the sum of $35 due by damage sustained," there being nothing in any other part of the proceedings to make it more certain, is fatally defective.[2] So where the action depends upon malice, it must be alleged.[3] So in an action against a sheriff for seizing a pianoforte, the allegation, that the plaintiff is a "pianist, and taught music within three months of the seizure," is not a sufficient allegation that music-teaching was his business.[4] So a plea, that the cause of action accrued in the furthering and countenancing of a company without any legal authority either by statute or royal charter, or having been duly registered under 7 & 9 Vict., ch. 110, pretending to raise transferable stock, and consisting of more than twenty-five members, and which was carried on to the grievance and nuisance of the queen's subjects, is bad, as the special averments do not show any illegality, and the general averments are not sufficient for that purpose.[5] So in an action against a judge of probate, for appointing, as guardian to a minor, a man who was insolvent, without security; the declaration that the plaintiff was owner and legal possessor of $2,000 worth of personal property, which was spent and unaccounted for by the guardian.[6] So where the petition charged the defendant, a constable, with wrongfully taking personal property of the plaintiff, and the answer alleged that he took it under an execution against A, in whose possession it was, but did not rebut the plaintiff's allegation that it was his property; held, the answer was properly stricken out.[7] So, to a complaint alleging quiet and peaceable possession, and a disseisin by the defendant under an illegal order of a magistrate having no jurisdiction, the answer should directly deny the allegations, or confess and avoid them, by stating new matter pertinent to the question raised by the complaint.[8] So, in an action for false imprisonment, the defendant sought to justify on suspicion of forgery, and stated, in his plea, that the plaintiff was *suspiciously* possessed of a note, and disposed of it in a *suspicious manner*, and in a *suspicious manner* left England

[1] Covington *v.* Powell, 2 Met. (Ky.) 226.

[2] Wagoner *v.* North Carolina, &c., 5 Jones, 367.

[3] Mooney *v.* Kennett, 19 Mis. 551.

[4] Tanner *v.* Billings, 18 Wis. 163.

[5] Hunt *v.* Hunter, 29 Eng. L. & Eq. 195.

[6] Phelps *v.* Sill, 1 Day, 315.

[7] Barley *v.* Cannon, 17 Mis. 595

[8] Ladd *v.* Stevenson, 1 Cal. 18

and went to Scotland. Held, the causes of suspicion should have been set forth.[1] So, in New York, while the Code abolished all technical rules of pleading, it did not abolish those dictated by good sense and necessary to carry into effect its own provisions; and, therefore, the facts relied on as a defence must be set forth with so much certainty, as to enable the court to say, that, if true, they constitute a bar to the action.[2] Though the denial of an answer may be general or specific, it must be direct and unequivocal, not matter of mere implication or inference. It is not sufficient to give a version of the transaction alleged, in some respects inconsistent with the complaint. As where the complaint alleged that the plaintiff, May 29th, 1861, owned a note, and employed the defendant to collect it, which he did, but failed to pay over the proceeds, though requested, and the answer, without a denial, set forth that the defendant was collecting agent in New York for the A. Bank, and as such received and held the note till maturity, when the proceeds were received by it as such agent, and afterwards, before July 1, 1861, it paid the same to the A. bank.[3]

§ 14. Sometimes, however, it will be sufficient to allege a fact, from which another material fact is necessarily inferred. Thus, where the time of a death, upon which the suit is founded, must be within two years after suit; the declaration is sufficient, if the time is named, and is actually within two years after verdict.[4] So a plea may be good as to one of several injuries, alleged in one count, though it does not answer the others. Or, though it professes to answer the whole, if other pleas which answer the other grounds of complaint also accompany it.[5] And the reasonable distinction is made, that less certainty is requisite with regard to facts which the opposite party is presumed to know. Thus, in an action for not repairing a private road through the defendant's ground, it is sufficient to allege that the defendant, by reason of his possession, ought to have repaired, &c., without adding by what right or obligation he was thus bound; the plaintiff being presumed ignorant of the defendant's title, while the latter has the power of distinctly stating it.[6] And an exception

[1] Mure v. Kaye, 4 Taun. 34.
[2] Gihon v. Levy, 2 Duer (N. Y.), 176.
[3] West v. American, &c. 44 Barb. 176.
[4] Hill v. New Haven, 37 Verm. 501. See Emmens v. Elderton, 26 Eng. L. & Eq. 1.
[5] Babb v. Mackey, 10 Wis. 371.
[6] 1 Chit. Pl. 238; 3 T. R. 767.

to strict certainty is found in the rule, that, "in an action for words spoken in England, which are slanderous according to the phrase of the county in which they are uttered, though the court may not in fact know what they signify, it is not necessary to aver their signification.[1]" So in general, "as it is an intendment of law, that a person is innocent of fraud, or any other imputation affecting his reputation, the party insisting upon the contrary must state it in pleading. Thus, in an action for words, as, for saying a man is a thief, the plaintiff has no occasion to aver that he is not a thief; and in an action on the case for maliciously suing out a commission of bankrupt, it is not necessary to state, in the declaration, that the plaintiff was not indebted to the defendant, or that he never committed an act of bankruptcy.[2]" So it is held, that, in the action for slander, "falsely" is equivalent to "maliciously."[3] So the words, "contriving and wrongfully and unjustly intending to injure the plaintiff, so as to deprive him of the benefit of" a judgment on appeal, are a sufficient allegation, in an action against a clerk for approving an insufficient bond, that he acted wilfully and maliciously.[4]

§ 14 *a*. The point of certainty, as necessary in pleading, often arises in connection with the allegation of *fraud*. (See Ch. IV.) It is held, that an allegation of fraud, either in the declaration or plea, must state the facts which constitute such fraud.[5] Thus, in an action on a premium note given to an insurance company, an allegation in general terms, that it was a fraudulent corporation, and not able to pay its losses, is not sufficient. The court remark: "There is no averment of fraud, or trick, or concealment, to induce the insured to enter into the contract of insurance. Nor are there any facts disclosed to show in what it was fraudulent. It is quite possible for a party to be of opinion that an inability to pay losses constitutes the corporation a fraudulent one. To different minds, different acts might be considered fair or fraudulent; hence the necessity of the rule which requires that the affidavit of defence shall 'state specifically and at length' the 'nature and character' of the defence, so that the court may

[1] 1 Chit. Pl. 224.
[2] Ibid. 227.
[3] 1 Saun. 242 a, n. 3.
[4] Billings *v.* Lafferty, 31 Ill. 318.
[5] Keller *v.* Johnson, 11 Ind. 387; Murphy *v.* Byrd, 1 Hemp. 221; Castle *v.* Bader, 23 Cal. 75.

be able to see that there is a defence that calls for trial."[1] So the declaration, in an action to set aside a patent, must state facts.[2] So a civil action, charging fraudulent embezzlement "as agent or attorney," is fatally defective in the alternative allegation, although the objection is not taken until after judgment by default.[3] And, where fraud lies at the basis of the action, it must be distinctly alleged. Thus the complaint in an action by attaching creditors, alleging that the defendants have a large amount of personal property, consisting of money, bills, notes, &c., deposited with them by, and belonging to, the defendants in the attachment suit, but not fraud, collusion or combination, obstructing the ordinary processes of the law, or that those processes have been exhausted or resorted to, or that the lien cannot be enforced without the aid of the court in the exercise of its equitable powers; does not sustain a suit for such interposition. The remedy is under § 238 of the (New York) Code.[4] But, on the other hand, where the facts alleged constitute a fraud, it is held not necessary to aver that they were done with intent to defraud.[5] So in a suit by heirs, to set aside the sale of lands, fraudulently made by one falsely assuming to act as administrator; the plaintiffs offered in evidence a deed from the grantor, in which he assumed to act as administrator. Objection was made, that the petition did not allege any violation of duty as administrator, and that, to set aside a deed, on its face executed in a fiduciary capacity, the failure to discharge the trust should have been alleged. Held, the allegation of fraud in assuming to act as administrator was sufficient.[6]

§ 15. The rule of directness and certainty precludes the statement of a mere legal inference or conclusion.[7] Thus the allegation of a duty in a declaration is of no avail, unless the facts necessary to raise the duty are alleged. It is but the statement of a legal inference, which is never traversable. And the defect is not cured by verdict, or by allegation that the acts of the defendants were done maliciously. The motive of a party, for doing that which is not in itself wrongful, is of no consequence. Thus, in a suit against a gas company for shutting off the gas

[1] Sterling *v.* Insurance Co. 32 Penn. State, 75; per Thompson J., ib. 77.

[2] Hill *v.* Miller, 36 Mis. 182.

[3] Porter *v.* Hermann, 8 Cal. 619.

[4] Skinner *v.* Stuart, 39 Barb. 206.

[5] McMahan *v.* Rice, 16 Tex. 385.

[6] McGaffey *v.* Millard, 17 ib. 365.

[7] See Judah *v.* The Trustees, &c. 23 Ind. 272; Hardy *v.* The Branch, &c. 15 Ala. 722; Merrill *v.* Plainfield, 45 N. H. 126.

from the plaintiff's rooms, the plaintiff alleged, that his rooms were furnished with gas-pipes and fixtures, which were connected with the main pipes of the defendants; that the defendants had for some time, and until the injury alleged, supplied him with gas, for which he had paid them; and that he was ready and willing to pay them for a continued supply, upon which he was dependent for the lighting of his rooms, and which he desired them to furnish; and that it became and was the duty of the defendants to continue to supply him with gas, but that they maliciously and wantonly shut off the gas, and refused to supply him; by means of which he was deprived of the means of lighting his rooms with gas, and put to great expense in procuring other means of lighting them. After verdict for the plaintiff, judgment was arrested, on the ground of the insufficiency of the declaration. If the declaration had alleged a contract to supply the plaintiff's rooms with gas until reasonable notice, the facts alleged might have gone to the jury as evidence tending to prove such a contract.[1] On the other hand, the law sometimes implies the right, for violation of which the action is brought, thereby dispensing with an express allegation of such right. "It is enough to state the facts from which a right or a duty arises." Thus a declaration, that the defendant wrongfully and improperly, and without leaving any proper or sufficient pillars or supports, worked coal-mines under and contiguous to the close of the plaintiff; and dug for and got and moved the coals, minerals, earth and soil of and in said mines, whereby the soil and surface of the close sank in, cracked, swagged, and gave way; need not further allege, that the plaintiff was entitled to have his close supported by the subjacent strata. "If the easement, which the plaintiff claims, exist, it does not arise from any special grant or reservation, but is of common right, created by the law, so that we are bound to take notice of its existence."[2] So it is a bad plea, that a party *lawfully* enjoyed the goods of felons.[3] So in an action for the negligent performance of duty in respect to

[1] McCune *v.* Norwich, &c. 30 Conn. 521.

[2] Humphries *v.* Brogden, 1 Eng. L. & Eq. 241 (*a*); per Ld. Campbell, C. J., ib. 242.

[3] 9 Co. 25; 1 Chit. Pl. 520.

(*a*) This case is said to have been very learnedly and ably argued, and contains an elaborate discussion of the question involved, and a copious citation of the leading authorities.

streets and sewers, an averment, that the defendant *wrongfully* refused to repair, and suffered, &c., states a legal conclusion, and is bad.[1] So a replication of a conclusion or inference of law is bad on demurrer.[2] So, under the Code of New York, the pleadings should be confined to a simple statement of facts, without the legal conclusions to be derived from them. Thus an answer, that "the plaintiff was not the real party in interest," &c., pursuing the words of the Code, but without stating the facts on which the allegation rested, was held bad on demurrer.[3] But general statements of facts, and statements of legal conclusions, as that an attachment was wrongfully sued out, are sometimes held good, on general demurrer, or on an objection to the admissibility of evidence, to prove the facts from which the conclusions would follow.[4] And it is sometimes held necessary to make use of a particular technical term. "As a general rule, it is inconvenient not to use the right legal word."[5] Thus, where a prescriptive right is relied on, the word "prescription" should be used in the pleadings.[6] And argumentative pleading is a mere formal defect, which is aided by a verdict.[7]

[1] Montgomery *v.* Gilmer, 33 Ala. 116.
[2] Roberts *v.* Albright, 2 Greene, 120.
[3] Russell *v.* Clapp, 7 Barb. 482.
[4] Black *v.* Drury, 24 Tex. 289.
[5] Per Dr. Lushington, 5 Eng. L. & Eq. 565.
[6] Knapp *v.* Parishioners, &c. 5 Eng. L. & Eq. 562.
[7] The People *v.* Warner, 4 Barb. 314.

CHAPTER II.

PARTIES.

§ 1. As a part of, or very closely connected with, the subject of pleading, it seems proper briefly to notice that of *parties*.[1] Inasmuch, however, as a wrong cannot itself be considered, without at the same time referring to the parties who respectively suffer and commit the wrong; the topic has been fully, though incidentally, treated, in the work to which the present is an addition.

§ 2. With reference to the plaintiff, the party injured is the proper party to the suit.[2] And "the general rule is, that the action should be brought in the name of the party whose legal right has been affected, against the party who committed the injury, or by or against their personal representatives." [3] (*a*)

[1] See Murphy *v.* Tilly, 11 Ind. 511; Munch *v.* Williamson, 24 Cal. 166.

[2] Bartges *v.* O'Neils, 13 Ohio St. 76.

[3] 1 Chit. Pl. 1.

(*a*) The plaintiff, a laundress, was in the habit of sending linen to London by the defendant's cart. A basket of linen belonging to A was thus sent, and on the way parts of the contents were lost or stolen. A did not pay for the carriage. Held, the plaintiff had sufficient title to maintain an action for the loss. Freeman *v.* Birch, 1 Nev. & M. 420.

The owner of property constructively attached, but who still retains actual possession, may maintain an action for its conversion. Mussey *v.* Perkins, 36 Verm. 690.

In a suit for conversion of property belonging to the plaintiff, the words "who sues for the use and benefit of P. D.," were inserted after the name of the plaintiff. Held, as these words had no legal effect on the rights of the parties, they should be rejected as surplusage. Turner *v.* Brooks, 6 Tex. 205.

The character in which a party sues must be determined from the body of the declaration, and not from his description of himself in its caption. If, therefore, he describes himself as administrator in right of his wife, and declares on a right of action accruing to him individually, he must be regarded as suing in his individual capacity, and the superadded words must be held a mere *descriptio personæ;* and upon his death, in such case, the suit should be revived with the name of his personal representative. Tate *v.* Shackelford, 24 Ala. 510. See Gould *v.* Clap, 19 Barb. 179.

§ 3. Under the Iowa Code, § 1676, providing that civil actions must be prosecuted in the name of the real party in interest, where a claim has been assigned, but not according to the provisions in the Code relating to assignments, the assignor is still the legal party in interest, and may sue.[1] And where a declaration in an action of trespass commenced, " A (who sues this action for the benefit of B) complains, &c. ; " held, while choses in action *ex delicto* were unassignable, this statement did not authorize the presumption of an assignment, nor of an agreement that B was to have the proceeds of the suit, and a demurrer on that ground was not well taken.[2]

§ 4. An action for trespass on lands alleged to belong to the State was brought in the name of the State " for the use of" a corporation. Demurrer, on the ground that, under the Code, the action was not brought by the party in interest. Held, the words " for the use of, &c.," were surplusage, and the demurrer was overruled.[3]

§ 5. The legal owner of real estate, attached as the property of another, who is a non-resident, has no right to be made a defendant, on his own motion ; nor is he a proper party, in order to oust the court of jurisdiction as to the other defendant.[4]

§ 6. In reference to the names and other descriptions of parties to a suit, the rules of law undoubtedly depend much upon local usage and express statutes.

§ 7. In Kentucky, in an action for injuries caused by a steamboat, the petition named the master as a party defendant, but did not designate the names of the owners, merely styling them " the owners," and they were not served with process. Held, the suit was against the master only.[5]

§ 8. In New Hampshire, where a tract of land was granted by the name of Saville to certain individuals, who went on and divided portions among themselves, leaving a part in common and undivided, and the name of the town was afterwards changed by the legislature to Wendell, and subsequently a portion of it was annexed to New London, and the name Wendell was afterwards changed to Sunapee ; held, an action by the proprietors for the

[1] State *v.* Butterworth, 2 Clarke, 158.
[2] Blankenship *v.* Cressillas, 10 B. Mon. 434.
[3] State *v.* Butterworth 2 Clarke, 158.
[4] Loving *v.* Edes, 8 Clarke, 427.
[5] Kountz *v.* Brown, 16 B. Mon. 577.

recovery of a portion of the tract should be brought in the name of "the proprietors of Saville."[1] (*a*)

§ 9. In New York, the plaintiff sued a constable to recover a horse, seized by virtue of an execution against A, who had possession. The plaintiff in the execution was, on his own motion, made a defendant.[2]

§ 10. The allegation in a complaint, that the defendant, being a canal commissioner, was bound to repair the banks of the Erie canal, at a certain place, in a division placed under his particular supervision, is sufficient to show that the action is brought against him in his private character; and it was not necessary to allege that he had in his hands funds sufficient to make the repairs, for not making which the action was brought.[3]

§ 11. The question of *joint* parties is one of very frequent occurrence.[4] (*b*)

§ 12. In an action of waste for injuries to the estate of a married woman, her husband must join.[5] (See § 15 *a.*)

§ 12 *a.* Petition by husband and wife, alleging that the defendant had by misrepresentation and deceit induced the husband to pay the defendant $1300 for a tract of land worth only $100, and that the land was conveyed to the wife; and claiming judgment for $1200 damages, as the amount of injury sustained. Demurrer to the petition, as not stating facts sufficient to constitute a cause of action. The demurrer being overruled, held, such overruling was erroneous, as the petition showed no joint cause of action.

[1] Sunapee *v.* Eastman, 32 N. H. 470.

[2] Conklin *v.* Bishop, 3 Duer, 646. See Davis *v.* The Mayor, &c. 2 ib. 663.

[3] Griffith *v.* Follett, 20 Barb. 620.

[4] See Herron *v.* Hughes, 25 Cal. 560; Pelberg *v.* Gorham, 23 Cal. 349; Fritz *v.* Fritz, 23 Ind. 388; 10 Allen, 460.

[5] Thacher *v.* Phinney, 7 Allen, 146.

(*a*) "Had the limits of the original grant never been changed, perhaps there would be no great difficulty in holding that the action could be maintained under the new name, on the ground that it is the same territory. . . . But a part of it having been annexed to New London, the proprietors of Sunapee are not the proprietors of Saville, but only the proprietors of a part of it; and where towns are divided into two or more, or where portions of them are taken off and annexed to adjoining towns, . . . it would evidently lead to much confusion, if not to difficulties that could not easily be remedied, to hold that actions like the present should be brought in the name of the new town. If the town be equally divided, in which name should the action be brought? The grant being to the proprietors and their heirs, it would seem that the action must, in such a case, be brought in their original name, or in both." Per Eastman, J., 32 N. H. 473.

(*b*) See Hilliard on Torts, chap. 33. In a late case it is held, that, in trespass against several, there cannot be a verdict for any of them, until the case for the plaintiff is finally closed by the complete examination of all his witnesses, nor so long as the cross-examination of any of them is reserved. Sinch *v.* Champion, 1 F. & F. 416.

Also, as judgment was rendered in favor of both plaintiffs, and the record did not show but that the defendant was thereby prejudiced, the judgment should be reversed.[1] (*a*)

§ 13. In Minnesota, an allegation, that one plaintiff holds the property in his own name, for the "joint use and benefit" of himself and the other, sufficiently shows an interest in the latter, to make him a necessary party.[2]

§ 14. In Pennsylvania, an action for the loss of a child, killed by the negligence or misconduct of a railroad company, is properly brought in the name of both parents.[3]

§ 15. Two persons, A and B, in joint possession, and claiming to be joint owners of wood, cut upon land which was originally owned by A, may maintain a joint action against a wrong-doer for its conversion, although no deed of conveyance of the land from A to B is proved.[4]

§ 15 *a*. All the owners of the land must join in an action of tort in the nature of waste.[5] (See § 12.)

§ 15 *b*. Where, in an action brought by two or more persons for an unlawful taking of property, the defendant answers, that the plaintiffs are not joint owners; that averment is material, and is new matter, requiring a reply. Such an allegation falls directly within the provision of § 144 of the New York Code of procedure, and, if not specifically controverted by the reply, it will be taken as true; no evidence will be required to establish it, and no evidence will be admissible to contradict it; nor will such evidence be of any avail, if admitted, unless it clearly appears that the defendant waives his rights under the pleadings; and the admission of such improper evidence in contradiction, without objection, is not conclusive evidence of such waiver.[6]

§ 16. One of two reversioners may, during the continuance of the particular estate, maintain an action on the case for an injury

[1] Bartges *v.* O'Neils, 13 Ohio St. 72. See Chase *v.* Chase, 6 Gray, 157.

[2] Hawke *v.* Banning, 3 Min. 67.

[3] Pennsylvania, &c. *v.* Zebe, 37 Penn. 420.

[4] Parker *v.* Parker, 1 Allen, 245.

[5] Bullock *v.* Hayward, 10 Allen, 460.

[6] Walrod *v.* Bennett, 6 Barb. 144.

(*a*) In this case it was remarked: "At common law, if the wife improperly join in action with her husband, who ought to sue alone, the defendant might, for that cause, demur to the declaration, or the same might be taken advantage of, after verdict, as a good cause for arrest of jud ment; or if judgment in such a case should be entered, if the objection appeared upon the record, the same would constitute good cause for a reversal of the judgment on a writ of error." Per Sutliff, C. J., Bartges *v.* O'Neils, 13 Ohio St. 76.

to the reversion, recovering only a moiety of the damages, unless nonjoinder be pleaded in abatement.[1] So one carrying on business in her own name, and in possession of goods, and claiming to own them, may recover of a railroad for their loss, although a third person is also interested in the business.[2] So a miller, employed by the owner of a mill to take charge of and tend the mill, receiving in compensation half the profits, but without agreement for any definite time, has no such title or possession as to require him to be joined in an action by the owner for an injury to the mill. "The plaintiff is to be taken to have been in the legal possession of the mill, and Butterworth in his employment as his miller, under an agreement that he should have one-half the earnings of the mill for tending the same. Butterworth was miller to the plaintiff and not lessee of the mill. There was no lease, no agreement for any particular time, in which Butterworth was to be employed in the mills, or have any interest in the mills, or have any interest in the income of them."[3]

§ 17. Where, in a lease, there is a reservation of a portion of the crops, the general property and right to them remain in the landlord, the tenant acquiring neither the ownership nor the right to sell; but, while the tenant retains possession of them, he is a tenant in common, and must join with the landlord in an action for an injury to them.[4] Otherwise, if he abandon the possession or assent to a sale of his interest, and relinquish further claim.[5]

§ 18. In New York, the owner in fee may maintain an action for the cutting of timber on the land, without joining the tenant for life or for years as plaintiff. The latter may bring a separate action.[6]

§ 19. In New York, when two or more join in bringing an action, and the facts alleged do not show a joint cause of action, a demurrer lies, upon the ground that the complaint does not state facts sufficient to constitute a cause of action. So when husband and wife are joined as plaintiffs, or the complaint shows that one alone must sue.[7]

[1] Putney *v.* Lapham, 10 Cush. 232.

[2] Mayall *v.* Boston, &c. 19 N. H. 122.

[3] Chandler *v.* Howland, 7 Gray, 348; per Dewey, J., ib. 351.

[4] Hatch *v.* Hart, 40 N. H. 93.

[5] Ibid.

[6] Van Deusen *v.* Young, 29 N. Y. (2 Tiffa.) 9.

[7] Mann *v.* Marsh, 35 Barb. 68 (distinguished by the court from the previous cases of Brumskill *v.* James, 1 Kern. 294; and Shumway *v.* Cooper, decided in 1856.)

§ 20. With reference to the joinder of *defendants*, in an action on the case against several as carriers of passengers, by whose neglect the plaintiff has received injury; the plaintiff need not prove that all were owners of the line, but may recover against such as he can prove to be owners and guilty of the alleged wrong. The court, in this case, give the following summary of the distinction, as to joinder of defendants, between tort and contract: "The declaration is founded upon the common law regulating common carriers; and this law imposes a duty upon them by reason of their calling, from considerations of public policy, and without regard to contract. It is true, that the law presumes or implies, from the fact of receiving, as common carriers, the passenger to carry for hire, a contract. But the plaintiff had his election to sue in assumpsit, declaring upon the contract, express or implied, or in case, for tort, declaring upon the breach of duty imposed by the law. . . . . It is urged as the declaration alleges, that all of the defendants were joint proprietors; unless this be proved, the *allegata* and *probata* do not correspond, and the plaintiff must therefore fail. This would be true were the contract declared on, or were it the substance of the cause of action. . . . . There is a class of cases arising out of contract, where, by reason of the contract, the law raises a duty, for the breach of which *duty* an action on the case may be maintained; and in such cases, the contract being the basis and *gravamen* of the suit, must be alleged and proved. Where, too, from the facts the duty arises, and there is also a contract which is alleged and made the substance and gist of the cause of the action, although the action be case, it being substantially founded upon contract, the rights of the parties will be governed by the law of contract."[1] So in an action on the case against owners of a steamboat, for the loss, by negligence, of a slave of the plaintiff hired to the defendants; a nonjoinder of a part of the owners, or a joinder of those not owners, will not affect the plaintiff's right to recover against those properly made defendants.[2]

§ 21. One injured by the concurrent negligence of two persons may maintain a joint action against them. Thus where the trains of two companies using the same track come in collision, an action is maintainable against them jointly for injuries incurred. "Had

[1] Frink *v.* Potter, 17 Ill. 406; per Skinner J., ib. 411.

[2] Swigert *v.* Graham, 7 B. Mon. 661.

the collision set in motion a third body, which in its movement had come in contact with and produced the same injury to the plaintiff, no good reason can be assigned against their joint liability; such a case is in principle like the one under consideration."[1]

§ 22. Declaration, that the defendants were owners of a coal mine, and the plaintiff was employed by them as a collier in the mine, and in the course of his employment it was necessary for him to descend and ascend through a shaft constructed by them; that, by their negligence, the shaft was constructed unsafely, and was, by reason of not being sufficiently lined or cased, unsafe, which they well knew; and by reason of the premises, and also by reason, as they well knew, of no sufficient or proper apparatus having been provided by them to protect the plaintiff from injuries arising from the unsafe state of the shaft, a stone fell from the side of the shaft on his head, and he was dangerously wounded. Plea, not guilty. It was proved that A, one of the two defendants, was manager of the mine, and that it was worked under his personal superintendence; and that the plaintiff was not aware of the state of the shaft. The jury found that the defendants were guilty of personal negligence. Held, on motion to enter a nonsuit, that on this finding A was liable, and therefore the other defendant was liable also. Also, on motion in arrest of judgment, that the declaration must be taken to allege personal knowledge in the defendants of the state of the shaft, and therefore the action was maintainable.[2]

§ 23. In a late case an action was brought for injury sustained by the falling of a party-wall, erected on the dividing line between two lots, owned respectively by the defendants. In giving judgment for the plaintiff the court remark: "The maintenance of an insecure party-wall was a tort in which they were both participants. The act was single, and it was the occasion of the injury. The case is not to be confounded with actions of trespass brought for separate acts done by two or more defendants. Then, if there has been no concert, no common interest, there is no joint liability. Here, the keeping of the wall safe was a common duty, and a

[1] Colegrove *v.* New York, &c. 20 N. Y. (6 Smith) 492; per H. Gray, J., ib. 493.

[2] Mellors *v.* Shaw, 1 Best & Smith, 437.

failure to do so was a common neglect."[1] So a joint action lies against two towns bound to support a bridge.[2]

§ 24. But where a complaint was brought against two defendants, that one of them erected a stone building across an alley, obstructing the plaintiff's right of way; and that possession of the building was then transferred by one defendant to the other, who continued such obstruction: held, ground for a separate, but not a joint action, and that the causes of action were improperly united. Also, that the objection of misjoinder might be made by a joint demurrer.[3] So case for deceit, in the nature of a conspiracy, can only be sustained, where some affirmation or representation, wilfully false, or some designed and positively fraudulent artifice, is directly proved, or necessarily to be presumed from the circumstances attending the transaction itself, to have been made or perpetrated by the defendants jointly, by means whereof a damage resulted to the plaintiff. Thus it cannot be sustained against a principal and his agent, jointly, for the unauthorized fraudulent acts and representations of the agent alone.[4]

§ 25. The general issue, in tort, is regarded as several, though in form joint.[5]

§ 26. If two defendants, in trespass and ejectment for land, join in pleading the general issue, evidence of title in one is a good defence for both.[6]

§ 27. An allegation of a joint freehold, in a notice, filed with a plea of the general issue in trespass, does not admit evidence of a several freehold in each defendant.[7]

§ 28. In trespass *de bon. aspor.* against several, they filed a special plea of justification, admitting that all took and carried away the property and converted it to their own use, but failed to make good their plea. Held, all were bound by the admission, though there was no evidence of the taking, &c., as to some of them.[8]

§ 29. In the New York Code, § 136, subd. 2, the words, "defendants severally liable," refer to all the defendants served, although jointly liable, if, as between them and other defendants not served,

[1] Per Strong, J., Klander *v.* M'Grath, 35 Penn. 129.

[2] Peckham *v.* Burlington, Brayt. 134.

[3] Hess *v.* Buffalo, &c. 29 Barb. 391.

[4] Page *v.* Parker, 40 N. H. 47.

[5] Downer *v.* Flint, 2 Wms. 527.

[6] Tripp *v.* Ide, 3 R. I. 51.

[7] Williams *v.* Holmes, 2 Wis. 129.

[8] Norris *v.* Norton, 19 Ark. 319.

the liability is several, as well as to the case where each and all are severally liable.[1]

§ 30. "A *cestui que trust*, or other person having only an equitable interest, cannot in general sue in the courts of common law, against his trustee, or even a third person, unless in cases where the action is against a wrong-doer, and for an injury to the actual possession of the *cestui*."[2]

§ 31. Where one conveys personal property in trust for the payment of a debt, and afterwards conveys the same property directly to the creditor, the legal title is in the trustee, and suit is properly brought against one in possession in the name of the trustee.[3]

§ 32. A executed a deed of slaves to trustees, for the benefit of himself and wife during their lives, and after their deaths to be divided among their children. A remained in possession of the slaves, removed to Missouri, and sold two of them to the defendant, who had notice of the deed. After the death of A and wife, the children brought a suit for the slaves. Held, the suit could not be sustained; it should have been brought in the name of the trustees, or their successors.[4]

[1] Pruyn *v.* Black, 19 N. Y. (7 Smith), 300.

[2] 1 Chit. Pl. 48.

[3] Bergesch *v.* Keevil, 19 Mis. 127.

[4] Gibbons *v.* Gentry, 20 Mis. 468.

CHAPTER III.

THE GENERAL ISSUE AND SUBSEQUENT PLEADINGS.

1. As a defence to the action.
4. In mitigation of damages.
6. What shall be construed as a denial; implied admissions.
8. Miscellaneous points.
11. Replication, &c.

§ 1. IT will be seen hereafter, in connection with particular forms of action, and actions for particular wrongs, what defences may be offered under the various pleas known to the law; more especially the plea of the *general issue* or *not guilty*. A few general points may properly be stated in the present connection.

§ 2. It is laid down, as the general rule, that, in actions *ex delicto*, matters in justification may be offered under the general issue.[1] That special matters may be given in evidence under the plea of not guilty; though it would be more in harmony with the general system of practice, to plead such matters specially.[2] Thus, in an action on the case, though for a tort, the defendant may justify under the general issue.[3] So *accident* may be offered in defence under the general issue.[4] So, in an action on the case for beating the plaintiff's horse, the defendant may show, under the general issue, that it was done to drive the horse from his own door, which he obstructed.[5]

§ 3. But it is also held, that new affirmative matter of avoidance or defence cannot be given in evidence under a general or special traverse, but must be specially pleaded.[6] And that, in actions for torts, matters in discharge or justification of the action must be specially pleaded, and cannot be given in evidence under the general issue.[7] Thus a defendant in trespass cannot show that the plaintiff has assigned his action, nor any interest in it, without having alleged the fact in his answer.[8] So a defence

[1] Collins *v.* Bilderback, 5 Harring. 133.
[2] Hunt *v.* Turner, 9 Tex. 385.
[3] Rust *v.* Flowers, 1 Har. 475.
[4] Gault *v.* Humes, 20 Md. 304.
[5] Slater *v.* Swann, 2 Str. 872.
[6] Marley *v.* McAnelly, 17 Tex. 658.
[7] Hahn *v.* Ritter, 12 Ill. 80.
[8] Goetz *v.* Ambs, 27 Mis. 28.

based upon fraud, to be admissible in evidence, must be specially pleaded.[1] And where notice is by statute substituted for a special plea, fraud cannot be set up to invalidate a contract, under the general issue, without notice, being consistent with the existence *in fact* of the contract, and therefore *matter of avoidance* within the terms of a statute.[2]

§ 4. Matter in mitigation of unliquidated damages, although not in total disproof of any of the items claimed, is admissible under a general denial.[3] (*a*)

§ 5. In an action by a father for the seduction of his daughter, the defendant offered to prove, not in mitigation but as a complete defence, though not set up in the answer, that the father knew of the intercourse between the defendant and his daughter, and connived at it. Held, although a good defence, not having been pleaded, it was inadmissible as such, though it might have been adduced in mitigation.[4]

§ 6. It is sometimes held, that a plea is to be construed as a denial, unless the fact is admitted.[5] Thus, under the laws of Indiana, a denial in general terms of all material allegations of the declaration puts the plaintiff to the proof of each of them.[6] So, in an action for obstructing a trade, the unlawfulness of such trade may be proved under the general issue.[7] So the general issue, in an action for fraud, denies both the act and the intent.[8] So, in an action for wrongful dismissal from service, a traverse of the allegation puts in issue the wrongfulness, as well as the fact, of dis-

[1] Fankboner *v.* Fankboner, 20 Ind. 62.
[2] Hoxie *v.* Home, &c. 32 Conn. 22.
[3] Harter *v.* Crill, 33 Barb. 283.
[4] Travis *v.* Barger, 24 Barb. 614.
[5] George *v.* Nelson, 23 Ind. 392.
[6] Spaulding *v.* Harvey, 7 Ind. 429.
[7] Tarleton *v.* M'Gawley, Peake, Cas. 207; acc. Harmam *v.* Mockett, 2 B. & C. 924.
[8] Mummery *v.* Paul, 8 Jur. 986; 2 Greenl. Evid. 190, § 232.

(*a*) In this case the following important distinction is made between *partial defence* and *mitigation of damages:* "Writers have confounded the distinction, to some extent, between *partial* defences and *circumstances of mitigation*, as both were admissible, under the old general issue, without pleading them, and there was no occasion for keeping up the distinction. But it is obvious that a defence, as understood in law language, is a full answer to the whole or to some part of the plaintiff's demand. Mitigating circumstances do not and never did amount to a defence to any part of the plaintiff's claim. They may diminish the *nominal* claim made by him, but do not diminish the *real* claim. . . . The amount of damages in this class of actions depends upon the circumstances as they appear before the jury. In this action they depend in a great measure upon the state of the relations subsisting between the parties (husband and wife); and although the parties lived together in the most unhappy state and condition, and in danger of their lives, it is no *defence* to the action. Certainly it is not *new matter* of defence." Per Morgan, J., Harter *v.* Crill, 33 Barb. 286.

missal.[1] So, in an action for damages sustained in falling into a ditch which the defendants had left open and unguarded by the highway, the declaration alleged that the plaintiff fell into it without any fault or want of care on his part. The answer denied that "the plaintiff, without any fault or want of care on his part, did fall therein." Held, a sufficient denial, both of the fact of falling in and due care on the part of the plaintiff.[2] So with a writ containing two counts in contract, one for the balance found due to the plaintiff by the parties on accounting together, and the other for a like sum for goods sold, and laying the damages at a less amount than the two sums added together, the plaintiff filed a bill of particulars, not in terms confined to either count, charging the defendant with a number of items of goods, mostly intoxicating liquors in less quantities than the law allowed to be sold without license; and the defendant answered that the goods alleged to have been sold were intoxicating liquors sold without license. Held, the plaintiff was not entitled to judgment on the first count for want of an answer.[3]

§ 7. But, on the other hand, it is not a sufficient denial in a plea, to say the defendants "do not admit" the allegations of the plaintiff. In such case, he need not prove them.[4] And an answer, which merely denies wrongfulness, is an admission of the fact.[5] So where the plaintiff, under a count for goods sold, files a bill of particulars, charging the defendant with many items, some of which are for goods unlawfully sold, and crediting him with payments made by the defendant generally, and applied by the plaintiff to the unlawful items; the defendant cannot, under an answer denying his liability on the single ground that all the goods were sold in violation of law, dispute this appropriation of payments.[6] So, under Mass. Stat. 1852, ch. 312, §§ 14, 15, the illegality of the contract declared upon, in an action on the common counts, or on an account annexed, cannot be given in evidence by the defendant, unless specified in his answer.[7] So to a declaration, "for that the defendant debauched and carnally knew the plaintiff's wife," the defendant pleaded not guilty.

[1] Horton *v.* McMurtry, 5 Hurl. & Nor. 767.

[2] Wall *v.* Buffalo, &c., 18 N. Y. (4 Smith), 119.

[3] Rundlett *v.* Weeber, 3 Gray, 263.

[4] Bomberger *v.* Turner, 13 Ohio St. 263.

[5] Lay *v.* Neville, 25 Cal. 549.

[6] Rundlett *v.* Weeber, 3 Gray, 263.

[7] Granger *v.* Ilsley, 2 Gray, 521.

Held, it was not necessary for the plaintiff to prove, that a female shown to have been debauched by the defendant was the wife of the plaintiff.[1] So fraud, if relied on, must be alleged in the answer.[2] So in an action for breaking and entering a close, and removing a fence; the defendant cannot disprove such removal under a denial merely of the breaking and entering.[3]

§ 8. Suit against the owners of a steamboat, to recover the value of a package of money, intrusted to the clerk of the boat, to be by him transported to another port. Held, an answer, averring want of authority in the clerk to receive and carry such packages, without compensation to the owners of the boat, and without their knowledge, was not bad as amounting to the general issue, there being no averment in the complaint that the defendants were engaged in the business of carrying packages of money for hire.[4]

§ 9. In an action of tort, the defendant pleaded "not guilty," with notice that he should prove a settlement. Held, after the jury were called, the defendant could not amend his notice, though it was defective in form, and therefore the court should not strike it out on motion, as it contained a substantial defence.[5]

§ 10. In an action for enticing away a servant, the defendant may show, under the general issue, a judgment against the servant for leaving the plaintiff, and satisfaction thereof since the bringing of the present suit. It was intimated that the court would stay the action on motion.[6]

§ 11. With reference to the pleadings subsequent to the plea or answer, a plaintiff is not bound to *reply* to averments in the answer, unsupported by proof, which set up new matter.[7]

§ 12. Declaration, that the plaintiff delivered to the defendants, as common carriers, a parcel, to be carried by them from London to Plymouth. Breach, non-delivery to the plaintiff at Plymouth. Plea, a tender on payment for the carriage, but that the plaintiff refused to pay the amount, whereupon the defendants refused to deliver the parcel. The plaintiff replied, that, within a reasonable time after the defendants had tendered the parcel,

[1] Kenrick *v.* Horder, 7 Ell. & B. 628.
[2] California, &c. *v.* Wright, 8 Cal. 585.
[3] Knapp *v.* Slocumb, 9 Gray, 73.
[4] The Cincinnati, &c. *v.* Boal, 15 Ind. 345.
[5] Whitehall *v.* Smith, 24 Ill. 178.
[6] Bird *v.* Randall, 3 Burr. 1345.
[7] Gouhenant *v.* Brisbane, 18 Tex. 20.

he offered at Plymouth to pay for its carriage, and requested the defendants to deliver it, but they refused to deliver it at Plymouth. The defendants having taken issue on this replication, the jury found that the allegations in it were proved. Held, that, if the defendants' having sent back the parcel to London excused its non-delivery, this should have been specially rejoined.[1]

§ 13. In an action in substance for the value of coal taken from a mine, a replication to the plea of the Statute of Limitations, that the wrongful taking was fraudulently concealed from the plaintiff until within six years before suit, was disallowed, on the ground that a court of equity would not restrain the defendant from setting up the defence, and that, if there was any right to equitable relief, it could only be by a bill for an account, in which the amount allowed would be different from the amount recoverable at law. "No case has decided that fraud is an answer in equity to the Statute of Limitations with respect to matters that occur in the way of wrong or contract between man and man. . . . If this replication of fraud were admitted . . . the defendant would indignantly deny its truth . . . and say, that though he may have taken under ground some coal not belonging to him, it was a mere mistake; . . . and nothing could be more unsatisfactory than an inquiry whether a man who fifteen years ago took some of his neighbor's coal, took it by mistake or by fraud."[2]

§ 14. The plaintiff sued to recover certain slaves, of which he alleged the defendant had illegally and fraudulently obtained possession, and had set up a fraudulent claim thereto. The defendant answered, that the plaintiff had voluntarily made to him a deed of gift of the slaves, and given him possession. The plaintiff gave evidence to show that the deed was a *donatio causâ mortis*. Held, the answer was in the nature of a plea of reconvention or cross petition, and the plaintiff ought not to have been allowed to give any evidence *dehors* the deed, without having first set up the matter to which it related by way of amendment to his original petition.[3]

§ 15. To a plea justifying an arrest under an execution, the plaintiff replied payment before the arrest, formally traversing that the judgment was then in full force, &c. Held, the traverse

[1] Great, &c. *v.* Crouch, 3 Hurl. & Nor. 183.

[2] Hunter *v.* Gibbons, 38 Eng. L. & Eq. 450; per Pollock, C. B., ib. 454.

[3] Thompson *v.* Thompson, 12 Tex. 327.

was to an immaterial matter, and a rejoinder, denying payment, was good.[1]

§ 16. Where a plea of fraud to a contract under seal set forth that the deed was executed and delivered to A, to be delivered to the plaintiff, in performance of a particular agreement between him and A, and that A and the plaintiff collusively made a different agreement, less beneficial to the defendants, and the deed was delivered on such new agreement; held, a replication, that the deed was not obtained by fraud and covin of A and the plaintiff, was bad, because, when a defence consists of several facts, the replication must deny only a single fact, or the facts making a single point of the defence.[2]

[1] Buck *v.* Blanchard, 20 N. H. 323.

[2] Watriss *v.* Pierce, 36 N. H. 232.

CHAPTER IV.

TORT AND CONTRACT. — FRAUD.

§ 1. QUESTIONS of pleading often arise from the settled distinction between torts and contracts. (*a*)

§ 2. A claim for unlawful conversion being founded on tort, and one for money had and received, upon contract, they are distinct causes of action, and cannot be joined in the same suit.[1] So an action growing out of a contract with A cannot be joined with a count on a tort of B; though the objection must be taken before joining issue.[2] So a count, upon an interference with the plaintiff's right to pass on a navigable stream, cannot be joined with a count for breach of a contract, which gives the plaintiff such right; each is a distinct cause of action.[3] And where contract and tort are joined, the plaintiff must elect upon the trial between them.[4]

§ 3. When non-assumpsit is pleaded to an action on the case in tort it may be stricken out on motion.[5]

§ 3 *a*. The law does not allow a set-off between tort and contract.[6]

§ 4. It is often difficult to determine whether an action is, in form, *ex contractu* or *ex delicto*. It is said, perhaps the best

[1] Cobb *v.* Dows, 9 Barb. 230.

[2] Wilson *v.* Thompson, 1 Met. (Ky.) 123. See Andrews *v.* Lynch, 27 Mis. 167.

[3] Rhodes *v.* Otis, 33 Ala. 578.

[4] Noble *v.* Laley, 50 Penn. 281.

[5] Wilkinson *v.* Moseley, 30 Ala. 562.

[6] The Indianapolis, &c. *v.* Ballard, 22 Ind. 448.

(*a*) In illustration of the connection between *tort* and *crime:* In a civil action for a felony, an allegation, that the grand jury of a certain county inquired and found no bill, is insufficient, as not showing that the criminal proceedings had been first had, unless it also show that the jury had jurisdiction. But the defect is amendable. Bell *v.* Troy, 35 Ala. 184. See Hilliard on Torts, Ch. II.

criterion is this: If the cause of action, as stated, arises from a breach of promise, the action is *ex contractu;* but if from a breach of duty, growing out of the contract, it is *ex delicto* and case.[1] Whether the action is for tort, depends on the substance of the declaration.[2]

§ 4 *a*. A declaration, that the plaintiff purchased of the defendant a note against one A, whom the defendant affirmed to be a person of good credit, when in fact he was poor, and the note was of no value, whereby the defendant deceived and defrauded him to his damage, &c., is bad in assumpsit, as no promise is averred, and bad in case, in not alleging a *scienter*. Neither is it a good declaration in case, upon a warranty, as it states no warranty.[3] But where the averment is, that the defendant engaged to safely keep, pasture, specially care for, and attend to certain horses of the plaintiff, for a reasonable compensation; and the breach, that, not regarding his duty in that behalf, he conducted himself so carelessly, negligently, and improperly, and by his absolute misuse and abuse, in and about the keeping and pasturing, caring for, and attending to, the horses, that they were injured; the declaration may be treated as in assumpsit, and the plea changed from not guilty to *non assumpsit*, payment, and set-off. So although proper care is averred to have been the duty of the defendant under the contract.[4] (*a*)

§ 5. Questions of pleading often arise in cases of alleged *fraud*, which is the intermediate ground, or the connecting link, between tort and contract.

[1] Wilkinson *v.* Moseley, 18 Ala. 288.
[2] Carter *v.* White, 32 Ill. 509.
[3] Bedell *v.* Stevens, 8 Fost. 118.
[4] Cook *v.* Haggerty, 2 Grant, 257; 36 Penn. 67.

(*a*) The rule against joining tort and contract is often changed by statute. In Kentucky, that the cause of action set up in an amended petition is in tort, while that set out in the original petition was in contract, is not ground of demurrer. Hord *v.* Chandler, 13 B. Mon. 403.

Under the Code, in Missouri, a plaintiff can only recover on the cause of action stated in his petition. Where the petition is for goods sold and delivered, and the evidence shows a trespass *de bon. asport.*, he cannot recover. Link *v.* Vaughn, 17 Mis. 585.

The statutory modification of the law upon the subject is strongly illustrated by a late case in Indiana, in which the declaration against a railroad corporation was as follows: "The Toledo, &c., to A. B., Dr. To one cow killed by your locomotive, within Clinton, &c., $50." On appeal, a judgment for the plaintiff was reversed, for the reasons, that the complaint was not sufficient under the statute, as it did not aver that the road was not fenced; nor as a charge of tort at common law, because it did not allege negligence; nor as a count in assumpsit, on waiver of the tort, for not alleging that the company used the dead animal, or derived any benefit from killing her, or promised to pay. Toledo, &c. *v.* Lunch, 23 Ind. 10.

§ 6. A count in assumpsit cannot be joined with a count for a deceit; and where, under a declaration containing only the latter, after an award and an appeal therefrom, the former was added, it was properly struck off upon the trial. The court remark: "That the same evidence will often support different forms of action there is no doubt, but cases which prove this cannot be resorted to, to prove the rightful joinder of inconsistent actions. The same evidence will often support trespass or case, deceit or trover, trover or replevin, *assumpsit* or debt, but it does not follow that you can join these several actions." [1]

§ 7. A complaint contained two or more counts confessedly on contract and well pleaded, and another, which set forth that the plaintiffs sold and delivered the defendant goods to a certain amount, on a credit of six months; that the defendant was insolvent at the time of said sales, and purchased the goods without any intent to pay for them and with the intent to defraud the plaintiffs of their value, and that by reason of said fraud the defendant became liable to pay for the goods immediately upon their delivery. The goods not having been paid for, the plaintiffs demanded judgment for the amount of the sales with interest. The action was brought before the expiration of the term of credit. The defendant demurred, for the joinder of improper causes of action in one complaint, and for want of any sufficient cause of action being set forth in the last count. Held, a good complaint, and demurrer overruled.[2]

§ 8. Held, also, that the cause of action set forth in the last count was upon contract; that fraud was sufficiently set forth to justify a rescission; that no specific act on the part of the plaintiffs, other than bringing this action, was necessary to manifest the plaintiffs' intent to rescind; that the facts justified the plaintiffs in making their election to sue in assumpsit rather than tort; and that they did not thereby adopt the express contract, but relied on the implied contract to pay, arising from the delivery and the defendant's possession of the goods.[3]

§ 8 *a*. The rules on the subject of pleading, stated in the first chapter, find frequent illustration in cases relating to fraud.

§ 9. It is held, in general, that the burden of *charging*, as well as *proving* fraud, is on the party who relies upon it; requiring facts and

[1] The Pennsylvania, &c. *v.* Zug, 47 Penn. 480; per Agnew, J., ib. 484.

[2] Roth *v.* Palmer, 27 Barb. 652.

[3] Ibid.

not conclusions; although it is unnecessary to state the *evidence*.[1] Thus, in an action for obtaining property under false pretences, a complaint, that the plaintiff was "satisfied" that the defendant procured certain property through fraud, &c., without any other allegations of fraud, is bad. So an action for obtaining property under false and fraudulent representations cannot be sustained, if it appears, on the face of the complaint, that the representations were made subsequent to the obtaining of the property.[2] So, in an action for deceit in making fraudulent representations, a count which does not allege any fraudulent representation by the defendants, nor any *scienter*, nor that the representation was made to the plaintiffs, is clearly defective.[3] So a declaration alleged, that the defendants falsely and fraudulently deceived the plaintiff in this, that "they, as brokers of the plaintiff, employed by him to purchase oil, falsely represented to him that they had purchased for him twenty-five tuns of palm oil, to arrive by the Celma, at the price of 30*l.* per tun;" whereas, in fact, the defendants purchased the oil on the terms "that the said twenty-five tuns were sold, and would be delivered to the plaintiff after and subject to the prior delivery of 800 tuns of palm oil from the said vessel;" that the vessel arrived with less than 800 tuns; and the consequent non-delivery to the plaintiff of the twenty-five tuns, and loss thereby. The facts were proved as stated, but it was conceded that there was no fraudulent intention on the part of the defendants. Held, an action was not maintainable.[4] "If the words 'falsely and fraudulently,' in the declaration can be struck out and a good cause of action left, they may be rejected, as in the case of a declaration for the warranty of a horse, or as where . . . this court held, that a plea to a declaration on a policy of insurance, averring a fraudulent misrepresentation as to the time of sailing . . . was supported without any proof of fraud, the misrepresentation affording a good defence, though not fraudulent. . . . . The averment that the defendants falsely and fraudulently deceived the plaintiff cannot be rejected without striking out the whole cause of action. All that follows is merely the explanation

[1] Butter *v.* Viele, 44 Barb. 166; Moore *v.* Clucas, 24 Eng. L. & Eq. 70; Fankboner *v.* Fankboner, 20 Ind. 62; Goodrich *v.* Reynolds, 31 Ill. 490; Jenkins *v.* Long, 19 Ind. 28; Swope *v.* Fair, 18 Ind. 300; Abraham *v.* Gray, 14 Ark. 301. See Union, &c. *v.* Mott, 27 N. Y. (13 Smith), 633.

[2] Snow *v.* Halstead, 1 Cal. 359.

[3] Behn *v.* Kemble, 7 C. B. (N. S.) 260.

[4] Thom *v.* Bigland, 20 Eng. L. & Eq. 467; per Parke, B., ib. 469.

of the deceit." So, to a suit on a note for the price of land, the plea was, that the plaintiff falsely represented, that there was on the land sufficient material to build a barn, whereas it was so insufficient that it cost the defendant $600 to buy enough more. Held bad, on special demurrer. The plea should have set out the value of the lumber as represented, and as it in fact existed at the time of the sale, that being the measure of damage. It seems, also, that the representation should have been alleged with more certainty; "enough to build a barn," is too indefinite. It seems, also, that the representation should have been alleged to have been fraudulent, as well as false.[1] So, if a county is induced to subscribe to the stock of a railway, in payment for which it issues negotiable bonds, by fraud and misrepresentation; fraud can be set up against an assignee of the bonds, only where it is alleged and proved that he is not a *bonâ fide* holder. The plea must allege why or how he is not a *bonâ fide* holder. In order to throw upon the plaintiff the burden of showing that he obtained the instrument *bonâ fide* and for value, the defendant must allege and prove that he took it overdue, or had notice, or gave no value.[2] So, in replevin for a mare, claimed to be exempt from execution, after the plaintiff had offered evidence of his residence in Iowa, the defendant offered to prove that the mare was sold by L. & L. of Chicago, Illinois, to N. & Co., of which firm the plaintiff was a member; that the plaintiff then resided in Illinois; that, in consideration of the sale, N. & Co. made their note to L. & L., which note was executed and payable in Illinois; that by the law of that State the mare was not exempt from execution; that, soon after the making of the note, the plaintiff, without the knowledge of L. & L., absconded from the State with the property, and came to Dubuque, in Iowa, where he was pursued by L. & L., who, to collect the note, sued out a writ of attachment against N. & Co.; and that under that writ the mare was attached. Held, the pleadings did not present the issue of fraud.[3] So an answer to an action upon a note, that "the note was obtained from him by fraud, covin, misrepresentations, and deceit," is bad for uncertainty.[4] And a plea of fraud should

[1] Kinney *v.* Osborne, 14 Cal. 112.

[2] Clapp *v.* Cedar, 5 Clarke (Iowa), 15.

[3] Newell *v.* Hayden, 8 Clarke (Iowa), 140.

[4] Honeywell *v.* Helm, 19 Ind. 321.

allege a *scienter*, and the pleader's reliance on the false representations.[1] Thus a complaint against a director, for falsely and fraudulently representing that the stock of a bank is worth par, by which the plaintiff was induced to purchase stock from the bank, when in truth the stock was worthless, &c.; must aver that the defendant knew that the stock was not worth what he represented it to be, and made the representations with intent to induce the purchase.[2] So, in an action upon a note given to a railroad, a plea that the note was given for a subscription to stock, and through misrepresentation of the company's agent as to the amount of stock taken and the time when the road would be finished, must allege that the representations were made by authority, and known to be false.[3]

§ 10. But there is a class of cases, partly depending, no doubt, upon statutory modifications of the common law, which adopt a less rigid rule. Thus the allegation of an answer, that the writing sued on was obtained from the defendants by fraud, covin, and misrepresentation of the plaintiffs, is held good. It is not a mere conclusion of law, but the averment of a substantive and traversable fact.[4] So, a release being pleaded, a replication, that the release was obtained by fraud and misrepresentation, without setting out particulars, is good.[5] So, in an action to recover goods obtained by a fraudulent purchase, the vendor may declare by a general claim of property, and give in evidence the facts showing the fraud.[6] So where the complaint, in an action for false representations, sets these forth as representations of fact made by the defendants of their own knowledge, and not as impressions of opinion or belief; alleges that they were false, and that the plaintiff relied on them, and suffered damage thereby, though not in terms any fraudulent, wilful, or intentional misrepresentation: the plaintiff may recover upon proof of those facts, unless the defendants can justify their representations. Upon these facts the law adjudges fraud.[7] So, in a declaration for a cheat in an exchange of horses, it is not necessary particularly to describe the

[1] White *v.* Watkins, 23 Ill. 480.

[2] Maybey *v.* Adams, 3 Bosw. 346.

[3] Goodrich *v.* Reynolds, 31 Ill. 490.

[4] Whitehead *v.* Root, 2 Met. (Ky.) 584.

[5] Hoitt *v.* Holcombe, 3 Fost. 535. (Containing an elaborate opinion, in which the old cases on the subject are cited. In some of them the ground of decision is, that *covin* is in its nature too secret to admit of knowledge on the part of the plaintiff as to its particulars.)

[6] Bliss *v.* Cottle, 32 Barb. 322.

[7] Sharp *v.* Mayor, &c. 40 Barb. 256.

unsoundness.[1] So it is a good declaration, that the defendant, the indorser of a note, with intent to deceive the indorsee, falsely represented that the maker was solvent, and, relying thereon, the plaintiff accepted the note.[2] So where the declaration alleged a "representation that a mortgage was good, and a valid security for payment of said note, and the plaintiff supposed and verily believed, at the time he bought the same as aforesaid, the said mortgage to be good, and that it was a valid and sufficient security;" held, a sufficient averment that the plaintiff bought on the faith of such representation.[3] So, in an action for fraud, the declaration alleged, that the defendant, to induce the purchase, fraudulently, &c., represented, &c., and warranted the premises to have and contain thereon three thousand spruce logs (meaning that there were spruce trees growing thereon that would cut and make three thousand spruce logs of the usual and customary size and quality), which the plaintiff believed to be true, and not knowing to the contrary, bought the premises, and paid for, and took a deed of them; and the representations were false and known to be false. Held good on demurrer. The plaintiff might prove, under the general issue, that the words were used and understood in the sense alleged by the *innuendo*, and in that sense they must be taken to have been used and understood. That the representation was mere opinion upon a point of which either party alike could judge, was matter of proof under a traverse.[4] So an action may be maintained, upon the declaration that the plaintiff bought hogs having the cholera, for a sound price, represented to be sound and healthy, but known to be otherwise; and the plaintiff bought relying upon the representations, and unable by reasonable diligence to ascertain that they were false.[5] So it is a good answer to an action upon a note, that it was given for the last instalment on a stock of goods, purchased of the plaintiff, who then represented it to be worth $3500, and that it would invoice that sum or more; that the defendants were ignorant of the amount and value, and requested an invoice, but the plaintiff said he had no time to make it; that the purchase was made on this representation, but it was knowingly false; and the goods invoiced and amounted to only $1500.[6] And it is held, that,

1 Reed *v.* Rogers, 3 Monr. 173.
2 Jamison *v.* Copher, 35 Mis. 483.
3 Hahn *v.* Doolittle, 18 Wis. 196.
4 Whitton *v.* Goddard, 36 Verm. 730.
5 Baker *v.* M'Ginniss, 22 Ind. 257.
6 Davis *v.* Jackson, 22 Ind. 233.

although it may be necessary, under English rules of pleading, to charge a fraudulent intent, where the fraud consists in the intention; yet it is not so in Texas, where fraud is a conclusion to be drawn from the facts specially alleged in the petition, and where the existence of those facts, and not the fraudulent intent, is the gist of the inquiry.[1]

§ 11. Questions on the same subject also arise, in reference to the *parties* who suffer or commit the wrong complained of.

§ 12. A complaint, in form a creditor's bill, praying that land conveyed away fraudulently as against creditors may be applied in payment thereof, must make the grantee a party to the suit. Thus five judgments were recovered by the plaintiffs against A, upon which were unsatisfied executions. Previous to the judgments, A owned certain real property, which he conveyed to B, without consideration, and with intent to defraud his creditors, and A had other equitable interests which ought to be applied on the judgments. Prayer to set aside the conveyance, and for equitable relief, &c. No equitable property was discovered, and it appeared that the real estate had been conveyed before suit commenced, to C, who was not made party. Held, C must be made a party.[2]

§ 13. For an injury against the common property of husband and wife, or the business carried on by means of such property, the husband should bring suit alone. Hence where a suit for deceit was brought by a husband and wife, averring that the plaintiffs had been induced to make a worthless purchase by false representations of the defendant; but not that the wife had any separate interest in the purchase-money, or in the business for which the purchase was made: held, a demurrer for misjoinder of parties was good.[3]

§ 14. But, upon a charge of fraud, the law does not require, as in case of contract, proof of *privity* between the parties to the suit. Thus a declaration alleged, that the defendant and others had formed a company, upon a principle known as *société anonyme*, in Spain, the capital of which was 96,000 shares of 1*l.* each, out of which 12,000 were to be appropriated to the public, at 12*s.* 6*d.*

[1] Carter *v.* Carter, 5 Tex. 93.

[2] Sage *v.* Mosher, 28 Barb. 287.

[3] Barrett *v.* Tewksbury, 18 Cal. 334.

per share, free from all further calls, and that the said 12,000 shares were actually offered to the public; that the defendant, as such promoter and managing director, intending to deceive the public, and to cause it to be publicly represented and advertised that the said company was likely to be a safe and profitable undertaking, and also to deceive the public who might become purchasers of the said 12,000 shares, and to induce them to become such purchasers, falsely, fraudulently, and deceitfully caused it to be publicly advertised and made known, in and by a prospectus issued by the defendant as such director (*inter alia*), that the promoters of the said company, in proposing to issue to the public the said 12,000 shares at 12*s*. 6*d*. per share, free from all further calls, did not hesitate to guarantee to the bearers of the said 12,000 shares a minimum annual dividend of 33*l*. per cent., payable in half-yearly dividends of 16*l*. 10*s*. per cent. each, and that the said guaranty should remain in force until the said 12*s*. 6*d*. per share should be thus repaid to the shareholder; that the defendant, by means of the said false, fraudulent, and deceitful representation, fraudulently induced the plaintiff to become, and the plaintiff, by reason thereof, became the purchaser and bearer of 2,500 of the said 12,000 shares at 12*s*. 6*d*. per share, and by means of the premises the plaintiff was induced to pay, and did pay 12*s*. 6*d*. for each of the said shares; whereas, in truth and in fact, at the time of making the said statement, the same was false and fraudulent, to the knowledge of the defendant, and the defendant had no ground whatever for offering such guaranty to the public, as the defendant well knew; by means whereof the plaintiff had lost the money so paid by him as aforesaid. Held, a sufficient allegation of a false representation by the defendant, and that the plaintiff was entitled to judgment, as there was no necessity for any privity between the parties. The court comment upon the argument, that the action could not be maintained, because it "did not arise from any public wrong or the neglect of any public duty. . . . The doctrine . . . cannot apply to an action founded, irrespective of a contract, upon a false representation fraudulently made by the defendant to the plaintiff, for the purpose of inducing the plaintiff to act upon it, the plaintiff showing that by so acting upon it he had suffered damage. Under such circumstances, although the parties be entire strangers to each other, the action lies."[1] (*a*)

§ 15. Questions also arise in reference to the *joinder* of parties. Thus, in an action against several, for fradulently inducing the plaintiff to buy an interest in a patented machine, an averment that the defendants conspired together to defraud the plaintiff need not be proved. "The gist of the action was not the conspiracy, but the damage."[2] But in an action against A & B, a partnership, for fraudulent representations made by A, one of its members; a declaration alleging that he, acting in behalf of the firm, procured a writ of replevin to be brought in the name of a third person, and signed his own name to the replevin bond as surety; and that he declared to the plaintiff, who was a deputy-

[1] Gerhard *v.* Bates, 20 Eng. L. & Eq. 129; per Lord Campbell, C. J., ib. 137. (Upon another count founded on *contract*, judgment was rendered for the defendant.)

[2] Hayward *v.* Draper, 3 Allen, 551; per Hoar, J., ib. 552.

(*a*) The counsel for the defendant asked: "Suppose a person coming from a colony were, with a view of inducing persons to emigrate there, to publish a book giving a false account of the colony, could any one who emigrated on the faith of what he there read bring an action against the author?" To which Lord Campbell replied in the affirmative, if he published it with the intention that it should be so acted upon. 20 Eng. L. & Eq. 134

A recent case in New York contains an elaborate opinion upon the important question, how far one party may be liable to another for false representations, not made directly to the latter, but influencing his action and resulting in pecuniary loss. The court remark: "The complaint does not state that these representations were made *to the plaintiff* . . . nor . . . that the plaintiff . . . came to the knowledge of them. . . . The representations . . . are charged to have been uttered in published reports and statements of the condition and property of this company, made and signed by him as one of its officers, and generally and publicly circulated and advertised. . . . A question very similar was presented to the Superior Court of the city of New York, in *Cross* v. *Sackett* (2 Bosw. 617), and although the doctrine of Lord Campbell was severely questioned by eminent counsel, it was substantially accepted. . . . The defendant had no interest in the stock which the plaintiff was induced to purchase, and reaped no benefit from the contract. The doctrine . . . is that a statement made to the public and designed to influence the public, is designed to influence every individual who is interested. . . . It is not necessary, however, to go as far as the courts have gone in these cases . . . since the defendant . . . was privy to the contract . . . and interested in the sale which was induced. The case of the *National Exchange Co.* v. *Drew* (32 Eng. L. & Eq. p. 1), is in this respect more nearly analogous. . . . That was a case in the House of Lords. . . . . It was held, . . . that a joint stock company would be bound by the fraudulent statements of their directors, whereby third parties were induced to contract with them, although . . . made in reports submitted by the directors to annual meetings. . . . . A liability was admitted; the only question was whether it attached to the company. . . . . In the present case the responsibility is cast upon the individual who made the representations, and the same individual profited by them. Another still more recent case in the House of Lords is *Bagshaw* v. *Seymour*, reported in 4 Com. B. Rep. (N. S.) 873, where an action was maintained against a chairman of a company who had procured its shares to be put on the stock list of the exchange by falsely stating in a prospectus, and in a letter to the committee of the stock exchange, that its capital was paid up. The action was by a person who had been induced to buy some of the shares." Per Emott J., Newbery *v.* Garland, 31 Barb. 128.

sheriff, that the firm was responsible, and that his signature to the bond bound the firm, and that he was authorized by the firm to bind it by his signature alone, and thus induced the plaintiff to accept the bond and to serve the writ, whereby the firm obtained and disposed of the goods replevied for its own benefit; and that judgment was rendered for the defendant in replevin, and the goods were not returned, and the firm was not bound by the signature to the bond, and the plaintiff has been held liable for taking an insufficient bond; — does not set forth sufficient facts to charge the other partner in the fraud. The declaration alleges facts, tending to show that the wrongful act of A became the tort of both defendants; but the fact intended to be put in issue is stated so indirectly and argumentatively, that the court cannot draw from the averments the legal inference that the defendant B is liable.[1]

§ 16. In an action for deceit in a sale of stock, by the defendant, through A, his agent, and to enforce the plaintiff's lien as vendor upon the land conveyed in payment; it appeared that A acted only as agent, that the stock was in fact sold by the defendant, and that the land conveyed to A had been conveyed to the defendant before the suit. Held, A was not a necessary party.[2]

§ 17. In the same connection may be considered the joinder of different causes of action.

§ 18. Several causes of action, all arising out of frauds alleged to have been practised by the defendant, a bank director, through misrepresentations made to the plaintiff and neglect of duties required by the statute, may be joined in one declaration.[3]

§ 19. It is the general rule, that a count for deceit in the sale of goods cannot be joined with one in assumpsit on a warranty of soundness.[4]

§ 20. Questions of *variance* often arise in connection with actions for fraud. In New York it is held, in a case of this nature, that a variance between the complaint and the case proved is material, and cannot be cured by conforming the pleadings to the facts proved. (Code, § 173.) And in such case the plaintiff cannot have judgment, under § 275 of the Code, because the relief which the proofs would warrant is not "consistent with the case made by the com-

[1] Gray *v.* Cropper, 1 Allen, 337.

[2] Newbery *v.* Garland, 31 Barb. 121.

[3] Maybey *v.* Adams, 3 Bosw. 346.

[4] Chamberlain *v.* Robertson, 7 Jones, 12. But see Patterson *v.* Kirkland, 34 Miss. 423.

plaint and embraced within the issue." Complaint, that the plaintiff employed the defendants, as brokers, to purchase for him on credit certain shares of stock, and delivered to them other stock as security for their indemnity, and that they afterwards rendered him an account of such purchase and of a subsequent sale, after notice, both of which transactions were not real, but fictitious. Also, that a charge in such account rendered, for negotiating a loan upon the stock, was also fictitious, and praying judgment thereupon, that defendants return the stock so delivered to them as security. It was found, that the defendants made the purchase according to their employment, and advanced the money therefor, and, in order to the holding of the stock for the period contemplated by the plaintiff, negotiated a loan thereon, but also, that the defendants had sold the stock for a price greater than that at which they accounted to the plaintiff. Held, the plaintiff was not entitled to damages for the value of the stock so purchased, as upon an illegal conversion of this stock.[1] So, in an action by the vendor of goods fraudulently obtained, against the consignees of the vendee, who has made advances upon the goods, it is not competent for the plaintiff, under an allegation that the consignees received the goods with knowledge of the fraud, and without paying any consideration therefor, to claim a recovery, on the ground that the advances were made upon a usurious contract; even though the usury appears by the defendants' own evidence. The court remark: "They had brought their action and rested their claim upon a totally distinct ground. The questions were, whether the defendants were cognizant of the fraud" (in the purchase of goods), "or had paid any consideration. Because proof incidentally appeared on the trial of those questions tending to show, that, though an advance had been made, it was under a usurious agreement, that was not a point in issue. The plaintiffs had not alleged it. The defendants did not come to trial to meet it. Incidental proof could not avail."[2] So if the averment of unsoundness, in an action for fraudulent misrepresentations as to the soundness of a horse, contain an allegation of the particular form of unsoundness; although unnecessary, it must be proved as laid.[3] So, in an action for deceit, a declaration, that the representations

[1] Saltus *v.* Genin, 3 Bosw. 250.

[2] Williams *v.* Birch, 6 Bosw. 299; per Woodruff, J., ib. 307.

[3] Lindsay *v.* Davis, 30 Mis. 406.

were well known by the defendant to be untrue, is not supported by proof of reasonable cause to believe that they were untrue.[1]

§ 21. But the fraud of an agent, authorized by his principal, is well pleaded as the fraud of the principal. "The same rule of law which imputes to the principal the fraud of the agent and makes him answerable for the consequences, justifies the allegation in pleading that the principal himself committed the wrong."[2] So a plaintiff may prove alleged misrepresentations in the sale of a certain described parcel of land, by a deed of this parcel and another annexed to his petition.[3] So, although he averred payment of $400 for the tract in dispute, and the deed mentioned $400 as the consideration for both; held, as the deed was not conclusive on this point, there was no variance.[4] So a declaration alleged, that the plaintiff assumed prosecution of a contract of work, commenced for the defendant by A, who had become unable to carry it on, being induced by the defendant's false and fraudulent representations that there would be no risk, and that the defendant had in his hands sufficient funds due to A. The evidence showed, that the defendant, being inquired of on behalf of the plaintiff, said that there would be funds enough to complete the undertaking, if A went on and finished it, and that the plaintiff was thereby induced to go on, though the plaintiff testified that he did not mean to assume the job, but only to assist the defendant. Held, sufficient to sustain the declaration. "Giving proper effect to the testimony, the conclusion might fairly be deduced from it, that the defendant did make the representations which are set forth."[5]

§ 21 *a*. In case for the loss of a slave who was killed while working on the defendant's house, if the declaration avers fraudulent concealment by the defendant of the dangerous condition of the house, and also fraudulent representations that it was safe; it is not demurrable for duplicity, but the latter averment may be stricken out as surplusage.[6]

§ 22. If the declaration, in an action of tort for deceit in the sale of property, sets forth some representations which are actionable, and some which are not; a new trial will not be granted,

1 Pearson *v.* Howe, 1 Allen, 207.

2 Bennett *v.* Judson, 21 N. Y. (7 Smith), 238; ib. 240, per Comstock, C. J.

3 Jones *v.* Smith, 6 Clarke (Iowa), 229.

4 Ibid.

5 Norton *v.* Huxley, 13 Gray, 285; per Merrick, J., ib. 291.

6 Perry *v.* Marsh, 25 Ala. 659.

after a verdict for the plaintiff, on account of an instruction to the jury, that "the plaintiff can maintain his action only by proof that he was induced to purchase the property by one or more of the representations alleged in the declaration to be false and fraudulent, and proved to be such;" if the judge did not further instruct them, that the plaintiff might maintain his action by proof of those representations which are not actionable.[1]

§ 22 *a*. Declaration, that the defendant requested the plaintiff to lend him a sum of money, and falsely, deceitfully, and fraudulently represented himself of full age, and that the plaintiff, confiding in the truth of that representation, lent him money on certain conditions; that the defendant at the time of making the representation was an infant, as he himself well knew, and refused to repay the loan or comply with the conditions, to the damage of the plaintiff. The court, suggesting that there was no cause of action, (*a*) granted leave to the defendant, under the 15 & 16 Vict. ch. 76, § 80, to demur to this declaration, and plead not guilty, with a traverse that the plaintiff confided in the alleged fraudulent representation, on an affidavit of the defendant's attorney, that he was informed and believed that the defendant had just cause to plead those pleas, and that the declaration would be held bad in substance on demurrer, and that the objections raised to it by the demurrer were good and valid objections in law.[2] (*b*)

§ 23. In reference to the *defence*, of fraud on the part of the plaintiff, it is held that, unless a party who sets up fraud, as a defence to an action on a contract, aver, in his answer, that he has done all in his power to restore the plaintiff to his former condition; he cannot show it at the trial.[3] But, in an action on a draft given for a horse, the defendant pleaded, that the plaintiff, intending, &c., did not perform his promise, but deceived and defrauded the defendant, in this, to wit: that the said horse, at the

[1] Pedrick *v*. Porter, 5 Allen, 324.
[2] Price *v*. Hewett, 18 Eng. L. & Eq. 522.
[3] Devendorf *v*. Beardsley, 23 Barb. 656.

(*a*) "Simple fraud gives no cause of action unless the party is damaged by it." Per Parke, B., 18 Eng. L. & Eq. 524. See Johnson *v*. Pye, 1 Sid. 258.

(*b*) The court remarked: "It would be a discredit to the defendant to admit on the record that he had made a fraudulent misrepresentation." The requisition of the statute referred to, — which enables the courts to authorize a plea and demurrer of the same matter, — that the party shall swear to the truth in substance and in fact of the matters proposed to be pleaded; applies only to pleas in confession and avoidance, not, as in this case, of denial.

time of making said promise, and at the time of said sale and delivery, was not sound, but on the contrary was unsound, whereby said horse became and was of no use or value to this defendant. Held, a sufficient averment of breach of warranty of soundness on general demurrer, though the plea contained no offer to return the horse.[1] And in a suit by a vendor to set aside a sale induced by the vendee's fraud, and for an account, the plaintiff being a partner of the defendant, and his interest being the property sold; an averment, that the defendant owes the plaintiff more than the sum paid for the interest, amounts to an offer to credit the defendant with that amount, and therefore sufficiently offers, upon rescission of the sale, to place the defendant *in statu quo*.[2]

[1] Palmer *v.* Wilks, 17 Tex. 105.

[2] Watts *v.* White, 13 Cal. 321.

CHAPTER V.

PLEADING IN TRESPASS.

§ 1. HAVING considered the subject of pleading in actions for torts, generally, we proceed to a view of pleading in the particular actions which have been appropriated to particular wrongs. The remark already made in another connection may be here properly repeated; that the statutory law, which has so extensively obliterated the technical distinctions or boundaries between different remedies, has still left untouched many of the principles upon which those distinctions depended.

§ 2. In no form of action are the rules of pleading more numerous, various, and precise, than that of trespass; which is a common remedy for immediate and forcible injuries to personal and real property, and to the person or body. This action will make the subject of the present chapter.

§ 3. Trespass laid with a *quod cum* or *whereas* is held bad on general demurrer, and cannot be amended after joinder.[1]

§ 4. In trespass for taking goods, the declaration must specify the goods.[2] Thus a declaration for taking fish, &c., or divers goods and chattels, is bad.[3]

§ 5. In trespass for taking "two cows at A., and also a load of wheat, the goods of the plaintiff there found;" the words "the goods of the plaintiff" refer only to the wheat; and therefore the trespass for taking the two cows is ill laid.[4]

[1] Holbrook *v.* Pratt, 1 Mass. 96.
[2] Bertie *v.* Pickering, 4 Burr. 2455.
[3] Com. Dig. Pleader, C. 21.
[4] Jose *v.* Mills, 6 Mod. 15.

§ 6. In actions for trespass to land, the *locus in quo* should be designated by abuttals, or other description, as it was at the time of the trespass, and not at the time of the declaration. (*a*) Therefore, where, in an action by a reversioner, the declaration described the *locus in quo* as "abutting on the south and east on a close in the occupation and possession of the defendants;" and the defendants (a railway company) pleaded that they took possession of part of the said close abutting on the south on the fence of their railway, under the provisions of the 8 & 9 Vict. ch. 20, §§ 32, 33, which was the trespass complained of; and it appeared at the trial, that, at the time of the trespass, the close in question abutted on the fence of the railway, but that afterwards the defendants took possession of and purchased, under the provisions of the above act, a small part of it adjoining the railway, so that the plaintiff's description was correct at the time of declaration, but not at the time of the trespass: held, the plaintiff could not recover for want of a new assignment.[1] But a declaration, that the defendant broke and entered "certain lands of the plaintiff covered with water, being the bed and channel of the river T., and under the same, in the several parishes of L. and L., in the county of G."; is good, on special demurrer.[2]

§ 7. The court cannot restrict the plaintiff in his proof to any less number of lots than he has described in his declaration.[3]

§ 8. A count in trespass for cutting down and carrying away a tree from the plaintiff's land, which commences like a count in trespass *quare clausum*, but concludes with an allegation that the trespass is "contrary to the statute in such case made and provided, whereby the plaintiff is entitled to recover of the defendant treble the aforesaid value of said tree, &c.," the statute is a count for the statute penalty (Verm. Comp. Stat. § 32, p. 550), and not a count in trespass at common law. The county court cannot allow an additional count in trover, either at common law, or by virtue of

[1] Humphrey *v.* The London, &c. 12 Eng. L. & Eq. 554.

[2] Duke of Beaufort *v.* Vivian, 12 Eng. L. & Eq. 564.

[3] Gardner *v.* Gooch, 48 Maine, 487.

(*a*) In New York, where a complaint shows no facts constituting a cause of action, the defendant may either demur or avail himself of the defect at the trial; and a bill of particulars under § 158 of the Code, or under § 160, in an action of trespass and ejectment, cannot be given, where the complaint omits to describe any premises; the proper course in such case is to dismiss the complaint, with leave to amend on terms. Budd *v.* Bingham, 18 Barb. 494.

the statute (Acts of 1856, p. 13), which allows the joinder of counts in trespass and trover, if for the same cause of action. And it is doubted whether, if the original count were simply for trespass *quare clausum*, the new count in trover could be added. In this case the following important distinction is taken with reference to the pleading of a statute: "The commencement of the count is in the appropriate form of a declaration in trespass upon the freehold, yet this is well enough, especially upon the general issue, although the pleader intends to go upon the statute and claim treble damages. To give a right of action founded upon the statute, the trees . . . must be standing, lying, or growing on the land of the plaintiff, and the entry . . . for such unlawful purpose necessarily constitutes a breaking of the plaintiff's close. . . . The statute in this declaration is *counted upon* by the pleader in the usual way, by an *express reference* to it, not only by declaring the transaction to be against the form of the statute, but" (as above stated) "showing clearly that the pleader goes for the penalty. If the facts are stated which bring a case within a statute, this is what is called *pleading a statute*, although no mention or notice is taken of the statute; but counting upon a statute . . . is by way of an express reference to it." [1]

§ 9. With reference to *time*, trespass for taking four loads of wheat, with a *continuando* of the trespass for a month, is good.[2] So trespass for breaking the plaintiff's close, treading down his grass, and hunting and killing his rabbits, on divers days and times from such a time to such a time, with a *continuando* of the said trespass as to all the particulars, is good; for, although one act cannot be continued from one day to another, yet an act may be daily continued.[3]

§ 10. The allegation of trespasses on a certain day, and on divers other days between that and another day, makes time a descriptive part of the trespass, and opens the door for proof as to any trespass committed within that time, and closes it as to all others.[4]

§ 11. In an action for trespass *quare clausum*, and with teams, carriages, and men, treading down and destroying the plaintiff's grass upon a certain day; evidence may be properly admitted of several separate and distinct acts or entries, each of which might alone

[1] Keyes *v.* Prescott, 32 Vt. 86; per Bennett, J., ib. 87.

[2] Wilson *v.* Howard, 5 Mod. 178.

[3] Monkton *v.* Ashley, 6 Mod. 38.

[4] Payne *v.* Green, 10 S. & M. 507.

technically constitute a breaking, when made upon the same close upon the same day, and in pursuance of the same general purpose. The court very justly remark: "The defendant cannot complain that, instead of two suits, or ten suits, if there had been as many loads of hay drawn, he has been chargedwith the whole in one suit. . . . No one probably ever knew a trespass charged with a *continuando*, from one hour or period in a day to some other hour or period of the same day; nor does the law favor the bringing of a multiplicity of suits, especially small ones of trifling amount, where one would as well settle all the questions of right, and the plaintiff could as well recover all his actual damage in one suit as in two or ten. And certainly the defendant cannot complain of this, though, perhaps, he might have done so with some reason, had the opposite course . . . been pursued."[1]

§ 12. In a second action for a continued trespass, the former verdict and judgment are evidence, but not conclusive, of title.[2]

§ 13. Under the Massachusetts Practice Act, time need not be stated in trespass *quare clausum*.[3]

§ 14. Trespass for taking and carrying away "mahogany tables and chairs," without specifying the number, was held well enough, after verdict; the court remarking: "The jury must have had evidence of the number of the several articles taken; at least they would have found damages only for so many as were proved."[4] So, in New York, where a declaration in trespass *de bon. asport.* omits to allege that the goods taken were the property of the plaintiff, and the defendant does not appear, and the plaintiff proves the trespass and his title; the declaration will uphold a judgment, although bad on demurrer.[5]

§ 15. But, in general, a declaration in trespass *de bon. asport.* is ill, even after verdict, and on motion in arrest of judgment, if it does not aver the plaintiff's title. The court make a distinction between this case and a title *defectively stated*, which may be cured by a verdict. But the plaintiff was allowed to amend, upon paying the costs accrued since the case went to the jury.[6]

§ 16. With reference to the *pleas* in trespass, whether the general issue, or a special justification, the general rule is laid down

[1] Cheswell *v.* Chapman, 42 N. H. 47; per Sargent, J., ib. 51.
[2] Nivin *v.* Stevens, 5 Har. 272.
[3] Knapp *v.* Slocomb, 9 Gray, 74.
[4] Richardson *v.* Eastman, 12 Mass. 505.
[5] Copley *v.* Rose, 2 Comst. 115.
[6] Carlisle *v.* Weston, 1 Met. 26.

as follows: (*a*) "In trespass *quare clausum fregit*, the defendant may give in evidence under the general issue any matter that contradicts the allegations which the plaintiff is bound to prove, or shows that the act complained of is not in its own nature a trespass. Thus he may give in evidence soil and freehold in himself, or in another by whose authority he entered, or that he has any other right to the possession. For he cannot be a trespasser in exercising a right which the law gives him, nor be bound to justify when he does not *primâ facie* appear to be a trespasser."[1] Accordingly he may give in evidence, under the general issue, that he is tenant in common with the plaintiff, or that he entered by license of such tenant.[2] In general, a license must be pleaded.[3] But the distinction is made, that the defence of license requires a special plea, only when such license was given by the plaintiff himself, and not by one claiming title as against the plaintiff.[4] So in trespass *de bon. asport.*, a defence, constituting a direct denial of, and inconsistent with, the allegations in the declaration, which are essential to be proved in order to maintain the action, may and ought to be given in evidence under the general issue. But if consistent with such a state of facts as would constitute a *primâ facie* case of trespass, and amounting only to an excuse or justification, the facts cannot be given in evidence under the general issue, but must be specially pleaded, or a brief statement filed under the statute.[5] And it is held in an old case, that, in trespass, the *right* cannot be given in evidence by the defendant, on the plea of *not guilty*, not even in mitigation of damages.[6] In other words, matters of defence which admit the original wrong must in general be specially pleaded.[7] Thus the defendant cannot justify, under the general issue, the cutting the posts and rails *of the plaintiff*, though erected upon the defendant's own land; there being no question raised as to the property remaining in the plaintiff.[8] So evidence of a former recovery is not admissible under the general issue.[9] So, as we have seen, a license to enter

[1] Per Morton, J., 4 Pick. 127.
[2] Rawson *v.* Morse, 4 Pick. 127.
[3] Haight *v.* Badgeley, 15 Barb. 499.
[4] Child *v.* Allen, 33 Verm. 476.
[5] Fuller *v.* Bounceville, 9 Fost. 554.
[6] Dove *v.* Smith, 6 Mod. 153.
[7] 2 Hill, 478.
[8] Welch *v.* Nash, 8 East, 394.
[9] Young *v.* Rummell, 2 Hill, 478; Hahn *v.* Ritter, 12 Ill. 80.

(*a*) The plea of not guilty is a waiver of all dilatory defences. Hill *v.* Morey, 26 Verm. 178.

Every plea in bar must be pleaded to the action, not to the damages merely. In trespass *de bon. asport.*, facts in mitigation cannot be specially pleaded, but must be given in evidence under the general issue. Hopple *v.* Higbee, 3 Zabr. 342.

the house of another should be pleaded.[1] So matters in discharge of the action must be specially pleaded; even though given in evidence by the plaintiff.[2]

§ 17. The common-law rules on this subject have been variously modified in the different States. But, in Texas, where to a petition, for entering on the plaintiff's close and tearing down and carrying away his fence, the defendant pleaded the general issue; held, under the common system of pleading, the plea of not guilty to an action of trespass *quare clausum* or *de bonis asportatis* did not put the plaintiff's title in issue, but the fact of the trespass; and that *à fortiori*, under the Texan form of pleading, a general denial of the petition did not put the petitioner's title in issue, but that the facts should be specially stated in the answer.[3] So, in Illinois, a plea of not guilty, in trespass *de bonis asportatis*, puts in issue only the wrongful taking; and the verdict, "not guilty," determines nothing as to the right of property.[4]

§ 17 *a*. And, in trespass, whatever admissions as to his own or the plaintiff's title, the defendant may make in his special pleas, have no effect as *estoppels in pais*, and do not estop him from putting the plaintiff to full proof of his title under the general issue. "It is always competent for a defendant, in trespass, to put the plaintiff on proof of his title under the general issue, however many special defences he may set forth on the record; and the special pleas have no effect by way of estoppel . . . unless the issues upon such special pleas shall become subjects of litigation; and then they estop only as admissions that operate to preclude proof in contradiction of the averment, or to dispense with proof of what is admitted by the pleadings."[5]

§ 17 *b*. On the other hand, in Vermont, if the defendant, in an action of trespass, give a special notice of his matter of justification under the general issue, in pursuance of the statute, the plaintiff, on trial, may avail himself of every matter, which he might have successfully new-assigned, if the defendant had pleaded his defence specially.[6]

§ 18. In *trespass to try title*, in Texas, a general denial puts in issue the plaintiff's right to recover.[7]

[1] Haight *v*. Badgeley, 15 Barb. 499.
[2] Walker *v*. Hitchcock, 19 Verm. 634.
[3] Carter *v*. Wallace, 2 Tex. 206.
[4] Harris *v*. Miner, 28 Ill. 135.
[5] Child *v*. Allen, 33 Verm. 476. Per Barrett, J., ib. 483.
[6] Keyes *v*. Howe, 18 Verm. 411.
[7] Harlan *v*. Haynie, 9 Tex. 459.

§ 19. In Massachusetts, an answer to an action of tort in the nature of trespass *qu. claus.*, which denies that the defendant entered the plaintiff's close, as described in the plaintiff's writ, puts the plaintiff's title in issue.[1]

§ 20. A license must be specially set up in the answer.[2]

§ 21. In South Carolina, in trespass for taking goods, the defendant may under the general issue prove that the goods were taken as a distress for rent.[3]

§ 22. In an action of tort in the nature of trespass to real estate, the defendant, under an answer, denying that the plaintiff is seized of the premises, may put in evidence a deed thereof to himself from a former owner, under whom the plaintiff also claims, which is prior in date to the title relied on by the plaintiff.[4]

§ 23. Under an answer in trespass *qu. claus.*, justifying under A, as owner, the defendant may show an estate in common in A.[5]

§ 24. In trespass for taking away goods, under a plea of property in a third person, evidence of such ownership at the time of the taking is admissible.[6]

§ 25. Where one alleges a particular title in excuse or justification for an act which would otherwise be a trespass, he is bound to prove the title precisely as he has alleged it.[7] Thus where, in an action for trespass on lands, the defendants in their answer set up a title to the premises in a third person, and justify their entry under a license from him; they cannot change their ground upon the trial, and show title in one of the defendants. Or that the plaintiff's grantor was estopped from denying the defendant's title.[8]

§ 26. Where the defendant pleads only soil and freehold in himself, and issue is joined thereon, he has the right of opening and closing. He thereby admits the act complained of, and undertakes to prove the property of the soil in himself. He has the affirmative, and, if he fails to make it out, the verdict must be against him.[9]

§ 27. It is very generally provided by express statute, that the

[1] Bennett *v.* Clemence, 6 Allen, 10.
[2] Hollenbeck *v.* Rowley, 8 Allen, 473.
[3] Reed *v.* Stoney, 2 Rich. 401.
[4] Walker *v.* Swasey, 2 Allen, 312.
[5] Jewett *v.* Foster, 14 Gray, 495.
[6] Anthony *v.* Gilbert, 4 Blackf. 348.
[7] Great, &c. *v.* Worster, 15 N. H. 412.
[8] Coan *v.* Osgood, 15 Barb. 583.
[9] Davis *v.* Mason, 4 Pick. 156.

question of *title to real estate* shall not be tried by *justices of the peace*. (*a*)

§ 28. In Massachusetts, in an action of trespass brought before a justice of the peace, the filing of a plea of title to real estate takes away his jurisdiction, and it cannot be restored by pleading over, and joining an issue not involving the question of title.[1]

§ 29. In an action of trespass, brought before a justice of the peace, for taking and carrying away the plaintiff's cow, the defendant pleaded that he was the owner of a close, and that the cow broke into the close, and that he thereupon impounded her. The plaintiff replied, that the defendant injured the cow. Issue was taken on the injury, and, after a trial upon that issue, the action was carried by appeal to the Court of Common Pleas, and there an amendment was allowed, putting in issue the title to the close. Held, the allowance of the amendment was erroneous.[2]

§ 30. Where, in trespass *qu. claus.* before a justice of the peace, the defendant pleads in bar that he entered into *his* adjoining close, and there erected a fence, &c.; the justice has jurisdiction.[3]

§ 31. The Mass. St. 1783, ch. 42, providing that an action of trespass brought before a justice of the peace may be removed into the Court of Common Pleas by a plea of title to real estate, comprehends all actions of trespass.[4]

§ 32. If the justice refuses to receive such plea, the defendant ought to appeal; but where, instead of appealing, he pleaded the general issue, and, after a trial and judgment against him, appealed from this judgment, and the Court of Common Pleas, upon motion, gave him leave to file his plea of title; held, the proceeding of that court was correct.[5]

§ 33. In an action of trespass brought before a justice of the peace, and removed into the Court of Common Pleas, by a plea of title to land; an appeal lies from the Court of Common Pleas to the Supreme Court, such action being a *real action* for the purposes of appeal.[6]

§ 34. In New Jersey, in an action of trespass *qu. claus.*,

[1] Kelley *v.* Taylor, 17 Pick. 218.
[2] Ibid.
[3] Wood *v.* Prescott, 2 Mass. 174.
[4] Blood *v.* Kemp, 4 Pick. 169.
[5] Ibid.
[6] Ibid.

(*a*) In Wisconsin, under the old practice, a justification of a trespass under a justice's execution must set out in detail the facts, to show jurisdiction. Roys *v.* Lull, 9 Wis. 324.

brought to the Supreme Court after plea of title before a justice, the defendant cannot plead "not guilty," or "leave and license," but those pleas will be struck out on motion, and he will be confined to his plea of title.[1]

§ 35. In Texas, the court may refuse *an order for a survey*, when defendants answer that they are the true and lawful owners of land described in the petition.[2]

§ 36. In trespass for taking the plaintiff's goods in Dale, the defendant cannot plead in justification, generally, that the place where is his freehold, and that the goods were then *damage feasant*.[3]

§ 37. Questions as to *joinder* have often arisen in the action of trespass.

§ 38. The causes of action in the old forms of trespass *qu. claus.* and *de bon. asport.* may be joined in one petition, under the pleadings in Texas, as they are not inconsistent rights of action.[4]

§ 39. An action for wilfully destroying a horse may be joined with a count for trespass in entering on the plaintiff's tenement.[5] But where, in trespass for breaking the plaintiff's close and carrying away his chattels, the declaration does not contain a count for only taking the chattels, he cannot recover for taking them, unless he proves a breach of the close.[6]

§ 40. In an action of trespass, the declaration contained two counts, one for breaking and entering a close with force and arms, and cutting down and carrying away sixteen stooks of rye, and the other for taking and carrying away sixteen stooks of other rye. The defendant pleaded, "as to the force and arms or anything against the peace and also the whole trespass and all the trespasses in the declaration mentioned, excepting the breaking and entering the close aforesaid and cutting down and carrying away sixteen stooks of rye then and there growing, she says she is not guilty thereof;" and justified the breaking the close and carrying away the rye, upon the ground of soil and freehold. Held, the plaintiff was not entitled to judgment on the second count as upon a *nihil dicit*, the plea being a sufficient answer to the whole declaration.[7]

1 Campfield *v.* Johnson, 1 N. J. 83.
2 Castro *v.* Marzbach, 13 Tex. 128.
3 Elwis *v.* Lombe, 6 Mod. 117.
4 Carter *v.* Wallace, 2 Tex. 206.
5 Ripley *v.* Miller, 1 Jones, 480.
6 Ropps *v.* Barker, 4 Pick. 239.
7 Parker *v.* Parker, 17 Pick. 236.

§ 41. Where there are several counts, and a general plea of not guilty, with leave to give special matter in evidence; the plea will be as broad as the declaration, and justify the counts collectively and separately, and each trespass, where the counts are so framed as to include more than one.[1]

§ 42. If a declaration in trespass contain two counts for the same trespass, and the defendant plead the general issue to both, and a special plea in bar to one, on which a verdict is found for him; he is entitled to a verdict on the general issue likewise. The court remark: "I am not aware of any rule of pleading by which the defendant can be considered as having admitted there were two supposed trespasses. He admits one and justifies it, and he denies the fact as to the other, if two were intended to be charged. It is not formally averred that there were two different trespasses; both counts charge the same trespass, the second count adding only some further matter of aggravation. . . . The inference is fair, that the same trespass was intended. . . . We do not, however, decide the point on this distinction, for we should come to the same result if it had been averred that the trespasses were committed at different times, the time in this action not being material. And it would make no difference if the law would permit the plaintiff to sustain two actions of trespass on the evidence introduced. For suppose he could maintain an action charging the defendant with taking and carrying away the plaintiff's goods in one count, and taking down the building in another, still, as the defendant has justified both charges, the plaintiff cannot recover without proof of another trespass not justified."[2]

§ 43. Trespass. First count, for seizing and carrying away certain goods, chattels, and effects of the plaintiff, to wit, &c. Fifth count, for tearing away, severing, and removing divers fixtures of the plaintiff. Pleas. First, not guilty; secondly, a justification to the first count, taking the goods and chattels as a distress for rent due on a tenancy. Replication, denying the tenancy; and issue thereon. The judge directed the jury, that the justification covered the whole declaration; but the jury found for the plaintiff, with one farthing damages. Held, the justification was *primâ facie* an answer to the seizing and carrying away in the first

[1] Payne *v.* Green, 10 S. & M. 507.

[2] Curl *v.* Lowell, 19 Pick. 25; per Wilde, J., ib. 28.

count; and the plaintiff, if he intended to rely on some of the articles being fixtures, ought to have replied that fact; but the justification was no answer to the trespasses stated in the fifth count. Also, as the jury had not acted according to the misdirection, but had given damages, the court would not grant a new trial on the ground of the misdirection.[1]

§ 44. To an action for breaking and entering, pulling down and destroying the plaintiff's house, whilst he and his family were therein, and assaulting the plaintiff, and by so pulling it down endangering the lives and injuring the persons of the plaintiff and his family, and ejecting them therefrom, and taking the materials of the house; the defendant, as to the breaking and entering and pulling down and destroying the house, and taking the materials, justified in the exercise of a right of common pasture over the land, on which the house was wrongfully erected, so that without pulling it down he could not enjoy the right. Held, no answer.[2]

§ 44 *a.* To a declaration for breaking open a gate and lock, the defendant pleaded, as an equitable defence, that, disputes having arisen between the plaintiff, defendant and other persons, about a right of way, an agreement in writing was entered into between the parties, that, without prejudice on either side to the question, of right, a way over the *locus in quo* should remain open for the passage of the defendant and the other persons, until the plaintiff's solicitor and the defendant should come to a definite understanding as to the course to be pursued in deciding the question in dispute; and that the trespasses were committed in the use by the defendant of the way, because the gate had been wrongfully, and contrary to the agreement, placed across it. Held, first, that the plea did not amount to a plea of leave and license at common law, as the locking of the gate was a revocation of the license. Second, that it was not good as an equitable plea, the circumstances in equity not entitling the defendant to have the plaintiff restrained by an unconditional injunction from prosecuting the action.[3]

§ 45. The pleas in trespass are answered by various *replications*. Where a defence sets up matter of positive and absolute right, as the levy of an execution, &c., a special replication is required;

[1] Twigg *v.* Potts, 1 Cromp. Mees. & Ros. 89.

[2] Jones *v.* Jones, 31 L. J., Exch. 506.

[3] Hyde *v.* Graham, 8 Jur. (N. S.) 1229; 11 W. R. 119 Exch.

but where the defence amounts to an excuse for the act complained of, &c., the general replication, *de injuriâ*, &c., is sufficient.[1]

§ 46. So where the defendant, in an action of trespass *quare clausum fregit*, pleads or insists upon a right, title, or interest in the close in question, the general replication *de injuriâ* is bad. Otherwise, if the title alleged is to something else, and is only stated as inducement to an excuse for entering. Thus where, to an action of trespass for entering the plaintiff's close and tearing down a dam there erected, the defendant pleads, that the dam caused an injury to the land of third persons, and that he entered as their servant, for the purpose of abating it; the plea insists upon no right, title, or interest, but sets up the title in the other lands as matter of excuse for the entry, or of inducement, to excuse or justify the entry; and the replication *de injuriâ* is sufficient.[2] So in trespass against an overseer of roads, for entering land, and cutting and carrying away timber, the defendant pleaded that he took the timber to repair bridges, "it being the nearest unimproved land to said bridges," &c. The plaintiff replied, that it was not the nearest unimproved land, &c. Held, the plea asserted two facts, and the replication traversed both, and was sufficient.[3]

§ 47. Where one abuses an authority or license which the law gives him, by which he becomes a trespasser *ab initio*, if the defendant plead the license or authority, the plaintiff should reply the matter showing the abuse. If he reply *de injuriâ*, generally, no question of excess is put in issue.[4]

§ 48. The remark, however, is justly made, that "it would be a useless labor to attempt to review all the cases where this replication has been sustained or overruled. To reconcile them all would be impossible. There are cases undoubtedly sustaining the rule . . . that this replication is proper, except where the plea justifies by matter of record; and yet, cases are not wanting, where a special replication has been required to a plea, setting up a defence in no way depending upon matter of record. . . . Many of these distinctions are more artificial than substantial."[5]

§ 49. In trespass *qu. claus.*, if the defendant excuse the entry,

1 Allen *v.* Scott, 13 Ill. 80.
2 Great, &c. *v.* Worster, 15 N. H. 412.
3 Austin *v.* Waddell, 10 Mis. 705.
4 Great, &c., *v.* Worster, 15 N. H. 412.
5 Per Caton, J., Allen *v.* Scott, 13 Ill. 84.

by alleging that he entered to remove a dam which flowed land of which he was lawfully in possession, the plaintiff cannot, in avoidance of the defence, set up a title to the land flowed, which was acquired by him subsequently to the removal of the dam.[1]

§ 49 *a.* In trespass for taking and driving the plaintiff's cattle, to which there was a justification, that the defendant was lawfully possessed of a certain close, and that he took the cattle there *damage feasant;* the plaintiff may specially reply title in another, by whose command he entered, &c.; and may also *give color* to the defendant.[2]

§ 49 *b.* A replication, in an action of trespass, that a tax was not legally assessed by the prudential committee on the lists of the district as averred, to a plea averring the organization and existence of a school district, an application and warning for, and holding of a meeting, the voting a tax, the plaintiff's liability in that district, a legal assessment, and an issue to the defendant, as collector, of his warrant, &c.; presents a single issue, and is good on special demurrer.[3]

§ 50. A form of replication, very commonly adopted in actions of trespass, is a *new assignment,* which is thus defined by a writer of high authority on the subject of pleading: "Though a replication must not *depart* from any material allegation in the declaration, yet where there is an *evasive* plea, either as to the whole or a part of the cause of action, the plaintiff may avoid the effect of it by *restating* the injury for which he meant to declare with *more particularity* and certainty, consistently, however, with the more general complaint in the declaration; and this is termed a *new* or *novel assignment,* and may be either as to time, place, or any other circumstance, when *material.* It is frequently necessary, in order that the defendant may have notice of the real ground upon which the plaintiff proceeds; and when from the nature of the action, as in trespass *quare clausum fregit,* the declaration is so framed as to be capable of covering several injuries, committed at different times or in different parts of a close, &c., the plaintiff may frequently reply, not only denying the right of common, or way, &c., stated in the plea, but also new-assigning

[1] Great, &c., *v.* Worster, 15 N. H. 412.
[2] Taylor *v.* Eastwood, 1 E. 212.
[3] Moss *v.* Hindes, 28 Verm. 279.

trespasses committed at different times or in different parts of the close, to those mentioned in the plea."[1]

§ 51. In the action of trespass *qu. claus.*, when the defendant pleads a right of way through the close, and justifies under it, the plaintiff may traverse the right, and at the same time newly assign for other trespasses committed *extra viam*.[2]

§ 52. The plaintiff may *newly assign*, as matter of right, in an action of trespass, commenced before a justice, and entered at the Court of Common Pleas, because of a plea of title to real estate.[3]

§ 53. Action for breaking and entering a close, particularly described in the declaration, and cutting certain trees therein. Plea, not guilty as to all, except a certain portion, described by specific boundaries, &c.; and, as to that portion, soil and freehold. The plaintiff traversed the justification, concluding to the country, and then new-assigned the trespass. Held, the pleas covered the whole declaration; that it was duly in issue for trial without the new assignment; and the latter was therefore bad. Leave to withdraw the new assignment.[4]

§ 54. Where the plaintiff names the close, and the defendant pleads *lib. ten.*, generally, without further description of the close, the plaintiff need not new assign, but may recover upon proving a trespass in a close in his possession bearing that name, although the defendant may have a close in the same parish known by the same name.[5]

§ 55. Where the defendant pleads a justification to trespass *qu. claus.*, the proof must be co-extensive with the plea; and, if he fails in proof of his justification to any part of the trespasses, the plaintiff is entitled to a verdict, without newly assigning the excess.[6]

§ 56. The plaintiff, having alleged in two counts, respectively, two acts of trespass, to which the defendant pleaded a justification, new assigns a trespass, which he avers to be different from those justified, and the defendant pleads the general issue to the new assignment. Held, the plaintiff was bound to prove a different trespass from those justified; and was estopped by the averment of a different trespass from sustaining the action, by proving the

[1] 1 Chit. Pl. 616.
[2] Cheswell *v.* Chapman, 42 N. H. 47.
[3] Janvrin *v.* Scammon, 6 Fost. 360.
[4] Smith *v.* Powers, 13 N. H. 216.
[5] Cocker *v.* Crompton, 1 B. & C. 489.
[6] Berry *v.* Vreeland, 1 N. J. 183.

trespass mentioned in one of the original counts, on the ground that the plea and justification was insufficient; for, if it was insufficient, he should have traversed it or demurred.[1]

§ 56 *a.* Under a plea of *lib. tenement.* to a novel assignment, in trespass *qu. claus.*, setting forth the *locus* to be a certain farm, the defendant need not show title to the farm generally, but only to that part on which the alleged trespass was committed.[2]

§ 56 *b.* Where, in trespass *qu. claus.*, after a new assignment, setting forth the *locus* as being a certain close called the A B farm, the defendant pleaded thereto that the *locus* was the freehold of the defendant, and no part of the A B farm; held, the plea was bad, as amounting to the general issue.[3]

§ 57. In connection with the subject of pleading in trespass, may be briefly considered the joining of a declaration in this form with the analogous remedies of *case* and *trover*.

§ 58. Independently of statute, trespass and case cannot be joined.[4] Thus, in Connecticut, a declaration contained a count in trespass, for the forcible ejection of the plaintiff by the defendants, a railroad, from their cars, and a count in case for the same injury by the negligence of the defendants as common carriers, in conveying him as a passenger, the latter count containing an averment that it was for the same cause of action with the former. The latter count also contained an allegation that the defendants, at the same time, assumed for a certain hire to also carry safely his tool-chest, but so negligently carried it that it became broken and greatly damaged. Held, on a motion in error from a judgment overruling a general demurrer to the declaration, that, although the latter count was averred to be for the same cause of action with the former, yet, as the injury to the chest was so set forth as to constitute an independent and substantial ground of recovery, both counts could not be for the same cause of action, and there was therefore a misjoinder of counts.[5] (*a*) And if, in

[1] Boynton *v.* Willard, 10 Pick. 166.
[2] Phillips *v.* Phillips, 1 N. J. 42.
[3] Ibid.
[4] Courtney *v.* Collet, 1 Ld. Raym. 272; Sheppar *v.* Furniss, 19 Ala. 760.
[5] Havens *v.* Hartford, &c. 26 Conn. 220.

(*a*) In a later case in the same State the court remark: "The statute" (providing that counts in trespass and case *for the same cause of action* may be joined) "does not alter at all the character of either form of action when joined. The principles of law, applicable to each when standing alone, are applicable to each when joined . . . In actions of trespass, by way of aggravation, the plaintiff may recover damages for that which, alone considered, might furnish a good cause of action in case." Per Park, J., 27 Conn. 516.

an action on the case, one count disclose injuries for which damages are recoverable in trespass, the other, for which they are recoverable in case, and part of the proof sustain the latter count; the court cannot treat all the injuries as resulting in damages recoverable in trespass, and not in case.[1] So a record of trespass *vi et armis* is not removed by a writ of error on a judgment in an action of trespass on the case.[2]

§ 59. In California, counts in trespass and in case, resulting from the same tort, may be joined.[3]

§ 60. In Kentucky, since the distinction between actions has been abolished by the Code, a petition, setting forth a claim for a forcible injury, should state such facts as would sustain an action of trespass at common law. If the trespass be waived, and the petition be for negligence or want of skill, it should state facts which would sustain an action on the case according to common-law principles.[4]

§ 61. The distinction between trespass and trespass on the case has been abolished in Maine by statute.[5] A declaration in trespass may contain one count in case and another of trespass *de bon. asport.*[6] But the statute applies only to the form of declaring, not the substance of the cases. Thus an allegation of breaking and entering into land is of substance, and not form merely. A count not containing this averment, but technically in case, for injuries to land, or in trespass *de bon.* for goods taken from it, is not sustained by proof of an unlawful entry. Nor can a declaration in trespass *qu. claus.*, alleging immediate acts of injury to land, be sustained by proof of an injury, consequentially resulting from acts done upon other land. And the declaration cannot be amended by a count in case, alleging consequential damages.[7]

§ 62. Whether an action is trespass or case, is to be determined from the facts alleged, and not from the name given to the action.[8] In general, if the plaintiff declare in trespass, where the action should be case, he will be non-suited at the trial. Otherwise, it seems, if the declaration contain enough to maintain case, though it commence by miscalling the action trespass. And facts, showing that the plaintiff has mistaken his remedy by bringing

[1] Scott *v.* Bay, 3 Md. 431.
[2] Kent's case, 6 Mod. 138.
[3] Fraler *v.* Sears, &c. 12 Cal. 555. And see Holly *v.* Boston, &c. 8 Gray, 130.
[4] Kountz *v.* Brown, 16 B. Mon. 577.
[5] Welch *v.* Whittemore, 25 Maine, 86.
[6] Moulton *v.* Smith, 32 ib. 406.
[7] Sawyer *v.* Goodwin, 34 ib. 419.
[8] Coggswell *v.* Baldwin, 15 Verm. 404.

trespass instead of case, cannot be pleaded at bar, but only in abatement.[1]

§ 63. A count, purporting to be in case, and alleging negligent wrongful acts, is not to be regarded as a count in trespass, simply because it alleges, among such acts, other acts of force, and which in themselves would have been proper matter for a count in trespass.[2] So, although counts in trespass and case cannot be joined, yet, if the count in case is bad on demurrer, it seems it may be regarded as surplusage, and be rejected, and the declaration stand.[3] And where a declaration contained several counts, some in trover and some in trespass, and it was stated in the commencement of the seventh count, which was the first count in trespass, that the preceding and following counts were for the same cause of action; held, as such averment was introduced for the purpose of justifying the joinder, under the Connecticut statute, the plaintiff was not confined, on the trial, to the proof of only one cause of action.[4]

§ 64. Under the California practice, a declaration in trespass and a prayer for injunction may be made in the same complaint, though not distinctly separated, provided they be not inseparably mixed.[5] But not trespass *quare clausum*, ejectment, and a prayer for equitable relief.[6] And in New York, where as great latitude is probably allowed in pleading, as in any other State, the court remark as follows upon the joinder of counts in trespass and ejectment: "To entitle him to recover for the trespass, he must show himself to have been in possession when the tortious acts were committed, and that he had regained the possession at the time of the commencement of the action; and to entitle him to maintain his action for the ouster and to recover the possession, he must show that the defendant had the possession when his action was instituted. . . . The plaintiff . . . was required to elect for which of the two claims he would proceed, . . . because the proof necessary to sustain them would be inconsistent, and incongruous."[7]

§ 64 *a*. In Massachusetts, "under our present system of pleading, an action of tort is sufficiently comprehensive to embrace all

[1] The Seneca, &c. *v.* The Auburn, &c. 5 Hill, 170.

[2] Havens *v.* Hartford, &c. 28 Conn. 69.

[3] Bell *v.* Troy, 35 Ala. 184.

[4] Munson *v.* Munson, 24 Conn. 115.

[5] Gates *v.* Kieff, 7 Cal. 124.

[6] Bigelow *v.* Gove, 7 Cal. 133.

[7] Per Brown, J., Budd *v.* Bingham, 18 Barb. 496.

the cases in which a remedy was formerly afforded, either by an action of trespass or an action of the case. An action of tort may therefore now be supported by proof of facts which would have been sufficient to maintain either of those actions."[1] In general, trover cannot be joined with trespass.[2] But in Texas, in an action which embraced both trespass and trover, the plaintiff was held entitled to recover, on proof of either cause of action.[3] So a declaration contained a count in trover, and one in trespass *de bon. asport.*, both relating to the same property. Not guilty was pleaded to both. Verdict for the plaintiff, and motion in arrest of judgment. Held, not such a misjoinder as to be fatal on this motion.[4] So a declaration contained counts in trover and trespass for the same goods, the causes of action being alleged to be the same. The latter count further averred, that the plaintiff was at the time in the peaceable possession of the goods in a store kept by her for their manufacture and sale, and that the defendant, by forcibly entering and taking possession of the store and seizing the goods, stopped her business for a long time, and caused her great expense in procuring other goods. Held, this was merely matter of aggravation, and the cause of action alleged in the latter count was not, by reason thereof, different from that alleged in the first count, so as to cause a misjoinder of the counts.[5]

§ 65. Trespass is the common-law form for recovery of mesne profits in case of disseisin ; but the statutory law has often changed the mode of proceeding. (See Book II.)

§ 66. In Delaware, in an action on the case for mesne profits, with a count in trespass for injury to the premises, evidence may be given of such injury.[6]

§ 67. The Code of Ohio has substituted for the action of trespass for mesne profits an action for "damages for withholding real property and for rents and profits." Such cause of action may be united with an action for the recovery of real property. But they are separate causes of action, and should be separately numbered and stated in the petition.[7]

§ 68. While forcible injuries to property are redressed by the

1 Per Merrick, J., Holly *v.* Boston, &c. 8 Gray, 130.

2 Crenshaw *v.* Moore, 10 Geo. 384.

3 Carter *v.* Wallace, 2 Tex. 206.

4 Williams *v.* Bramble, 2 Md. 313.

5 Belden *v.* Grannis, 27 Conn. 511.

6 Gooch *v.* Geery, 3 Har. 423.

7 McKinney *v.* McKinney, 8 Ohio (N. S.), 423.

actions of trespass *qu. claus.* and trespass *de bon. aspor.*, trespass is also the remedy for violence *to the person*, or *assault and battery;* the pleadings in which may therefore be most properly considered in the present connection. (*a*)

§ 69. In an action for an assault, the day is immaterial; proof of an assault on any day before action is sufficient.[1]

§ 70. The allegation of *alia enormia* is not necessary.[2]

§ 71. Legal and natural consequences need not be specially alleged. Otherwise, with damages of a different description, such as loss of health, or destruction of clothing.[3]

§ 72. In a civil action for rape, an allegation is sufficient, that "the defendant made an indecent assault upon the plaintiff, and then and there debauched and carnally knew her." [4]

§ 73. Where there is but one count, the plaintiff cannot waive one assault, of which he has offered evidence, and prove another.[5] And evidence is admissible only of the number of assaults alleged in the declaration.[6]

§ 74. Matters in justification, or which might be pleaded, cannot be given in evidence under the general issue in mitigation of damages;[7] as, that the beating was inflicted by way of punishment for misbehavior.[8] But, under the general issue, the defendant, in mitigation of damages, may rely on any part of the *res gestæ*, even though a justification, if properly pleaded; as the plaintiff cannot be surprised by evidence of what passed at the time.[9] (*b*)

[1] Palmer *v.* Skillenger, 5 Har. 234; Sellars *v.* Zimmerman, 18 Md. 255.

[2] 1 Chit. Pl. 348.

[3] Ib. 346.

[4] Koenig *v.* Nott, 2 Hill, 323.

[5] Stante *v.* Pricket, 1 Camp. 473.

[6] Gillon *v.* Wilson, 3 Monr. 217.

[7] Lair *v.* Abrams, 5 Blackf. 191.

[8] Watson *v.* Christie, 2 B. & P. 224 Corning *v.* Corning, 2 Seld. 97.

[9] Bingham *v.* Garnault, Bull. N. P. 17; 2 Greenl. Ev. 71, § 93.

(*a*) "If two persons fight in France, and both happening casually to be here, one should bring an action of assault against the other, it might be a doubt whether such an action could be maintained here; because . . . it must be laid to be against the peace of the king." Per Ld. Mansfield, Fabrigas *v.* Mostyn, Cowp. 176.

In general, however, this action is not local.

(*b*) The answer to an action for assault alleged, that the plaintiff was a niece and adopted daughter of the defendant, and had been educated and supported by him; that, immediately before the assault, he unexpectedly met her in a public street, where his relations to her were well known; riding with a man of bad character, by whom she had been enticed from his house about a year before, and taken to a house of ill fame, kept by him, and where she had since lived and was still living; and, in the sudden impulse of the moment, he struck with his whip at the man in question, with the intention of hitting him, and the blow accidentally fell on her. Held, the answer was immaterial, except so far, as it showed the injury to be an accident; and the other facts were inadmissible even in mitigation of damages. The court make a distinction between this case and tha

§ 75. The plea of *son assault demesne* is a sufficient answer to a declaration for assault and battery, though the latter aver personal injuries to the plaintiff, showing the assault to have been of a very aggravated character. The question, whether the defendant used an excess of force in his own defence, is in general to be determined only upon the evidence, and this issue is raised by the replication of *de injuriâ*.[1] But this answer must show that the first assault justified or excused the other.[2]

§ 76. In trespass, for a simple assault and battery, a plea is sufficient, that the defendant *molliter manus imposuit*, &c., in his reasonable efforts to prevent the plaintiff from breaking the peace by an assault upon a third person. Otherwise, when the declaration alleges extraordinary or aggravated force.[3]

§ 77. Trespass, for that the defendant "assaulted the plaintiff, and beat, bruised, pushed, dragged, and pulled about, kicked, wounded, and ill-treated him, and then knocked down and prostrated him on the deck of a certain vessel, and then hit and struck him numerous blows." Plea, "as to the assaulting, beating, and ill-treating" the plaintiff, a justification by the defendant as captain of a vessel on board of which the plaintiff and others were passengers, and alleging that the plaintiff made a great noise, disturbance, and affray on board the said vessel, and was then fighting with another person, "then also being a passenger in and on board of the said vessel, and whose name was to the defendant unknown," and was striving to beat and wound the said person; wherefore the defendant, as such captain, to preserve peace and order, and prevent the beating and wounding of such person, gently laid his hands upon the plaintiff, which was the trespass complained of. Held, the plea would have been good, without the statement that the person with whom the plaintiff was fighting was a passenger, &c.; that such statement did not necessarily contain matter of description, and consequently,

1 Mellen *v.* Thompson, 32 Verm. 407.
2 Schlosser *v.* Fox, 14 Ind. 365.
3 Mellen *v.* Thompson, 32 Verm. 407.

cited, in which it was held, that, where material matter is informally alleged, or material matter is omitted in a pleading otherwise formal, if the party does not demur, but goes to trial, he is concluded by the verdict.

"The defendant does not set up that he was provoked, by any act of the plaintiff, or of any other person, at any time, to commit the alleged violence upon her. It was virtually disclaimed by his answer, . . . that she was the object to which the blows . . . were aimed, or that she had in any manner provoked him to violence." Corning *v.* Corning, 2 Seld. 97; per Jewett, J., ib. 102.

require proof; and that the knocking down and prostrating of the plaintiff was alleged as a distinct trespass, and was not covered by the plea.[1]

§ 78. To a declaration in trespass for forcibly ejecting the plaintiff from a railroad train, the defendant pleaded specially, in justification, that he was the conductor of the train; that the plaintiff had no ticket, and refused to pay his fare; that he required the plaintiff to leave the train, and thereupon the plaintiff did leave the train accordingly, which was the same ejecting complained of. Held, this was no admission of the alleged trespass, and the pleas were therefore bad, as amounting only to the general issue.[2]

§ 79. If the declaration contain two counts, alleging different assaults and batteries, and the plea justify only one, the plaintiff by replying *de injuriâ*, waives the benefit of one of the counts, and cannot give evidence of an assault and battery different from the one justified.[3]

§ 80. If, to a declaration for an assault containing but one count, a justification be pleaded, and the plaintiff reply *de injuriâ*, he cannot introduce testimony relating to any other assault than the one specified in the plea. He should new assign.[4]

§ 81. If *son assault demesne* be pleaded, the plaintiff may, under the replication *de injuriâ*, &c., prove that the defendant's battery was excessive, without specially replying the excess.[5]

§ 82. The declaration averred an assault on the plaintiff "while sitting in his gig." The replication represented the defendant in the gig, "and the plaintiff gently laid hands on him and put him out," and then the assault. Held, this was not a departure; for both allegations, though apparently discrepant, might be true, as they did not necessarily refer to the same exact point of time.[6]

§ 83. The plea to assault and battery was *son assault demesne*, which the replication confessed and avoided. The rejoinder substantially reiterated the plea. Held, it was bad for not traversing the replication.[7]

§ 83 *a*. Under the plea of *son assault*, &c., and the replication *de injuriâ*, &c., the burden of proof is on the defendant.[8]

[1] Noden *v.* Johnson, 2 Eng. L. & Eq. 201.
[2] Blood *v.* Adams, 33 Verm. 52.
[3] Berry *v.* Borden, 7 Blackf. 384.
[4] Carpenter *v.* Crane, 5 ib. 119.
[5] Fisher *v.* Bridges, 4 ib. 148.
[6] McFarland *v.* Deane, 1 Cheves, 64.
[7] Ibid.
[8] Crogate's case, 8 Co. 66; Timothy *v.* Simpson, 1 Cr., M. & R. 757; Guy *v.* Kitchiner, 2 Str. 127.

§ 84. The replication puts in issue only the allegations of the plea. Hence the plaintiff cannot, under it, prove new facts showing that the plea, though true, is not a justification. As that the defendant, being in his house, abused his family and refused to leave; and, upon the plaintiff's gently laying hands on him to put him out, furiously assaulted and beat him.[1] So under this replication to a plea, that the acts were done in defence of the master of the defendant, the plaintiff cannot justify his own assault upon the master.[2]

§ 85. If a party justify a trespass upon a slave upon the ground that he was a patrol, and the plaintiff reply that the punishment was excessive; the replication admits the justification as alleged, and precludes the plaintiff from offering any evidence to disprove it.[3]

§ 86. In trespass for ejecting the plaintiff from a railroad station, where the defence is that it was rightfully done, the replication, setting up the purchase of a ticket, and that the plaintiff was waiting in the station to take a train, must allege that the train was expected soon to leave. But not, necessarily, that the plaintiff went into the station-house for the purpose of travelling upon the cars, if it appear that such purpose was formed after his entry and before the assault.[4]

§ 87. In trespass for assault and battery, the declaration contained only one count, and the pleas were, 1. Not guilty; 2. *Son assault demesne.* The plaintiff new assigned, and the defendant pleaded not guilty to the new assignment. Held, the plaintiff was not obliged to prove two trespasses; but only a trespass differing from that justified, and agreeing with the new assignment.[5]

[1] King *v.* Phippard, Carth. 280.

[2] Webber *v.* Liversuch, Peake's Add. Cas. 51; acc. Sayre *v.* Rockford, 2 W. Bl. 1165.

[3] Tomlinson *v.* Darnall, 2 Head, 538.

[4] Harris *v.* Stevens, 31 Verm. 79.

[5] West *v.* Rousseau, 7 Blackf. 450.

CHAPTER VI.

PLEADING IN THE ACTION ON THE CASE, INCLUDING TROVER.

§ 1. ANALOGOUS to the action of trespass is that of *trespass on the case*, or, as it is more commonly termed, the *action on the case*.

§ 1 *a*. Although an action be described in the writ as trespass on the case, yet, if the declaration show a cause of action of trespass *de bon.*, the plaintiff may require the action to be so considered.[1] "The declaration ought not in general to state the injury to have been committed *vi et armis*, nor should it conclude *contra pacem*, in which respects it principally differs from the declaration in trespass. In other points the form of the declaration depends on the particular circumstances . . . and consequently there is greater variety in this than in any other form of action."[2]

§ 1 *b*. In an action on the case against a surgeon for unskilfully performing an operation, a count may be joined, averring that he maliciously pretended that he would improve the appearance of, and restore, the eye of the plaintiff, with the intent to defraud her of her money.[3]

§ 1 *c*. The rules of pleading in this action are comparatively few and simple. "An action upon the case is founded upon the mere justice and conscience of the plaintiff's case, and is in the nature of a bill in equity, and, in effect, is so. Whatever will, in equity and conscience according to the circumstances of the case, bar the plaintiff's recovery, may, in this action, be given in evidence, because the plaintiff must recover upon the justice and conscience of his case."[4] "The plea . . . is usually the genera

[1] The White, &c. *v*. Dow, 1 Cart. 141.
[2] 1 Chit. Pl. 147.
[3] Cadwell *v*. Farrell, 28 Ill. 438.
[4] Per Lord Mansfield, Bird *v*. Randall 3 Burr. 1353.

issue, not guilty; and under it (except in an action for slander and a few other instances) any matter may be given in evidence, but the Statute of Limitations."[1]

§ 2. We shall hereafter consider the specific injuries for which this action is the prescribed remedy. In the present connection it may be stated, that, in general, it is brought either for *nuisance*, *negligence*, or *conversion*.

2 *a*. As we have already seen (Chap. IV.), the points of distinction between case and trespass are often very nice. They are illustrated by a recent decision in Massachusetts, relating to an action for nuisance.

§ 3. Declaration, that the plaintiff was lawfully possessed of a certain close, and the defendant, "well knowing the premises, wrongfully and injuriously kept and continued a building projecting and overhanging the plaintiff's said close, and before then wrongfully erected and built, projecting as aforesaid, for a long space of time." Held, an action of tort for a nuisance, and, the plaintiff having prevailed, that the defendant could not except to an order of court entering judgment that it be abated. The court remark in reference to this declaration: "It has not the peculiar characteristics of an action of trespass. . . . There is no allegation that the wrong or injury was committed 'with force and arms' or 'forcibly.' It may be that an action of trespass might have been brought for the erection and continuance of the structure . . . and that, on proof of the plaintiff's title, and of the facts and circumstances . . . such action would be the only appropriate and proper remedy. But that is not the question before us on this record. We are not called on to decide a question of variance . . . but only to determine the nature of the action."[2]

3 *a*. In another recent case, where a declaration in case alleged that a railroad engine, by the negligence of the defendants' servants, was run upon the intestate, whereby he was killed, the court remark: "The defendants . . . urge that, as the action is case, consequential damages are necessary as the gist of the action, while there are none here alleged, inasmuch as the plaintiff's intestate was killed instantly. . . . Although the form of action is case, as it must be, of course, if the defendants are liable at all

[1] 1 Chit. Pl. 147.

[2] Codman *v.* Evans, 7 Allen, 431; per Bigelow, C. J., ib. 433.

. . . the injury is none the less direct and positive than if trespass was the form."[1] And the declaration need not show that the plaintiff has a freehold estate in the premises affected by the nuisance; but it is enough that he is in possession.[2]

§ 4. It is not necessary to give a local description to the nuisance, in an action on the case for diverting the water of a navigation; and therefore if it be doubtful whether the place, where such navigation is stated to be, is laid in the declaration as a venue or as local description, it will be referred merely to venue, and need not be proved to be at such a place; but it is sufficient if it be at any other place within the county.[3]

§ 5. Where the count, in an action of nuisance, alleged that the nuisance was *below* the plaintiff's land, and the proof was that it was *adjoining* and *on* the plaintiff's land; held, the variance was fatal.[4]

§ 6. In case for the disturbance of a ferry, a count, alleging that the plaintiffs were entitled to a certain ferry across the Thames, and that the defendant conveyed passengers and goods across the river near to the plaintiffs' ferry, and that, by reason thereof, the plaintiffs lost profits, and were prejudiced and disturbed in the possession and profit of their ferry; was held, after verdict for the plaintiffs, to disclose a sufficient cause of action.[5]

§ 7. To a declaration in case for an injury arising from smoke issuing out of the defendant's factory chimneys, the defendant justified under a prescriptive right. This plea was traversed, and the plaintiff new assigned. It was proved that one of the chimneys had been erected for more than twenty years. Held, upon the issue raised by the traverse, the defendant was entitled to the verdict.[6] The remarks of the judges will show the particular grounds of the decision: "If this were an action of trespass and this a plea of justification, it would not be sufficient to entitle the plaintiff to recover, because a justification being pleaded, the defendant would have a right to apply that justification to the trespass proved; and then, if there were any excess, the plaintiff ought to have new assigned. . . . But it is said, that there is a distinction between an action of trespass and an action

[1] Per Ellsworth, J., Murphy *v.* N. Y., &c. 30 Conn. 187.

[2] Cornes *v.* Harris, 1 Comst. 223.

[3] Mersey, &c. *v.* Douglas, 2 East, 497.

[4] Brown *v.* Woodworth, 5 Barb. 550.

[5] Blacketer *v.* Gillett, 9 Com. B. 26.

[6] Bennett *v.* Thompson, 37 Eng. L. & Eq. 51.

like this upon the case; and that as the action upon the case stood formerly, the plaintiff was not bound to prove the whole of the declaration. But since the new rules a party relying upon an easement must plead that specially, which makes it the same as trespass. . . . We must consider this as an action of trespass to which a plea of justification is pleaded and proved . . . otherwise the plaintiff might recover for the whole . . . whereas . . . as to part the defendant was justified."[1] "The defendants plead that they had an easement for the smoke, and this easement is traversed and found for the defendant [s]. . . . The replication traverses the easement . . . as to some part of the subject-matter; and if it had said that they had a right to an easement for the smoke from the four chimneys, that would have been divisible, but they only claim an easement as to one, and that being traversed is found for the defendants."[2]

§ 8. In an action for a nuisance originally brought on the 1st of April, but the declaration in which had been amended under a judge's order by making it the 19th of April, the defendant pleaded, except as to alleged grievances committed by him before April 15, not guilty, and paid money into court in respect of the grievances before that date. A rule to show cause, why these pleas should not be struck out or amended, was refused.[3]

§ 9. In trespass on the case for destroying the plaintiff's common in six acres, a justification, in three acres only, is ill.[4]

§ 9 *a*. A statute provided as follows: "The plaintiff may unite injuries with or without force to the person; injuries with or without force, to the property, &c. But the causes of action . . . must belong to one only of these classes." Under this statute, injuries both to person and property, from an act of negligence, may be joined in the same complaint. "The plaintiff has not united several causes of action. . . . He has stated only one. . . . The legislature . . . must have had reference to the causes of action as they were then bounded, limited, and defined by the common law. . . . This 167th section, instead of severing causes of action . . . was intended to lessen suits, by allowing the plaintiff to bring into the same suit any number of assaults committed upon distinct and independent occasions. And so he may

[1] Per Coleridge, J., ib. 53.
[2] Per Crompton, J., ib.
[3] Fountain *v.* Chamberlain, 37 Eng. L. & Eq. 260.
[4] Mosse *v.* Bennett, 8 Mod. 120, 121.

join in the same action with assault and battery, any other injury to the person. . . . The Code does not abolish . . . the causes of action . . . nor . . . define what shall constitute a cause of action . . . The 69th section has abolished the forms of the action, but it leaves . . . the causes as they were."[1]

§ 10. A declaration for negligence, generally, is held good.[2] So it is not necessary to aver *gross* negligence. When the right of recovery depends on the degree of negligence, it is a matter of proof, and not of pleading.[3] In actions for personal injuries, resulting from negligence, it is sufficient to allege in general terms that the injury was occasioned by the carelessness of the defendant, without setting forth the circumstances to show it. An allegation of the extent of the injury, and of the manner in which it was inflicted, is sufficient. Thus a petition by an administratrix, alleging that the defendant, by means of his wilful neglect, shot and killed her said husband, to her great damage, &c.[4]

§ 10 *a*. It is held that a declaration in case, alleging both negligence and malice, is sustained by proof of the former alone.[5] So a complaint, that the defendants' reservoir, by reason of some fault in its construction, or some carelessness and mismanagement on the part of the defendants, broke away, &c., is good under the practice of California. Negligence in the construction and in the management need not be set out as distinct causes of action, in distinct counts.[6]

§ 10 *b*. In an action for injury caused by the careless driving of a servant, the court refused an order for particulars of the injury.[7]

§ 11. In declaring, under the Code of Alabama, for neglecting to use due diligence in the collection of a judgment, out of the proceeds of which, when collected, the defendant had promised in writing to pay a specified amount; it is not necessary to aver in what respect he had failed to use due diligence; an allegation, that "he has failed and omitted to do so from mere neglect," is sufficient.[8]

§ 11 *a*. Declaration, that the defendant had received money and

[1] Howe *v.* Peckham, 10 Barb. 656; per Mason, J., ib. 658.
[2] Indianapolis, &c. *v.* Keeley, 23 Ind. 133.
[3] Chicago, &c. *v.* Carter, 20 Ill. 390.
[4] Chiles *v.* Drake, 2 Met. (Ky.) 146; Strain *v.* Strain, 14 Ill. 368.
[5] Panton *v.* Holland, 17 Johns. 92.
[6] Hoffman *v.* Tuolumne, &c. 10 Cal. 413.
[7] Wicks *v.* Macnamara, 3 Hurl. & N. 568.
[8] Gliddon *v.* McKinstry, 25 Ala. 246.

given his receipt therefor to the plaintiff, specifying that certain land was to be entered therewith; that, relying on the assurance of the defendant, the plaintiff had conveyed the same to B, for whose use the action was brought, and that since that time one G had entered the land. The defendant demurred, for the reason that it did not appear that the plaintiff had been dispossessed, nor that the original receipt had been assigned to B, nor whether he had given a warranty deed to B. Held, these facts need not appear; that the *gravamen* of the action was, that, by the defendant's neglect to enter the land, the plaintiff had never had any title or possession; and that, though suing for the use of B, B's claims need not appear, as the nature of them could not affect the right of the plaintiff to maintain the action.[1]

§ 11 *b*. The second count of a declaration stated that a messuage and land, the reversion whereof belonged to the plaintiff, were supported by the land adjoining; yet the defendant wrongfully and negligently dug and made excavations in the land adjoining, without sufficiently shoring the messuage and land, and thereby deprived them of their support, whereby they sank and were injured. The third count stated, that the plaintiff, by reason of her said interest in the messuage and land, was entitled to have the messuage supported laterally by certain land adjoining; yet the defendant wrongfully and negligently dug and made divers excavations in the land adjoining, without sufficiently shoring the said messuage and land, and thereby deprived the messuage of the support to which the plaintiff was so entitled, whereby the messuage and land sank and were injured. Held, the second count was good, although it did not allege any right to support; for, as it did not appear that the defendant was the owner of the adjoining land, he must be taken to be a stranger and a wrongdoer. Also, that the third count was good.[2]

§ 12. More especially, in a count for negligence, the particulars in which such negligence consisted are not required, where they lie more properly in the knowledge of the adverse party.[3] And any defect in this respect will be cured by verdict. Thus, in an action against an attorney, for negligence, it was alleged that "the defendant did obtain judgment for the plaintiff, on said notes and accounts, and did, without the consent of the plaintiff,

[1] Scott *v.* Granger, 3 Clarke (Iowa), 447.
[2] Bibby *v.* Carter, 4 Hurl. & N. 153.
[3] Eldridge *v.* Long Island, &c. 1 Sandf. 89.

and contrary to his express directions, undertake to settle and adjust such claims with said P., and did not follow the instructions of the plaintiff; but so carelessly and negligently conducted the said trust, that the said debt has never been paid or collected, and the plaintiff has wholly lost the attachment," &c. On motion in arrest of judgment, held, that, if the declaration was defective, in not setting out any specific, particular act of negligence, the defect was cured by the verdict.[1]

§ 12 *a*. But a declaration against a city, that they wrongfully suffered a street to be out of repair, and wrongfully suffered water to run on to the plaintiff's land, does not show, as it should, that it is from negligent want of repair that the water is suffered to run on the plaintiff's land.[2] So, in case against an attorney for negligence, the declaration alleged a retainer to examine a title, and to cause and procure an estate in fee-simple to be conveyed to the plaintiff, and alleged as a breach that the attorney advised the plaintiff to purchase without having an unincumbered title. Held, the existence of incumbrances did not disturb the fee, and the retainer as alleged was not broad enough to cover the breach. Also, that the declaration should state what the incumbrances were.[3] So in an action to recover money, which was advanced on cotton, received and stored by the plaintiff, and destroyed by fire before repayment of the advance, without his fault or negligence; all these facts should be averred in the petition, and not merely an advance and promise of repayment.[4] So an allegation in a suit against a constable, that the plaintiff "believes the defendant has collected, &c.; if he has not, it is his own neglect," is insufficient. A constable is liable for failure to collect a debt, when by proper diligence he might have collected it; but an averment that, "if he did not collect it, it was his own fault," does not bring the case within the above provision.[5]

§ 13. Where the plaintiff sues to recover the value of horses shipped on the defendants' boat, and alleged to have died of a disease, contracted in consequence of the negligence and want of skill of those in charge of the boat, in removing the horses from one part of the boat to another; under the general denial, it is competent for the defendants to give in evidence all circumstances

[1] Wilson *v.* Coffin, 2 Cush. 316.
[2] Montgomery *v.* Gilmer, 33 Ala. 116.
[3] Elder *v.* Bogardus, Hill & Denio, 116.
[4] Grimes *v.* Hagood, 19 Tex. 246.
[5] Walters *v.* Chinn, 1 Met. (Ky.) 499.

going to relieve the act of removal of the character of a tortious violation of the contract between the parties, by assigning a reasonable necessity for such removal.[1]

§ 14. An answer to a complaint for injury caused by the negligence of the defendant's agents, which denies every allegation in the complaint, but does not allege that the injury was done by other persons, who were responsible therefor, and not the defendant, puts in issue his liability.[2]

§ 15. It is a good answer to a complaint for negligently leaving building materials on the highway, which alleges the defendant's right so to leave them, and the negligence of the plaintiff in driving carelessly upon them.[3]

§ 16. The plaintiff in an action on the case, instituted before the new (Missouri) Code of Practice, alleged that the defendant, on a specified day of the month, not naming the day of the week, wrongfully and negligently set fire on his own land, which extended to the plaintiff's land, and burned his fence. At the trial, he brought to the notice of the court, that the specified day of the month was Sunday, and, the act being unlawful, the defendant was responsible for all the consequences. Held, under this declaration, that ground of recovery could not be made available.[4]

§ 17. Declaration against the defendants, ship-owners, for negligently and carelessly stowing salt-cake, whereby it sustained damage. Fourth plea; that the damage complained of arose from the salt-cake being delivered by the plaintiffs in bulk and not in casks, and being shipped by the plaintiffs in bulk, and consequently stowed by the defendants in bulk, and not in casks, and between and amongst other goods; and that the same was stowed in the manner in which the same was actually stowed, with the knowledge, and by the direction and license of the plaintiffs to the defendants given before and during such stowage, &c. Held, this plea did not amount to an allegation, that the negligent stowage took place by the authority of the plaintiffs, and was no answer to the action.[5]

§ 18. Fifth plea; that salt-cake was a corrosive substance, rotting casks and other substances being in contact with it, which

[1] Elliot *v.* Steamboat, &c. 12 La. An. 212.

[2] Schular *v.* Hudson, &c. 38 Barb. 653.

[3] Wood *v.* Mears, 12 Ind. 515.

[4] Martin *v.* Miller, 20 Mis. 391.

[5] Hutchinson *v.* Guion, 5 C. B. (N. S.) 149.

the plaintiffs knew, but which the defendants, without any default on their part, did not know, and could not reasonably be expected to know, until after the happening of the damage; that it was the duty of the plaintiffs to have informed the defendants of the destructive nature of salt-cake, in order to its proper and safe stowage by them; that the plaintiffs did not so inform the defendants, or ascertain that they were so informed, but, on the contrary, negligently delivered the salt-cake to the defendants in bulk, and thereby and otherwise represented to the defendants and induced them to believe, and they did reasonably believe, that the said salt-cake might be placed in contact with casks, &c.; that, under this reasonable belief, and induced as aforesaid, the defendants stowed the said salt-cake in contact with and between and amongst casks of salt provisions, being, as they reasonably believed, a safe and proper mode of stowing the same; and that afterwards, and without default of the defendants, the said salt-cake corroded, rotted, and destroyed the said casks, and the hoops thereof, and the brine therefrom damaged the salt-cake, and caused the default in the delivery thereof complained of in the declaration. Replication: that salt-cake is an article of merchandise well known in trade and commerce, and the nature and properties of which are well known in trade and commerce, and is an article of merchandise commonly carried in ships, and the nature and properties of which are commonly and well known to persons carrying on the trade and business of carriers by water, and that, at the time of the shipment, the defendant well knew that the goods were salt-cake. Held, that the fifth plea was good, and the replication no answer to it; for, if the defendants' ignorance arose from the wilful misrepresentation of the plaintiffs, such ignorance was justifiable.[1]

§ 19. A demurrer to a declaration admits the facts alleged, for the sole purpose of raising the question of law whether the declaration presents a cause of action. Upon a hearing in damages, after the overruling of a demurrer, the case stands, with reference to the evidence necessary for the plaintiff and admissible for the defendant, precisely as it would have stood upon a default. In the absence of proof of actual damage on such a hearing, the plaintiff is entitled to nominal damages only. And the admissions

[1] 5 C. B. (N. S.) 149.

of the demurrer are applicable even to the principal wrongful act, only in its relation to the question whether there is a cause of action, and not at all in its relation to the question of damages. Where, therefore, in an action on the case for damages caused by the negligent acts of the defendant, the plaintiff had alleged in detail sundry acts of the defendant going to constitute the principal wrongful act; held, it was incumbent upon him, on such a hearing in damages, to prove these facts, and the defendant might introduce evidence in contradiction, and might show that wrongful acts of the plaintiff himself entered into the transaction, and that some portion of the damage claimed was attributable thereto.[1]

§ 19 *a*. Trover, the action brought for the injury of conversion, is technically an action on the case. Case and trover may be joined in different counts in the same declaration.[2] It is sometimes necessary, however, to distinguish one from the other. Thus a count alleging that under a contract, by which the defendant hired a slave from the plaintiff, to be used and employed as a cook in a specified city, it became the defendant's duty to employ the slave there in that capacity, and not otherwise or elsewhere; that the defendant, disregarding his duty in that behalf, employed said slave as a field-hand on a plantation; and that by means thereof said slave died, and was wholly lost to the plaintiff; is a count in trover and not in case.[3] So in New York, a conversion and a breach of duty are distinct causes of action, and therefore proof of one, under an allegation of the other, is a fatal variance, not to be cured under the Code by amendment.[4] (*a*) The remarks of the court explain the nature of the case, the grounds of distinction between these causes of action, and the proper limitations in construing the statute referred to: "An action for conversion will not lie against an agent, for selling under the price fixed, . . . else the purchaser would get no title. No one . . . would pretend that the purchaser did not get a good title." . . . Therefore "the sale could not be tortious. . . . It is not the want of authority, but the exercise of it contrary to the measure pre-

[1] Havens *v.* Hartford, &c. 28 Conn. 69.
[2] Wilkinson *v.* Moseley, 30 Ala. 562.
[3] Ibid.
[4] Moore *v.* McKibbin, 33 Barb. 246; per Johnson, J., ib. 248.

(*a*) Under 1st subdivision of § 107 of the Code, a cause of action against a carrier for waste or conversion may be joined with a claim to recover back freight overpaid on the same goods. Adams *v.* Bissell, 28 Barb. 382.

scribed, which constitutes the wrong. . . . If the evidence had proved a conversion of the property by some act of the defendant other than that alleged, . . . it would have been a variance, and amendable within the provisions of the Code. But . . . it was just the case of a failure of proof of the allegation of the cause of action, in its entire scope and meaning. Although forms of action are abolished by the Code, causes of action are not. They remain distinct and distinguishable as they ever were, and ever must be, while legal rules regulate the conduct and dealings of men with each other." But in an action by the reversioner, against one having the life-estate and another, for injuries to the inheritance and reversion, the complainant may state a cause of action for wrongfully cutting, removing, and converting wood, and also a cause of action for drawing off the wood which had been cut, and converting it. The distinction is made, that these causes of action, followed by averments of injury to the inheritance and reversion, may be united, under the New York Code, if they affect all parties to the action. But if either cause of action is against only one of the defendants, it cannot be united with that against both.[1]

§ 20. Trover is a transitory action, and the venue may be laid in any county, even though the conversion were committed out of the jurisdiction of the State courts.[2]

§ 21. It is always necessary to allege the time of taking the goods, although not the true time.[3]

§ 21 *a*. The defendant is not entitled as of right, under the New York Code, to a particular statement or description of the goods. But the ordering of such a statement is a matter in the discretion of the court.[4]

§ 21 *b*. An omission to aver the value of the property is cured by verdict.[5] But a count, not stating that the plaintiff is possessed of the thing as of his own property, is defective, and not cured by verdict.[6]

§ 22. Where trover was brought by trustees, in whom the legal title was vested, for conversion of the trust property, and they alleged in their declaration that they sued "for and in behalf" of the *cestuis que trust;* held, the trustees were the real party

[1] Rodgers *v.* Rodgers, 11 Barb. 595.

[2] Robinson *v.* Armstrong, 34 Maine, 145.

[3] Glenn *v.* Harrison, 2 Harr. 1; Dietus *v.* Fuss, 8 Md. 148.

[4] Blackie *v.* Neilson, 6 Bosw. 681.

[5] Carter *v.* Wallace, 2 Tex. 206.

[6] Sevier *v.* Holliday, 1 Hemp. 160.

plaintiffs, and the words "for and in behalf," &c., were surplusage.[1]

§ 23. A declaration in trover, after describing a promissory note of the plaintiff's, its loss, and its finding by the defendant, proceeded, with a "and whereas also," to state another note, its loss and finding in like manner, and a conversion of both notes. The defendant, treating it as containing two distinct counts, demurred to the first. Held, the declaration was to be deemed as containing a single count, and was good; and the words "whereas also" might be treated as surplusage.[2]

§ 24. Where the only cause of action alleged is one accruing by the unlawful conversion of the property when the plaintiff owned it; the plaintiff cannot avail himself, at the trial, of a conversion by the defendant when another person was owner, and before sale of the property, by such owner, to the plaintiff.[3]

§ 24 *a*. If the complaint admits, that, before the plaintiff became entitled to possession of the property, it had been seized under an attachment issued at the suit of the defendant, under the laws of another State, but does not show nor aver that the attachment was void, either absolutely or as against the plaintiff; the defendant was, upon the face of the complaint, justified in refusing to deliver possession on the demand of the plaintiff, and the complaint will be held bad on demurrer.[4]

§ 25. In trover, "it is not usual to plead any other plea than the general issue, not guilty, except the plea of the Statute of Limitations and a release."[5] Hence under the general issue, in trover, the defendant may show a taking of the animal in question as a distress, damage feasant.[6]

§ 26. A complaint alleged that, on or about the 31st day of May, 1851, the complainant was possessed, as of his own property, of a gold watch, of the value of $125, and lent it to the defendant for four days, he promising that within said time it should be returned; that the defendant knew that the watch was the property of the plaintiff, but, fraudulently intending to defraud him, had not delivered it to the plaintiff, but had converted it to his own use. Answer, that "he is not informed and cannot state

[1] Schley *v.* Lyon, 6 Geo. 530.

[2] Oakley *v.* West, 1 Sandf. 96.

[3] Bowman *v.* Eaton, 24 Barb. 528.

[4] Fairbanks *v.* Bloomfield, 2 Duer, 349.

[5] Per Bell, C. J., Drew *v.* Spaulding, 45 N. H. 478.

[6] Ib. 472.

whether the plaintiff, on or about, &c., was possessed, as of his own property," of a gold watch; and a specific denial that "on or about the 31st day of May the plaintiff did leave said watch as aforesaid with the defendant for any period, with the promise of the defendant to return it." Also, that the plaintiff sold the watch to the defendant, and denial of all unlawful conversion thereof. The plaintiff, in reply, denied that he ever sold the watch to the defendant. Held, the allegation, in the complaint, that the watch was lent, was material and issuable; that the denial, that the plaintiff, "on or about the 31st day of May," &c., was bad in form, being a negative pregnant, but the answer negatived the lending, and put that fact in issue; and, as no objection was made to the informality, that was waived; that the allegation in the answer, that the defendant "was not informed and could not state," &c., was not warranted by the Code; that the averment, in the answer, of a sale of the watch was not a denial of the bailment, it not appearing, from the pleadings, that the sale was not subsequent to the bailment; and that a denial of all "unlawful conversion," was not a denial that the defendant actually converted the property to his own use.[1]

§ 27. In trover, the defendant pleaded that A, being lawfully possessed, lost the goods, which came into the hands of B, and the defendants, as servants of A, took them from B. Held, that, under a replication *de injuriâ*, the plaintiff might set up a conveyance from A to the parties under whom he claimed.[2]

§ 28. In trover by assignees for four hundred bales of cotton, the defendant pleaded, as to the converting of three hundred and, four bales, parcel of the cottons in the declaration mentioned that they were purchased by one A, as agent for the bankrupts, and paid for by him, and shipped for and on account of the bankrupts, and that, they becoming insolvent, and the cottons coming to the hands of the defendant as owner of the vessel, A stopped them *in transitu*. To this plea the plaintiffs new assigned, that they issued their writ and declared thereupon, not for the supposed conversion in that plea mentioned, but for that the defendant converted and disposed to his own use divers bales of cotton, "different to and other than the said bales of cotton in the introductory part of that plea mentioned;" and also for that the

[1] Elton *v.* Markham, 20 Barb. 343.

[2] Eyre *v.* Scovell, 5 Com. B. 702.

defendant converted and disposed of the last-mentioned bales of cotton "on other and different occasions and times, and for other and different purpose, and in another and different manner than in the said plea mentioned." Plea, not guilty. Held, however objectionable in form, the new assignment in substance alleged another and different conversion of the same subject-matter as that mentioned in the plea; and, a verdict having passed for the defendant, upon the assumption that the plaintiffs were bound to prove a conversion of cottons other than those mentioned in the plea, the court directed a new trial.[1]

[1] Brancker *v.* Molyneux, 1 Scott, N. 553.

CHAPTER VII.

PLEADING IN ACTIONS FOR INJURIES TO THE PERSON. — FALSE IMPRISONMENT.

§ 1. Having now completed our view of the general rules of pleading, and of pleading in the general forms of action *ex delicto;* we proceed to a consideration of the same subject, in connection with some of the principal wrongs to person, character, and property. A portion of these wrongs it has been necessary to treat, in illustration of the principles which apply to forms of action. Thus pleading in the action on the case involves the subject of nuisance; and, in trover, that of conversion. And with regard to the injury of assault and battery, the technical identity of the remedy — trespass *vi et armis* — with that for forcible and immediate injuries to property, seemed to recommend a consecutive statement of the rules of pleading in trespass in all its several branches, of *quare clausum*, *de bonis asportatis*, and *assault and battery.*

§ 2. In pursuance of the arrangement heretofore adopted, we proceed to a consideration of *injuries to the person*, exclusive of assault and battery.

§ 3. We have heretofore adverted to the points of resemblance and of difference between *false imprisonment*, including wrongs to *the person*, and *malicious prosecution*, classed with wrongs to *character.* The following cases further illustrate this connection.

§ 3 *a.* The defendant appeared before a justice, and on affidavit charged the plaintiff with having taken or stolen a breast-chain, and procured the justice to issue a warrant against him, and maliciously, &c., caused him to be arrested and imprisoned twelve hours. Held, good ground for an action of trespass, though not for malicious prosecution. "The affidavit, being in the disjunctive, 'taken or stolen,' charges no criminal offence, and this being the case, the justice had no right to issue the warrant; it was void process; void on its face, because it recites the defective affidavit . . . and all who were directly engaged in its procurement or execution were trespassers." [1] So a count, that the defendant caused the plaintiff to be arrested and imprisoned without reasonable or probable cause, on a false and malicious charge of felony, is a count in trespass for an assault and false imprisonment, and not an informal count for a malicious prosecution; and therefore requires no evidence of malice, or want of reasonable and probable cause.[2] So in an action for maliciously, and without probable cause, going before a magistrate, and procuring the plaintiff to be held to bail to keep the peace, it is not necessary, as in an action for malicious prosecution, to aver that the proceeding was determined in favor of the plaintiff, it being *ex parte*, and the truth of the statement made by the applicant to the magistrate not being controvertible.[3] So a declaration alleged, that the defendants (the one, A, acting as attorney for B, the other) recovered a judgment against the plaintiff for 30*l.* 7*s.* 4*d.*, that the plaintiff paid and satisfied to B the debt recovered, except 15*s.* 8*d.*, and that they sued out a *ca. sa.* upon the judgment, and wrongfully and maliciously, and without any reasonable or probable cause, indorsed the writ with directions to levy 5*l.* 14*s.* 8*d.* and interest and 1*l.* 7*s.* for the costs of execution; that the plaintiff tendered and offered to pay to the defendants 3*l.* 8*s.*, which was sufficient to pay and discharge all that was recoverable against the plaintiff upon the judgment and writ, together with the costs of the writ of executing, and all other legal and incidental expenses; and that they wrongfully and maliciously, and without any reasonable or probable cause, procured the sheriff to arrest the plaintiff, and detain him until he paid 7*l.* 6*s.* 9*d.*, whereas the sum of 3*l.* 8*s.*, and no more, was due, &c. Held, the declaration disclosed a good cause of action, and without alleging that the plaintiff had obtained his discharge by order of the court, or a judge, so as to show that the proceedings had terminated in his favor.[4]

[1] Steele *v.* Williams, 18 Ind. 161.

[2] Brandt *v.* Craddock, 27 L. J. Exch. 315; 3 Hurl. & N. 958.

[3] Steward *v.* Gromett, 7 C. B. (N. S.) 191; 6 Jur. (N. S.) 776.

[4] Gilding *v.* Eyre, 10 C. B. (N. S.) 592.

§ 4. An action for abduction and false imprisonment is not maintained by proof that the defendant, by misrepresentations, threats of a criminal prosecution, and payment of money for expenses, but without using or threatening force, induced the plaintiff to go to another place and remain in concealment for a time. "It is at most a case where she yielded voluntarily to the defendant's misrepresentations and threats . . . and absented herself from court and from her home for a time."[1]

§ 5. In an action for maliciously and without reasonable or probable cause causing the plaintiff to be arrested, under a *ca. sa.* issued upon a judgment obtained by the defendant against him, and upon which the defendant maliciously and without reasonable or probable cause indorsed a direction to levy the whole amount recovered by the judgment, whereas a portion of that amount had been previously satisfied; the declaration alleged, as damage, that the plaintiff was, after he was taken, during his detention, and before his discharge, able and willing and offered to pay, and always afterwards during his detention was willing to pay, and was finally discharged from imprisonment upon paying the smaller sum; and that the plaintiff, by reason of the premises, was necessarily put to and incurred divers costs and expenses in and about obtaining his discharge. Held, the declaration sufficiently showed special damage, inasmuch as the plaintiff must show, not merely that he was arrested and kept in custody for a greater amount than was due, however improperly indorsed, but also that, by reason thereof, his imprisonment was prolonged, or the expense of obtaining his discharge increased.[2]

§ 5 *a*. In trespass for assault, battery, and false imprisonment, on a certain day, the defendant cannot plead the suing out of a warrant against the plaintiff on a preceding day in justification, without traversing a trespass on any other day before or after.[3]

§ 6. The defendant, under the plea of "not guilty," may give in evidence the excuse, if it merely goes in mitigation of damages, but not if it amounts to a justification.[4] Thus, in an action of trespass *vi et armis* against a magistrate, not so styled in the declaration, for false imprisonment; a justification must be pleaded.[5]

[1] Payson *v.* Macomber, 3 Allen, 59; per Chapman, J., ib. 73.

[2] Jennings *v.* Florence, 2 C. B. (N. S.) 467.

[3] Halliday *v.* Noble, 1 Barb. 137.

[4] Linford *v.* Lake, 3 Hurl. & Nor. 276. See 5 Harring. 462.

[5] Bailey *v.* Wiggins, 5 Harring. 462.

But where the declaration avers that the arrest was made without affidavit or warrant, the defendant may prove the contrary, though he has not pleaded it in justification.[1]

§ 6 *a*. In trespass for an assault and battery and false imprisonment, a plea, that the defendant made oath before a justice of the peace that he had been threatened by the plaintiff, &c., and prayed surety of the peace; and the justice thereupon issued his warrants, &c.; amounts to the general issue.[2]

§ 7. To an action for arresting the plaintiff on two writs for the same cause of action, the answer does not set up inconsistent defences, within Mass. St. 1852, ch. 312, § 20, by denying the allegations of the declaration, and averring that, if the plaintiff was arrested on two writs, as alleged, he was rightfully arrested, because the first action was discontinued by reason of his representations, and notice given him of the discontinuance, before the commencement of the second action. "Here is no denial, and then confession and avoidance; the facts stated in the answer tend to show that there never existed a cause of action, because there was no false or illegal imprisonment or detention. The defendant does not say, 'you were illegally arrested, but you have discharged or released the cause of action;' but he says, 'under the facts, the arrests were not illegal, and the plaintiff had no cause of action.'"[3] But if the defendant, by special plea, set up legal process in justification, and then aver that he did not arrest the plaintiff, but that he voluntarily gave bail; the plea is bad for duplicity.[4]

§ 8. To a complaint, that the defendant without any justifiable cause caused the plaintiff to be arrested and detained and imprisoned until the enforced payment of a sum of money, it is a good answer, under the New York Code, if in proper form, that the plaintiff was brought before the defendant, then mayor of New York, duly elected and qualified, and acting as such mayor, charged with a violation of a certain ordinance of the city; further alleging an examination into and determination of the charge; the making of a record of the proceedings and judgment, the issuing of process pursuant to, and to carry the decision into effect; that the offence was within the jurisdiction of the defend-

[1] Boynton *v.* Tidwell, 19 Tex. 118.

[2] Crookshank *v.* Kellogg, 8 Blackf. 256.

[3] Jewett *v.* Locke, 6 Gray, 233; per Thomas, J., ib. 235.

[4] Stanton *v.* Seymour, 5 McLean, 267.

ant as mayor, and that he acted throughout as such and in good faith, and in the discharge of his duty as mayor, and by virtue of certain acts and ordinances to which the answer refers.[1]

§ 9. Suit for false imprisonment. Answer, that the defendant, acting as city marshal, arrested the plaintiff, on view, for intoxication and noise in the streets on Sunday, in violation of the city ordinances, whereof three were set out, (1.) fixing a fine for intoxication; (2.) against improper noise; (3.) authorizing the marshal to arrest and conduct before the mayor's court persons found guilty of breach of city ordinances. The mayor's court not being in session on Sunday, the defendant kept the plaintiff in custody five hours, then released him on promise of his appearance in court the next day, when he did appear and was fined for drunkenness. Held, that no statute made drunkenness a crime or misdemeanor, and, though the city might recover a forfeiture or penalty in a suit at law, yet this did not authorize the imprisoning of a man for an uncertain time, by a ministerial officer, of his own volition; the duty of such officer being to take the prisoner forthwith before a tribunal having jurisdiction, and then prefer a complaint against him. The answer was held bad on demurrer.[2]

§ 9 *a*. A replication to a plea of justification under legal process, that the plaintiff was detained in prison until he paid other money than that for which the process issued, or submitted to other conditions against his will, is a good answer to the plea. Such a replication is not a *departure*, since, if true, it supports the declaration.[3]

§ 10. In connection with the action for false imprisonment, it has been recently held, that an action will lie in England for a tort committed abroad, if, by the law of the foreign place, a compensation or damages could be recovered. And that, in a transitory action, a plea in abatement of an action pending in a foreign court is bad.[4]

§ 11. To a declaration for trespass and false imprisonment, the defendant pleaded (except as to the imprisonment), that the trespasses were committed at Naples, where the plaintiff and the defendant were then resident, and that, at the instance of the plaintiff, proceedings were there taken before a correctional judge, sit-

[1] Willis *v.* Havemeyer, 5 Duer, 447.

[2] Low *v.* Evans, 16 Ind. 486.

[3] Breck *v.* Blanchard, 2 Fost. 303.

[4] Scott *v.* Seymour, 8 Jur. (N. S.) 568.

ting according to the articles of the penal procedure laws of that country, and having jurisdiction; and that, by the laws there in force, the defendant was not liable to be sued by the plaintiff in any civil action or other proceedings to recover damages for the said trespasses, nor liable to any other proceedings except those taken, and which were still pending. Held, this plea did not negative that the proceedings taken were proceedings in which a compensation or damages might be recovered, and was therefore bad. So a plea, that, by the laws of Naples, until the defendant has been criminally condemned for the matter complained of, no action can be maintained against him for damages, and that he has not been so condemned, is bad, as setting up a matter of procedure which is to be governed by the *lex fori*.[1]

§ 12. In trespass for breaking and entering the plaintiff's house and taking his goods, the defendant justified under a *fi. fa.*, and warrant of execution against the goods of one A, which warrant was delivered to the defendant, a bailiff, to be executed. The plaintiff replied *de injuriâ*, admitting the writ, the warrant, and its delivery to the bailiff. Held, the existence of a warrant was admitted by the replication, and the defendant was not bound to prove it.[2]

§ 13. In trespass for assault and false imprisonment, the defendant justified under an order made by the judge of the sheriff's court of London, for committing the plaintiff for non-payment of an amount recovered against him in that court, and ordered to be paid by instalments. The plea first stated the various proceedings in the cause and court, necessary to give jurisdiction, except that it did not allege that the plaintiff had been summoned to show cause against the order of commitment; but it stated that the judge duly and according to the form of the statute made the order. The replication averred, that the judge did not order the plaintiff to be committed in the manner and form as alleged in the plea. Held, this traverse only put in issue the fact of the order, and not its validity, or the question whether the plaintiff had been duly summoned. "Supposing that the traverse was in the formal terms, that the order was not made duly and according to the form of the statute, we do not think that such a replication would be considered as including a denial that the plaintiff was

[1] Scott *v.* Seymour, 8 Jur. (N. S.) 568.

[2] Hewitt *v.* Macquire, 7 Eng. L. & Eq. 571.

duly summoned and neglected to appear. . . . It is clear on such an issue as this, where divers facts essential to the validity of the order are stated, and an opportunity to traverse each is afforded, that the denial of the order does not involve the denial of any one of those facts; as, for instance, where it is averred that one was seized in fee and demised, the plea of *non demisit* does not involve the question of the seisin in fee."[1]

[1] Buchanan *v.* Kinning, 7 Eng. L. & Eq. 455; per Parke, B., ib. 460.

CHAPTER VIII.

PLEADING IN ACTIONS FOR LIBEL AND SLANDER, AND MALICIOUS PROSECUTION.

§ 1. THERE is no action, in which the niceties of pleading have been more frequently or more strictly applied, than that for libel and slander. The pleadings accordingly constitute so essential and inseparable a part of the general subject, that they have been much more extensively considered, in connection with the wrong itself, than those relating to any other injury. (See Hilliard on Torts, Ch. XV.) The present work, however, would be quite incomplete, without a further and more separate view of this particular part of the law relating to a topic so important and extensive.

§ 2. In an action for words imputing an offence criminal by statute only, the statute need not be referred to.[1]

§ 3. Under the Mass. St. of 1852, ch. 312, a declaration in slander must set forth substantially the words spoken.[2]

§ 4. In an action by husband and wife for slander, imputing incontinency to the wife, the declaration alleged that, by reason thereof, the wife became ill and unable to attend to her necessary affairs and business, and that the husband was put to expense in endeavoring to cure her. Held, on demurrer, the declaration showed no cause of action.[3]

§ 5. In an action of slander, for charging the plaintiff with incest, the words alleged were to the effect that the plaintiff had carnal intercourse with his daughter, but without alleging that he had any knowledge of the relationship. Held, demurrable.[4]

[1] Elam *v.* Badger, 23 Ill. 498.
[2] Lee *v.* Kane, 6 Gray, 495.
[3] Allsop *v.* Allsop, 5 Hurl. & Nor. 534.
[4] Griggs *v.* Vickroy, 12 Ind. 549.

§ 6. A declaration is demurrable under Mass. Gen. Sts. ch. 129, §§ 2, 11, 12, as containing superfluous, impertinent, and scandalous allegations, which, in averring that the defendant, while arguing as a counsellor at law a case to the jury in which the plaintiff was a party, imputed insanity to the plaintiff, states in detail numerous occupations of the plaintiff, with an advertisement annexed of his actions and discourses; the occupation of the defendant; the political creed of both parties; and the fact that in several public orations the plaintiff has denounced the creed of the political party to which the defendant belongs as traitorous, and thereby made that party enemies of the plaintiff.[1]

§ 7. If the complaint states that the publication was a libel, it is unnecessary to aver that it is false and malicious.[2] So, when words spoken are actionable *per se*, malice is implied, and no express averment of it is required; but, if spoken in the exercise of some public or private duty, or of some right, express malice must be proved.[3]

§ 8. In an action for libel, an averment that the defendant is proprietor of the paper, and that the libellous matter was published in his paper, is a sufficient averment of a publication by him.[4]

§ 9. A declaration in slander, that "the defendant publicly, falsely, and maliciously accused the plaintiff of the crime of larceny, in word, substantially as follows: 'He is a thief,'" is bad, for not showing that the words were spoken of the plaintiff.[5]

§ 10. Words relied on as actionable, because spoken of the plaintiff in his profession, must be expressly alleged by proper averments of inducement and colloquium to have been so spoken of him.[6] So an action does not lie for the charge of insolvency, without an averment that it was made concerning the plaintiff's trade or business, and was false.[7] But, in an action for slander, the declaration was amended, by inserting an allegation, that the words were spoken of the plaintiff in his character as an auctioneer, and that he had had a transaction with a third party, in the way of his business as an auctioneer, to which the words might apply. Held, sufficient to support the allegation.[8]

[1] "Joannes" *v.* Burt, 6 Allen, 236.
[2] Hunt *v.* Bennett, 19 N.Y. (5 Smith) 173.
[3] Weaver *v.* Hendrick, 30 Mis. 502.
[4] 4 E. D. Smith, 647.
[5] Baldwin *v.* Hildreth, 14 Gray, 221.
[6] Carroll *v.* White, 33 Barb. 615.
[7] Redway *v.* Gray, 31 Verm. 292.
[8] Ramsdale *v.* Greenacre, 1 F. & F. 61.

§ 11. In an action for libel, imputing to the plaintiff that he was a "truckmaster," there being no innuendo to explain the meaning of the word; held, although the word was not to be found in any English dictionary, yet, as it was composed of two well-known English words, the plaintiff was not bound to give evidence of its meaning, nor the judge to explain it to the jury; but that it was properly left to them to say, whether, under all the circumstances, it was used in a defamatory sense.[1]

§ 12. A new count for another slander cannot be added, where the action therefor is barred by the Statute of Limitations.[2]

§ 13. The first two counts of a declaration alleged a slander, in regard to the sale of intoxicating liquor by the plaintiff; and the other, slanderous words, imputing adultery, &c. The declaration contained no allegation of special damages, as resulting from the words charged in the first and second counts; but, at the close of the declaration, there was an allegation of general damages, resulting from "the aforesaid grievances" and "by reason of the premises;" and also an allegation, that the plaintiff had been subjected to a prosecution for violation of the law prohibiting the sale of intoxicating liquor. Held, on general demurrer, the damage occasioned by such prosecution was not such a natural and immediate consequence of the slander, alleged in the first and second counts, as would justify the court in referring it to those counts.[3]

§ 14. When a declaration contains several counts, each setting forth a distinct and separate slander; each must be perfect in itself, and the omission of a material statement in one cannot be supplied by reference therein to another. Thus the absence of a *colloquium*, showing by extrinsic matter that the words are actionable, is not supplied by an innuendo attributing to those words an actionable meaning.[4]

§ 15. It is allowable to include in the same declaration divers distinct words of slander, of different import.[5]

§ 16. So, in a single count, words spoken at different times, and to different persons, in relation to the same subject.[6]

§ 17. Though it is not proper to join in the same counts, as

[1] Homer v. Taunton, 5 Hurl. & Nor. 661.
[2] Smith v. Smith, 45 Penn. 403.
[3] Holton v. Muzzy, 30 Verm. 365.
[4] Ibid.
[5] Hall v. Nees, 27 Ill. 411.
[6] Hoyt v. Smith, 32 Verm. 304.

ground of recovery, a slander and a libel, yet, when the latter is matter of inducement and preliminary to the former, it may be set forth as such.[1]

§ 18. Injuries to character by simple slander, and also by a false and malicious charge made under oath, before a grand jury, whereby several matters of special damage occurred, which the complaint sets forth, but not alleging want of probable cause, are embraced in the 4th sub-division of § 167 of the N. Y. Code, and may properly be joined.[2]

§ 19. In slander, where the words laid are not *per se* defamatory in their ordinary sense, or have no meaning at all in ordinary acceptation, there must be an innuendo, in order to admit evidence that in a peculiar sense they are defamatory.[3] The office of an innuendo is to explain matter already expressed, words doubtful or double in their meaning, or which do not of themselves show the slander intended.[4] It cannot enlarge ambiguous words, not necessarily of themselves importing crime, beyond the averment of the speaker's intention.[5]

§ 20. The innuendoes, "meaning to insinuate and falsely represent," "meaning to insinuate and be understood," or "meaning and intending to represent," "that the plaintiff had stolen the money aforesaid," indicate that the charge against the plaintiff was that he had stolen the money, and are therefore sufficient.[6]

§ 21. Averment, that the defendant, intending to have it understood that the plaintiff intended to produce a child, and pretend that it was born of herself, spoke, &c. Innuendo, that he thereby intended to charge the plaintiff with "attempting" to produce a false child, &c. Held, the words must be taken as charging the criminal intent, not the criminal attempt, they being such as to bear that construction.[7]

§ 22. Averments were introduced into the declaration, of words imputing dishonesty to L., "meaning the plaintiff's agent and clerk;" but there was nothing else showing any connection between L. and the plaintiff. Held, insufficient.[8]

§ 23. Words, charging that the plaintiff and one A were caught together in the packing-room, no special damage being charged,

1 Hoyt *v.* Smith, 32 Verm. 304.
2 Hull *v.* Vreeland, 42 Barb. 543.
3 Rawlings *v.* Norbury, 1 F. & F. 341.
4 Evans *v.* Tibbins, 2 Grant, 451.
5 Weed *v.* Bibbins, 32 Barb. 315.
6 Hoyt *v.* Smith, 32 Verm. 304.
7 Weed *v.* Bibbins, 32 Barb. 315.
8 Smith *v.* Hollister, 32 Verm. 695.

are not actionable. Otherwise, if with an innuendo of fornication.[1]

§ 24. As we have seen, an innuendo cannot alter, enlarge, or extend the natural and obvious meaning of the words. Where the words may be taken in a double sense, the innuendo is used to attach such meaning to them as the plaintiff claims was intended, or may think necessary to render them actionable. And if, in such case, the actionable quality of the words arises from circumstances extrinsic of them; averments are essential to show of record that such circumstances existed, and connect the words with the circumstances.[2] Where the actionable quality of the words depends on circumstances, they must be alleged and proved by way of *colloquium*.[3] (*a*)

§ 25. It is held, that no colloquium or innuendo is necessary to explain words which import a charge of fornication.[4] So a charge of perjury is actionable without a colloquium, showing that it was in the course of a judicial proceeding.[5] So it seems that words spoken by the defendant of the plaintiff as follows: "He (the plaintiff) acknowledged that he swore to a lie about the money, and had taken seventy-five dollars out of F. more than he ought to; he acknowledged to me, that he swore falsely in the trial with F., and that he swore falsely in reference to the money, and that he never let F. have any money as he swore he did, and that he must go to State prison;" construed all together, are actionable in themselves, without a colloquium to show that they were uttered with reference to a judicial proceeding.[6] But in a late case the distinction was taken, that, on demurrer, the following words, standing by themselves, are not actionable: "In my opinion the bitters that A fixed for B were the cause of his

[1] Evans *v.* Tibbins, 2 Grant, 451.

[2] Gosling *v.* Morgan, 32 Penn. 273. See Stancell *v.* Pryor, 25 Geo. 40.

[3] Little *v.* Barlow, 26 Geo. 423.

[4] Elam *v.* Badger, 23 Ill. 498.

[5] Waggstaff *v.* Ashton, 1 Har. 503.

[6] Cass *v.* Anderson, 33 Verm. 182.

(*a*) In New York, where the words are ambiguous in themselves, there must be *innuendos* even under the Code. But extrinsic facts, which are the inducement, need not be averred; it is sufficient, in their place, that the speaking be averred to be of the plaintiff. Van Slyke *v.* Carpenter, 7 Wis. 173.

Under § 16 of the 15 & 16 Vict. ch. 76, and forms 32, 33 in Schedule (B.) to that act, the declaration need not state any colloquium, but may set out the words complained of, and put any construction upon them by innuendo. Whether the words were spoken with such meaning is for the jury. Hemmings *v.* Gasson, El. Bl. & El. 346; 4 Jur. (N. S.) 834; 27 L. J. Qu. B. 252. See Barnett *v.* Allen, 3 Hurl. & Nor. 376.

death;" as not involving a charge of murder. While with a colloquium as to the profession of the plaintiff these words were held slanderous: "The bitters that Dr. A gave to B caused his death; there was poison enough in them to kill ten men."[1]

§ 26. When the statement of material facts in the colloquium is defective in form, the defect cannot be taken advantage of by motion in arrest of judgment. After verdict, the court will supply by intendment all such averments as may fairly and reasonably be presumed to have been proved, and which the general, though defective, allegations of the declaration embrace. As where the action was for words imputing perjury on a certain trial, and the words were connected with that trial, and the trial described, only by way of argument and recital. So, although the declaration contained no direct averment that the plaintiff was legally sworn as a witness, but only that the words were "uttered concerning the plaintiff, and his testimony given as a witness on that trial;" as the court would construe it, that the testimony was given in the usual manner, under oath. So, although the declaration did not directly aver that the defendant charged the plaintiff with perjury, when the words, explained by the colloquium were actionable, and the innuendo showed that they were uttered in an injurious sense. So it is immaterial, whether the words are a direct averment that the plaintiff swore falsely, or what their form is, if as spoken they would generally be understood, in their ordinary and natural import, to convey the slanderous idea or meaning.[2]

§ 26 *a*. Under Mass. St. 1852, ch. 312, the objection that a declaration in slander, which sets forth a general charge in itself imputing a felony, and states the words spoken, is insufficient, by reason of not stating the circumstances necessary to show the sense in which the words were spoken, must be taken by demurrer.[3]

§ 27. Where slanderous words are uttered in a foreign language, the declaration should aver that the persons in whose presence they were spoken understood the language.[4] The words must be set out in the original, and with a translation. Even under the Indiana Code, to allege in English and prove the speaking in

[1] Jones *v.* Diver, 22 Ind. 184.
[2] Cass *v.* Anderson, 33 Verm. 182.
[3] Clay *v.* Brigham, 8 Gray, 161.
[4] Amann *v.* Damm, 8 C. B. (N. S.) 597; 7 Jur. (N. S.) 47.

German, is a variance.[1] But, after verdict, an averment of the publication of a libel in a foreign language, to the injury, &c., is good, without an averment that the language was understood by the person to whom it was published.[2]

§ 28. A wife who has left her husband cannot maintain an action in her own name for slander, though he refuse or neglect to support her in her separation, the pleadings showing only a causeless desertion.[3]

§ 29. A complaint is not demurrable upon the ground of privilege, unless it state the facts which constitute such privilege, and which the defendant would be bound to state in a plea of privilege.[4]

§ 30. Slander cannot be laid with a *continuando*.[5] But on a declaration, in which the words are alleged to have been uttered "on the 1st day of November, 1856, and on divers other days and times before the purchase of the plaintiff's writ;" the plaintiff may prove a single uttering on any day prior to the date of the writ.[6]

§ 31. It is necessary, in actions of slander, for the plaintiff to prove the actual words alleged, or enough of them to sustain the action, and it will not be sufficient to prove other words of similar meaning, and involving the same charge.[7] The distinctions are made in a late case, that the substance of the alleged charge must be proved in substantially the same words laid in the declaration. (*a*) Any mere variation, in the form of expression only, is not material, but the words alleged cannot be proved by showing that the defendant expressed the same meaning in different words. It is not necessary, however, to prove all the words, unless the identity of the charge depends upon them.[8]

§ 32. The action cannot be sustained, where the declaration is

[1] Kerschbaugher *v.* Slusser, 12 Ind. 453.

[2] Kiene *v.* Ruff, 1 Clarke (Iowa), 482.

[3] Smith *v.* Smith, 45 Penn. 403 (containing some caustic remarks as to the rights and duties of husband and wife, and the wife's making her abode with his mother and sisters, by Lowrie, C. J. Ib. 404.)

[4] Perkins *v.* Mitchell, 31 Barb. 461; Little *v.* Barlow, 26 Geo. 423.

[5] Swinney *v.* Nane, 22 Ind. 178.

[6] Rice *v.* Cottrel, 5 R. I. 340.

[7] M'Connell *v.* M'Kenna, 10 Ir. Com. Law, 511.

[8] Smith *v.* Hollister, 32 Verm. 55.

(*a*) A declaration in the form prescribed by Mass. St. 1852, c. 312, that the defendant charged the plaintiff with a certain crime, "by words spoken of the plaintiff substantially as follows," is supported by proof, that the defendant spoke words substantially, though not precisely, like those set out. Baldwin *v.* Soule, 6 Gray, 321.

affirmative, and the proof interrogative;[1] nor if the declaration allege, that the defendant charged the plaintiff with a crime, and the proof is, merely that he said he supposed the plaintiff to be guilty of such crime;[2] nor upon a count, that the defendant charged upon the plaintiff an act of fornication, witnessed by A, and proof of charging an act witnessed by B, or of words implying a charge of habitual fornication and lewdness with A; nor a count, that the defendant charged the plaintiff, who was an unmarried woman, with having had a child, and proof of words expressing the opinion, that, at the time of speaking them, she was pregnant.[3]

§ 34. As in case of slander, if a portion of the article claimed to be libellous is omitted in the declaration, but the substance of the charge remains the same, it is no variance.[4] So a variance of one day between the date of the libel as set forth, and the date as shown in evidence, is held immaterial, if the defendant be not thereby misled.[5] So an alleged discrepancy between the title of a paper offered in evidence, and the title alleged, was held not to require its rejection.[6] But where the words charged were, "the girl that hired with us, &c.," and those proved, "the girl that lived with us, &c.;" held, not a material variance.[7]

§ 35. An instruction in an action of slander, hypothecated upon the belief of the jury, "that the slanderous words set forth in the petition, or any part of them," were spoken, but which fails to inform the jury what words set out in the petition were slanderous and actionable, is misleading, especially if the petition contain expressions charged to have been spoken which are not slanderous.[8]

§ 36. It is held in a late case, that the court has a general jurisdiction, applicable to every species of action, to order a plaintiff to furnish the defendant with further particulars, if the circumstances of the case and the course of justice require it. Therefore where, in an action for slander, the defendant moved the court to order the plaintiff to furnish "the names, descriptions, and addresses of the persons in whose presence the slanderous words were spoken, and the time or times when, and the place or

[1] King v. Whitley, 7 Jones, 529.
[2] Dickey v. Andros, 32 Verm. 55.
[3] Payson v. Macomber, 3 Allen, 69.
[4] Smart v. Blanchard, 42 N. H. 137.
[5] Thrall v. Smiley, 9 Cal. 529.
[6] State v. Jeandel, 5 Harring. 475.
[7] Robinet v. Ruby, 13 Md. 95.
[8] Letton v. Young, 2 Met. (Ky.) 558.

places where, the words were spoken ; " held, that the plaintiff should furnish a statement of the occasion or occasions on which the words were spoken, though not of the names, descriptions, and addresses of persons present.[1]

§ 37. In an action for libel, where the allegation is merely that the defendant is proprietor of the certain newspaper, without alleging that he published it, and this is proved without objection on the trial, according to the New York Code, § 171; the objection cannot prevail on appeal.[2]

§ 38. A motion in arrest of judgment will not lie, where, the declaration being examined in connection with the whole record, though imperfect in itself, the imperfection is supplied by an admission in the plea.[3]

§ 39. With reference to the pleadings in the action for libel or slander, subsequent to the declaration ; many and various changes have been introduced by the statutory law of the different States, and the recent cases, founded in part upon the statutes, are not harmonious or reconcilable.[4]

§ 40. The plea of the general issue in an action for libel admits the falsehood of the words.[5] So the truth of the words spoken, in an action for slander, cannot be proved under the general issue ;[6] nor any circumstances to disprove malice, or mitigate the damages, if they *tend* to establish the truth ;[7] (*a*) though the defendant expressly admit the words to be false.[8]

§ 41. In slander, the defendant, under the general issue, may show, as evidence of accord and satisfaction, that the plaintiff agreed to waive the action in consideration of the defendant's destroying certain papers, which he did.[9]

§ 42. With reference to the plea of justification,[10] although the strict rules of pleading have been much relaxed by statutory provisions, it is held, in New York, that the Code has only abol-

[1] Early *v.* Smith, 12 Ir. Com. Law, App. XXXV. Q. B.

[2] Hunt *v.* Bennett, 19 N. Y. (5 Smith), 173.

[3] Hoyt *v.* Smith, 32 Verm. 304.

[4] See Hagan *v.* Hendry, 18 Ind. 177.

[5] Thomas *v.* Danaway, 30 Ill. 373.

[6] Kinney *v.* Hosea, 3 Har. 397.

[7] Parke *v.* Blackiston, 3 Har. 373.

[8] Waggstaff *v.* Ashton, 1 Har. 503.

[9] Lane *v.* Applegate, 1 Stark. R. 97.

[10] See Bryan *v.* Gurr, 27 Geo. 378; George *v.* Lemon, 19 Tex. 150; Thomas *v.* Dunaway, 30 Ill. 387.

(*a*) In Indiana, circumstances of mitigation may be set forth in the answer, though not required to be. Swinney *v.* Nane, 22 Ind. 178. And the rule is held applicable to no other action except for libel and slander. Smith *v.* Lisher, 23 Ind. 500.

ished those rules of pleading which are technical and formal; those which have their foundation in reason and good sense, and lend an important aid in the investigation of truth, retain all their original force and authority. An answer is insufficient, in the sense of the Code, not only when it sets up a defence groundless in law, but when, in the mode of stating a defence, otherwise valid, it violates the essential rules of pleading. Of the rules of pleading, none is better established than that a defamatory charge, made in general terms, can only be justified by a specification, on which the defendant relies to establish its truth.[1] And in a late case it is held, that a justification cannot be set up under an answer which merely denies the allegations of the complaint, and alleges that the words charged are true. Under the Code, as before, a justification must state the facts which establish it, with the time, place, and circumstances. Thus, in an action for the charge of false swearing, the answer must state the evidence, and what the plaintiff swore to. "It should present, substantially, an indictment against the plaintiff, for the alleged perjury."[2] And in another recent case it is held, that the law as to the pleading of a justification remains under the Code. The provision, that new matter in an answer must be in ordinary and concise language, without repetition, does not authorize a mere repetition of the libellous words and an averment of their truth, without any fact to show it. And the same construction is to be given to the section of the Code, which allows at the same time a justification and circumstances in mitigation. And the plaintiff may object to the introduction of evidence under an answer thus defective, though he might also have compelled an amendment by motion.[3]

§ 42 *a*. Where the only plea justifies the words as true, the affirmative of the issue being on the defendant, he has the right to open and reply in evidence and argument.[4]

§ 43. Not guilty and a justification may be jointly pleaded.[5] In Massachusetts, a denial of having spoken the words charged, and an averment of their truth, are consistent defences, and may be separately stated in the same answer.[6] But to a declaration containing three counts for three distinct libels, the court re-

[1] Fry *v.* Bennett, 5 Sandf. 54.

[2] Tilson *v.* Clark, 45 Barb. 178; per Miller, J., ib. 181.

[3] Wachter *v.* Quenzer, 29 N.Y. (2 Tiffa.), 547; Sorrell *v.* Craig, 15 Ala. 789.

[4] Moses *v.* Gatewood, 5 Rich. 234.

[5] Smith *v.* Smith, 39 Penn. 441.

[6] Payson *v.* Macomber, 3 Allen, 69.

fused to allow the defendant to plead one general plea of justification.[1]

§ 44. The plaintiff alleged that, he having advertised his goods for sale by auction, the defendant published a libel, whereby, after reciting the advertising and that the plaintiff unlawfully detained goods of the defendant, and which, as the defendant was informed, the plaintiff intended to dispose of, the defendant gave notice that the goods were his absolute property, and did forbid the purchase of them; by means whereof the sale failed altogether. Plea, that the plaintiff did unlawfully detain, &c., that the defendant was informed and believed, &c., and therefore the defendant published the said words for the purpose of warning all persons from purchasing the goods so unlawfully detained. Held good, on demurrer, as amounting to the general issue. Also, by one Justice, as showing the truth of the statements.[2]

§ 45. Declaration, that the plaintiff was cashier to A, and the defendant, in a letter to A, falsely, &c., the words, "I conceive there is nothing too base for him to be guilty of." Justification, that the plaintiff signed and delivered to the defendant an I. O. U., and afterwards, on having sight thereof, falsely and fraudulently asserted that the signature was not his, and that the libel was written and published solely in reference to this transaction. Held, the libel must be interpreted by the subject-matter, and the justification was sufficient.[3]

§ 46. The defendant is bound to make out the defence which he has chosen. Thus where, in an action for charging false swearing, the defendant, by his plea, has based his defence on the fact that the plaintiff was guilty of perjury; he will be required to prove the perjury.[4] So a justification must be an answer to the exact charge. Thus words charging the plaintiff with having begotten a bastard child, and thereby having committed adultery with the child's mother, are not answered by a plea alleging adulterous intercourse with the mother.[5] So where a plea justified words which charged the sale of intoxicating liquor contrary to law, by setting forth several distinct sales; held, not sufficient, on general demurrer, because it did not allege that such sales were contrary to the laws of the State.[6]

[1] Honess v. Stubbs, 7 C. B. (N. S.) 555.
[2] Carr v. Duckett, 5 Hurl. & Nor. 783.
[3] Tighe v. Cooper, 7 Ell. & B. 639.
[4] Hicks v. Resing, 24 Ill. 566.
[5] Holton v. Muzzey, 30 Verm. 365.
[6] Ibid.

§ 47. In an action for libel; that the publication is not a libel, is a good plea.[1] So it is a good defence, under the plea of not guilty, that the publication consists of a fair, correct, and impartial report of a trial in a court of justice.[2]

§ 48. Where the charge is not matter indictable, a plea of justification may be allowed, in a general form, the defendant rendering particulars of the charges intended to be justified.[3]

§ 49. If a plea may justify a part only of distinct charges, it will, at all events, be bad on general demurrer, if, where the libellous matter is all charged in one count, it do not deny or justify the whole or all the charges which it professes to cover.[4] And where, in an action for libel, the defendant had charged the plaintiff with having on a certain occasion acted from motives of spite and lucre, and pleaded a justification, which failed as to the latter feature of the charge; held, the libel being entire, the defendant was not entitled to a verdict on the plea as it stood, or as to any part of it.[5]

§ 50. The court refused leave to plead, to a declaration containing three counts for separate libels, a general plea of justification, that the libels in the several counts were true.[6]

§ 51. A plea, justifying the repetition of a slander, because the plaintiff had first said the same of himself, will not let in evidence tending to prove the charge. Under such plea, the defendant is confined to declarations of the plaintiff prior to the slander.[7]

§ 52. If there be evidence of express malice, the jury may give exemplary damages. The plea of justification on the truth, wholly unsupported, is evidence of express malice. But this plea is held not necessarily evidence of express malice. As where the defendant, having good grounds and reasonable cause to believe the plaintiff guilty, on evidence creating a strong presumption of guilt, pleads a justification for the purpose of getting these circumstances in evidence, and not for the purpose of repeating the slander.[8]

§ 53. With reference to the action for malicious prosecution,

[1] Nixon *v.* Harvey, 8 Ir. Com. Law, 446, Exch.

[2] Lewis *v.* Levy, 4 Jur. (N. S.) 970; 27 L. J. Qu. B. 282.

[3] Behrens *v.* Allen, 8 Jur. (N. S.) 118.

[4] Ames *v.* Hazard, 6 R. I. 335.

[5] Cory *v.* Bond, 2 F. & F. 241.

[6] Honess *v.* Stubbs, 7 C. B. (N. S.) 555. 6 Jur. (N. S.) 682; 29 L. J., C. P. 220.

[7] Kinney *v.* Hosea, 3 Har. 397.

[8] Parke *v.* Blackiston, 3 Har. 373.

wrong usually classed with libel and slander, as done to character or reputation; little needs to be added, in the present connection, to what was said in treating of the injury itself. (See Hilliard on Torts, Ch. XVI.) The remedy is an action on the case, the pleadings in which, as already explained, are less technical than in other actions, and give rise to comparatively few questions and decisions.

§ 54. It is held, that a variance between the day alleged in the declaration as that of the plaintiff's acquittal, and the day of trial mentioned in the record which is offered in evidence, is not fatal, unless the day is alleged by way of description of the record. Otherwise with a misdescription in this respect, or of the teste or return of process.[1]

§ 55. Under a declaration which avers the wrongful and vexatious suing out of an attachment, and the seizure of the goods of the plaintiffs, whereby they have lost the advantage and benefit of their business as merchants, been forced to abandon the same, and been "wholly ruined in their circumstances," &c.; the plaintiffs may recover the actual injury done to the goods by their seizure.[2]

§ 56. Declaration, that, the plaintiff being possessed of premises, the defendant and S. maliciously contrived to get possession of a portion of them, and to set up illicit stills there; and thereupon, in pursuance of the conspiracy, they, by falsely and fraudulently representing to the plaintiff that S. required such portion for making ink, induced the plaintiff to permit S. to enter thereon; and thereupon the defendant and S., in further pursuance of the conspiracy, entered thereupon and set up illicit stills; and, in further pursuance of the conspiracy, maliciously represented, and made it appear and be believed, that it was the plaintiff who had so set up the stills; and also that, in further pursuance of the conspiracy, the defendant and S. manufactured in that portion of the premises exciseable articles, contrary to the statute; and then, in further pursuance, &c., maliciously represented, and made it appear and be believed, that it was the plaintiff who manufactured such articles, and that he was knowingly aiding and concurring in the manufacturing, &c.; by means whereof an officer of the excise found in the said portion of the premises manufacturing, and in the course of manufacturing, divers goods, and did at the same

[1] 1 Chit. Pl. 385.

[2] Donnell v. Jones, 17 Ala. 689.

time discover in and about such place the plaintiff, who, by reason of the premises, appeared to be assisting in the manufacture, &c., whereupon the officer arrested the plaintiff, and the plaintiff was convicted by a magistrate in the penalty of 30*l*. Held bad, as neither stating a good cause of action in the nature of conspiracy, nor of an action for malicious prosecution.[1]

[1] Barber *v.* Lesiter, 7 C. B. (N. S.) 175; 6 Jur. (N. S.) 654.

CHAPTER IX.

PLEADINGS IN ACTIONS FOR INJURIES TO PROPERTY.

§ 1. FOLLOWING the order of topics heretofore adopted, we pro ceed to consider the pleadings in actions for *injuries to property*. Of course these have been largely, though incidentally, treated in other connections,— as under the heads of trespass, nuisance, negligence, and conversion,— and comparatively little remains to be added with reference to the particular subjects of ownership or possession.

§ 2. A plaintiff cannot recover for injuries to his possession, when the complaint negatives such possession. The remarks of the court show the nature of the case and grounds of decision. "There is no averment . . . that the plaintiff . . . had the actual possession of the land . . . or that being then disseised he had since regained the possession. . . . Possession . . . would sufficiently appear from an allegation of title . . . for if the land is vacant . . . the title will . . . draw after it the possession. . . . The plaintiff deprived himself of this effect of his allegation of title, by averments . . . showing that before and at the time he acquired title the land was in the actual possession of the defendant, and has so remained ever since. These allegations . . . cannot be rejected as surplusage; for if the complaint is to be regarded as in ejectment, they or some of them are necessary to show a cause of action; and if as in trespass, then . . . the plaintiff shows on the face of his own pleading that he has no cause of action."[1]

§ 3. We have heretofore considered, at much length, the subject of *watercourses and mills*.[2] (See Hilliard on Torts, Ch. XX.)

[1] Cowenhoven *v.* Brooklyn, 38 Barb. 9; per Scrugham, J., ib. 12.

[2] See Tyler *v.* Mather, 9 Gray, 177.

§ 4. In an action for diverting water from the plaintiff's mill, the declaration must allege, that by such diversion the quantity of water which continued to flow to the mill was insufficient, or that the plaintiff was thereby injured.[1]

§ 5. It is no ground for arresting judgment, in an action for stopping a watercourse and thereby flowing the plaintiff's land, that the declaration, which alleges that the plaintiff was seised and possessed of a certain lot of land, from which the water which fell and flowed thereon was accustomed to flow off through this watercourse in the land of the defendant, does not more particularly describe the plaintiff's right.[2]

§ 6. Complaint that the defendants built dams, &c., whereby they kept back the water, and also opened gates whereby mud washed out with the water, and filled the plaintiff's ditches, and rendered the water worthless. Held, merely two ways of diverting the water, and therefore properly set out in the same count.[3]

§ 7. The remedy for an obstruction of a watercourse, and preventing the water from flowing to the land of an owner below, as it has been accustomed to flow, by erecting a dam, and closing the gates at night for the purpose of collecting the water, is by an action of tort, and not by a complaint under the Massachusetts mill acts.[4]

§ 8. Under the California practice, words which are technical, but not important, may be rejected as surplusage, if they do not lead to misapprehension as to the material facts of the case, which are otherwise clearly stated. Thus, in a suit for damages occasioned by the overflow of water from the defendant's land, bringing with it gravel, stones, &c., the averment of "with force and arms broke and entered" is immaterial and need not be proved.[5] So where the complaint alleges that the defendant wrongfully and injuriously diverted water, while the testimony shows the injury to be the result of the act of another, preventing its return to its channel, as designed by the defendant, after its use; this is no variance.[6] So, A and B being owners of lands and mills on opposite sides of a river, which mills were operated by the waters raised by a dam across it, A brought an action on the case against B, for unlawfully raising the dam on his side of the

[1] Burden *v.* Mobile, 21 Ala. 309.
[2] Ashley *v.* Ashley, 4 Gray, 197.
[3] Gale *v.* Tuolumne, &c. 14 Cal. 25.
[4] Thompson *v.* Moore, 2 Allen, 350.
[5] Darst *v.* Rush, 14 Cal. 81. See Pickett *v.* Condon, 18 Md. 412.
[6] Stein *v.* Burden, 29 Ala. 127.

river, in such a manner as to inundate A's wheel and mill; alleging that he was entitled to the free course of the waters, and to the use of them for his mill, by means of the dam, free and undisturbed. In support of this allegation, A gave in evidence an indenture, from which both parties derived their titles, providing, that, when there should be water enough in the pond, all the mills might be improved, without let or hindrance; but, when there should be want of water, the party under whom B claimed should have the sole power of drawing the water out of the pond, for his mills, three whole days in four, and the party under whom A claimed should have the like power one day in four. Held, there was no fatal variance; for the indenture proved the right alleged, either for the whole time, or for one day in four; and, in either case, A was entitled to recover to the extent of the injury proved.[1] But where, in an action for diverting water, the declaration alleged, that the plaintiff was entitled to all the water in a dam which should rise above a certain mark, and the evidence showed that he was entitled only to such part as should remain after a prior use by the defendant; held, on error, a fatal variance.[2] So, under a complaint for obstructing a stream, and causing the water to flow back upon and over land of the plaintiff, the plaintiff cannot show that raising the stream interfered with the natural drainage of the land, so that the rain-water did not soak away, but remained until it dried away.[3] So a declaration, for the obstruction of "a small stream of water" running through the plaintiff's land, is not sustained by evidence, that the flow, through a ditch, of water which has accumulated from rains or the melting of snow or the undermining of the land, has been obstructed.[4] So a declaration, for the diversion of a watercourse running through the plaintiff's cedar swamp, by digging a ditch from the channel thereof, above the swamp, on land not belonging to the plaintiff, and diverting the water into it, and thereby injuring the swamp; is not sustained by proof, that the defendant dug a ditch which diverted the water from flowing in an ancient stream into a large swamp, of which the plaintiff's land was a portion, if no watercourse of the plaintiff is thereby disturbed; although it does not appear that the defendant had authority for his acts.[5]

1 Burdick *v.* Glasko, 18 Conn. 494.
2 Wilbur *v.* Brown, 3 Denio, 356.
3 Pixley *v.* Clark, 32 Barb. 268.
4 Dickinson *v.* Worcester, 7 Allen, 19.
5 Griffith *v.* Jenkins, 2 ib. 589.

§ 9. To an action for wrongfully keeping and maintaining a weir at a height beyond its ordinary level, whereby the plaintiff's lands were flooded, the defendant pleaded, that "he did not wrongfully keep and maintain the weir at a height greater than its ordinary level." The issue followed the words of the plea. Held, the plea only put in issue the maintenance of the weir, and evidence on behalf of the defendant, that such maintenance was rightful, was inadmissible.[1]

§ 10. Under an answer to a complaint for flowing land, which claims the right to maintain the dam at its present height, without compensation, the burden of proof is on the respondent.[2]

§ 11. In an action for diverting a stream, by cutting ditches on the defendant's lot above that of the plaintiff; the defendant cannot set up, by way of equitable defence, a parol agreement between them relative to the deepening of the channel on their respective premises, made several years before, and having no connection with, the diversion. Nor could such an agreement have been set up as a counter-claim under the New York Code of 1852. Nor by way of recoupment of damages. Nor could the defendant claim damages for breach of the agreement, as a set-off, under the Revised Statutes, or the Code prior to 1852.[3]

§ 12. Under a canal act, mill-owners, within a specified distance of the canal, were entitled to use the water for the purpose of condensing the steam used for working their engines. In an action against such a mill-owner, the declaration charged, that he abstracted more water than was sufficient to supply the engine with cold water for the purpose of condensing the steam, and that he applied the water to other and different purposes than condensing steam. The plea alleged an user by the defendant, as occupier of the mill, of the water, as of right and without interruption for twenty years, for other purposes than condensing steam, to wit, for supplying the boiler of the engine, and of generating steam for working the engine, and of supplying a certain cistern, to wit, a cistern on the roof of a certain engine-house. The replication traversed such user. The evidence was, that the defendant was the occupier of two mills, adjoining to each other and occupied together, each having a separate steam-engine. The

1 Blood *v.* Keller, 11 Ir. Com. Law Rep. 132 Exch.

2 Jackson *v.* Harrington, 2 Allen, 242.

3 Pattison *v.* Richards, 22 Barb. 143.

"old mill" was erected in 1823, since which time the defendant had used the water from the canal for twenty years, for the purposes mentioned in the plea, in respect of the "old mill." The "new mill" was built in 1829, and the water had been used, as alleged in the plea, for less than twenty years in respect of that mill. There was no cistern on the roof of any engine-house, but there were various cisterns in and about the engine-house in the old mill, through which the water passed. The jury found that the two buildings formed one mill, and that there had been a twenty years' user as of right by the defendant. Held, the issue was divisible, and the defendant was entitled to the verdict, except as to the supplying a cistern on the roof of the engine-house, as to which the plaintiff was entitled to a verdict, with nominal damages. Held, also (upon motion for judgment *non obstante veredicto*), that the plea was bad, as the canal company had no right to grant the water for other purposes than for condensing steam, and that no such right could consequently be inferred from a twenty years' user. "This is a claim by the defendant to impose a servitude on the canal, by the effect of a twenty years' adverse user. . . . Twenty years' adverse user will not establish such a right unless the owner of the servient tenement is capable of giving such a right by express grant. Now, if there had been such a grant here, . . . the plaintiffs, who are trustees for public purposes, would, nevertheless, have a right to the flow of the water." [1]

§ 13. The plaintiff was entitled, for the purposes of his mill, to a supply of water, by means of a stream running through and over the lands of the defendant. The defendant, in working the minerals lying under the bed of the stream, had caused a subsidence of the bed, to the extent of four feet, for some distance. In order to maintain the original level of the stream, the defendant had constructed embankments on either side, and there was no actual diminution in the supply of water to the mill. Upon a bill for an injunction, the court refused to make a hostile decree against the defendant. But, by reason of the subsidence, he was required to give an undertaking, not to work the mineral in such a way, as to obstruct or interfere with the flow and passage of the water to the mill; staying further proceedings; giving no costs;

[1] The Rochdale, &c. *v.* Radcliffe, 12 Eng. L. & Eq. 409; per Erle, J., ib 418.

but reserving liberty to the plaintiff to apply, if occasion should require.[1]

§ 15. With reference to the subject of *lights* and other *easements;* in an action for injury to the reversion by obstructing ancient lights, it is sufficient for the declaration to show an obstruction which may cause such injury, especially if it is alleged that, by means thereof, the plaintiff's reversionary estate was injured. And such declaration is not bad, on demurrer, because the obstruction is one which is capable of being shown, at the trial, to be only temporary, and not injurious to the reversion.[2]

§ 16. An averment, that the plaintiff owned a dwelling-house, in which there were, and still of right ought to be, four ancient windows, through which the light and air ought to have entered, and still ought to enter of right, allows proof of a prescriptive right, of one founded on grant, or on adverse user.[3]

§ 17. Where a bill stated, that the erection of a proposed building would materially affect the comfort and enjoyment, in respect of light and air, of the inhabitants of an adjoining house, of which there had been uninterrupted enjoyment for twenty years and upwards; the court granted an injunction to restrain the erection of such building, the plaintiff undertaking to bring an action within one month.[4]

§ 18. To an action for obstructing the plaintiff's lights, and depriving him of support to his buildings, the defendant pleaded an equitable plea; that the grievances complained of were occasioned by his pulling down a house and erecting another in its place, which he did with the acquiescence and consent of the plaintiff, and on the faith of such acquiescence and consent he incurred expenses. Replication, that the plaintiff acquiesced and consented on the faith of false representations of the defendant; that is, that the grievances complained of would not result from his works. Held, the plea and the replication were respectively good.[5]

§ 19. Declaration, that the defendants wrongfully raised, made, and formed, and caused to be raised, made, and formed, a certain embankment of earth near the plaintiff's house, and wrongfully

[1] Elwell *v.* Crowther, 8 Jur. (N. S.) 1004; 6 L. T. (N. S.) 596.

[2] Metropolitan, &c. *v.* Petch, 27 L. J. C. P. 330; 5 C. B. (N. S.) 504.

[3] Ward *v.* Neal, 35 Ala. 602.

[4] Arcedeckne *v.* Kelk, 5 Jur. (N. S.) 114; 7 W. R. 194; 32 L. T. 331.

[5] Davis *v.* Marshall, 7 Jur. (N. S.) 1247.

continued the same, &c., by reason whereof, &c., divers large quantities of water ran and flowed to and into the said house, whereby the same became greatly injured, wetted, and damaged. Plea, that the said embankment was raised, under and by virtue of certain acts of Parliament granted in that behalf, to wit, &c. Replication, that the running and flowing of the water to and into the plaintiff's messuage, as in the declaration mentioned, was and is occasioned by the wrongful construction, negligent and improper raising, making, and forming of the said embankment, and the want of proper and sufficient drains to the same. Held, by Crompton and Mellor, JJ. (*dubitante* Cockburn, C. J.), that the replication was no departure.[1]

§ 20. A plea of right of common for "one cow, and three-fourth parts of a right of common of pasture for another cow," with an averment "that one L. had one-fourth part of a right of common of pasture for one cow," and that the defendant in respect of his right of common for one cow and three-fourth parts of the right of common for another cow in his own right, and in respect of one-fourth part of a right of common as the servant of L. put two cows, and no more, on the common; was held bad.[2]

§ 21. In an action for the infringement of a patent, the court (since the Common-law Procedure Act) allowed the defendant to plead, first, not guilty; secondly, that the patentee was not the inventor; thirdly, *non concessit;* fourthly, that the invention was not a manufacture; fifthly, that the invention was not new; and sixthly, that no sufficient specification was enrolled.[3]

[1] Brine *v.* Great, &c. 8 Jur. (N. S.) 410; 2 B. & S. 402.

[2] Nichols *v.* Chapman, 5 Hurl. & Nor. 643.

[3] Platt *v.* Else, 20 Eng. L. & Eq. 304.

CHAPTER X.

PLEADINGS IN ACTIONS FOR INJURIES TO RELATIVE RIGHTS; OFFICERS OF THE LAW.

1. Justices.
2. Clerk.
3. Sheriffs, &c.

§ 1. DECLARATION against the defendants, as justices of the peace, that the plaintiffs were rated to a church rate, and were summoned before the justices, to answer a complaint that they had refused to pay it; that they duly attended, and in good faith, &c., disputing and intending to dispute the validity of the said rate, upon the hearing gave to the defendants, then being and acting as such justices as aforesaid, notice that they disputed the validity of the rate, and required the defendants, as such justices, to forbear from and not to give judgment in respect of the matter of the complaint; and that there was no evidence given to or before the defendants, that the plaintiffs did not in good faith dispute the validity of the said rate, or that they did not in good faith give such notice to the defendants as aforesaid; yet the defendants, disregarding the said notice, and assuming to act as justices when they well knew they had not jurisdiction to make any order upon the matter of the complaint, made an order for the payment of the amount of the rate, together with a sum for costs. Demurrer, on the ground that the declaration ought to have alleged that the defendants committed the grievances maliciously. Held, that, assuming the plaintiffs did *bonâ fide* dispute the rate, and gave notice to the justices, the jurisdiction was ousted; and, the action being against justices for acting in excess of their jurisdiction, the declaration was good, without an allegation that they acted maliciously and without reasonable and probable cause.[1]

§ 2. The clerk of a county court, against whom an action of

[1] Pease *v.* Chayton, 8 Jur. (N. S.) 482.

trespass is brought, may give special matter in evidence under a plea of "not guilty by statute," by virtue of the 13 & 14 Vict. ch. 61, § 19.[1]

§ 3. A complaint against a sheriff, for not executing a deed to the plaintiff, and claiming special damages for the failure to get possession of the land sold, is bad, without an averment that the plaintiff's failure to get possession was caused solely by the want of the deed.[2]

§ 4. If, in an action against a sheriff for the default of his deputy, the declaration does not allege that he is sheriff, the defect will not be aided by verdict.[3]

§ 5. In an action against an officer for the unlawful taking of property, it is not necessary to aver that such property was exempt from execution.[4]

§ 6. In an action against an officer for taking, on an attachment against A, goods mortgaged to B; the declaration need not allege that the demand made by the plaintiff on the officer, as required by the Mass. Rev. Sts. ch. 90, § 79, contained a just and true account of the mortgage-debt.[5]

§ 7. A complaint, which, after stating the due commitment of a prisoner by the defendant as sheriff to the county jail, then proceeds to state the expiration of the term of the defendant's office, the election of a new sheriff, the due qualification of the latter, and the service upon the defendant of the certificate of the county clerk that such new sheriff had qualified and given the security required by law (2 N. Y. Rev. Sts. 438), and avers that the defendant did not, within ten days after such service, deliver to the said new sheriff the prisoner, then in the defendant's custody on the said execution, and confined within the jail liberties; shows a clear and explicit neglect of duty and violation of the statute, for which the defendant is liable, and is enough to put him to his defence.[6]

§ 8. An averment in a declaration, that an execution was returnable according to the statute, is to be understood as meaning, that the execution was returnable, on its face, to the term of the court, to which by law it should have been made returnable; and

1 Dews *v.* Ryley, 7 Eng. L. & Eq. 469.
2 Knight *v.* Fair, 12 Cal. 296.
3 Low *v.* Tilton, 19 N. H. 271.
4 Stevens *v.* Somerindyke, 4 E. D. Smith, 418.
5 Gassett *v.* Sanborn, 8 Gray, 218.
6 French *v.* Willet, 4 Bosw. 649.

if, when offered in evidence, it appears returnable at a time different from that, it should be excluded on account of the variance.[1] But where, in an action of trespass, the defendant justifies the taking by a writ directed to him as an officer, and the action is brought before the term of the court to which such writ is returnable; the special plea need not allege that the writ was returned at the term of the court to which it was made returnable.[2]

§ 9. A declaration against a sheriff stated in detail, that five several writs of *fi. fa.* against the plaintiff were delivered to the sheriff; that he afterwards, under the said several writs respectively, seized the plaintiff's goods, to the value of the said writs; and took for executing the said writs a large sum, to wit, 52*l.* 12*s.* 3*d.*, the same being more than he was entitled to by 35*l.* 18*s.* 6*d.* To this was a special demurrer, for not setting out with particularity the amounts taken, and in respect of what fees the excess arose, and that it was not averred that the extortion took place within one year before the commencement of the suit. Suggesting, that the declaration did not sufficiently show whether there were one or more seizures, the court held that this objection was not sufficiently taken by the demurrer, and that in other respects the declaration was good.[3]

§ 9 *a.* If one assume to justify by special process of *capias*, he should in his plea state such facts as authorize that form of process.[4]

§ 10. A complaint, in an action against a sheriff for the escape of a person arrested by him upon a process for contempt, which alleges that the sheriff "suffered and permitted such person to escape and go at large," states a voluntary and not a negligent escape. An answer to such a complaint, which in terms is stated to be "a further separate and distinct defence," and which avers that such person "may have wrongfully and privily, and without the knowledge, permission, or consent of this defendant, escaped," &c., and that, "if he did so escape, he afterwards" returned into custody, &c., is insufficient as a pleading, as it does not deny, either generally or specifically, the allegation that the sheriff permitted the prisoner to escape. The New York statute requires, as

1 Forward *v.* Marsh, 18 Ala. 645.

2 Briggs *v.* Mason, 31 Verm. 433.

3 Berton *v.* Lawrence, 1 Eng. L. & Eq. 453.

4 Wright *v.* Hazen, 24 Verm. 143.

essential to the sufficiency of an answer to such a complaint, that it contain averments, whatever may be the words used, amounting to a clear and distinct allegation that the alleged escape "was made without the consent of the defendant."[1]

§ 11. In an action against a constable for neglecting to execute process, he cannot plead the defectiveness of his writ, unless it be for want of jurisdiction.[2]

§ 12. Where a sheriff justifies, in trover, under an attachment and order of sale therein issued; an averment in these words, "of which proceedings under said order of sale, said defendant made due return to said court, according to the mandate thereof," is not sufficient, the facts not being stated.[3]

§ 13. In an action against an officer, for refusing to serve a writ, and make an attachment thereon of property which was pointed out to him, and which was then held by him on another precept, and afterwards sold for more than sufficient to satisfy the same; the defendant cannot prove, as a bar to the action, a settlement made after the action was commenced, and not set forth in the answer, by which the surplus was paid over to other creditors, with the plaintiff's consent.[4]

§ 14. Where, in an action of trespass for taking goods, the defendant pleaded in justification that he took them by virtue of a writ directed to him as an officer; a replication, that he did not attach said goods by virtue of said writ, upon special demurrer was held to be a negative pregnant, and therefore bad.[5]

§ 15. To a plea by the sheriff, in an action against him for neglecting to return a writ of attachment, that the execution defendant was worthless; fraud in the bill of sale offered to sustain this plea need not be replied, but may be shown by evidence.[6]

§ 16. To a declaration, that, the plaintiffs having bailed and let to P. divers wagons for a term, and being entitled to and the owners of the wagons, subject to the interest of P. thereupon, during the term, and while the plaintiffs and P. were so interested, the defendant converted them to his own use, and sold the same, whereby the plaintiffs were injured in their title to the wagons, and the same became lost to them; it is a good plea, that the defendant sold, but not in market overt, the wagons, as sheriff, in the execution

[1] Loosey *v.* Orser, 4 Bosw. 391.
[2] Coverdale *v.* Fowler, 4 Har. 358.
[3] Young *v.* Davis, 30 Ala. 213.
[4] Wolcott *v.* Root, 2 Allen, 194.
[5] Briggs *v.* Mason, 31 Verm. 433.
[6] Smith *v.* Tooke, 20 Tex. 750.

of a *fi. fa.*, and that at the time of the sale he had not any notice of the plaintiffs' interest in the wagons. Another plea, that the defendant seized and sold the wagons, not maliciously, and not in market overt, as sheriff, in execution of a *fi. fa.;* and that the plaintiffs had not sustained and will not sústain any damage. New assignment to both pleas: that the defendant converted the wagons by absolutely selling the plaintiffs' interest and delivering the wagons to divers persons in pursuance of the sale, and thereby causing the same to be used by those persons and worn by such users. Held, that the plaintiffs were entitled to judgment on the new assignment to both pleas.[1]

§ 17. A defendant, failing to justify under a *habere*, the judgment in ejectment having been set aside as irregular, may, either under a plea that the plaintiff was not possessed, or that a third party was, prove the title upon which he recovered in ejectment.[2]

§ 18. A justification of breaking an inner door, in order to search for and arrest the party, must allege a demand of the key, or that no one was present of whom a demand could be made. It is not sufficient to allege that the door was locked, so that without breaking it the officer could not enter.[3]

§ 19. In a suit for false imprisonment, if the defendant plead that he was sheriff, and arrested the plaintiff by virtue of process; a replication, of the tender of a bail-piece to the defendant, which he refused to accept, is bad.[4]

§ 20. Whenever new matter is introduced in any of the pleadings in a suit, the plea should conclude with a verification. Thus where the defendant, in an action of trespass, justifies the taking of the property by virtue of a rate-bill and warrant, and the plaintiff replies a tender of the amount of the tax and interest; a rejoinder, that the defendant was entitled to and claimed travelling fees, in addition to the tax and interest, and that therefore the tender was insufficient, being new matter, should conclude with a verification.[5]

§ 21. The attorney of P., who had obtained judgment in an action against W. F., caused a *fi. fa.* to issue against W. F., and indorsed on the writ, "The defendant is a ——, and resides at

[1] Lancashire, &c. *v.* Fitzhugh, 6 H. & N. 502.

[2] Bilcker *v.* Beeston, 2 F. & F. 410, Wilde.

[3] 1 Chit. Pl. 518; 3 Bos. & P. 223.

[4] Yingling *v.* Hoppe, 9 Gill, 310.

[5] Joslyn *v.* Tracy, 19 Verm. 569.

R. in your bailiwick." The writ was delivered to the sheriff, who seized the goods of W. F., the son, he being the only person of that name who resided at R. The real defendant, W. F. the father, resided at C., which adjoined R. An action having been brought by the son against the sheriff, in which the sheriff had to pay damages, he sued the attorney to recover compensation. It was agreed that both the attorney and the sheriff acted *bonâ fide*. A first count alleged that the defendant, by an indorsement on the writ, and with the intent that the plaintiff should act on the statement contained in the indorsement, falsely stated and represented to the plaintiff, that the W. F. against whose goods the writ was directed resided at R. The second count alleged the indorsement to have been negligently, carelessly, and improperly made. The third count alleged that the defendant, having issued the *fi. fa.*, directed and required the plaintiff, to wit, by the indorsement on the writ, to execute the writ by seizing the goods of W. F., who resided at R., as and for the goods of the W. F. in the writ named. Held, by Cockburn, C. J., Hill and Blackburn, JJ., that the first count, which was simply for a misrepresentation, could not be supported; that the second count was defective in not showing any obligation or duty on the part of the attorney, as between him and the sheriff, to make the indorsement; and the third count could not be supported, inasmuch as the indorsement on the writ was no more than a statement by the attorney for the purpose of affording information to the sheriff, leaving the sheriff to his own discretion as to how he would act. But by Wightman, J., that the indorsement was a direction to the sheriff to take the goods of W. F., who resided at R., and therefore the plaintiff was entitled to judgment on the third count. Also held, by the court, that the sheriff was not entitled to recover so much of the damages, as were given in respect of his officer's having remained in possession after he had notice that the execution was wrong.[1]

[1] Childers *v.* Wooler, 6 Jur. (N. S.) 444; 29 L. J. Q. B. 129; 8 W. R. 321; 2 L. T. (N. S.) 49.

CHAPTER XI.

PLEADINGS IN ACTIONS AGAINST RAILROADS, TOWNS, AND IN CASES OF MASTER AND SERVANT, BAILMENT, LANDLORD, &C., SEDUCTION.

§ 1. In an action against a railroad [1] for causing the death of a person, it is sufficient to allege that the defendants "did carelessly and negligently run over," &c., without stating the facts.[2] So in an action against a railroad company for personal injuries, where the facts stated show a common-law liability, independent of any charter or statute, an averment that the injury was occasioned by the defendants' negligent management of the cars and engines of "a railroad" in Jersey City, of which the defendants then had possession, is sufficient, on demurrer.[3]

§ 2. A railroad servant, suing for personal injuries, need not, in his complaint, negative knowledge or notice by him of the alleged defects in the road and machinery.[4]

§ 3. In an action against a railroad company for loss of a trunk, the declaration need not allege that the owner was a passenger; that he was a passenger, and that he owned the trunk, will be *primâ facie* presumed from the production by him of the baggage-check, which would only be given to a passenger.[5]

§ 3 *a*. In an action against a railroad for a personal injury, an averment in the declaration, that the plaintiff was struck by their locomotive engine while travelling in the highway, is not sustained by proof, that, by means of the defendants' negligence in the man-

[1] See 18 Ind. 168; 9 Allen, 557; 23 Ind. 553; 21 ib. 10; 23 ib. 81, 101, 340; 20 ib. 229.

[2] The Indianapolis, &c., *v.* Keeley, 23 Ind. 133.

[3] Austin *v.* New York, &c. 1 Dutch. 381.

[4] Indianapolis *v.* Klein, 11 Ind. 38.

[5] Illinois, &c. *v.* Copeland, 24 Ill. 332.

agement of their train, the plaintiff's horse was frightened, and ran or was driven out of the highway, five or six rods before reaching the railroad crossing, upon land owned by the defendants, and the plaintiff was there struck, while attempting to cross the railroad. And the declaration cannot be amended after verdict so as to cure this variance.[1]

§ 4. A declaration against a railroad for killing stock may contain one count describing the stock as *common*, and another as *of the full blood;* and the plaintiff cannot be required to elect between them.[2]

§ 5. In Indiana, the declaration must allege that cattle killed upon a railroad were killed in the county.[3]

§ 6. In Illinois, in an action for injury done to animals by a railroad, the plaintiff should aver, that, when injured, they were not within the limits of a town, village, &c.[4]

§ 7. In actions to recover damages for the killing of stock by the cars of a railroad company, the complaint must show either carelessness, or that the road was not properly fenced.[5] And a complaint against a railroad, for killing animals by its rolling-stock, is bad, even after verdict, unless it allege negligence, or that the road was not fenced.[6]

§ 8. The first count of the declaration stated, that the defendants were the owners and occupiers of a railway, and of a station thereon for the loading, &c., of cattle carried thereby, and of a yard adjoining the station, through which yard the cattle were accustomed to pass in going from the station to a certain common highway near thereto; and that the defendants, by reason of the premises, ought to have maintained sufficient fences between the said yard and the railway, so as to prevent cattle lawfully being in the yard from straying thereout into and upon the railway; but that they omitted to maintain such fences, whereby a bull of the plaintiff, lawfully being in the yard, on his way to the highway, without default or negligence on his part, strayed from the yard on to the railway, and was killed by a passing train. Held, there was no liability upon the company, either by the common law or by the Sts. 8 & 9 Vict. ch. 20, § 68, to fence their yard

[1] Shaw *v.* Boston, &c. 8 Gray, 45.

[2] The Toledo, &c. *v.* Daniels, 21 Ind. 256. See Presdt. &c. *v.* Smith, 19 ib. 42; Story *v.* O'Dea, 23 ib. 326.

[3] Indianapolis, &c. *v.* Wilsey, 20 ib. 229.

[4] Chicago, &c. *v.* Carter, 20 Ill. 390.

[5] Indianapolis, &c. *v.* Sparr, 15 Ind. 440; Same *v.* Williams, ib. 486.

[6] The Indianapolis, &c. *v.* Brucey, 21 ib. 215.

from the railway, and consequently the count disclosed no cause of action.[1] The second count alleged, that a certain bull of the plaintiff was lawfully in a close, adjoining a railway, of which the defendants were owners and occupiers, and along which railway they had not made any fences for preventing cattle being in the close from straying thereout upon the railway, and that, whilst the bull was lawfully in the close, the defendants and their servants negligently and wrongfully chased and frightened the bull, and so caused it to run upon the railway, where it was killed. The bull, with other cattle which had been brought by the railway, being in the station-yard, a place unlighted and not fenced from the railway, a porter came out of the office with a lantern, such as were ordinarily used by porters, in his hand, and the light startled some of the beasts, and caused the plaintiff's bull to run upon the line, where it was knocked down and killed by a passing train. Held, no evidence for the jury, that the company's servants had been guilty of negligence.[2]

§ 9. The distinction, however, is made, that, in an action on the case at common law against a railroad company for killing cattle, negligence should be averred and proved; but it is otherwise, if the action is brought under the statute.[3] So a declaration alleged, that the defendants neglected to keep a suitable fence along their track, and that "for want of such fence the plaintiff's horse escaped from his pasture and went at large, and by means of going at large, as aforesaid, the horse was greatly injured; whereby an action, &c." Held, though this declaration might have been bad on demurrer, it was sufficient on a motion in arrest of judgment.[4]

§ 10. In a suit against a railroad company to recover for stock killed, the allegation that the road was not fenced is a material one, and must be proved.[5]

§ 11. To an action for forcibly entering upon land, digging, excavating, making embankments, &c., whereby a mill-seat and buildings were destroyed; it is a sufficient answer on demurrer, that the defendants entered as the servants of a railroad, which had legally appropriated the property for its line; even though the

[1] Roberts v. Great, &c. 4 C. B. (N. S.) 506.

[2] Ibid.

[3] Terre Haute, &c. v. Augustus, 21 Ill. 186.

[4] Holden v. Rutland, &c. 30 Verm. 297.

[5] Indianapolis, &c. v. Wharton, 13 Ind. 509.

company might be liable to a suit for any personal property not taken for the construction of the road.[1]

§ 12. In an action for injury to land, the defendants (a railway company) pleaded, that they entered on the land under § 85 of the Land Clauses Consolidation Act, before the expiration of the prescribed period for exercising their compulsory powers; and, having so entered and being lawfully in possession, that they, after the expiration of the prescribed period, continued in possession, and, in the due and lawful exercise of the powers of the said act, committed the grievances complained of. The plaintiff replied (admitting the statute) *de injuria absque residuo causæ.* Held, the replication was bad, as the plea claimed an interest in land, and the replication traversed an authority in law by the denial of acting under the statute.[2]

§ 13. Where two highways lead across a waste, in which and near the highways there is a quarry unfenced and unguarded, and a person crossing from one highway to the other, in the dark, falls into the quarry and is injured; no action lies against the owner of the quarry, without showing that the quarry is so near the highway as to be a public nuisance. Nor is it sufficient to aver that "all persons, having occasion to cross or pass over the waste land, have been used and accustomed to go upon, along, and across the same, without interruption or hindrance from, and with the license and permission of, the owners of such waste land; and that the quarry was and is situate near to and between two public highways leading over and across the waste land, and was and is precipitous, and of great depth and width, and dangerous to persons who might have occasion to cross over the waste land, for the purpose of passing from one of such roads to the other of them, beside or near the quarry."[3]

§ 14. The want of a sufficient railing, barrier, and protection, to prevent travellers passing upon a highway from running into some dangerous excavation or pond, or against a wall, stones, or other dangerous obstruction, without its limits, but in the general direction of the travel thereon, may properly be alleged as a defect in the highway itself.[4]

§ 15. In a declaration against a town for special damage hap-

1 Green *v.* Boody, 21 Ind. 10.

2 Worsley *v.* South, &c. 4 Eng. L. & Eq. 223.

3 Hounsell *v.* Smith, 7 C. B. (N. S.) 897; 29 L. J. C. P. 303; 8 W. R. 277.

4 Davis *v.* Hill, 41 N. H. 329.

pening by reason of the insufficiency of a highway, it is not necessary to allege that the highway was established in one of the modes authorized by statute.[1]

§ 16. In an action brought against a town, upon the Connecticut statute "concerning highways and bridges," for injuries by reason of a defect in the bridge; averments respecting an injury to the person of the plaintiff can be united, in each count of the declaration, with averments respecting an injury to his property, although damages for these different injuries are given by different sections of the statute.[2]

§ 17. An averment, that there was in the highway "a ditch or uncovered drain running across the same," is supported by testimony, that there was a water-bar about six inches high across the highway, with a deep rut or "cradle-hole" above it.[3]

§ 18. An averment, that the plaintiff's horse, by reason of the narrowness of the highway and the want of a sufficient railing, was precipitated off the steep side of the highway into a pond among certain timbers, and the shoulder of the horse was so broken that it became necessary to kill him; is supported by proof, that the horse, by the insufficiency and giving way of the rail, struck his shoulder against the stone post on which the rail had rested, and so broke his shoulder, before falling into the pond.[4]

§ 19. It is not competent to declare, with a *continuando*, for injuries occasioned by the obstruction or insufficiency of a highway, or to allege a repetition of such injuries upon divers days and times between a day specified and the commencement of the suit. It is the *per quod* which is the *gravamen* of the action, and not the insufficiency of the road; and the injury sustained at any one time cannot be continued or repeated. In such case the plaintiff, without any waiver on his part, may, upon the objection of the defendant, be confined in his proof to a single injury; or it might be ground for a special demurrer.[5]

§ 20. An excavation was made by the defendant on his own land, a short distance from a sidewalk, and was left unguarded, he having removed a fence which had been standing between his

[1] Hurley *v.* Manchester, 39 N. H. 289.

[2] Seger *v.* Barkhamsted, 22 Conn. 29.

[3] Goldthwait *v.* East Bridgewater, 5 Gray, 61.

[4] Ibid.

[5] Baxter *v.* W'nooski, &c. 22 Verm. 114.

land and the street. The night following, A, passing along the sidewalk, got off the walk, and fell in and was injured. A general statute made it the duty of the city to protect the sidewalk by a railing where necessary, and A recovered damages against the city. In a suit brought by the city to recover indemnity from the defendant, held, 1. That the liability of the defendant did not depend upon how near the excavation was to the sidewalk, but upon the question whether, in the circumstances, it rendered travelling upon the sidewalk dangerous [one judge dissenting]. 2. That the defendant was liable, on the ground of his personal connection with the wrongful acts, and that it was not necessary that he should have been in the occupancy of the land. 3. That it was not necessary, in consequence of the allegation of a general duty on the part of the city to protect the sidewalk by a railing, to allege a particular duty on the part of the defendant to erect the railing in this instance, but the general allegation of the defendant's negligence in leaving the excavation exposed, and the subjection of the city to damages in consequence of it, was sufficient.[1]

§ 21. A declaration against a city is sufficient, which alleges the existence of a street within its limits without a sewer, whereby stagnant water flowed upon the plaintiff's land.[2]

§ 22. A petition is not bad on demurrer, on the ground of *respondeat superior*, which alleges a wrong committed by the defendant while in another's employ, but not that it was done within the scope of his employment. An answer, denying that the defendant committed the act, and alleging that it was done by another, is a mere special denial, requiring no reply.[3]

§ 23. In an action by a guest against an innkeeper for the value of goods stolen, the allegation of carelessness, if necessarily made, will at any rate be proved sufficiently by proof of the loss of the goods from the room in which the guest lodged.[4]

§ 24. An innkeeper cannot, under the New York act, avoid responsibility for goods stolen, when the guest failed to bolt his door, unless he sets up this fact in his answer.[5]

§ 25. In an action against a carrier, for breach of duty as such,

[1] Norwich *v.* Breed, 30 Conn. 535.
[2] Smith *v.* Milwaukee, 18 Wis. 63.
[3] Hoffman *v.* Gordon, 15 Ohio St. 211.
[4] Gile *v.* Libby, 36 Barb. 70.
[5] Ibid.

although negligence be averred, it is not necessary to show any positive misconduct.[1]

§ 26. In an action against a carrier for loss of baggage, the plaintiff alleged and proved that he was a carrier, and took him and his baggage to be carried, and in the same count alleged a special contract to carry safely. Held, the special allegation might be stricken out as surplusage, and the plaintiff could recover on the general allegations, under Minnesota Rev. Sts. ch. 86.[2]

§ 27. In an action against a steamboat, as a common carrier, it is not necessary that the petition should expressly state that the steamboat is a common carrier, if it clearly appear, from the whole petition, that the contract was entered into with her in that capacity.[3]

§ 28. In trover against a carrier, the declaration need not set forth the duty of the defendant as carrier; if it allege his business, negligence, and the loss caused thereby.[4]

§ 29. In an action against a common carrier for non-delivery of goods, intrusted to him under an agreement, by which he was only to be responsible for loss or damage occasioned by his fraud or negligence; the objection, that the complaint did not allege any such fraud or negligence, cannot be taken after trial and verdict. Nor that the legal effect of the contract proved varied from that described.[5]

§ 30. The answer to a petition, to recover for a loss by a jettison of goods by the carrier, must show all the facts necessary to justify him. The averment, that the loss occurred by the dangers of the river, is but a conclusion of law, and not sufficient. But if a justification is alleged in general terms, which embrace the particular facts necessary to be proved, and is held good on demurrer, and the parties go to trial upon that issue, and the evidence conduces to prove facts, upon which the jury might have found for the defendants, and a judgment thereon would have been sustained; the defendants are not precluded from questioning the judgment against them, on the ground of errors in the trial, which may have prevented a verdict in their favor.[6]

§ 31. To an action on the case, in which the declaration stated that the defendants were common carriers, and that they received

[1] Merritt *v.* Earle, 31 Barb. 38.
[2] War Eagle *v.* Nutting, 1 Min. 256.
[3] Smithers *v.* War Eagle, 29 Mis. 312.
[4] Wright *v.* McKee, 37 Verm. 161.
[5] Newstadt *v.* Adams, 5 Duer, 43.
[6] Bentley *v.* Bustard, 16 B. Mon. 643.

from the plaintiff, as such, a package, to be safely carried and delivered for him at a place mentioned, and that they did not safely carry the package, but through their negligence it was lost; the defendants pleaded, with a verification, that, at the time they received the package, they gave the plaintiff notice that they would not be responsible for packages of a particular description, under which this particular package fell, unless their contents were declared; and that the contents of this package were not declared; and that the defendants did not consent to be responsible contrary to the terms of such notice. Held, an argumentative denial of the bailment as alleged in the declaration.[1]

§ 32. It is no defence, in a landlord and tenant process, that the plaintiff has taken possession, unless pleaded *puis dar. con.*; even though it appear in an agreed statement.[2]

§ 33. First count, that the plaintiff was the owner of goods, which had been let to hire to one T. for a term, and that the defendant sold the goods and dispersed them, so as to prevent their being followed or found, whereby the plaintiff was injured in her reversionary estate. Second count, similar to the first, except that it alleged that the goods were let to T. "to be used in a certain house, and not otherwise or elsewhere; that T. had the use of the goods, subject to the expiration of the term, and subject to the determination of the term by the violation of the terms thereof." Pleas, that the defendant seized and took and sold the goods, not in market overt, but as sheriff under a writ of *fi. fa.* against T., and that the plaintiff had not sustained, and would not sustain, any damages by reason of the premises. Held, as the damages sustained by the plaintiff were the foundation of the action, the pleas were an answer.[3]

§ 34. To an action of trespass, for breaking and entering the plaintiff's house and seizing his goods, the defendant pleaded, that one Thomas held a house as tenant to one Payne, at a certain rent; that the rent was in arrear; that the said goods, being the goods of Thomas, were fraudulently and clandestinely conveyed by him from his house to prevent a distress, and were, with the plaintiff's consent, placed in the plaintiff's house; whereupon

[1] Crouch *v.* The London, &c., 14 Eng. L. & Eq. 498.

[2] Hayden *v.* Ahearn, 9 Gray, 438.

[3] Tancred *v.* Allgood, 4 Hurl. & Nor. 438.

the defendant, as bailiff of Payne, and by his command, seized the goods as a distress. Replication, that the said goods were not the goods of Thomas, nor were they fraudulently and clandestinely conveyed away by Thomas to prevent a distress. It seems the replication is not multifarious, but a good answer.[1]

§ 35. In a complaint for *crim. con.*, it is a sufficient averment of marriage, that the female was the wife of the plaintiff at the time when the act was committed.[2]

§ 36. Want of virtue in the plaintiff and his wife, is not a defence. But, without being pleaded, it may be proved in mitigation of damages.[3]

§ 37. An action for seduction of a daughter, brought in the form of trespass to the dwelling-house of the plaintiff, need not allege a *per quod serv.*, &c.[4]

§ 38. A promise of marriage, as the means of seduction, may be alleged in the declaration.[5]

§ 39. To an action for seduction, with promise of marriage, an answer of the infancy of the defendant is bad on demurrer.[6]

[1] Thomas *v.* Watkins, 14 Eng. L. & Eq. 489.

[2] Hanck *v.* Grantham, 22 Ind. 53.

[3] Harrison *v.* Price, ib. 165.

[4] Donohue *v.* Dyer, 23 Ind. 521.

[5] Lee *v.* Hefley, 21 ib. 99.

[6] Lee *v.* Hefley, ib. 98.

BOOK IV.

EVIDENCE IN ACTIONS FOR TORTS.

CHAPTER I.

GENERAL RULES OF EVIDENCE.

1. Proof of the affirmative of the issue; exceptions to the general rule.
3. Affirmative proof of wrong or illegality; fraud; official neglect or misconduct, &c.
5. Proof as to possession.
7. Burden of proof; to what it extends.
8. Change in the burden of proof.
9. Nonsuit for want of proof.
10. Presumptions.
11. Presumption of innocence as to official conduct; possession, &c.
12. Reasonable doubt.
14. Miscellaneous.
16. Rebutting evidence.

§ 1. It is the general rule of evidence, that "the obligation of proving any fact lies upon the party who substantially asserts the affirmative of the issue. It is generally deemed sufficient, where the allegation is affirmative, to oppose it with a bare denial, until it is established by evidence." [1]

§ 2. There are, however, some exceptions to this rule. (*a*) Where the plaintiff grounds his right of action on a negative allegation, the establishment of which is an essential element in his case, he is bound to prove it.[2] Thus, in the action for malicious prosecution, the want of probable cause, though a negative

[1] 1 Greenl. Evi. 147, § 74. See People *v.* Third, &c. 45 Barb. 63.

[2] Nash *v.* Hall, 4 Ind. 444.

(*a*) "The general statement that the party who alleges the affirmative shall prove it, will not much aid us. The point will often arise, who has the affirmative." Per Dewey, J., Pond *v.* Gibson, 5 Allen, 20; overruling Emmons *v.* Haywood, 11 Cush. 48, so far as that case decides that the burden of proving a defence under the Statute of Limitations is upon the defendant.

In this connection, we may allude to the question which frequently arises, with reference to the comparative weight of positive and negative testimony. In a late case, in an action for damages occasioned by collision with cars at a crossing, positive evidence that the bell was rung and whistle sounded, was held entitled to more weight, than the negative evidence of those who testified that they did not hear the bell or whistle. Chicago, &c. *v.* Still, 19 Ill. 499.

allegation, must be affirmatively proved.[1] So where the plaintiff complained that the defendants, charterers of his ship, put on board a highly inflammable and dangerous article, without notice to the master or others in charge of the ship, whereby it was burned; held, the latter averment, though negative, must be affirmatively proved. The court remark: "That the declaration . . . imputes to the defendants a criminal negligence, cannot well be questioned. In order to make the putting on board wrongful, the defendants must be conusant of the dangerous quality of the article . . . and, if being so, they yet gave no notice, considering the probable danger thereby occasioned to the lives of those on board, it amounts to a species of delinquency . . . for which they are criminally liable."[2] So an allegation, that a theatre was not duly licensed; or goods not legally imported; or of non-compliance with the act of uniformity; or of not taking the sacrament; must be affirmatively proved.[3] So, in an action against an officer for false return, it is presumed in his favor to be true, and the plaintiff must prove it to be false, though negative.[4] So in a suit to recover double the value of goods distrained for rent, when no rent is due, under Indiana Rev. Sts. 1843, ch. 45, § 220, the averment that no rent was due is material, and, though negative, the burden is on the plaintiff to prove it.[5]

§ 2 *a*. And where the plaintiff has established a *primâ facie* case, the defendant is bound to meet it, though by proof of a negative. Thus, in an action for the infringement of a patent, the burden of proof is upon the defendant, to show that the patentee was not the inventor of what he patented.[6]

§ 3. In general, an allegation of wrong or illegality must be affirmatively proved. (*a*) Thus, in an action for injury arising

[1] Purcell *v.* Macnamara, 1 Camp. 199; Gibson *v.* Waterhouse, 4 Greenl. 226.

[2] Williams *v.* East, &c. 3 E. 192; per Ld. Ellenborough, C. J., ib. 200.

[3] Rodwell *v.* Redge, 1 C. & P. 220; Sissons *v.* Dixon, 5 B. & C. 758; Powell *v.* Milburn, 3 Wils. 355; Rex *v.* Hawkins, 10 E. 211.

[4] Clark *v.* Lyman, 10 Pick. 47; Boynton *v.* Willard, ib. 169.

[5] Smith *v.* Downing, 6 Ind. 374.

[6] Pitts *v.* Hall, 2 Blatch. Ct. 229.

(*a*) In a suit for tythes in the spiritual court, the defendant pleaded, that the plaintiff had not read the XXXIX. Articles; and the court put the defendant to prove it, though a negative. Whereupon he moved the court for a prohibition, which was denied; for in this case the law will presume that a person has read the Articles, for otherwise he is to lose his benefice; and when the law presumes the affirmative, then the negative is to be proved. Monke *v.* Butler, 1 Rol. Rep. 83; cited in 3 E. 199.

In the case of Central, &c. *v.* Butler, 2 Gray, 132, a distinction is made between the burden of proof and the weight of evi-

from an accident, evidence of the mere happening of the accident is not enough, without affirmative evidence of negligence, to prevent a nonsuit.[1] Even in an action against a railroad company for negligence, though the rule of liability is perhaps more strict than in ordinary cases, the occurrence of an injury, not necessarily importing negligence, if it be *primâ facie*, is not conclusive proof of such negligence.[2] Thus, in an action against a railroad company for killing cattle, the plaintiff should negative by proof that there was a public crossing where the killing occurred; and should show that the company was bound to fence at that point.[3] So, in an action against a railroad for injury to goods through its negligence; the plaintiff must prove, either directly or by circumstances, that they were in good condition when delivered to the defendants, not merely that they were injured when delivered by them. Though, in a case of connecting railroads, proof of condition of the goods on delivery to the first road is sufficient.[4]

§ 4. The same rule is applied in cases of alleged *fraud*. Thus, where an actual purchase, payment, and possession are shown on the part of a vendee, the burden of proof is on the party who seeks to impeach his title on the ground of fraud.[5] So where a defendant, seeking to avoid a deed of trust, avers in his answer, that it was made to hinder, delay, and defraud creditors, and therefore void, the burden of proof rests on him.[6] And the testimony of a single witness called to prove fraud, who testified as to a conversation in which he did not participate, when his attention was not requested or particularly attracted to it, should be received with caution, and subjected to severe scrutiny.[7] So where, by the terms of a building contract, if the contractor failed to comply therewith, the engineer might declare it forfeited; and, on the engineer's making such declaration, the contractor brought suit, alleging that it was wrongfully made: held, the proof of the allega-

[1] Hammack *v.* White, 8 Jur. (N. S.) 796.

[2] Bird *v.* Great N. R. Co. 4 Hurl. & Nor. 842; Robinson *v.* Fitchburg, &c. 7 Gray, 92.

[3] Ohio, &c. *v.* Taylor, 27 Ill. 207; Illinois, &c. *v.* Williams, ib. 48.

[4] Smith *v.* N. Y. &c. 43 Barb. 225.

[5] Salmon *v.* Orser, 5 Duer, 511; Martin *v.* Drumm, 12 La. An. 494; Lesseps *v.* Weeks, ib. 739.

[6] Hempstead *v.* Johnston, 18 Ark. 123.

[7] Hall *v.* Layton, 16 Tex. 262.

dence. The former remains on the party affirming a fact in support of his case, and does not change; the latter changes from one side to the other during the trial, according to the nature and strength of the proofs offered for or against the main fact to be established.

tion devolved upon him.[1] So, in an action to recover the price of intoxicating liquors, the burden of proof is upon the defendant to show that they were unlawfully sold. The court remark: "There is no legal presumption that the sale is unlawful, and there should hardly be, in favor of a defendant who has himself joined in the contract. As against the Commonwealth, the legisture have required that the defendant in a criminal prosecution shall prove the authority under which he acts, when charged with a violation of the statutes; but they have interposed no such obligation upon parties who seek the enforcement of contracts."[2] So, where goods are seized for an alleged forfeiture under the revenue laws, the seizure is presumed unlawful until proved lawful.[3] So where certain liquors, seized by an officer of the law, and held by him, a portion having been condemned as forfeited, were all illegally seized by another officer under a second warrant; held, in a suit against the latter, the burden was upon the former, to show the actual extent of his damages, taking into consideration the forfeiture of a part of the property.[4] So a party, complaining of a breach of official duty in the clerk of a court, must show every fact necessary to constitute such breach. Damages will not be presumed.[5] So every presumption is in favor of the regularity of the proceedings of probate courts, they being placed on the footing of superior courts, and, nothing appearing in the record to the contrary, an order of sale and conveyance of a slave belonging to minors will be presumed to have been authorized, on a sufficient showing, and for the benefit of the minors.[6] So, in Massachusetts, if the use of steam-engines and furnaces has been regulated by an order of the municipal authorities, duly made and recorded, under St. 1845, ch. 197; the burden is on a party, who complains of the works as a nuisance, to prove non-compliance with the terms of the order, or an unlawful or improper use of the works.[7]

§ 5. Upon a similar principle, the burden of proof is on the party claiming title by adverse possession against one showing a clear documentary title, and he must prove such possession beyond a reasonable doubt.[8] (*a*) Whenever the possession of one person is

[1] State *v.* McGinley, 4 Ind. 7.
[2] Wilson *v.* Melvin, 13 Gray, 73.
[3] Aitcheson *v.* Maddock, Peake, 162.
[4] Jones *v.* Fletcher, 41 Maine, 254.
[5] Craig *v.* Adair, 22 Geo. 373.
[6] Redmond *v.* Anderson, 18 Ark. 449.
[7] Call *v.* Allen, 1 Allen, 137.
[8] Rowland *v.* Updike, 4 Dutch. 101.

(*a*) Generally, a person who takes property from a mere temporary bailee must

shown to have once been in subordination to the title of another, it will not be adjudged afterwards adverse to such title, without clear and positive proof of its having distinctly become so.[1]

§ 6. It is a somewhat analogous rule, that he who avers a fact, in excuse of his own misfeasance, must prove it.[2]

§ 7. A party having the burden of proof is bound to prove each essential circumstance, in the same manner as if the whole issue had rested on it.[3] And the jury cannot find for the plaintiff on the ground of preponderance of evidence, unless the evidence is sufficient to prove, to their satisfaction, the truth of all the facts upon which the right to recover depends.[4]

§ 8. As we have seen (§ 1), "the general rule is, that things once proved to have existed in a particular state, are to be presumed to have continued in that state until the contrary is established by evidence either direct or presumptive."[5] But, if the plaintiff establishes a *primâ facie* case, the burden of proof is thereby shifted, and he is entitled to recover, unless his *primâ facie* case is destroyed by proof from the defendant.[6] Thus, in an action for slander, where the speaking of the words is admitted, the burden of proof is on the party offering evidence in justification or mitigation of damages, and he is entitled to open and close.[7] So where a machine sold is found not to work well, the burden of proof is upon the vendor to rebut the *primâ facie* presumption that the fault is in the machine, and not in the buyer and user.[8] So, where a railroad agent offered to pay for certain cattle killed, but the owner thought the offer too small, and brought a suit; held, the *onus* of disproving negligence was thereby put upon the railroad.[9] So the burden of showing probable cause or belief in a trespasser, that the land on which a trespass was committed belonged to him, is on the defendant, though it need not be set up in his plea or answer.[10] So, in a case often cited, memorable for its decisive promptness, and perhaps as striking an application of the maxim

1 Hood *v.* Hood, 2 Grant's Cas. 229.

2 Finn *v.* Wharf. Co. 7 Cal. 253.

3 Henderson *v.* State, 14 Tex. 503.

4 Duncan *v.* Watson, 28 Miss. 187.

5 Per Johnson, J., Smith *v.* N. Y., &c. 43 Barb. 228.

6 Ogletree *v.* State, 28 Ala. 693.

7 Gaul *v.* Fleming, 10 Ind. 253.

8 Parker *v.* Hendrie, 3 Clarke (Iowa), 263.

9 Georgia, &c. Co. *v.* Willis, 28 Geo. 317.

10 Walther *v.* Warner, 26 Mis. 143.

give it up to the owner, upon such proof as would suffice against the bailee. Pugh *v.* Calloway, 10 Ohio, (N. S.) 488.

"*omnia presumuntur contra spoliatorem,*" as can be found in the books; the plaintiff, a chimney-sweeper's boy, found a jewel and carried it to the defendant's shop (who was a goldsmith) to know what it was, and delivered it into the hands of the apprentice, who, under pretence of weighing it, took out the stones, and calling the master to let him know it came to three half-pence, the master offered the boy the money, who refused to take it, and insisted to have the thing again; whereupon the apprentice delivered him back the socket without the stones. In trover against the master, as to the value of the jewel, several of the trade were examined to prove what a jewel of the finest water that would fit the socket would be worth; and the Chief Justice (Lord Parker) directed the jury, that unless the defendant did produce the jewel, and show it not to be of the finest water, they should presume the strongest against him, and make the value of the best jewels the measure of their damages; which they accordingly did.[1] So every imprisonment of a man is *primâ facie* a trespass; and, in an action to recover damages therefor, if the imprisonment is proved or admitted, the burden of justifying it is on the defendant.[2] So, in trespass brought by the owner of land against a railroad corporation, the plaintiff having proved his title, the entry of the defendants, and construction of the road upon the land; they are bound to prove that the land is covered by their authorized location of the road.[3] So, in the case of common carriers by water, when the damage is established, the burden lies upon them to show, that it was occasioned by one of the perils from which they are exempted in the contract of shipment or bill of lading.[4] So, in a suit against an administrator for a sum of money deposited with his intestate, proof that, at the time of his death, the deceased had in his house a bag in which was a purse containing the exact sum claimed, both labelled in the handwriting of the deceased, with the name of the plaintiff, and that it was delivered to the administrator, makes a *primâ facie* case for the plaintiff.[5] So, in an action against an assessor for imprisonment for non-payment of a school-district tax, claimed to be illegal for want of legal districts; the arrest being admitted or proved, the burden is on the defendant to prove a legal districting

[1] Armory *v.* Delamirie, 1 Str. 505.

[2] Per Metcalf, J., Bassett *v.* Porter, 10 Cush. 429.

[3] Hazen *v.* Boston, &c. 2 Gray, 574.

[4] Steamer Niagara *v.* Cordes, 21 How. 7.

[5] Grimes *v.* Booth, 19 Ark. 224.

of the whole town by territorial limits; and this, although *de facto* districts had existed more than forty years, and a lost town-record book contained a record of such districting; it not appearing that such record was made after the statute which required territorial districts.[1] So, in a suit by a creditor, to follow the assets of an estate, against one standing in a confidential relation to an intemperate executor; the defendant must prove a fair purchase and payment of the price.[2] So, in an action against a surveyor of highways for trespassing on a close bounded "westerly by the road;" although the plaintiff proves that he owned and occupied a close, in other respects corresponding to the declaration, the defendant is not bound to prove that the *locus* of the trespass was part of the highway. The burden of proof throughout is on the plaintiff. A highway duly located being shown along the same general line, the word *road*, as a generic term, is to be construed *highway*.[3] So under a declaration, alleging that the defendants are a corporation owning a railroad, and the plaintiff was a passenger thereon, and the defendants, by their agents, assaulted him and expelled him from their cars; if the assault is proved, the burden of justifying it rests upon the defendants, as in ordinary cases. "The case set forth . . . is nothing more than an action for an assault and battery upon the person of the plaintiff while he was a passenger, or occupying a place in the cars. It does not present the question as it would have arisen, if the declaration had alleged that the plaintiff was a passenger . . . having a legal right to be carried therein from, &c., . . . and the defendants, by force . . . deprived him of the enjoyment of this legal right. In such case the burden might have been on the plaintiff to show . . . his legal right."[4] So to a declaration, for that the defendant debauched and carnally knew the plaintiff's wife, the defendant pleaded not guilty. Held, that under this plea it was not necessary for the plaintiff to prove that the female debauched was his wife.[5] (*a*) So, in an action for slander, the

[1] Bassett *v.* Porter, 10 Cush. 418. See Dickinson *v.* Billings, 4 Gray, 42.

[2] Barnawell *v.* Threadgill, 3 Jones, 50.

[3] Holbrook *v.* McBride, 4 Gray, 215.

[4] St. John *v.* Eastern R. Co. 1 Allen, 544; per Dewey, J., ib. 545.

[5] 7 Ell. & B. 628.

(*a*) In reply to the argument, that, if the person debauched be not the wife of the plaintiff, no wrong is done to him; Crompton, J., said: "It might as well be said that, if the horse converted be not the plaintiff's horse, no wrong is done to him."

answer averred among other things, that the cause of action did not accrue within two years next before the suing out of the plaintiff's writ, and issue was joined thereon. Held, the burden of proof was on the plaintiff to prove that the words were spoken within the two years.[1] So, if the owners of a privilege in surplus water bring a bill in equity, praying for relief by injunction and otherwise, for the disturbance of it by the owners of the prior privileges, the burden of proof is on the plaintiffs to show that their rights have been invaded, although, since they acquired their privilege, the defendants have lawfully changed the places and manner of using the water to which they are entitled in priority to the plaintiffs.[2]

§ 8 *a*. It may be added, as a further modification of the general rule relating to the burden of proof, in the words of the court reported in a recent case: "The general rule undoubtedly is, that the burthen of proof is always upon the party who asserts the existence of any fact which infers legal responsibility. But the exception is equally well established, that the *onus probandi* lies upon the party who is interested to support his case by a particular fact which lies more particularly within his knowledge."[3]

§ 9. In an action for a personal injury arising from alleged negligence of a corporation, the court may order a nonsuit, though there is some evidence from which negligence may be inferred, unless there be evidence on which a jury might reasonably and properly conclude that there was negligence.[4]

§ 10. The rules of law relating to the burden of proof are of course closely connected with those pertaining to *presumption; burden of proof* meaning the evidence necessary to overcome an antecedent presumption. (*a*)

[1] Pond *v.* Gibson, 5 Allen, 19.
[2] Pratt *v.* Lamson, 6 ib. 457.
[3] Smith *v.* N. Y., &c. 35 Barb. 225.
[4] Beaulieu *v.* Portland Co. 48 Maine, 291.

And Lord Campbell, C. J., upon the same point, remarks: "Not guilty, pleaded to such a count (for conversion) does not put in issue the fact that the goods were the goods of the plaintiff, or in his possession, but merely denies the defendant's act." 7 Ell. & B. 628. This was under a rule that, in an action for violation of a private right, the defendant shall consider whether he will deny both the right and the violation of it, or only one of these.

(*a*) In trover, *possession* of the defendant is not presumptive evidence of ownership, as against the recent previous possession and ownership of the plaintiff. Weston *v.* Higgins, 40 Maine, 102.

Ownership of personal property, once proved, is presumed to continue until an alienation is shown;—merely parting with the possession is not conclusive evidence of a change of title. Possession, with the consent of the true owner, does not raise a

§ 11. The well-established maxim, "the law presumes every man innocent,"[1] though primarily applicable to the charge of *crime*, may still be regarded as, in general, equally true of private wrongs. Thus official acts done by an officer are, *primâ facie*, evidence of his authority to do them.[2] (See § 14.) So the return of an officer, "executed," raises a presumption that the process was rightly executed. Though, if the manner of the execution is set forth, its correctness may be examined by the court.[3] So it is to be presumed that a sale by an officer of the law, invested with authority to sell, was regularly conducted with the necessary preliminary formalities.[4] So the omission of wax, in sealing, by a public officer in another State, raises a presumption that such is the law or custom there.[5] So the return of an officer of the levy of an execution, and of the sale of personal property thereunder, stated that he "advertised the property as the law directs," and then proceeded to state the places where it was to be sold, and was sold. Held, the court would presume that the property was advertised at the same places where it was sold; and the return was held sufficient.[6]

§ 11 *a*. But where the consequences of an act are injurious, the act itself is sometimes presumed to be wrongful. Thus the fact, that a blast injured a house near by, raises a presumption that it was not properly covered.[7]

§ 12. The point of *reasonable doubt*, as sufficient to justify ac-

[1] Greenl. Ev. 37, § 34.
[2] Shelbyville *v.* Shelbyville, 1 Met. (Ky.) 54.
[3] Case *v.* Colston, ib. 145.
[4] Vincent *v.* Eaves, ib. 247.
[5] Roberts *v.* Pillow, 1 Hemp. 624.
[6] Drake *v.* Mooney, 31 Verm. 617.
[7] Ulrich *v.* McCabe, 1 Hilt. 251.

legal presumption of title against such owner. Magee *v.* Scott, 9 Cush. 148.

But, on the other hand, the possession of personal property is *primâ facie* evidence of title. Thus the possession of persons claiming to be owners of a vessel is, in all cases, presumptive evidence of their ownership; and it is only when the title is rendered doubtful by contradictory proof, that production of the register is necessary. Fish *v.* Skut, 21 Barb. 333; Stacy *v.* Graham, 3 Duer, 444; Bailey *v.* New World, 2 Cal. 370.

And a prior possession, which has not been legally devested, is sufficient *primâ facie* evidence of title, against a defendant who has proved no title. Clifton *v.* Lilley, 12 Tex. 130.

The *primâ facie* evidence of ownership, arising from possession, is not overcome by the bare assertion of the possessor that the thing belonged to another. Roberts *v.* Haskell, 20 Ill. 59.

Twenty years' possession of land, under a deed from an administrator, raises a conclusive presumption that all the legal formalities of the sale were observed. Winkley *v.* Kaime, 32 N. H. 268.

In favor of long possession, almost every variety of written evidence will be presumed, the defective links in the chain of title will be supplied by presumption, and the title declared perfect. Nixon *v.* Carco, 28 Miss. 414.

quittal in criminal prosecutions, is sometimes raised in civil actions for tort or wrong.

§ 13. In *trover*, for goods stolen, it is not necessary to prove the guilt of the defendant beyond a reasonable doubt, but the jury is to give a verdict according to the weight of evidence, as in other civil cases.[1] (*a*) So, in an action of trespass for shooting a horse, there is no presumption of innocence on the part of the defendant, and the plaintiff is not bound to prove his liability beyond a reasonable doubt.[2]

§ 14. Where the evidence, as to the exercise of care by an officer, is evenly balanced, the presumption is that he has done his duty.[3] (See § 11.)

§ 15. Where it appeared from the evidence on the part of the plaintiff, that he testified as a witness on the trial in which the false testimony was said to have been given by him, but there was no express evidence that he was *sworn;* held, the former fact tended to prove the latter, and in the absence of evidence to the contrary was sufficient proof of it.[4] (*b*)

[1] Sinclair *v.* Jackson, 47 Maine, 102.
[2] Wells *v.* Head, 17 Ill. 204.
[3] Mills *v.* Gilbreth, 47 Maine, 320.
[4] Cass *v.* Anderson, 33 Verm. 182.

(*a*) In the recent case which settles this point, the court give the following abstract of other authorities, and recognize a distinction somewhat nice and technical, but probably well founded:

"In cases of insurance, it is said, in 2d Greenl. Ev. 408, when the defence is, that the property was wilfully burned by the plaintiff himself, the crime must be as fully and satisfactorily proved to the jury as would warrant them in finding him guilty on an indictment. . . . The same rule has been held to be the law in this State. . . . Butman *v.* Hobbs & Tr. 35 Maine, 227. But in Schmidt *v.* New York M. F. I. Co. 1 Gray, 529, which was an action on a policy . . . and where one of the grounds of defence was, 'that the fire was set by the plaintiff, and was his own fraudulent and wilful act,' the judge was requested to instruct the jury, that the defendants must satisfy them, beyond a reasonable doubt, that the plaintiff purposely set fire to the property . . . before they could find for the defendants. The judge declined so to instruct, and his ruling was sustained. In civil cases, when the rule contended for by the defendant is required, the criminal act must be so set out in the pleadings as to raise that distinct issue. . . . But when no such criminal act is raised by the pleadings, the jury are authorized to decide upon the preponderance of the evidence. 1 Greenl. Ev. 537; Schmidt *v.* Ins. Co. 1 Gray, 529. No such issue was presented by the pleadings in this case. Nor was it necessary that the jury should find that a larceny had been committed to entitle the plaintiff to a verdict. Though the taking might have been felonious, it was not necessarily so. The only issue . . . was one of conversion. . . . The fact that testimony was introduced tending to show that the defendant had committed a larceny . . . cannot change the result." Per Rice, J., 47 Maine, 107.

(*b*) The point in this case was the correctness of an instruction to the jury, that they not only *might*, but were *bound to*, infer one fact from proof of the other. The reasoning of the court might, perhaps, lead to results somewhat impracticable, and not strictly accordant with the established rules of evidence. "The fact that he testified tends to prove that he was sworn, and as the jury might find that fact from the evidence so tending to prove it, and as there was no evidence to the contrary, they were bound to find that fact as proved. . . . Such is the natural and legal inference, and jurors are not at liberty to disregard the necessary result of undisputed facts." Per Aldis, J., 33 Verm. 185.

§ 16. Evidence is sometimes admitted in *rebuttal*, which might not otherwise be strictly admissible.[1] Thus in an action against an officer, to recover the value of attached property which has been stolen, if evidence has been introduced to show that in particular instances his keeper was careless, in leaving the room in which the property was kept with the door unlocked, he may show, in reply, that it was the habit of the keeper to lock the door when about to leave the room. "The probability that the property was taken away when the door was open might certainly have been lessened by the evidence."[2] So, in an action for a personal injury, if the surgeon who attended the plaintiff testify, on cross-examination, that he should judge the plaintiff to have been a man of intemperate habits, and that injuries such as he had received would be aggravated by intemperance; the plaintiff may introduce the testimony of other surgeons as to the nature, severity, and ordinary duration of an injury such as the plaintiff had received. "If the defendants had a right to rely on the fact that the bad habits of the plaintiff aggravated the consequences of the injury . . . then the evidence of surgeons as to the effect of predisposing causes on similar injuries was clearly competent. If, on the other hand, a tortfeasor cannot avail himself of proof of the health or condition of the plaintiff at the time of the injury . . . then the evidence introduced by the plaintiff was irrelevant. And in either view its introduction worked no harm to the defendants."[3] So if, in an action for breaking and entering a shop and destroying articles therein, the plaintiff, while testifying in his own behalf, has volunteered the statement that no liquors were in the shop at the time; it is competent for the defendant to introduce evidence in reply, that liquors were found in the shop at the time of the alleged trespass, although the plaintiff disclaims seeking damages for their destruction.[4] So, when one party gives in evidence the statements of a deceased agent of a former owner in regard to a division line, it is competent for the other party to prove, by another witness, the declarations of the same man about the same thing; the court remarking, "it was not unfair to fight the adversary with his own weapons."[5] So where the plain-

[1] See Union, &c. *v.* Crary, 25 Cal. 507.

[2] Dorman *v.* Kane, 5 Allen, 38; per Metcalf, J., ib. 40.

[3] Linton *v.* Hurley, 14 Gray, 191; per Bigelow, J., ib. 192.

[4] Brown *v.* Perkins, 1 Allen, (Mass.) 89.

[5] O'Reilly *v.* Shadle, 33 Penn. 489; per Thompson, J., ib. 490.

tiff in an action of trespass produced a mortgage from F. to himself, in order to prove constructive possession, and the defendant replies that F. at that date had divested himself of all title by a previous mortgage to B.; the latter mortgage becomes admissible evidence.[1] So, in an action for personal property, where the defendants have, under the New York Code (§ 211), put in an "undertaking" requiring a return to them of the property; the undertaking is competent evidence for the plaintiff, as disproving the allegation in the answer, that the defendants did not detain the property; its weight being for the jury.[2] So, in an action against a railroad corporation, for damages sustained by the negligence of an engineer, who is alleged by the plaintiff to have been employed by the defendants at low wages because of his want of skill; the defendants may prove by their president that he employed him as a competent and safe engineer.[3] And, assuming that it is *primâ facie* evidence of negligence in a railway company that a train has got off the line, such evidence is entirely rebutted by proof that the accident arose from the wilful and wrongful act of a stranger.[4] So where, in an action for assault and carnal intercourse, the plaintiff is asked whether she had not held the same intercourse with others, and answers in the negative; the defendant may prove the contrary, in order to repel the charge of force.[5] So where the question was, whether one J. was making a reasonable and proper use of his land within the limits of a highway, in piling lumber there, and the plaintiff had introduced evidence that J. claimed a piece of land near by, not in the highway, on which he might have piled it; it was competent for the defendant to show that a part of such land was claimed by another person, or that he claimed a right of way over it to a building of his own, as tending to rebut the plaintiff's evidence.[6] So, in an action for infringement of a patent, the defendant contended that the plaintiff had abandoned his discovery, and urged, as proof of abandonment, the lapse of time between the granting of the patent and the commencement of the suit. Held, the plaintiff might show acts prosecuting or asserting his discovery; as the filing of drawings in the patent-office.[7]

1 Howe *v.* Farrar, 44 Maine, 233.
2 Black *v.* Foster, 28 Barb. 387.
3 Robinson *v.* Fitchburg, &c. 7 Gray, 92.
4 Latch *v.* Rumner, &c. 3 Hurl. & Nor. 930.
5 Watry *v.* Ferber, 18 Wis. 500.
6 Chamberlain *v.* Enfield, 43 N. H. 356.
7 Emerson *v.* Hogg, 2 Blatch. 1.

§ 17. But a newspaper advertisement, which furnished the occasion of a conversation testified to, but which neither formed part of, nor explained the conversation, is not admissible.[1] So possession of property is not a fact that entitles the party holding it to give his own declarations in evidence, either to establish his title, or to contradict the witnesses of the other side.[2] So, to rebut the inference of malice from statements made by the defendant of the plaintiff's difficulties with his wife, it is not competent for the defendant to prove, that "the plaintiff's wife had in fact complained of his abuse in connection with her leaving him at a certain time."[3] So, in an action of tort against a city for obstructing a stream by the erection of a bridge, to the injury of a mill, evidence that one of the then owners of the mill, at the hearing before the committee of the city council, objected to the construction of the bridge, as likely to obstruct the water, is inadmissible for the plaintiff; although the defendants have been allowed to show, upon cross-examination of the other owner, that he was one of that committee, and approved of the bridge.[4] So declarations of a defendant in an attachment suit cannot be explained, by others subsequent to the attachment.[5] So a witness, who has testified to the use of a way across a piece of land, cannot be contradicted, by proof that there was a nearer route over a public road which he might have used.[6]

[1] Bell *v.* Troy, 35 Ala. 184.
[2] Swindell *v.* Warden, 7 Jones, 575.
[3] Collins *v.* Stephenson, 8 Gray, 438.
[4] Sprague *v.* Worcester, 13 Gray, 193.
[5] Tucker *v.* Frederick, 28 Mis. 574
[6] Blake *v.* Everett, 1 Allen, 248.

CHAPTER II.

EVIDENCE OF OPINION, REPUTATION, CUSTOM, ETC.

§ 1. THE *opinions* of witnesses cannot ordinarily be received as evidence, unless they relate to matters of skill and science.[1]

§ 1 *a.* Upon a question of damages, evidence of opinion is not admissible, unless governed by some pecuniary standard or rule of law.[2] Thus the opinion of the plaintiff, testifying as a witness, is not sufficient evidence to sustain a judgment for trespass done upon his land by cattle and horses, where there is no other evidence of the amount of damage or by which it can be properly determined. The court, in reference to cases cited, in which opinions had been admitted as evidence, remark as follows: "Opinions in such a case are received *ex necessitate*, for the reason that the minute appearances upon which they depend cannot be so perfectly described as to enable a jury to draw a just conclusion from them. They are likened to opinions of witnesses which are receivable in proving handwriting, identity, and intoxication. . . . It would have been competent for the witness to state the quantity of hops, &c., . . . the fields would have produced in the year 1864, if the defendant's cattle had not trespassed upon them, and how much less each field would produce in consequence of the injury; . . . and to have followed up such statements with other facts until his final conclusions would approximately show the amount of damages, . . . or the witness could have been

[1] Spear *v.* Richardson, 34 N. H. 428; Rich *v.* Jones, 9 Cush. 329.

[2] Chamberlain *v.* Porter, 9 Min. 260.

confined . . . to a statement of the facts. . . . It would also have been proper . . . to state the market value . . . at the time of the trial, and the ordinary fluctuations in such values, between the times the trespasses were committed, and the times the crops would have been ready for market, if they had not been injured."[1] And in another recent case it is said, that the opinions of *experts* are admitted "in matters of skill, science, or trade . . . because the matter of inquiry is one on which the jury are not supposed in general to possess information sufficient to enable them to draw proper inferences from facts; and the witnesses, being persons of skill, whose business or profession leads them to an habitual application of principles to such facts, and to the weigh ing of such facts with reference to the results which they indicate, are able, by their opinions, to afford the jury the means of making a proper application of the facts."[2] When the subject of inquiry "so far partakes of the nature of science as to require a course of previous habit or study in order to attain the knowl edge of it, the opinion of witnesses acquainted with the subject of inquiry may be received." But not "when the inquiry is in rela tion to a subject-matter, the nature of which is such as not to require any peculiar habits of study in order to qualify a man to understand it."[3] And another distinction of equal importance, though relating to the *effect*, rather than the *competency*, of this kind of evidence, is forcibly expressed in a recent case, as follows "While the opinion of the experienced, skilful, and scientific witness, who has a competent knowledge of the facts involved in the case on which he speaks, affords essential aid to courts and juries, that of unskilful pretenders, quacks, and mountebanks, who, at times, assume the character of experts, not unfrequently serves to becloud and lead to erroneous conclusions."[4]

§ 1 *b*. Such evidence is not admissible, to prove that a rule of navigation, recognized by the general maritime law, does not exist in a particular locality.[5]

§ 1 *c*. And the opinions of witnesses will not be allowed to control the effect of the facts proved, which show that the plaintiff

1 Armstrong *v.* Smith, 44 Barb. 120; per Balcom, J., ib. 124.

2 Per Bosworth, J., Buffum *v.* N. Y. &c. 4 R. I. 223.

3 1 Smith, Lead. Cas. 286. See Com. *v.* Cooley, 6 Gray, 350; Keener *v.* State, 18 Geo. 194; Dawson *v.* Callaway, ib. 573; Redf. on Railw. 398, n.

4 Per Rice, J., Heald *v.* Thing, 45 Maine, 398.

5 The Clement, 2 Curt. 363.

has no cause of action, even so far as to require submission of the case to the jury. Thus the staircase, leading from a station of the defendants' railway, was about six feet in width, had a walk on each side, but no hand-rail; and, on the edge of each step, a strip of brass, originally roughened, but from constant use worn and slippery. The plaintiff, a frequent passenger, while ascending the stairs, slipped, fell, and was injured. Two persons testified that in their opinion the staircase was unsafe; and one of them, a builder, suggested that brass nosings were improper; that lead, being less slippery, would have been better; and that there should have been a hand-rail. Held, there was no evidence of negligence to go to the jury.[1]

§ 2. But a question to *experts* requires no particular form.[2]

§ 3. There is no class of cases, in which the competency and effect of opinion, as evidence, more frequently come in question, than those growing out of the taking of land by railroad corporations, counties, towns, and cities.[3] Upon this subject it is remarked in a late case: "If the true value of an estate immediately before and immediately after the location of a road over it could be accurately ascertained, such a discovery would afford the most exact means of determining what was the real pecuniary damage. The market value is a near and perhaps the closest approximation to it; and, therefore, any evidence which is competent in its general character to prove such value, is apposite and admissible. There can be no absolute standard by which the value of land or real estate can be measured; and, of course, when it cannot be tested by the fact of a recent sale, the nearest approach to it which can be attained is a knowledge of the opinion and judgment of intelligent practical men, who are best acquainted with the property."[4] And with regard to the general admissibility of mere opinions upon questions of value, it is remarked in a late case: "Questions of value are always more or less questions of opinion. They are always resorted to in actions for breach of warranty of soundness to test the value between a sound and an unsound animal; and so far as I know,

[1] Crafter *v.* Metropolitan, &c. (Eng.) Law Rep., 1 C. P. 300; Am. Law Rev. Oct. 1866, p. 147.

[2] Hunt *v.* Lowell, &c. 8 Allen, 169.

[3] See Brown *v.* Corey, 43 Penn. 495; Shaw *v.* Charlestown, 2 Gray, 107.

[4] Per Merrick, J., Dwight *v.* County, &c. 11 Cush. 203.

the rule is universal . . . after a proper foundation . . . by showing the acquaintance of the witness with this species of property.[1]"

§ 4. One who has been an assessor eighteen years may testify to the value of land and an easement connected therewith, taken for a railroad the first year of his official position, though prior to such taking he had no personal knowledge thereof.[2] So a witness may give his opinion as to the value of the land affected, both before and after the location.[3] So one residing and owning land within half a mile of the land, which he has known for six years, and who has heard of sales of land in the vicinity, may testify to his opinion of the value of the land taken.[4] So in a hearing to assess damages occasioned by laying out a highway, the opinion of competent witnesses, as to the comparative value of the land before and after the laying out, is admissible evidence, its weight and value being determined by the jury.[5] So a farmer, who has bought and sold other land, may be asked his opinion of the value of the land before and after the location of the way.[6] So on the hearing, before a jury, of a petition for the assessment of damages sustained by the taking of land for a highway, an expert in the value of land, who testifies that the laying out of the street was a benefit to the estate of the petitioner, may be asked by the respondents how much, in his opinion, it benefited the estate; how much more per foot the remaining land would be worth in consequence of such laying out; and what would be the difference per foot between the value of the land on the street, as laid out, sixty feet wide, and the value of the same land on a street forty feet wide, as proposed on a plan shown to the jury by the petitioner.[7]

§ 5. But the policy of admitting opinions as evidence, in this class of cases as well as others, is often seriously questioned. The remark is applied to them, made in an early case in Massachusetts: "Although the opinions of professional gentlemen, on facts submitted to them, have justly great weight attached to them, yet they are not to be received unless predicated upon facts testified to either by them or by others."[8] And in a recent

[1] Per Hogeboom, J., Van Deusen *v.* Young, 29 Barb. 20.

[2] Whitman *v.* Boston, &c. 7 Allen. 313.

[3] Cleveland, &c. *v.* Ball, 5 Ohio (N. S.), 568; Evansville, &c. *v.* Cochran, 10 Ind. 560.

[4] Russell *v.* Horn, &c. 4 Gray, 607.

[5] Dwight *v.* County, &c. 11 Cush. 201.

[6] West, &c. *v.* Chase, 5 Gray, 421. See Fowler *v.* County, &c. 6 Allen, 92; Shattuck *v.* Stoneham, &c. ib. 115; Flint *v.* Flint, ib. 34.

[7] Shaw *v.* Charlestown, 2 Gray, 107.

[8] Dickinson *v.* Barber, 9 Mass. 225.

case it is said: "Opinions are not evidence, according to the rule of the common law, except in a limited class of cases. In this country, a greater latitude is allowed in some of the States than in others, in permitting opinions to go to the jury, when accompanied by the facts on which they are based . . . In those States where the greatest latitude is allowed, very little weight is attached, however, to these opinions, unless supported, in the opinion of the jury, by the facts on which they are based. We do not see the propriety of admitting opinions of witnesses . . . in cases in which, from the nature of the subject, they may be deemed as capable as the witnesses of forming opinions."[1] Accordingly it is held, that the opinions of witnesses as to the value of land taken by a railroad company, the damage done to it by the location and construction of the road, or the benefits derived to other land of the claimant, not taken, when attempted to be set off against the damages, cannot be admitted, merely because such witnesses reside near, and are acquainted with the land, and the manner in which it is crossed; unless they are experts.[2] And where, under the Ohio statute of July 30, 1852, land was taken for constructing a railroad, it was held, that the opinions of witnesses as to the amount of damage sustained were not competent evidence.[3]

§ 6. In an action against a railroad for land damages, the plaintiff cannot inquire of a witness whether the roads crossing and recrossing the railroad rendered it more or less dangerous for horses, cattle, teams, &c. The question is immaterial.[4]

§ 7. A witness may testify as an expert to damage to land, though not a farmer, if acquainted with property and the value of lands in the neighborhood.[5] But in an action for damage caused by negligently burning brush, the opinions of witnesses, whether the day was a suitable one, are inadmissible: "There could be no difficulty . . . in the witnesses stating to the jury the position of the fires . . . their number and magnitude; the direction and course of the wind; the position, distance, and character of the plaintiff's property, and its exposure to injury from that source. The jurors, upon the question whether the defendant exercised proper care, could form as definite an opinion from the facts stated

[1] Per Bosworth, J., 4 R. I. 222.

[2] Buffum *v.* New York, &c. 4 R. I. 221.

[3] Cleveland, &c. *v.* Ball, 5 Ohio (N. S.), 568; Evansville, &c. *v.* Fitzpatrick, 10 Ind. 120; Same *v.* Stringer, ib. 551; Atlantic, &c. *v.* Campbell, 4 Ohio (N. S.), 583.

[4] Pinneo *v.* Lackawanna, &c. 43 Penn. 361.

[5] Van Deusen *v.* Young, 29 Barb. 9.

by the witnesses as the witnesses themselves. . . . The case should be tried and decided upon the opinion of jurors, and not . . . of witnesses."[1] So, in an action for damage done to the plaintiff's land by a fire negligently set by the defendant, it is not competent to ask a witness, from what he saw, how much damage the fire did. The question belongs to the jury.[2]

§ 8. The opinion of a land-surveyor, as to the true location of land in controversy, is not competent evidence.[3]

§ 9. A witness may testify who was in possession of the land in controversy at a time indicated, if he afterwards point out particular acts of possession.[4]

§ 10. Another class of cases, involving the competency of opinions, are those relating to injuries sustained upon highways and railroads from alleged neglect of the defendant corporation. "The running and management of railroad locomotives and trains is so far an art, outside of the experience and knowledge of ordinary jurors, as to render the opinions of persons acquainted with the running and management of such locomotives and trains, as experts, admissible and proper testimony."[5]

§ 11. In a suit against a town for injury sustained by a defective highway, the opinion of a witness, as to the state of repair of the road between two and three months before the accident, is incompetent.[6]

§ 12. In an action against a railroad, for the killing of the plaintiff's horses by negligence in the running and management of a locomotive and train, the engineer, who saw the horses when they came upon the track, and has been engaged in running locomotives and trains for five years, is competent to testify, as an expert, in reference to their management, and to give an opinion whether, in view of the distance between the engine and the horses when the latter came upon the track, it was possible to avoid the injury. "If the witness had been a stranger to the actual facts, it would have been necessary to assume a state of facts. But . . . it is fairly presumable that he knew something of the distance between the engine and the horses when they

1 Fraser *v.* Tupper, 3 Wms. 409; per Isham, J., ib. 411.

2 Simons *v.* Monier, 29 Barb. 419.

3 Blumenthal *v.* Roll, 24 Mis. 113.

4 Jones *v.* Merrimack, &c. 11 Fost. 381.

5 Per Brinkerhoff, J., 11 Ohio (N. S.), 335.

6 Hutchinson *v.* Methuen, 1 Allen, 33.

came upon the track; the velocity and weight of the train; and the time and distance which would be required to check the progress of, or stop the train."[1] And the following statement of a witness was held admissible, as being an account of the actual condition of a road, not a mere opinion: "A bad place at the side of the road; there had been a culvert put across. The condition of it was bad. At the mouth of the culvert, it was a steep right down; a culvert that I thought a dangerous place."[2] But, in an action against a railroad, for an injury occasioned by their locomotive to a man delivering wood from a wagon by the side of their track, a witness cannot be asked his opinion, whether the only mode of approach by a wagon to the place of delivery was by way of the track.[3] And the following question and answer are inadmissible as to a defect in a road: "What cause or occasion he saw for the accident?" "Did not see any."[4]

§ 13. In an action against a railroad corporation, by a passenger, for a personal injury, after several experts, called by the plaintiff, have testified, upon a statement of the facts and circumstances of the accident, what, in their opinion, threw the cars from the track; the defendants may ask a machinist, connected for many years with railroads, and with the running of cars and engines upon them, and who was in the cars at the time, and saw all these facts and circumstances, "What, in your judgment, threw off the cars at the time of the accident?"[5]

§ 14. In an action for injury caused by sparks from an engine, a witness cannot be asked whether he considers it dangerous to usè a steam-dredge without a spark-catcher; it not being a question of science or skill, and not falling within the rule relating to evidence by experts, and being itself, in fact, the very "issue to be tried."[6]

§ 15. Other cases of opinion are those relating to bodily health and disease, as connected with the injury for which the suit is brought.

§ 16. A physician, who has attended a party as such, on his being assaulted and bruised, may, as an expert, testify as to the effect produced thereby upon his health and mind.[7]

[1] Bellefontaine, &c. v. Bailey, 11 Ohio (N. S.), 333; per Brinkerhoff, J., ib. 337.

[2] Lund v. Tyngsborough, 9 Cush. 36.

[3] Robinson v. Fitchburg, &c. 7 Gray, 92.

[4] Patterson v. Colebrook, 9 Fost. 94.

[5] Seaver v. Boston, &c. 14 Gray, 466.

[6] Teall v. Barton, 40 Barb. 137.

[7] Anthony v. Smith, 4 Bosw. 503.

§ 17. Medical works, admitted or proved to be standard with the profession, are held admissible as evidence, with proper explanation of technicalities or phrases not generally understood.[1]

§ 18. The opinion of a witness, not shown to have any peculiar skill or knowledge in such a case, that a wound which he saw inflicted upon a horse was sufficient to cause his death, is not competent evidence.[2]

§ 19. What constitutes unsoundness in a horse is a technical question. So whether a horse has a particular disease. And a witness, not an expert, cannot testify that a horse was or was not sound, or that he had or had not the heaves. But whether a horse appeared well and free from disease, in a general sense, is matter of common experience; and a witness, not an expert, may testify to that extent.[3]

§ 20. What is a cruel whipping, or what are the appearances of one, is not a question for experts. But witnesses of experience may testify what number of stripes a slave has in their judgment received, judging from the marks upon him; and the common practice of slave-owners in correcting their slaves may be shown.[4]

§ 21. In an action for injuries to the body, a person not a physician is competent to testify that it was necessary for a physician to attend a patient as long as he did in fact attend him. "Any person of intelligence is capable of judging of the necessity of medical advice and services. . . . When it comes to determine the nature or the effects of disease it is different. These are scientific questions." [5]

§ 22. Although the opinion of a physician as to the length of time a disease has existed, predicated upon present symptoms, is not equal to positive proof; yet, where he testifies to the existence of certain diseases from personal examination, and thence infers the length of time, it is a wrong instruction, that "the testimony of physicians is matter of opinion merely." [6]

§ 23. Opinions are sometimes offered in evidence *hypothetically*, or as predicated upon a supposed or assumed state of facts.

§ 24. Medical testimony is admissible, as to the personal injuries likely to be produced under a certain state of facts, the

[1] Stoudenmeir *v.* Williamson, 29 Ala. 558.

[2] Harris *v.* Panama, &c. 3 Bosw. 7.

[3] Spear *v.* Richardson, 34 N. H. 428. See Willis *v.* Quimby, 11 Fost. 485.

[4] Hall *v.* Goodson, 32 Ala. 295.

[5] Chicago, &c. *v.* George, 17 Ill. 170; per Walker, J., ib. 516.

[6] Bennett *v.* Fail, 26 Ala. 605.

precise facts being stated by the witness, and the question whether they were proved being also left to the jury.[1] So in trover for a manufactured article, which the defendant has declined to exhibit on the trial, a witness who testifies that he is not acquainted with its market value, but that he could form an opinion of the workmanship if he could see it, may be asked by the plaintiff his opinion of the value of the article, as described by other witnesses. The court remarked: "After it became manifest that it was the purpose of the defendant to conceal the articles, which were of rather a peculiar character" (being a double-barrelled gun, pistols, a gold watch and chain), "and especially after he had admitted them to be the plaintiff's; it was the right of the plaintiff to have such directions from the judge as would prevent the defendant from profiting by his own wrong in getting the property undervalued."[2] So an experienced grazier is a competent witness, on a hypothetical statement of certain disturbances and frightening of cattle, to testify as to the effect of such disturbances upon their fattening properties, though not, as matter of opinion, that the construction of a railroad through the pasture where they were feeding would disturb them; such opinion not falling within his peculiar qualification.[3] So, after evidence of the contents and value of certain trunks alleged to have been converted by the defendant, the testimony of experts may be received to prove the value of similar articles, although the particular goods have never been seen by such witnesses.[4] So, in an action on a policy of insurance, the defence was, that the vessel was unseaworthy. Evidence of the condition of the ship at that time having been given in the hearing of an expert; the defendant offered in evidence his opinion, that a ship in such condition could not be seaworthy; and the evidence was held to be competent. In answer to the suggestion, of the prejudice which might arise from asking the opinion of a witness, on a statement which might be false, Lord Ellenborough remarked, that "the prejudice might be removed by asking, in cross-examination, what the witness would think on the statement of facts contended for on the other side."[5] So, in a case for running down the plaintiff's ship, a nautical witness may be asked, whether, having heard the evidence, and admitting the facts

[1] Wendell *v.* Mayor, &c. 39 Barb. 329.

[2] Beecher *v.* Denniston, 13 Gray, 354; per Shaw, C. J.

[3] Baltimore, &c. *v.* Thompson, 10 Md. 76.

[4] Mish *v.* Wood, 34 Penn. 451.

[5] Beckwith *v.* Sydebotham, 1 Camp. 116.

proved by the plaintiff to be true, he is of opinion that the collision could have been avoided by proper care on the part of the defendant's servants.[1] But, in an action for running down the plaintiff's vessel, it is held, that an expert cannot be asked, whether, having heard the evidence, he thought the conduct of the captain of the defendant's vessel was right or not.[2] And experts must give their opinion on an ascertained or supposed state of facts, not upon reading depositions.[3]

§ 25. The following miscellaneous cases illustrate the admissibility of testimony derived from so-called *experts;* where, either the witness is claimed to be such from his general occupation, or his special familiarity with the case in controversy; or the report or statement of such party, though not a witness, is offered on the same ground.

§ 26. Engineers, who have taken the comparative levels of a fountain of water, and of certain agricultural drains laid in the same lot of land in which the fountain is situated, and have examined the character of the subsoil intervening between them, are, as experts, competent to testify to their opinion that the drains do not lessen the quantity of water in, or injuriously affect, the fountain, giving the facts upon which their opinion is founded. A well-digger, who, from the exercise of his business in the vicinity, has become acquainted with the character and qualities in that respect of the intervening subsoil, is, for the same reason, competent to testify to his opinion, whether a given thickness of such intervening subsoil, if undisturbed, is impervious to water. And a farmer and a gardener, who have attended to and practised the draining of lands for the purpose of making them productive, are competent, as experts, to testify to their opinion, whether a certain piece of land, examined by and known to them, requires to be drained to fit it for cropping.[4]

§ 27. In an action for a nuisance, upon the question whether a privy and pig-sty, placed by the defendant near the dwelling-house of the plaintiff, are nuisances; witnesses who have examined the premises, and are acquainted by personal observation

[1] Fenwick *v.* Bell, 1 Cas. & Kir. 312 (47 E. C. L. 311).

[2] Sills *v.* Brown, 9 C. & P. 601. See Redf. on Railw. 398, n.

[3] The Clement, 2 Curt. 363.

[4] Buffum *v.* Harris, 5 R. I. 243.

with the effect upon the air in such cases, may testify, in connection with the facts, to their opinions founded on the facts, that the effluvia must necessarily render the house uncomfortable as a place of abode.[1] So evidence of opinion is admissible in relation to a trespass upon crops by cattle.[2]

§ 28. It is held that witnesses, acquainted with the *value* of personal property, may testify to their opinion of its value. The rule, that witnesses must state facts, and not opinions, has no application to such cases.[3] (See § 3.) Thus a witness, who testifies that he knows a particular stove, and is acquainted with the value of stoves, is qualified to testify to its value.[4] So, in replevin on a distress for rent in arrear at a share rent, a witness who examined the crop, to form an opinion as to quality, may give that opinion in evidence.[5] But, in a late case, the court rejected the opinion of a witness as to the value of horses.[6]

§ 29. Upon the question of reason to believe a debtor insolvent, a witness, though well acquainted with his business, cannot be asked whether, from his knowledge of the debtor, the business was or was not profitable.[7] But where a witness, in answer to the question, whether at a certain time A was able to pay his debts, answered, "No, so far as I know, I know he was not;" and went on to state facts in regard to A's property and liabilities, showing an intimate acquaintance with A's condition, and his utter insolvency: held, as the question did not call for a mere opinion, but, in form, for a fact, the witness was justified in stating such fact, and the evidence was competent.[8]

§ 30. A stock-raiser may testify to the extent of an injury received by cattle from falling through a wharf.[9]

§ 30 *a*. Individuals, who, by their personal observation, had acquired a knowledge of the character of a stream and of the dam erected thereon, were permitted to testify, whether in their opinion the dam was sufficiently strong to withstand the stream; not on the ground that they were technically experts, acquainted professionally with the force of water in streams, and the strength of dam required to resist it, but on the ground that, as practical and

[1] Kearney *v.* Farrell, 28 Conn. 317.
[2] Watry *v.* Hiltgen, 16 Wis. 516.
[3] Rogers *v.* Ackerman, 22 Barb. 134.
[4] Smith *v.* Hill, 22 Barb. 656.
[5] Townsend *v.* Bonwill, 5 Harring. 474.
[6] Low *v.* Connecticut, &c. 45 N. H. 370
[7] Bartlett *v.* Decreet, 4 Gray, 111.
[8] Thompson *v.* Hall, 45 Barb. 214.
[9] Polk *v.* Coffin, 9 Cal. 56.

observing men, having knowledge of facts which such men would observe and understand, their judgment and opinion in connection with the facts so observed were admissible. The court remarked, that to preclude them from giving their opinion would close an ordinary and important avenue to the truth.[1]

§ 31. A witness, though not an expert, may testify what *hard pan* is, and whether any was found in excavating; the questions not relating to a matter of science, art, or skill.[2]

§ 32. In an action against common carriers for delay in carrying a quantity of potatoes, whereby they were frozen; the opinion of a witness may be given in evidence, upon the question whether it was cold enough to freeze them in the cars or storehouse.[3]

§ 33. But a witness cannot estimate the injury inflicted by *flowage*, unless he be an expert.[4] So a witness, who had on two occasions examined cotton that had been under water, he did not know how long, is not an expert as to the injury which twelve to twenty-four hours' submersion would probably cause.[5]

§ 34. In an action for the burning of a dry-house and personal property, the plaintiff cannot offer the evidence of experts, to prove whether the placing of wet staves upon the outside of an arch, in which a fire is kindled, is a safe and prudent mode of drying them. It is a question depending on the degree of heat produced by the fire, a point of conflicting evidence; and a question which the common experience of the jury would enable them to determine.[6]

§ 35. A witness cannot state his opinion as to the amount of injury caused by an attachment, though he also state the facts within his own knowledge on which his opinion rests.[7]

§ 36. The opinions of innkeepers and others, that it is negligence to keep money in a locked trunk or portmanteau, are not admissible in evidence.[8]

§ 37. Upon a question as to the sufficiency of the number of officers and hands on a steamboat, at a particular time, to run her on a particular river, the judgment of ordinary persons, having an opportunity of personal observation, and of forming a correct opinion, and testifying to the facts derived from that observation,

[1] Porter *v.* The Pequonnoc, &c. 17 Conn. 249.
[2] Currier *v.* Boston, &c. 34 N. H. 498.
[3] Curtis *v.* Chicago, &c. 18 Wis. 312.
[4] Sinclair *v.* Roush, 14 Ind. 450.
[5] Weaver *v.* Alabama, &c. 35 Ala. 176.
[6] White *v.* Ballou, 8 Allen, 408.
[7] Clardy *v.* Callicoate, 24 Tex. 170.
[8] Taylor *v.* Monnot, 4 Duer, 116.

is admissible.[1] So in an action brought by the owner of a ship for damages arising from a collision, after the witness has testified concerning the position of the vessels and the character of the night, he may be asked, whether a vessel, on such a night and in such a place, could be seen at a considerable distance from a vessel approaching the shore; and, if so, how far?[2]

§ 38. A pilot who knows the place of a disaster, and one in charge of the boat at the time, may testify whether it was proper to suffer the latter to pilot the boat at the time and place of the accident.[3]

§ 39. Evidence of opinion as to the location of a railroad, founded on a line run and stakes set up, is inadmissible to show fraud in a release of a right of way, on the ground that the location was changed.[4]

§ 40. In an action against a railroad corporation for injuries occasioned by their locomotive engine to a traveller in the highway, at a place where the county commissioners had authorized the corporation, upon certain conditions, to cross upon a level; the record of the county commissioners, stating that in their opinion no flagman at the crossing was necessary, is not competent evidence of due care on the part of the corporation.[5]

§ 41. The report of a State fair committee upon agriculture, as to the value of a patented drill, is mere hearsay, and inadmissible.[6]

§ 42. The official valuation of assessors is incompetent evidence of the value of land in controversy.[7]

§ 43. In an action by a town against the owners of a dam, alleged to have broken away from insufficiency, the examination and report of persons, found by the jury to have been competent, made to the defendants before the breaking away of the dam, as to its condition and safety, is competent evidence for the defendants, as tending to show their care and prudence.[8]

§ 43 *a*. Somewhat analogous to evidence of opinion, as distinguished from facts, is that relating to *intention*. A striking application of the relaxed rule, in regard to the competency of parties to testify in their own favor, is found in a very late decision; that a plaintiff, charged with an intent to defraud his creditors, may

1 McCreary *v*. Turk, 29 Ala. 244.
2 Innis *v*. Steamboat Senator, 4 Cal. 5.
3 Hill *v*. Sturgeon, 28 Mis. 323.
4 Ohio, &c. *v*. Bath, 11 Ind. 538.
5 Shaw *v*. Boston, &c. 8 Gray, 45.
6 Gatling *v*. Newell, 9 Ind. 572.
7 Flint *v*. Flint, 6 Allen, 34.
8 Shrewsbury *v*. Smith, 12 Cush. 177.

himself testify to his own intention. "It was a matter concerning which he would have the means of positive knowledge, and the only question would be as to his veracity."[1]

§ 44. Frequent questions arise as to the competency of evidence concerning *reputation* and *character*.

§ 45. It is said that generally, in actions of tort, whenever the defendant is charged with fraud from mere circumstances, evidence of his general good character is admissible to repel it.[2]

§ 46. Evidence of bad character is also under some circumstances admissible. Thus evidence of the general bad character and unfitness of a servant of a corporation, if material to the issue, cannot be objected to, by reason of its tendency to prejudice the jury against the corporation, and to increase the damages against them.[3] So reputation as a negro-trader is evidence, on a question of selling a slave to be exported.[4]

§ 47. But it is held, in general, that evidence of character can be offered only when it is in issue, and with special reference to the nature of the question raised.[5] Thus character cannot be set up as a defence, unless directly in issue, and material to the question of damages — as in slander and seduction; even though the case is virtually one of alleged embezzlement.[6] And numerous cases are found in which such evidence has been rejected. Thus, in an action against the owner of a horse and cart, for the negligence of his servant, resulting in injuries to a horse belonging to the plaintiff; evidence of the general reputation of the servant as a reckless driver, or that he has been careless on other occasions, is inadmissible.[7] So in an action against a railroad corporation, to recover damages sustained by a person in a carriage on a highway, by means of collision with a locomotive engine of the defendants; the carelessness of the driver of the carriage cannot be proved by common reputation.[8] So evidence is inadmissible of the professional reputation of the physician, who was employed by the plaintiff to dress his wounds and effect a cure; though it would be competent to prove that the plaintiff's injuries were wholly or partially the

[1] Graves *v.* Graves, 45 N. H. 323; per Sargent, J., ib. 324; Hale *v.* Taylor, ib. 405.

[2] 1 Greenl. Ev. 123.

[3] Vicksburg, &c. *v.* Patten, 31 Miss. 156.

[4] Taylor *v.* Horsey, 5 Harring. 131.

[5] Church *v.* Drummond, 7 Ind. 17.

[6] Wright *v.* M'Kee, 37 Verm. 161.

[7] Jacobs *v.* Duke, 1 E. D. Smith, 271.

[8] Baldwin *v.* Western, &c. 4 Gray, 333

result of improper treatment on the part of the physician.[1] So evidence, that the general reputation of the plaintiff among his neighbors was that he was a tricky man, and would take liberties with paper in his hands, thereby altering its character, is not sufficient to prove that he had perpetrated a fraud on the defendant; nor is it, when followed by testimony showing that the note given in evidence had been altered, sufficient or admissible to prove forgery or alteration of the note by the plaintiff.[2] So, in a suit against an officer to recover goods attached, and which are claimed by the plaintiff to have been purchased from him by fraud, evidence of the good reputation, for honesty and moral worth, of the purchaser, who has testified in the case, is inadmissible.[3] So, in an action by the assignee of an insolvent debtor for property alleged to have been fraudulently conveyed, evidence is not admissible of the defendant's general reputation for honesty and integrity.[4]

§ 48. In an action against a railroad, the plaintiff having attempted to prove that a flagman employed by the company was a careless and intemperate person, the defendants may show, by persons who have seen his conduct, though not experts, that he was careful, attentive, and temperate.[5] And similar evidence is sometimes admitted, as responsive to the averments of the declaration. Thus, in a suit against an officer for "carelessly, negligently, wilfully, and corruptly" taking insufficient sureties in a replevin bond, evidence that he acted honestly and in good faith, believing the security taken to be sufficient.[6] But in an action against a steamboat for the loss of a horse by explosion of the boiler, alleged to be caused by racing; the good condition of the boiler, and good management of the boat, cannot be shown.[7]

§ 49. In an action to recover damages for an assault and battery, committed by the son of the owner of a house, upon one who had wrongfully intruded into the house, but, in compliance with orders given to him, had left and was going away; evidence is incompetent, in mitigation of damages, that the plaintiff was of bad repute in the community, and was accompanied by his paramour, who was also of bad repute in the community;

1 Thorne *v.* California, &c. 6 Cal. 232.
2 Martin *v.* Good, 14 Md. 398.
3 Atwood *v.* Dearborn, 1 Allen, 483.
4 Heywood *v.* Reed, 4 Gray, 574.
5 Gahagan *v.* Boston, &c. 1 Allen, 187.
6 Howe *v.* Mason, 12 Iowa, 202.
7 Agnew *v.* Steamer, &c. 27 Cal. 428.

although the plaintiff's counsel, in opening his case, and throughout the trial, has claimed damages, on the ground that the assault and battery were an indignity calculated to injure the plaintiff's standing and reputation in the community. Upon the points involved the court remarked as follows: "The fact that a man bears a bad character, or keeps company with persons of evil repute, furnishes no just provocation or palliation for doing violence to his person. He may forfeit the good opinion of his fellow-men, and become an object of pity and contempt, . . . but we know of no principle of law or ethics on which for such a cause impunity is to be granted to those who inflict injury upon another, or full indemnity is to be denied to a party for a violation of the sanctity of his person. The facts which took place in the house . . . had no such connection with the assault as to form part of the *res gestæ*. . . . The plaintiff had left the house. . . . The motive which led the defendant to order the plaintiff to leave the house was wholly immaterial. He had a right to give such an order, and the plaintiff was bound to obey it. . . . Counsel often make exaggerated and unfounded claims in behalf of their clients. These are to be corrected by countervailing statements, . . . and by proper instructions."[1]

§ 50. Somewhat analogous to character or reputation, is public *rumor* or *report*.

§ 51. In an action for killing a slave, after proof that the defendant shot some one in the night-time, near a particular spot, at a stated hour, and that the slave was found about that time, near the place, badly wounded with gunshot; it is competent to show, that there was no rumor or report in the neighborhood, that any other person had been shot about that time and near that place.[2] But, on a question whether a defendant had introduced slaves into the State for sale contrary to the statute, it is not admissible to show a general ignorance, among the public and the bar, of the existence of the statute, in order to prove that the defendant, a slave-trader, was ignorant of it, so as to show that his declarations were made in good faith, and not with intent to evade the statute.[3]

§ 52. To prove that a mortgage was taken without reasonable

[1] Bruce *v.* Priest, 5 Allen, 100; per Bigelow, C. J., ib. 102.

[2] Newby *v.* Jackson, 7 Jones, 351.

[3] Holman *v.* Murdock, 34 Miss. 275.

cause to believe the mortgagor insolvent, the mortgagee may show inquiries made of competent persons, and their replies thereto.[1] So a preferred creditor may prove, that he had no reasonable cause to believe the debtor insolvent, by his pecuniary standing among his neighbors, creditors, and all others having business with him.[2]

§ 53. Questions also arise as to evidence of *custom* and *usage*. Of course a party cannot, in general, set up his own habitual wrong or negligence as a justification of any particular act for which a suit is brought. But, in a late case, and in justification of this decision, the following important distinctions were laid down by the court: "It was not allowed, for the purpose of showing that the company exerted the same degree of diligence in this as they did in other like instances; nor was it ruled that they would be exonerated from responsibility on the occasion complained of, if they acted up to the standard which they had themselves established. If this had been the object of the evidence, it ought to have been rejected. But upon the more broad and general ground of exhibiting their system and plan of action, the means provided for conducting the great enterprise confided to their management, the evidence proposed seems to be peculiarly fit and appropriate, if, indeed, it is not to be regarded as absolutely indispensable. Without it, it is difficult to see how . . . the jury could determine . . . whether the defendants were supine and negligent, or acted with the vigor and efficiency demanded by the rule requiring the exercise of ordinary care and prudence."[3] Accordingly, in defence of an action against a gas company for injury occasioned by their neglect in repairing a leak in their pipes, evidence of their system and course of business in regard to complaints of such leaks was held admissible.[4]

§ 54. But evidence of a custom that shipping-masters act merely as owners' agents, and are not themselves responsible, is inadmissible, in an action against a shipping-master for neglect in notifying the plaintiff, who had shipped for a voyage, of the time of sailing, so that he lost his employment.[5] So when, in a suit against a railroad company for an injury received while passing along a

[1] Boardman *v.* Kibbee, 10 Cush. 545.

[2] Bartlett *v.* Decreet, 4 Gray, 111; Heywood *v.* Reed, ib. 574.

[3] Per Merrick, J., Holly *v.* Boston, &c. 8 Gray, 134.

[4] Ibid. 123.

[5] Maguire *v.* Woodside, 2 Hilt. 59.

highway, an issue is made upon the unreasonable or negligent conduct of the company in the use of the highway at the time complained of; its usage at other times has no legitimate bearing upon this issue; and evidence respecting such usage is incompetent.[1] So, in an action against a master for the excessive punishment of a scholar, evidence is not admissible in defence, that the defendant's ordinary management is mild and moderate.[2] Though it may be otherwise in regard to the question, whether the punishment was wanton and malicious. And upon this question it is competent to show that the same instrument of punishment was used in other schools in the vicinity.[3] So, in an action for shooting a colt, evidence that the colt was in the habit of trespassing on neighboring cornfields, when unsupported by further evidence, is not admissible, as showing, that the colt was shot by some person so trespassed on.[4]

§ 55. Character must be proved by evidence of general reputation, or general bad conduct, not by particular facts.[5] Thus character for care, skill, truth, &c., though growing out of the special acts of a party, cannot be established by proof of such acts, but only by evidence of general reputation. It is truly remarked: "Character grows out of special acts, but is not proved by them. Indeed, special acts do very often indicate frailties or vices that are altogether contrary to the character actually established, and sometimes the very frailties that may be proved against a man may have been regarded by him in so serious a light as to have produced great improvement. . . . Ordinary care implies occasional acts of carelessness, for all men are fallible in this respect, and the law demands only the ordinary."[6]

§ 56. In a suit in equity, to recover damages for a nuisance to buildings, arising from the unlawful erection and maintenance of steam-engines and furnaces, as well as for an injunction, evidence of the general character of the neighborhood, of the various kinds of business carried on there, and of the class of tenants by whom dwelling-houses in that vicinity are usually occupied, is competent upon the question of damages; but not that a particular insurance company had increased the rate of insurance on the houses.[7]

[1] Gahagan *v.* Boston, &c. 1 Allen, 187.
[2] Lander *v.* Seaver, 32 Verm. 114.
[3] Ibid.
[4] Dean *v.* Blackwell, 18 Ill. 336.
[5] Swift *v.* Dickerman, 31 Conn. 285.
[6] Frazier *v.* Pennsylvania, &c., 38 Penn. 104; per Lowrie, C. J., ib. 110.
[7] Call *v.* Allen, 1 Allen, 137.

§ 57. A right of way, claimed by prescription in a particular line, cannot be disproved by evidence that strangers were accustomed to cross the land in different courses.[1]

[1] Smith *v.* Lee, 14 Gray, 473.

CHAPTER III.

ADMISSIONS AND DECLARATIONS.

§ 1. THE *admissions* of a party to the suit against himself are competent evidence for the other party. (*a*) In general, the relation of the former to the subject of admission, at the time of making it, is held to determine the question of competency. Thus, the plaintiff sued the defendant for entering and digging a ditch upon his land. The defendant justified, on the ground that he only cleared out an ancient ditch, as he had a right to do, to drain his own land above the plaintiff's. The plaintiff formerly owned the defendant's land, and sold it to him; and A formerly owned the plaintiff's land. Held, declarations of the plaintiff to the defendant, while owner of the defendant's land, and while negotiating the sale of it to the defendant, and made, apparently, as an inducement to purchase, that he had a right to drain it over A's land, were admissible in evidence. It was properly left to the jury, whether he intended something which would pass by the conveyance.[1] So declarations of a party, as to his title to property in controversy, made in the pleadings in a prior suit between

[1] Stetson *v*. Howland, 2 Allen, 591.

(*a*) But in an action of trespass, by a minor, through his father as next friend, the father's declarations were excluded from the evidence, having been offered by the defendant. Hammer *v*. Pierce, 5 Har. 304.

him and another party, are admissible against him, not as an estoppel, but as evidence, in favor of a person not a party to that suit.[1]

§ 2. The effect of an admission, though in its terms direct and unqualified, may be controlled by proof of the circumstances under which it was made. (See § 4.) Thus, in an action for injury to a passenger on a railroad car, testimony, that at the time of the accident, and shortly afterwards, the plaintiff said the accident was attributable to his own fault; that if he had been in his seat it would not have occurred; is admissible, but not conclusive, the plaintiff at the time suffering severe bodily injuries, and not knowing the state of the road.[2] So, in an action for assault and battery, there being no direct evidence that the injury was caused by the defendant, two witnesses testified, that shortly after the injury they heard the plaintiff charge the defendant with causing it, and did not hear the defendant deny it. Two other witnesses testified, that about an hour before this they heard the same charge made by the plaintiff, and the defendant denied it. Held a correct instruction, that, if the plaintiff charged the defendant with having committed the assault, and he at the same time denied it, this furnished no evidence against him; but, if he remained silent, the jury might regard it as an admission, or give it such weight as they might think it entitled to; that the jury would not probably conclude that the defendant, after he had once emphatically denied the accusation, would be called upon to deny it again, if the accusation were repeated; but that it was left to the jury, under the rules which had been stated as to remaining silent, to give such weight to the defendant's silence, when the charge was repeated, as they thought it entitled to.[3]

§ 3. But, on the other hand, a mere implied admission may control the effect of *direct* testimony. Thus, to prove delivery of a lost trunk, the defendants adduced the deposition of the clerk of a steamer, running from Montgomery to New Orleans, where the trunk was directed, who stated that it was delivered, and a receipt taken, which was subsequently lost. The address of the trunk received was different from that alleged to have been delivered; and, in reply to numerous inquiries, the defendants said,

[1] Warfield *v.* Lindell, 30 Mis. 272.

[2] Zemp *v.* Wilmington, &c. 9 Rich. 84.

[3] Jewett *v.* Banning, 23 Barb. 13; 21 N. Y. (7 Smith), 27.

"We have written all along the line, and will get it to you as soon as possible." Held, that delivery was not proved.[1] So admissions by an innkeeper, of the loss of the goods of a guest, are sufficient evidence thereof to authorize proof of their value, though the innkeeper, called by the plaintiff, testifies that he made the admissions relying solely on the guest's statements.[2]

§ 3 *a*. Where the plaintiff has made an equivocal admission as to the identity of a prior invention with his own; the question of identity is for the jury, not for the court.[3]

§ 4. Implied admissions are liberally construed, with reference to their relevancy or pertinency to the point in question. (See § 2.) In trespass against a school-master for *excessive* punishment of a scholar, on account of misconduct out of school; it is competent to show, that, at a former trial, no such claim was made, but only that the master had no right to punish for such misconduct; as tending to prove that such claim on the then pending trial was unfounded.[4] So in an action of trespass against the officers of a school district, for the taking and sale of personal property in payment of a school-house tax, the defendants may offer in evidence a bond for the delivery of the property, executed by the plaintiff.[5] So a lease of a mill to A, containing stipulations as to the amount of water-power to be furnished to the lessee, and as to the height to which B, the defendant, shall have the right to raise another dam lower on the same stream, is admissible in evidence against the lessor, on the trial of a complaint for flowing occasioned by raising the dam too high.[6] But, that one threatened with a suit for slander gave money to another, to indemnify him against loss by such a suit, and took from him a bond to save him harmless, is not competent as an admission of guilt.[7] So evidence that the defendant, sued for instigating his slave to fire a building, some time previously, when purchasing a negro, had said, "I like these smart negroes; one or two more would steal me rich in a short time," is inadmissible.[8] So a letter addressed to a railroad corporation, claiming damages of them, and read at the meeting of their stockholders, who thereupon vote to lay it on the table, is

[1] Stadlacker *v*. Combs, 9 Rich. 193.
[2] Kitchens *v*. Robbins, 29 Geo. 713.
[3] Turrill *v*. The Michigan, &c. 1 Wall. 491.
[4] Lander *v*. Seaver, 32 Verm. 114.
[5] Higgins *v*. Reed, 8 Clarke (Iowa), 298.
[6] Nutting *v*. Page, 4 Gray, 581.
[7] Lucas *v*. Nichols, 7 Jones, 32.
[8] Bell *v*. Troy, 35 Ala. 184.

inadmissible in evidence against the corporation.[1] So in an action against a carrier for the loss of a sealed package, alleged to contain money; a receipt, "said to contain" so much money, is not even *primâ facie* evidence.[2]

§ 5. Admissions are held competent evidence, though relating to facts which appear by a written instrument. Thus, in replevin of goods distrained, held, the plaintiff's admissions as to the terms upon which he occupied were competent evidence, though he held under a written agreement, which was not produced.[3]

§ 6. Admissions are often objected to, as made in the course of an attempt at *compromise*. It is said, in a late case: "Peace is of such worth that a reasonable man may well be presumed to seek after it even at the cost of his strict right, and by an abatement from his just claim. The offer which a man makes to purchase it is to be taken, not as his judgment of what he should receive at the end of litigation, but what he is willing to receive and avoid it."[4] But the distinction is well established, between an offer of settlement itself, and an admission of independent facts, made in connection with such offer. Thus the selectmen of a town, in the course of conversation with a person claiming damages for an injury occasioned by a defect in a highway, with a view to a compromise, offered to pay for his loss of time and actual expenses, and asked him what they would amount to. Held, his statements in reply, of the amount of those items, if not made as offers upon which he was willing to settle, were admissible in evidence against him. But not an admission to a third person of the amount for which he had offered to compromise the action.[5] So in an action by a father for the seduction of his daughter, an agreement in writing between the defendant and the daughter, in which he admitted the seduction, and agreed to pay her a sum of money, and she released and discharged him from all actions of damages, and all claims, is admissible, not as showing the amount of damages or extent of injury, but as an admission of the facts necessary to make out the right of action.[6]

§ 7. A party's admission of record in a former proceeding is evidence against him. Thus the plea of *guilty* in a prosecution for the same assault.[7]

[1] Robinson *v.* Fitchburg, &c. 7 Gray, 92.

[2] Fitzgerald *v.* Adams, &c. 24 Ind. 447.

[3] Howard *v.* Smith, 3 Scott, N. 574.

[4] Per Thomas, J., 4 Gray, 567.

[5] Harrington *v.* Lincoln, ib. 563.

[6] Travis *v.* Barger, 24 Barb. 614.

[7] Birchard *v.* Booth, 4 Wis. 67.

§ 8. It is laid down, that "where the acts of the agent will bind the principal, his representations, declarations, and admissions, respecting the subject-matter, will also bind him, if made at the same time, and constituting part of the *res gestæ*."[1]

§ 9. The question whether mere admissions, independent of facts, are competent, sometimes arises in reference to corporations. Thus, in an action against a city for partial destruction of a vessel, occasioned by the action of health officers, while they were officially in charge of the vessel; the declarations of an alderman, relative to the detention of the vessel in quarantine, are not admissible in evidence against the city, where the alderman was not a member of, and did not represent, the board of health, nor the city government.[2] So the report of a committee, that a town way is unsafe, though duly accepted, is not evidence against the town in an action for injuries arising from a defect in the way.[3]

§ 10. In an action against a carrier for failing to deliver goods, evidence is competent, that his servant requested the person from whom he received them to make out a bill of the goods "said to have been lost."[4] So, in an action against a carrier, the answer of his coachman or driver, to an inquiry for the goods.[5] So, in an action against a railroad corporation by a passenger for the loss of his trunk, the admissions of the conductor, baggage-master, or station-master, as to the manner of the loss, made in answer to inquiries on behalf of the passenger the next morning after the loss. "It was part of the duty of those agents to deliver the baggage of passengers, and to account for the same, if missing, provided inquiries for it were made within a reasonable time."[6] So declarations by the captain of a steamer, as to damage to crops on shore by fire from the steamer, made while she was running under his command and the fire was being communicated, are admissible against the owners.[7] (*a*) But in an action against a rail-

[1] Story on Agency, § 134 *et seq.*; 1 Greenl. Ev. 191, § 113.

[2] Mitchell *v.* Rockland, 41 Maine, 363.

[3] Wheeler *v.* Framingham, 12 Cush. 287. Acc. Collins *v.* Dorchester, 6 Cush. 396.

[4] Ingledew *v.* Northern, &c. 7 Gray, 86.

[5] Mayhew *v.* Nelson, 6 C. & P. 58.

[6] Morse *v.* Connecticut, &c. 6 Gray, 450; per Bigelow, J., ib. 451.

[7] Gerke *v.* California, &c. 9 Cal. 251.

(*a*) Where suit is brought against a steamboat, and the master and his securities have been substituted as defendants in place of the boat, under the 9th section of the Missouri act concerning boats and vessels (R. C. 1845, p. 180), depositions and admissions of the master will be treated in the same way as if the suit had been originally instituted against him. Withers *v.* Steamboat, &c. 24 Mis. 204.

road corporation for damages sustained by the negligence of their engineer, his statements as to the accident, made a few days afterwards, are inadmissible against the corporation. So also of statements of their president to the plaintiff, that he thought the defendants would give him something, or pay him something.[1]

§ 10 *a*. Declarations, other than admissions by a party against his own interest, are in general incompetent evidence, being mere *hearsay*, and wanting the sanction of an oath and the test of cross-examination. The general rule of exclusion, however, does not apply to declarations *accompanying acts*, or making part of the *res gestæ*.[2]

§ 11. Perhaps the most frequent application of the general rule referred to is found in the case of declarations, by persons suffering under bodily injury or disease, made either to their physicians or others, with reference to their bodily or mental condition. (*a*) It is remarked in a late case: "This species of evidence was undoubtedly admitted originally and mainly because parties could not testify, but it is equally admissible now, though the necessity is less."[3] And, in another State, "If made to a physician, surgeon, or other medical attendant, they are of greater weight; but if made to any other person, they are not on that account rejected. They are received as indications or concomitants of the disease, malady, or injury, in some sort as going to elucidate and explain the condition of the person making them, and so part of the disease, malady, or injury itself."[4] Accordingly, the representations of a sick or injured person, as to the nature, symptoms, and effects of the disease or injury under which he is suffering at the time, are competent evidence of his condition.[5] Whenever the bodily or mental feelings of an individual,

[1] Robinson *v.* Fitchburg, &c. 7 Gray, 92.

[2] See Woodwell *v.* Brown, 44 Penn. 121; McLemore *v.* Pinkston, 31 Ala. 266; Hall *v.* Young, 37 N. H. 174.

[3] Per Poland, J., Kent *v.* Lincoln, 32 Verm. 598.

[4] Per Fowler, J., Howe *v.* Plainfield, 41 N. H. 136.

[5] Ibid. 135.

(*a*) In questions of insanity, it is held that the acts and *declarations* of the party, the condition of whose mind is the subject of investigation, may be given in evidence. A case of this nature is somewhat remarkable for the disagreement of eminent judges in seven successive hearings. Wright *v.* Tatham, 5 Clark & Fin. 670; 7 Ad. & Ell. 313.

A striking application of the general rule is found in a case, where, from necessity, the declarations of a slave were held admissible to show the effects of a blow upon his head, though in general he would not be a competent witness against a white man. Biles *v.* Holmes, 11 Ired. 16.

at a particular time, are material, the usual expressions of such feelings, made at the time, are admissible as evidence of such feelings. They are classed with natural evidence, as distinguished from personal evidence, and whether they were real or feigned, is for the jury to determine.[1] Thus one who has brought an action for personal injuries may prove, as tending to show their nature and extent, his own statements made, while suffering under such injuries, to an examining physician, in regard to his inability to move certain portions of his frame, and the pain produced by other motions, notwithstanding such examination was made after commencement of suit, and with a view to this testimony.[2] So in an action for assault and battery, the plaintiff may prove that, about two years after the assault, in which he was wounded in the breast, side, head, and neck, he lay down and complained that his head, neck, and back hurt him.[3] So in an action against a town, by husband and wife, for damages sustained by the wife, in consequence of a defect in the highway; her representations as to the nature, symptoms, and effects of the injury, made to her physician, are admissible and competent evidence tending to show her actual condition.[4]

§ 12. As already suggested, declarations of a sick person are competent, though not made to a physician.[5]

§ 13. The declarations of a physician, on leaving home and taking medicines with him, as to the person whom he is going to visit, are admissible as part of the *res gestæ*.[6]

§ 14. But declarations of this nature are confined to somewhat narrow limits. They are sometimes excluded upon the ground that "they tended to qualify no act done."[7] It is said to be well settled, that the declarations of a person, injured when no one else who can be a witness is present, are not evidence to show the manner in which the injury occurred, however nearly contemporaneous they may be with the injury itself.[8] Although a party's declarations as to his health are admissible evidence to some purposes in his own behalf, they must be restricted to his health at the time of speaking, and cannot be taken with relation to past

[1] Phillips *v.* Kelly, 29 Ala. 628.
[2] Kent *v.* Lincoln, 32 Verm. 591.
[3] 29 Ala. 628.
[4] Howe *v.* Plainfield, 41 N. H. 135.
[5] Wilkinson *v.* Moseley, 30 Ala. 562.
[6] Autauga, &c. *v.* Davis, 32 Ala. 703.
[7] Per Shaw, C. J., 5 Gray, 459. See Ford *v.* Haskell, 32 Conn. 489.
[8] Per Redfield, C. J., State *v.* Davidson, 30 Verm. 377.

matters.[1] Thus representations of a slave, made to a physician or other person, must be confined to the malady under which she is laboring. A representation, without any question, that she had become diseased after the plaintiff purchased her, and in consequence of ill-treatment, is not admissible.[2] So, in an action by an administrator, to recover property on the ground that a transfer made by A, the deceased, in his last sickness, was fraudulent, and that he was insane when he executed it; the plaintiff cannot give in evidence the declarations of A's wife, made to a creditor who called to see him in his last sickness, that his mind was affected by his disease.[3] Nor, where insanity is relied upon to avoid a sale, can a physician, who a short time before the sale had visited the party in consultation with his attending physician, testify to the declarations made to him at that time by either the wife, physician, or other attendant, as to previous symptoms or condition.[4] In the same case, with reference to the offer of the physician's opinion in evidence, founded upon the excluded declarations, Mr. Justice Rice remarks as follows: "While it excludes declarations . . . it receives . . . an *opinion*, based upon that incompetent testimony, thus attempting to elevate the stream above the fountain, to make a corrupt tree bring forth good fruit. The declarations of the nurse and wife may have been only mere inferences on their part, and on those inferences the doctor is desired to draw an inference, and this last inference, being called the *opinion of an expert*, is made to assume the character of competent and substantial evidence. . . . The opinion of medical men is evidence as to the state of a patient whom they have seen. . . . So where . . . they have heard the symptoms and particulars of his condition detailed by other witnesses. . . . We permit experts to testify as to the genuineness of handwriting by comparison, but . . . it must be admitted or *proved* that the specimen with which the comparison is made is genuine."[5]

§ 15. Declarations are often introduced, as part of the *res gestæ*, upon questions of *title to land*. Thus they are held admissible upon a question of *boundary*.[6] So the declaration of a public surveyor, when running a line, that he was running

[1] Hunt *v.* People, 3 Parker, 569.
[2] Nored *v.* Adams, 2 Head, 449.
[3] Kimball *v.* Currier, 5 Gray, 458.
[4] Heald *v.* Thing, 45 Maine, 392.
[5] Ibid. 395.
[6] George *v.* Thomas, 16 Tex. 74.

a division line.[1] Or, upon the question of title, the declarations of the purchaser at the time of purchase.[2] But evidence that the owner of a dam, when rebuilding it, gave instructions to mark the height of the old dam, and make the new one of the same height, is not admissible in his favor to show that it was so built. Such instructions had no tendency to explain the act done, which was a fact susceptible of direct proof. Moreover, the acts were disconnected from the instructions, and in point of time subsequent.[3] So declarations of the owner of land, since deceased, while standing on his land, are not competent evidence, in favor of a person claiming under him, to prove a right of way over adjoining land.[4] Mr. Justice Thomas thus enumerates the supposable cases in which such evidence might be competent; at the same time questioning the broad proposition on the subject laid down in 1 Greenl. on Evidence, § 109: "It is not evidence of the party under whom the defendant claims, tending to show an admission of the right of way in disparagement of his own title. It is not evidence of the plaintiff's grantor in disparagement of his title. It is not the declaration of one in possession of land or in the use of an easement, qualifying that possession or use. It is not the declaration of a party against his interest. It is not a declaration made by an owner of land now deceased, while on the land, and pointing to its boundaries, in relation to such boundaries. The declaration was accompanied by no act, which it qualified and gave character to; it was not of the *res gestæ*. It is not evidence of reputation. It is, on the other hand, but the naked declaration of the owner of land, standing on his own land, and in favor of himself and his estate, claiming an easement over land in the possession of another." [5]

§ 16. The rule of *res gestæ* is not unfrequently applied in connection with the *execution of legal process*. Thus an admission by a husband, while holding a slave, that it was a loan to the wife from her father, is evidence against a purchaser at an execution sale, under a judgment subsequently rendered against the husband.[6] So in an action by A against B, for taking his property in satisfaction of an execution against C, evidence of declarations of C, while acquiring the property as the agent of A, that he was

[1] George *v.* Thomas, 16 Tex. 74.
[2] Brush *v.* Blanchard, 19 Ill. 31.
[3] Nutting *v.* Page, 4 Gray, 581.
[4] Ware *v.* Brookhouse, 7 Gray, 454.
[5] Ibid. 455.
[6] Cole v. Varner, 31 Ala. 244.

purchasing it for himself, is admissible.[1] So what was said by a constable at the time of a levy, as to the fact of the levy, as corroborative of his return.[2] So in an action against a constable, for selling hogs of the plaintiff, as the property of A, the person in possession; the declaration of A, that the hogs belonged to the plaintiff, made before the levy; — as showing the character of the possession, and as against the defendant claiming under A.[3]

§ 17. As miscellaneous examples of the rule in question, it was held that the plaintiff, for the purpose of showing that the offensive smells from a privy and pig-sty were an annoyance to his family, might introduce evidence of complaints made by his wife, since dead, while *suffering* (upon which word, as used technically, particular stress was laid) from the offensive smells, and at a time when the smells were perceived by others.[4] So, in an action against a sheriff for the escape of one J. G. W., it was proved that J. G. W. was captain of the ship H., which was towed out to sea on a certain day, and that a person on board, who was addressed as "Capt. W.," replied thereto and acted as captain. This was held to be *primâ facie* evidence that W. left the country as captain of the H., upon which the case should have been left to the jury.[5] So, that a carrier by water, whose boat had stranded, telegraphed up the river to ascertain the stage of the water, may be proper evidence of diligence, and therefore its admission is not necessarily error.[6] So in an action by bailor against bailee for loss by negligence, the declarations of the latter, contemporaneous with the loss, are admissible in his favor, to show the nature of the loss.[7] So in an action for enticing away a servant, his declarations made at the time of leaving the master are admissible, as part of the *res gestæ*, to show the motive of his departure.[8]

§ 18. The admission or rejection of such evidence is not, however, discretionary in the particular case, but is governed by fixed principles of law.[9] The declarations of a third person, explanatory of contemporaneous acts, are not admissible, unless the acts are

[1] McNeely *v.* Hunton, 24 Mis. 281.
[2] Grandy *v.* McPherson, 7 Jones, 347.
[3] Sharp *v.* Miller, 3 Sneed, 42.
[4] Kearney *v.* Farrell, 28 Conn. 317.
[5] Jackson *v.* Orser, 2 Hilt. 99.
[6] Johnson *v.* Lightsey, 34 Ala. 169.
[7] 1 Greenl. Ev. 185, n.; Story, Bailm. § 339.
[8] Hadley *v.* Carter, 8 N. H. 40.
[9] Per Fletcher, J., Lund *v.* Tyngsborough, 9 Cush. 36.

themselves relevant and material,[1] independently of what was said; nor unless the declaration relates to those acts, and is explanatory of them.[2] And an offer of evidence of what was said by a party, accompanying his act, must be limited to what was said relative to or connected with the act, or it may be properly rejected.[3]

§ 19. In a late case it is remarked: "Two things must concur. 1. The facts themselves must be relevant and material, independently of what was said; and 2. The declaration must relate to those facts, and must be explanatory of them. So that if the declaration is material, but the act is important only as it furnished the occasion for making the statement; or if the act is not material without the declaration, and the only connection of the act with the case grows out of the declaration; or if the statement relates to a matter in no way connected with the act, except that it occurred at the same time, the evidence is not admissible." [4] And these rules were applied to the somewhat peculiar facts of the case. In order to show that A and B, two of the heirs of C, a former owner of the land in question, under whom all parties claimed, conveyed their interest in the estate of their father to D, under whom the defendant claimed; the defendant offered the following evidence. A witness, sixty-three years old, testified, that about the year 1804 or 1805 E, who married B, came to the house of F, where the witness lived, in the winter, with a lumber-box and two horses, and also went to the house of D, from which place he returned with his lumber-box filled with sugar, tea, and other necessaries for a family. In the evening he said to F, that he had been to all the heirs, and they had signed an acquittance of the land, desiring it might be sold, and the price applied to the support of their mother, and that he had got all his pay, a part in the articles, and the rest in money. In commenting upon this somewhat remarkable attempt to apply the doctrine of *res gestæ*, Mr. Justice Bell remarks: "Taking the whole statement of the witness, exclusive of the story told by Kimball, there is no act of any person, no fact of any kind, in the slightest degree material in the case. It was absolutely immaterial and irrelevant, that Moses Kimball came to Thompson's with a sleigh and horses, and

[1] Fail *v.* McArthur, 31 Ala. 26.

[2] Morrill *v.* Foster, 32 N. H. 358; S. C. 33 ib. 379.

[3] Wiggin *v.* Plumer, 11 Fost. 251.

[4] Per Bell, J., Morrill *v.* Foster, 32 N. H. 360.

went to Wheeler's, and came back with his sleigh filled with sugar, tea, and other necessaries for a family. However explanatory of those facts, and whatever elucidation or character might be given to them by the statements made by Kimball, those facts were inadmissible, because they had of themselves no bearing on the case."[1]

§ 20. And in a late case such declaration is held competent, "only when the thing done is equivocal, and it is necessary to render its meaning clear and expressive of a motive or object."[2] And the general rule was held not to render admissible the reason given by a pauper for not paying a tax.[3]

§ 21. As may be inferred from what has already been said, declarations, to be admissible as explanatory of acts or transactions, must generally be made at or about the same time at which the acts were done or the transactions occurred. They are not competent, if merely narrative, as in the familiar case, referred to by Mr. Justice Fletcher (in *Lund* v. *Tyngsborough*, 9 Cush. 36), where the holder of a check went into a bank, and when he came out said he had demanded payment. So declarations of a defendant in execution, while in possession of the chattels in controversy, and explanatory of this possession, are admissible evidence against the claimant; but not his declarations respecting the source of his title, as that he claimed them as a distributee of his father's estate.[4] So, in trover by A for a negro, carried by his wife to his son-in-law B's house, her declarations, while carrying, are inadmissible to rebut the presumption of a gift from three years' subsequent possession by B. So her declarations made several months after his possession commenced.[5] So where the question is the good faith of the sale of goods, whatever is said in the progress of the negotiations, and contemporaneous with the sale, and having a tendency to give a character to it, and which derives credit from it, is admissible. But not a recital of past transactions; as where the sale had been completed, and one of the parties, during the afternoon of the day of the sale, at another place, stated what had been done.[6] So an *agreement*

[1] Per Bell, J., Morrill *v.* Foster, 32 N. H. 360.

[2] Per Bigelow, J., Nutting *v.* Page, 4 Gray, 584. See Jacobs *v.* Whitcomb, 10 Cush. 255.

[3] North, &c. *v.* Stonington, 31 Conn. 412.

[4] Brice *v.* Lide, 30 Ala. 647.

[5] Raiford *v.* French, 11 Rich, 367.

[6] Banfield *v.* Parker, 36 N. H. 353.

cannot be proved by declarations accompanying an act, although they may be competent as to the subject or result of the agreement. Thus declarations of a wife, contemporaneous with the delivery of money to another person, that it was her separate property, are admissible evidence as a part of the *res gestæ;* but not her declarations that the money was the proceeds of her own labor, under an agreement with her husband that she might retain it.[1] So the declarations of a ticket-agent, made after the transaction of selling the ticket was closed, are not admissible.[2] Nor statements of a conductor, made after the malfeasance of the railroad complained of, and unauthorized by his principal.[3] So the declaration of a third person, not made at the time, is not admissible evidence of the motive for an act.[4]

§ 22. One party, in order to rebut the effect of his declarations and admissions, cannot show contrary declarations made at a different time, and in the absence of the other; although connected with certain acts and circumstances, which, of themselves, would not tend to prove the issue. Thus where it is sought to charge the defendant as a partner; after evidence of his admissions, it is not competent for him to prove by the same witness that at another time he denied the partnership, though in connection with the act of refusing to execute a lease of the store; nor a conversation concerning the parties to a writ made in the name of the firm, or the insolvency of the firm.[5]

§ 23. Declarations of a plaintiff in an action for an assault and battery, made at a distance of two or three hundred yards from the *place* of the assault, the interval of time not being fixed, are not admissible.[6]

§ 24. Questions often arise, as to the competency and effect of admissions or declarations made by one of several parties who are jointly interested in the subject-matter of suit. Upon this point it is the general rule, that, where several persons are proved to have combined together for the same illegal and fraudulent purpose, any act done by one, in pursuance of the original concerted plan, and with reference to the common object, is, in contemplation of law, the act of all; and any writings or verbal expressions, being

1 McLemore *v.* Pinkston, 31 Ala. 266.

2 Milwaukee, &c. *v.* Finney, 10 Wis. 388.

3 Griffin *v.* Montgomery, &c. 26 Geo. 111.

4 North, &c. *v.* Stonington, 31 Conn. 412.

5 Hunt *v.* Roylance, 11 Cush. 117.

6 Cherry *v.* McCall, 23 Geo. 193.

acts in themselves, or accompanying and explaining other acts, in furtherance of the common design, and so part of the *res gestæ*, which are brought home to one, are evidence against the others, if made and used in furtherance of the common purposes; but the joint conspiracy and common design must be proved.[1] So, in an action for conspiracy, proof of a division of the profits is sufficient evidence of combination, in the first instance, to render admissible the declarations of one conspirator against the rest.[2] So, in case of fraud, to render such declarations admissible, it is not necessary that the person making them should have been a party at the original concoction of the fraud, if he attempt subsequently to reap the benefit of it.[3] So, after proof of collusion between a debtor and one to whom he has conveyed property, conversations of the grantee with a third party, in the presence of the debtor, are admissible against the debtor to show fraudulent intent in the conveyance.[4] So where a sheriff, at a sale on execution, acts under the direction of two creditors, holding different executions, the instructions given to him by either, in presence of the other, are properly received in evidence, in a suit between them growing out of the sale.[5]

§ 25. But where no common object or motive is imputed, as in actions for negligence, the declaration or admission of one joint defendant is not evidence against the others.[6] "It is only acts and declarations of a conspirator in furtherance of the common design, or during the prosecution of it, that can affect his confederates."[7] Nor the declarations of one against others not present, made after the offence was committed, and merely a narration of a past transaction, and not made for the purpose of furthering the illegal or criminal design.[8] So in an action of trespass against a sheriff for selling the property of A, a non-resident, under an execution against B (which property was found in the possession of B, who claimed to hold it as the agent of A), the declarations of B are not admissible as evidence of fraud and collusion between him and A, without some evidence of a common purpose or design between them.[9] So the admissions of one defendant, as

[1] Page *v.* Parker, 40 N. H. 47; Lee *v.* Lamprey, 43 ib. 13; 37 Penn. 330.
[2] Kimmell *v.* Geeting, 2 Grant, 125.
[3] Peterson *v.* Speer, 29 Penn. 479.
[4] O'Neil *v.* Glover, 5 Gray, 144.
[5] Smith *v.* Hill, 22 Barb. 656.
[6] Daniels *v.* Potter, 1 M. & M. 501.
[7] Per Strong, J., Thomas *v.* Maddan, 50 Penn. 265.
[8] 30 Verm. 100.
[9] McDowell *v.* Bissell, 37 Penn. 164.

to his own illegal and improper conduct, should not be received in evidence, after his death, in an action for conspiracy, which is tried against his surviving co-defendants only.[1] And admissions of one tort-feasor are evidence against himself, but not against others joined in the same action, where the cause of action is the negligence of only one of the parties.[2] So the admissions of one of several *cestuis que trust* of real estate are inadmissible to defeat the title of their trustee.[3] So declarations of one of two defendants in an action of trover, made while in possession of the property, that the plaintiff formerly owned it, though admissible against himself, are not admissible against the other, to prove title in the plaintiff.[4]

§ 26. A party's own acts, declarations, or omissions, are not in general admissible in his favor. Thus a party sued for an alleged loan cannot show, that he made no entry in his books of the receipt of the money; or his own declarations, about the time of the alleged loan, as to the condition of his pecuniary obligations.[5] But the effect of an implied admission by acts may be qualified by accompanying declarations. Thus, where a steamer ran into a flat-boat, sunk it, picked up and carried forward a portion of the cargo, claimed salvage, and received a large sum of money; in an action against the steamer for the collision, the shipper may show that he paid the money, protesting that no salvage was due, and in order to get possession of the goods, and under a special agreement that the claim for salvage, damages, &c., was to be left to legal decision.[6]

§ 27. The declarations of parties are sometimes received in their own favor, when they accompany acts, or make part of the *res gestæ*.[7] Thus where two drovers, A and B, came to an inn together, and A told the hostler not to tie the horses, but he did tie them, and B's horse was strangled; held, in an action against the inn-keeper, such direction was admissible in evidence.[8] So in an action by a town against the owners of a dam, alleged to have broken away from insufficiency, the declarations of the defendants, when leaving home in a direction towards the dam,

[1] Gaunce *v.* Backhouse, 37 Penn. 350.
[2] De Benedetti *v.* Mauchin, 1 Hilt. 213.
[3] Pope *v.* Devereux, 5 Gray, 409.
[4] Edgerton *v.* Wolf, 6 Gray, 453.
[5] Douglass *v.* Mitchell, 35 Penn. 440.
[6] Weaver *v.* Alabama, &c. 35 Ala. 176.
[7] See Antoine, &c. *v.* Ridge, &c. 23 Cal. 219; Wadsworth *v.* Harrison, 14 Iowa, 272.
[8] Jones *v.* Hill, 26 Geo. 194.

that they were going to the dam to take care of it, are competent, as part of the *res gestæ*.[1]

§ 27 *a*. Upon this point the following distinctions are made: "The declarations of a party, giving character to and qualifying his acts, and deriving a credit from them, are admissible in favor of the party making them, as part of the *res gestæ*, when the acts themselves are material to the issue. . . . The fact was material, as being the foundation of the plaintiff's claim, constituting the service for which he seeks to recover compensation. . . . But it is not material in the sense that as evidence it would tend to establish the point in controversy in favor of one party or the other. The question at issue was, whether there had been a change in the location of the line of the road. The act of the plaintiff, in doing the work at the sand-hill, was equally consistent with the conflicting positions taken by the parties . . . whether in doing that work he was grading the original line or a new one."[2]

§ 28. Admissions sometimes operate by way of *estoppel*, rather precluding the party from setting up facts in his own favor, than constituting evidence of facts against him. Thus, where one assumes to act in an official character, this is an admission of his appointment or title to the office, so far as to render him liable for official misconduct or neglect.[3] So in an action for charging an attorney with swindling, and threatening to have him struck off the roll of attorneys; held, the threat imported an admission that he was an attorney.[4] So one, who has officiously meddled with the goods of a person recently deceased, is estopped to deny his own executorship, as against creditors.[5] So where the proprietors of a coach took up more passengers than were allowed by statute; in an action for an injury alleged to be thereby caused, held, this excess was conclusive proof of such allegation.[6] So where the plaintiff signed a railroad receipt for the carriage of goods, containing certain provisions, under the head of "conditions," which he did not read, nor know their terms; he was presumed to have known the effect of the paper, and was held bound by its con-

[1] Shrewsbury *v.* Smith, 12 Cush. 177.

[2] Per Sawyer, J., 34 N. H. 505.

[3] 1 Greenl. Ev. 298, 299.

[4] Cummin *v.* Smith, 2 S. & R. 440. But see Smith *v.* Taylor, 1 N. R. 196. See also, Wilson *v.* Carnegie, 1 Ad. & Ell 695.

[5] Reade's case, 5 Co. 33.

[6] Israel *v.* Clark, 4 Esp. 259.

ditions.[1] So where goods in possession of a debtor were attached as his property, though belonging to one, who received them from the sheriff for safe-keeping as the debtor's property, without notice of his own title, the debtor having at the time other attachable goods ; held, in an action by the sheriff, the bailee was estopped to claim the goods as his own.[2] So the defendants, brokers, instructed to effect insurance, falsely wrote in reply, that they had effected two policies. In trover against them for the policies, held, they were estopped to deny their own statement, and should be treated as themselves insurers.[3] So it is held that a sheriff is estopped from denying his own return that he had taken bail.[4]

§ 29. But, in general, there can be no admission by way of estoppel, unless other parties have acted upon the strength of such admission. Thus, in an action by a tenant for selling grain in the ground upon executions against the landlord; the defendant cannot rely, as an estoppel, upon declarations of the plaintiff as to the tenancy, made to third persons, there being no proof that the defendant acted upon, or was misled by, such declarations.[5] So, in *crim. con.*, an admission by the defendant that the woman was the wife of the plaintiff is not conclusive against him.[6]

§ 30. The acts and declarations of third persons, not in the party's presence, are not admissible against him.[7] Thus, the declarations of a physician with respect to the health of a slave.[8] So (in Iowa) in an action of trespass for killing a bull, it appeared that the defendant committed the act. The defendant then offered to prove, that A and B had told the witness, that the defendant had nothing to do with killing the bull; that they themselves had done the act; that A and B, at the time of the conversation, were leaving the State, in consequence thereof; that this conversation took place about the time the bull was killed; that B left the State previously to the trial before the justice, and A some tw months after the trial; that B was then dead, and A resided in the State of Illinois. Held, the evidence was incompetent.[9] But if

[1] Lewis *v.* Great, &c. 5 Hurl. & Nor. 867.

[2] Davey *v.* Field, 4 Met. 381.

[3] Harding *v.* Carter, 1 Greenl. Ev. 316; Park on Ins. 4.

[4] Simmons *v.* Bradford, 15 Mass. 82; Eaton *v.* Ogier, 2 Greenl. 46.

[5] Ream *v.* Harnish, 45 Penn. 376.

[6] Morris *v.* Miller, 4 Burr. 2057.

[7] Barker *v.* Coleman, 35 Ala. 221.

[8] Blackman *v.* Johnson, 35 Ala. 252.

[9] Ibbitson *v.* Brown, 5 Clarke (Iowa), 532.

the law prescribes a penalty for the failure of a certain class of persons to perform a duty; the fact of its omission by an individual, and that it was not complained of by the community where he resided, is admissible, on the question whether he belonged to that class or not.[1]

§ 31. The declarations of third persons as to possession are often offered in evidence.

§ 32. The declaration of a person, while in possession of a slave, to the effect that her father gave it to her, is not explanatory of possession, but relates to title.[2]

§ 33. The statements of one in possession of land are admissible evidence of the manner of possession.[3]

§ 34. In trover against the bailee of a sheriff, the declarations of his bailor, tending to show a conversion made after suit brought, are not admissible evidence against him.[4]

§ 35. Questions often arise, as to the declarations of persons in some way connected with a party, in reference to the subject-matter of the suit.

§ 36. In an action by a minor, through his father as next friend, the father's declarations were excluded.[5]

§ 37. The declarations and admissions of a slave, made at the time of his arrest as a runaway, are not competent evidence for the party making the arrest, in an action against the owner to recover the statutory penalty;[6] nor can confessions of a slave, that he had committed wrongful acts, be heard as evidence against the master.[7] But declarations of a mother and guardian, as to the right to certain property claimed by her minor children, made when she was a *feme sole*, are competent evidence against her husband after her death.[8] So the declarations of an intestate, that certain slaves were held by him as trustee for his wife, and not as her husband, are admissible in evidence against his administrator, in a suit brought by him aga nst the wife for the slaves.[9]

§ 38. Where the defendant, in an action of trover, relies on paramount title outstanding in A, the admissions and declarations of A, disclaiming title, are admissible in behalf of the plaintiff.[10]

1 Bryan *v.* Walton, 20 Geo. 480.
2 Allen *v.* Prater, 30 Ala. 458.
3 Young *v.* Adams, 14 B. Mon. 127.
4 Spencer *v.* Godwin, 30 Ala. 355.
5 Hammer *v.* Pierce, 5 Harring. 304.
6 Thorpe *v.* Burroughs, 31 Ala. 159.
7 Doty *v.* Moore, 16 Tex. 591.
8 Brush *v.* Blanchard, 19 Ill. 31.
9 Lide *v.* Lide, 32 Ala. 449.
10 White *v.* Dinkins, 19 Geo. 285.

§ 39. Declarations are often offered in evidence to prove or disprove alleged *fraud.*

§ 40. Statements by a vendor, made after a sale and conveyance to a creditor, concerning his indebtedness to the vendee before the sale, and in the absence of the vendee, are not competent, in a suit by other creditors, to prove the conveyance fraudulent.[1] (*a*) A grantee is not to be bound, as to the fraudulent nature of the transaction, by the declarations of the grantor, until shown *aliunde* to be cognizant of, or implicated in, the fraud.[2] But to prove an assignment for the benefit of creditors fraudulent, it is competent to show the declarations of the assignor, made after the assignment was delivered, but before the schedules were made out and attached, and while the assignor was engaged in preparing them.[3]

§ 41. To show that the sale of a stock was made in the regular course of legitimate business, *bonâ fide*, and not in fraud of creditors, it is competent to prove previous declarations of the seller to the witness of his desire to sell out.[4]

§ 42. An insolvent debtor's statement of the terms of a previous agreement, under which certain machinery was put into the building of another, are inadmissible, to show that a subsequent sale of the machinery to the owner of the building was made in good faith.[5] So the statements of an insolvent debtor, whether made before or after a sale alleged to be fraudulent, as to the value of the property, and of his other property, are inadmissible against his assignee in insolvency, to show that the sale was in good faith.[6]

§ 43. Where it is stipulated, in a deed of trust, that the grantor may remain in possession until the debt secured shall become due, when, if not paid, the trustee shall have the right to take possession and sell; and the grantor continues in possession, and sells the goods conveyed in the usual course of business: in a suit by attachment against the grantor by a creditor, on the

[1] Short *v.* Tinsley, 1 Met. (Ky.) 397.
[2] Ewing *v.* Gray, 12 Ind. 64.
[3] Wyckoff *v.* Carr, 8 Mich. 44.
[4] Heywood *v.* Reed, 4 Gray, 574.
[5] Ibid.
[6] Ibid.

(*a*) In late cases the distinction is made, that, in favor of an execution creditor, the declarations of a vendor are competent to prove fraud against himself, and also against the vendee, if made before completion of the sale, or if the vendee had notice of the fraudulent intention. Gallagher *v.* Williamson, 23 Cal. 331; Gregory *v.* Frothingham, 1 Neva. 253.

ground of a fraudulent conveyance, the declaration of the *cestui que trust*, he not being a party to the suit, and a competent witness for either of the parties, made in the absence of the grantor, that the grantor had a right to sell the goods conveyed in the deed in the ordinary course of business, is inadmissible.[1]

§ 44. In an action brought by a purchaser of chattels against the sheriff, for seizing them under an execution in favor of a creditor of the vendor, upon the ground that the sale was merely colorable; to prove the good faith of the sale, the wife of the vendor cannot be asked, among other questions, "Did you hear anything said before you heard the sale talked of?"[2]

§ 44 *a*. Another subject, concerning which declarations are frequently offered, is that of *title to real property*.

§ 45. In an action by A, as owner, for overflowing lands at the time and for many years in the possession of B; the declarations of B, while in possession, are inadmissible for A, to prove that B was a tenant for life in right of his wife, and A the remainder-man.[3] So the declarations of a person deceased, made while living on land, that he had an estate in fee therein, are not admissible evidence for one claiming under him.[4] So, in ejectment, the admissions of an occupant are incompetent, unless there be some privity between him and the defendant; and even then, if he can be called as a witness.[5] So in an action for trespass on land, the declarations of a person, who formerly occupied it under a bond for a deed from the defendant, that he did not own the land, are inadmissible, if he has not been called as a witness, and no evidence introduced that he ever did own the land.[6] So it is incompetent for a defendant in ejectment to show, by the declarations of his ancestor, the circumstances of his previous possession; though he may thus show how and what he claimed at the time of his speaking.[7]

§ 46. But the declarations of an occupant under a bond for a deed are evidence of the boundaries of the land against a stranger, in favor of one who afterwards takes an assignment of the bond and a deed from the obligor.[8] So where an adverse possession of twenty years is claimed by the tenant, it is competent to show by contemporaneous declarations of those whose possession is relied

1 Reed *v.* Pelletier, 28 Mis. 173.
2 Salmon *v.* Orser, 5 Duer, 511.
3 Wardlaw *v.* Hammond, 9 Rich. 454.
4 Watson *v.* Bissell, 27 Mis. 220.
5 Hanley *v.* Erskine, 19 Ill. 265.
6 Niles *v.* Patch, 13 Gray, 254.
7 Hood *v.* Hood, 2 Grant, 229.
8 Niles *v.* Patch, 13 Gray, 254.

upon, and by their payment of rent to the demandant's predecessor, and, if the possession relied upon is traced through executors who held for the benefit of heirs, by the admissions of the heirs, that the possession was not adverse.[1] But such declarations must be *ante litem motam*.[2] So the declarations of one in possession of land, in disparagement of his own title, are admissible in evidence against him and those claiming under him ; though declarations in favor of his own title, or made after a sale, are inadmissible ;[3] upon the ground that such (former) declaration gives character to the possession.[4] So declarations of a former owner of land, made during his ownership, and tending to prove a right of way over it, are competent evidence against the present owner ; though those tending to disprove the right of way are incompetent in his favor.[5] So declarations of a grantor before the grant, to the effect that he had previously sold the land to another, are admissible against the grantee and all who claim under him.[6] So the declarations of one in relation to the boundary of land he once owned are held competent evidence.[7] (*a*)

§ 47. As we have already intimated, an *act* may generally be proved as an admission against the party doing such act.[8] Thus in an action brought for an assault, by one woman against another, the two living in different parts of the same house ; the defence being set up, of an accidental collision, evidence is competent for the plaintiff, that, although she was several days confined to her bed from the effects of the injury, and under the care of a physician, the defendant did not visit her, or show her any attention or sympathy.[9] And the acts of an agent will bind the principal. Thus a ship-owner may be held liable for all acts of the alleged master, done in the ordinary scope of his employment, by

[1] Hale *v.* Silloway, 1 Allen. 21.
[2] Leger *v.* Doyle, 11 Rich. 109.
[3] Osgood *v.* Coates, 1 Allen, 77 ; Canler *v.* Fite, 5 Jones, 424 ; Ferguson *v.* Staner, 33 Penn. 411.
[4] Fellows *v.* Fellows, 37 N. H. 75.
[5] Blake *v.* Everett, 1 Allen, 248.
[6] Dickerson *v.* Chrisman, 28 Mis. 134.
[7] Dawson *v.* Mills, 32 Penn. 302.
[8] Warner *v.* Scott, 41 Penn. 274. See Bradley *v.* Pike, 34 Verm. 215.
[9] State *v.* Alford, 31 Conn. 40.

(*a*) One boundary in a deed was described as running from a monument, "thence in said wall as it now stands," to another monument. The wall extended from each monument straight towards the other, but with an interval of several rods in the middle. Held, for the purpose of showing that a wooden fence, built circuitously across the interval, so as to include less land than a straight continuation of the wall would have included, was the true boundary, declarations as to the fence, made by the grantee upon the land soon after the delivery of the deed, and even nine years after, were admissible. Davis *v.* Sherman, 7 Gray, 291.

evidence of his having actual command of the ship.[1] So the acts of an agent, in perpetrating a fraud under instructions from his principal, are admissible against the principal.[2]

§ 48. The acts of a party are sometimes received in his own favor. Thus, in an action against a sheriff for carrying away the plaintiff's property as another's, it is competent for the plaintiff to show acts of ownership, and tending to prove possession.[3] So in an action by a consignee of goods against a carrier for failing to deliver them, the fact that the plaintiff, after the goods should have been delivered, made inquiries for them of the carrier, is admissible in evidence of the loss.[4] But, in an action for money lost at play by a clerk of the plaintiff, he cannot prove, that the clerk omitted to enter money collected for him in the clerk's collection-book, by such book.[5]

§ 49. In general, written documents, as mere declarations, are regarded as only hearsay, and on that ground inadmissible in evidence.

§ 50. In an action of trespass for placing rocks and rubbish on the plaintiff's land, the boundaries being in dispute; a photograph of the land, offered merely as a "chalk representation," and not verified by the oath of the artist, though other parties testify to its correctness, is not of course admissible in evidence, but its admission is a question of discretion.[6]

§ 51. A deed or bill of sale is competent evidence, though it does not show the identity between the property mentioned therein and that sued for; because the identity must be shown by other proof.[7]

§ 52. And different rules apply to documents of an official character, from those which govern the admission or exclusion of other writings. Thus, where a sheriff justifies the taking of personal property under a writ, the writ and return must be given in evidence; or, if it has not been returned, proof must be made that the property was taken under it.[8] So in an action of trespass for breaking a close and carrying off liquors, where the defence is justification under a warrant issued by a justice, under the act for prevention of the illegal sale of liquors, the record of the

[1] Story on Agency, § 116–123; 2 Greenl. Ev. 48, § 64.

[2] Lunday v. Thomas, 26 Geo. 537.

[3] Fitch v. Brockman, 3 Cal. 348.

[4] Ingledew v. Northern, &c. 7 Gray, 86.

[5] Comer v. Pendleton, 8 Md. 337.

[6] Hollenbeck v. Rowley, 8 Allen, 473.

[7] Sadler v. Anderson, 17 Tex. 245.

[8] Glascock v. Nave, 15 Ind. 457.

warrant and of the proceedings before the justice is competent evidence.[1] So in an action by the assignee of an insolvent debtor against an officer, to recover the value of property attached and sold by him on mesne process against the debtor, the defendant, after proving a demand upon him for the property by a mortgagee thereof, may give in evidence a writ subsequently sued out against him by the mortgagee, containing a bill of particulars of the property, for the purpose of showing that the mortgagee was still insisting on his rights.[2] So in an action against the assignee of an insolvent debtor, by one claiming under a conveyance alleged to be void as a preference made by the debtor within six months of the commencement of the proceedings in insolvency, the record of the proceedings is admissible in evidence for the defendant, for the purpose of proving the time of the commencement of proceedings.[3] So it has been held (though since questioned), that the schedule, proofs, and list of debts in insolvency are competent evidence to prove the debtor's insolvency, in an action brought by his assignee to recover property alleged to have been fraudulently conveyed.[4] So letters of administration are competent evidence of the due appointment of the administrator, where a title to real estate is set up under an administrator's deed.[5] So, for the purpose of proving that the defendant has fraudulently conveyed his real estate to third persons, copies of the deeds thereof from the registry are admissible, as the originals are not presumed to be in the possession of either party to the suit.[6] So where, in an action for real estate, the defendants claim title, in support thereof they may offer a record of proceedings, under a petition by the administrator of the plaintiff's father, against the widow and heirs, to sell lands; and it appearing, by the record, that it was shown "to the court, that due notice had been given to the defendants," the plaintiff, an heir, cannot oppose the record, by evidence that he had never been served with process in such proceeding, nor appeared, and that the court had therefore no jurisdiction as to him.[7] So, in ejectment, the plaintiff, claiming under execution sale, may offer in evidence, to prove the judgment, the journal entry, the

[1] Plummer *v.* Harbut, 5 Clarke (Iowa), 308.

[2] Caverly *v.* Gray, 7 Gray, 216.

[3] Bartlett *v.* Decreet, 4 Gray, 111.

[4] Heywood *v.* Reed, ib. 574.

[5] Remick *v.* Butterfield, 11 Fost. 70.

[6] Blanchard *v.* Young, 11 Cush. 341.

[7] Richards *v.* Skiff, 8 Ohio (N. S.), 586.

charge of a new fraud, but was corroborating evidence of the fraudulent intent already charged. It was evidently known to the defendant. . . . He should have anticipated the disclosure, at the hearing, of so important a fact, and have been prepared to meet it in advance."[1]

§ 3. There are many cases, however, where evidence of this nature has been held not admissible.[2] And though, in questions of fraud, great latitude is given to the admission in evidence of collateral facts tending to prove the fraud, yet those facts must be proved, precisely as in other cases.[3]

§ 4. In an action to recover possession of property, upon the i sue whether the title passed by delivery to the defendant, who failed soon afterwards, evidence of other purchases made by him at about that time, for which he also failed to pay, is inadmissible, there being no proof of fraud.[4] So on trial of an issue whether a bank-bill, inclosed and mailed to a party at A, was r eived by him; evidence is not admissible, that there were found secreted in the house, occupied at that time by the mail-carrier, over whose route the letter might have come, various opened letters directed to persons in A.[5] So in an action by a vendor to recover the goods from the buyer for his fraudulent representations; the plaintiff cannot prove that the defendant said he did not intend to buy more goods of other parties, because they refused to trust him without security.[6]

§ 5. In an action to set aside as fraudulent against creditors a sale made by A & company in August; evidence is competent of an assignment made by A to his son in the previous May, after the company had become embarrassed, and appearing to be part of a general plan of A to put his property out of the reach of his creditors; also of the consideration and mode of payment therefor. But not that notes given by purchasers at the alleged fraudulent sale had been paid since the commencement of the suit. Such "payment . . . could not change the character of the transaction. The defendants cannot make evidence to purge the fraud at so late a period."[7]

§ 6. Upon inquiry whether a vendee procured the sale of the

1 Ballard *v.* Fuller, 32 Barb. 68; per Leonard, J., ib. 72.

2 See Murfey *v.* Brace, 23 Barb. 561.

3 Douglass *v.* Mitchell, 35 Penn. 440.

4 Durbrow *v.* McDonald, 5 Bosw. 130.

5 Pike *v.* Crehore, 40 Maine, 503.

6 Murfey *v.* Brace, 23 Barb. 561.

7 Angrave *v.* Stone, 45 Barb. 35; per Leonard, J., ib. 36.

goods through fraud, evidence is admissible, of purchases made by him at or about the same time, involving similar frauds, and also of contemporaneous sales procured by affirmative representations of his solvency, though the issue is on fraudulent concealments of facts material to his credit; but not statements made to a creditor whose claim was not due, for the purpose of quieting his alarm about his security, accompanied by an offer to return the goods, which offer was declined in consequence of the statements.[1]

§ 7. For the purpose of proving that a party would not have been likely honestly to have the amount of money shown to be in his possession, and as tending to confirm other evidence of dishonesty, in appropriating the money of his employer; evidence is admissible to show that he has for several years been living at a rate of expenditure far beyond his apparent means.[2] So, in a suit by an assignee, for property alleged to have been conveyed in fraud of the insolvent law, evidence that the debtor had expensive habits, and was inattentive to business, and that these facts were known to the defendant, and of the debtor's general reputation as to insolvency, is competent, for the purpose of proving that the defendant had reasonable cause to believe the debtor insolvent. "All experience shows that such courses . . . are commonly, if not inevitably, destined to end in failure and bankruptcy. . . . The conduct of a party and his habits — whether of frugality or of extravagance in his expenditures — are among the first things which men of ordinary care and prudence usually consider in forming a judgment respecting his pecuniary credit and responsibility."[3]

§ 8. Evidence is admissible, in a suit against a mandatary, for the loss of personal property entrusted to him and alleged by him to have been lost, of his pecuniary circumstances, and of his good character before the alleged loss, in rebuttal of testimony that he was seen in possession of property, buying and selling, &c., subsequent to such loss.[4]

§ 9. In an action against a postmaster for negligence, by means of which a money-letter, addressed to the plaintiff, and proved to have reached his office, was there lost; evidence of the exposed

[1] Hall v. Naylor, 18 N. Y. (4 Smith) 588.

[2] Hackett v. King, 8 Allen, 144.

[3] Simpson v. Carleton, 1 Allen, 109; per Merrick, J., ib. 118.

[4] McNabb v. Lockhart, 18 Geo. 495.

manner in which the office was kept is admissible. "If the postmaster had kept his office in the street, or left it open at nights in his absence . . . it might reasonably be inferred that the loss was caused by such exposure."[1]

§ 10. In an action against a carrier for delay in carrying potatoes, whereby they were frozen, evidence is admissible, that the witness saw them in the consignee's warehouse, and as to their condition a week or more after shipment.[2]

§ 11. Where the defence to a promissory note is, that it was given for liquors, to be resold, as the plaintiff knew, and aided in effecting, in violation of law; bills for liquors previously sold by the plaintiff to the defendant, though not shown to be the liquors which were the consideration of the note in suit, are admissible in evidence, to show the course of dealing between the parties, in connection with the plaintiff's knowledge that the defendant was a dealer in liquors.[3]

§ 12. Questions of this nature have often arisen, in actions against towns and railroad corporations, for injuries arising from their alleged negligence in the maintenance or management of their roads. (*a*)

§ 13. In an action against a turnpike company for an accident caused by not keeping their road in repair, evidence is competent of its condition in other places in the vicinity.[4] "One of the issues . . . was upon the condition of the road. Had the defendant negligently suffered it to become broken and indented with ruts and fissures, or was the fissure where the horse was injured a mere accidental indentation recently made, and which the defendant had no opportunity to fill up and repair? . . . Upon the question of the omission of the defendant to keep (the road) in repair, it was proper and right to show its condition elsewhere in the vicinity."[5] So in an action against a town for injuries attributed to the insufficiency of a highway; evidence of the effect on car-

[1] Ford *v.* Parker, 4 Ohio (N. S.), 576; per Kennon, J., ib. 582.

[2] Curtis *v.* Chicago, &c. 18 Wis. 312.

[3] Hubbell *v.* Flint, 13 Gray, 277.

[4] Cox *v.* Westchester Turnpike, 33 Barb. 414.

[5] Per Brown, J., 33 Barb. 418.

(*a*) The cases upon this subject are not wholly reconcilable. For an interesting and important case, involving the question of statutory forfeiture by the process of *scire facias*, on the ground of neglect in relation to a road, and the competency of evidence to sustain the complaint; see Pres. &c. *v.* State, 19 Md. 241.

riages, driven by other persons than the plaintiff, over the same road, has a tendency to show its fitness or unfitness for public travel, and is therefore competent, whether such carriages are like that driven by the plaintiff or not, and without evidence as to the speed or care with which they were driven. "All these effects produced in going over the road were in the nature of experiments, to show the actual condition of the road at the time, and whether it was safe or unsafe. The more minutely and clearly each one was understood by the jury, the rate and manner of the driving, the kind of the carriage used, and the exact effect produced upon it, the more valuable would the evidence become, but neither party could make such evidence improper by omitting inquiries that would elicit all these particulars."[1] So it is proper to show that a railroad crossing was in an improper condition at the time of an accident, by proof of its condition immediately after, where there is no pretence of change.[2] But in determining the sufficiency of a road, the practice of other towns is not admissible in evidence.[3] Nor, in an action against a railroad for negligent management of their locomotive, evidence of specific acts of negligence of the engineer on other occasions, previous and subsequent. "It would not only lead to collateral inquiries, and so distract and mislead the jury from the true issue; . . . but it had no legal or logical tendency to prove the point in issue. Because a man was careless or negligent of his duty in one or two specified instances, it does not follow that he was so at another time and under different circumstances. Collins *v.* Dorchester, 6 Cush. 396."[4] So in an action for an injury caused by a defective bridge; it is not competent for the defendants to ask the question, how the bridge compared on the day of the accident, in respect to its safety and state of repair, with other bridges of like character on roads of like amount of travel.[5]

§ 14. In an action for injury caused in the upsetting of an omnibus by a defective highway, it appeared that for three or four rods the side of the road was depressed towards a ditch, that the road was narrow and the ditch on its margin, that the track was covered with ice and snow, and that the condition of the road

[1] Kent *v.* Lincoln, 32 Verm. 591; per Poland, J., ib. 597.

[2] Milwaukee, &c. *v.* Hunter, 11 Wis. 160.

[3] Littleton *v.* Richardson, 32 N. H. 59.

[4] Robinson *v.* Fitchburg, &c. 7 Gray, 92; per Bigelow, J., ib. 96.

[5] Bliss *v.* Wilbraham, 8 Allen, 564.

was substantially the same for the whole distance. Held, it was not a valid objection to evidence, offered by the plaintiff, that, on the next day, and before any change in the road, a cart was upset in the same manner, within the limits above stated; that the place was fifteen or twenty feet from the place of the other accident; although perhaps the whole evidence might have been excluded, as raising a collateral issue, if generally objected to.[1]

§ 15. In an action against an abutter on a public street, for damages received by falling into a survault therein, evidence of another defect, unconnected with the plaintiff's injury, is admissible as a description of the premises, and as tending to show the negligence of leaving such premises unprotected.[2]

§ 16. In an action for burning caused by a dredge, a witness cannot be asked, whether he had ever known any accident to happen from sparks from a dredge at the same distance from the dredge.[3]

§ 16 *a*. In an action against a railroad corporation for the destruction of property by fire communicated from its engine; if it is relied upon as a ground of defence, that no burning sparks could reach so far as to set fire to the property, evidence is competent to show, that the same engine, using similar fuel, has emitted burning sparks which have fallen at as great a distance; and if evidence has been introduced in defence, to show that other similar engines upon other roads did not emit sparks which would set fire to buildings, evidence is competent in reply, to show that such engines upon one of such roads have emitted sparks which communicated fire.[4]

§ 17. The point in question has arisen in recent cases relating to injuries caused by *gas*.

§ 18. In an action against a gas company for injury caused by an escape of gas, evidence that the plaintiff and other members of his family, who occupied the same house, had been in good health before the time complained of, and that afterwards they all became ill, and that one of his daughters died, is competent; but evidence in defence, that the illness of the plaintiff and his family was typhoid fever; that prior occupants of the same house had been much afflicted with illness of the same class; that many families

[1] Bailey *v*. Trumbull, 31 Conn. 581.
[2] Grier *v*. Sampson, 27 Penn. 183.
[3] Teall *v*. Barton, 40 Barb. 137.
[4] Ross *v*. Boston, &c. 6 Allen, 87.

had removed from it on that account; that its location was low, and upon made land; and that it was generally regarded and reputed to be unhealthy; is incompetent.[1]

§ 18 *a*. In an action against a gas-light company for an injury to health caused by an accidental escape of gas from a main pipe in a public street, from which it passed through various sewers and drains into the plaintiff's cellar and house, evidence is inadmissible of the escape of gas into other houses at the time alleged, and that the defendants were negligent in relation thereto, before it has been shown that gas came into the plaintiff's house. Nor can a physician, who has been in practice for several years, but who has had no experience as to the effects upon the health of breathing illuminating gas, be allowed to testify thereto as an expert, notwithstanding his experience in attending upon other persons who, it is alleged, were made sick by breathing gas from the same leak.[2]

§ 19. In an action against a gas company for an injury to health caused by an escape of gas from a main pipe in the street, and thence through sewers and drains into the plaintiff's cellar and house, evidence is admissible, that all the other occupants, previously healthy, became sick; and it is immaterial whether this arose from inhaling the gas of the defendants, or other gases from the sewers and drains which it set in motion; provided the plaintiff was, and the defendants were not, guilty of negligence. Mr. Justice Chapman remarked, upon the latter point, "The defendants' negligence was as much the proximate cause of the injury as if their own gas had occasioned it. It would be like the case of a mill-owner who should negligently suffer his dam to give way, whereby the meadow of his neighbor below him is overflowed. If the flood should in its course take up stones and gravel, and carry them upon the meadow, the mill-owner would be liable as well for the damage caused by the stones and gravel as for the damage caused by the water."[3]

§ 20. In an action for injury to land by gas from a copper-mill, evidence is not admissible, except from experts, of like injury from the same cause to neighboring lands, or as to the produce of other neighboring lands, not thus affected.[4]

[1] Hunt *v.* Lowell, &c. 1 Allen, 343.
[2] Emerson *v.* Lowell, &c. 6 Allen, 146.
[3] Hunt *v.* Lowell, &c. 8 Allen, 169, 172.
[4] Lincoln *v.* Taunton, &c. (Mass.) Law Reg. Dec. 1865, p. 125.

§ 21. Where, in an action for injury to land by copper gas, an expert testifies that he has obtained copper from the grass on such land, the defendant may show in the same way that copper has been obtained from grasses not thus affected.[1]

§ 22. With more special reference to the point of *time;* the remoteness or nearness of time of threats and declarations, pointing to an act subsequently committed, makes no difference as to their competency in evidence. All the facts, upon which any reasonable presumption or inference can be founded as to the truth or falsity of the issue, are admissible in evidence.[2]

§ 23. In an action against a railroad corporation for an injury occasioned by their locomotive engine to a man delivering wood by the side of their track, the plaintiff, after having introduced evidence tending to show that there was, at the time of the accident, a travelled crossing at that place, cannot show that such a crossing was there previously to the accident, and also at the time of the trial.[3] But in an action for breaking the plaintiff's leg, where evidence of a second breaking, by slipping down on the sidewalk, has been admitted without objection, evidence of the subsequent state of the leg is admissible, to show its condition before and after the second breaking, so that the jury may determine for how much injury the defendant is liable.[4] So in an action for a continuing nuisance, by obstructing or altering the flow of water; evidence may be received of the condition of the premises at or about the time of the trial, not for the purpose of recovering damages for injuries sustained after commencement of the suit, but of furnishing the most precise and reliable information as to the nature and extent of the injury, and thus enabling the jury, by comparison, to judge of the amount of damages resulting from the alleged nuisance, prior to the commencement of the action.[5]

§ 23 *a.* Where land is taken for a railroad, a petitioner for damages may be asked, on cross-examination, for what price he sold the rest of the lot, seventeen years afterwards.[6]

§ 24. The same point is sometimes connected with evidence of *common reputation.* Thus in trespass *qu. claus.* the defendant

[1] Lincoln *v.* Taunton, &c. (Mass.) Law Reg. Dec. 1865, p. 125.
[2] Keener *v.* State, 18 Geo. 194.
[3] Robinson *v.* Fitchburg, &c. 7 Gray, 92.
[4] Wright *v.* New York, &c. 28 Barb. 80.
[5] Morris, &c. *v.* Ryerson, 3 Dutch. 457.
[6] Whitman *v.* Boston, &c. 7 Allen, 313.

pleaded a prescriptive right of common, and the plaintiff replied, a prescription in right of his messuage to use the land for tillage with corn during harvest, traversing the defendant's prescription. Many persons besides the defendant having a right of common there, held, evidence was admissible, coming from persons conversant with the neighborhood, of reputation as to the plaintiff's right.[1] Lord Ellenborough questioned the competency of the evidence, upon general principles, and independently of the established practice to admit it with reference to public rights; remarking that "the right in question may be said in some sense to partake of the nature of a public right, . . . a question between the plaintiff and a multitude of persons." Mr. Justice Bailey remarks: "I take it that where the term public right is used it does not mean public in the literal sense, but is synonymous with general; that is, what concerns a multitude of persons."[2] So in a suit in equity, to recover damages for a nuisance to buildings, arising from the unlawful erection and maintenance of steam-engines and furnaces, as well as for an injunction to prevent their further continuance; evidence of the general character of the neighborhood, of the various kinds of business carried on there, and of the class of tenants by whom dwelling-houses in that vicinity are usually occupied, is competent, upon the question of damages. But not that a particular insurance company had increased the rate of insurance on his houses.[3]

§ 25. We shall hereafter have occasion to consider, under the title of *Damages*, what facts and circumstances may be proved in the various forms of action, as increasing or diminishing the amount to be recovered. In the present connection, we may briefly notice the question of *value*, as a matter of evidence; remarking, in general terms, that whatever is admissible in evidence may affect the amount of damages; and, on the other hand, that whatever (and that only) has a proper bearing upon the damages may properly be offered in evidence.[4]

§ 25 *a*. To prove the value of land, evidence of what a witness

[1] Weeks *v.* Sparke, 1 M. & S. 379.
[2] Ibid. 686, 690.
[3] Call *v.* Allen, 1 Allen, 137.
[4] See Ward *v.* Reynolds, 32 Ala. 384; Kingsbury *v.* Moses, 45 N. H. 422.

had offered for other land, on the opposite side of the street, is not competent.[1]

§ 25 *b*. An estimate, not on oath, of damages that would be sustained by a party over whose land a railroad was afterwards laid out, made by a committee of a town, while a petition of the town for a change of the route of the railroad was before the legislature, and merely stating those damages as the least the party would take, is not admissible in evidence to a jury impanelled to appraise damages caused by laying out the railroad over the land, although such estimate was made at the request of an agent of a railroad company.[2]

§ 26. In an action for breaking and entering the plaintiff's close and tearing down his unfinished building, he cannot offer evidence of what the building would have cost or rented for, if finished according to the plan.[3] So, in trespass for mesne profits, evidence is not admissible, of the profits of a proprietor adjoining the defendant, to show how much was made by the defendant.[4]

§ 26 *a*. Under a declaration for injury, by building on the next lot, and driving spikes into the plaintiff's wall, it is not competent to show that the market value of the plaintiff's house has been lessened by the fact of the defendant's erecting the building in question.[5]

§ 27. In an action for a personal injury, by which the plaintiff is prevented from following his usual employment; he may offer in evidence the amount he was thus earning or realizing from fixed wages, and may himself testify what was his net income for services for the year preceding the injury.[6]

§ 28. In trespass for the taking and detention of slaves, the expense of recovering them may be proved, without proof of its reasonableness or necessity.[7]

§ 29. The fact, that sales of patent rights have been made in one State, is admissible to show the value of the patent in another State, where the suit is brought.[8]

§ 30. A witness, having testified as to the value of a patent for a certain county, may further testify that he, though having no authority to sell, had been offered a like sum by an unknown person.[9]

[1] Davis *v.* Charles, &c. 11 Cush. 506.
[2] Webber *v.* Eastern, &c. 2 Met. 147.
[3] Bennett *v.* Clemence, 6 Allen, 10.
[4] Mitchell *v.* Mitchell, 10 Md. 234.
[5] Wilson *v.* Hinsley, 13 Md. 64.
[6] Grant *v.* Brooklyn, 41 Barb. 381.
[7] Williams *v.* Newberry, 32 Miss. 256.
[8] Gatling *v.* Newell, 9 Ind. 572.
[9] Ibid.

§ 30 *a*. The defendant assigned to the plaintiff a claim upon the United States in payment for goods sold in California just before its annexation, but prevented the plaintiff from collecting such claim. In an action for damages, held, the plaintiff might show the first cost of the goods in the United States, the expenses of transportation to California, the duties there, and the usual and proper profits; also sales of like articles for cash within three or four months before and after the sale, and a repurchase of some of the goods for cash by the plaintiff, at advanced rates, within two months afterwards; in connection with other evidence of the market value at that time and place.[1]

§ 30 *b*. Where the price paid for one animal was another animal, the age, appearance, and qualities of the latter, and the price for which it sold, are competent evidence of the value of the former; "upon the almost axiomatic principle, that things which are equal to the same thing, are equal to one another."[2]

§ 31. In an action on the case for injury to property, and especially to a well, by rendering the water impure, all the circumstances may be proved and considered; and, to ascertain the damages, the cost of furnishing water to the family, having regard to quality and quantity, also the difference in value of the property, owing to the erection of gas and other offensive structures in its vicinity.[3]

§ 32. Where A and B had exchanged lands; in a suit by A for false and fraudulent representations of B, as to the quality and description of his land, evidence as to the value of the land and the improvements conveyed to B is immaterial, and properly excluded.[4]

§ 33. Where the plaintiff delivered to the defendant gold, to be made up into jewelry; in an action for making and delivering plated articles, evidence of the amount of gold it would take to make them solid is irrelevant.[5]

§ 34. Similar remarks to those made on the subject of *value* are also applicable to that of *motive*, *intent*, or *malice;* which has a double connection with *Evidence* and *Damages*. See Book V., Chap. V.

§ 35. In an action of trespass, where the general issue is

[1] Eaton *v.* Mellus, 7 Gray, 566.

[2] Carr *v.* Moore, 41 N. H. 131; per Fowler, J., ib. 33.

[3] Ottawa, &c. *v.* Graham, 28 Ill. 73.

[4] Likes *v.* Baer, 8 Clarke (Iowa), 368.

[5] Harris *v.* Bernard, 4 E. D. Smith, 195.

pleaded, all the acts and circumstances directly connected with and attendant upon the transaction are competent for either party to prove, as tending to favor or rebut the presumption of malice, but for no other purpose.[1]

§ 36. In trespass *quare clausum*, and for tearing down the plaintiff's house, evidence, that the house was occupied by lewd females, and that persons, a short time before the trespass, in visiting the house, passed over the defendant's land and left his bars down, struck the defendant, and disturbed a religious meeting at his house, swore at him, &c.; is not admissible, under the general issue, to rebut the presumption of malice, or in answer to a claim for exemplary damages.[2]

§ 37. In an action of trespass, the declarations of the defendant at the time are evidence to show the *quo animo*, and admissible as part of the *res gestæ*.[3]

§ 38. In trespass *quare clausum*, where the malice of the defendant may be the ground of exemplary damages, he, being a competent witness, may testify what his motive and purpose were.[4]

§ 38 *a*. In trespass against an overseer of the highway for cutting down a tree therein, evidence of improper motives, and that the act was done maliciously, is admissible. But only the state of feeling between the parties at the time, not the cause or history of the quarrel.[5]

1 Perkins *v*. Towle, 43 N. H. 220.
2 Ibid.
3 Emory *v*. Collings, 1 Har. 325.
4 Norris *v*. Morril, 40 N. H. 395.
5 Winter *v*. Peterson, 4 Zabr. 524.

CHAPTER V.

PAROL EVIDENCE.

§ 1. "PAROL contemporaneous evidence is inadmissible to contradict or vary the terms of a valid written instrument;"[1] though it may be read by the light of surrounding circumstances, to understand the intent of the parties.[2] "Where written instruments are appointed, either by the immediate authority of law, or by the compact of parties, to be the permanent repositories and testimonies of truth, it is a matter both of principle and of policy to exclude any inferior evidence from being used, either as a substitute for such instruments, or to contradict or alter them. Of *principle*, because such instruments are in their own nature and origin entitled to a much higher degree of credit than that which appertains to parol evidence; of *policy*, because it would be attended with great mischief and inconvenience if those instruments upon which men's rights depended were liable to be impeached and contradicted by loose collateral evidence."[3]

§ 2. Parol evidence to prove the issuing of a warrant and the arrest of a person thereon is incompetent, unless it be shown that neither the warrant nor a copy of it can be produced.[4]

§ 3. Parol evidence is admissible, of fraud in a written agreement.[5] Or to contradict the terms of a note, where it goes to establish either usury or illegality in the contract.[6] But not that the writing, at the time of its execution, was agreed to be a sham, to defeat creditors, or for other purposes.[7] And in an action for

[1] 1 Greenl. Ev. 398, § 275. See Harbold *v.* Kuster, 44 Penn. 392.
[2] Emery *v.* Webster, 42 Maine, 204.
[3] 3 Stark. Ev. 994.
[4] Hackett *v.* King, 6 Allen, 58.
[5] Lunday *v.* Thomas, 26 Geo. 537; Pierce *v.* Wilson, 34 Ala. 596.
[6] Newsome *v.* Thighen, 30 Miss. 414.
[7] Conner *v.* Carpenter, 2 Wms. 237.

deceit in a sale, the contract, if written, must be proved by the writing itself, or its absence accounted for.[1]

§ 4. In an action for fraudulent representations on a sale at auction, the declarations of the vendor, after the premises have been struck down, but before the terms of the sale have been reduced to writing, are admissible.[2] So where a bill in chancery charges, in a sale of land by written contract, misrepresentation and fraud, which are denied in the answer, parol evidence of the fraud is admissible.[3] And, in general, where the *gravamen* of an action is fraud in inducing the plaintiff to enter into a contract, the rule does not apply, that anterior and accompanying stipulations and representations are merged in the contract, but they may be proved by parol evidence. Thus, in case of sale by sample to one acting as broker to the plaintiff, the purchaser, the plaintiff may offer parol evidence of the statements of the defendants, the sellers, to such broker, previous to the sale, respecting the quality of the bulk of the article, as compared with the sample, notwithstanding a written memorandum, signed by the broker, and containing nothing in reference to the quality.[4]

§ 4 *a*. Parol evidence is not admissible, to prove a contemporaneous understanding and agreement contrary to the terms of a conveyance.[5] Thus a defendant in ejectment cannot prove that a deed, professing to convey a certain number of acres, was intended to convey more;[6] nor introduce parol evidence, to control an absolute deed of the demanded premises, given by him.[7] So the declarations of a husband, after the date of a deed by himself and wife of the wife's land, cannot be given in evidence against the grantee, to impeach the validity of the conveyance, or to prove that it was dishonestly obtained.[8] So a declaration by one executor is not admissible to vary the date of an executor's deed, in ejectment founded on the deed.[9] So a deed cannot be contradicted or varied by parol evidence, that part of the premises included was intended to be excepted, for the purpose of negativing any breach of the covenants contained in it; the conclusive presump-

[1] Gwynn *v.* Setzer, 3 Jones, 382.

[2] Haight *v.* Hayt, 19 N. Y. (5 Smith), 464.

[3] Harrell *v.* Hill, 19 Ark. 102.

[4] Koop *v.* Handy, 41 Barb. 454.

[5] Trullinger *v.* Webb, 3 Ind. 198; Burns *v.* Jenkins, 8 Ind. 417; New, &c. *v.* Fields, 10 Ind. 187; New, &c. *v.* Slaughter, ib. 218.

[6] Doe *v.* Swails, 3 Ind. 329.

[7] Lincoln *v.* Parsons, 1 Allen, 388.

[8] Kirkland *v.* Hepselgefser, 2 Grant, 84.

[9] Pratt *v.* Phillips, 1 Sneed, 543.

tion being, that the whole engagement of the parties, and the extent and manner of it, were reduced to writing.[1] So a grantee, who has voluntarily, and without fraud or mistake, destroyed the conveyance, cannot resort to parol evidence of its contents in support of his title.[2] But where, in ejectment, the defence set up is an outstanding title in another, extrinsic evidence is admissible to show that the description in the deed relied upon, and that in the plaintiff's deed, cover the same premises, unless repugnant to each other.[3] So the term "old" in a deed, when applied to the channel of a stream flowing through alluvial lands, as a boundary, may be explained by parol evidence of the language or acts of the parties, at the time of, or subsequent to, the conveyance.[4] So the identical monument referred to in a deed.[5] Facts, tending to show that a "stake" is such a monument, are proper for the consideration of the jury, but raise no binding presumption of law.[6] More especially if the description in a deed be doubtful, or lines or monuments lost or destroyed, parol evidence of the practical construction given by parties is admissible.[7] Or to remove uncertainty, arising in the application to the subject-matter of definite terms of the description;[8] as, to show the position of monuments erected by commissioners, whose return fixed the disputed boundary with a latent uncertainty.[9] Or to explain the certificate of a surveyor, containing a general description of land by bounds, in order to identify the land.[10]

§ 5. The defendant, C, having a lease of a store, underlet to A the whole of the first floor, excepting a portion thereof which was then partitioned off, and which consisted of the stairway, with a hatchway in front, leading to the upper stories of the building. There were two doors in the front, the one opening opposite the stairway, and the other into the lower room, into which there was also access through a door in the partition. A, with the consent of C, removed the partition, agreeing to restore it when requested. Afterwards A sold out to S, with whom C agreed in writing, that "the present lessee and occupant of the first floor

[1] Nutting *v.* Herbert, 35 N. H. 120.

[2] Parker *v.* Kane, 4 Wis. 1; Speer *v.* Speer, 7 Ind. 178.

[3] Schultz *v.* Lindell, 30 Mis. 310.

[4] Emery *v.* Webster, 42 Maine, 204.

[5] Afferty *v.* Connover, 7 Ohio (N. S.), 99.

[6] Robinson *v.* White, 42 Maine, 209.

[7] Fletcher *v.* Phelps, 2 Wms. 258.

[8] Patch *v.* Keeler, ib. 332.

[9] Ibid.

[10] Spears *v.* Burton, 31 Miss. 547.

of the house may continue to use and occupy the said premises as long as I hold the lease thereof." In an action by S against C, for putting up the partition, held, parol evidence was competent that S took the agreement from C with knowledge of the rights and obligations of A.[1]

§ 6. The same principles are applied to written *contracts*. Thus, if a bill of lading does not require the master to take a certain route, such obligation cannot be established by proof of any preliminary conversation.[2] But, in an action for procuring the arrest and imprisonment of the plaintiff, on an execution against him and a former partner, in favor of A, but assigned to the defendant, in which there is evidence that the plaintiff had sold out his interest in the firm to B, and that, as part of the consideration, B agreed to indemnify him against all the outstanding debts, and that the new firm had accordingly paid the execution; it is competent to prove by parol, that the defendant authorized B to make the contracts of purchase and indemnity, as his agent, before the assignment and arrest, for the purpose of showing knowledge on his part that the execution was paid. "This was not the purpose" (to vary the contract) "for which it was offered, nor could it, if received, have had any such effect. It was offered because the fact . . . would have some tendency to show that the defendant must have known of the payment . . . if it had been made."[3] And a bill of lading or railroad receipt, stating that the goods were received in apparent good order, does not exclude parol proof of their real condition.[4]

§ 7. Upon petition to vacate the levy of an execution for want of notice to the debtor to choose an appraiser, the fact may be shown by parol, though the officer states in his return of the levy that notice was given.[5]

§ 8. Questions as to parol evidence arise from the alleged *loss* of the written instrument.

§ 9. The issuing of a warrant, and arrest thereupon, cannot be proved by parol evidence, without proving that neither the warrant nor a copy can be produced. So held, in a late case for conversion, where the warrant in question was not returned

1 Steffens *v.* Collins, 6 Bosw. 223.
2 White *v.* Van Kirk, 25 Barb. 16.
3 Paget *v.* Cook, 1 Allen, 522; per Merrick, J., ib. 525.
4 Blade *v.* Chicago, &c. 10 Wis. 4.
5 Briggs *v.* Green, 33 Verm. 565.

into court, and not produced, though the plaintiff had notified the defendant to produce it. The defendant claimed the property for which the suit was brought under a release or bill of sale from the plaintiff; to which the plaintiff replied that the release was obtained from him through duress and fraud. The plaintiff testified, that he was arrested upon a charge of larceny from the defendant, upon a warrant which was never returned.[1]

§ 10. Action to recover the amount of a note alleged to have been left with the defendant for collection. The defendant offered to prove, that the plaintiff had written him instructions not to attempt to collect the note of the maker, but to exchange it for the note of another person named, if he could, which he had done. This proof he offered to make, by proving the contents of the letters of instruction, having first clearly shown that he had deposited the letters with another, to be kept during his absence from home, and that, while so on deposit, they had been accidentally destroyed. The proof was objected to, not as being irrelevant, but for want of sufficient proof of loss. Held admissible.[2]

§ 11. In an action of trespass for levying a tax, to establish the assessment, the defendants offered to prove the loss and contents of the district records. The witnesses, in speaking of the records, described them as being kept on half sheets and quarto sheets of paper, not bound in book form. To all this testimony the plaintiff objected, for the reason that the evidence did not show such a record as a school district was required to keep, and that the existence and contents of a public record could not be proved by parol. Held, that, after proof of the loss of a record, its contents may be proved, like any other document, by secondary evidence; that, if a copy can be produced, its production should be required; but, if the existence of better evidence is not disclosed, then the contents may be proved by parol.[3] (*a*)

§ 12. In Georgia, it being the duty of the sheriff, after levying under a tax execution, to return it to the office of the solicitor-

1 Hackett *v.* King, 6 Allen, 58.

2 Littler *v.* Franklin, 9 Ind. 216.

3 Higgins *v.* Reed, 8 Clarke (Iowa), 298.

(*a*) The defendants offered in evidence a paper, in the handwriting of the secretary of the district (but whether in that of one of the defendants did not appear), showing the amount of tax due from the several citizens of the district, containing the names of the plaintiffs and others, with memorandums as to who had paid, which paper was the only written evidence remaining of the tax-list of 1855. Held, if the paper was a copy of the assessment-roll provided for in § 1130 of the Iowa Code, or one of the lists posted up, as provided for in that section, it was admissible. 8 Clarke, 298.

general; it is to be presumed that he did so, and inquiry for it must be made at such office, before secondary evidence of its contents can be admissible.[1]

§ 13. In an action against selectmen for refusing to receive a vote, parol evidence that the plaintiff's name was on the list is inadmissible, without notice to produce the list, or a *subpœna duces tecum*.[2]

§ 14. In an action on the case, by a town, for illegally transporting A, a pauper, into the town; where the question was, whether A had formerly gained a settlement in Vermont, under the statute which provides, that every person who shall inhabit in any town or place within said State, and have been charged with and paid his share of the public rates or taxes for two years, shall acquire a settlement; and it appeared that such taxes were assessed and collected in much the same manner as in Connecticut, but there was no record evidence before the court, that a tax claimed to have been paid by A had been legally assessed, and no foundation had been laid for dispensing with such evidence: held, secondary evidence was not admissible.[3]

§ 15. The question of parol evidence often arises in determining the *application* of a writing. Thus, in case of a former judgment, the precise object and effect of which become material, as bearing upon the pending action.

§ 16. Parol evidence is admissible, that an obstruction, for which damages were recovered in a former action against another defendant, is the same for which damages were claimed in a subsequent suit; but not that there was a claim for false imprisonment in the former suit, and that, on appeal from a justice, in the Superior Court, upon a suggestion that the false imprisonment was the plaintiff's only cause of action, he thereupon, desiring to amend, was told by the court that it was unnecessary, that the trial might go on as if the amendment were made, and that the amendment was disallowed; and therefore it cannot thus be shown that the judgment of the Superior Court, affirming that of the justice, should not be a bar to the present action for the obstruction, against another defendant.[4]

§ 17. In case of sale of a certain amount of standing timber,

[1] Davenport *v.* Harris, 27 Geo. 68.
[2] Harris *v.* Whitcomb, 4 Gray, 433.
[3] Marlborough *v.* Sisson, 23 Conn. 44.
[4] Federal, &c. *v.* Mariner, 15 Md. 224.

by a contract partly reduced to writing; parol evidence is admissible to show, what did not appear by the writing, from what tract the timber was to be cut.[1]

[1] Pinney *v.* Thompson, 3 Clarke (Iowa), 74.

CHAPTER VI.

MISCELLANEOUS POINTS OF EVIDENCE. — VARIANCE; TESTIMONY OF PARTIES.

1. Variance.
9. Testimony of parties.

§ 1. It has already been explained, under the head of *Pleading*, that the facts proved must conform to the facts alleged. Otherwise there is a *variance* which is fatal to the action or defence. A few leading cases upon this subject are here subjoined.

§ 2. In trespass, the *locus in quo* must be proved to be within the hundred laid.[1]

§ 3. Voluntary waste cannot be proved, upon the issue of permitting the premises to be out of repair.[2]

§ 4. An action for malicious prosecution before Baron Waterpark, of *Waterfook*, is not sustained by proof of such prosecution before Baron Waterpark, of *Waterpark*.[3] So, in trespass for breaking and entering, the defendant pleaded a justification under a search-warrant granted by a justice of the county of *Stafford*, and gave in evidence a search-warrant granted by a justice of the borough of *Wolverhampton*, acting as such, but who was also a justice of the county of Stafford. Held, the evidence did not support the plea.[4]

§ 5. An immaterial averment need not be proved. Thus an action for removing earth from the defendant's land, thereby injuring the foundation of the plaintiff's house, does not depend on intention, which, therefore, though alleged, need not be proved.[5]

§ 6. Whether an allegation is mere surplusage, not requiring to be proved, is often a point of much nicety.

§ 7. An action for deceit in a sale against two is not sustained by proof of a sale by one of them.[6] So in trespass for breaking and

[1] Emory *v.* Collings, 1 Har. 325.
[2] Edge *v.* Pemberton, 12 M. & W. 187.
[3] Walters *v.* Mace, 2 B. & Ald. 756.
[4] Webb *v.* Ross, 4 Hurl. & Nor. 111.
[5] Panton *v.* Holland, 17 John. 92; acc. Twiss *v.* Baldwin, 9 Conn. 291.
[6] Weall *v.* King, 12 E. 452; Lopes *v.* De Tastet, 1 B. & B. 538.

entering a several fishery, if the replication prescribe for a sole right of fishing in four places, upon which issue is taken, proof in only three places is a fatal variance. So a plea in trespass, justifying under a prescriptive right of common on five hundred acres, is not sustained by evidence, showing that the ancestor of the defendant had released five of them. So, in replevin of cattle, and avowry of taking *damage feasant*, a plea by the plaintiff of a prescriptive right of common for all the cattle is not sustained by proof of a right for a part.[1] So an allegation, in an action by landlord against tenant for negligently keeping his fire, of a demise for seven years, is not sustained by proof of a lease at will; though an allegation of a tenancy, generally, would have been sufficient.[2]

§ 8. But in trespass, for driving against the cart of the plaintiff, an allegation that he was in the cart need not be proved.[3] So, in an action for an injury to a reversionary interest in land, an allegation that the close "continually from thence hitherto hath been, and still is," in the possession of A. B., is surplusage, and need not be proved.[4] So, in an action for disturbance of a right of common by opening stone quarries, the declaration alleged a common by reason of a messuage and land, in possession of the plaintiff. The general issue was pleaded, and a common proved by reason of the land only. Held, the proof was not of a different allegation, but of the same allegation in part, and the declaration was sustained, and damages might be given accordingly.[5] So if a declaration discloses a state of facts, upon which an action is maintainable without either malice or fraud, the plaintiff is not bound to prove either, although both are alleged, and may recover though both fraud and malice are disproved.[6]

§ 9. "The general rule of the common law is, that a *party to the record* in a civil suit *cannot be a witness* either for himself, or a co-suitor."[7]

§ 10. Exceptions to this rule, however, are adopted in some cases; more especially in courts proceeding according to the Roman law; "first, where it has been already proved that the party against whom (such evidence) has been offered has been

[1] 1 Greenl. Ev. 144, § 71; Bull. N. P. 299.

[2] Cudlip *v.* Rundle, Carth. 202.

[3] Howard *v.* Peete, 2 Chit. R. 315.

[4] Vowles *v.* Miller, 3 Taun. 137.

[5] Rickets *v.* Sabrey, 2 B. & A. 360. See Bushwood *v.* Pond, Cro. Eliz. 722.

[6] Swinfen *v.* Chelmsford, 5 H. & N. 890.

[7] 1 Greenl. Ev. 475, § 329.

guilty of some fraud, or other tortious and unwarrantable act of intermeddling with the complainant's goods and no other evidence can be had of the amount of damages; and, secondly, where, on general grounds of public policy it is deemed essential to the purposes of justice."[1] In reference to cases of the latter description it is remarked: "This rule is repudiated in some of the States, and it can only be defended on the alleged necessity of the case. We have always endeavored to restrain the rule within the narrowest possible limits, and to caution juries when they receive such testimony."[2]

§ 11. In an action against a railroad company, for the value of a trunk and its contents lost on the railroad, the party may prove himself or wife the contents, but not the value.[3] The jurors, when the property is described, may have a proper measure of damages in their knowledge of values.[4]

§ 12. This rule has been sometimes affirmed by statute.

§ 13. The provision of Mass. St. 1851, ch. 47, § 5, that, in any action "brought by a passenger against any railroad corporation, steamboat proprietor, or other common carrier," the plaintiff, after proof of the bailment of his trunk to the defendants, and of its loss "by the fault of such carrier, or of the agents of such carrier," shall be allowed to put in evidence a descriptive list of its contents, sworn to by himself; applies to the case of the loss of a trunk left by the passenger with the baggage-master of a railroad corporation, after arriving at his place of destination. The court remark: "The statute makes no distinction, if there be one, between the larger liability of carriers whilst the baggage is *in transitu* . . . and that more limited duty which devolves on them as bailees for hire after it is received at the depot. . . . Whatever may be the nature and extent of the duties of carriers, whether they be liable for all losses, or only for such as proceed from negligence and carelessness, . . . or from failure in the performance of all duties incumbent on all bailees for hire, the relation of passenger and carrier, in regard to baggage, continues until the carriers have performed their whole duty."[5]

§ 13. In the United States, by express statute, the common-

[1] 1 Greenl. Ev. 492, § 348.
[2] Per Breese, J., 24 Ill. 336.
[3] Illinois, &c. *v.* Taylor, 24 Ill. 323.
[4] Illinois, &c. *v.* Copeland, ib. 332. See Stadhecker *v.* Combs, 9 Rich. 193.
[5] Harlow *v.* Fitchburg, &c. 8 Gray, 237; per Shaw, C. J. ib. 240.

law rule has been still further relaxed, and parties are very generally allowed to testify, in most cases, in their own favor. Some questions have arisen in the application of these statutory provisions.

§ 14. In an action against selectmen for refusing to put a name upon the voting-list and rejecting a vote, the plaintiff may prove his own statements concerning his residence made to the defendants under oath, for the purpose of furnishing evidence of his qualifications. So he may testify to his own intention in previously leaving the town for a prolonged absence.[1] So the plaintiff in an action of tort in the nature of trespass *qu. claus.* may testify, how long his use and occupation of the premises have continued.[2]

§ 15. It is no ground for a new trial, that, the plaintiff having been asked, while under cross-examination, whether he was the author of a pamphlet, which contained expressions of opinion on religious subjects altogether at variance with those generally received among Christians, and having declined to answer, on the ground that his answer in the affirmative might subject him to a criminal prosecution; the counsel for the defendant was permitted for a considerable time (obviously with a view to prejudice the plaintiff with the jury), to read various passages of a similar tendency from other printed documents, each time repeating the inquiry whether the plaintiff was the author, or whether the passage read expressed his notions on the subject; the jury being entitled to have before them all the facts and circumstances, from which they might be enabled to judge of the degree of credit due to the party as a witness.[3] So, in an action for false imprisonment, the plaintiff, who was arrested on a charge of stealing from the defendant's house, may testify as to the statement made to the policeman by the defendant's sister, who was the owner of the stolen property, that the defendant ordered the arrest to be made.[4] So in an action against an officer, for the conversion of property, attached by him on a writ against one under whom the plaintiff claims title by a prior purchase; the plaintiff, while testifying in his own behalf, may

[1] Lombard *v.* Oliver, 7 Allen, 155.

[2] Bennett *v.* Clemence, 6 Allen, 10.

[3] Bradlaugh *v.* Edwards, 11 C.B. (N. S.) 377.

[4] Harris *v.* Dignum, 5 Hurl. &. Nor. 943.

be asked by his counsel if he took possession of the property; and a notice given by him to the defendant, in which he claimed ownership thereof, and demanded its return, is also admissible.[1]

§ 16. After the defendant, in an action for obstructing the highway with building materials, has sworn positively that he received the materials in person, and that they were put in the particular place according to his direction; he cannot offer evidence that under the contract of purchase they were to have been delivered in another place.[2]

§ 17. A statute authorizing the testimony of parties was by a liberal construction held applicable in the case of corporations, though not expressly mentioned. The court remark: "It may well be that the present case did not occur to the legislature when the statute was enacted; but the design was to admit, as a witness, a party to an action, whenever the adverse party or person in interest could also be a witness. A corporation could never be a witness, but a corporation is composed of a person or persons, who are natural persons and are interested in the corporation, and they can be witnesses."[3]

[1] Rand *v.* Freeman, 1 Allen, 517.
[2] Clark *v.* Kirwan, 4 E. D. Smith, 21.
[3] Per Marvin, J., 28 Barb. 84.

CHAPTER VII.

TORT AND CONTRACT. — FRAUD AS A GROUND OF ACTION OR DEFENCE.

§ 1. In an action on the case for falsely recommending a person as fit to be trusted, the knowledge of his insolvency, as well as the fraudulent intent, must be proved.[1]

§ 2. In an action for false representation as to the value of a business, the question will not be merely whether it was ever made, but whether the defendant kept it up, and whether, even if he did, the plaintiff was thereby induced to complete the purchase.[2]

§ 3. In cross actions between the vendor and vendee of a ship, the question in both being fraud in obtaining a classification as A 1, which had been obtained by trickery on the part of an agent of the vendor; the jury must, to find against the vendor, believe him to have been a party to this fraud; and letters from the agent to him are admissible to show his *bona fides*.[3]

§ 4. In an action for falsely representing that a good living might be got at a certain public house, evidence is admissible, that, a year or two before the plaintiff took it, some one else found it impossible to get a living; the character of the house not having since changed.[4]

§ 5. In an action for a false representation that a third party to the best of his knowledge was responsible, the defendant may be asked in chief whether, at the time of the representation, he believed the debtor to be in good credit; and other persons residing in the neighborhood may be asked a similar question.[5]

§ 6. Parol evidence is admissible of false representations as to what passed by a lease. Thus, in case of a lease of a ferry-ship, using the words, "or so much thereof as belongs to the" lessor;

[1] Fooks *v.* Waples, 1 Har. 131.

[2] Incledon *v.* Watson, 2 F. & F. 841.

[3] Tindall *v.* Baskett — Baskett *v.* Tindall, ib. 644.

[4] Penn *v.* Steadman, ib. 546.

[5] Sheen *v.* Bumpstead, 8 Jur. (N. S.) 702; 10 W. R. 740, Exch.

evidence is competent, of representations that he owned nearly the whole ship.[1]

§ 7. Upon a question of fraudulent conveyance, the reputation of the grantee, as to means or property, in the town or neighborhood where he resided, is competent evidence upon the point of *bona fides* or *mala fides*.[2]

§ 8. "Generally, to establish an allegation of fraud, and perhaps to repel it, large latitude is allowed to the admission of evidence, but the evidence must have some bearing upon the matter in controversy."[3] Thus, in an action for falsely representing a person as entitled to credit, evidence is not competent for the defendant of declarations of a different character made by him to other persons at about the same time. It tends in no degree to disprove the specific fraud charged in the declaration, to excuse, or lessen the defendant's responsibility for damages.[4]

§ 9. In an action, for fraudulent conspiracy in the transfer of property, against A and B, testimony is not admissible, that before the alleged fraudulent transfer A had endeavored to sell his property; having no tendency to prove the honesty of the arrangement with B.[5]

§ 10. In an action to set aside a conveyance as fraudulent against creditors, evidence is admissible to show what other property the grantor had at or before that time, and its value, and that he had conveyed it to different persons without consideration and with fraudulent intent. First, for the purpose of showing his situation at the time in question, and what he had done with his previous property. Secondly, to prove the fraudulent intent alleged in the complaint.[6]

§ 11. In case of a sale, alleged to have been made for the purpose of defrauding creditors, the fraud of the vendor may be proved by statements and admissions, made by him before the sale, in the absence and without the knowledge of the vendee.[7] But not by such acts subsequent to the sale.[8]

§ 12. A debtor's declaration of intention, though competent evidence to prove his fraudulent disposition of property in order to avoid the payment of his debts; must not have been made at

1 Sharp *v.* Mayor, &c. 40 Barb. 256.
2 Amsden *v.* Manchester, ib. 158.
3 Per Strong, J., Graham *v.* Hollinger, 46 Penn. 56.
4 Ib. 55.
5 Tams *v.* Lewis, 42 Penn. 402.
6 Amsden *v.* Manchester, 40 Barb. 158.
7 White *v.* Chadbourne, 41 Maine, 149.
8 Dennison *v.* Benner, ib. 332.

so remote a period as to prevent them from becoming part of the *res gestæ;* and this question of time is held to rest in the sound discretion of the judge at *nisi prius.*[1]

§ 13. In replevin, for goods alleged to have been obtained by fraud and false pretences from the plaintiff, against one claiming them as a subsequent purchaser; the intent to defraud cannot be shown by declarations, other than the alleged false pretences, subsequently made by one A, to whom the plaintiff was referred by the purchaser for information; nor by proof that the plaintiff found on inquiry that a person, whom the vendee subsequently introduced to him as doing business at a certain place, did not do business there.[2]

§ 14. Fraudulent misrepresentations, as to the price paid for real estate by the vendor, do not sustain an action for deceit in the sale. Such representations are to be regarded in the same light as those respecting the value. A purchaser ought not to rely upon them.[3]

§ 15. Upon a question of fraudulent conveyance, the grantor may testify to his actual intent.[4]

§ 16. A plaintiff, who has received from the defendant letters, which, if existing, would be admissible, may prove their contents by secondary evidence, where the destruction of them is shown to have arisen from misapprehension, and without fraudulent purpose, notwithstanding their destruction was the plaintiff's own voluntary act. To repel the inference of fraud, a witness, who was present and advised the destruction of the letters, may be allowed to state, as part of the *res gestæ*, his declarations made to the party at the time. The destruction of the letters was a question for the court; and from the evidence the court was also to decide that they were not dishonestly destroyed.[5]

§ 17. In replevin, for goods alleged to have been obtained by fraud and false pretences, against one claiming as subsequent purchaser, it may be shown, by cross-examination of the plaintiff, that a few days before the trial he made a complaint against the alleged fraudulent party, and caused him to be arrested on the morning of the trial.[6]

[1] Hardee *v.* Langford, 6 Florida, 13.
[2] Easter *v.* Allen, 8 Allen, 7.
[3] Hemmer *v.* Cooper, ib. 334.
[4] Mathews *v.* Poultney, 33 Barb. 127.
[5] Tobin *v.* Shaw, 45 Maine, 331.
[6] Easter *v.* Allen, 8 Allen, 7.

§ 18. In an action upon a contract, fraud is admissible as a defence.[1]

§ 19. Where goods are obtained by fraud and false pretences, in an action by the owner against a subsequent purchaser, the burden of proof is upon the latter to show that he was a purchaser for a valuable consideration, without notice.[2]

§ 20. An agent, employed by seller and purchaser, on the purchase of a business, may be liable to the purchaser for false representations as to its value, and, if he declares that he has personal knowledge of the facts, and his statements are found to be false, that is evidence that they are false to his knowledge.[3]

§ 21. In an action for false representation, other false statements than those laid may be proved and considered by the jury, with reference to the question whether those laid were made fraudulently. But the declaration will not be amended by introducing them as distinct causes of action; at all events without allowing, if necessary, time for their consideration by the defendant.[4]

[1] Robertson *v.* Reed, 47 Penn. 115.
[2] Easter *v.* Allen, 8 Allen, 7.
[3] Wright *v.* Self, 1 F. & F. 704.
[4] Huntington *v.* Massey, ib. 690.

CHAPTER VIII.

INJURIES TO THE PERSON; ASSAULT AND BATTERY; FALSE IMPRISONMENT; INJURIES TO HEALTH.

§ 1. In an action for assault and battery, the plaintiff may prove previous threats, both for the purpose of showing that the defendant made the assault, and that it was malicious. Such a threat may have become of little importance, either from the time elapsing before the assault, or from other causes; but upon principle a threat to do an act can never be rejected as irrelevant, where the issue is whether the party making the threat did the act. And where it is material to show the *animus*, both the prior and subsequent declarations, as well as those which accompany the act, are admissible, whether the plaintiff knew of the threats before the assault or not.[1]

§ 2. It is not competent, in such a suit, to prove that the plaintiff is a turbulent man, and of desperate disposition; nor that the defendant is a quiet man and of peaceful demeanor.[2] Nor is evidence admissible of hostile feelings or a previous assault.[3]

§ 3. Where the defence of property is set up as a justification, lawful possession is sufficient, without proof of title; as where the house was vacant, but a servant of the defendant had the key.[4] So where the stewards of a musical festival occupied a county hall, the title of which was in the county justices, according to a custom for several years, but without evidence of express permission.[5]

§ 4. In trespass for assault and battery, words uttered by the plaintiff against the defendant, on a former occasion, are not ad-

[1] Bartram *v.* Stone, 31 Conn. 159.
[2] Smithwick *v.* Ward, 7 Jones, 64.
[3] Dole *v.* Erskine, 37 N. H. 316.
[4] Hall *v.* Davis, 2 C. & P. 33.
[5] Thomas *v.* Marsh, 5 C. & P. 596.

missible in mitigation. Nor statements made by third parties to the defendant of such words. The defendant's condition in life and occupation may be put in evidence.[1]

§ 5. Though the defendant offers evidence, not objected to, of previous provocation, by charging him with a crime, evidence for the plaintiff of the truth of such charge is incompetent.[2]

§ 6. In an action for false imprisonment, on suspicion of stealing the property of an inmate of the house of the defendant, with whom the plaintiff lived as his servant; the fact that the defendant signed the charge-sheet, and appeared before the magistrate, is strong though not conclusive evidence that he authorized the arrest.[3]

§ 7. In an action for malicious arrest, the plaintiff need not prove the whole of the proceedings before the magistrates.[4]

§ 8. The defendant cannot show, under the plea of not guilty, a judgment and execution against the plaintiff, even for the avowed purpose of proving that he was not guilty of the trespass.[5]

§ 8 *a*. To establish reasonable and probable cause in the action for false imprisonment, it is not necessary to prove that the defendant believed the facts stated in his plea, and that he acted upon that belief; but it is sufficient to prove such facts, as, in the opinion of the judge, amount to reasonable and probable cause. Reasonable and probable cause is a question for the judge and not for the jury.[6]

§ 9. In an action for false imprisonment, the plaintiff may be asked what the owner of the article, an inmate of the defendant's house, stated, in the presence of the policeman, as to what the defendant had said to her, on her going to ask him what she should do as to giving the plaintiff into custody.[7]

§ 10. Upon the question whether a release of personal property was obtained by duress by means of a criminal arrest; the declarations of the party, prior to the complaint, are admissible evidence against him, for the purpose of showing probable cause.[8]

[1] Jarvis *v.* Manlove, 5 Har. 452.

[2] Mowrey *v.* Smith (Mass.), Law Reg. Dec. 1865, p. 121.

[3] Harris *v.* Dignum, 29 L. J. Exch. 23.

[4] Biggs *v.* Clay, 3 Nev. & M. 464.

[5] Coats *v.* Darby, 3 Comst. 517.

[6] Hailes *v.* Marks, 9 W. R. 808; 4 L. T. (N. S.) 805, Exch.

[7] Harris *v.* Dignum, 5 Hurl. & Nor. 943; 29 L. J. Exch. 23.

[8] Hackett *v.* King, 8 Allen, 144.

§ 11. Where no justification is pleaded, upon the question of damages and wrong motives, evidence is admissible of grounds of suspicion.[1]

§ 12. Upon a question made as to the professional skill of the defendant, a surgeon, as compared with that of the profession in general, the opinion of the physician with whom he studied his profession is not competent evidence; nor the general reputation among the profession of the medical institution at which he attended lectures upon surgery; nor his declarations made to a physician, as to cases alleged to have been treated by him, and their symptoms, and the course of treatment pursued, and the opinion of the physician, derived from the statements and from the symptoms observed by himself, as to the propriety of the course pursued by the defendant; nor his manner of treatment of surgical cases, two years after the treatment of which complaint is made in the action, and eight or ten months after the commencement of the action. The fact, that a surgeon of acknowledged skill assisted the defendant in the treatment of the case, a part of the time, but not by his procurement, during which time, however, the defendant had the charge and control of the case, and the consulting surgeon disagreed with him as to the course of treatment in relation to which the unskilfulness was alleged; is not competent proof to show either skill or diligence.[2]

§ 13. In an action against a physician for unskilful treatment of a cut upon the plaintiff's thumb, several physicians testified that the disease of the thumb was a felon, which often resulted from a punctured wound. Held, that it was not competent to inquire of the plaintiff's nurse, who had attended her during all the time, when she first heard of a punctured wound in connection with the injury, it not appearing that the defendant had ever assigned that cause as the origin of the disease.[3]

§ 13 *a*. A declaration, by a husband and wife against a physician for malpractice, alleged that the defendant fraudulently represented to the female plaintiff that she was doing well, in consequence of which she did not apply to other physicians, and thereby lost the use of her hand; but there was no evidence that the plaintiff desired

[1] Brown *v*. Chadsey, 39 Barb. 253.
[2] Leighton *v*. Sargent, 11 Fost. 119.
[3] Twombly *v*. Leach, 11 Cush. 397.

to call in any other physician. Held, a witness could not be asked what effect was produced upon his mind by the declarations of the defendant concerning another physician in the same town. In such action, evidence is not competent for the plaintiff, to show the effect of the remedies, prescribed by the defendant for the wife, upon a person entirely well; nor to prove that the husband was unable to labor, and dependent upon his wife for his support; there being no allegation in the declaration of a loss of the wife's services. There was evidence tending to show that the defendant did not communicate to the plaintiff the nature of the disease, but that he opened her thumb, giving as a reason that there was a nerve partly cut off, and it would be better to cut it entirely off. Held, other physicians could not be asked: "Is it good medical practice to say you opened a thumb to cut off a nerve, because it is already partly cut off?" But it is competent for the defendant to prove, that physicians, in addressing their patients, often call the tendon of the thumb a nerve; and that it is good medical treatment in some cases for physicians to withhold from patients the extent of their disease and their actual condition; and that the treatment of the disease, as detailed by the principal witness for the plaintiffs, was proper in the opinion of medical men.[1]

[1] Twombly *v.* Leach, 11 Cush. 397.

CHAPTER IX.

EVIDENCE IN ACTIONS FOR LIBEL AND SLANDER.

§ 1. It is more peculiarly true of libel and slander than of almost any other wrong, that a consideration of the wrong itself necessarily involves a view of the evidence relating to it; which accordingly has been somewhat fully treated in other connections.[1] The plan of the present work requires a brief additional notice.

§ 1 *a*. In an action for slander, other words than those for which the suit is brought may be proved, as showing the intent.[2] "Every uncalled for utterance of a defamatory charge is more or less indicative of the speaker's malice at the time." [3] So the plaintiff's answer to the slanderous words at the time they were uttered.[4] The whole conversation may be proved.[5] But not words spoken after suit brought, to explain the others.[6]

§ 2. In an action for a libel, the declarations of the defendant at the time of publication are evidence, as a part of the *res gestæ*, and to show the *quo animo*.[7] But not a verbal explanation of the libel at the time of publication.[8]

§ 3. It is held that evidence may be given of the sense in which the words were understood by the hearers, unless their meaning was clear.[9] So, although the mere opinions of witnesses as to the meaning of a libel, or that it was of and concerning the plaintiff, are not admissible; yet, when the words are ambiguous, and the

[1] See Hilliard on Torts, Chap. XV.
[2] Taylor *v.* Moran, 4 Met. (Ky.) 127.
[3] Per Sanford, J., Swift *v.* Dickerman, 31 Conn. 291.
[4] Bradley *v.* Gardner, 10 Cal. 371.
[5] Barton *v.* Holmes, 16 Iowa, 252.
[6] Lucas *v.* Nichols, 7 Jones, 32.
[7] Rice *v.* Simmons, 2 Har. 309.
[8] Hagan *v.* Hendry, 18 Ind. 177.
[9] Barton *v.* Holmes, 16 Iowa, 252; Garret *v.* Dickerson, 19 Md. 418; De Moss *v.* Haycock, 15 Iowa, 149.

application doubtful, it must be shown that they were used in their actionable sense, and were applied to the plaintiff, and that the hearers so understood them, and therefore the testimony of the hearers, as to how they understood the words, is admissible.[1]

§ 4. But the understanding of the by-standers cannot be shown to make words slanderous, which, as stated in the declaration, are not *per se* actionable.[2] And it is held, in Pennsylvania, notwith standing some cited cases to the contrary, that the opinion of a witness, that the plaintiff was the person intended, is not competent evidence. "A party cannot thus aid the *innuendo* by the opinion of the witness. . . . If this could be done there would be no use for an *innuendo*. Its office would be supplied by the oath of witnesses, who would draw the inference from precedent facts instead of the jury. . . . It is the business of witnesses to state facts, and the province of the jury to draw such inferences or conclusions from them as they shall conscientiously believe to be warranted."[3] Nor can it be shown that the words were used in a sense different from their natural one, unless accompanied with proof that such different meaning was explained at the time they were uttered.[4] It is for the jury, not for an expert, to judge of the meaning of the words. Thus, where the words were, that the plaintiff was "getting up a bogus baby-affair," a "Mrs. Cunningham affair," evidence, as to what was generally understood by a "Mrs. C. affair," was rejected.[5]

§ 5. In an action for slander of a physician in his profession, the currency of the slander in the place of his practice, following the utterance, may be given in evidence, as well as its effect upon his professional gains, in aggravation or proof of damages, without strict proof connecting the current report with the slander of the defendant; the fact of such connection being a question for the jury.[6] So evidence is admissible, in enhancement of damages, that the plaintiff suffered great anxiety and distress of mind by reason of the slander, though the charge was against him in his professional and not in his private character.[7] So where the plaintiff, in an action for a libellous publication in a newspaper charging her with theft, had alleged as special damage, that she

[1] Smart *v.* Blanchard, 42 N. H. 137.
[2] Smith *v.* Gaffard, 33 Ala. 168.
[3] Raigler *v.* Hummel, 37 Penn. 130; per Thompson, J., ib. 133, 134.
[4] Dempsey *v.* Paige, 4 E. D. Smith, 218.
[5] Weed *v.* Bibbins, 32 Barb. 315.
[6] Rice *v.* Cottrell, 5 R. I. 340.
[7] Swift *v.* Dickerman, 31 Conn. 285.

had in consequence of the libel been discharged by one A from his employment as a seamstress in a neighboring town; held, she might prove, that a few days after the publication A had said to her, that there were flying reports in the newspapers about her and her sister, and that it would injure his shop to have such girls there, and had thereupon discharged her; although there was no other evidence, either that A had seen the particular publication in question, or as to what reports and what newspapers he referred to.[1] But one charged with theft cannot show that he is a minister, in order to enhance the damages, where there is no averment of that fact, and no allegation of special damage to him in his profession.[2] So where the plaintiff, a surgeon, sued for a slander, charging him with having had a bastard child by a female servant, alleging that the words were spoken to A, whereby A would not employ him, and that he was otherwise injured in his business; held, he could not recover for damages to his general business occasioned by repetitions of the slander, but which did not follow directly from the speaking of the words to A.[3] So in an action for libels of and concerning the plaintiff as an opera manager; the question, "What was the effect upon the house (the plaintiff's Opera House) or the filling of the house, of the articles that were published in the Herald, and which are now complained of," is not competent, the answer being a mere opinion.[4]

§ 6. It is held that, on a statement of special damage by loss of custom, the customers themselves must be called.[5]

§ 7. In an action for libels, published in the defendant's newspaper, although the complaint alleges that the defendant boasted of a circulation of 20,000 copies daily, and although this allegation is not denied by the answer; copies published by him, at about the date of the libels, stating a greater circulation at that time, are competent evidence to prove that fact.[6]

§ 8. Upon the subject of *variance* between the words alleged and those proved, some late cases adopt a strict rule, though doubting its policy. The rule is attributed to the fact, that "the action of slander has not been regarded with any great favor by the courts."[7] Thus, in an action for slander, so many of the

1 Moore *v.* Stevenson, 27 Conn. 14.
2 Gandy *v.* Humphries, 35 Ala. 617.
3 Dixon *v.* Smith, 5 Hurl. & Nor. 450.
4 Fry *v.* Bennett, 3 Bosw. 200.
5 Wood *v.* Jones, 1 F. & F. 301.
6 Fry *v.* Bennett, 3 Bosw. 200.
7 Per Walker, J., 29 Ill. 459.

words complained of must be proved as will establish the slander; not other words of similar import, or equivalent words. More words may be proved, provided they do not change the meaning. A difference in the tense of the word proved, and that alleged, will defeat a recovery,— as the use of "has" for "had."[1]

§ 9. It is held calculated to mislead the jury, to refer it to them to determine, whether the defendant, "in substance," spoke or published the words charged, without explaining the meaning which the law would attach to that expression in connection with the proof of the slander charged.[2]

§ 9 *a*. Where the plaintiff alleges an office or special character, it is generally held sufficient to prove actual possession and enjoyment of the office, or actual exercise of the employment or profession.[3] But an allegation of the mode of the plaintiff's appointment must be proved; as in case of the allegation that he has taken a medical degree.[4] If the charge itself assumes the alleged office or employment, it need not be proved.[5]

§ 10. In an action for slanderous words, *malice* is an essential fact, and should always be proved.[6] The defendant's manner, and other circumstances accompanying the slander, may be proved on the question of malice.[7] And, while malice is doubtless to be inferred from falsehood, evidence of *actual* malice is admissible upon the question of damages.[8]

§ 11. *Repetition* of the slanderous or similar words, after suit brought, is held admissible proof of malice, but not of other words, amounting to a distinct slander.[9] And when words, oral or written, actionable in themselves, other than the publication declared on, are offered in evidence to prove malice, the court must caution the jury that they are not to increase the damages on that account.[10] Thus A, and B his wife, sued C, and D his wife, for the slander of B by D, and introduced evidence to prove the words, and that they were similar to those contained in an anonymous letter, said to have been written and sent by B to D;

[1] Wilborn *v.* Odell, 29 Ill. 456. See Maybee *v.* Fisk, 42 Barb. 326.

[2] Atteberry *v.* Powell, 29 Mis. 429.

[3] Jones *v.* Stevens, 11 Price, 235; Berryman *v.* Wise, 4 T. R. 66. See Sellers *v.* Till, 4 B. & C. 655; McPherson *v.* Chedeall, 24 Wend. 24; Smith *v.* Taylor, 1 N. R. 196.

[4] Moises *v.* Thornton, 8 T. R. 303.

[5] Berryman *v.* Wise, 4 T. R. 366; Yrisarri *v.* Clement, 3 Bing. 432; Cummen *v.* Smith, 2 S. & R. 440.

[6] Harry *v.* Constantin, 14 La. An. 782.

[7] Parke *v.* Blackiston, 3 Har. 373.

[8] Fry *v.* Bennett, 3 Bosw. 200.

[9] Parmer *v.* Anderson, 33 Ala. 78.

[10] Letton *v.* Young, 2 Met. (Ky.) 558.

which letter contained libellous statements against both B and her daughter. Held, admissible for the purpose of showing malice, though not to affect the damages, provided the jury were cautioned by the court upon this latter point; that portion, however, relating to the daughter being evidence for no purpose whatsoever. An instruction was given to the jury, to the effect that the letter was only admissible to show malice, and for no other purpose, and that they had a right to award such damages to the plaintiffs as they thought them entitled to from all circumstances proved in the case. Held, the caution to the jury was not sufficient.[1]

§ 12. *Passion* does not disprove malice.[2]

§ 13. Where the plaintiff, to show malice, proves an admission of the defendant as to a conversation with the defendant's brother; the defendant, to rebut the inference of malice, may show what he actually did say, and the circumstances of the conversation.[3]

§ 14. When the libel is *primâ facie* a privileged communication, it is open to the plaintiff to put in evidence subsequent statements made by the defendant, as tending to show malice at the time of publication. The judge ought, especially if there be a considerable interval between such statements and the publication, to direct the jury to consider, whether such subsequent statements might not refer to something which happened subsequently to the libel, so as not to show malice at the time of publication.[4]

§ 15. Circumstances tending to disprove malice are admissible, in a slander suit, in mitigation of damages, but not evidence of the apparent good humor of the defendant, when uttering language clearly slanderous.[5] And where mitigating circumstances are offered in evidence, for the purpose of repelling the presumption of malice, it should be shown that he knew of them at the time he made the charge.[6]

§ 16. The act of 1855, of Connecticut, with regard to libels, provides, that, "in every action for an alleged libel, the defendant may give proof of intention, and unless the plaintiff shall prove malice in fact he shall recover nothing but his actual damage proved and specially alleged in the declaration." Held, the former provision was only an extension of a previous rule; such evidence having been always admissible in reduction of damages,

1 Letton *v.* Young, 2 Met. (Ky.) 558.
2 Hosley *v.* Brooks, 20 Ill. 115.
3 Smith *v.* Gaffard, 3 Ala. 168.
4 Hemmings *v.* Gasson, 1 Ell. B. & E. 346
5 Weaver *v.* Hendrick, 30 Mis. 502.
6 Swift *v.* Dickerman, 31 Conn. 285.

and the only difference here being, that, in the absence of rebutting proof on the part of the plaintiff, it prevents the recovery of general damages. The latter provision was not intended to prescribe any new rule as to the kind and degree of malice to be proved, or as to the evidence by which it was to be shown, but only to require other evidence than mere legal presumption from the fact of publication. That the motives of the defendant were improper and unjustifiable, may be shown by the character of the publication itself, and by all the circumstances, without proof of any actually hostile motive. This construction of the act reconciles it with the provision of the constitution, that "every person, for an injury done him in his person, property, or reputation, shall have remedy by due course of law, and right and justice administered without sale, denial, or delay."[1]

§ 17. Evidence is not admissible, on the part of the defendant, of previous harsh language of the plaintiff's wife at the time.[2] Nor, in mitigation, that in other conversations he spoke of the plaintiff less offensively.[3]

§ 18. Evidence is not admissible, that the alleged slander was a mere repetition of what had been said by another, unless the authority was given.[4] So if the defendant would avail himself, in mitigation of damages, of the fact, that, at the time he told the injurious story, he mentioned the name of the author, it must not only appear that he did so mention his author, but also that he did so receive the story.[5]

§ 19. It is held, that, in an action for slander, the defendant may show, in order to disprove malice and in mitigation of damages, that, when the words were uttered, a general report existed, that the plaintiff had committed the act charged.[6] (See § 21.) So for the purpose of proving that the owner of a building, set on fire, had reason to believe that a particular person was the incendiary, and used good faith in making statements charging him with the crime; evidence that he was informed of declarations and acts of the suspected person, tending to show his guilt, is competent.[7]

§ 20. But other cases hold the contrary.[8] Thus it is held, that

[1] Hotchkiss v. Porter, 20 Conn. 414; acc. Moore v. Stevenson, 27 ib. 14.

[2] Hosley v. Brooks, 20 Ill. 115. See Thomas v. Dunaway, 30 ib. 373.

[3] Bradford v. Edwards, 32 Ala. 628.

[4] Elliott v. Boyles, 31 Penn. 65.

[5] Rice v. Cottrell, 5 R. I. 340.

[6] Wetherbee v. Marsh, 20 N. H. 561; Morris v. Barker, 4 Har. 520.

[7] Lawler v. Earle, 5 Allen, 22.

[8] Richardson v. Roberts, 23 Geo. 215.

the defendant cannot, under the general issue, prove that the words were but a repetition of common reports, either to rebut malice or mitigate damages. Nor, for either purpose, acts of the plaintiff tending to excite suspicions that he was guilty of the crime charged, but stopping short of actual proof of such guilt; although it is also proposed to show, that, at the time the words were uttered, a public investigation was going on, involving an inquiry into the plaintiff's conduct, and was a subject of public remark.[1] So it cannot be proved, that the plaintiff was the object of general suspicion in the neighborhood in relation to the act charged.[2] Nor that another person had previously made the same charge, and the plaintiff did not deny it.[3] Nor, in case of an alleged libel in a newspaper, that a similar article had recently appeared in another paper.[4] More especially, if the libellous matter be stated positively in the publication, and not as resting in rumor merely; the mere existence of the rumor, known to all parties, is not admissible in mitigation of damages.[5]

§ 21. It is generally held, that evidence of character is admissible.[6] Thus, in mitigation of damages, of the plaintiff's bad character.[7] Hence, in an action of slander, charging the defendant with having accused the plaintiff of adultery, it is competent for the defendant, in mitigation of damages, to prove that the plaintiff was commonly reputed to be unchaste and licentious.[8] Other cases, however, hold the contrary.[9] And in a recent case in England it is held, that, in an action for libel, where there is no plea of justification, questions cannot be asked, tending to show the plaintiff's previous bad character, in mitigation of damages.[10] And the distinction is made, between evidence of the plaintiff's bad character, and that of particular reports, relating to the charge in question.[11] (See § 19.) Thus, in an action by a female for a charge of general unchastity, upon a plea of the general issue, evidence is admissible for the defendant of the bad general reputation of the plaintiff for chastity, but not of reports of particular acts of incontinency. The court remark: "Without undertaking to review at length

[1] Knight *v.* Foster, 39 N. H. 576.
[2] Fuller *v.* Dean, 31 Ala. 654.
[3] Ibid.
[4] Sheahan *v.* Collins, 20 Ill. 325.
[5] Haskins *v.* Lumsden, 10 Wis. 359.
[6] See Bryan *v.* Gurr, 27 Geo. 378.
[7] Fuller *v.* Dean, 31 Ala. 654; 20 Ill. 325; Conroe *v.* Conroe, 47 Penn. 198; Burton *v.* March, 6 Jones, 409; Waples *v.* Burton, 2 Har. 446.
[8] Bridgman *v.* Hopkins, 34 Verm. 69.
[9] Parke *v.* Blackiston, 3 Har. 373.
[10] Bracegirdle *v.* Bailey, 1 F. & F. 536.
[11] Sheahan *v.* Collins, 20 Ill. 325.

the numerous decisions made, especially in the English, Massachusetts, and New York courts, upon the question how far, in actions of slander, the defendant may, under the plea of not guilty, attack the character of the plaintiff, it may be safely said to be almost everywhere settled, that evidence of general bad reputation is admissible in mitigation of damages. Whether reputation in that department of character which the alleged slander has assailed may be given in evidence is perhaps not so well established by authority. In many of the cases the question has been embarrassed by the pleadings. There has been no plea of not guilty, or it has been accompanied with a plea or notice of justification."[1] So, in an action for charging a female with unchastity, evidence that the plaintiff's general reputation is bad, independently of the slander of which she complains, and that it was bad ten years before, and at another place, is admissible in mitigation of damages, although no such ground of defence is set up in the answer. But evidence of particular instances of her misconduct is not admissible.[2] And it cannot be shown in mitigation of damages that the plaintiff was quarrelsome.[3]

§ 22. It is held, that no evidence can be offered of the plaintiff's good character, till it has been attacked.[4] The law presumes his character to be good.[5] And this notwithstanding the proof of circumstances under the general issue, which may have awakened suspicion of the plaintiff's guilt in the mind of the defendant.[6]

§ 23. In an action for a libel upon the plaintiff, in connection with a donation party which she had attended, the character of that party, and the conduct of its members, cannot be proved by the defendant under the general issue.[7]

§ 24. It is held, that the *wealth* of the defendant cannot be offered in evidence;[8] nor his poverty;[9] nor, in general, his circumstances as to property.[10] But evidence of the rank, profession, or standing of either party is admissible.[11]

§ 25. The *truth* is a good defence to an action for libel or

[1] Conroe *v.* Conroe, 47 Penn. 198; per Strong, J., ib. 200.
[2] Parkhurst *v.* Ketchum, 6 Allen, 406.
[3] Hosley *v.* Brooks, 20 Ill. 115.
[4] Tibbs *v.* Brown, 2 Grant, 39; 3 Har. 373; 34 Penn. 314.
[5] Parke *v.* Blackiston, 3 Har. 373.
[6] Chubb *v.* Gsell, 34 Penn. 114.
[7] Smart *v.* Blanchard, 42 N. H. 137.
[8] Palmer *v.* Haskins, 28 Barb. 90. Contra, Humphries *v.* Parker, 52 Maine, 502.
[9] Pool *v.* Devers, 30 Ala. 672.
[10] Morris *v.* Barker, 4 Har. 520.
[11] Parke *v.* Blackiston, 3 Har. 373.

slander;[1] and this, notwithstanding malice.[2] But when a defendant in slander pleads the general issue, he admits that the plaintiff is innocent of the charge. The truth can only be shown under a plea of justification.[3] The defendant cannot, upon plea of the general issue, prove the truth of the words charged, for the purpose of disproving malice or of mitigating damages;[4] though it is held, that he is not to be denied; the benefit of mitigating circumstances, merely because they *tend* to prove the truth of the charge, while they fall short of it; and may show by way of excuse anything short of a justification, which repels the presumption of malice, but does not *necessarily* imply the truth of the charge, or *necessarily* constitute evidence of it.[5] And, in an action for slanderous words, the defendant cannot in the same answer deny and also justify the words. So an answer justifying the speaking must confess it. And an answer, merely stating that the words spoken are true, is not sufficient as a justification; it should state the facts constituting the crime or offence imputed, so that an issue either of law or fact may be found.[6] And evidence is sometimes held not admissible in mitigation of damages, which tends to prove the truth; "such as would, in the mind of a prudent man, justly awaken suspicions of guilt of the crime imputed. The purpose of the testimony is to mitigate the legal imputation of malice, on the ground of misapprehension, as to the character of the acts out of which the imputation of guilt was made, and consequently the damages. It must not tend, at the same time, to prove the truth . . . and hence that there was no misapprehension."[7]

§ 26. But although the truth of the charge cannot be proved in mitigation of damages; it is sometimes held, that for this purpose the defendant may prove, under the general issue, a belief of its truth, and the facts upon which such belief is founded. Thus, in an action for the charge of poisoning a cow, the defendant may prove an actual poisoning; the hostility of the plaintiff; that the defendant had poisoned his dog, and the plaintiff had threatened to pay him in his own coin; and that the defendant had attempted

1 Rayne v. Taylor, 14 La. An. 406; 3 Bosw. 200.

2 Fry v. Bennett, 3 Bosw. 200.

3 Sheahan v. Collins, 20 Ill. 325.

4 Swift v. Dickerman, 31 Conn. 285; Knight v. Foster, 39 N. H. 576.

5 Swift v. Dickerman, 31 Conn. 285.

6 Atteberry v. Powell, 29 Mis. 429.

7 Per Thompson, J., Smith v. Smith, 39 Penn. 442.

to instigate a malicious prosecution against the plaintiff.[1] So where the words spoken charged the plaintiff with attempting to produce a "bogus" baby; the defendant, admitting their falsity, and setting up in mitigation of damage, that, in common with others, he believed the charge, may show, on the question of damages, as tending to prove absence of malice and a well-founded belief, that the physical condition of the father was such, as to induce a sincere belief that at the time he was incapable of procreation.[2] (*a*) And it is held in New York, that, if the defendant fails to prove his plea of justification, he may still offer evidence in mitigation, if the mitigating facts are stated in the answer.[3] But it is no defence to an action for slander, by words imputing unchastity to a woman, to show that the defendant spoke the words to her, and was led to do so by her general conduct, and especially by her deportment with a particular man, believing the same to be true.[4] So a belief of the truth is held no defence to an action for libel;[5] more especially if the party was indifferent whether it were true or false.[6]

§ 26 *a*. It is held, that, where the defendant pleads, and offers evidence tending but failing to prove, the truth; if this defence is made *bonâ fide*, and not with the purpose of spreading and perpetuating the original slander, it ought not to aggravate the damages; and whether the defence is made with a fair or malicious purpose, is a question for the jury.[7] (*b*)

§ 27. It is held, that, under a plea of the truth, evidence must be offered which would *convict* of the crime charged.[8] Thus, in an action for charging perjury, the plea of justification must be established by such amount of evidence as would authorize a conviction for that crime.[9] So it is held, that the truth cannot be established by indirect and remote evidence.[10] And the justification must apply

[1] Hutchinson *v.* Wheeler, 35 Verm. 330.
[2] Weed *v.* Bibbins, 32 Barb. 315.
[3] Russ *v.* Brooks, 4 E. D. Smith, 644.
[4] Parkhurst *v.* Ketchum, 6 Allen, 406.
[5] Fry *v.* Bennett, 3 Bosw. 200.
[6] Moore *v.* Stevenson, 27 Conn. 14.
[7] Pallet *v.* Sargent, 36 N. H. 496.
[8] Forshee *v.* Abrams, 2 Clarke (Iowa), 571.
[9] Gorman *v.* Sutton, 32 Penn. 247.
[10] Forshee *v.* Abrams, 2 Clarke (Iowa), 571.

(*a*) It is held in a late English case, that, in an action by an optician against a newspaper proprietor, for inserting an advertisement alluding to him as a licensed hawker and quack in spectacle secrets; evidence that this was true is admissible under the general issue, as showing that the advertisement was not a libel. Keyzor *v.* Newcomb, 1 F. & F. 487.

(*b*) Upon the point, whether an attempted justification aggravates the slander, or whether, if set up *bonâ fide*, it is no aggravation; see Gorman *v.* Sutton, 32 Penn. 247; Richardson *v.* Roberts, 23 Geo. 215; Pool *v.* Devers, 30 Ala. 672; Rayner *v.* Kinney, 14 Ohio St. 283.

to the very charge complained of. Thus, where the same offence was committed only once, instead of repeatedly, as charged, the justification was held bad.[1] So where, in slander, the words laid in the declaration charged that the plaintiff committed an offence with one person; evidence that he had committed a like offence with other persons will not be received, either as a defence or in mitigation of damages. Nor evidence that he had committed a different offence either with the same or with other persons. Thus, where the words laid charged that the plaintiff had committed a rape on a particular person, named in the declaration; evidence will not be received, that he had attempted to commit a rape on the same, and also on another person, either as a defence or in mitigation of damages. Nor will evidence be received in mitigation, that the plaintiff had admitted and boasted that he had committed, with other persons, offences of a like character with that charged upon him by the words laid in the declaration.[2] So under a plea of justification, in a suit for charging the plaintiff with fornication with a certain man, evidence that her child is a bastard is not sufficient.[3] So where the charge was, that the plaintiff, a physician, had no professional knowledge or skill, and lost almost all his patients; held, proof of particular instances, in which the plaintiff had shown want of knowledge and skill, was inadmissible, for the purpose of mitigating damages, or showing the professional reputation of the plaintiff. Reputation can only be proved by the direct testimony of those who are acquainted with it, and not by particular facts.[4] So the plaintiff was charged in a newspaper with having "made himself invisible on account of too much borrowing and not paying; that is to say, ran away." Innuendo, that he had borrowed articles of property, and then ran away and absconded, without paying for or returning the same. General justification, without specification of particulars. Held, the charge was not met by evidence of the plaintiff's absconding in debt.[5] So in an action for slander, in accusing the plaintiff of buying and selling by unsealed weights and measures, and also of the crime of gross fraud and cheating at common law, a justification of the truth cannot

[1] Burford *v.* Wible, 32 Penn. 95. See Forshee *v.* Abrams, 2 Clarke (Iowa), 571.

[2] Pallet *v.* Sargent, 36 N. H. 496.

[3] Richardson *v.* Roberts, 23 Geo. 215.

[4] Swift *v.* Dickerman, 31 Conn. 285.

[5] Washten *v.* Quenzer, 29 N. Y. (2 Tiffa.) 547.

be supported by evidence, that the plaintiff "applied to a person to take some damaged meat and sell it, without letting it be known that the plaintiff was connected in the transaction."[1] So the defendant published of the plaintiffs, coal-merchants, what purported to be a report of an inquiry before a board of guardians respecting the fraudulent conduct of the plaintiffs' agent, who, in performance of a contract for "best coals," had delivered at the workhouse coals of an inferior description, and (by falsifying the weighing machine by means of a wedge) deficient in weight. The libel commenced, "The way in which Messrs. P. (the plaintiffs) do things at Guildford. Inserting the wedge;" and ended with a recommendation of one of the guardians to "have nothing more to do with Messrs. P.," innuendo, "the defendant meaning thereby that the plaintiffs were cognizant of, and had sanctioned improper and fraudulent conduct by their agent at Guildford, and were accustomed to carry on their said trade there improperly and fraudulently." The defendant pleaded a justification, following the innuendo, and saying that the coals delivered, as mentioned in the libel, were inferior in quality, as the plaintiffs well knew, and deficient in weight. Held, the defendant, having by his plea alleged that the fraud of their agent was sanctioned by the plaintiffs, must prove that the libel imputed personal misconduct and fraud to the plaintiffs, and the jury were bound to find for the plaintiffs, unless satisfied that the defendant had shown some complicity on their part in the misconduct and fraud imputed to their agent.[2] But an action of slander for charging a man with having the venereal disease, and, with that disease upon him, contracting marriage, and communicating the disease to his wife, cannot be maintained, if the plaintiff immediately after his marriage had the disease in fact, even by proof that his wife, whom he married without knowing that she had the disease, communicated it to him.[3]

§ 27 *a*. Where the defendant, to an action for slander, pleads the general issue and a justification, he may give evidence in mitigation of damages under the general issue; though it may be doubted whether he can do it when a justification is pleaded alone.[4]

§ 27 *b*. Where alleged libels imputed to the plaintiff, an opera

[1] Chapman *v.* Ordway, 5 Allen, 593.

[2] Prior *v.* Wilson, 1 C. B. (N. S.) 95.

[3] Golderman *v.* Stearns, 7 Gray, 181.

[4] Pallet *v.* Sargent, 36 N. H. 496.

manager, cruel treatment towards his artists, and the defendant justified; evidence of the opinions of third persons, as to such conduct, was held inadmissible. The acts of the plaintiff, which are relied upon as a justification, must be proved, and, upon the evidence given, the truth or falsity of the charge determined by the jury. And evidence of the plaintiff's conduct towards some other person, employed by him during a prior season, and in a previous year, is inadmissible.[1]

§ 28. In an action of slander, for charging the plaintiff with fornication, while a medical student in the city of New York, the defendant having attempted to prove the charge to be true, evidence is not competent for the plaintiff in rebuttal, "that he was at the time in straitened pecuniary circumstances, and had hardly the means of supporting himself." "Such a man in such a place might readily find other means than money, which would enable him to commit the acts charged."[2]

§ 29. In an action of slander, where the general issue alone is pleaded, the plaintiff cannot, in the first instance, give evidence tending to prove the defendant's knowledge of the falsity of the words spoken. A plaintiff cannot give such evidence, except for the purpose of rebutting the defence.[3]

§ 30. Where the slander imputes larceny, and the circumstances of the alleged larcenous taking referred to have been proved by the defendant, the plaintiff may show in rebuttal, that, in taking the property, he acted upon the advice of counsel, that he had a legal right so to do.[4]

§ 31. If, in an action for slander, a verdict has been found for the defendant on the ground that the words were privileged; questions arising in the course of the trial, as to the admission or exclusion of evidence in reference to the truth, and the defence of justification on that ground, are immaterial.[5]

§ 32. The court will not permit the plaintiff to exhibit interrogatories to the defendant, the answer to which, if in the affirmative, would tend to show that he composed or published the libel, and would therefore criminate him.[6]

§ 33. It is doubted whether, in an action for malicious prosecu-

[1] Fry v. Bennett, 3 Bosw. 200.
[2] Orcutt v. Ranney, 10 Cush. 183–185.
[3] Hartranft v. Hesser, 34 Penn. 117.
[4] Gandy v. Humphries, 35 Ala. 617.
[5] Lawler v. Earle, 5 Allen, 22.
[6] Tupling v. Ward, 6 H. & N. 749.

tion, the defendant can be asked in chief if he had any other motive in view than to further the ends of justice? [1]

§ 34. In case for malicious prosecution, the plaintiff must prove the prosecution, acquittal, want of probable cause, and malice of the defendant.[2]

§ 35. The waiving of an examination before a magistrate, and giving bail for appearance at court, is not such an admission of guilt as will preclude an action for malicious prosecution.[3]

§ 36. A discharge of a person arrested, by the prosecuting attorney, is the usual mode of terminating a prosecution, in Illinois. A bill need not be ignored, before he may maintain an action for a malicious prosecution.[4]

§ 36 *a*. The discharge, by an examining magistrate, of a person accused of a crime, is not such evidence of want of probable cause, as will maintain an action for malicious prosecution.[5]

§ 37. The notes of a magistrate, taken on the hearing of a criminal charge, and never read to, or signed by the witness, are not a deposition; and are not evidence to impeach or contradict such party.[6]

§ 38. In an action for malicious prosecution, the record of an action of replevin, brought by the plaintiff for the property alleged to have been stolen, is not competent evidence. It was for a different cause of action. All that the plaintiff could have recovered in that suit was the value of the property and damages for taking it, aggravated perhaps by the accompanying circumstances. He could have recovered nothing for the personal injury. This is an action for a personal wrong.[7]

[1] Hardwick *v.* Coleman, 1 F. & F. 531.
[2] Rhodes *v.* Silvers, 1 Har. 127.
[3] Schoonover *v.* Myers, 28 Ill. 308.
[4] Ibid.
[5] Thorpe *v.* Ballvett, 25 Ill. 339.
[6] Schoonover *v.* Myers, 28 ib. 308.
[7] Scofield *v.* Ferrers, 47 Penn. 194.

CHAPTER X.

MISCELLANEOUS INJURIES TO PROPERTY.

§ 1. In an action against a city, for obstructing a culvert for a watercourse under a highway, the burden of proof is upon the plaintiff, to show that the injury was caused solely by the defendant's negligence in not removing the obstruction. Upon such proof, and in the absence of any proof of neglect or want of care in the plaintiff or a third person, contributing to the obstruction, the action is maintainable.[1]

§ 1 *a*. The plaintiff owned a mill and water-privilege, subject to a right in the defendant to take from the flume all the water necessary for his mill below. In an action for diversion of the water, by taking more than the defendant was entitled to, the plaintiff alleged, that he had a right to a *flow of the water in great abundance and plenty to his mill.* Held, that this was not *descriptive* of his right, and therefore proof of the limited right which he held was not a variance; also, that the taking, by the defendant, of more water than was necessary for his mill, was a *diversion* of the water of the plaintiff; also, that, under the allegation that the defendant had diverted the water and prevented it from flowing to the plaintiff's mill, the plaintiff might show that the trough, by which the defendant conveyed the water from the flume to his mill, was leaky, in consequence of which much water was wasted, and that his water-wheel was out of repair, and required more water to move it than if it was in a proper condition.[2]

§ 2. Evidence that, since the commencement of an action against the owner of land for obstructing a *way* claimed over it

[1] Parker *v.* Lowell, 11 Gray, 353. See Union, &c. *v.* Crary, 25 Cal. 507.

[2] Wier *v.* Covell, 29 Conn. 197.

by prescription in a definite line, the plaintiff broke down the defendant's wall and crossed the land in another direction; is inadmissible for the defendant.[1]

§ 3. A refusal to instruct the jury, that the closing of a way claimed by prescription, by agreement of the claimant of the way with the owner of the land over which it is claimed, and the subsequent use of a new way instead, may be deemed evidence that it was a way of necessity, shifting at the pleasure of the owner of the land; is no ground of exception, especially if the jury are correctly instructed as to the nature of ways of prescription and of necessity.[2]

§ 4. In an action against a *common carrier* for failure to stop according to previous notice, at a time specified, at A, and take the plaintiff on his vessel as passenger, which failure occasioned great bodily exposure and mental suffering; the peculiar bodily condition of the plaintiff may be proved in aggravation of damages.[3]

§ 5. Where a passenger applied to the agent of a railroad for a ticket, who gave him a certificate that the tickets "were all out," which he showed to the conductor; the testimony of the agent is competent, to show that the passenger applied for a ticket, and the certificate, to show that the conductor knew that the fault of the passenger's not having a ticket lay with the company and not with the passenger.[4]

§ 6. In an action for lost baggage, the fact that the plaintiff was a passenger may be proved, without an averment, by the possession of a baggage check and ticket; and by the check alone, if it appears that such checks are not given until the passenger-tickets are shown.[5]

§ 7. In an action on a bill of lading for non-delivery of goods, alleged to be lost by the defendant's negligence; there being no evidence that the loss could have been prevented if the collision which caused it occurred, the proper question for the jury is, whether the collision was caused by negligence.[6]

§ 8. In an action for injury caused by the *negligence* of persons having charge of a ship at a public dock, under the care of a

[1] Smith *v.* Lee, 14 Gray, 473.
[2] Ibid.
[3] Heirn *v.* McCaughan, 32 Miss. 17.
[4] St. Louis, &c. *v.* Dalby, 19 Ill. 353.
[5] Ill. Cent. &c. *v.* Copeland, 24 ib. 332.
[6] Grill *v.* General, &c. Law Rep. 1 C. P. 600; Amn. L. Rev. Jan. 1867, p. 288.

ship-keeper, there being no evidence by whom the keeper was appointed; held, the jury might infer from the ship's register, bearing the defendant's name as owner, that he employed the negligent parties.[1]

§ 9. In an action to recover the value of leather delivered to the defendant to be made into shoes, the plaintiff alleging *conversion* of a portion of the leather, and the defendant that it had all been returned in the shoes manufactured; some of the defendant's witnesses having described leather which they supposed had been received by the defendant of the plaintiff, the defendant cannot ask another witness, called as an expert, how much leather, such as was described by the above witnesses, it would take, to make a certain number of pairs of shoes; it not appearing that the witness had the means of forming the opinion desired.[2]

§ 10. If goods, alleged to have been converted, have been mixed by a mortgagee with other similar goods, which the defendant, as mortgagee, had a right to retain under his mortgage, and it is left for the jury to determine whether or not he had means for making a discrimination, which the other party had not; evidence of a general demand by the plaintiff for the goods mortgaged, and of a reply by the defendant, that "he was sorry he could not accommodate him, and that he had been expecting this demand for some days," is competent to be submitted to the jury, with the other testimony, to show a conversion. But if all the goods so intermixed have been sold by the defendant, no proof of demand is necessary.[3]

§ 10. In an action for infringement of a *patent*, for which there is no established patent or license fee, the value of the thing used may be determined by all the evidence as to its character, operation, and effect.[4]

§ 11. On the trial of issues in a patent case, if the defendant set up a prior user, the plaintiff may offer rebutting evidence. But after the defendant's evidence has been summed up, he cannot offer further evidence in answer to the plaintiff's evidence in reply.[5]

[1] Hibbs *v.* Ross, Law Rep. 1 Q. B. 534; Amn. Law Rev. Jan. 1867, p. 315.

[2] Rich *v.* Jones, 9 Cush. 329.

[3] Simpson *v.* Carleton, 1 Allen, 109.

[4] The Suffolk Co. *v.* Hayden, 3 Wall. 315.

[5] Penn. *v.* Jack, Eng. Law Rep. 2 Eq. 314; Amn. Law Rev. Jan. 1867, p. 309.

CHAPTER XI.

EVIDENCE IN ACTIONS RELATING TO PUBLIC OFFICERS.

§ 1. PROOF that an individual is reputed to be, and has notoriously acted as, a public officer, is *primâ facie* evidence of his official character. This exception to the general rule, requiring the best evidence, is founded upon the strong presumption which arises from the exercise of a public office, that the appointment to it is valid; and upon the general inconvenience of requiring full and strict proof of the appointment or election of public officers.

§ 2. In an action against a person, for an act which he had no right to do unless he were an officer, he must show that he was *primâ facie* an officer *de jure*. Proof, of acting as such under color of authority, and of reputation, is admissible evidence for that purpose; and is sufficient, in a collateral proceeding, to establish that character. The uniform practice has been, where officers have been sued for their official acts, and have sought to justify as such, to admit proof of their reputation and action as officers.[1]

§ 3. But in an action against a sheriff, for the misconduct of his bailiff, the plaintiff must prove the original warrant of execution from the former to the latter. It is not sufficient to prove official acts of the bailiff, he not being a general officer of the defendant.[2] "The under-sheriff is the general deputy of the high-sheriff for all purposes; but this is not the case with the bailiff."[3]

[1] Colton *v.* Beardsley, 38 Barb. 29. See Briggs *v.* Taylor, 35 Verm. 57. (In this case the subject was very elaborately discussed, and the court were not unanimou in their opinion.)

[2] Drake *v.* Sykes, 7 T. R. 113.

[3] Per Ld. Kenyon, C. J., ib. 116.

"The bailiff gives a bond to execute such warrants as shall be directed to him; when a warrant is granted to him, he becomes the special officer of the sheriff. . . . It did not appear that the sheriff had granted any warrant to this officer." [1]

§ 3 *a*. An action of trespass against a sheriff, in which he is directly charged, will be supported by proof, that the alleged trespass was committed by one who was acting as his deputy, for whose misfeasance he is by law answerable, although there is no such averment in the writ. And evidence that the trespasser was the deputy of the defendant, in connection with the defendant's brief statement justifying the act, makes out a *primâ facie* case for the plaintiff.[2]

§ 4. While an officer *de facto* is, in many cases, presumed to be such *de jure;* by an extension of the same principle, the doings of an officer are presumed to be conformable to law, and the burden of proof is on the party alleging the contrary.[3]

§ 5. In an action for neglecting to attach property, the burden is upon the plaintiff to prove that it was attachable, although the defendant claims it by purchase from the debtor.[4] So, where the sheriff's return and the deed made by him to a purchaser set forth notice of seizure, the burden of proof rests on the party attacking the sale to show the falsity of such recitals, although it involves the proof of a negative.[5] So in trover, for levying on a tool protected by an exemption act, the *onus* is on the plaintiff to prove that the value of all his tools, &c., including the one in question, did not exceed the sum exempted.[6] So the presumption is, that a sheriff, who sells property on execution, has done his duty in previously making a levy, and the fact will be deemed admitted, if no objection is made at the trial.[7] So, where the law requires a sheriff to appraise property taken and sold on execution, it is not incumbent on one claiming title under such sale to show that such appraisement was made. In the absence of proof, the sheriff will be presumed to have done his duty.[8]

§ 6. But the general rule of presumption and the burden of

1 Per Lawrence, J., ib. 117. See Yabsley *v*. Doble, 1 Ld. Ray. 190; (a case, upon the authority of which the court seriously doubted, before deciding as stated in the text.)

2 Pratt *v*. Bunker, 45 Maine, 569.

3 But see Keane *v*. Cannovan, 21 Cal. 291. Also, ch. 1, § 11.

4 Phelps *v*. Cutter, 4 Gray, 137.

5 Morse *v*. McCall, 13 La. An. 215.

6 Chambers *v*. Halsted, Hill & Denio, 384.

7 Smith *v*. Hill, 22 Barb. 656.

8 Mercer *v*. Doe, 6 Ind. 80.

proof may be changed by circumstances. Thus where a sheriff is shown to be guilty of negligence, in failing to serve a writ, the onus of showing that the defendant in the writ was insolvent devolves on him.[1] So, in a suit by the original plaintiff in a replevin for the sheriff's negligence in the custody of the property, no proof of title need be made, where it does not appear that any other person has made a claim of title.[2]

§ 7. The *return* of a sworn officer, in reference to facts which the law requires him to state, and as between the parties and privies to the suit, and others whose rights are necessarily dependent upon it, is conclusive, till vacated or set aside in due course of law. But, as to all others, it is only *primâ facie* evidence. *Privies* are those who might maintain an action for false return. But, in a suit by a purchaser of property, against an attaching creditor and officer, for attaching the property upon an order against the seller, though on the ground of fraud in the sale; the officer's return is open to contradiction by the plaintiff.[3]

§ 8. In an action against an officer for the conversion of property attached by him on a writ against a third person, his return upon the writ, showing a sale of the property under the statutes as perishable, the certificate of the appraisers, and a schedule of prices received for the property at the auction sale, which were annexed to the return as a part thereof; are competent evidence against him, on the question of damages.[4] So in an action against an officer, for not maintaining possession of personal property, which he has returned as attached upon a writ; his return is evidence of possession, that will render him liable, if the case discloses nothing to show that such return was made under misapprehension, and the creditor in the suit omits no duty required on his part, to fix the liability of the officer.[5]

§ 9. In an action by an execution creditor against a sheriff for false return, the defendant having set up title in the assignees of

[1] Murphy *v.* Troutman, 5 Jones, 379.

[2] Moore *v.* Westervelt, 21 N. Y. (7 Smith), 103. In this case the important question arose as to the degree of care required from an officer in the keeping of property. The court remark: "A sheriff, marshal, or other officer of like character, who takes property by virtue of legal process, is under some obligation to see to the protection of such property against injury or loss; but to what precise degree of care he is bound under the various circumstances which may attend such a taking, is not very well settled." Per Selden, J., 21 N. Y. 105. See Story, Bailm. § 130; Jenner *v.* Joliffe, 6 John. 9; Burke *v.* Trevitt, 1 Mass. 96.

[3] Phillips *v.* Elwell, 14 Ohio St. 240.

[4] Sanborn *v.* Baker, 1 Allen, 526. But see Bailey *v.* Capelle, 1 Har. 449.

[5] Wetherell *v.* Hughes, 45 Maine, 61.

the debtor under a bill of sale, with delivery, prior to the levy; evidence is admissible of an indebtedness of the debtor as a consideration of the sale; but only upon the question whether the sale was fraudulent in fact. If there were no indebtedness, the sale was a fraud in fact. Otherwise, and in case of a secret trust for the debtor, though valid between the parties, it was a fraud in law, and void against creditors. The plaintiff may also offer rebutting evidence that there was no indebtedness.[1] So it is held that an officer may *explain* his return.[2] And where an officer's return showed a levy on a wagon, but no disposition thereof; and the plaintiff charged him with negligently permitting it to be stolen: held, the officer, having joined issue on this charge, might introduce proof that it was stolen from his bailee.[3] So, in defence of an action against a sheriff by a stockholder of a manufacturing corporation, for arresting him on an execution against the corporation; it may be shown that he was a stockholder, although the return on the execution states that he was arrested as "now or formerly an officer of the within named corporation."[4]

§ 10. In a summary proceeding against a sheriff for non-return of a summons, the inquiry is confined to the face of the return. Extrinsic evidence is not admissible.[5]

§ 11. In general, evidence is not admissible to contradict a return.[6] Thus the sheriff's return of service cannot be contradicted, except for fraud or collusion.[7] So the officer cannot be a witness to falsify his return.[8] Thus an officer, who had returned on an execution the taking of a yoke of oxen and a yoke, cannot be permitted to testify, on a trial in trespass, that he did not take the yoke; though he may be permitted to amend his return according to the facts.[9]

§ 12. One who claims by virtue of a sale on execution may show that the sale was made in a different manner from that stated in the officer's return.[10] So as between the purchaser at a sheriff's sale, and one who claims as mortgagee, the sheriff's return on the execution is not conclusive as to the time of the levy, but such mortgagee has a right to show that the levy was

1 Connelly *v.* Walker, 45 Penn. 450.
2 Langdon *v.* Summers, 10 Ohio, (N. S.) 77.
3 Harper *v.* Moffit, 11 Iowa, 527.
4 Richmond *v.* Willis, 13 Gray, 182.
5 Hill *v.* Hinton, 2 Head. 124.
6 Johnson *v.* Stone, 40 N. H. 197.
7 Tillman *v.* Davis, 28 Geo. 494; Brown *v.* Way, ib. 531; Wilson *v.* Spring, &c. ib. 445.
8 Eastman *v.* Bennett, 6 Wis. 232.
9 Johnson *v.* Stone, 40 N. H. 197; Hatch *v.* Bartle, 45 Penn. 166.
10 Drake *v.* Mooney, 31 Verm. 617.

not made till after the time stated in the return, and after his right, as mortgagee, accrued. Such evidence would show, that there was no privity between the mortgagee and the judgment debtor, and that the sheriff had no right to make a return affecting the mortgagee or the property. And where a purchaser, knowing of a mortgage, colludes with the sheriff, and procures from him a false return of a levy before the giving of the mortgage, and purchases on condition that such false return shall be made in a suit between the mortgagee and the purchaser; this fraudulent collusion may be shown, and any effect of the return on the rights of the mortgagee defeated thereby.[1]

§ 13. In a suit brought to quiet title, the complainant cannot, to defeat the defendant's title made under a sheriff's sale, and to show that the defendant had notice of his (the complainant's) rights, offer in evidence a notice to the sheriff of his rights under a deed, and an indorsement thereon by the sheriff, that he had read the notice at the sale; it being no part of an officer's duty to read the notice or make such return.[2]

§ 14. The declarations of the person, in whose hands property is attached as belonging to him, respecting his ownership, are evidence for the defendant, in a suit by a third party, claiming the property, against the sheriff.[3]

§ 15. Declarations by an execution defendant, before levy, are admissible to disprove property in the sheriff after levy.[4]

§ 16. In trover against a sheriff for levying an attachment against a partnership on goods claimed by the plaintiff, under a purchase from one of the partners, individually, the declarations of the others, that they had sold out to him, are mere hearsay, and therefore incompetent evidence.[5]

§ 17. The admissions of one in possession of property, against his title, are admissible against an officer who has subsequently attached and taken possession of the property as his, in a suit brought against the officer to try the title, by one claiming adversely both to the officer and the person who has made such admissions.[6]

§ 18. Inquiry made by a creditor, of a claimant of property

[1] Nall *v.* Granger, 8 Mich. 450.
[2] Wickersham *v.* Reeves, 1 Clarke (Iowa), 413.
[3] Ross *v.* Hayne, 3 Iowa, 211.
[4] King *v.* Wilkins, 11 Ind. 347.
[5] Hartshorn *v.* Williams, 31 Ala. 149.
[6] Hayward, &c. *v.* Duncklee, 30 Verm. 29.

alleged to be transferred to such claimant in fraud of creditors, relative to the claimant's business standing, and his reference to the business men of the place where he had formerly done business, do not make them agents with authority to speak, and their declarations evidence in favor of an officer who afterwards attached the property on a suit by the creditors.[1]

§ 19. In an action of trespass by a father against an officer for seizing and selling property as belonging to his son, the defendant offered evidence of the plaintiff's declarations that the property belonged to the son. Held, it was competent for the plaintiff to prove, in rebuttal, that prior to the execution the plaintiff had turned out to the sheriff the same property, in the son's presence, upon an execution against the plaintiff himself.[2]

§ 20. "The admissions of an under-sheriff are not evidence against the sheriff, unless they tend to charge himself, he being the real party in the cause. He is not regarded as the general officer of the sheriff, to all intents;[3] though the admissibility of his declarations has sometimes been placed on that ground.[4] At other times they have been received on the ground, that, being liable over to the sheriff, he is the real party to the suit.[5] And where the sheriff has taken a general bond of indemnity from the under-officer, and has given him notice of the pendency of the suit, and required him to defend it; the latter is in fact the real party in interest, whenever the sheriff is sued for his default, and his admissions are clearly receivable, on principle, when made against himself. It has elsewhere been said that the declarations of an under-sheriff are evidence to charge the sheriff, only where his acts might be given in evidence to charge him; and they rather as acts, than as declarations, the declarations being considered as part of the *res gestæ*."[6]

§ 21. In an action against an officer for serving an attachment, the record of that attachment is competent evidence for him.[7]

§ 22. To admit an execution in evidence, the judgment must be produced,[8] except in a few particular cases.[9]

§ 23. In trespass against a sheriff, he cannot show that the title

[1] Rosenbury *v.* Angell, 6 Mich. 508.

[2] Roberts *v.* Young, 42 Penn. 439.

[3] Snowball *v.* Goodricke, 4 B. & Ad. 541.

[4] Drake *v.* Sykes, 7 T. R. 113.

[5] Yabsley *v.* Doble, 1 Ld. Raym. 190.

[6] Wheeler *v.* Hambright, 9 S. & R. 396. 1 Greenl. Ev. 283, n. 3.

[7] Sneed *v.* Wegman, 23 Mis. 263.

[8] Tindall *v.* Murphy, 1 Hemp. 21.

[9] Campbell *v.* Strong, ib. 265.

was not in the plaintiff, because acquired by a fraudulent sale from an execution defendant, without first alleging and proving his execution and justifying under it.[1]

§ 24. In an action against the sheriff for not paying over money collected on execution, the defendant marked the case "not for the jury," and asked a continuance, which was refused, and judgment entered for the plaintiff, and the case continued for assessment of damages. Held, upon the trial on this issue, the plaintiff's right to recover was established by the judgment, and, upon proof by him that the sheriff had collected and not paid over the amount of the execution, he was entitled to recover that sum.[2]

§ 25. In an action by the execution debtor against an officer, to recover the balance of proceeds of sale after satisfying the execution, a bill of sale from the debtor to a third person, who had recovered against the officer in an action for wrongfully levying on the property, is competent evidence.[3]

§ 26. A purchaser of logs at a sheriff's sale, valid as to part only, must, in order to maintain trover, identify these logs.[4]

§ 27. In an action against an officer for levying an execution, against a former owner of a saw-mill improvement erected upon leased land, upon a part of the machinery; the vendor of such improvement, by assignment and quitclaim indorsed on the lease, without warranty, is a competent witness for the plaintiff, because, if the machinery was a fixture, it passed by the assignment without warranty; if detached, and personalty, it was not included in the assignment, and there was no implied warranty.[5]

§ 28. In an action for neglect to serve a writ, the plaintiff must prove a cause of action against the defendant in such writ, which he may do by the same evidence as in the action itself;[6] as by the debtor's admission.[7] Evidence must be given of ability to serve the writ; as, of notice that the party was within the officer's precinct, and might have been arrested; or that he had attachable property in his possession.[8]

§ 29. In an action for failure to seize goods, the officer may

[1] Beaty *v.* Swarthout, 32 Barb. 293.

[2] Bradley *v.* Chamberlain, 31 Verm. 468.

[3] Etters *v.* Wilson, 12 Rich. 145.

[4] Brown *v.* Pratt, 4 Wis. 513.

[5] M'Invoy *v.* Dyer, 47 Penn. 118.

[6] Alexander *v.* Macauley, 4 T. R. 611; Riggs *v.* Thatcher, 1 Greenl. 68; Gunter *v.* Cleyton, 2 Lev. 85.

[7] Gibbon *v.* Coggon, 2 Camp. 188; Dyke *v.* Aldridge, 7 T. R. 665; 4 ib. 611.

[8] Beckford *v.* Montague, 2 Esp. 475; Frost *v.* Dougal, 1 Day, 128.

show that they did not belong to the debtor, or reasonable doubt as to the title, and that the plaintiff refused to indemnify him.[1] In case of an execution, he may show that the judgment was fraudulent, and that he held the process of another judgment creditor,[2] or prior attachments to the full value of the goods.[3] But where an officer levies on goods, and leaves them with a receiptor, who rightly claims to own them, and against whom, upon his retaining them, the officer recovers a judgment for their value; in an action by the execution plaintiff, the officer is estopped to deny that they belonged to the debtor, although, in consequence of the receiptor's insolvency, the judgment against him was worthless.[4]

§ 29 *a*. The sufficiency of bail is presumed to be known to the officer; hence slight evidence of their insufficiency will sustain an action against him; as that they have been pressed by creditors, and repeatedly broken their promises to pay.[5] The officer is liable, without proof of knowledge on his part; though he may show in defence that the bail were apparently responsible and in good credit.[6]

[1] Canada *v.* Southwick, 16 Pick. 556; Bond *v.* Ward, 7 Mass. 123; Marsh *v.* Gold, 2 Pick. 285.

[2] Clark *v.* Foxcroft, 6 Greenl. 296; Pierce *v.* Jackson, 6 Mass. 242.

[3] Commercial, &c. *v.* Wilkins, 9 Greenl. 28.

[4] The People *v.* Reeder, 25 N. Y. (11 Smith), 302.

[5] Gwyllim *v.* Scholey, 6 Esp. 100; Saunders *v.* Darling, Bull. N. P. 60.

[6] Jeffery *v.* Bastarel, 4 Ad. & Ell. 823; Concanen *v.* Lethbridge, 2 H. Bl. 36; Hindle *v.* Blades, 5 Taun. 225.

CHAPTER XII.

EVIDENCE IN CASE OF HUSBAND AND WIFE, AND PARENT AND CHILD.

§ 1. INDEPENDENTLY of express statutory provisions to the contrary, it is the general rule that, in the action for criminal conversation, actual marriage must be proved.[1] Thus a reply of the defendant, to the inquiry where the plaintiff's wife was, that she was in the next room, is not sufficient proof.[2] It has been held otherwise, however, with a serious and solemn admission; as that the defendant committed the wrong with full knowledge of the fact.[3] Proof of marriage according to any prevailing form of religion is held sufficient.[4] (*a*)

§ 2. With regard to the proof of adultery, most of the decided cases have arisen upon applications for divorce. Independently of statutory provision, however, the same rules are substantially applicable to actions at common law.

§ 3. "In every case, almost, the fact is inferred from circumstances that lead to it by fair inference as a necessary conclusion: . . . The only general rule that can be laid down upon the subject is, that the circumstances must be such as would lead the guarded discretion of a reasonable and just man to the conclusion."[5] In

[1] Morris *v.* Miller, 4 Burr. 2059; 1 Doug. 174.

[2] Bull. N. P. 28.

[3] Rigg *v.* Curgenver, 2 Wils. 399. See People *v.* Anderson, 26 Cal. 132.

[4] Bull. N. P. 28.

[5] Per Lord Stowell, Loneden *v.* Loneden, 2 Hagg. Con. 2.

(*a*) A and B, residing at S., left S. together, saying that they intended to get married at G.; and returned to S., saying that they had been married at G. On the day they left S., there was an entry of the marriage in a book at G., signed by A, the man; and, after their return to S., they lived there many years as husband and wife. On a suit for dissolution of marriage, held, in the absence of better evidence, sufficient proof of the marriage. Patrickson *v.* Patrickson, Law Rep. 1 P. & D. 86; Amn. Law Rev. Oct. 1866, p. 143.

general, *proximate* circumstances must be proved.[1] General cohabitation is of itself sufficient.[2] So, after proof of a criminal disposition, the finding the parties together in a bedroom.[3] Adultery of a man may be proved by his visiting a brothel; by the birth, support, and acknowledgment of a child. Of a woman, by the birth of a child, the husband being out of the realm.[4] (*a*) But neither the confessions of the wife, nor the opinion of a physician who had attended on her, as to her fondness for the defendant, are admissible.[5] (*b*)

§ 4. The language and deportment of husband and wife to each other, their correspondence with each other and with strangers, are competent evidence.[6] But not letters written after the alleged misconduct of the wife, upon the ground of possible collusion;[7] nor after an attempt of the defendant to seduce the wife.[8]

§ 5. The wife's declarations, prior to the alleged seduction, as to the husband's cruel treatment of her, are admissible in mitigation of damages.[9]

§ 6. The defendant may prove, in mitigation of damages, the bad character of the wife, or particular acts of unchastity; that she made the first advances; the unchaste conduct of the plaintiff, and his ill-treatment of the wife, which (as we have seen, § 5) has sometimes been shown (and more especially by way of rebuttal) by her own declarations. But not her misconduct since the alleged adultery.[10]

§ 7. It has been held, that, where a certain time is alleged, acts prior to that time may be proved as explanatory of subsequent

[1] Williams *v.* Williams, 1 Hagg. Con. 299.

[2] Cadogan *v.* Cadogan, 2 ib. 4 n.; Turton *v.* Turton, 3 ib. 356.

[3] Soilleaux *v.* Soilleaux, 1 ib. 373.

[4] Astley *v.* Astley, 1 Hagg. Ecc. 719; Kenrick *v.* Kenrick, 4 ib. 114; D'Aguilar *v.* D'Aguilar, 1 ib. n.; Richardson *v.* Richardson, ib. 6.

[5] McVey *v.* Blair, 7 Ind. 590.

[6] Trelawney *v.* Coleman, 2 Stark. 191.

[7] Edwards *v.* Crock, 4 Esp. 39; 1 Phil. Ev. 190; Milton *v.* Webster, 7 C. & P. 198.

[8] Wilton *v.* Webster, 7 C. & P. 198.

[9] Palmer *v.* Crook, 7 Gray, 418.

[10] Bull. N. P. 296; Gardiner *v.* Jadis, 1 Selw. N. P. 24; Bromley *v.* Wallace, 4 Esp. 237; Winter *v.* Wroot, 1 M. & Rob. 404; Hodges *v.* Windham, Peake, Cas. 39; Elsam *v.* Fawcett, 2 Esp. 562.

(*a*) A suit by a wife for judicial separation cannot be sustained solely by the testimony of a woman of loose character. Ginger *v.* Ginger, Law Rep. 1 P. & D. 29; Amn. Law Rev. Oct. 1866, p. 100. Contrary to the general rule of evidence, *impression and belief* are held competent in cases of adultery. Crewe *v.* Crewe, 3 Hagg. Ecc. 128.

(*b*) In a suit for dissolution of marriage, a decree *nisi* may be founded solely upon admissions of the respondent and co-respondent. Williams *v.* Williams, Law Rep. 1 P. & D. 29; Amn. Law Rev. Oct. 1866, p. 100.

ones, though beyond the period of limitation, which is set up in defence.[1]

§ 8. In an action by a husband for enticing away his wife, her declarations, made shortly before, are admissible for the plaintiff, as showing the state of her affections towards him up to that time; and whether prior or subsequent to the marriage. But her declarations, as to the words and acts of the defendant, and tending to sustain the petition, are mere hearsay, and inadmissible.[2]

§ 9. In an action, for enticing away the wife of the plaintiff, against a part of the persons alleged to have conspired together for that purpose; the declarations of any of them are admissible in evidence to prove their own participation, but not against the others, without satisfactory proof of the conspiracy, nor unless the declarations are in furtherance of the objects of the conspiracy.[3]

§ 10. In an action by a father for the seduction of his daughter, some proof of service by the latter, or the right to service from her, is required; but service, however trivial, will sustain a verdict. Where a claim is made for expenses in curing the seduced, but there was no proof to sustain it, if there is a general verdict, the presumption will be that the jury allowed nothing on such claim.[4]

§ 11. Evidence of promise of marriage is not admissible as a ground of damage; but may be given to explain the daughter's conduct, if she is attacked. The defendant's condition as to property may be inquired into. And the plaintiff's dissolute habits; but not his general reputation in this respect. The character of the daughter is in issue. The damages may be exemplary or punitive in aggravated cases.[5]

§ 12. In an action by husband or father for seduction, evidence is admissible against the character of the female for chastity. Also evidence to rebut it. But not if referring to a time subsequent to the seduction.[6] So, in an action for seduction, evidence is admissible of particular acts of unchastity with other persons.[7] But, in an action for seduction of a daughter, she cannot be

[1] Duke of Norfolk v. Germaine, 12 How. St. Tr. 929.

[2] Preston v. Bowers, 13 Ohio St. 1.

[3] Ibid.

[4] Doyle v. Jesup, 29 Ill. 460; 5 Har. 335.

[5] Robinson v. Burton, 5 Har. 335.

[6] 1 Greenl. Ev. 122, § 54.

[7] Kerry v. Watkins, 7 C. & P. 308.

asked, even on cross-examination, and with reference to the time near the alleged deduction, whether she had connection with other men, for the purpose of showing her bad character, or of contradicting her in case of denial. The court say, " true enough, the parent is entitled to damages for the disgrace brought upon the family by this stain upon the general good character or reputation of the daughter, but is entitled to damages only for the loss of service, if her previous reputation for chastity was bad. . . . But reputation is a fact that is to be directly proved, and not inferred from special acts. . . . The law does not inquire whether the reputation is well founded or not; for, to do so, it would have to investigate the whole life." [1]

§ 13. A father may maintain an action, for harboring or secreting his minor daughter, and persuading her to remain absent from his family and service without his consent, and in such action may recover for his mental suffering thereby caused; though he may not introduce evidence thereof, distinct from and in addition to that which shows the nature and extent of the injury.[2]

[1] Per Lowrie, C. J., Hoffman *v.* Kemerer, 44 Penn. 453; 5 Har. 335.

[2] Stowe *v.* Heywood, 7 Allen, 118.

BOOK V.

DAMAGES.

CHAPTER I.

GENERAL RULES OF DAMAGES.

§ 1. In case of tort, two entirely distinct questions arise with respect to damages. First, is the injury one which justifies an action for damages; or is it so slight, so remotely connected with the act or neglect of the defendant, or so far attributable to the fault of the plaintiff himself, that no action can be maintained. The other question is, supposing the action to be maintainable, to what amount of damages is the plaintiff entitled, or by what standard, if any, is that amount to be governed. The former of these questions has been considered at some length in the third and fourth chapters of the work to which the present is a supplement. The latter we propose now to consider. Of course it has been incidentally treated in connection with the subject of *evidence*; — inasmuch as all facts legally admissible in evidence may affect the damages; and, on the other hand, everything which has a legitimate bearing upon the damages may also be offered in evidence. In a less degree, also, damages are connected with *pleading*; because the amount which the plaintiff is entitled to recover is often determined by the allegations of the writ. The subject, however, is a distinct one, by itself, and, as a branch of the general topic of *remedies*, requires a full and detailed consideration.

§ 1 *a*. It hardly need be added, that the subject of damages, in actions for torts, is of very great and peculiar importance. The amount of damages for *breach of contract* is in many, perhaps a majority of cases, determined by the contract itself. A party, who neglects or refuses to pay a certain sum of money, or to deliver certain property, which he has expressly or impliedly *agreed* to pay or deliver, will, in a suit at law, suffer a verdict and judgment against him for that sum or for the value of that property; not unfrequently, it is true, with incidental accompaniments, but still only as accompaniments to a fixed standard or basis. But, on the other hand, an action for tort is in many cases said to *sound in damages;* that is, the damages themselves, as determined by a jury, constitute the first defined pecuniary claim and liability between the parties. Under these circumstances, it of course becomes proportionably important, that *the law* should substitute some at least approximate standard of damages for that which in case of contract the parties furnish for themselves.

§ 1 *b*. In an action for a wrong, whether arising out of trespass or negligence, the jury, in estimating the damages, may take into consideration all the circumstances attending it;[1] such as circumstances in aggravation, "which give character to the transaction."[2] And it is held, that the jury may give such damages as the case requires in equity.[3] Thus where one obstructed a way, whereby another was prevented from repairing his dam when necessary; the measure of damages was held not necessarily the reasonable cost of removing the obstruction; but the decision of the jury, considering the motives of the parties and all the circumstances, was the only standard.[4] So in an action for injury caused by an accident upon a railroad, damages may be allowed for the plaintiff's mental sufferings, the dismay and consequent shock to the feelings, without reference to the question of vindictive damages. "His mind is no less a part of his person than his body; and the sufferings of the former are oftentimes more acute and also more lasting than those of the latter. . . . The dismay, and the consequent shock to the feelings, which is produced by the danger

[1] Emblin *v.* Myers, 6 Hurl. & Nor. 54; 30 L. J. Exch. 71. See Bell *v.* Midland, &c. 9 W. R. 612, C. P.; Jones *v.* Allen, 1 Head, 626.

[2] Bateman *v.* Goodyear, 12 Conn. 575.

[3] Leland *v.* Stone, 10 Mass. 459, 462; Weld *v.* Bartlett, ib. 470; Aldrich *v.* Palmer, 24 Cal. 516; Boyce *v.* California, &c. 25 ib. 467; St. Paul *v.* Kuby, 8 Min. 154 Allison *v.* Chandler, 11 Mich. 542.

[4] McTavish *v.* Carroll, 13 Md. 429.

attending a personal injury, not only aggravate it, but are frequently so appalling as to suspend the reason and disable a person from warding it off."[1] And, in general, in an action for a personal injury resulting from negligence, the jury may allow damages for the plaintiff's natural anxiety and mental suffering at the time, caused by the danger.[2]

§ 2. In general, the remedy shall be commensurate with the injury.[3] If there be a legal rule for the measurement of damages, the jury must follow it; as, for example, in an action of trover.[4] And if a judge at *nisi prius* does not inform the jury what is the proper measure of damages, on an issue on which it is admitted that the plaintiff is entitled to a verdict and to damages, the court will direct a new trial, although the point was not taken by counsel at the trial.[5] (*a*) So, in an action for running over the plaintiff with a train of coal-cars, by reason of which the amputation of his foot became necessary, the court charged the jury, "that there was no certain rule by which to estimate the damages for the personal injury to the plaintiff, and that the jury will fix them at such sum as they think right and proper under the evidence." Held, the injury not being wilful, *compensation* was the measure of damages, and the instruction was erroneous for want of precision upon this point.[6]

[1] Seger *v.* Barkhamsted, 22 Conn. 290; per Storrs, J., ib. 298.

[2] Masters *v.* Warren, 27 ib. 393.

[3] Rockwood *v.* Allen, 7 Mass. 254; Swift *v.* Barnes, 16 Pick. 194; Bussey *v.* Donaldson, 4 Dall. 206.

[4] Ryan *v.* Baldrick, 3 M'Cord, 498; Baker *v.* Wheeler, 8 Wend. 505.

[5] Knight *v.* Egerton, 12 Eng. L. & Eq. 562.

[6] Heil *v.* Glanding, 42 Penn. 493.

(*a*) Where property is in question, the value of the article, as nearly as it can be ascertained, furnishes a rule, from which the jury are not at liberty to depart. Hillebrant *v.* Brewer, 6 Tex. 45.

In an action for forcibly bricking up the entrance of a restaurant kept by the plaintiff, and thereby breaking up his business, evidence that "the plaintiff did a pretty large business," that "the business was good and profitable," and that "one-half of the receipts were clear profit," is admissible, to show in some manner the nature and extent of the injury. Marquart *v.* La Farge, 5 Duer, 559.

Where coffee was damaged on its voyage from Boston to New Orleans, and in its damaged state was shipped up the river to St. Louis; the original cause of damage being established, and there being no evidence of any additional damage received in its last voyage; held, the amount of damage ascertained to have been received, on examination at St. Louis, might be received as a fair criterion of the amount received on its arrival at New Orleans. The Norman, 1 Newb. Adm. 525.

A peculiar question as to the measure of damages is presented by the separation of the property in question from the realty, of which it made a part before the wrongful act complained of. The value of *gold* thus separated is to be estimated as of the time when it becomes a chattel. Antoine, &c. *v.* Ridge, &c. 23 Cal. 219.

The value of an orchard is to be estimated, with reference to what, in its growing state, it is worth to the premises. Mitchell *v.* Billingsley, 17 Ala. 391.

The actual value of growing timber is not its supposed worth to the owner, but the price for which it would sell at the time in the neighborhood in which it is situated. Ivey *v.* McQueen, ib. 408.

§ 3. But, as is truly remarked in a very recent case: "It is often much easier to discover when an assumed rule for damages will lead to erroneous results, than to point out in all cases in advance, what the true rule should be."[1]

§ 4. The nature of damages, and the distinction between general and special damages, are thus explained by an approved writer: "All damages must be *the result* of the injury complained of. Those which *necessarily* result, are termed *general damages*, being shown under the *ad damnum*, . . . for the defendant must be presumed to be aware of the necessary consequences of his conduct, and therefore cannot be taken by surprise in the proof of them. . . . But where the damages, though the *natural* consequences of the act complained of, are *not* the *necessary* result of it, they are termed *special damages;* which the law does not imply; and therefore, in order to prevent a surprise upon the defendant, they must be particularly specified in the declaration, or the plaintiff will not be permitted to give evidence of them. But where the special damage is properly alleged, and is the natural consequence of the wrongful act, the jury may infer it from the principal fact."[2]

§ 5. A mere *possible* injury furnishes no ground of damages.[3] But every trespass to property gives a right, at least, to nominal damages.[4] It is held that the maxim, "*de minimis non curat lex*," when properly applied to prevent a right of recovery, has reference to the *injury*, and not to the *resulting damages*. That it is never properly applied to a wrongful and positive invasion of property, when damages result which are capable of estimation. That to give a right of action there must be both an injury and a damage; but every violation of a right imports some damage; and, if none other be proved, the law allows nominal damages. Thus, in levying an execution upon, and removing machinery from a building, in order to disengage it from the bands by which it was connected with the shafting, which bands did not belong to the owner of the machinery, but to the plaintiff, the mortgagee of the building; the defendants cut the thongs by which the bands were laced together, which thongs could have been easily untied and taken out without cutting. The testimony tended to show that these thongs were considerably worn and of small value.

[1] Per Thompson, J., McKnight *v.* Ratcliff, 44 Penn. 169.

[2] 2 Greenl. Ev. 209, § 254.

[3] Massey *v.* Craine, 1 M'Cord, 489; Bond *v.* Quattlebaum, ib. 584.

[4] Champion *v.* Vincent, 20 Tex. 811.

The court charged the jury, that, if they found that the thongs were old, worn out, and nearly worthless, the defendants would not be liable for cutting them, unless they did so wantonly, and advised them, as the suit appeared to be brought to try the defendants' right to enter the building and take the machinery, not to decide it upon the ground of a trifling damage of this kind to the thongs, provided the officer acted in good faith. Held, these instructions were erroneous, because the damage, though small, was still capable of estimation, and the plaintiff was entitled to recover for such damage, and therefore a new trial was granted.[1]

§ 6. In many cases, the law gives a liberal construction in favor of the plaintiff to the right of recovering damages for injuries. Thus a party, who appropriates to his own use another's land, is liable in damages for the value of the land *to one who has a use for it*.[2] So where, from the circumstances of the case, the defendant, but not the plaintiff, has it in his power to show the amount of damage sustained, heavy damages are justified.[3] So, in an action for conversion of property fluctuating in value, the plaintiff is entitled to the highest value at or after the time of conversion.[4] And a plaintiff is not restricted, in the amount of damages, to the sum which he demanded of the defendant for the injuries.[5] But a court of equity, in assessing damages resulting from a wrongful taking and detention of property, will give neither vindictive nor speculative damages, but compensation only for the actual loss and injury.[6] And it is said, "What the law seeks to secure in an assessment of damages to an injured party is compensation. He can ask no more than to be made whole."[7] More especially, "In all *actions on the case*, the question is, what is the amount of damages sustained?"[8] And it is sometimes held, in *trespass*, where there is no aggravation that damages shall be given only for the actual injury.[9] Thus, where the judge instructed the jury, in an action of trespass for levying an execution upon property which the plaintiff had conditionally sold to the execution debtor, to find the value of the

1 Fullam *v.* Stearns, 30 Verm. 443.
2 M'Carthy *v.* Cabrera, 17 Tex. 629.
3 Antoine, &c. *v.* Ridge, 23 Cal. 219.
4 Douglass *v.* Kraft, 9 ib. 562.
5 Western, &c. *v.* Carlton, 28 Geo. 180.
6 Sanders *v.* Anderson, 10 Rich. Eq. 232.
7 Per Strong, J., M'Inroy *v.* Dyer, 47 Penn. 121.
8 West *v.* Rice, 9 Met. 564.
9 Conard *v.* Pacific, &c. 6 Pet. 262.

property and interest, and such further amount, as, under all the circumstances of the case as argued by the counsel, they might think the plaintiff entitled to demand, if any; held erroneous; the court remarking: "This is giving them a discretionary power without stint or limit, highly dangerous to the rights of the defendants. . . . Nothing appears which should swell the damages beyond the value of the interest which the vendee (vendor) had in the property." [1]

§ 7. In case of default, the ordinary mode of ascertaining damages is by a *writ of inquiry*. And it is held, that the record must show such writ.[2] Thus, where the defendant in trespass *qu. claus.* becomes defaulted, he has a right to be heard in damages. And, if the jury assess them at the request of the plaintiff, either party may except to the instructions of the judge as to the principles which should govern them.[3] (*a*) So in *trover*, after default, the defendant is entitled to be heard in the assessment of damages by the court, he having moved for a hearing before the final adjournment of the court, and before judgment had been entered up. "In the English practice, upon default, the plaintiff is entitled, as of right, to a writ of inquiry, and an assessment of damages by a jury, unless he consents that they be assessed by a master or a prothonotary appointed by the court. The defendant . . . has no such election. He has no right to a jury to assess damages." [4]

§ 8. Where the jury have found a verdict for the defendant, with leave given to the plaintiff to enter a verdict for a sum at which his damages have been without objection contingently

[1] Rose *v.* Story, 1 Barr, 191.

[2] Wetzell *v.* Waters, 18 Mis. 396.

[3] Crommett *v.* Pearson, 6 Shep. 344.

[4] Begg *v.* Whittier, 48 Maine, 314; per Appleton, J., ib. 315.

(*a*) In New Hampshire, when a default is entered, the court assess the damages, unless, for special reasons, it is deemed expedient to order an inquiry of damages by the jury. If one defendant be defaulted, and another plead, the jury, if they find for the plaintiff, assess damages, for which judgment is rendered against all. Bowman *v.* Noyes, 12 N. H. 302. See Pratte *v.* Corl, 9 Mis. 163; Evans *v.* Bowlin, ib. 406; Chambers *v.* Lathrop, 1 Morris, 102; Davis *v.* Morford, ib. 99; Parvin *v.* Hoopes, ib. 294; Romaine *v.* Commissioners, &c. ib. 357; Kahoon *v.* Wisconsin, &c. 10 Wis. 290; Keeler *v.* Campbell, 24 Ill. 287; Van Dusen *v.* Pomeroy, ib. 289; Nobles *v.* Christmas, 2 How. Miss. 885; Grigsby *v.* Ford, 3 ib. 184; Clemson *v.* State Bank, 1 Scam. 45.

It is held, that no writ of inquiry is allowable for a defendant. Hopewell *v.* Price, 2 Har. & G. 275.

In an action to recover a penalty under Rev. Stat. of Maine, ch. 158, § 17, for falsely and corruptly certifying as a witness, the amount to be recovered may be assessed by the jury. Kennedy *v.* Wright, 34 Maine, 351.

assessed, the court will not grant a new trial, in order that there may be a fresh assessment.[1]

§ 9. Where there is an issue of law and an issue of fact in the same cause, and the latter is first tried, there is no need of assessing damages contingently, if the issue of fact goes to the whole declaration.[2]

§ 9 *a*. Upon an agreed statement of facts, not fixing or providing for the assessment of damages; a judgment for the plaintiff will be for nominal damages.[3]

§ 10. In trials at common law, all testimony must be delivered orally in presence of the jury, who are to try a cause or assess damages, except where the statute provides for the admission of depositions. Therefore the evidence spread on the record, in a case in which a demurrer is offered to evidence, cannot be allowed to go to a second jury, impanelled to assess damages after the demurrer is overruled.[4]

§ 11. Upon a writ of inquiry, the defendant cannot set up a substantive defence.[5] (*a*)

§ 12. By consent (in Ohio), the court may leave a question of damages to *arbitrators*.[6]

§ 13. In Indiana, where the report of persons appointed to assess damages sustained for draining a creek was set aside, the application for a second assessment cannot be made seven years thereafter.[7]

[1] Booth *v.* Clive, 4 Eng. L. & Eq. 374.
[2] Bates *v.* Green, 19 Wend. 630.
[3] McAneany *v.* Jewett, 10 Allen, 151.
[4] Young *v.* Foster, 7 Port. 420.
[5] South, &c., *v.* Foster, 20 Ill. 296
[6] Conner *v.* Drake, 1 Ohio St. 166.
[7] Brake *v.* The Board, &c. 2 Cart. 606.

(*a*) In Illinois, the defendant cannot set up any new defence, but he may cross-examine witnesses, offer testimony in reduction of the sum claimed, and ask instructions of the court. Herrington *v.* Stevens, 26 Ill. 298.

CHAPTER II.

AMOUNT OF DAMAGES; NOMINAL DAMAGES; MITIGATION OF DAMAGES.

§ 1. WE have already stated the general principle, that a party is entitled to damages corresponding with the amount of injury suffered, however small. With more special reference to what are technically termed *nominal damages*, (*a*) it is the prevailing rule, that, where an invasion of a right is established, though no actual damage be shown, the law imports damage, and nominal damages will be given. As where the unlawful act might have an effect upon the right of a party, and be evidence in favor of the wrong-doer, if the right ever came in question; or where a continuance of the wrong might result in an easement or incumbrance on land. So when one wantonly invades another's rights for the purpose of injury. Though not for a trespass to personal property, when no unlawful intent, or disturbance of a right or possession is shown, and when the property sustains no injury.[1] Thus, in an action of slander, where there is no real injury, the jury may find for nominal damages; and, it seems, may consider the question of costs. As, in an action by the master of a workhouse, for words imputing to him that he dishonestly got honest men turned out of employment there, in order to get in creatures of his own, for his own purposes. The words were held actionable; but, being spoken in angry altercation, and without malice, the

[1] Paul *v.* Slason, 22 Verm. 231; Bassett *v.* Salisbury, &c. 8 Fost. 438; Whipple *v.* Cumberland, &c. 2 Story, 661.

(*a*) It is hardly necessary to remark, that the question whether nominal damages, *at least*, can be recovered, is but another form of the question, whether an action is maintainable, and therefore appertains to the general subject of torts, rather than to the special head of damages.

jury were directed that they might, if they thought there was no real injury, give nominal damages, so as not to carry costs; and the defendant's counsel was allowed to ask, on cross-examination, what would be the probable amount of costs to the defendant if a verdict for more than a nominal amount were given.[1] So it is the prevailing rule, that, in an action for flowage, if the damage is so small that it cannot be estimated, the plaintiff is still entitled, at common law, to nominal damages.[2] (*a*) Damage is implied, but "the lowest damage."[3] So where an action is brought for damages to personal property, and damages are proved, but not the amount, judgment should be for the plaintiff, with nominal damages.[4] But, in a summary proceeding under a penal statute, nominal damages are not recoverable.[5]

§ 1 *a*. In late English cases, it is held, that, on an inquiry whether any, and what, damage has accrued from the unlawful use of a trade-mark, the plaintiff must prove special damage; and it will not be presumed that, but for such use, the plaintiff would have sold the amount of goods sold by the defendant.[6] So an action cannot be maintained against one who digs a well near the land of another, which thereby is caused to sink, and a building, not twenty years old, to fall; if without the building the land would have sunk, but without appreciable damage.[7]

§ 2. *Mitigation* or *reduction* of damages is a subject which gives rise to very nice and numerous questions.

§ 3. *Recoupment* is a familiar mode of reducing damages. Recoupment is defined as "the right and the act of making a set-off, defalcation, or discount, by the defendant, to the claim of the plaintiff."[8] Recoupment is distinguished from *set-off*, as being a

[1] Wakelin *v.* Morris, 2 F. & F. 26.
[2] Cory *v.* Silcox, 6 Ind. 39.
[3] Pastorius *v.* Fisher, 1 Rawle, 27.
[4] Brown *v.* Emerson, 18 Mis. 103.
[5] Hamilton *v.* Ward, 4 Tex. 356.
[6] Leather, &c. *v.* Hirschfield, Law Rep. 1 Eq. 299; Amn. Law Rev. Oct. 1866, p. 170.
[7] Smith *v.* Thackerah, Law Rep. 1 C. P. 564; Amn. Law Rev. Jan. 1867, p. 297.
[8] Bouvier's Law Dict. "Recoupe." See Keyes *v.* Western, &c. 34 Verm. 81; King *v.* Woodbridge, ib. 565; McLure *v.* Hart, 19 Ark. 119; Stow *v.* Yarwood, 20 Ill. 597; Gilmore *v.* Cook, 33 Mis. 25; Snow *v.* Carruth, Sprague, 324; Nichols *v.* Tremlett, ib. 361; Grand, &c. *v.* Knox, 20 Mis. 433.

(*a*) It is said (2 Greenl. Ev. 210, 255), "if they (the jury) are unable to agree, and the plaintiff has evidently sustained some damages, the court will permit him to take a verdict for a nominal sum." (This, however, cannot be regarded as the prevailing rule. The case cited is Feize *v.* Thompson, 1 Taun. 121. This was an action for general average, and, the jury being about to render a general verdict for the defendant, because they could not ascertain any definite sum as the plaintiff's proportion, a nonsuit was taken, and, on motion, the court ordered a verdict for the plaintiff, with 6*d*. damages.)

reduction of the claim upon which the action is founded; while the term set-off is applicable only to a claim which grows out of an independent transaction.[1] Thus, in an action to recover back advances made by the plaintiff on cotton delivered him by the defendant, where the cotton had been destroyed by fire; if the defendant would be entitled to damages of the plaintiff for the loss of the cotton, he may *recoup* such damages; and, for this purpose, may prove the destruction of the cotton, and the manner in which it occurred.[2] So, in an action for foreclosure of a mortgage, with a note, to secure rent; the defendant may recoup his claim for misrepresentations as to the quantity and productiveness of the farm leased.[3]

§ 4. But evidence to prove damages by way of recoupment is not competent, where no claim to such recoupment is set up in the answer.[4] So where A contracted with B to build a steamboat, and have it completed at a certain time; the price to be paid in instalments; and the vessel was not delivered until two months after the agreed time, but B made no objections at the time of delivery: in an action by A for that part of the purchase-money which remained unpaid, held, B could not recoup the amount which he lost as freight during the two months; because the damages were speculative.[5] So, in an action for injuries done to hogs, which had broken into the defendant's inclosure, the defendant cannot recoup for damages done to his crop by the hogs, when it is shown that his fence was not a "lawful fence," agreeably to the statute.[6] And where A hired slaves of B, and gave his note therefor, and C, as coroner, took the slaves on execution, and, in a suit by B on the note, A elected to recoup the damages he had sustained; held, A had thereby precluded himself from suing for damages for the loss of the hire of the slaves, but might still maintain an action for a trespass, which could not have been recouped in the former action.[7]

§ 5. Action upon a bond to procure the discharge of a vessel attached to enforce a lien for repairs. The defendants claim to recoup for delay in repairing. Held, the measure of damages was not the probable profits of the vessel, but the rent or price

1 Avery *v.* Brown, 31 Conn. 393.
2 Hatchett *v.* Gibson, 13 Ala. 587.
3 Avery *v.* Brown, 31 Conn. 393.
4 Crane *v.* Hardman, 4 E. D. Smith, 448.
5 Taylor *v.* Maguire, 12 Mis. 313.
6 Woodward *v.* Purdy, 20 Ala. 379.
7 McLane *v.* Miller, 12 ib. 643.

which would have been paid for the charter, as the vessel was used or chartered at the time.[1]

§ 6. There are other, less technical, grounds of deduction from the damages proved on the part of the plaintiff, sometimes depending upon express statute. (*a*) Thus, in Kentucky, § 152 of the Code authorizes a *counter-claim* on behalf of one of several defendants, to be set up in answer to the action; but such counter-claim must be a cause of action arising out of the transaction set forth in the petition, or be connected with the subject of the action. Where the petition states the occupation of the land, pending an injunction against the execution of a judgment for restitution, and claims damages therefor; any interference by the plaintiff, rendering such occupation less profitable or less valuable to the occupant, even though amounting to a trespass or other tort, is a good counter-claim, and the taking of the growing crop by the plaintiff is a good defence to the demand of rent for that year, and shall go in reduction of damages, claimed for the withholding of the possession for that year. But, as the injunction protects the occupant during its pendency, and the injunction bond secures the other party for rent during the occupancy, the occupant, when his original entry is lawful, is a *quasi* tenant during the pendency of the bond; and, as the duration of this is uncertain, he is entitled to emblements, and the taking and disposing of them by the plaintiff, when he obtained possession, constituted a good counter-claim under the Code.[2] (*b*)

§ 7. Action for damages, occasioned by the filling up by the defendants of their land, lying adjacent to that of the plaintiffs whereby the free flow of water off the plaintiff's land, as formerly existing, had been obstructed. Instructions to the jury, that "they should take into consideration the evidence on both side bearing on this point, and, if they were satisfied that the filling up had actually benefited the plaintiff's estate in any particular, they would, in assessing the damages, make an allowance for such benefit, and give the plaintiff such sum in damages as they found upon the evidence would fully indemnify and compen-

[1] Rogers *v.* Beard, 36 Barb. 31.

[2] Tinsley *v.* Tinsley, 15 B. Mon. 454.

(*a*) As to the set-off, in assumpsit, of damages for not delivering all the goods contracted for, see Fishell *v.* Winans, 38 Barb. 220.

(*b*) As to *counter-claim* in Ohio and New York, see Wiswell *v.* First, &c. 14 Ohio St. 31; Barhyte *v.* Hughes, 33 Barb. 320; Tyler *v.* Willis, ib. 327.

sate him for all the damage he had actually sustained." Held correct.[1]

§ 8. Against a claim for *mesne profits*, the value of the improvements made by the defendant is a fair set-off, provided he took possession of the premises *bonâ fide*. Trespassers are not entitled to the benefit of this principle, except where the profits have been increased by the repairs or improvements. In that case, it is proper for the jury to take into consideration the improvements or repairs, and diminish the profits by that amount; but not below the sum which the premises would have been worth without them. Whether the defendants are trespassers, is a question for the jury.[2]

§ 9. In case of obstruction of a road by a railroad, any benefit accruing to the plaintiff from the railroad may be shown in mitigation of damages.[3] So, in estimating the damages of locating a railroad over land, and filling up an adjacent canal in which the owner had a privilege; the jury may properly be instructed, that, if the value of the remaining land was so increased in consequence of some peculiar advantages conferred upon it, not shared by neighboring estates not lying upon the canal, that the remainder of the land wrs worth as much as the whole lot previously, the owner has no claim for damages; though they are further instructed, that the benefit to be set off is some increased value of the estate, in consequence of becoming better adapted to and more valuable for some specific purpose than the other estates where the land had not been taken, and illustrations of such benefits are given.[4]

§ 10. In tort for conversion of machinery in a workshop, consisting merely in refusal to allow a removal, without appropriation to the defendant's own use, removal, or actual possession except by rightful possession of the shop; the defendant may set up, in mitigation of damages, a notice to the plaintiff that he had relinquished all claim to the machinery.[5]

§ 11. The general rule, that the value of property wrongfully taken shall be the measure of damages in an action by the owner, may be controlled by circumstances, which make this too large a measure, and require an equitable deduction. Thus, where the

[1] Luther *v.* Winnisimmet Co. 9 Cush. 171.

[2] Beverly *v.* Burke, 9 Geo. 440.

[3] Porter *v.* North, &c. 33 Mis. 128.

[4] Whitman *v.* Boston, &c. 7 Allen, 313.

[5] Delano *v.* Curtis, ib. 470.

creditor of a husband took certain property, belonging to the trust estate of his wife, on execution against him, and the husband bid off such property for the trustees, when it was sold at the port, paying less for it than its value; held, in an action of trover brought by the trustees against the creditor, that proof of such fact was admissible in mitigation of damages; the real damage, which was the sum paid at the port, furnishing the rule of damages.[1] And although, in an action of trespass for taking goods, if the plaintiff is liable over for them, he may recover their full value; yet the defendant may show, in mitigation of damages, under the general issue, that the goods at the time of the letting belonged to a third person, and that the plaintiff was not liable for them to the owner.[2] Or, that the goods did not belong to the plaintiff, and that they have gone into the hands of the owner, or been taken for his debts.[3] (See § 15.) So, in trover, it may be shown, in mitigation of damages, that the goods were not the plaintiff's, and have gone to the owner's use. "The reason why a party having possession should maintain trespass is, that he may have sustained injury by being deprived of the goods; nor should his claim to damages be construed strictly. Ordinarily, he is either the owner or answerable over to the owner; and in either case he is entitled not only to damages for the taking, but also for the value of the goods. . . . But here . . . the plaintiff is not answerable over. The real damage sustained by him arises from the injury to his special property."[4] So where a purchaser of property brings an action against an officer, who seizes and sells it upon an execution against the former owner; if it appears that he himself bought the property at the execution sale, and remained in possession, the value with interest is not the measure of damages, but the sum bid at the sale with interest.[5] So where the purchaser of a vessel from B, who bought it of A, sued an officer for taking it without legal process, although he subsequently sold it on a *fi. fa.* against B and C, as the property of B; held, the defendant might show, in mitigation of damages, that the proceeds were applied to the satisfaction of the judgments against B and C. Also, as foundation for this proof, that the sale by B and A was fraudulent

[1] Baldwin *v.* Porter, 12 Conn. 473.
[2] Anthony *v.* Gilbert, 4 Blackf. 348.
[3] Criner *v.* Pike, 2 Head, 398.
[4] Squire *v.* Hollenbach, 9 Pick. 551, 552.
[5] M'Inroy *v.* Dyer, 47 Penn. 118.

as to the creditors of B.[1] So where, upon a wrongful tax sale, the owner purchases the property, in an action for damages, the amount of the tax must be deducted.[2]

§ 12. And the same general point is hypothetically illustrated by Chief Justice Shaw, as follows: " A factor has a lien on goods to half their value. The principal becomes bankrupt, and the property vests in his assignees, subject of course to all legal liens. The assignees, denying and intending to contest the factor's lien, get possession of the goods and convert them. The factor brings trover, establishes his lien, and recovers. How shall damages be assessed? If he recover the full value of the goods, he will be responsible directly back to the defendants themselves for a moiety of the value. To avoid circuity of action, why should not damages be assessed to the amount of his lien? He is fully indemnified, the balance of the value is in the hands of those entitled to it, and the whole controversy is settled in one suit." [3]

§ 13. Upon a similar principle it is held, that, in an action for conversion of a promissory note, the insolvency of the maker may be proved in mitigation of damages.[4] So where a carrier, having a lien for freight, wrongfully sells the goods, the measure of damages is the market value, deducting the amount of the lien, though not the expenses of making the sale, which was an unlawful act.[5]

§ 14. There are many cases, however, where no such claim of an alleged equitable deduction from the value will be allowed. Thus, in an action of trespass, brought by B against A, for taking, by attachment, B's growing grass; the expenses of cutting, curing, and storing the hay, though included in the costs taxed against B, in the suit brought by A against B, and collected and applied on the execution, shall not be deducted from the value of the hay, as damages.[6] So where a slave, confined in jail for rape and murder, was taken out and hung by the defendants; it was held, that the measure of damages was not what any particular person would give for him, if this charge were true, but his market-value, determined from age, appearance, and health; also, that from motives of public policy the jury might give vindictive damages.[7] So A, having recovered in ejectment against

[1] Cotton *v.* Reed, 2 Wis. 458.
[2] Alexander *v.* Helber, 35 Mis. 334.
[3] Chamberlin *v.* Shaw, 18 Pick. 283.
[4] Latham *v.* Brown, 16 Iowa, 118.
[5] Briggs *v.* Boston, &c. 6 Allen, 246.
[6] Benjamin *v.* Benjamin, 15 Conn. 347.
[7] Polk *v.* Fancher, 1 Head, 336.

B, sued him for mesne profits, and obtained judgment on demurrer. While that suit was pending, B brought an ejectment against A for the premises, and recovered. On A's executing his writ of inquiry, held, B could not offer his judgment in evidence in mitigation of damages, the record not showing the date of the demise, and that B's title had commenced before A's cause of action.[1] So, in trespass for assault and battery, the circumstance, that the defendant entered the house for the purpose of making an attachment, is not admissible in evidence in mitigation of damages. "It ought rather to aggravate the damages, for the defendants had no legal right to break open a dwelling-house for such a purpose, and it was an abuse of legal process."[2] So, in an action of trespass, it is a correct instruction to the jury, that one could not trespass upon another's rights, and allege in defence that there was no market for the property taken, or that it was on that account of less value, but the measure of damages was the full and fair value of the property; that if, at the time of the trespass, the market was depressed, too much importance should not be given to that fact, and that to the trespasser must be meted out an assessment in damages commensurate to the injury he had done. "If at any particular time there be no market demand for an article, it is not of course, on that account, of no value. What a thing will bring in the market at a given time is perhaps the measure of its value then, but it is not the only one."[3]

§ 15. The return or recovery of the property in question, or its appropriation to the use and benefit of the owner, though not effectual to "purge the trespass or bar the action,"[4] is often set up in mitigation of damages.[5] It is said, in trover, "it is quite common for the courts to make a rule, stopping the action on a redelivery and payment of costs."[6] Thus, in trover, where the property converted has been sold, and the proceeds applied to the payment of the plaintiff's debt, or otherwise to his use, it goes in mitigation of damages.[7] (See § 11.) So, in trover, for tortious taking of personal property by a collector of taxes, the proceeds having been

[1] Buntin v. Duchane, 1 Blackf. 255.

[2] Sampson v. Henry, 11 Pick. 379; per Wilde, J., ib. 389.

[3] Trout v. Kennedy, 47 Penn. 387; per Strong, J., ib. 393.

[4] Per Shaw, C. J., 10 Met. 319.

[5] See Robinson v. Barrows, 48 Maine, 186; M'Inroy v. Dyer, 47 Penn. 121; Smith v. Perry, 18 Tex. 510.

[6] Stevens v. Low, 2 Hill, 132. Doubted in Sedgwick on Damages, 504, n.

[7] Pierce v. Benjamin, 14 Pick. 356; Prescott v. Wright, 6 Mass. 20; Caldwell v. Eaton, 5 ib. 399.

applied in part payment of the taxes, the measure of damages is the value of the property at the time of the conversion, deducting the amount of such payment.[1] So, in an action of trespass against a collector of the customs, for seizing and detaining the plaintiff's vessel, for a pretended breach of the registry laws; the vessel having been restored, held, the difference between the price at which the vessel would have sold, at the time of seizure, and the price for which she actually sold at public auction, immediately after her restoration, together with the actual expenses incurred, with interest on the amount, constituted a proper estimate of damage.[2] So, in an action of trespass *quare clausum* and *de bonis*, against a justice, for issuing an attachment against the goods of the plaintiff as an absent or absconding debtor, without legal proof of the fact of concealment; the restoration of the property, before the suit, to the plaintiff, cannot be pleaded in bar of the action, nor *puis darrein continuance*, but may be admitted as evidence in mitigation of damages.[3] So A, a deputy sheriff, levied an execution, against B, on certain live stock and produce on a farm occupied by B. C forbade the sale, claiming that all the property belonged to him, and, at the sale, he bid in most of the stock, including a certain cow. A gave C a bill of sale of all the property purchased by him, including this cow, but refused to take pay for the cow, excepting her in the receipt at the foot of the bill, and reciting that the price of her was tendered him by C. In an action of trespass, brought by C against A, to recover the value of the property sold by the latter, A specified in defence that, after the sale, the cow was returned by him to C, and accepted by C in full of all damages, if any, he was entitled to; and, a verdict having been rendered for C for the value of the property, including the cow, held, that he could have judgment, only on condition that he should remit expressly on the record the price of the cow, and take judgment only for the balance. "The plaintiff has got his cow, and also a verdict for the value of her. . . . The plaintiff, while he has the cow in his possession, will take from the defendant, as a trespasser, the value of the cow, and then the plaintiff, as a purchaser, will pay back the defendant, as the vendor of the cow, the same money. . . . What occurred . . . was a sufficient

1 Pierce *v.* Benjamin, 14 Pick. 356.
2 Woodham *v.* Gelston, 1 Johns. 134.
3 Vosburgh *v.* Welch, 11 ib. 175.

acquittance . . . of all claims to the purchase-money, so that the plaintiff . . . would have no right of action for the value of the cow."[1]

§ 16. In an action of trespass for goods, which the plaintiff demanded before action, and the defendant promised to return, but which were attached on a writ against the plaintiff while the defendant was preparing to return them; the measure of damages is the same that it would have been if the defendant had returned the goods.[2] So A brought trover against B, for goods which A had surreptitiously taken from B, and which had been, by consent of A, transferred to B as his, which goods were afterwards levied upon as the goods of A, by his direction. Held, A could only recover nominal damages, if anything, against B for a detention of such goods; and that the presumption was, in the absence of proof to the contrary, that the goods either went to satisfy the execution, or were returned to A.[3] But, in trespass for taking the plaintiff's only cow on execution, the value of the cow is the measure of damages, though the proceeds of sale have been applied to the execution. "The provision exempting a man's only cow from attachment was intended for the relief of the poor, and ought to be so construed as to give all which the legislature intended; and the value of the cow, at least, ought in all cases to be given in damages. There will then be no inducement to a creditor to take his debtor's last cow."[4] So, in an action for excluding a wife from her house, it cannot be shown in mitigation of damages, that the house was obtained by fraud of her husband; more especially unless it occurred so near the act complained of as to show excitement arising from that cause.[5] And in trespass against a sheriff, for seizing and selling the plaintiff's goods under a judgment against another person, the amount paid out of the proceeds of sale for rent of the premises cannot be received in evidence to abate the damages.[6]

§ 17. In an action of trespass for pulling down a building, evidence that the building was peaceably taken down and its materials preserved, in conformity with the directions of the commissioners of the township, during a period of great public

[1] Long v. Lamkin, 9 Cush. 361; per Fletcher, J., ib. 368.

[2] Kaley v. Shed, 10 Met. 317.

[3] Perkins v. Freeman, 26 Ill. 477.

[4] Hill v. Loomis, 6 N. H. 263, 264.

[5] Jacobs v. Hoover, 9 Min. 204.

[6] Dallam v. Fitter, 6 W. & S. 323.

excitement and disorder, with the view of saving the neighborhood from threatened violence, is admissible in mitigation of damages. But not that the commissioners had by law the power to abate and remove nuisances, and that a grand jury, after instructions by a competent court, presented the building as a public nuisance and recommended its abatement. "It sometimes happens, in the mountainous region of Pennsylvania, that there is no other way of arresting the progress of the flames and saving property, but by firing against the fire: although those who fire against the fire are liable for the actual damage . . . they certainly might . . . in mitigation of damages show that the act was . . . induced by the necessity of their situation to protect their property and that of their neighbors from inevitable destruction. Houses are frequently pulled down in towns and cities to arrest the progress of . . . fire."[1]

§ 18. In an action against an officer for negligently levying only a part of the execution debt, judgment was entered for the whole debt, and the plaintiff released the part levied.[2]

[1] Reed *v.* Bias, 8 W. & S. 189; per Burnside, J. ib. 190.

[2] Maccubbin *v.* Thornton, 1 Har. & M'H. 194.

CHAPTER III.

DAMAGES IN REFERENCE TO TIME.

§ 1. THE question of *time* is one of great importance in settling the amount of damages. It involves the various inquiries, *from* what time and *to* what time the damages are to be estimated; at what time the valuation is to be made, in case of a change of value; and especially in what cases and upon what principles prospective and contingent damages may be added to those which are certain and immediate. The cases, as might be expected, are numerous, various, and by no means entirely reconcilable. The fixed standards of damages, which it has been the prevailing purpose and tendency to establish, must be admitted still to have left much latitude to the discretion of a jury.[1]

§ 2. The rule of damages for the wrongful taking of goods is the market value at the time, not the price paid.[2] Thus, in trover, the measure of damages is the value of the property at the time of conversion, with interest to the time of trial; as, for example, against a bailee;[3] or in case of conversion by sale.[4] And if, before conversion, the plaintiff, as vendee, paid the defendant for the article, and he, before trial, resold it at an advanced price, the rule is the same.[5] So, in trespass *de bon. aspor.*, the value at the time of taking is the measure of damages.[6] And in trespass for severing and carrying away coal from the plaintiff's mine, the proper measure of damages, in re-

[1] See Bishop *v.* Williamson, 2 Fairf. 504; Story *v.* N. Y. &c. 1 Seld. 85.
[2] King *v.* Orser, 4 Duer, 431.
[3] Vaughan *v.* Webster, 5 Harring. 256.
[4] Dorsett *v.* Frith, 25 Geo. 537.
[5] Kennedy *v.* Whitwell, 4 Pick. 466; Watt *v.* Potter, 2 Mas. 77; Lillord *v.* Whitaker, 3 Bibb, 92.
[6] Schurdel *v.* Schurdel, 12 Md. 108.

spect of the coal taken, is its value as soon as it existed as a chattel, that is, as soon as severed.[1] So for taking land to widen a street, the measure of damages is the value of the land at the time of taking.[2] And damages caused by the construction of a canal must be estimated as of the time of such construction. A subsequent purchaser cannot maintain an action for injury done to him.[3] So, in case of a railroad, the land damage is predicated upon the value at the time, with interest.[4] So, on the question of fraud in the sale of land, evidence of the value of the land to fix the damages should be confined to the time when the sale took place.[5]

§ 3. In trover, for the capture and detention of a cargo, bound to A, on the high seas, the proper rule of damages is the value of the cargo, at the time and place of capture, estimated upon the prices at A, with interest; and deducting a reasonable premium of insurance from the place of capture to A, also the value of such part of the cargo, or of the avails thereof, as had been restored.[6]

§ 3 *a*. In an action against an association for refusing to permit a transfer of stock; the measure of damages is its actual value at the time of such refusal.[7]

§ 4. The general rule is laid down, that *prospective damages* may be recovered, where the cause accrues before the commencement of the action.[8] That, in an action for trespass, the plaintiff may prove special damages, if strictly the consequence of the trespass, or if the act causing such special damages constitutes part of an entire transaction, of which the principal trespass was the commencement.[9] That, where the act complained of is admitted to have been done with force, and to constitute a proper ground for an action of trespass *vi et armis*, all the damage to the plaintiff of which such injurious act was the efficient cause, and for which the plaintiff is entitled to recover in any form, may be recovered in such action, although, in point of time, such damage did not occur till some time after the act was done.[10] Thus, in an action brought in 1833, for harboring and conveying away a slave bound to serve until 4837, damages may be recovered for the

1 Morgan *v.* Powell, 2 Gale & Dav. 721.
2 Parks *v.* Boston, 15 Pick. 198.
3 Zimmerman *v.* Union, &c. 1 W. & S. 346.
4 Whitman *v.* Boston, &c. 7 Allen, 313.
5 Gaulden *v.* Shehee, 24 Geo. 438.
6 Hallett *v.* Novion, 14 Johns. 273.
7 Building, &c. *v.* Sendmeyer, 50 Penn. 67.
8 Tarleton *v.* M'Gawley, Peake, 205.
9 Damron *v.* Roach, 4 Humph. 134.
10 Dickinson *v.* Boyle, 17 Pick. 78.

whole term.[1] So A pulled down the fence of B, whereby the cattle of B escaped and were lost. Held, the loss was strictly the consequence of the trespass, and evidence thereof admissible in an action of trespass for throwing down the fence and permiting the cattle to escape.[2] So, for making a railroad through a farm, the measure of damages is the market value of the land taken, with an allowance for the disadvantages resulting from the mode of dividing the farm.[3] Evidence is admissible of what the property would have sold for, before and after the road was made and went into successful operation; and the difference may be considered in estimating the damages.[4] So, in trespass for breaking down and destroying part of a mill-dam, damages may be allowed for the cost of repairs, and interruption to the use of the mill, or diminution of profits caused by the flow of water through the break, and its thereby falling too low for the working of the mill.[5] So, in an action of the case by the owner and operator of a cotton-mill, against the owner of a mill on the same stream, for the unlawful raising of a dam below, and causing backwater, and thereby diminishing the profits of the plaintiff; evidence of the profits lost from the interruption may be submitted to the jury, as a basis, if not as the measure, of damages. The court remark: "Evidence as to profits, as a general rule, is rejected; because, generally, they are uncertain and contingent; depending upon other circumstances than the injurious act of the defendants, and not the natural result of it. Nevertheless, the general rule is subject to many exceptions. . . . Whenever a loss of profits is the natural and necessary result of the act charged, — such as the party probably would have made, not what by chance he might have made, but what any prudent man must naturally have made, — evidence has been, if not always, most usually admitted as to them."[6] So in trespass *qu. cl.*, the plaintiff may claim for damage to his crop by driving away his negroes.[7] So, in an action against a railroad for personal injury caused by the negligence of the company, evidence is admissible of consequent loss in business, and therefore of the nature and extent of such business, and the importance of the plaintiff's personal oversight. But the opinions

[1] Stille *v.* Jenkins, 3 Green, 302.

[2] Damron *v.* Roach, 4 Humph. 134.

[3] East, &c. *v.* Hottenstine, 47 Penn. 565.

[4] Ibid.

[5] White *v.* Mosely, 8 Pick. 356; acc. Allison *v.* Chandler, 11 Mich. 542.

[6] Simmons *v.* Brown, 5 R. I. 299; per Brayton, J., ib. 302.

[7] Johnson *v.* Courts, 3 Har. & M'H. 510.

of witnesses as to the amount of loss are not competent.[1] So, to an action against an attorney for negligence in the examination of securities, whereby the plaintiff had suffered great loss, the defendant pleaded the Statute of Limitations. The examination occurred in 1814, but the defect was not discovered till 1820, up to which time the interest was paid. Upon the ground, that, if the action had been brought immediately after the neglect occurred, the plaintiff might have recovered damages for the probable future loss, the defence was sustained, the statute being held to run from 1814, not from 1820.[2] So where a toll-bridge was carried away by the defendant's fault, the rule for assessing damages is the value of the superstructure, or so much of it as was carried away and lost, and the loss of tolls during the time that was reasonably necessary to repair or rebuild.[3] So where the defendant's horse, driven by his servant, ran against and injured the horse of the plaintiff; held, the cost of cure, the value of the services of the horse while being cured, and his depreciation in value, constituted the measure of damages.[4] And, in general, where the chief value of the thing injured is its daily use, damages are not confined to interest on the value.[5]

§ 5. It is the result of the rule of damages above stated, that, for an injury *continuous* in its nature, the party is entitled to recover for all damages done *previously to the trial*.[6] Thus a libel, the subject of the action, appeared in the defendant's newspaper in the form of an advertisement, on the 4th of October. Placards containing copies of the advertisement were also extensively posted, and distributed through the town. The defendant was served with the writ on the 5th of October. Held, evidence of injury was admissible, to increase the damages, accruing to the plaintiff after action brought. Also, that the jury were rightly instructed to consider what was the natural consequence of the defendant's act, without reference to other publications.[7] So the hirer of a slave for a specified time may recover, from one who takes the slave from him, the value of the slave's services for the entire term, though the suit is brought pending the term.[8] So, in actions of trespass for injuries continued after the actions are

[1] Lincoln *v.* Saratoga, &c. 23 Wend. 425.

[2] Howell *v.* Young, 5 B. & C. 259; acc. Smith *v.* Fox, 12 Jur. 130.

[3] Sewall's, &c. *v.* Fisk, 3 Fost. 171.

[4] Streett *v.* Lanmier, 34 Mis. 469.

[5] Williams *v.* Phelps, 16 Wis. 80.

[6] Puckell *v.* Smith, 5 Strobh. 26.

[7] Harrison *v.* Pearce, 4 Hurl. & Nor. 863.

[8] Moore *v.* Winter, 27 Mis. 380.

brought, damages may be recovered up to the time of trial.[1] (*a*) So, in an action by a town for removing paupers into such town, and thereby throwing upon it the burden of their support, the rule of damages is the amount necessarily and in good faith expended in supporting the paupers from the time of their removal to the time of trial.[2] But, in an action of trespass, &c., to recover freedom, the plaintiff is held not entitled to damages after the institution of the suit.[3] And where, in trover for a negro woman, a jury gave damages for the value of her child, born after the action was commenced, a new trial was granted.[4]

§ 6. The plaintiff had pledged a depreciation note, in the nature of a certificate of public debt, nominally worth $2,629.48, for a loan of $600, a part of which was subsequently paid. The pledgee, without demand of payment or notice of sale, sold the certificate for $625, which was then its highest market value. Eleven years after, the administrator of the pledgor went to the house of the pledgee to demand it, but made no demand, in consequence of the incapacity of the pledgee to attend to business. The administrator then brought his action to recover the value of the certificate. Held, the measure of damages was the price of the certificate at the time of the proposed demand.[5] So, in an action for wrongful conversion of shares in a corporation, the plaintiff having commenced and prosecuted it with reasonable diligence, but the case being protracted, and the stock having risen from $5,962 to $8,175 ; he was held entitled to recover the latter sum as damages.[6]

§ 7. In a late case, being an action against a common carrier, damages were allowed *beyond* the time of trial.[7]

§ 8. The rule above stated, as to special or prospective damages, of course involves the consequence, that no subsequent action can be maintained for damages resulting from the wrongful act for which a former action was brought, though subsequent to

[1] Pepoon *v.* Clarke, 1 Con. Ct. 137.
[2] Stratford *v.* Sanford, 9 Conn. 275.
[3] Tramell *v.* Adam, 2 Mis. 155.
[4] Craig *v.* Todd, 2 Const. (S. C.) 757.
[5] Cortelyou *v.* Lansing, 2 Caines's Cas. in Er. 200.
[6] Romaine *v.* Van Allen, 26 N. Y. (12 Smith), 309.
[7] Russ *v.* Steamboat, &c. 14 Iowa, 363. See Hicks *v.* Herring, 17 Cal. 566.

(*a*) The plaintiff in a second suit, on account of a continuing nuisance, can recover only for damages since the commencement of the former suit. Beckwith *v.* Griswold 29 Barb. 291.

the former action.[1] Thus, where the leg of a slave was broken by another, and damages given to the owner for the deteriorated value of the slave in consequence of this permanent injury; held, such damages were in lieu of loss of service, as being in full compensation for the wrong.[2] So, in estimating the value of land condemned for the use of the Chesapeake and Ohio Canal Company, it is the right and the province of the jury to consider all damages which the owner would sustain, whether immediate, remote, or contingent; and the legal presumption is, that the jury awarded damages to the extent of their authority, and to all persons who might be affected by their finding. An action of trespass cannot therefore be sustained by an owner of land for such damage, he having already received an adequate remuneration.[3] So where one town recovers judgment against another, for damages caused by the leaving of a pauper in the limits of the former town, the damages being assessed up to the time of trial; and, having unsuccessfully notified the defendant to remove the pauper, brings another suit for subsequent damages: the former judgment is a bar to such action. The case is not like that of the continuance of a nuisance, which is a constantly renewed cause of action. In this case the whole injury was, in contemplation of law, done by the original wrong, although the future damages were contingent.[4]

§ 9. There is, however, a class of cases which reasonably qualify the general rules above stated. It is said, if remote damages were allowed, the rules would become so numerous, complex, and uncertain, as to be impracticable.[5] And this principle is more especially applied to damage caused, in any degree, by third persons.[6] (See pp. 425, 431.) In other cases, it is said, "the damage must be a natural consequence of the principal injury."[7] "The negligence must be the immediate and not the remote cause of damage. The plaintiffs are entitled to recover the actual damage, of which such negligence is the direct and efficient cause, and no other."[8] And in a late case in Pennsylvania, relating to a mine, the court remark: "These damages would depend on a thousand contingen-

[1] See Herriter v. Porter, 23 Cal. 385.

[2] Johnson v. Perry, 2 Humph. 569.

[3] Canal Co. v. Grove, 11 Gill & Johns. 398.

[4] Marlborough v. Sisson, 31 Conn. 332.

[5] Per Marvin, J., Jones v. N. Y. &c. 29 Barb. 644. See Nightingale v. Scannell, 18 Cal. 315.

[6] Fitzsimons v. Inglis, 5 Taun. 534; Sedg. on Dam. 67.

[7] Phillips v. Hoyle, 4 Gray, 571.

[8] Waite v. Gilbert, 10 Cush. 178.

cies. The success in working the mine against the ever-resisting laws of nature to efforts to disembowel the earth. These, to be successful, would depend on the management of its affairs. After this would come the contingencies of a market, of transportation, of the demand for the particular product, the abundance or scarcity of money, the crops, and the state of the country."[1] So the actual damage at the time and place of injury, and not probable profits at the port of destination, is the measure of damages, in cases of collision as well as insurance.[2] So, in an action for forcibly bricking up the entrance of a restaurant or refreshment saloon kept by the plaintiff, and thereby breaking up his business; he is entitled at least to a full indemnity, and the value of the business is a proper subject of estimate for the jury. But not, it seems, the possible or probable profits.[3] So in an action for injury to the plaintiff, personally, damage is not recoverable for loss of profit on contracts which might have been entered into by him. Such damage is too remote.[4] So, in an action for assault and battery, evidence is not admissible, in aggravation of damages, that, in consequence of the injury, the plaintiff lost a place to which he was about to be appointed, having withdrawn his application; though specially alleged in the declaration. The assault is not the proximate cause of the loss. "It is somewhat like the case of a merchant who should offer to prove that, in consequence of an assault and battery, he was unable to go to his store, and thereby lost the opportunity to close a particular bargain which would have been profitable; or of a farmer who should offer to prove that, in consequence of such an act, he was unable to gather in his crop of grain, and thereby lost it. One of the intervening causes of the loss of the office appears to have been a voluntary act of the plaintiff's own will, and there must also have been the concurrent voluntary acts of other men."[5] (See pp. 424, 431.) So the defendant caused the plaintiff to be apprehended upon an unfounded charge, and to be detained from half-past one until two o'clock. In support of a claim for special damage in an action for false imprisonment, the plaintiff proved that he would have been engaged as a journeyman if he had presented himself

[1] Per Thompson, J., M'Knight *v.* Ratcliff, 44 Penn. 169.

[2] Smith *v.* Condry, 1 How. 28; 17 Pet. 20.

[3] Marquart *v.* La Farge, 5 Duer, 559.

[4] Priestley *v.* Maclean, 2 F. & F. 288.

[5] Brown *v.* Cummings, 7 Allen, 507, per Chapman, J., ib. 509.

at the factory at two o'clock on the day in question; but that, being unwell from the treatment he had received, he went home and did not go to the factory until the next morning, when he found that his intended employer had engaged another man. Held, that this damage was too remote.[1] So but one action can be maintained to recover damages for an injury to the person. The party is not obliged to wait until all the consequences of the injury are fully developed; he may sue whenever he thinks proper, and recover damages for both past and future pain of body, as well as for past and future deprivation of health or of any of his bodily powers. But nothing prospective should be conjectural. Thus, in an action against a railroad corporation, to recover damages for an injury, it is not erroneous to charge the jury that, in ascertaining the amount of damages, it would be proper for them to consider the bodily pain and suffering which had occurred, or was likely to occur, in consequence of the injury, but that they could not act on conjecture as to the prospective condition or situation of the plaintiff; they could only regard, in respect to the future, what the evidence rendered reasonably certain would necessarily and inevitably result from the original injury.[2] So, where imported wool of the plaintiff, on which the duties had been paid, was injured by reason of the negligence of the defendant's servants, and in consequence it became necessary to take it out of the original packages, and in a few weeks afterwards an act of Congress was passed, under which, if the wool had remained in the original packages, the plaintiff would have been entitled to a return of duties; held, the plaintiff was not, on this ground, entitled to additional damages.[3] So it is held, generally, that, in trespass for an injury to property, the value of property at the time of the injury, with interest, is the measure of damages;[4] that, in actions of trespass, the measure of damages is the value of the property destroyed, unless the trespass is wanton and malicious, which is a question entirely for the jury, who may give vindictive damages;[5] and that, in actions of tort for the destruction of property, its value furnishes the measure of damages, from which, if the jury materially depart, the court will order a new trial.[6]

[1] Hoey *v.* Felton, 11 C. B. (N. S.) 142; 8 Jur. (N. S.) 764; 31 L. J. C. P. 105. See, as to the damages in case of imprisonment of a slave, Woodfolk *v.* Sweeper, 2 Humph. 88.

[2] Curtis *v.* Rochester, &c. 20 Barb. 282.

[3] Stone *v.* Codman, 15 Pick. 297.

[4] Brannin *v.* Johnson, 1 App. 361.

[5] Wylie *v.* Smitherman, 8 Ired. 236; Bradley *v.* Geiselman, 22 Ill. 494; Alston *v.* Huggins, Const. Rep. 688.

[6] Bailey *v.* Jeffords, 2 Spear, 271.

Hence where, in trespass for taking personal property, without malice and under a claim of right, to which the controversy solely relates, the plaintiff claims that, by the taking of the property, he has been broken up in his business; a charge that the defendant must make the plaintiff good for all the actual damage sustained by him at the defendant's hands, resulting directly and naturally from the injury, is erroneous.[1] So, in trespass for taking away a yoke of oxen, the jury ought not, in estimating the damages, actually sustained by the plaintiff, to add to the value of the oxen any sum for their services.[2] So, in an action for removing a belt by which water-power was communicated to the plaintiff's machinery, and placing it so as to run the defendant's machinery, accompanied with a claim of right so to do, and with such forcible acts and threats as to lead the plaintiff to believe that such interruption would be continued; the plaintiff cannot recover, as damages, for the expense and delay of fitting up another wheel to drive his machinery.[3] So, in an action of trespass for obstructing a ditch running through the plaintiff's land, damages can only be recovered up to the commencement of the suit.[4] So, in an action for breaking and entering the plaintiff's close and tearing down his unfinished building, he cannot show, for the purpose of proving damages, what the building would have cost, or rented for, if it had been finished according to the plan.[5] So, in an action against a railroad company for injury to a mill, caused by the construction of the road, the injury to the unused and surplus water-power of the plaintiff, and its actual market value for any useful purpose, constitute the measure of damages, the mill remaining as it was when the mill was made. But evidence is not admissible of the power which might be gained by erecting a new dam further down the stream, making a shorter race, and other alterations. Such damage is merely theoretical and speculative.[6] So loss by delay, resulting, in consequence of intervening badness of the roads, from the taking in execution of an emigrant's horses and wagon, is not such a natural, proximate consequence of the act as will constitute legal damage.[7] So in an action against an officer for taking

[1] Oviatt *v.* Pond, 29 Conn. 479.
[2] Anthony *v.* Gilbert, 4 Blackf. 348.
[3] Sibley *v.* Hoar, 4 Gray, 222.
[4] Shaw *v.* Etheridge, 3 Jones, 300.
[5] Bennett *v.* Clemence, 6 Allen, 10.
[6] Dorlan *v.* East, &c. 46 Penn. 521.
[7] Vedder *v.* Hildreth, 2 Wis. 427.

a vessel of the plaintiff under a writ of attachment against a third person, there being some evidence that she was preparing for a voyage, but no proof of malice, the jury were directed to estimate her value at the time of taking, and "the additional damage sustained, if any." Held, the jury were not authorized to allow damages for the breaking up of the voyage.[1] So where the navigation of a river is unlawfully obstructed by a gas-pipe, upon which a vessel, navigated with due care, in passing, is caught, subjecting the charterer to expense in getting her off; in an action against the gas company, he may recover such expense, but not for delay in his business or other consequential damage.[2] So, in an action against a railroad for an oblique fracture of the plaintiff's leg, caused by a collision, it appeared that the nature of the injury made probable another fracture. But the court remarked: "The present and probable future condition of the limb were proper matters for inquiry; but the consequences of a hypothetical second fracture were obviously beyond the range of it, and calculated to draw the minds of the jury into fanciful conjectures;" and decided accordingly.[3]

§ 10. It is said, the rule of damages for personal injuries, inflicted by negligence, is loss of time during the cure, and expense incurred in respect of it, the pain and suffering undergone by the plaintiff, and any permanent injury, especially when it causes a disability for future exertion, and consequent pecuniary loss.[4] But where, by reason of the negligence of the lessors, an opera-house was not completed in season, whereby one of the singers took cold, and the lessee lost the anticipated receipts of the performance; held, the sickness of the performer was too remote to be the subject of damages.[5] So, in an action against a railroad corporation for injuries to a horse from a defect in the highway caused by the defendants, a proper measure of damages is the diminution in the market value of the horse at the commencement of the suit, reasonable expenditures for the purpose of curing him, and a reasonable compensation to the plaintiff for attempting to cure him, and for the loss of use of the horse while under such treatment; not exceeding, however, the value of the horse.[6]

§ 11. In an action of trespass against the New York collector

[1] Boyd *v.* Brown, 17 Pick. 543.
[2] Benson *v.* Malden, &c. 6 Allen, 149.
[3] Lincoln *v.* Saratoga, &c. 23 Wend. 425.
[4] Peoria, &c. *v.* Loomis, 20 Ill. 235.
[5] Academy, &c. *v.* Hackett, 2 Hilt. 217.
[6] Gillett *v.* Western, &c. 8 Allen, 560.

of customs, it appeared that the plaintiff's vessel was illegally seized, and detained nearly eleven months, when she was restored. Six months before the seizure, the plaintiff bought the vessel for $12,474 ; and, the day before, contracted to sell her for $9,500. Eight days after the restoration, the vessel was sold at auction for $4,288. Held, the measure of damages was $9,500, with interest and marshal's fees, deducting the sum of $4,288.[1]

§ 12. In an action against a railroad for non-delivery of goods in reasonable time, the measure of damages is not the decline of price at the time of delivery.[2] The court remark, upon the general subject, in connection with a full examination of the cases: "The bailor may, in such a case, undoubtedly recover an indemnity for any *legitimate* damages . . . the natural and proximate consequence of the breach of the contract or duty . . . damages that naturally result from the breach, and which are not too remote, speculative or contingent. This may include interest upon the value of the property during the time the owner was deprived of it ; or if it should be property he could use, the value of the use of it. Many special circumstances may exist entitling him to damages, within the principles referred to."[3]

§ 12 *a*. The measure of damages is held to be the highest value of the property at any time between conversion and the day of trial.[4] But if, in case of non-delivery, the article advances in price, but goes back to its former value, the advance cannot be recovered, without showing that the plaintiff could have sold for the increased price.[5]

§ 13. In trover by a mortagee against a purchaser from the mortgagor, who has himself sold the property ; the measure of damages is the value of the property, with interest from the latter sale, not the former.[6]

§ 14. The plaintiffs made a conditional sale of brown cottons to a printing company, who, after printing them, transferred them to the defendant, without having complied with the conditions. In trover, held, the measure of damages was the value of the goods before being printed.[7]

§ 15. It is held, that an injured party cannot recover for damages

[1] Woodham *v.* Gelston, 1 Johns. 134.
[2] Jones *v.* N. Y., &c. 29 Barb. 633.
[3] Per Marvin, J., 29 Barb. 643.
[4] Wilson *v.* Mathews, 24 Barb. 295.
[5] Williams *v.* Phelps, 16 Wis. 80.
[6] Barry *v.* Bennett, 7 Met. 354.
[7] Dresser, &c. *v.* Waterston, 3 Met. 9.

which, at a trifling expense, or by reasonable exertion, he might have prevented;[1] especially if remote, speculative, and contingent.[2] It is incumbent upon any person subjected to an injury to use such means as are reasonably in his power to make the evil consequences as light as possible. And where an injured party, by reasonable efforts, succeeds in reducing his actual damages, his claim for redress must be reduced accordingly.[3] Thus where a trespass consisted in removing a few rods of fence, the measure of damages is the cost of repairing it, and not an injury arising to the subsequent year's crop from the defect in the fence.[4] So, in Pennsylvania, in an issue under the act of 19th February, 1849, to assess the damages done to a water-power by the construction of a railroad; it is error to reject evidence, that the cause of mischief complained of could be removed for $140, a verdict being returned for $3,472. "It was much more certain proof in its nature, than those speculative views on which damages in such cases are too often assessed."[5] So in trover for a bond, the condition of which was, that, if the plaintiff would remove to the town of P., and dwell there a year, he should have certain lands; he not having removed, the measure of damages is the value of the lands, deducting what it would have cost to perform his part of the condition.[6] So the measure of damages in an action for injuries, arising to house, grounds, &c., by water diverted from its course, upon the plaintiff's land, by the defendants in constructing a railroad, is the difference between the value of the premises before the injury and the value immediately after, resulting from the defendants' acts, and which could not be prevented by reasonable care and diligence on the part of the plaintiff.[7] So, where animals fit for beef are not killed, nor so injured but that they are of value for food, it is the duty of the owner to dispose of them to the best advantage; he has no right to abandon them wantonly, and then claim their full value. The criterion of damages in such a case is the value of the cattle as injured, and their value before the injury.[8] So if B unnecessarily throws cotton, left on his land, without his consent, by A, into the water, and A gets it again; A's measure of damage is only the injury to the cotton by B's act and the cost of getting it

1 Douglass *v.* Stephens, 18 Mis. 362.
2 Loker *v.* Damon, 17 Pick. 288.
3 Chandler *v.* Allison, 10 Mich. 460.
4 17 Pick. 284.
5 Barclay, &c. *v.* Ingham, 36 Penn. 194; per Woodward, J., ib. 199.
6 Rogers *v.* Crombie, 4 Greenl. 274.
7 Chase *v.* New York, &c. 24 Barb. 273.
8 Illinois, &c. *v.* Finnigan, 21 Ill. 646.

back, which he is bound to prove. And A can recover nothing or only nominal damages against B, if it belonged to C, and C afterwards got possession without any expense or trouble to A.[1] So damages cannot be recovered for detention of a steamboat. seized for a small debt, but which could have been released on bond.[2] So, upon a somewhat analogous principle, in an action of tort for the conversion, by the assignee of an insolvent debtor, of property claimed by the plaintiff under a conveyance from the debtor; if the jury find the conveyance void as a preference, the plaintiff cannot recover cash paid by him to the debtor for the difference in value between such property and the debt which the conveyance was made to secure.[3] And special damages cannot be recovered, where the wrong complained of was produced by the improper act of a third person, remotely induced by the wrong.[4] (See pp. 424–5.) So, although it is no defence to an action for corrupting the water of a well, that the injury has been partly produced by other causes than the one complained of; this may be shown in mitigation of damages.[5] But in case for unfastening a vessel from a dock, by means of which it floated off and was injured, the damages will not be mitigated, by proof that the plaintiff had subsequently neglected to take such measures as were in his power to recover and secure it.[6] So, in an action for the falling in of land, consequent on the excavation of the adjoining land by the defendant, the measure of damages is, not what it would cost to restore the lot to its former situation, or to build a wall to support it; but what is the lot diminished in value, by reason of the acts of the defendant.[7] And in an action for depositing earth on the plaintiff's land; if removal of the earth would cost more than the value of the land, the measure of damages is the value of the land.[8] So where a plaintiff recovers damages for the obstruction caused by the stone and earth of a bridge, falling, and damming up a canal which turned his mill; he may also include the loss occasioned by the shutting off of the water by a third party in order to clear the canal.[9] (*a*)

1 Grier *v.* Ward, 23 Geo. 145.
2 Biggs *v.* D'Aquin, 13 La. An. 21.
3 Bartlett *v.* Decreet, 4 Gray, 111.
4 Crain *v.* Petrie, 6 Hill, 523.
5 Sherman *v.* Fall River, &c., Mass., Law Reg. Oct. 63, p. 768.
6 Heeney *v.* Heeney, 2 Denio, 625.
7 McGuire *v.* Grant, 1 Dutch. 356.
8 Harney *v.* Sides, 1 Neva. 539.
9 Dayton *v.* Pease, 4 Ohio, (N. S.) 80.

(*a*) That an action lies for nuisance by reason of the vapors from smelting works,

§ 16. The plaintiffs delivered to the defendants, who were carriers, ten tons of cotton, to be carried from Liverpool to Oldham. In the usual course the cotton should have been received on the following day, but it did not arrive till four days afterwards. In consequence of the delay, a new mill of the plaintiffs was stopped for want of cotton. At the time of the delivery of the cotton to the defendants, nothing was said as to this particular inconvenience likely to result from the delay. But on the previous day, and repeatedly on each succeeding day until it arrived at Oldham, one of the plaintiffs called to inquire about it; and on each occasion told the manager of the goods department at the Oldham station, that the mill was at a stand solely on account of the non-delivery of the cotton. In an action against the defendants for neglect, the plaintiffs proved, that while the mill was at a stand they had paid in wages 7*l.*; and that the profit if the mill had been at work would have been 7*l.* 10*s.* The judge told the jury, that when, as in the present case, by the neglect of a carrier, a man had no material to carry on his business, he had a right to charge as legal damage such loss as naturally and immediately arose from stopping the mill; that the plaintiffs were entitled to the money they had actually paid as wages, 7*l.*, and that the profit which the plaintiffs would have made was a fair subject of calculation; and the jury should therefore give, over and above the sum of 7*l.*, such amount as would be the actual loss and detriment the plaintiffs had suffered by the non-arrival of the cotton in due course. Held, a misdirection, and that the plaintiffs were not entitled to the above sums as *legal damages*, inasmuch as it assumed that the stoppage of the mill arose entirely from the non-delivery of the cotton, when in fact it arose partly from that, and partly from the plaintiffs' having no cotton to go on with; though it seems the jury might have properly given the amount of the wages and loss of profit as damages, if they had found as a fact that the stoppage of the mill was a consequence of the non-delivery of the cotton, which, either from express notice, or the course of business in the district, might have been anticipated by the parties at the time of making the contract.[1]

[1] Gee *v.* L. & Y., &c. 6 Hurl. & Nor. 211.

though in a manufacturing neighborhood; see St. Helen's, &c. *v.* Tipping, Law Reg. Dec. 1865, p. 104; House of Lords; affirming the judgments of the Queen's Bench and Exchequer Courts.

CHAPTER IV.

MEASURE OF DAMAGES IN ACTIONS FOR PARTICULAR WRONGS.

§ 1. As we have seen, the measure of damages is not for the most part materially affected by the nature of the injury or the form of the action. There are, however, some peculiarities, depending on one or both of these circumstances, which require to be particularly mentioned.

§ 2. In an action for *deceit*, the defendant may claim a deduction from the damages on account of the value of the article sold, or of its use, if kept by the purchaser.[1] So, in an action for false affirmations in the sale of a horse, no damages can be recovered for the keep of the horse, previous to an offer by the plaintiff to return him.[2] So, where the plaintiff employed the defendant to manufacture jewelry from gold which the plaintiff furnished, and the defendant fraudulently made and delivered plated articles; in an action for such fraud, the plaintiff having failed to return the base jewelry, its value must be deducted from his judgment.[3] So the damages, for selling as a slave a man who was free, are found by estimating the yearly services, during the time he was held by the plaintiff, and deducting his clothing and other necessary expenses.[4]

§ 3. In a leading case in New York, the general question, what is the proper measure of damages, "the rule for ascertaining the sum which the injured party ought to recover, in all cases where *personal property is wrongfully taken or detained*, whether

[1] M'Laren *v*. Long, 25 Geo. 708.
[2] West *v*. Anderson, 4 Conn. 107.
[3] Harris *v*. Bernard, 4 E. D. Smith, 195.
[4] Jones *v*. Conway, 4 Yea. 109.

by force, by fraud, or by process of law," is examined and considered on principle and the adjudged cases. It is there held, that the amount to be recovered will be ascertained by adding to the value of the property, when the right of action accrued, such damages as shall cover every additional loss which the owner has sustained, and also every increase of value which the wrong-doer has obtained, or has it in his power to obtain. The highest price which the property has borne, at any time between its conversion and the trial, cannot, *in all cases*, be the measure of damages, since, when it does not appear that this price would have been obtained by the owner, or has been obtained by the wrong-doer, the damages, measured by this rule, would be vindictive, instead of remunerative. With still less reason can the value of the property at the time of the trial be assumed as the true and sole measure of the damages, since this would cast the risk of depreciation, deterioration, or destruction of property upon the innocent owner. The principles above laid down, although not explicitly stated, are said to be not only consistent with, but deducible from, the adjudged cases in England and the United States, with the exception of a few which must be regarded as anomalous.[1]

§ 3 *a*. In a later case, in the same State, it is held no bar to an action of trover or trespass, that the plaintiff has recovered his property. In this case, the sum paid to recover the property is the measure of damage.[2]

§ 4. Some cases have occurred, involving the measure of damages for the taking of property *connected with the realty*, whether in trespass or trover.

§ 4 *a*. In trespass, for wrongfully entering upon lands, and taking and carrying away the soil, &c., the proper measure of damages is not the actual damage sustained, but the value of the land removed.[3]

§ 5. In an action for injury to a coal-mine, the measure of damages is the actual loss by delay, loss of time, damage to machinery, &c.; and, if the mine was irreclaimable, the value of the estate and property; but not merely speculative profits. An instruction is erroneous, that, " if the mine was rendered entirely

[1] Suydam *v.* Jenkins, 3 Sandf. 614. See West *v.* Wentworth, 3 Cow. 82; Clark *v.* Pinney, 7 ib. 681; Carpenter *v.* Stevens, 12 Wend. 589.

[2] Ford *v.* Williams, 24 N. Y. (10 Smith) 359.

[3] Mueller *v.* St. Louis, &c. 31 Mis. 261.

useless, then the profits that have been made out of the coal would be a fair basis" of damages.[1]

§ 6. In trover for coal mined upon and carried away from the plaintiff's land by mistake; the measure of damages is the fair value of the coal *in place*, and the injury to the land caused by the mining.[2]

§ 7. The measure of damages for taking petroleum oil is its value at the instant of separation from the freehold.[3]

§ 8. In an action for the destruction of all the fruit-trees in an orchard through negligence of the defendant; the measure of damages is the value of the trees, though having no market value independent of the land, as they stood upon the land, when burned; not the diminished value of the land. The value may be determined by the opinion of witnesses.[4]

§ 9. The measure of damages in trover is in general the value of the goods at the time and place of conversion, with interest; subject, however, to many miscellaneous qualifications, which we proceed to notice.[5] (*a*)

§ 10. Where the owner of a chattel, who has transferred possession to another person, with the agreement that it should become his property on payment of a certain sum in monthly instalments, brings an action against a third person for a conversion of the chattel after payment of some of the instalments and a failure to pay the remainder; the title to the property not having passed from the plaintiff, and for the purpose of his full indemnity, the measure of damages is the whole value of the property, with interest from the time of conversion.[6]

§ 11. In trover for tallow, evidence being given tending to prove it to have been merchantable, testimony is admissible, in fixing

1 McKnight *v.* Ratcliff, 44 Penn. 156.
2 Forsyth *v.* Wells, 41 ib. 291.
3 Kier *v.* Peterson, ib. 357.
4 Whitbeck *v.* N. Y. &c. 36 Barb. 644.
5 Kennedy *v.* Strong, 14 Johns. 128; Douglass *v.* Kraft, 9 Cal. 562; 1 Head, 626; 26 Conn. 389, 483; 13 Gray, 313; Greenfield, &c. *v.* Leavitt, 17 Pick. 1; Stirling *v.* Garritee, 18 Md. 468; Stevens *v.* Low, 2 Hill, 133; Clement *v.* Brown, 30 Ill. 43; Yater *v.* Mullen, 24 Ind. 277; Robinson *v.* Barrows, 48 Maine, 36.
6 Angier *v.* Taunton, &c. 1 Gray, 621.

(*a*) The rule of damages in trover does not apply in Texas. Pridgin *v.* Strickland, 8 Tex. 427.

It is said, by a writer of authority, "if he elects to sue in trover, he can ordinarily recover no more than the value of the property, with interest; whereas, if he should bring trespass, he may recover not only the value of the goods, but the additional damages occasioned by the unlawful taking." 2 Greenl. Ev. 218, § 265.

the amount of damages, to show what was the retail price of merchantable tallow at the time and place of conversion.[1]

§ 12. The plaintiff may recover the enhanced value of the property taken, with interest; as where logs are taken and converted into boards and plank.[2]

§ 13. The jury are held not at liberty to give additional damages, in consideration of the plaintiff's trouble and expenses incurred in the prosecution of his suit.[3]

§ 14. Upon the ground that the plaintiff is entitled to no more than his actual damage; where the property is returned to him, he can recover only for the detention.[4]

§ 15. In trover for a slave, brought by an administrator, he may recover the value of the slave and her descendants, with damages for their detention from demand and refusal.[5] But damages for *detention* can only be computed from the time of demand, and, if no demand is proved, only from the date of the writ.[6]

§ 16. In trover for money, damages may be allowed as interest.[7]

§ 17. Where an action of replevin was instituted, but, the holder of the property refusing to deliver it up, the action was changed to trover; held, the general rule of damages must prevail.[8]

§ 18. A refusal to instruct the jury, in addition to a statement of the general rule of damages, that the plaintiff is entitled to recover only the value at the time and place of conversion, is no ground of new trial.[9]

§ 19. Where the defendant in trover conceals the article till a late stage of the trial, but finally produces it; it is not an erroneous instruction, that the plaintiff ought not to be prejudiced by an intentional withholding of the chattel, calculated and intended to prevent him from showing its actual value; and that they ought to give the full value, no more and no less.[10]

§ 19 *a*. In case of sale by the defendant, the measure of damages was held to be the price, which did not exceed the value.[11]

[1] Waters *v.* Langdon, 16 Verm. 570.

[2] Baker *v.* Wheeler, 8 Wend. 505.

[3] Hurd *v.* Hubbell, 26 Conn. 389; Cook *v.* Loomis, ib. 483.

[4] Cook *v.* Loomis, ib.; Hogan *v.* Kellum, 13 Tex. 396.

[5] Fishwick *v.* Sewell, 4 Har. & J. 393.

[6] Colvit *v.* Cloud, 14 Tex. 53.

[7] Commercial, &c. *v.* Jones, 18 Tex. 811.

[8] McGavock *v.* Chamberlain, 20 Ill. 219.

[9] Selkirk *v.* Cobb, 13 Gray, 313.

[10] Beecher *v.* Denniston, ib. 354.

[11] Symes *v.* Tucker, 13 Mich. 9.

§ 20. For conversion of plates for printing labels or advertisements, of great value to the plaintiff, though of trifling value to others; the measure of damages is the former value, estimating the cost of replacing the plates.[1]

§ 21. In an action for conversion, the amount of damages is not affected by the defendant's having afterwards attached the property, discontinued the action, and offered to restore the property to the plaintiff, who refused to receive it.[2]

§ 22. Under special circumstances, the jury are held to have an arbitrary discretion as to the amount of damages.[3]

§ 22 *a*. The law presumes damages from a *trespass*, and an instruction to the jury, that, if no damage was done, they should find for the defendants, is error.[4]

§ 23. In trespass *quare clausum*, the jury may give damages for the conduct of the defendant in entering the premises, knowing they were not his, and for his subsequent acts after such entry.[5]

§ 24. Where it appeared, in an action of trespass for the seizure and detention of the plaintiff's vessel, that the plaintiff, afterwards, but some time before the date of his writ, purchased her under a decree of court; it was held, that damages might be given for the detention, after she was so in the plaintiff's possession, down to the date of the writ, as she was restored only by the substitution of the plaintiff's money for her value as sold.[6]

§ 25. In an action for burning a house, in mitigation of damages, the defendant may show it to be a house of ill-fame, by the actions of persons visiting the house, when going to and from it, and in its immediate neighborhood.[7]

§ 26. An act of the legislature authorized a corporation to make a canal, and provided that any person, damaged thereby, might apply to the Superior Court, and have his damages adjudged to him. Held, this provision was not intended to give a remedy from time to time, as the damages might actually arise, but to give a remedy at once for all the damages that might be sustained by having the lands perpetually incumbered.[8]

1 Stickney *v.* Allen, 10 Gray, 352.
2 Ibid.
3 Jones *v.* Allen, 1 Head, 626; Backentoss *v.* Stahler, 33 Penn. 251.
4 Attwood *v.* Fricot, 17 Cal. 37.
5 Ridgely *v.* Bond, 17 Md. 14.
6 Denison *v.* Hyde, 6 Conn. 508.
7 Abrams *v.* Ervin, 9 Iowa, 87.
8 Woods *v.* N. M. Co. 5 N. H. 467.

CHAPTER V.

SPECIAL, EXEMPLARY, AND VINDICTIVE DAMAGES; MALICE, ETC.

§ 1. DAMAGES additional to the amount of direct and immediate injury are often termed *special*. It is said, special damage is that which may "be given in evidence to aggravate the damages in one action, or be itself the substantive cause of action, as in the case of trespass *quare clausum*, and carrying away plaintiff's goods; the carrying away the goods may be a ground of special damage, or be the cause of a separate action."[1]

§ 2. The right to recover special damages often depends upon the allegations in the writ. Such damage must be specially alleged, solely for the purpose of giving the defendant notice of the plaintiff's claim with regard to it; while he is held to take notice of such damage as is the necessary consequence of his act, without any special allegation,[2] and without any statement of the particular circumstances of aggravation.[3] Thus, in a suit to recover for injury done to a horse through the unskilfulness of the defendant, the expense of doctoring and taking care of it cannot be recovered, unless declared for as special damage.[4] So, in an action for falsely and maliciously giving information that the plaintiff was about to offer for sale unwholesome meat, the jury cannot assess damages for an injury to the plaintiff's reputation, without an averment that the defendant stated that the plaintiff knew the meat to be unwholesome.[5] So an allegation, that the defendant caused by the erection of a mill-dam "an unhealthy pond of standing water," does not authorize evidence

[1] Per Shaw, C. J., Smith *v.* Sherman, 4 Cush. 413.

[2] Bristol, &c. *v.* Gridley, 28 Conn. 201.

[3] Heirn *v.* M'Caughan, 32 Miss. 17.

[4] Patten *v.* Libbey, 32 Maine, 378.

[5] Hemmenway *v.* Woods, 1 Pick. 524.

of sickness caused by the pond.[1] So, in an action for injury to real estate, loss of rents, not being a necessary result of the act complained of, must be specially alleged.[2] And, upon the same ground, special damages for the obstruction of a way must be specially alleged.[3] So, in an action against the commissioner of patents, for refusing to give copies of patents, in his office, on demand and tender of fees, special damage, if not alleged in the declaration, cannot be proved.[4] So, in trespass for killing a mare, damages for taking care of the wounded beast, and rearing two colts she was suckling, not the direct necessary results of the trespass, cannot be given, unless specially alleged. And where evidence to the above effect was given, and the jury gave much more than the average estimated value of the mare, and more than the highest estimate in the testimony, it was presumed that they gave the above improper damages.[5] So an unmarried woman cannot recover damages, on account of her prospects of marriage being lessened by injury which she has received, unless alleged and proved.[6] So, in trespass for a ship, more especially unless specially alleged, the plaintiff cannot show that a writ of replevin for the ship, taken out by one A in his own name, was procured by the plaintiff for his benefit.[7] So, under a declaration for loss of the benefit and profit from working a mill, and the custom and trade thereof, by a disturbance, the plaintiff can only recover the value of the use of the mill. Special damages, as that he was obliged to transport the grain he raised to a distant mill, must be alleged, to admit of evidence as to them.[8] So, in trespass for *mesne profits*, after ejectment for a house used as an inn, the plaintiff cannot recover the loss sustained by shutting up the inn and destroying the custom, unless specially stated.[9] (*a*)

[1] Morris *v.* McCarney, 9 Geo. 160.
[2] Parker *v.* Lowell, 11 Gray, 354.
[3] Adams *v.* Barry, 10 ib. 361.
[4] Boyden *v.* Burke, 14 How. 575.
[5] Teagarden *v.* Hetfield, 11 Ind. 522.
[6] Hunter *v.* Stewart, 47 Maine, 419.
[7] Hempstead *v.* Bird, 2 Day, 293.
[8] McTavish *v.* Carroll, 13 Md. 429.
[9] Dunn *v.* Large, 3 Doug. 335.

(*a*) The omission to lay damages in a declaration, though in an action sounding altogether in damages, will be cured after verdict by the (Virginia) statute of jeofails. Stephens *v.* White, 2 Wash. 203.

A judgment for a sum greater than the *ad damnum* is bad. It seems, if no specific *ad damnum* be alleged, a verdict not exceeding the stating part of the declaration may stand. Walcott *v.* Holcomb, 24 Ill. 331.

And, it is said, damages may exceed the value alleged in the body of the count. 2 Greenl. Ev. 214, § 260.

Where unauthorized damages are claimed, and a general judgment rendered; an arrest is held to be lawful. Stirling *v.* Garritee, 18 Md. 468.

§ 3. As we have seen, in the absence of proof of aggravation, *compensation* is the proper measure of damages. Thus, in an action of trespass, where the defendant has suffered a wall to remain, after a recovery by the plaintiff in a former action for the same cause, but not from a wanton disregard of the plaintiff's rights, or disregard of his comfort and convenience, but for the proper purpose of again trying the question of title; it is not a case for aggravated damages.[1]

§ 4. It remains to be stated, that in numerous cases, (*a*) according to the weight of authority, *exemplary* damages may be given; and the question is for the jury,[2] resting altogether in their discretion, and dependent on the complaint stated in the declaration and the proof offered to support it.[3] More especially vindictive damages *for personal injuries* can be recovered, where they are accompanied with circumstances of aggravation.[4]

[1] Nivin *v.* Stevens, 5 Har. 272.

[2] Nagle *v.* Mullison, 34 Penn. 48; Major *v.* Pullain 3 Dana, 582; Allison *v.* Chandler, 11 Mich. 542; Snively *v.* Fahnestock, 18 Md. 391.

[3] Nivin *v.* Stevens, 5 Har. 272.

[4] Chiles *v.* Drake, 2 Met. (Ky.) 146.

In Connecticut, in an action of trespass, removed from a justice of the peace upon plea of title, treble damages are allowed, though they exceed the amount claimed. Hart *v.* Brown, 2 Root, 301.

And, in an action of tort, after a verdict for the plaintiff, the damages will be presumed to have been assessed according to the case proved; and, if improper circumstances were alleged as aggravation, the presumption is, that no damages were given on such ground. Richards *v.* Farnham, 13 Pick. 451.

(*a*) No question relating to damages has been so prolific of discussion, and still remains so unsettled, as the one, whether, in any case, and if so in what cases, exemplary damages may be given. There are several reasons for not entering at large upon this discussion in the present work. In the first place, it would be foreign from the brief and compendious plan of the work, and would occupy a space altogether disproportionate to the consideration of other equally or more important topics. Another reason is, that the question still remains an open one; the reports abounding with direct decisions and incidental dicta, which, notwithstanding the labored and ingenious efforts of opposing elementary writers to explain them away, respectively adopt both sides of the question;—and the expression of another individual opinion would add no weight to either. And finally, with great deference it is suggested, that the practical importance of the subject has been very much overrated. In a large proportion of cases where exemplary damages can even plausibly be claimed, the plaintiff may at any rate claim full indemnity or compensation, and this will include, in the discretion of the jury, precisely the same elements, of wounded feeling on the one side, and malice on the other, which would enter into a verdict ostensibly rendered for the sake of individual punishment or public example. The term *vindictive* is often used as synonymous with exemplary; and, without reference to example or punishment, a jury may feel bound and authorized to award an amount of damages which will *vindicate* the authority of the law, and *avenge*, with reference to the plaintiff, the wrong complained of.

It may be added, in this connection, that, as the terms are generally used, the distinction between *special* damages, whether *exemplary* or not, and *prospective* or *contingent* damages, which we have already considered, though perhaps not always very precisely observed, would seem to be this: Special damages are predicated chiefly on the circumstances of *aggravation* attending the injury complained of, as connected with the conduct or motives of the defendant; while damages of the other class pertain more particularly to the effects of such injury upon the plaintiff. Damages of both kinds may and often do co-exist; but nei ther necessarily involve the other.

§ 5. Punitive, vindictive, and exemplary damages are, in legal contemplation, synonymous terms.[1] In a late case it is said, "Exemplary damages would seem to mean, in the ordinary and proper sense of the words, such damages as would be a good round compensation, and an adequte recompense for the injury sustained, and such as might serve for a wholesome example to others in like cases."[2] Malice is the usual requisite for exemplary damages;[3] as in case of insult;[4] (*a*) disposition to annoy, harass, or tease;[5] oppression, outrage, or vindictiveness;[6] wanton or malicious motives, or a reckless disregard of the rights of others; circumstances of great hardship and oppression;[7] or circumstances of contumely or indignity. Malice is not merely the doing of an unlawful or injurious act; but implies that the act was conceived in the spirit of mischief, or of criminal indifference to civil obligations.[8] And it is held, in an action for a trespass, that the defendant must be presumed to have intended the legitimate effects of such trespass.[9] And the plaintiff in trespass may give in evidence, to enhance damages, or for punishment, such circumstances accompanying the wrong as may have occasioned him especial inconvenience or injury.[10]

§ 6. Malice of the defendant may be proved by his own testimony.[11]

§ 7. It is sometimes held that malice can be shown to increase the damages only in questions of *character*.[12] And there is no doubt of the rule, that, for the speaking of words actionable *per se*, the jury may give *smart-money*.[13] So it is sometimes laid down, that exemplary damages may be recovered for injuries to *person* or *character*.[14] Thus, for an aggravated and unprovoked assault.[15] (*b*)

1 Chiles *v.* Drake, 2 Met. Ky. 146. See Graham *v.* Roden, 5 Tex. 141.

2 Per Holmes, J., Freidenheit *v.* Edmundson, 36 Mis. 226.

3 Fry *v.* Bennett, 3 Bosw. 200; Etchberry *v.* Levielle, 2 Hilt. 40; Schindel *v.* Schindel, 12 Md. 108.

4 Wilkins *v.* Gilmore, 2 Humph. 140; Anthony *v.* Gilbert, 4 Blackf. 348.

5 Etchberry *v.* Levielle, 2 Hilt. 40.

6 Nagle *v.* Mullison, 34 Penn. 48.

7 Dorsey *v.* Manlove, 14 Cal. 553; Kennedy *v.* North, &c. 36 Mis. 351.

8 Philadelphia, &c. *v.* Quigley, 21 How. 202.

9 Allison *v.* Chandler, 11 Mich. 542.

10 Snively *v.* Fahnestock, 18 Md. 391.

11 Norris *v.* Morrill, 40 N. H. 395.

12 Stallings *v.* Corbet, 2 Speers, 613. See M'Cune *v.* Norwich, &c. 30 Conn. 321.

13 Guard *v.* Risk, 11 Ind. 156.

14 Bell *v.* Morrison, 27 Miss. 68.

15 Foote *v.* Nichols, 28 Ill. 486; Birchard *v.* Booth, 4 Wis. 67.

(*a*) To allow damages for insult is said to prevent duelling. Merest *v.* Hamey, 5 Taunt. 442.

(*b*) In a late case in Maine, being an action of trespass *vi et armis*, for maiming and disfiguring the plaintiff, a majority of

§ 8. But the prevailing rule now is, without restriction to any particular classes of injuries, that, in actions *sounding in tort*, whether to person or property, if the injury was inflicted wilfully, wantonly, or maliciously, the jury are not limited, in assessing damages, to mere compensation, but may give exemplary (including in this term the evil example of the act) or vindictive damages, in view of the degree of malice or wantonness, and, as is sometimes held, may take into consideration the plaintiff's expenses in the prosecution of his suit.[1] In a very late case in Pennsylvania, it is said, "In wanton and aggravated trespasses more than mere compensation may be allowed by way of punishment.[2]" So in another late case it is held, that exemplary damages may be recovered in actions for injuries caused by the gross negligence of the defendant, as well as in actions for forcible injuries.[3] And in actions for injuries to personal property, whether trespass or case, the jury are not restricted to the pecuniary loss, but may take into consideration the circumstances of aggravation. Thus, where it was alleged and proved, in an action on the case, that the plaintiff, a clothier, being the owner of one moiety of certain clothier's works, with the land and privileges connected therewith, which he had mortgaged to a third person, and had paid the mortgage debt, leaving the legal title outstanding, the defendants, proprietors of an adjoining manufactory of cloths, purchased the other moiety, and

[1] Dibble *v.* Morris, 26 Conn. 416; Tillotson *v.* Cheatham, 3 Johns. 56; Milburn *v.* Beach, 14 Mis. 104. McWilliams *v.* Bragg, 3 Wis. 424; Wilkins *v.* Gilmore, 2 Humph. 140; Edwards *v.* Beach, 3 Day, 447; Hatch *v.* Pendergast, 15 Md. 251; Dennison *v.* Hyde, 6 Conn. 508; Williams *v.* Reil, 20 Ill. 147; Peoria, &c. *v.* Loomis, 20 Ill. 235; Day *v.* Woodworth, 13 How. 363, 371; Treat *v.* Barber, 7 Conn. 274; Ously *v.* Hardin, 23 Ill. 403; Wylie *v.* Smitherman, 8 Ired. 236.

[2] Per Thompson, J., McKnight *v.* Ratcliff, 44 Penn. 168.

[3] Kounts *v.* Brownz, 16 B. Mon. 577.

the court held, that the jury are authorized to give exemplary or punitive damages, if they find the defendant wantonly committed the injury. The instructions to the jury "that, in such case, they were authorized, if they thought proper, in addition to the actual damages the plaintiff has sustained, to give him a further sum, as exemplary or vindictive damages, both as a protection to the plaintiff and as a salutary example to others, to deter them from offending in like cases," was held to be in accordance with the weight of judicial authority in this country, in the courts of the United States and in those of the several States. On the other hand, Mr. Justice Rice remarked, that, "in actions of tort, damages are given as a compensation for injuries received, and should be commensurate with those injuries; no more, no less. Exemplary, vindictive, or punitive damages are something beyond, given by way of punishment. This rule of damages is presented in the ruling in this case distinctly and without any ambiguity. Hitherto it has not been adopted in this State. Deeming it unsound and pernicious in principle, I cannot concur in engrafting it upon our law, nor in adopting it as a rule of practice in our courts." Pike *v.* Dilling, 48 Maine, 539.

then, with a view to break up the plaintiff's business, and get rid of him as a competitor, bought in the outstanding legal title, and, under color of that title, appropriated the whole of the water privileges and clothier's works to their own use, and expelled the plaintiff therefrom; it was held, that the jury, in estimating the damages, might consider the motives and objects of the defendants, in committing the act complained of.[1] So exemplary damages may be given, in case of an entry in good faith, under a belief of right, for wilful damage to goods.[2] So in an action for obstructing a public way, the jury may allow punitive damages.[3] So in an action for wilful trespass in carrying away the plaintiff's wheat, the jury may give "smart-money."[4] So exemplary damages may be recovered in actions of trespass *qu.claus.*, when there are such circumstances of aggravation, insult, or malice, as would warrant them any other form of action.[5] Thus, where the defendants were part of a body of armed men, which forcibly broke and entered a store, put the plaintiff in bodily fear, and carried away most of his goods and injured his business; the value of the goods was held not to be the measure of damages.[6] And the court will not disturb a verdict on the ground of excessive damages, in a case of trespass, and exposing a crop to be destroyed by cattle, where the jury gave the highest price for which the crop might have been sold.[7] (*a*) So in an action of tort against a common carrier, for a personal grievance, by fraud, gross negligence, or oppression, the jury may in their discretion award such damages by way of punishment or for the sake of example, as they may think that the peculiar circumstances justify.[8] So exemplary damages may be given against an overseer of a highway, who cuts down a tree therein without authority and maliciously.[9]

[1] Merrill *v.* Manufacturing Co. 10 Conn. 384; Tillotson *v.* Cheetham, 3 Johns. 56.

[2] Best *v.* Allen, 30 Ill. 30.

[3] Windham *v.* Rhame, 11 Rich. 283; Jefcoat *v.* Knotts, ib. 649.

[4] Bull *v.* Griswold, 19 Ill. 631.

[5] Perkins *v.* Towle, 43 N. H. 220.

[6] Freidenheit *v.* Edmundson, 36 Mis. 226.

[7] Denby *v.* Hairson, 1 Hawks. 315; Allen *v.* Craig, 1 Green, 294.

[8] Heirn *v.* M'Caughan, 32 Miss. 17.

[9] Winter *v.* Peterson, 4 Zabr. 524.

(*a*) It is sometimes held, that exemplary damages may be given in trespass, even if it is not shown that the defendant was actuated by ill-will and hostility. Goetz *v.* Ambs, 27 Mis. 28.

The Pennsylvania statute of March 29, 1824, § 3, giving treble damages, does not apply to an innocent purchaser of timber cut from another's land. O'Reilly *v.* Shadle, 33 Penn. 489.

§ 9. Another very important point of inquiry is, how far actual punishment, or mere liability to punishment, in a criminal prosecution, is to affect the amount of damages in a civil action for the same wrongful act. Upon this point it has been held, that, in a civil action for assault and battery, vindictive or exemplary damages may be given, though the act may be punishable in a criminal prosecution.[1] So, notwithstanding the defendant has been convicted and fined in a criminal prosecution for the same offence.[2] And, it seems, the fact that the defendant has been punished criminally cannot be given in evidence to mitigate damages. And although, it seems, after a criminal conviction, the court may, with a view to the measure of punishment, suspend judgment until the decision of a civil action pending for the same cause; yet, it seems, the proceedings in the civil action will not be stayed for the purpose of awaiting the event of the criminal prosecution.[3] And, in assessing damages for an assault, it is competent for the jury to consider the effect which the finding of trivial damages may have, to encourage disregard of the laws and disturbance of the peace.[4]

§ 10. There is, however, another class of cases, which hold a different doctrine. It is this. While, on the one hand, forcible injuries are those in which the element of malice is most likely to be found, and are therefore peculiarly the subjects of exemplary damages; on the other hand, being liable to prosecution as criminal offences, they are held to be, for this reason, exempted in a civil action from anything more than the actual damages.[5]

§ 11. In a case in Massachusetts, Mr. Justice Metcalf remarks: "Whether exemplary, vindictive, or punitive damages, that is, damages beyond a compensation or satisfaction for the plaintiff's injury, can ever be legally awarded, as an example to deter others from committing a similar injury, or as a punishment of the defendant for his malignity, or wanton violation of social duty, in committing the injury which is the subject of the suit, is a question upon which we are not now required nor disposed to express an opinion. The arguments and the authorities on both sides of

[1] Wilson v. Middleton, 2 Cal. 54.

[2] Corwin v. Walton, 18 Mis. 71; Jefferson v. Adams, 4 Harring. 321; Cook v. Ellis, 6 Hill, 466; Roberts v. Mason, 10 Ohio (N. S.), 277.

[3] Cook v. Ellis, 6 Hill, 466.

[4] Beach v. Hancock, 7 Fost. 223.

[5] Taber v. Hutson, 5 Ind. 322; Ormsby v. Johnson, 1 B. Monr. 80; Humphries v. Johnson, 20 Ind. 190; Austin v. Wilson, 4 Cush. 273.

this question are to be found in 2 Greenl. Ev. tit. Damages, and Sedgwick on Damages, 39 et seq. If such damages are ever recoverable, we are clearly of opinion that they cannot be recovered in an action for an injury which is also punishable by indictment; as libel and assault and battery. If they could be, the defendant might be punished twice for the same act. See Thorley *v.* Lord Kerry, 4 Taunt. 355; Whitney *v.* Hitchcock, 4 Denio, 461; Taylor *v.* Carpenter, 2 Woodb. & Min. 1, 22."[1] Accordingly, in Indiana, one liable to a penalty under the liquor law of 1853, cannot also be liable for vindictive damages in a civil action.[2] So it is held, that the record of a judgment upon a criminal complaint for assault and battery should, if proved in a civil action, be a sufficient defence against exemplary damages.[3] So, for a malicious trespass, exemplary damages cannot be given. A criminal prosecution is the proper remedy.[4] It is to be observed, however, that in cases of this description, as remarked in a recent case, the jury may consider "every circumstance of the act which injuriously affected the plaintiff;"[5] and thus, probably, reach the same point of damages, as if they were termed exemplary.

§ 12. With reference to injuries to property, in general not the subjects of criminal prosecution; in an action of trespass for cutting and carrying away timber, where the defendant had wilfully or through gross negligence cut over the line, it was held, that the damages were not to be confined to mere compensation, but the jury might give such damages as would be also adequate, in their judgment, for prevention.[6] So in a case of aggravated trespass, resulting in the loss of the plaintiff's slave, the jury are authorized to give exemplary damages.[7] So vindictive damages may be given in trespass, for a wanton violation of the plaintiff's rights, by killing hogs that wandered repeatedly into an insufficiently fenced potato patch.[8]

§ 13. In an action for *wilful negligence*, the jury may take into consideration the motives of the defendant, and, if the negligence is accompanied with a contempt of the plaintiff's rights and convenience, may give exemplary damages.[9]

§ 14. In order to recover special damages, for loss by disease

[1] Austin *v.* Wilson, 4 Cush. 274.
[2] Struble *v.* Nodwift, 11 Ind. 64.
[3] Cherry *v.* McCall, 23 Geo. 193.
[4] Butler *v.* Mercer, 14 Ind. 479.
[5] Nossaman *v.* Rickert, 18 Ind. 350.
[6] Kolb *v.* Bankhead, 18 Tex. 228.
[7] Hedgepeth *v.* Robertson, 18 ib. 858.
[8] Champion *v.* Vincent, 20 ib. 811.
[9] Emblen *v.* Myers, 6 Hurl. & Nor. 54.

communicated to another part of his flock, from sheep purchased of, and warranted by, the defendant, the plaintiff need not allege nor prove that the defendant knew at the time that they were intended to be placed with the other sheep.[1]

§ 15. A physician who, in what was called a frolic, put in the plaintiff's glass of wine a potion of cantharides, from the effects of which he was not free for months, was held liable to pay very exemplary damages.[2]

§ 16. It is held, that, while damages should be *full and ample*, but not vindictive, or beyond what has been really suffered; and the language used by the judge to the jury was "*exemplary* damages:" yet, if the jury appear not to have gone beyond the actual injury, the verdict will not be disturbed.[3]

§ 17. Vindictive damages should never be allowed against the representative of a deceased *tort-feasor*.[4] So, in an amicable action, to try the respective rights to a division wall, part of which has been wrongfully used by the defendant; it is error to instruct the jury, that, if there had been a wanton invasion of the plaintiff's rights, they were not confined to the actual damages.[5] So, in Maine, vindictive damages are not intended to be given, by Rev. Sts. ch. 154, § 23, against a shipmaster transporting an infant. The measure is the value of the child's services up to the time of bringing the suit, or if the child die previously, up to his death.[6] So, in an action for nuisance, the plaintiff cannot have exemplary damages, if the defendant exercised due care and prudence himself, and the damage occurred by reason of the neglect of his workmen to follow his directions.[7] Nor vindictive damages against a master or principal for the act of his servant or agent, unless expressly or impliedly authorized or ratified.[8] Nor exemplary damages, in an action of trespass, for building a house on the land of the defendant, whereby the plaintiff's house is darkened and its value greatly diminished.[9] Nor for mere failure to pay over money collected; though it seems it would be otherwise in a case of special damage and deception.[10]

§ 18. In an action of trespass, for the wrongful taking and detention of slaves, it is competent to show malice, and thus in-

1 Packard *v.* Slack, 32 Verm. 9.
2 Genay *v.* Norris, 1 Bay, 6.
3 Taylor *v.* Carpenter, 2 W. & M. 1.
4 Rippey *v.* Miller, 11 Ired. 247.
5 Amer *v.* Longstreth, 10 Barr, 145.
6 Nickerson *v.* Harriman, 38 Maine, 277.
7 Morford *v.* Woodworth, 7 Ind. 83.
8 Hagan *v.* Providence, &c. 3 R. I. 88.
9 Hays *v.* Askew, 7 Jones, 272.
10 Neill *v.* Newton, 24 Tex. 202.

crease the damages; but not to prove a fact which is legal in itself, and has no tendency to show that the act was unjustifiable or wantonly done. As, for example, the institution of and failure to prosecute an action by the defendant, for the recovery of the slaves.[1]

§ 19. While the motives and disposition of the *defendant* are often an important subject of inquiry; on the other hand, although the plaintiff has a right of action, the jury may look at all the circumstances, and at the conduct of both parties, and if, in going on with the action, the plaintiff has acted in an obstinate and perverse manner, they may take that into consideration when estimating the damages. Thus, the plaintiff delivered to a railway company certain goods to carry from A to B, paying the carriage, to be delivered to a party there. Part of the transit was effected by another railway company, which refused to deliver up the goods to the consignee without payment of an additional specified sum; but, an action having been threatened against the contracting company, an offer was made to deliver them up without that payment. The action was, however, persevered in, the plaintiff declaring against the company as carriers, with a count in trover for the conversion of the goods, subsequently to which they were given up in a damaged state. Held, that the additional sum demanded for the goods was not the measure of damage. It was also questioned whether the plaintiff could recover for deterioration of, and damage done to, his goods while detained by the company, or for loss of profits arising from his being deprived of the use of them during that time.[2] So in an action of trespass, for breaking the plaintiff's close, and taking certain liquors, adjudged to be forfeited in a judicial proceeding, to which he was a party; he cannot recover the value of the liquors; and, if the defendants acted in good faith, believing their doings to be authorized, he can recover only nominal damages.[3] So, in trespass, for removal of goods from, and destruction of, a store; the defendant may show, in mitigation of damages, that the chief business was an unlawful traffic with slaves.[4] So, in trespass, for an injury to a vicious and annoying animal, only nominal damages can be recovered, unless actual damage is proved.[5]

[1] Williams *v.* Newberry, 32 Miss. 256.

[2] Davis *v.* North-Western, &c. 4 Hurl. & Nor. 855; 4 Jur. (N. S.) 1303, Exch.

[3] Plummer *v.* Harbut, 5 Clarke, 308.

[4] Boulard *v.* Calhoun, 13 La. An. 445.

[5] Custard *v.* Burdett, 15 Tex. 456.

CHAPTER VI.

DAMAGES FOR FRAUD, ETC.

§ 1. HAVING completed our view of those general rules and principles relative to damages, which seem for the most part indiscriminately applicable to all subjects, injuries, and forms of action, we proceed to a consideration of the separate wrongs, in relation to which the same class of questions arise. From the nature of the case, some repetitions must occur of what has already been more generally stated.

§ 2. In conformity with the plan heretofore adopted, we proceed to consider, first in order, the subject of damages for that injury which connects tort and contract, namely, *fraud.* (*a*)

§ 3. The general rule is laid down, that the proper measure of damages, in an action for fraud and deceit in the sale or exchange of property, retained by the purchaser, is the difference between its actual and represented values at that time; the price paid being strong, but not conclusive, evidence of the latter.[1] So where the purchaser retains the property, and where numerous misrepresentations in relation to it, or in relation to several distinct particulars or qualities of it, were made by the vendor, some of which may be material and others immaterial, some fraudulent and others honest, though all false; the rule of damages is the difference between the actual value and the value as it would have

[1] Carr *v.* Moore, 41 N. H. 131; Page *v.* Parker, 40 ib. 47; Likes *v.* Baer, 8 Clarke (Iowa), 368. See Stevenson *v.* Greenlee, 15 Iowa, 96.

(*a*) In California, a complaint may set forth a breach of contract on the part of the defendants, a steamship company, to convey the plaintiff, and also wrongs and injuries, resulting in physical and mental hardship, committed in connection with such breach. The plaintiffs may also show fraud at the inception of the contract, in a predetermination not to carry it out, and this may be considered by the jury in connection with the subsequent tortious acts. Jones *v.* Cortes, 17 Cal. 487.

been if the representation had been true, in those particulars, concerning which the false and fraudulent representations were made, on which the verdict was founded. In such case the price paid is strong, but not conclusive, evidence of the value of the property as it was represented to be, whether such representations were fraudulent or honest, provided they were material.[1]

§ 4. The same rule of damages is adopted in case of fraudulent misrepresentations in the sale of real estate.[2] So, A and B being co-tenants in common of a vessel, C agreed to buy the whole vessel of A for a certain price. A afterwards bought of B his share at a less rate, by means of alleged fraudulent representations. In an action of B against A for such fraud, held, on the question of damages, evidence was admissible, that the sum paid B was the full value of his share; but that the price to be paid by C was strong, though not conclusive, evidence of the value.[3] So, in a suit in equity for relief from a contract into which the plaintiff has been induced to enter by fraud, the court, in ascertaining the value of the consideration fraudulently obtained from him, will adopt the price fixed by the parties themselves as the value of shares in a mining company transferred by him as a part thereof, if the price fixed does not appear to have been unconscionable, and he has practised no fraud, and both parties had equal opportunities to judge of their value.[4] So, by the laws of Louisiana and Kentucky, the fraudulent vendor of goods is not liable to vindictive damages, nor to the costs of transportation to and from the place of delivery. The measure of damages is the difference between the real value and the contract price.[5]

§ 5. In an action of deceit for knowingly selling and conveying to the plaintiff more land than the defendant had title to, the measure of damages is the *pro ratâ* value of that part of the land to which the plaintiff could get no title, and the expense of perfecting his title to another part.[6]

§ 6. The measure of damages, in an action against directors of a company for false representations as to its affairs, whereby they induced the purchase of shares which were worthless; is the

1 Page *v.* Parker, 43 N. H. 363.
2 Likes *v.* Baer, 8 Clarke (Iowa), 368.
3 Matthews *v.* Bliss, 22 Pick. 48.
4 Franklin *v.* Greene, 2 Allen, 519.
5 Singleton *v.* Kennedy, 9 B. Monr. 222.
6 Parker *v.* Walker, 12 Rich. 138.

difference between the purchase-money paid and a fair price at the time.[1]

§ 7. But on the other hand it is held, that, in cases of fraud, the jury may give exemplary or *smart* damages.[2] More especially where the fraud is not indictable.[3] Thus, for deceit in a sale, the purchase-money, with interest, is not the proper measure of damages.[4] So where a horse having a contagious disease is sold, and the seller, though having knowledge of the fact, fails to give information of it, he is liable for the injury caused by communication of the disease to other horses of the buyer.[5] So a railroad corporation, who fraudulently put an end to a contract for grading their road, pretending to act under a power reserved to them therein to terminate the same, if, in their opinion, not complied with by the contractor; are liable to the contractor in damages, including any loss of profit sustained by him by the breaking off of the contract.[6] So, in an action for deceit in selling a vessel as British, when she was not, nor entitled to a British national character; the plaintiff may recover the difference of value of the vessel, as sold, and her value, if her real character had been known, and also the amount of such repairs made on her, on the faith of the representation, as had not been remunerated by her earnings, or in any other way.[7]

§ 8. Where a ship-master received divers casks of lime on freight, consigned to him for sale, which had been duly inspected and branded, and were represented by the owner as good lime, and accordingly sold as such by the master, but in fact were filled with substances of little or no value; whereupon he was sued by the vendee, and obliged to respond to him in damages, having given the owner immediate notice, and faithfully and prudently defended the suit: held, he might recover of the owner the amount of the judgment recovered against himself, with all necessary costs and expenses, and that a copy of the judgment was admissible evidence.[8]

§ 9. One obliged to take steps to relieve himself from another's fraud may generally recover his attorney's fees as special dam-

[1] Huntington *v.* Massey, 1 F. & F. 690.

[2] Oliver *v.* Chapman, 15 Tex. 400; Nye *v.* Merriam, 35 Verm. 438.

[3] Millison *v.* Hoch, 17 Ind. 227.

[4] Brown *v.* Shields, 6 Leigh, 440.

[5] Faris *v.* Lewis, 2 B. Monr. 375.

[6] Philadelphia, &c. *v.* Howard, 13 How. 307.

[7] Sherwood *v.* Sutton, 5 Mas. 1.

[8] Henderson *v.* Sevey, 2 Greenl. 139.

ages. Otherwise, where he sets up fraud in a contract as a defence to an action thereon.[1]

§ 10. A sold to B a bill, representing it as unpaid, when he knew it had been paid. B transferred it to C, and afterwards, having it in his possession, he sued A for the fraudulent sale. Held, B's possession enabled him to sustain the action, and the measure of damages was the amount of the bill, with interest.[2]

§ 11. Action by C, in the name of A, against B, on a promissory note payable by B to A. At the time the note was given, A had secretly given a defeasance to B, with intention to defraud whoever might purchase the note. C had purchased the note, in ignorance of the defeasance, paying for it partly in money and partly by his own note to B, which B had sold to D for its full value, D also being ignorant of the fraud. Held, the rule of damages to C was the amount of the note in suit and interest; B, a party to the fraud, not being entitled to any deduction, on the ground that C, when sued on his note by D, in B's name, could avoid it.[3]

§ 12. In an action for misrepresenting the location of a mill, privileges, and land described in a deed, the vendee retaining so much as actually passed; the measure of damages is the expense of obtaining by writ *ad quod damnum*, or other equally cheap and speedy remedy, the land falsely represented to pass.[4]

§ 13. Where a printer, having contracted to print for his employer a thousand copies of a book, and no more, printed from the same types, while set up at the expense of his employer, five hundred other copies, for his own disposal; he was held liable to refund to his employer one-third part of the expense of setting up the types, no actual damage having been proved.[5]

§ 14. The laws of Alabama permit the defendant, in an action on a sealed instrument, to impeach the consideration, as if the writing were not under seal; they also permit such instrument to be assigned by indorsement, and the assignee to sue in his own name, allowing the defendant the benefit of all payments, discounts, and set-offs, made, had, or possessed against the same, previous to notice of the assignment, in the same manner as if the suit were brought by the obligee or payee. Held, the defend-

[1] Flack *v.* Neill, 22 Tex. 253.
[2] Spikes *v.* English, 4 Strobh. 34.
[3] Lyon *v.* Summers, 7 Conn. 399.
[4] Reynolds *v.* Cox, 11 Ind. 262.
[5] Williams *v.* Gilman, 3 Greenl. 276.

ant, in a suit brought by the assignee of a bond given for the price of a chattel, might prove, in reduction of damages, that the sale was effected by means of false representations on the part of the payee as to the value of the chattel, although the chattel had not been returned or tendered to the plaintiff.[1]

§ 15. In an action for deceit in procuring a receipt, where the defendant, as agent of the maker of a note payable to the plaintiff, by fraud and misrepresentation prevailed on the plaintiff to accept notes against insolvent persons, and give a receipt in full discharge of his note; the plaintiff is entitled to recover nominal damages, although the maker of the note which he gave up was also insolvent.[2]

§ 16. Lands fraudulently transferred, by means of a judicial sale, descended to the heirs of the alienee, who, without notice of the fraud, assigned them in partition to A, one of such heirs. A took possession, paid the annual taxes, and *bonâ fide* made valuable and permanent improvements. A judgment-creditor filed his petition against the alienor and the heirs, to set aside the transfer for fraud, and subject the lands to payment of the judgment. Held, A was entitled, in this proceeding, to equitable compensation for his expenditures from the proceeds of any sale which might be ordered; and an answer, claiming such compensation, was good, on demurrer; and that a decree, merely saving the rights of A under the *occupying claimant* law, and ordering that the property be appraised and sold, was erroneous.[3]

[1] Withers *v.* Greene, 9 How. 213, 661.

[2] Ledbetter *v.* Morris, 3 Jones, 543.

[3] Bomberger *v.* Turner, 13 Ohio 263.

CHAPTER VII.

INJURIES TO THE PERSON; ASSAULT AND BATTERY; FALSE IMPRISONMENT; INJURIES TO HEALTH.

§ 1. THE damages in an action for an injury to the person may include bodily pain and suffering.[1] So, in estimating damages for an unintentional but reckless assault, the jury may consider the pain as well as the wounded feelings of the female plaintiff.[2] And for an unprovoked and aggravated assault exemplary damages may be given.[3] So, as we have already seen (Chap. V.), damages may be allowed for circumstances of insult, &c.[4] So, also, for any natural and necessary consequences, even those subsequent to the trial;[5] including expense, loss of time, of hearing, of peace of mind, and individual happiness.[6] Thus a verdict for $85, for a violent beating and wounding with an axe, was held not excessive; nor would a much higher verdict be considered extravagant, especially where it was proved that the defendant was amply able to pay it.[7]

§ 2. But it is sometimes held, that the court cannot instruc the jury to allow "smart money" in an action for assault and battery.[8] And in trespass for an assault and battery upon the child or servant of the plaintiff, the measure of damages is the actual loss of the plaintiff; and exemplary damages cannot be given, though the assault be of an indecent character, upon a female, and under circumstances of great aggravation.[9] (*a*)

[1] Ransom *v.* New York, &c. 15 N. Y. (1 Smith), 415.

[2] West *v.* Forrest, 22 Mis. 344.

[3] Foote *v.* Nichols, 28 Ind. 486.

[4] Bracegirdle *v.* Orford, 2 M. & S. 77; Tullidge *v.* Wade, 3 Wils. 19.

[5] Fetter *v.* Beale, 1 Ld. Ray. 339; Moor *v.* Adam, 2 Chit. 198.

[6] Cox *v.* Vanderkleed, 21 Ind. 164.

[7] Gore *v.* Chadwick, 6 Dana, 477.

[8] Mooney *v.* Kennett, 19 Mis. 551.

[9] Whitney *v.* Hitchcock, 4 Denio, 461.

(*a*) In a suit for assault and battery, the plaintiff alleged that he had been "obliged to pay" large sums to get cured. His physician testified, that his services had

§ 2 *a*. In an action for assault and battery, the defendant may prove, in mitigation of damages, that the plaintiff, immediately before the assault, charged him with a crime. But the plaintiff cannot, in reply, go into proof that the charge was true. Nor the defendant, that the charge was false. The evidence is admissible solely for the purpose of showing that the defendant acted under the sudden provocation of the charge, and not from premeditated malice.[1] And provocation, to be admitted in mitigation of damages, must be so recent and immediate, as to induce a presumption that the violence done was committed under the immediate influence of the feelings and passions excited by it. The defendant cannot give evidence of acts or declarations of the plaintiff at a different time, or any antecedent facts which are not fairly to be considered as part of one and the same transaction, however irritating and provoking.[2] And no provocation, amounting to less than justification, will render the defendant liable in less than compensatory damages.[3]

§ 3. It is competent, for the purpose of mitigating vindictive damages, to show that the defendant has been convicted and punished at the suit of the State.[4]

§ 4. That the plaintiff had prosecuted the defendant's child for malicious mischief, whereupon the defendant committed the assault, is not matter in mitigation of damages.[5]

§ 5. Where the defendants accused the plaintiff of stealing a watch, and whipped him to get it back; held, he might show, upon the question of damages, that he was (to the knowledge of the defendants) of weak mind.[6]

§ 6. In an action for malicious arrest, *injury to credit* is not ground of special damage.[7]

§ 7. It is held, that damages may be awarded by way of *punishment*, but not to an arbitrary amount. Thus a verdict for $2,000 for a short detention in the police-office, the plaintiff being discharged for want of any appearance against him, was set aside as excessive.[8]

[1] Bartram *v*. Stone, 31 Conn. 159.

[2] Lee *v*. Wolsey, 19 Johns. 329. See Corning *v*. Corning, 1 Seld. 97.

[3] Birchard *v*. Booth, 4 Wis. 67.

[4] Smithwick *v*. Ward, 7 Jones, 64.

[5] Schlosser *v*. Fox, 14 Ind. 365.

[6] Ously *v*. Hardin, 23 Ill. 403.

[7] Macfarlane *v*. Ellis, 1 F. & F. 288.

[8] Brown *v*. Chadsey, 39 Barb. 253.

been worth a few dollars, which he had charged to the plaintiff, and of which none had been paid. Held, the evidence did not support the allegation. Ward *v*. Haws, 5 Min. 440.

§ 8. In New York, evidence may be given, in mitigation of damages, without having filed any answer, on the execution of a writ of inquiry.[1]

§ 9. In an action for assault and false imprisonment, it is no ground of new trial, that the plaintiff had expended 7*l.* 14*s.* in procuring a discharge from custody, but the jury awarded him only a farthing.[2]

§ 10. Where the defendant caused the plaintiff to be arrested upon an unfounded charge, and detained from 11½ to 2 o'clock; held, damages could not be allowed upon the ground that the plaintiff would have been engaged as a journeyman by A if he had presented himself at the factory at two o'clock; but, being unwell from the imprisonment, he did not go to the factory till the next morning, when another had been engaged. In this recent case, the court suggested some considerations in reference to remote damages, which are of general applicability and of much value: "The damage does not immediately, and according to the common course of events, follow from the defendant's wrong; they are not known by common experience to be usually in sequence. The wrong would not have been followed by the damage, if some facts had not intervened for which the defendant was not responsible. Thus, there was the act of the plaintiff, who returned home instead of going to the factory and explaining; and, although it was said he was unwell, . . . it was not suggested that he was so unwell as to be unable to go. There was also the act of the intended employer, changing his purpose in respect of the plaintiff." [3]

§ 11. In an action against a *surgeon*, the increased amount paid to another surgeon, to effect a cure, by reason of injuries resulting from the unskilful treatment of the defendant, may properly be considered by the jury; and that is the proper limit.[4]

[1] Hays *v.* Berryman, 6 Bosw. 679.

[2] Bradlaugh *v.* Edwards, 11 Com. B. (N. S.) 376.

[3] Hoey *v.* Felton, 11 C. B. 140; per Erle, C. J., ib. 146.

[4] Leighton *v.* Sargent, 11 Fost. 119.

CHAPTER VIII.

LIBEL, ETC., AND MALICIOUS PROSECUTION.

§ 1. In an action for libel, the actual damages are to be determined by the jury, upon a careful consideration of the charge against the plaintiff, the circumstances of the publication, the extent of its circulation, and the natural and necessary consequences of such a publication, according to the results of human experience.[1] It is held, that the jury are at liberty to give punitive damages.[2] (See Chap. V.) So in an action of slander, in case of actual malice, it is held, that exemplary damages may be given.[3] And this, more especially, if accompanied by another form of actionable injury. Thus, in a late case, where the defendant charged a female with larceny, commenced a criminal prosecution against her, and had her arrested for that offence, and persisted in the prosecution after being advised by able and learned counsel to desist; a verdict for $1,400 was held not excessive. The court remarked: "The result will probably make the defendant wiser for the future, and have a good influence upon others who are tempted to gratify feelings of revenge at the expense of female character."[4]

§ 2. In an action against a railroad corporation for a libel, the jury cannot find damages for a publication made after the commencement of the suit; nor exemplary damages, without proof that the act was done maliciously or wantonly.[5]

§ 3. Where, in an action for slander, no special damages are claimed by the petition, and there is no evidence of actual dam-

[1] Fry *v.* Bennett, 3 Bosw. 200.
[2] Hunt *v.* Bennett, 19 N. Y. (5 Smith), 173.
[3] Knight *v.* Foster, 39 N. H. 576.
[4] Humphries *v.* Parker, 52 Maine, 502; per Walton, J., ib. 508.
[5] Philadelphia, &c. *v.* Quigley, 21 How. 202.

age, a new trial cannot be allowed, because the jury gave only nominal damages.[1]

§ 4. In an action of slander, the following instructions, taken together, were held correct; being given after stating the different kinds of damages: "Compensatory damages are given, where the words were spoken without malice, but under circumstances which show a want of caution, and a proper respect for the rights of the plaintiff. Compensatory damages are such as will pay the plaintiff for his expenses and trouble in carrying on the suit, and disproving the slanderous words; the character of the plaintiff can never be considered, until the jury come to the question of giving vindictive or exemplary damages."[2]

§ 5. In case of slander of a physician, as such, the currency of the slanderous report in the place of his practice, following its utterance by the defendant, may be given in evidence, as well as the effect of such report upon the professional gains of the plaintiff, in aggravation or proof of damages, without strict proof connecting the current report with the slander of the defendant; the fact of such connection being for the jury, and not for the court, to pass upon.[3]

§ 6. In an action by a surgeon for slander, imputing that a female servant had had a bastard child by him, whereby D. would not employ him as an accoucheur, and the plaintiff was otherwise injured in the way of his business; it was proved that the words were spoken by the defendant in conversation with D. Held, that the plaintiff was not entitled to recover such damages, in respect of a general loss of business, as might have been caused by repetitions of the slander, but could not have arisen directly from the speaking of the words by the defendant to D.[4]

§ 7. In an action of slander, for charging the plaintiff with having illicit intercourse with a married woman, and thereby committing the crime of adultery; the defendant may prove, in mitigation of damages, that, before the speaking of the words, the plaintiff's general character and reputation in the community for chastity was bad, and that he was generally reputed in the community to be an unchaste and licentious man. Such evidence is

[1] Irwin *v.* Cook, 24 Tex. 244.

[2] Armstrong *v.* Pierson, 8 Clarke (Iowa), 29.

[3] Rice *v.* Cottrel, 5 R. I. 340.

[4] Dixon *v.* Smith, 5 Hurl. & Nor. 450.

not restricted to the reputation of the plaintiff in reference to the crime of adultery.[1] (See § 12.)

§ 8. It is held, in late cases, that in an action for slander the plaintiff may prove the pecuniary condition of the defendant to increase the damages.[2] The wealth of the defendant is said to be "an element which goes to make up his rank and influence in society, and therefore his power to injure the plaintiff by his speech."[3]

§ 9. Anxiety and distress of mind caused by a slander may be proved in aggravation of damages, though the charge was made against the plaintiff as a physician only.[4]

§ 9 *a*. L., a step-brother of the wife of K., spoke slanderous words to K., imputing to Mrs. K. gross levity, and asserting that she had been all but seduced by another man before marriage. The husband thereupon dismissed her, and sent her to her father. She (joining her husband, as co-plaintiff, for conformity) brought an action against L., alleging her loss of the husband's consortium as special damages. Held, whether or not the action lay, the damages were too remote; not being the natural and probable consequence of the injury complained of; seeing that no husband, acting reasonably, would dismiss a wife on an unsupported charge of gross levity, when no actual adultery was imputed.[5] (*a*)

§ 10. It is held, that a plea of the truth, in slander, made in good faith, under an honest belief in the truth of the words

[1] Bridgman *v.* Hopkins, 34 Verm. 532.

[2] Karney *v.* Paisley, 5 With. (13 Iowa), (questioned in Law Reg. August, 1863, p. 639); 52 Maine, 502.

[3] Humphries *v.* Parker, 52 Maine, 502; ib. 508, per Walton, J.

[4] Swift *v.* Dickerman, 31 Conn. 285.

[5] Lynch *v.* Knight, 5 L. T. (N. S.) 291 — H. L.

(*a*) In this case, the several judges incidentally expressed their views as follows: Lords Campbell and Cranworth, that, where a person imputes to a married woman adultery, which he pretends to know and assert as a fact, and the husband, reasonably believing the charges to be true, dismisses her, the wife is entitled to maintain an action (joining her husband for conformity) against the slanderer for the special damage caused to her by the loss of the husband's consortium. Lords Wensleydale and Brougham, that a married woman cannot maintain an action for being deprived of the society of her husband by the slander of another upon her character, though the husband deserts her in consequence. Lord Wensleydale, that, although no action lay, yet the desertion by the husband was properly laid as special damage; for, to make words actionable by reason of special damage, the consequence must be such, as, taking human nature as it is, with its infirmities, and having regard to the relationship of the parties concerned, might fairly and reasonably have been anticipated to follow from the speaking of the words, and need not be such as would reasonably follow. Lords Campbell and Brougham, that the law of England is barbarous in holding that an imputation by words, however gross, on an occasion however public, upon the chastity of a modest matron or pure virgin, is not actionable without proof that it has actually produced special temporal damage to her.

uttered, and with reasonable grounds for such belief, furnishes no cause for exemplary damages. "The motive with which the justification was pleaded, is for the consideration of the jury. If they find that it was done with the intention to injure the plaintiff, they may rightfully consider it an aggravation of damages; but where no wrongful intention is found, there is no just ground for the punishment of the defendant."[1]

§ 11. In an action of slander, circumstances which disprove malice, but do not tend to establish the truth of the charge, may be given in evidence in mitigation of damages.[2] And it is sometimes held, that evidence may be available in mitigation of damages, though it *tends* to prove the truth, but does not necessarily prove it.[3] (See § 7.)

§ 12. In an action for a libel, the defendant cannot prove, in mitigation of damages, an independent libel on himself by the plaintiff. Otherwise, where such libel by the plaintiff affords a reasonable presumption that it provoked the libel by the defendant, or where it impliedly refers to it, or explains the meaning of it or the occasion of writing it.[4]

§ 13. To authorize proof of mitigating circumstances, as rebutting the presumption of malice, it must appear that they were known to the defendant at the time.[5]

§ 14. In an action of slander, for saying that the plaintiff, a physician, had no professional knowledge or skill, and lost almost all his patients; evidence is inadmissible, in mitigation of damages, of particular instances of ignorance or want of skill.[6]

§ 15. Under a declaration that the defendant, without probable cause, maliciously sued out a writ against the plaintiff from a court which had no jurisdiction of the plaintiff, and attached his property thereon, and kept and detained the property from the plaintiff for twenty days; the plaintiff may recover damages for the trespass to his property.[7]

§ 16. If the holder of a promissory note, after suing out a writ against the maker, and procuring thereon a return of *non est*, under a mistake as to his legal rights, sues out an attachment

[1] Raymond *v.* Kinney, 14 Ohio St. 283 per Wilder, J., ib. 287; Clement *v.* Brown 30 Ill. 43.

[2] Gilman *v.* Lowell, 8 Wend. 573. See Porter *v.* Henderson, 11 Mich. 20.

[3] Swift *v.* Dickerman, 31 Conn. 285.

[4] Child *v.* Homer, 13 Pick. 503.

[5] Swift *v.* Dickerman, 31 Conn. 285.

[6] Ibid.

[7] Whiting *v.* Johnson, 6 Gray, 246.

against the indorser; in an action for wrongfully and vexatiously suing out this latter process, the proceedings against the maker are admissible in evidence in mitigation of damages.[1]

§ 17. In an action for commencing a suit against the plaintiff without authority, evidence of express malice on the part of the defendant towards the plaintiff, although not necessary, is still competent.[2]

§ 18. If the plaintiff in such action disclaims any damages for injury to his character, the defendant cannot attack such character, either to rebut the evidence of malice, or in mitigation of damages.[3]

§ 19. If no specific instructions as to damages are requested, it is a sufficient instruction, that, in case they find for the plaintiff, the jury are to give such a sum as will indemnify him for the injuries he has sustained by the wrongful acts of the defendant.[4]

[1] White *v.* Wyley, 17 Ala. 167.

[2] Smith *v.* Hyndman, 10 Cush. 554.

[3] Ibid.

[4] Leach *v.* Wilbur, 9 Allen, 212.

CHAPTER IX.

NEGLIGENCE; NUISANCE; WATERCOURSES; RAILROADS; TOWNS.

§ 1. THE measure of damages for *negligence* is held to be the actual damage suffered.[1] Thus where property, bought in one place, and delivered by the seller to be carried to another place, is lost on the way by his negligence, the value of it at the latter place is the measure of damages.[2] So where a prize had been offered, for the best plan and model of a machine for loading colliers from barges, and plans and models intended for the competition were to be sent by a certain day; and the plaintiff sent a plan and model accordingly by a railway, but, through negligence, it did not arrive at its destination until after the appointed day: held, it seems, the proper measure of damages is the value of the labor and materials expended in making the plan and model, and not the chance of obtaining the prize, as the latter is too remote a ground for damages.[3] The judges remarked as follows: "The plaintiff had put his damages upon a right principle, for he said the goods were made for a special purpose, which has been defeated by the negligence of the defendants, and they have become useless."[4] "He says he has lost the chance of one hundred guineas. I have great doubts whether that chance was not too contingent and remote . . . but we are here as a court of appeal, and the case laid before us does not advert to that point. . . . We give no opinion as to the remoteness of the damages."[5] So in an action against a boatman, for negligently permitting the plaintiff's tobacco to be sunk in the river, whereby the value was diminished,

[1] Goetz *v.* Ambs, 27 Mis. 28.
[2] Bailey *v.* Shaw, 4 Fost. 297.
[3] Watson *v.* Ambergate, &c. 3 Eng. L. & Eq. 497.
[4] Per Patteson, J., ib. 501.
[5] Per Erle, J., ib. 501.

the measure of damages is the difference between the value of the tobacco before and after its submersion.[1] So in an action against the publishers of a newspaper, for neglecting to insert an advertisement of a public sale of real estate, for which they received payment in advance; the measure of damages, in the absence of fraud, is the amount paid. They are not liable to speculative damages.[2]

§ 2. It is sometimes held, however, that exemplary damages may be given for negligence.[3] Thus, where the proprietor of a newspaper published a false and unfounded libel on a tailor, stating that he had been flogged; and, although it was complained of at once, and the falsehood shown, delayed publishing any contradiction until after action: these circumstances were left to the jury as evidence of negligence, and a verdict sustained for very large damages.[4] So, in an action for negligence, the damages may be aggravated by the conduct of a defendant having been reckless, or accompanied by expressions showing a disregard for the safety or property of others. Thus, in an action for negligence in pulling down a wall, whereby a portion of the bricks fell upon the plaintiff's stable, broke down the roof, and damaged his horse, the jury may take into consideration, as a ground of damages, expressions of the defendant to the workmen, that they should not take any care to guard against mischief to the plaintiff's property in so doing.[5]

§ 3. But special damages must be expressly claimed in the declaration and warranted by the evidence; as in an action against a common carrier, for an injury arising from his negligence. Thus an unmarried woman, receiving an injury by the neglect of a carrier in whose carriage she was upset, cannot recover damages for impaired prospect of marriage, such damages not being specially alleged in the writ, nor sustained by the evidence.[6]

§ 3 *a*. It is held in a late English case, that one who for his own purposes brings, collects, and keeps on his land anything likely to do mischief if it escapes, must keep it at his peril, and, without proof of negligence, is *primâ facie* liable for all damage naturally resulting from its escape.[7]

§ 3 *b*. In a suit to abate a *nuisance*, caused by digging a ditch

1 Stark *v.* Porter, 4 J. J. Marsh, 211.
2 Eisenlohr *v.* Swain, 35 Penn. 107.
3 Huntley *v.* Bacon, 15 Conn. 267.
4 Smith *v.* Harrison, 1 F. & F. 565.
5 Emblin *v.* Myers, 8 M. R. 665, Exch.
6 Hunter *v.* Stewart, 47 Maine, 419.
7 Fletcher *v.* Rylands, Law Rep. 1 Ex. 263; Amn. Law Rev. Jan. 1867, p. 294.

on the plaintiff's land, and for damages, the court cannot properly order an abatement, and a sum sufficient to pay for the filling of the ditch, &c. The case is not one for prospective damages, and the plaintiff cannot recover beyond the injury sustained.[1]

§ 4. The law implies damage from the flooding of the ground of another, though it be in the least possible degree, and without immediate actual prejudice. Hence a mere reversioner may maintain an action therefor. "In contemplation of law, the rent issues out of the land; and whatever impairs the productiveness of it, decreases the landlord's security; but compensation recovered by the tenant would be a poor substitute for the means of payment derived from an unimpaired enjoyment of the premises. Besides, the market value of the reversion would be greatly lessened by an apparent injury which would permanently affect the property, or saddle the purchaser with a lawsuit."[2]

§ 5. It has been sometimes held, in an action for obstructing a watercourse, that the jury must find the full value of the land overflowed in damages.[3] And where the damages of overflowing land were not equal to what was sworn to by some of the witnesses, the court refused to set aside the verdict, though they seemed high.[4]

§ 6. In trespass for destroying a mill-dam, &c., the plaintiff may give evidence of damage sustained by the stoppage of the mills. The court remark: "In an action of trespass, for destroying a *mill-dam* (not merely a dam which may be for other purposes), the stoppage of the mills supplying its means with water-power seems to fall within the description of such a damage as naturally or necessarily results from the act. . . . These words have received a large construction, so as to embrace consequential injuries not specifically mentioned in the declaration, but ordinarily flowing from the act complained of. Under the . . . *alia enormia*, damages naturally arising may be given in evidence . . . though not stated."[5]

§ 7. Where one riparian proprietor had, by means of a water-wheel, raised and diverted from the premises of another about one-fortieth part of the volume of a stream; held, that it was for

[1] De Costa *v.* Massachusetts, &c. 17 Cal. 613.

[2] Ripka *v.* Sergeant, 7 W. & S. 9; per Gibson, C. J., ib. 14. See Miller *v.* Laubach, 47 Penn. 154.

[3] 4 Dall. 147.

[4] Winans *v.* Brookfield, 2 Smith, 847.

[5] Spigelmoyer *v.* Walter, 3 W. & S. 540; per Sergeant, J., ib. 542.

the jury to consider whether he had thereby inflicted on the other any sensible or material injury.[1]

§ 8. In the assessment of damages caused by diversion of a river, the tenant of a mill will be entitled to damages for his loss during the unexpired term of his lease.[2]

§ 9. The owner of a mill-dam cannot, in an action against the owner of a mill above, for forcibly taking down more of the plaintiff's dam than was necessary to remove the defendant's mill, recover, as part of his damages, anything paid for counsel fees or to engineers for making surveys.[3]

§ 10. A conveyed a mill to B, and covenanted with him to keep one-half of the dam in repair. The dam was afterwards carried away by a flood, and B duly requested A to aid him in rebuilding it. A refused, and B repaired it at his own expense. Held, B could not recover damages for loss of the profits of the mill by reason of the delay caused by A's refusal, but only for one-half of the expense of repairing it. Mr. Justice Dewey remarks: "It being the duty of the plaintiff to make one-half of the repairs, and it being a right which he might at once exercise, to proceed to make the whole repairs, after neglect and refusal of the defendant, upon reasonable notice, to aid in the repairs; if the plaintiff delayed to exercise that right, and thereby sustained a loss, it is one which he alone must bear."[4]

§ 10 *a*. To indemnify a *patentee* in damages, the jury may allow actual costs in suits relating to the patent, and also reasonable counsel fees; and the Circuit Court, under the act of Congress, will award treble what is found by the jury as damages, if deemed proper to protect useful inventors from combination and ruin.[5]

§ 10 *b*. Under a reference to a master, to ascertain and report the amount of profits realized, or which might with due diligence have been realized, by a defendant to a bill in equity, to restrain the infringement of a patent, for work done by mechanics similar to the plaintiff's; the plaintiff is entitled only to the actual profits realized by the defendant, and not to any greater amount of damages sustained by the plaintiff.[6]

[1] Norbury *v.* Kitchin, 3 F. & F. 292.

[2] Matter of Water Commissioners, 4 Edw. Ch. 545.

[3] Day *v.* Woodworth, 13 How. 363.

[4] Thomson *v.* Shattuck, 2 Met. 615, 619.

[5] Allen *v.* Blunt, 2 W. & M. 121. See Earle *v.* Sawyer, 4 Mas. 1.

[6] Livingston *v.* Woodworth, 15 How. 546.

§ 10 *c.* In a suit to recover damages for infringement of a patent, the plaintiffs are entitled to recover all the actual profits which the defendant has made by the use of the principle of the plaintiff's combination, the law presuming, that, if the defendant had not put his machines into the market, the demand would have been for the plaintiff's, and he would have received the profits. The interest on the capital, the risk of bad debts, and the expenses of selling the machines, are all to be taken into account. Vindictive or exemplary damages are not to be allowed.[1]

§ 10 *d.* In a very recent English case, where a bill in equity had been filed to restrain the infringement of a *trade-mark*, and a decree obtained for an injunction; the court offered a decree for an account of profits, but the plaintiffs elected an inquiry as to damages. Held, the law would not presume that they would have sold the amount of goods sold by the defendant, but the burden of proof was on them to show special damage by loss of custom or otherwise. The remarks of the court have an important bearing upon the subject to which in various connections we have so often referred, — remote or contingent damages: "How can the court assume that the persons who bought what the plaintiffs aver were inferior articles at an inferior price, would necessarily, if they had not done so, have bought the superior articles at the higher price, . . . and that in the absence of any evidence that any of the purchasers had at any time been customers of the plaintiffs. But even supposing that such an assumption were possible, why is the court to assume that, even if the purchasers would have bought the higher-priced article, they would have bought it of the plaintiffs? There were or there may have been persons licensed by the plaintiffs to use their trade-mark and to sell goods manufactured by their process, or there may have been, and doubtless were, persons who had purchased from the plaintiffs with a view of selling again. How can the court assume that the supposed purchasers would have . . . purchased direct from the plaintiffs."[2]

§ 11. The measure of damages, in actions against *railroads*, of

[1] Wilbur *v.* Beecher, 2 Blatch. Ct. 132; Hall *v.* Wiles, ib. 194; Pitts *v.* Hall, ib. 229; McCormick *v.* Seymour, ib. 240.

[2] Leather, &c. *v.* Hirschfield (Eng.), Law Rep. Eq. Series, Feb. 1867, pp. 298–301.

course depends upon the nature of the particular injury complained of.

§ 12. A person ejected from the cars three or four miles from a station, but without any aggravating circumstances, he having refused to pay his fare, and offered without any explanation a ticket which was void by the usages of the road, and his intention being to ride from one station to another, is entitled to only nominal damages.[1]

§ 13. In an action by a passenger against a railroad company for carrying him beyond his station, the verdict was for $4,500 damages. The court thought the verdict very large, but held, that, as the action sounded in tort, the jury could give punitive damages, and so refused to set aside the verdict.[2] So it is held that the jury may in their discretion give exemplary damages, where a personal injury has been caused by the gross carelessness of a railroad in the management of its trains.[3]

§ 14. It has been held that, in an action brought against a railroad for a personal injury occasioned by their negligence, damages may be recovered for loss of business.[4] So, in an action against a railroad for injury done to a child of the plaintiff, the damages may include all such prospective loss as must necessarily result from the injury.[5] But a verdict for damages occasioned by a railroad collision, of more than twice the amount limited by law if the accident had occasioned the death of the plaintiff, will be set aside, on motion for a new trial. As where, in a case said to involve no peculiar aggravation or gross negligence, although the plaintiff was crippled for life, a verdict was given for eleven thousand dollars. (In this instance, adopting a practice not unusual in cases of contract, but rarely applied to torts, the motion for a new trial was denied, if within twenty days a stipulation is given to reduce the verdict to five thousand dollars.)[6] So the measure of damages, in an action against a railroad for negligence, whereby certain slaves of the plaintiff were permitted to escape, is not the full value of the property. It lies in the discretion of the jury, after a consideration of the circumstances.[7] And in a case, afterwards referred to by the same

[1] Terre Haute, &c. *v.* Vanatta, 21 Ill. 188. But see Sanford *v.* the Eighth, &c. 23 N. Y. (9 Smith) 343.

[2] New Orleans, &c. *v.* Hirst, 36 Miss. 660.

[3] Hopkins *v.* Atlantic, &c. 36 N. H. 9.

[4] Kinney *v.* Crocker, 18 Wis. 74.

[5] Drew *v.* Sixth, &c. 26 N. Y. (12 Smith) 49.

[6] Collins *v.* Albany, &c. 12 Barb. 492.

[7] O'Neall *v.* South, &c. 9 Rich, 465.

court as being very carefully considered, it was held, that a female teacher, injured, when travelling on the highway, by the engine of a railroad, cannot claim damages with reference to her occupation and means of earning support, unless specially alleged in the writ. The court remark: "Under the (Mass.) Practice Act, St. 1852, ch. 312, a general allegation of damages at the end of the declaration will not entitle a party in an action of tort to prove special damages; that is, such damages as are not implied by law, because they do not necessarily arise from the act complained of. The rule of the common law, which requires a plaintiff, for the purpose of guarding against surprise, . . . to set out any particular damage, . . . remains unchanged. There is no specific provision . . . which authorizes any alteration. . . . On the contrary, it is expressly provided in § 6, that the rules of evidence and the measure of damages shall remain unchanged, 'except so far as . . . herein specially provided for.' Besides, to the forms of declarations, . . . there is this significant note: 'The *ad damnum* is a sufficient allegation of damage in all cases in which special damages are not claimed.' . . . The evidence offered by the plaintiff to show her education and learning, and that she was a school-teacher . . . did not tend to show an injury falling within the class of general damages, . . . such damages as any other person . . . might, under the same circumstances, have sustained from the acts set out. . . . This part of the plaintiff's claim could be founded only upon a peculiar loss, . . . by reason of the interruption to her occupation." (The learned judge also suggested it as "a more difficult question, whether the evidence would be admissible under any form of declaration.")[1]

§ 15. In an action against a railway company, for carelessly letting sparks fly from their engine, so as to set the herbage and pasturage on fire, the compensation should be measured as in the case of an *unwilling vendor*.[2]

§ 16. A judgment for the plaintiff against a railroad, for the destruction of a building by fire communicated from an engine, is a bar to a subsequent action for the destruction of other buildings by fire communicated from the building first destroyed, although the subsequent action is brought and prosecuted for the

[1] Baldwin *v.* Western, &c. 4 Gray, 333; per Bigelow, J., ib. 335.

[2] Gibson *v.* S. E. Railway, &c. 1 F. & F. 23.

benefit of an insurance company which has paid to the plaintiff the amount of a policy thereupon. "The loss of the shop and of the dwelling-house and shed were distinct items or grounds of damage, but they were both the result of a single and indivisible act. The plaintiff therefore does not show any right to maintain another action to recover additional damages merely by showing that, in consequence of his omission to produce upon the trial all the evidence which was admissible, . . . he failed to obtain the full amount of compensation to which in that event he might have been entitled. . . . To protect their interest, the insurance company should have seasonably intervened and supplied . . . the evidence which would have shown that the plaintiff ought to recover . . . for the burning of the dwelling-house and shed." [1]

§ 17. With reference to another class of actions against railroads; *land damages* cannot be recovered of a railroad for neglect to remove the stones thrown upon land by blasting, while grading the road; though damage by the blasting itself may be. The duty of the road was to remove the stones in reasonable time, and the jury were bound to presume that they would do it. "They can only embrace, in their estimate, injuries caused by the acts of the company which are authorized by their charter." The remedy for the neglect in question is an action at common law.[2]

§ 18. In case of a *lateral* railroad, in Pennsylvania, the measure of land damages is the injury done to the tract as a whole, or the difference between its value at the time of the entry and its value after completion of the road.[3]

§ 18 *a*. In a very recent English case, it is held that the owner of a house, whose lands have not been taken by a railroad company, cannot, under the Lands Clauses Consolidation Act, or the Railway Clauses Consolidation Act, of 1845, recover damages for depreciation of the house caused by the vibration, smoke, and noise incident to the ordinary use of a railroad. The case was very elaborately argued, and numerous decisions were cited. The remarks of one of the judges, who gave their opinions at length, show the grounds of adjudication, and illustrate the general subject. "The claim to compensation is subject to two

[1] Trask *v.* Hartford, &c. 2 Allen, 331; per Merrick, J., ib. 332.

[2] Whitehouse *v.* Androscoggin, &c. 5 Maine, 208.

[3] Brown *v.* Corey, 43 Penn. 495.

important limitations. . . . The land must be injuriously affected in this sense . . . that the injury must be one for which an action would have lain, had the act of the company not been authorized by the statute. . . . The land must be 'injuriously affected by the execution of the works,' which is the expression used in one of the acts. . . . The words . . . in their ordinary and proper sense, mean nothing more than the construction of the railway. . . . The 6th section of" the other act "is preceded by the following heading: 'And with respect to the construction of the railway and the works connected therewith.' Therefore, one would suppose, the clauses which are about to follow that heading would be clauses relating to the construction of the railway, and would have no reference to it afterwards. Section 6th then goes on to enact . . . 'The company shall make to the owners and occupiers of, and all other parties interested in, any lands, taken or used for the purpose of the railway, or injuriously affected by the construction thereof, full compensation for the value of the lands so taken or used, and for all damage sustained by such owners, occupiers, and other parties, by reason of the exercise, as regards such lands, of the powers by this or the special act, or any act incorporated therewith, vested in the company.' . . . The legislature uses the words 'by the construction thereof' as equivalent to, or synonymous with, 'by the exercise of the powers of the act.' . . . What was intended was no more than was intended by the form in the 68th section of the Lands Clauses Consolidation Act, namely, the exercise of the power given to execute the works, that is, in the present case, to construct the railway; so that the compensation must be limited to such damage as was occasioned to the property by reason of the construction of the railway. All the damage which is caused to the claimant was damage occasioned . . . by the use of the railway . . . legalized by the act of parliament."[1]

§ 19. The damages recoverable against *a town* in Massachusetts, under the Rev. Sts., ch. 25, § 22, are for an injury to the person or property only, and not merely on account of a risk or peril which causes fright and mental suffering. But, where an actual injury to the person is sustained, however small, which causes

[1] Brand *v.* Hammersmith, &c., (Eng.) Law Rep. Com. L. Feb. 1866, p. 130; per Lush. J., ib. 146.

mental suffering, that suffering is a part of the injury for which the town is liable.[1]

§ 20. In an action against a city for personal injury caused to the plaintiff, a practising physician, by its neglect to repair a bridge, the plaintiff may show the nature and extent of his business, and the loss arising from his being disabled by the injury to pursue it, as affecting the amount of damages.[2]

§ 21. In an action for injury caused by a defective highway, the jury cannot add interest to the damages.[3]

§ 22. It is held, by a late case in Kentucky, that, in condemning land for a bridge, damages cannot be allowed for injury to a ferry, but only the value of the land taken, and incidental or collateral injury to other land.[4]

§ 23. In estimating damages to property by act of a city on the highway, the cost of restoring a building to a condition as good as before should be considered, and also the loss of the use of the house.[5]

§ 24. For the location and opening of a highway through land, the measure of damages is the difference between its market value at the time with and without the highway.[6]

[1] Canning *v.* Williamstown, 1 Cush. 451.

[2] Nebraska, &c. *v.* Campbell, 2 Black, 590.

[3] Sargent *v.* Hampden, 38 Maine, 581.

[4] Richmond *v.* Rogers, 1 Duv. (Ky.) 135.

[5] Freeland *v.* Muscatine, 9 Iowa, 461.

[6] Sedener *v.* Essex, 22 Ind. 201.

CHAPTER X.

DAMAGES IN ACTIONS AGAINST OFFICERS.

§ 1. No class of cases has given rise to more questions, relating to damages, than those brought against officers (*a*) for neglect or misfeasance in the service of process entrusted to them, whether by seizure of property, or by arrest and commitment.

§ 2. For wanton violation or neglect of duty, officers are liable to a very rigid accountability. (*b*) Thus, in a very late case, it was remarked by the court in Pennsylvania: "Nothing could be more irregular or unwarrantable than the sheriff's conduct.

(*a*) In an action before a justice, under the (Iowa) Code of 1851, § 509, against a *county treasurer* for the wrongful sale of land for taxes; the measure of damages is the sum paid to him by the plaintiff, with interest. The measure of damages fixed by the act of 1858, ch. 152, § 63, is not applicable in cases of sale made before that act took effect. Costs incurred in foreclosing the tax title are not recoverable in an action under this act. Traer *v.* Filkins, 10 Iowa, 563.

In an action against public officers for injury done in *the construction of a road*, by building a causeway instead of a bridge, it is competent for one of the defendants to prove, as showing the absence of malice, that before commencement of the work he had received a message from the supervisor of the adjoining township, a co-defendant, that he would not join in building a bridge because the people of his township were opposed to it. Yealy *v.* Fink, 43 Penn. 212.

A *magistrate*, who has rendered judgment for the plaintiff in an action pending before him, and, on request for an execution, has issued one which is invalid on its face, is liable for such damages as are the natural, necessary, and proximate consequences of his wrongful act; but not for the costs of levying the execution, or losses to which the plaintiff has been subjected by reason of attempting to enforce it. And he may show, in mitigation, that the condition and circumstances of the judgment-debtor were such, that nothing could have been collected upon a valid execution. Noxon *v.* Hill, 2 Allen, 215.

(*b*) The defendants, bailiffs, in serving an execution, found money secreted in a wall, and took it away and embezzled it, and did great spoil to the debtor's goods. Held, they were liable, not only for the money, but for any other damage to which the plaintiff would make oath. Childrens *v.* Sarby, 1 Vern. 207. See E. Ind. Co. *v.* Evans, ib. 308.

Indemnified by the plaintiff, it was his duty to sell the goods under the *fi. fa.* If he found them claimed by adverse parties, there was the Interpleader Act for his guidance and protection. To lie still until the last days of the life of the *vend. exp.*, and then to take a bond from strangers to the writ, to protect him against the consequences of his official delinquency, was a gross breach of duty, which he ought to have been ashamed to offer as a legal return to the writ of *vend. exp.*"[1] So, in an earlier case, it is said: "It is to be regretted that officers, having a plain path before them, will not pursue it. If they deviate from it, it must be at their own peril; and they cannot protect themselves, against the damages arising from a breach of official duty, by any collateral stipulation for indemnity."[2]

§ 3. But, on the other hand, it was said, in an early case in Massachusetts: "It is peculiarly the right of the jury to assess the damages, and in this they are not restricted to any precise sum. They may give more than the former judgment, if they believe that the wrong was wilful on the part of the officer; for they may, and sometimes do, add to the amount of the first judgment the expenses and costs not taxable, in actions against the officers by way of damages. And as they may exceed, so they may fall short of the former judgment; the great object of the action being to restore the plaintiff to what he has lost by means of the misdoings of the officer. If it should be apparent to the jury that the wrong on the part of the officer was not the result of a design to injure, and also that by the wrongful act of the officer the plaintiff is put in no worse situation than he would have been in, had the officer done his duty; the jury would be at liberty, indeed it would be their duty, to see that a humane or mistaken officer is not made to pay more than the party has really suffered by his wrong."[3] And in a much later case it is held, that an officer, who is not guilty of gross and wilful neglect in not serving process, but acts in good faith, though erroneously, is only liable for the actual damage.[4]

§ 4. In other late cases the distinctions are made, that an officer

[1] Per Woodward, J., Connelly *v.* Walker, 45 Penn. 450.

[2] Per Parsons, C. J., Denny *v.* Lincoln, 5 Mass. 389.

[3] Per Parker, J., Weld *v.* Bartlett, 10 Mass. 473.

[4] Blodgett *v.* Brattleboro', 30 Verm. 579. See Hodsdon *v.* Wilkins, 7 Greenl. 113; Ackley *v.* Chester, 5 Day, 221; Potts *v.* Commonwealth, 4 J. J. Marsh. 202; Commonwealth *v.* Bradley, ib. 209.

of the law, committing a malicious trespass, under color of process, is liable in vindictive or exemplary damages. Otherwise, though there be malice on the part of the party putting an execution into the hands of an officer, if the acts of the officer be honest and *bonâ fide*.[1] Damages for an illegal seizure, made in good faith and upon reasonable cause, and without circumstances of aggravation, cannot exceed compensation or the value of the property and interest, although the execution is void. If the plaintiff asks for consequential or vindictive damages, the defendant may show all the circumstances which bear upon his motives and intention.[2]

§ 5. For misfeasance in office by a sheriff, each creditor can recover only what he has lost by it, and one who could have got nothing, if the sheriff had done his duty, can demand nothing for the breach of it.[3]

§ 6. Though an officer conduct the service of an execution irregularly, yet, if the goods are fairly sold, and the proceeds applied to the execution, only nominal damages can be recovered. But he is liable for the amount of any difference between the value of the goods and the sum for which they were sold.[4]

§ 7. The plaintiff, the grantee of an equity of redemption, caused the equity to be sold on execution against the grantor, for the purpose of strengthening his title, bid it off himself, took a deed from the officer, and paid the officer only his fees and expenses. In consequence of the officer's neglect the sale was ineffectual, but the plaintiff's title was valid independent of the sale. In an action against the officer for his default, the measure of damages was held to be only the amount of fees and expenses actually paid by the plaintiff, with interest.[5]

§ 8. In an action for *not returning* process, the measure of damages is the actual injury; and they will be merely nominal if the debt was not collectable.[6] Thus, to an action for not making return in a suit upon a note, the officer may set up the invalidity of the note as a defence.[7] So, to an action for not returning a writ, the officer may show the existing ability and liability of

[1] Nightingale *v.* Scannell, 18 Cal. 315.

[2] Van Pelt *v.* Littler, 14 ib. 194; Dorsey *v.* Manlove, ib. 553.

[3] Hamner *v.* Griffith, 1 Grant, 193.

[4] Daggett *v.* Adams, 1 Greenl. 198.

[5] Sexton *v.* Nevers, 20 Pick. 451. See further, as to the general liability of an officer, Brooks *v.* Hoyt, 6 Pick. 468; Shackford *v.* Goodwin, 13 Mass. 187; Burrell *v.* Lithgow, 2 ib. 526; 9 Conn. 387; Rich *v.* Bell, 16 Mass. 294.

[6] Hamilton *v.* Ward, 4 Tex. 356.

[7] Woolcott *v.* Gray, Brayt. 91.

the debtor in mitigation of damages.[1] So, in an action for non-return of an execution, the plaintiff must show the amount of damages. The measure is not the amount of the execution.[2]

§ 9. For non-return of an execution for Commonwealth's notes, the officer is liable for the value of the notes, with interest and damages. Without proof of value, the judgment is erroneous.[3]

§ 10. In an action against a sheriff for a *false return* on a *fi: fa.*, the measure of damages is, *primâ facie*, the execution debt. He may show that other executions in his hands would have taken the proceeds of a sale, in mitigation of damages.[4]

§ 11. Where an officer sold an equity of redemption on execution, without having given notice of the place of sale, but falsely returned that he had, whereby a subsequently attaching creditor was prevented from obtaining satisfaction of his demand; in an action for the false return, the measure of damages is the debt and interest, if the value of the property attached amounts to so much.[5]

§ 12. In an action by a creditor against an officer, for falsely returning that he had served upon the creditor a copy of the notification that a debtor intended to take the poor debtor's oath (the copy actually served being such that the creditor, if he had chosen, might have been present at the examination), the officer may give in evidence, in mitigation of damages, that the debtor had no attachable or visible property; and if this, in connection with other evidence, satisfies the jury that the debtor was entitled to take the oath, the plaintiff ought to recover only nominal damages.[6]

§ 13. In a suit against an officer, who had attached property and taken a receipt, for not delivering either the property or the receipt, it is not competent to show, in mitigation of damage, that the property was of a value less than that which he alleged in his return.[7]

§ 14. In an action against an officer, for attaching tools of trade, and disturbing the plaintiff in the use and occupation of his barn; if, by the attachment, the plaintiff wholly lost the tools, he may recover their value, with interest; if for a time only, the amount

[1] Woolcott *v.* Gray, Brayt. 91.

[2] Bennet *v.* Vinyard, 34 Miss. 216. See Sanders *v.* Bank, &c. 2 Met. (Ky.) 327; Goodrum *v.* Root, ib. 427.

[3] Williams *v.* Hall, 2 Dana, 97.

[4] Forsyth *v.* Dickson, 1 Grant, 26.

[5] Whitaker *v.* Sumner, 9 Pick. 308.

[6] Woods *v.* Varnum; 21 ib. 165.

[7] Allen *v.* Doyle, 33 Maine, 420.

of injury from the loss of their use; and if the property was kept in the barn, to the exclusion of the plaintiff, then for the loss of the use and occupation of such part of the barn as was not occupied by the tools.[1]

§ 15. In an action on the case, for an illegal sale of property lawfully attached; if the property deteriorate without the officer's fault, the value at the time of sale is the measure of damages. The court make the following remarks, involving an important distinction as to forms of action: "If the defendant had . . . made a valid sale of the mare . . . upon the writ, he would have been accountable only for what he got . . . upon the sale. . . . An officer is not liable for accidents and injury to property held by him under attachment . . . which happen without any fault of act or neglect on his part . . . It is claimed, that . . . the defendant became trespasser *ab initio*, and, therefore, the measure of damages is the value of the property at the time it was taken. . . . Whatever might have been the rule, if the plaintiff had brought *trespass* . . . he cannot . . . insist upon that measure of damages in the present case."[2]

§ 16. If, after seizure and levy at the suit of the plaintiff, the sheriff permit the property to be "run off or eloigned," he or his sureties are liable to the plaintiff for the debt, interest, and costs in his execution, if the property was of so much value.[3]

§ 17. Where property attached by a deputy is stolen, being left in an unsafe place, the sheriff is liable, not the deputy. Refusal to deliver the property is no conversion by the deputy.[4]

§ 18. If the sheriff, following his instructions, not wilfully, wantonly, or with any unnecessary oppression, without malice or aggravating circumstances, on the part of either officer or creditor, *seize the property of a stranger;* the measure of damages is the actual loss, being the value thereof and interest to the time of the verdict;[5] the cash value of the articles in the market at the time they were taken, or the amount of money it will take in the market to replace the articles.[6] So where the sheriff, acting in good faith and with good discretion, takes goods not the property

[1] Clapp *v.* Thomas, 7 Allen, 188.

[2] Walker *v.* Wilmarth, 37 Verm. 289; per Barrett, J. ib. 294.

[3] Mitchell *v.* Commonwealth, 37 Penn. 187.

[4] Buck *v.* Ashley, 37 Verm. 475.

[5] Phelps *v.* Owens, 11 Cal. 22; 18 ib. 372; 14 Penn. 96, 1 Baldw. 138; Smith *v.* Putney, 6 Shepl. 87; Walker *v.* Borland, 21 Mis. 289; Relberg *v.* Gorham, 23 Cal 349.

[6] Cassin *v.* Marshall, 18 Cal. 689.

of the defendant, no exemplary damages can be allowed; the measure is the legal interest upon the value while the owner was out of possession (they having been replevied), compensation for depreciation, if any, and the expense of replacing them.[1] Thus, in a suit against a sheriff for an illegal attachment upon a stock in trade, proof of injury to the plaintiff's business as a merchant is inadmissible as a basis of damages.[2] So in trespass against one furnishing an execution to an officer, and against the officer, for taking a stock in trade, with a charge of malice, and claim of vindictive damages: evidence of the retail value of the goods is inadmissible; the market cost of replacing them is the proper basis for damages.[3]

§ 19. If goods attached, on a writ against a person not owning them, are delivered to the owner, and by him receipted, he may yet sue the officer in trespass, and the measure of damages is the value of the goods at the time of the attachment, without interest. But, in an action by the officer, the owner would be estopped to set up property in himself.[4]

§ 20. The rule of damages, in case of articles of merchandise, allows interest from the expiration of the usual term of credit on sale. If an auction sale has become necessary in consequence of the levy, the plaintiff will be entitled to recover the expenses of such sale; as also the amount of the premium for insurance against fire effected on the goods. But not counsel fees or other expenses incurred in prosecuting the suit.[5]

§ 21. When an officer is liable in trespass to the assignee of a mortgage of personal property, for taking it on an execution against the mortgagor, and holding it until the assignee paid the amount of the execution and officer's fees, the measure of damages is the amount paid, and interest, and reasonable compensation for the taking and detention.[6]

§ 22. A mortgage estops one who joins in it from asserting his title only as against the mortgagee; and he may recover the full value in trespass against an officer who attaches the property as the mortgagor's, notwithstanding a settlement, without the mortgagor's consent, between the attaching creditor and the mortgagee.[7]

[1] Beveridge *v.* Welch, 7 Wis. 465.
[2] Dexter *v.* Paugh, 18 Cal. 372.
[3] Nightingale *v.* Scannell, ib. 315.
[4] Robinson *v.* Mansfield, 13 Pick. 139.
[5] Ins. Co. *v.* Conard, 1 Bald. 138.
[6] Carpenter *v.* Cummings, 40 N. H. 158.
[7] Cram *v.* Bailey, 10 Gray, 87.

§ 23. For attaching, in an action against a third person, property which remains in the owner's possession until judgment and execution, the measure of damages is the value at the time of taking.[1]

§ 24. For neglect seasonably to *collect and return an execution*, the amount of the execution is the measure of damages, unless the defendant can show that the debtor had no property upon which it could be levied.[2] Substantially the same rule is laid down in other language. The measure of damages against an officer or his sureties, for neglect to seize property, is the actual loss.[3] (*a*)

§ 25. A declaration in case against a sheriff alleged, that although he could have levied of goods of the execution debtor within his bailiwick the moneys indorsed on the writ, yet, disregarding his duty, he did not levy of the said goods the moneys, or any part thereof; and, further disregarding his duty, falsely returned, &c. Held, though the execution debtor had other goods, which the sheriff had not seized or not sold, the measure of damages was what the goods would have realized if sold for the best price which the sheriff could have obtained.[4]

§ 26. In an action against an officer for making an insufficient levy, the measure of damages is the actual injury, and not the amount of the execution, unless that measures the injury.[5]

§ 27. When a sheriff levies upon goods and refuses to sell, the plaintiff in the execution is entitled to recover from him the value of the goods or the amount of the execution, whichever is least. His only remedy is against the sheriff to the amount of the goods.[6]

§ 27 *a*. In an action against an officer for not serving and returning an execution, he may show the insolvency of the debtor in mitigation of damages, notwithstanding he does not return the precept, nor allege that it is lost. It is incumbent on the plaintiff to show that the precept has never been returned.[7]

§ 28. For refusal to levy upon and sell property, mortgaged for

[1] Henshaw *v.* Bank, &c. 10 Gray, 518.
[2] Bowman *v.* Cornell, 39 Barb. 69.
[3] Marshall *v.* Simpson, 13 La. An. 437.
[4] Mullett *v.* Challis, 2 Eng. L. & Eq. 260.
[5] Commonwealth *v.* Lightfoot, 7 B. Mon. 298.
[6] Hanmer *v.* Griffith, 1 Grant, 193.
[7] Varril *v.* Heald, 2 Greenl. 91.

(*a*) In Alabama, upon a suggestion against a sheriff, that the money could have been made on an execution by due diligence, the measure of damages is the amount of the judgment and interest thereon to the time of the issuance of the execution, together with ten per cent. on that amount. Bondurant *v.* Lane, 9 Port. 484.

more than its value, upon executions against the mortgagor, the officer is liable only to nominal damages.[1]

§ 29. Where property of a party is sold under illegal process, and bid off for his benefit, for the precise sum demanded by the process, the measure of damages, in an action of trespass, is the amount of the bid, and interest, not the value of the property.[2] And, in general, upon a wrongful sale by an officer, if the owner buys the goods, the measure of damages is the price paid.[3] So, in trover, if the property has been applied to an execution at the plaintiff's request, only nominal damages are recovered.[4] So, in a suit brought by A, one of two partners, to recover his interest in property taken wrongfully on an execution against the firm, B, the other partner, refusing to join as plaintiff, was joined as defendant. Held, a recaption of the goods, whether before or after suit brought, by B, was in legal effect a recaption on joint account of himself and A, and to this extent would reduce the damages.[5] So, in an action against a sheriff, by the surety of a defendant in an elder execution, for applying the proceeds of such defendant's property upon a junior execution, whereby such surety's property was taken upon the elder; the officer is only liable for so much of the surety's property as was sold for the sum so misapplied.[6]

§ 30. But, in an action of trespass for a wrongful levy upon personal property, evidence of the application of part of the proceeds of sale to the plaintiff's rent is inadmissible in reduction of damages.[7] So, in an action against the sheriff for an illegal levy, although the plaintiff was himself about to have sold the goods at auction, evidence is not admissible that they brought full and fair auction prices, and what these prices actually were; or that the sale was by a competent auctioneer.[8] So an attachment in favor of K, containing only the common counts, was vacated as against F, a subsequent attaching creditor, by an amendment introducing a new and fraudulent cause of action, on which, as well as on an honest cause of action, judgment was recovered, although F was admitted to defend the action. After notice from F, without any offer of indemnity, the officer sold the articles under K's

[1] Cooper *v.* Wolf, 15 Ohio St. 524.
[2] Baker *v.* Freeman, 9 Wend. 36.
[3] Alexander *v.* Hellber, 35 Mis. 334.
[4] Perkins *v.* Freeman, 26 Ill. 477.
[5] Nightingale *v.* Scannell, 18 Cal. 315.
[6] Staton *v.* Commonwealth, 2 Dana, 397.
[7] Graham *v.* McCreary, 40 Penn. 515.
[8] Cassin *v.* Marshall, 18 Cal. 689.

execution, and returned F's execution unsatisfied. In an action therefor by F against the officer, it was held, that the measure of damages was the amount of his execution (being less than the proceeds of the goods), with interest, and that the amount of K's honest demand was not to be deducted from the value of the goods.[1] And the *tender*, by an officer, of a part of the value of property sold under void process, does not entitle him to a miti gation of damages.[2]

§ 31. In an action against a sheriff for *neglecting to take the body* of a defendant in execution, he should be allowed, by way of mitigating damages, to prove the pecuniary circumstances and condition of such defendant. The court say: "It is urged, on behalf of the plaintiff, that the body of a defendant in execution, being in law the highest form of satisfaction of a judgment, is equally so, whether the defendant is rich or poor; and that it is nothing to the sheriff what kind of satisfaction the plaintiff may elect. . . . But the conclusive answer to this is, that an action of this kind is given against the sheriff by statute, 'at the suit of any party aggrieved, for the *damages sustained* by him.' This means pecuniary damages. Hence, if it should be made to appear that satisfaction in that form alone could be of no pecuniary advantage to the plaintiff by reason of the poverty of the defendant, that fact would seem to be competent on the question of damages."[3]

§ 32. The measure of damages, in an action against an officer for an *escape*, (*a*) seems somewhat unsettled; depending in part upon the form of action, which may be either *debt* (unless abolished by statute) or *case*.

§ 33. It is laid down as the general rule, that, in the action of debt for an escape, the measure of damages is the debt and costs, with interest from the date of the writ.[4] Or, as is sometimes held, in escape from an execution, the amount of the execution, with interest from the time of escape.[5] Thus, in New York, in

[1] Fairfield *v.* Baldwin, 12 Pick. 388.

[2] Clark *v.* Hallock, 16 Wend. 607.

[3] Dininny *v.* Fay, 38 Barb. 18; per Johnson, J: ib. 23.

[4] Whitehead *v.* Varnum, 14 Pick. 523. See Griffin *v.* Brown, 2 ib. 304.

[5] Bowen *v.* Huntington, 3 Conn. 423; Seymour *v.* Harvey, 8 ib. 63.

(*a*) A person was taken upon an attachment for non-payment of money. The sheriff, without taking bail, allowed him to go at large on his promise to surrender. The sheriff's officer having called on him to surrender, he shot himself before a recapture, but the officer retained his body. Held, the sheriff was liable as for an escape. Moore *v.* Moore, 25 Beav. 8.

case of the escape of one arrested on a *ca. sa.*, the sheriff is liable for the debt, damages, or sum of money for which such prisoner was committed; and this may be recovered of the sheriff since the Code, where the complaint states all the facts essential, according to the former practice, to a good declaration in debt, and prays judgment for the amount of the judgment.[1]

§ 34. But the prevailing rule now seems to be, that, in an action on the case against a sheriff, for neglecting to arrest, or permitting an escape after arrest, the measure of damages is the injury thereby sustained.[2] So the liability, in equity, of a sheriff for an escape, is the loss actually sustained, and the court will ascertain the amount of damages, by charging the sheriff with the debt, and throwing on him the *onus* of proving that less would have been recovered if the debtor had remained in custody or had given bail.[3]

§ 35. In a late case in Ohio, it is held that in case of escape, whether voluntary or negligent, it may be shown, in mitigation of damages, that the debtor was either insolvent, or wholly destitute of property. The court remark: "In this country the following rules seem now to be settled by the preponderating weight of authority: 1. On proving the judgment, arrest, and escape, the plaintiff is, *primâ facie*, entitled to recover the whole amount of his debt. 2. To reduce the recovery below the amount of the debt due from the escaping prisoner, the *onus probandi* rests upon the defendant. 3. For this purpose the defendant may not show that the amount of the debt is still capable of being collected from the escaped prisoner; but may show his partial or total insolvency or pecuniary worthlessness at the time of the escape. 4. That on proving judgment, arrest, and escape, the plaintiff, in all cases, is entitled to recover at least nominal damages. 5. Where the jury find the escape to have been not only voluntary on the part of the officer, but that, in permitting the same, he was actuated by malice, fraud, or corruption, they are not restricted to the amount of pecuniary injury actually sustained, and may include reasonable exemplary damages; but, with this exception, where evidence in mitigation is given, the actual injury sustained is the measure of recovery."[4]

1 Renick *v.* Orser, 4 Bosw. 384; McCreery *v.* Willett, ib. 643.

2 Pugh *v.* M'Rae, 2 Ala. 393.

3 Moore *v.* Moore, 25 Beav. 8; 4 Jur. (N. S.) 250; 27 L. J. Ch. 385.

4 Hootman *v.* Shriver, 15 Ohio St. 43; per Brinkerhof, C. J., ib. 46.

§ 36. In case of the escape of a person committed for contempt, who is to stand committed until a fine is paid, the true measure of damages against the sheriff is, *primâ facie*, the value of the custody of the person at the time of the escape. But upon proof of his insolvency and utter inability to pay, the damages will be only nominal.[1]

§ 37. The important rule is adopted, in a very late English case, that not only the party's own means, but all reasonable chances, founded on his position in life and surrounding circumstances, that but for the escape any part of the debt would have been paid, are to be considered in damages.[2] (*a*)

§ 38. In an action against an officer for taking insolvent sureties on a prison-bounds' bond, after commitment upon a *ca. sa.*, the measure of damages is held to be the amount of the execution. The solvency of the defendant cannot be inquired into.[3]

§ 39. In an action for *taking insufficient bail*, the measure of damages is the injury actually sustained by the judgment-creditor; and evidence is competent, of the pecuniary condition of the debtor three months before he was liable to be taken in execution; any objection to such evidence affecting its weight and effect, not its competency.[4] And, in such case, "the fact that the principal debtors were out of the Commonwealth, and could not be arrested on execution, may be important in its bearing upon the amount of damages sustained by the default of the sheriff, but it does not affect the rule of damages, or the competency of evidence tending to show the entire inability of the debtor to satisfy the demand. In all actions on the case, the question is, what is the amount of damage sustained.[5] . . . The

[1] Loosey *v.* Orser, 4 Bosw. 391.

[2] Macrae *v.* Clarke, Law Rep. 1 C. P. 403; Amn. Law Rev. Jan. 1867, p. 298.

[3] Jones *v.* Blair, 4 M'C. 281.

[4] Danforth *v.* Pratt, 9 Cush. 318. See Metcalf *v.* Stryker, 31 Barb. 62.

[5] Brooks *v.* Hoyt, 6 Pick. 469.

(*a*) In an action by the sheriff against the county commissioners for failing to provide a jail; the measure of damages is the sum recovered from him for the escape thereby caused. Commrs., &c. *v.* Butt, 2 Ham. 348. See Dennie *v.* Middlesex, 1 Root, 278.

Where an action for an escape is decided against the officer, in an action by him against the prisoner, he may recover the costs of the former suit. Griffin *v.* Brown, 2 Pick. 304.

In an action against a town for the omission of a constable to arrest a party upon a writ delivered to him with that instruction, and with the necessary affidavit, the constable supposing that a bond of indemnity was requisite, and giving back the writ for want of such bond, with a statement of this reason; evidence is admissible, in mitigation of damages, of these facts, and also that the party remained in the State subject to arrest for several months. Blodgett *v.* Brattleboro', 30 Verm. 579.

statute (Rev. Sts., ch. 92, § 71), abolishing the action of debt for an escape, is strongly in affirmance of this rule of damages. Indeed, the only object of such enactment was, to allow, in all cases of this nature, the application of this principle, and not to permit the plaintiff, by changing the form of his action, to evade this rule of damages."[1]

§ 40. In an action by a judgment-creditor against the sheriff for *not delivering over the bail-bond*, the judgment-debtor having avoided on the execution, the sheriff will not be allowed to give in evidence, in mitigation of damages, that the debtor has been insolvent from the time of the rendition of the judgment against him.[2] "Such evidence would not be admissible on the part of the bail, if the officer had filed the bail-bond, and the action had been brought against them; and the officer, who has prevented the plaintiff from bringing that action, ought to leave him another remedy, at least as good as that of which he has been unjustly deprived. The officer, by such a proceeding, voluntarily assumes the situation of the bail; and is subject to all their liabilities, although he may not have all their privileges." The officer having falsely returned that he had taken bail, the court proceed to remark: "When the officer returned that he had taken bail, which he knew was not literally true, he must be understood as intending that he would himself be the bail, or surety for the debtor."[3]

§ 41. In an action against an officer for not returning the bail-bond; if he deliver or offer it to the plaintiff in season for a *scire facias* against the bail, he is liable for only nominal damages.[4]

§ 42. In an action, *by an officer*, against a person who has taken goods seized by virtue of an execution, the plaintiff can only recover the amount of the execution.[5] Thus, where property levied on is taken from the officer by a mortgagee, whose mortgage is void against creditors, the officer can recover only the amount of the execution, not the value of the property.[6]

§ 43. In an action by a sheriff against a person by whose com-

1 Per Dewey, J., West *v.* Rice, 9 Met. 564.

2 Seeley *v.* Brown, 14 Pick 177; Simmons *v.* Bradford, 15 Mass. 82.

3 Per Jackson, J., Simmons *v.* Bradford, 15 Mass. 84, 85.

4 Glezen *v.* Rood, 2 Met. 490.

5 Spoor *v.* Holland, 8 Wend. 445.

6 Linville *v.* Black, 5 Dana, 176.

mand he had made an attachment and sold on execution certain goods, the value of which he has been obliged to pay to their real owner in another action; the defendant is liable for the whole amount thus recovered, though some of the counts included the breaking open of the owner's store, with which this defendant had nothing to do; the whole being but one transaction in the eye of the law.[1]

[1] Nelson *v.* Cook, 19 Ill. 440.

CHAPTER XI.

DAMAGES IN CASE OF PRINCIPAL AND AGENT, MASTER AND SERVANT; BAILMENT.

§ 1. THE measure of damages, in an action against a factor for selling goods in violation of instructions, is the difference between the price obtained and the minimum price limited by the instructions.[1]

§ 2. A, a merchant at Seville, wrote to B, his agent at Liverpool, desiring him to insure a cargo of fruit to that place. B, acting *bonâ fide*, instructed C, who had occasionally acted as A's agent in London, to get a policy there. C, for that purpose, employed D, an insurance-broker, who effected the insurance in his own name, and afterwards received the amount of a loss from the underwriters, but retained it, claiming a lien for a debt due to him from C, in respect of former premiums and commissions. In an action by A against B, for neglecting to effect a good and available insurance, and to take steps to get the money, and for money had and received, the judge, — treating it as immaterial whether the letter of instructions from B to C had been shown to D or not, — ruled, that B had violated his duty as agent, by employing another agent in London, instead of effecting the policy himself, and was responsible for the whole amount received from the underwriters by D. Held, erroneous; that, if B's letter had been thus shown, D could acquire no lien upon the proceeds, and his unlawful detention of the money could not give A a right of

[1] Blot *v.* Boiceau, 1 Sandf. 111.

action against B for the whole amount, though B might be liable for some nominal damages for breach of duty as agent.[1]

§ 3. And, in general, where an agent fails to execute orders faithfully, damages are not recoverable for any speculative loss, but only for positive and direct loss, resulting from the breach of orders.[2]

§ 4. In an action against a notary, for failing to give notice of the dishonor of paper, according to his undertaking, the measure of damages must be the injury sustained by the neglect; in estimating which, the solvency of the party to whom notice should have been given is a material element.[3]

§ 5. In an action against bankers for refusing to pay a trader's checks, though having sufficient assets of the trader, he may recover substantial damages, without proof of actual damage.[4]

§ 6. Exemplary damages cannot be recovered for malicious acts of an agent, unless authorized or ratified. As against a railroad, for a wrongful expulsion from a car by the conductor.[5] So a stage-coach proprietor cannot be mulcted in exemplary damages for the negligence or fault of his servant, though the jury may award more than the damages actually sustained.[6]

§ 7. One employed for a definite time, if improperly dismissed during the time, is *primâ facie* entitled to recover the agreed price for the whole term. But it may be shown, in mitigation of damages, the burden of proof being upon the defendant, that the plaintiff was otherwise profitably employed, or refused an offer of such employment.[7]

§ 8. In an action for enticing away an apprentice, where there has not been a loss of service during the entire apprenticeship, and where the apprentice is not taken out of the State, prospective damages cannot be recovered.[8]

§ 9. Where goods are *bailed*, to be exchanged for others which the bailee converts to his own use; the value of the latter, not the former, is the measure of damages.[9]

[1] Cahill *v.* Dawson, 3 C. B. (N. S.) 106.
[2] Bell *v.* Cunningham, 3 Pet. 69.
[3] Bank, &c. *v.* Marston, 7 Ala. 108.
[4] Rolin *v.* Steward, 25 Eng. L. & Eq. 341.
[5] Milwaukie, &c. *v.* Finney, 10 Wis. 388.
[6] Wardrobe *v.* Stage Co. 7 Cal. 118.
[7] King *v.* Steiren, 44 Penn. 105; 2 Greenl. Ev. § 261; Costigan *v.* The Mohawk, &c. 2 Denio, 609.
[8] Moore *v.* Love, 3 Jones, 215. See Gray *v.* Crocheron, 8 Port. 191.
[9] Chase *v.* Blaisdell, 4 Min. 90.

§ 10. Any neglect or omission of the bailee of goods entrusted to him for sale, or his wilful or negligent sale for a sum less than their real value, should, in a suit against him, be alleged, made the ground of a claim for special damages, and, on denial, proved; the damages depending upon the value of the property in the hands of the plaintiff at the time of the neglect complained of. If the acts of the bailee amount to a conversion, the damages will be the full amount of the original owner's interest in the property, less the charges contemplated in the agreement.[1]

§ 11. Where goods *pledged* were attached, and taken from the possession of the pledgee, at the suit of a creditor of the pledgor, without payment or tender of the amount for which they were pledged, as provided by statute; the attachment being void, and the plaintiff liable to the pledgor for all beyond the debt, the pledgee is entitled to recover of the officer the full value of the goods, and not merely the amount due from the pledgor.[2] So in Maine, where property pledged was taken and sold on execution, before the statute of 1835, ch. 188, as the property of the pledgor; in an action by the pledgee to recover the goods, the measure of damages is the value of the property, and not the amount of his lien as against the pledgor only.[3]

§ 12. In trover, by a pledgee against the pledgor, for the conversion of a pledge, delivered by the former to the latter for a special purpose, the measure of damages is the value of the pledge, with interest, unless such amount exceeds the sum due the pledgee, in which case that sum is the proper measure of damages.[4]

§ 13. The plaintiffs, a bank, received from A a pledge of stocks to secure a debt. Under a power of attorney from A, the stocks were afterwards transferred to them, the next year A credited therewith, for a less sum than the amount of the debt at the time of the pledge, and the following year the stocks were sold and transferred by the bank to its own officers without notice or judicial sale. Subsequently to the pledge, A gave two notes to the bank, indorsed for his accommodation by the defendant, who set up, as a defence thereto, a wrongful conversion, and increase in the value, of the stocks, to an amount exceeding A's whole indebtedness.

[1] Chase *v.* Blaisdell, 4 Min. 90.
[2] Pomeroy *v.* Smith, 17 Pick. 85.
[3] Soule *v.* White, 2 Shep. 436.
[4] Hays *v.* Riddle, 1 Sandf. 248.

Held, the pledge covered the notes in question; that the plaintiffs, before selling, were bound to call for a redemption, and notify the sale, and were guilty of gross neglect of duty in failing to do so; that the private sale to their own officers was illegal; and that the defence was good.[1]

§ 14. In an action against a *carrier* for not delivering goods according to contract, more especially if the place is within his route, or if expressly informed of a favorable market for the goods at the particular time and place; the measure of damages is the net value of the goods at the place of delivery, or the end of the carrier's route, being the value less the freight, and at the time when they should have been delivered, with interest.[2] The value of the goods at such place is the price for which they can be got *to*, not *at* that place.[3]

§ 15. The rule is applied in case of railroads. The measure of damages in an action against a railroad corporation for the non-delivery, within a reasonable time, of goods intrusted to them for transportation, without actual conversion, is not the value of the goods, but the difference in value at the place where they were deliverable, at the time when in fact they were delivered, from their value when they should have been delivered. In case of refusal to carry such goods, however unlawful, the measure of damages is the difference between the value of goods, at the point of destination, when they should have arrived, and at the same time at the place of detention, including necessary expenses incurred by such detention, and deducting reasonable charges of transportation.[4] In another case, where a railroad failed to deliver flour at a day agreed upon, the measure of damages was held to be the difference between the contract price of the flour on that day and the price actually realized.[5]

§ 16. The defendant contracted with the plaintiff to carry pease from Canada to New York by water, but, through negligence

[1] Sitgreaves *v.* Farmers', &c. (Penn.) 13 Wright; Law Reg. Feb. 1866, p. 250.

[2] Spring *v.* Haskell, 4 Allen, 112. See Van Winkle *v.* United States, &c. 37 Barb. 122; Zeigler *v.* Wells, 23 Cal. 179; Hayes *v.* Wells, ib. 185 (a case relating to *drafts*); Dean *v.* Vaccaro, 2 Head, 488; Michigan, &c. *v.* Caster, 13 Ind. 164; Taylor *v.* Collier, 26 Geo. 122; Davis *v.* New York, &c. 1 Hilt. 543; King *v.* Woodbridge, 34 Verm. 565.

[3] Rice *v.* Baxendale, 7 H. & N. 96.

[4] Galena, &c. *v.* Rae, 18 Ill. 488; Ingledew *v.* Northern, &c. 7 Gray, 86; Briggs *v.* N. York, &c. 28 Barb. 515.

[5] Medbury *v.* New York, &c. 26 Barb. 564.

and needless delay, could carry them that season only to Burlington, the lake being frozen. He refusing either to forward them by railroad, or deliver them to the plaintiff but on payment of freight, the plaintiff replevied and sent them to Boston, to market, which was a judicious disposition of them. Held, the plaintiff should recover the difference between the net amount realized from the sale of the pease in Boston, and the net amount they would have sold for in New York, at the time when they should have arrived there, had the defendant properly discharged his contract.[1]

§ 17. The defendant, a carrier from Buffalo to Albany, agreed with the plaintiff to carry barrels of apples from A and B, two of its stations, to Albany, and there deliver them to the S line. The barrels were directed to the plaintiff, in the city of New York, care of the S line, Albany. The apples, with the knowledge of the defendant, were purchased for the New York market. After delivery by the defendant to the S line at Albany, they were immediately forwarded to New York, where they were opened, and the apples found injured by frost, in consequence of delay. Held, if the damages should have been measured by the value or depreciation at Albany, such value or depreciation in the New York market might also be shown as a basis of the former. Also that, in the absence of any allegation or proof of a difference, or that the depreciation was after leaving Albany, the jury might be instructed to find the value to be that proved at New York, deducting the freight from Albany.[2]

§ 18. The measure of damages against a common carrier, for delay in the delivery of machinery, is the value of its use during the time of such delay. If notice of the intended use had been given to the carrier, special damages may be recovered, under proper averments in the declaration.[3]

§ 19. In an action against a carrier for injuries to cattle through his neglect, the measure of damages is the diminution of their value while they were in his charge.[4]

§ 20. The measure of a carrier's liability for property destroyed by his negligence, which has not been the subject of traffic, is the fair value of the property at or near the place of its destruction. But it would seem that the jury may consider the fact, that the

[1] Laurent *v.* Vaughn, 30 Verm. 90.

[2] Marshall *v.* New York, &c. 45 Barb. 502.

[3] Priestly *v.* Northern, &c. 26 Ill. 205.

[4] Black *v.* The Camden, &c. 45 Barb. 40.

property has a market value, at another place to which it was destined, and towards which the carrier, in the course of the usual and regular communication, was then taking it, in connection with the hazards and expenses attendant upon the residue of the intended voyage.[1]

§ 21. Where goods are injured on shipboard, the measure of damages is the difference, between their value in their damaged state, and their value at the port of destination, if they had been delivered in good order; which should be ascertained by a public sale.[2]

§ 22. In a case against a carrier for negligence, only such damages can be recovered, as result necessarily from the act complained of, unless special damages are alleged and proved.[3]

§ 23. A carrier who at first wrongfully refuses to deliver, but afterwards delivers, goods consigned to a manufacturer, is not liable for consequential damages arising from delay to the consignee's works, or for a loss of profits caused by such refusal; though he is liable for the expense of sending to the carrier's office a second time for the goods.[4] So where the plaintiff sent goods from A, by railroad, to his traveller at B, which through its negligence were not delivered before the traveller left B; held, the profits, which the plaintiff would have made by a sale at B, could not be recovered as damages from the corporation.[5] So where, by default of a common carrier in transporting coal according to contract, a manufacturer suffered loss by reason of a necessary suspension of business, there being no other reasonable means of supply, evidence of the amount of profit which might have been realized is not admissible.[6] So a party delivered to a railway company goods to carry from A to B, paying the carriage, to be delivered to a party at B. Part of the transit was effected by another railway company, which refused to deliver up the goods to the consignee without payment of an additional specified sum; but, an action having been threatened against the contracting company, an offer was made to deliver them up without that payment. The action was, however, persevered in, the plaintiff declaring against the company as carriers, with a count in trover, subsequently to which the

[1] Harris *v.* Panama, &c. 3 Bosw. 7.

[2] Henderson *v.* Maid, &c. 12 La. An. 352.

[3] Hunter *v.* Stewart, 47 Maine, 419.

[4] Waite *v.* Gilbert, 10 Cush. 177.

[5] Great, &c. *v.* Redmayne, Law Rep. 1 C. P. 329; Amer. Law Rev. Oct. 1866, p. 108.

[6] Cooper *v.* Young, 22 Geo. 269.

goods were given up in a damaged state. Held, the additional sum demanded for the goods was not the measure of damage. It was questioned whether the plaintiff could recover for deterioration of, and damage to, his goods, or for loss of profits, while detained by the company. It was remarked by the court: "It is impossible to hold that a person, who really has sustained an injury of which he complains, is at all times entitled to act in an obstinate and perverse manner and say, 'I care nothing in reality about the real loss occasioned to me by this injury, but I have a claim against the other party, and I will let my action go on.' On the other hand, all persons are responsible for all the natural and legal consequences resulting from acts done by them in violation of the rights of others, although they are not for damage which might have been avoided. The jury are entitled to look at the circumstances and at the conduct of both parties in every case, see where blame is, and adjudicate in what way the actual mischief shall be borne, according to the way the parties have conducted themselves. That is entirely within the province of the jury."[1]

§ 24. The plaintiff, a hop-grower in Kent, sent to London, by railway, some pockets of hops, consigned to a purchaser. The company kept the hops for some days on their premises in an open van, whereby a small portion was stained by wet, and the purchaser rejected the whole, as he was entitled to do by the custom of the market. The plaintiff dried the stained hops, and they were rendered as good as ever for actual use, but the staining had depreciated the market value of the bulk. The plaintiff sent the hops to a factor for sale, but at that time the market price of hops had considerably fallen from what it was at the time the hops ought to have been delivered. Held, he was entitled to recover the amount of such depreciation in value, not merely in the value of the portion actually damaged. Also the difference in the market price above referred to.[2]

§ 25. It is held that, as a common carrier owes indemnity to the shipper of goods for delay in transportation, legal interest upon the price during the delay may be recovered, as the measure of such indemnity.[3] But, in an action against a carrier for negli-

[1] Davis *v.* N. W. Railway, 4 Jur. (N. S.) 1303; Exch. 4 H. & Nor. 855; per Pollock, C. B., ib.

[2] Collard *v.* S. E. Railway Co. 7 H. & N. 96.

[3] Murrell *v.* Dixey, 14 La. An. 298.

gence, it is error to instruct the jury, *as matter of law*, that the plaintiff is entitled to interest on the damages.[1]

§ 26. In an action against a carrier, for damage to goods in his hands, it is enough to prove their condition and value when delivered to him and when received by the consignee; the fact that the damage was partly caused by bad packing goes only to the amount of damages.[2]

§ 27. The receipt of the proceeds of sale from a factor making it, to whom the carrier had, contrary to orders, delivered the goods, is no bar to the recovery of damages from the carrier.[3]

§ 28. Where an article was delivered to a common carrier, to be delivered to a factor, at a certain market, who had been instructed not to sell until ordered, and such carrier delivered it to a factor at a different market, who had no instructions concerning it, and it was by him immediately sold, and the article rose in price from that day until the suit was brought; held, in a suit against the carrier, brought within a reasonable time, the plaintiff was entitled to recover the highest price attained within that period.[4]

§ 28 *a*. A *passenger-carrier* may become liable for special damages to one not a passenger. Thus the plaintiff went on board a steamboat on the Mississippi river, at one of her intermediate landings, and, while transacting business with the boat, was taken off to a landing below, against his remonstrance. Held, he was entitled to a reasonable time to transact the business (to take charge of a lady passenger), and to damages amounting to the reasonable value of the time lost and expense incurred in being taken to and returning from the place at which he was landed; and if the master of the boat could have caused him to be landed at any point easy of access between the places where he was taken off and where he was finally landed, but maliciously or wantonly and wrongfully refused so to do, to such further damages as would be reasonable punishment for such malicious conduct.[5]

§ 28 *b*. In an action for negligence as a common carrier, whereby the plaintiff's arm was broken, the declaration was for damages arising from pain, loss of time, and expenses. The plaintiff offered to show the number of his family, and that they were dependent upon him for support, and that in consequence

[1] Black *v.* The Camden, &c. 45 Barb. 40.

[2] Higginbotham *v.* G. N. Railway Co., 2 Fost. & Fin. 796, 10 W. R. 358.

[3] Arrington *v.* Wilmington, &c. 6 Jones. 68.

[4] Ibid.

[5] Stoneseifer *v.* Sheble, 31 Mis. 243.

of the injury he became embarrassed; but the evidence was rejected. The court remarked: "In estimating damages, the jury may consider, not only the direct expenses incurred by the plaintiff, but the loss of his time, the bodily suffering endured, and any incurable hurt inflicted; for these may be classed among the necessary results. But alleged damages sustained by the plaintiff, from the circumstance of his being the head of a family dependent upon him, have no necessary connection with the injury done to his person."[1]

§ 29. A carrier, who is responsible for the safety of the cargo, may have damages for the injury thereto, as well as for that to his vessel, occasioned by a collision.[2]

§ 30. In a late case, elaborately and learnedly argued, being an action brought by a pawnbroker for an illegal distress of goods pledged to him; the plaintiff was held entitled to recover the value of the goods, not merely of his interest in them. The case was distinguished from that of Johnson *v.* Slear, 15 C. B. (N. S.) 330, where the plaintiff had a mere nominal interest, and therefore was entitled to but nominal damages. The court remark: "He may retain out of that the sums he has advanced upon them and the interest, and he will be liable to hand over the surplus to the respective owners of the goods."[3] And while, in general, in case of any *lien* the measure of damages is held to be the value of such lien;[4] yet the distinction seems well established, that in trover or trespass, brought by one having a lien, a bailee, or special property-man, against the general owner, the plaintiff can recover the value of his special property only; but if the suit is against a stranger, then he recovers the value of the property and interest according to the general rule, and holds the balance, beyond his own interest, in trust for the general owner.[5] Thus, in an action for the conversion of sheep held by the plaintiff as estrays, their value will be the measure of damages, in a suit against any person who cannot show a superior right to the possession of them.[6]

[1] Laing *v.* Colder, 8 Barr, 497.

[2] Commerce, 1 Black, 574.

[3] Swine *v.* Leach, 18 C. B. (N. S.) 478; per Erle, C. J., ib. 492.

[4] Ingersoll *v.* Van Bokkelin, 7 Cow. 670; 5 Wend. 315.

[5] White *v.* Webb, 15 Conn. 502. See Horton *v.* Reynolds, 8 Tex. 284; Sedg. on Damages, 509, 3d ed.; Outcalt *v.* Durling, 1 Dutch. 443.

[6] Hendricks *v.* Decker, 35 Barb. 298.

§ 31. But a different rule has been applied in case of conditional sale. Thus A entrusted to B goods to peddle, but to remain the property of A till sold. B had a right to return them, and A to retake them, at will. When sold, B was to account at specified prices, and he left with A, as collateral security, money equal to the value of the goods. B sold a portion of the goods and took more on the same terms, paying thirty-nine dollars, the value of the last lot, wanting four dollars and twelve cents, and took a bill, on which the thirty-nine dollars was credited as so much paid. The goods were attached as B's property. Held, that A could maintain trespass for the goods, but could only recover the balance unpaid on the second bill, deducting the thirty-nine dollars and interest.[1]

[1] Chaffer *v.* Sherman, 26 Verm. 237.

CHAPTER XII.

LANDLORD AND TENANT; MORTGAGE.

1. Action by reversioner against a third person.
5. By lessee against a third person.
6 *a.* By a third person against lessee.
7. By lessee against landlord.
13. For distress.
18. For fraud.
19. By landlord against tenant.
20. Mortgage.

§ 1. In many cases, a reversioner may maintain an action for injury to his reversionary estate; and the damages are determined by the peculiar nature of such an interest.[1]

§ 2. In an action on the case by a reversioner, the measure of damages is the amount of injury to the reversion.[2]

§ 3. In an action for damages done to a reversion, by cutting off the eaves of a building, and erecting a wall with a drip over the premises; as there may be repeated actions for continuing the nuisance, evidence is not competent of diminution in the salable value of the premises.[3]

§ 3 *a.* In an action by a landlord against an officer, for taking under execution and removing goods of his tenant, without paying the arrear rent due the landlord, the measure of damages is the value of the goods.[4]

§ 4. The plaintiff was tenant for life, in possession, of a long term, A having the remainder, and the plaintiff the reversion after the term. The plaintiff brings an action against a stranger for cutting and carrying away trees, with a *per quod.* Held, the entire value of the timber might be recovered, and A could not claim any part of it, though he also might maintain an action for the injury to his remainder.[5]

§ 5. On the other hand, a lessee or particular tenant may often bring an action.[6]

[1] See Jackson *v.* Fisher, 1 M. & S. 234; Tucker *v.* Newman, 11 Ad. & Ell. 40; Baxter *v.* Taylor, 4 B. & Ad. 72; Dobson *v.* Blackmore, 9 Qu. B. 991.

[2] Dutro *v.* Wilson, 4 Ohio (N. S.), 101.

[3] Bathishill *v.* Reed, 37 Eng. L. & Eq. 317.

[4] Crawford *v.* Jarrett, 2 Leigh, 630.

[5] Burnett *v.* Thompson, 6 Jones, 210.

[6] See Attersoll *v.* Stevens, 1 Taun. 182.

§ 6. In an action for a continuing trespass, a tenant can recover only for injury to his possession, not to the reversion.[1]

§ 6 *a*. Where a tenant from year to year falsely represents to the plaintiff that he had authority from his landlord to let in a new tenant, and thereby induces him to pay 100*l*. for allowing him to enter into possession, and also to take the stock at a valuation; but, the landlord refusing to accept him as a tenant, he is compelled to leave after a year's occupation: it being doubtful, on the evidence, whether on the whole the plaintiff had become a loser or gainer, and the defendant having paid the first half of the year's rent to the landlord; the jury, in an action for the false representation, may find for the plaintiff a sum less than the 100*l*., or even nominal damages; and, in a cross action, for half a year's rent, for money paid, should find for the plaintiff.[2]

§ 6 *b*. A lessee of premises, hired and used for a livery stable, may maintain an action against one who has laid gas-pipes, in neighboring streets, so imperfectly, that gas escapes therefrom through the ground and into the water of a well upon such premises, and thereby renders it unfit for use, and makes the enjoyment of his estate less beneficial; although the nuisance may have existed in a less degree when the premises were hired. Also for the inconvenience to which he has been thereby subjected, and expenses incurred in reasonable and proper attempts to exclude the gas; but not for injury caused by allowing his horses to drink the water after he knew that it was corrupted by the gas.[3] The fact, that other causes have contributed to render the water impure and unfit for use, is no bar to such action; but it may be shown to affect the amount of damages.[4]

§ 7. Actions may also arise between the landlord and tenant themselves.

§ 8. In an action by a tenant for taking grain in the ground upon execution against the landlord; the measure of damages is the full value of the grain, the lease providing that the landlord should receive his share of the grain, to be delivered in the bushel, at the mill, and no title therefore resting in him till delivery.[5]

[1] Nivin *v*. Stevens, 5 Harring. 272.
[2] Cracknell *v*. Davy, 1 F. & F. 57.
[3] Sherman *v*. Fall River, &c. 2 Allen, 524.
[4] Ibid. 5 Allen, 213.
[5] Ream *v*. Harnish, 45 Penn. 376.

§ 9. Where a lessee covenants to spend or consume hay and fodder upon the farm, if the lessor attaches it, in a suit by the lessee against the officer, damages cannot be measured in part by the plaintiff's disability thereby caused to comply with his covenant. The disability being caused by the act of the lessor himself, the latter could not claim upon the covenant.[1]

§ 10. Where a landlord enters and ejects his tenant without right, the latter, in an action of trespass for the injury, may recover damages for his improvements before expulsion; as, for example, the value of vegetables and grape-vines which he had planted.[2]

§ 11. In a suit for the destruction of a store occupied by the plaintiff, whereby he was put out of possession and deprived of the use and benefit of the store, &c.; held, evidence of the underletting, by the plaintiff, of parts of the store, and the rates thereof, was admissible, as tending to show, whether or not his holding was favorable, and how much his rights were really worth. Also, that the cost of repairing certain damages inflicted by the first attempt at trespass, by which the plaintiff was not fully ousted, was admissible evidence, as a very obvious measure, of a principal branch of damages. Also, that under his count, alleging that he had been hindered and prevented from carrying on his business, as, &c., and his count that he had been deprived of the use and benefit of his store, the plaintiff might show that he had hired another store, the best he could obtain, but inferior, as a stand for his business, to that from which he had been ejected. But not the cost of repairs, no tenancy being alleged.[3]

§ 12. A tenant at will, evicted without notice, may recover damages from the landlord up to the time when the latter might have terminated the tenancy, being the direct result of the expulsion, though the action is brought before that time; but for no longer period.[4]

§ 13. For a *wrongful distress*, actual damage may be recovered, the rent being deducted, if thus paid.[5]

§ 14. The owner of sheep, seized and sold under a distress for rent, which was unlawful because there were other goods on the

[1] Clapp v. Thomas, 7 Allen, 188.

[2] Fox v. Brissac, 15 Cal. 223; Ricketts v. Lostetter, 19 Ind. 125.

[3] Chandler v. Allison, 10 Mich. 460; Allison v. Chandler, 11 ib. 542.

[4] Ashley v. Warner, 11 Gray, 43. See Bartlett v. Greenleaf, 11 Gray, 98.

[5] Mickle v. Miles, 1 Grant, 320.

premises which might have been distrained, is entitled to recover the full value of the sheep.[1]

§ 15. In trespass for damages upon the execution of a distress warrant, the plaintiff may recover exemplary damages, and special damages, if stated in the declaration; under which, evidence of loss from the interruption of business is proper; also, the unnecessary or malicious taking of books of peculiar value, and files of papers indispensable to such business, but of little value in the market. The parties issuing a distress warrant may show in mitigation of damages, even though there be a written lease, that they were recognized by the tenant as landlords. Also the record of a judgment for rent in a distress proceeding.[2]

§ 16. Damages may be recovered for an excessive distress, although the sale, less the expenses, does not equal the rent due; as where, in an action for trespass and for an excessive distress, it appeared that the plaintiff, a landlord of a warehouse, let with heavy machinery, had levied a distress of ten times the amount, and locked the tenant out, and that the proceeds of the sale did not, less expenses, equal the rent due.[3]

§ 17. In case for selling goods distrained for rent without appraisement, the measure of damages is the real value of the goods sold, *minus* the rent due.[4]

§ 18. In an action by a lessee against his lessor, for a fraudulent representation as to the territorial extent of the lessor's right, the proper measure of damages is the sum which the lessee in good faith is obliged to pay to a third person, to obtain what the lease would have given him if the representation had been true.[5]

§ 19. Where a tenant by lease holds over, and is removed by execution under the landlord and tenant process, he is liable to the landlord in an action of tort, alleging forcible entry and keeping out the plaintiff, for all damages caused to the latter by exclusion from the property, from the expiration of the lease to the time of such removal. The (Mass.) statute, providing the landlord and tenant process, also provided, that the judgment should not bar an action for trespass on the premises. "The plaintiff has the same remedy which was formerly open to a demandant, after

[1] Keen *v.* Priest, 4 Hurl. & Nor. 236.
[2] Sherman *v.* Dutch, 16 Ill. 283.
[3] Smith *v.* Ashforth, 5 Hurl. & Nor. 962.
[4] Knight *v.* Egerton, 12 Eng. L. & Eq. 562.
[5] Whitney *v.* Allaire, 1 Comst. 305.

a recovery in a writ of entry; namely, an action of trespass for mesne profits." Whether a count upon the covenants in the lease could be sustained, was considered a doubtful question.[1]

§ 20. In an action by the *mortgagee* of a mill-privilege for flowing the water back so as to render it useless, the measure of damages is the interest of the value of the privilege, if unobstructed, from the time of taking possession.[2]

§ 21. The measure of damages for timber cut on land, held as security, is the amount of injury to the security, not the value of the timber.[3]

§ 22. A mortgagee may recover, for a levy upon the property as the mortgagor's, at least the amount of the debt, if not the value of the property, subject to restriction in equity.[4]

§ 23. In an action by a second against a first mortgagee of personal property for conversion, the measure of damages is the amount due the plaintiff.[5]

§ 24. In trover, by a second mortgagee against a stranger, the measure of damages is the value of the property, without deducting the amount of the first mortgage.[6]

§ 25. To a suit by a mortgagee to obtain a sale of the mortgaged property, upon a mortgage given for the purchase-money; the defendant may set up in defence a counter-claim for fraud in the sale. "The counter-claim . . . must be one existing in favor of a defendant, and against a plaintiff, between whom a several judgment might be had in the action, and arising out of the contract or transaction set forth in the petition as the foundation of the plaintiff's claim, or connected with the subject of the action."[7]

1 Sargent *v.* Smith, 12 Gray, 426; per Metcalf, J., ib. 427.

2 Hatch *v.* Dwight, 17 Mass. 289.

3 State *v.* Weston, 17 Wis. 107.

4 Peek *v.* Inlow, 8 Dana, 192.

5 Chadwick *v.* Lamb, 29 Barb. 518.

6 White *v.* Webb, 15 Conn. 502.

7 Allen *v.* Shackelton, 15 Ohio St. 145.

CHAPTER XIII.

DAMAGES FOR THE TAKING OR CONVERSION OF NOTES AND OTHER PAPER SECURITIES.

§ 1. QUESTIONS have often arisen, as to the measure of damages for wrongful appropriation of notes and other papers, which derive their value from being evidences of property.

§ 2. In an action for unlawful appropriation of a paper security, the measure of damages is the amount of the debt of which the paper is the evidence.[1] Thus, in a suit for conversion of a promissory note, in the absence of proof, the presumption is, that the instrument is worth the sum payable on it.[2] The measure of damages is not the amount of property in the hands of the maker liable to execution; but if the defendant offer evidence that the maker is in debt and unable to pay his debts, the plaintiff may then prove him to be an honest man, who would pay when he should be able, and that he was working for the plaintiff, and expected to be able to pay; and may thereupon recover the amount of the note.[3]

§ 2 *a*. Where the payee of a note, more than six years old, pledges it for a debt, which he pays, and demands the note; in an action against the pledgee, for not returning the note, he may recover its full amount, no inability of the promisor to pay it being shown, and although the defendant files in court an obligation to indemnify the plaintiff against any act done or to be done by the defendant in relation to the note.[4]

[1] Romig *v.* Romig, 2 Rawle, 241.

[2] Menkens *v.* Menkens, 23 Mis. 252; Ingalls *v.* Lord, 1 Cow. 240.

[3] Rose *v.* Lewis, 10 Mich. 483.

[4] Thomas *v.* Waterman, 7 Met. 227.

§ 3. An officer who, upon arresting a person charged with larceny, takes from him other property than that alleged to have been stolen, and refuses to give it up on demand, and retains it for two years after the person arrested has been convicted, is liable in damages; and if the property so taken is a promissory note, the maker of which becomes insolvent before the offer to restore it, the measure of damages is the value of the note at the time of the conversion, and interest thereafter.[1]

§ 4. Deposit of notes by the plaintiff with the defendant, as collateral security for the discharge of certain mortgages; one being that of the defendant himself, the others notes of A, given to the plaintiff in payment of land, which the latter had conveyed to him, by a deed conditioned to be valid upon payment of the notes. A quitclaimed the land to the defendant, who agreed with him and the plaintiff to pay the notes. Afterwards, the plaintiff deposited the notes as security, and conveyed the land to the defendant, who subsequently, with the plaintiff's consent, conveyed it to A. Held, after the plaintiff had so removed the mortgages as to be entitled to have the notes back, the rule of damages in trover for them was the full amount due upon them.[2]

§ 4 *a*. In a leading case, already cited in another connection, April 29, 1786, the plaintiff's intestate, A, deposited with the defendant a depreciation note, nominally worth $2,629, to be delivered to A on payment of $600 and interest. In 1788, the defendant sold the note for the best price he could get, but less than the debt. In 1791, or 1792, A died, and, in 1799, the plaintiff, as his administrator, went to the defendant's house to redeem, but was prevented by his illness from seeing him. In an action of assumpsit, held, the measure of damages was the value of the certificate at the time last mentioned.[3]

§ 5. The rule of damages, in an action by an indorsee and owner of a promissory note, against a justice, or his sureties, for negligence, whereby the collection of the note intrusted to the justice for collection was lost, is the actual loss occasioned by such neglect.[4]

1 King *v.* Ham, 6 Allen, 298.

2 Robbins *v.* Packard, 31 Verm. 570.

3 Cortelyou *v.* Lansing, 2 Caines, Cas. in Er. 200.

4 Dehn *v.* Heekman, 12 Ohio (N. S.), 181.

§ 6. The payee of a note left it for collection with a banking firm in A, who transmitted it to their correspondents at B, the residence of the maker, where it was protested by them for non-payment, but the indorser was not notified by them. The payee afterwards transferred the note, and after divers negotiations it came again into his hands, when he sued the banking firm for negligence. Held, the measure of damages was *primâ facie* the face of the note, and was not changed by the fact that the plaintiff bought it at a discount. Also, that the plaintiff must make out the insolvency of the maker, and the solvency of the indorser; that the defendants might mitigate damages by showing the solvency of the maker, insolvency of the indorser, partial or entire security for the note, or any other fact that would lessen the actual loss to the plaintiff, which was the fact to be arrived at by the jury. But the plaintiff might show solvency of the indorser, not only on the day of maturity, but on any day between that and the commencement of the action; and the defendant could show only such facts as the indorser could have availed himself of in defence to a suit against him, or as would have rendered wholly or partially valueless a judgment against him.[1]

§ 7. In an action against a banker for neglect to demand payment of a note and charge the indorser; the instruction to the jury, as to damages, should have reference to the pecuniary means of the indorser. The worth of such a claim, against "such a man as the indorser was shown to be," is not the proper measure of damages. This is *primâ facie* the amount of the note, but it may be shown, in mitigation, that the indorser was insolvent, or not worth enough to pay the judgment, and entire insolvency is a defence to the action. The court significantly remarked: "Fulda may be a very mean man, and yet the claim be collectable against him. The rule laid down by the judge admitted of the construction, that Fulda, being contemptible, denying himself when called on for the payment of the drafts, the jury might find that nothing could be collected from him."[2]

§ 8. Questions have arisen as to the measure of damages for

[1] Borup *v.* Nininger, 5 Min. 523.

[2] Bridge *v.* Mason, 45 Barb. 37; per Leonard, J., ib. 39.

wrongfully refusing to transfer stock. (*a*) In Massachusetts, where an insurance company, bound to enter on its books a transfer of assigned shares, refused to enter such transfer, and attached and sold them as the property of the assignor; the measure of damages, in a suit by the assignee, was held to be the value of the shares at the time of refusal, with interest. This decision, however, was not the unanimous opinion of the court, and was admitted not to be in conformity with the rule in New York.[1] So, in New Hampshire, where, upon a sale on execution of shares in a corporation, a certificate is demanded of the corporation, by the purchaser, and refused; the measure of damages is the value of the stock at the time of the demand, with interest, and not the value at the time of trial, or at any intermediate period.[2] But in Pennsylvania, for withholding bank stock, if the consideration has been paid, the measure of damages is the highest market value between the breach and the trial, with the bonus and intermediate dividends. If the consideration has not been paid, the difference between it and the value, with the difference between the interest on the consideration and the dividends.[3]

§ 9. In trover for *East India Company warrants* for cotton, which had risen, from sixpence per pound at the time of conversion, to ten and a half pence; it was held, that the jury in their discretion might measure the damages by the value at the time of conversion or any subsequent time, at their discretion.[4]

§ 10. In case of the conversion of *title-deeds* or other evidences of title to real property; if the title is not affected, and the injury occurred from mistake, slight negligence, or omission; the measure of damages is the actual loss, and the trouble and expense of establishing and perpetuating the title by law. But if the act is wanton or malicious, punitive damages may be given; and if the defendant vexatiously withhold the instrument, to the full value of the land or more.[5]

1 Sargent *v.* The Franklin, &c. 8 Pick. 90; acc. Gray *v.* Portland, &c. 3 Mass. 364. See Clark *v.* Pinney, 7 Cow. 681.

2 Pinkerton *v.* Manchester, &c. 42 N. H. 424.

3 Bank, &c. *v.* Reene, 26 Penn. 143.

4 Greening *v.* Wilkinson, 1 Car. & P. 625; (substantially overruling Mercer *v* Jones, 3 Camp. 476.)

5 Mowry *v.* Wood, 12 Wis. 413.

(*a*) See Jarvis *v.* Rogers, 15 Mass. 389, a case relating to 150,000 acres of *Mississippi scrip.*

§ 11. Where the defendant had falsely represented to the plaintiff, his principal, that he had effected an insurance; held, the former was bound by this representation, and, in trover for the policy, the plaintiff's loss being proved, the measure of damages was the same, as if express proof had been given of the insurance.[1]

[1] Harding *v.* Carter, Park on Ins. 4; Sedg. on Dam. 3d ed. 517. See Kolme *v.* The Insurance Co. &c. 1 Wash. C. 93.

CHAPTER XIV.

WRONGS CONNECTED WITH SALE.

§ 1. ALTHOUGH the sale of property is itself a *contract*, yet the question of damages often arises from some wrong connected with such sale.[1]

§ 2. Notwithstanding the title to goods may have passed from seller to buyer, yet, if the former will not surrender them, the latter may, in a special action on the case, recover the difference between the price agreed on and the market value of the goods at the time and place when and where they should have been delivered.[2] So, in trover for goods bought by the plaintiff of the defendant for an agreed price, the value, not the price, is the measure of damages.[3] So A, having bought sheep on credit, left them in the custody of the vendor. Without any default on the part of A, though the price had not been paid or tendered, the vendor resold them. Held, a conversion, and A was entitled to maintain trover. Also, that the measure of damage was, not the value of the sheep, but the loss sustained by A by not having them delivered to him at the price agreed on.[4]

§ 3. In trover by assignees of a bankrupt, for goods purchased by him under an agreement, that the purchase-money be paid by instalments, and an assignment of the property executed when the whole had been paid, with power to reënter upon default in payment; they are entitled to recover the full value of such goods against a mere wrong-doer, notwithstanding default had been made in some of the instalments, and the vendor had to that extent an interest in the goods.[5]

[1] See Kent *v.* Ginter, 23 Ind. 1; Weymouth *v.* C. & N., &c. 17 Wis. 550.

[2] Biggers *v.* Pace, 5 Geo. 171.

[3] Stevens *v.* Dow, 2 Hill, 132.

[4] Chinery *v.* Viall, 5 Hurl. & Nor. 288.

[5] Turner *v.* Hardcastle, 11 C. P. (N. S.) 683; 31 L. J., C. P. 193.

§ 4. Where goods were sold at an agreed price, to be paid in notes, and were delivered conditionally, the condition not being performed, the seller brought trover for the goods. Held, the price was not the measure of damages, but the defendant might offer evidence that the price exceeded the value.[1]

§ 5. The plaintiff sold to A, in February, a pair of oxen, for $120, to be paid for in the following September,—"to remain the property of" (the plaintiff) "until paid for." A, having sent $60 to the plaintiff, in part payment, sold the oxen to the defendant, who converted them to his own use. Held, in trover, the measure of damages was the value of the oxen at the time and place of conversion, not deducting the amount of the payment. The court remark: "He might sell the same and the purchaser would acquire a perfect title. The oxen might be attached as his, and the attachment would be held valid. The plaintiff might replevy them from any person in whose possession they might be found. His rights are not impaired by any attempt on the part of some one to purchase on conditions which have never been complied with. The vendee has no attachable interest in the property or its increase, until performance of the condition. . . . If the plaintiff had resumed possession . . . for non-performance . . . he would have been under no legal obligation to repay the sums received in part payment." The court remark upon the points of distinction from this case of other cases, involving *a return of the property*, *special property* of the plaintiff, a *lien* of the defendant, or an increase of value by *work done on the property;* in all which cases a deduction is allowed from the damages.[2]

§ 6. A purchaser may plead fraud to an action for the price, and thereby defeat the action or reduce the damages. Fraud may also be set up as a counter-claim, and any excess of damages thereupon recovered by the defendant.[3]

§ 7. Where a cow was sold by the defendant to the plaintiff, with the false and fraudulent representation that she was free from infectious disease, and was placed with others, which took and died of the disease; held, the plaintiff might recover, as damages, the value of all the cows.[4]

[1] Stevens *v.* Low, 2 Hill, 132.

[2] Brown *v.* Haynes, 52 Maine, 578; per Appleton, C. J. ib. 581.

[3] Love *v.* Oldham, 22 Ind. 51.

[4] Mullett *v.* Mason, Law Rep. 1 C. P. 559; Amn. Law Rev. Jan. 1867, p. 294.

CHAPTER XV.

INTEREST, COSTS, COUNSEL–FEES, EXPENSES.

1. Interest.
3. Costs and expenses.

§ 1. It is held that, in actions for tort, the jury may in their discretion calculate interest on the damage actually sustained, and add it to their verdict.[1] But when, in an action for unliquidated damages, interest may be considered by the jury, it is not recoverable as such in addition to the sum found due, but must enter into and form part of the estimated amount.[2]

§ 2. A late case in New York gives the following view of decisions upon the subject in that State: "It has for a long time been a controverted question whether in actions of tort interest could be given as matter of right, in addition to the damages. In Dana *v.* Fiedler (2 Kern. 42), it was held, that, in an action for damages on a breach of a contract, the plaintiff was entitled to interest on the damages awarded for the breach from that time until the trial. So in actions of trespass for taking the plaintiff's property (1 John. 136; 1 Baldwin, 138). And in trover (4 Cowen, 58; 7 Wend. 354), the plaintiff has been considered as entitled to interest on the value of the property taken or converted, from the time of conversion; but this rule has not, as far as I am aware of, been applied to other classes of torts, where there was no property taken or converted, and where the question was one of damages purely, unliquidated and to be assessed by a jury. The rule in such cases has been to leave the question to the jury, not only as to the amount of damages, but as to the question of interest. This rule was recognized in Walrath *v.* Redfield (18 N. Y. Rep. 462). Selden, J., says: 'The jury were not instructed to allow

[1] Hogg *v.* Zanesville, &c. 5 Ham. 410; Derby *v.* Gallup, 5 Min. 119; Beals *v.* Guernsey, 8 John. 446; Hyde *v.* Stone, 7 Wend. 354; Handley *v.* Chambers, 1 Litt. 358. But see Green *v.* Garcia, 3 La. An. 702.

[2] Dozier *v.* Jerman, 30 Mis. 216.

interest, but its allowance was submitted to their discretion. There was no error in this. In general, in actions *ex delicto*, it is in the discretion of the jury whether to allow interest by way of damages or not.' This was so held in an action against a carrier. (Richmond *v.* Bronson, 5 Denio, 55; Lakeman *v.* Grinnell, 5 Bosw. 625)."[1]

§ 3. The jury, in estimating damages, have no right to take into their consideration what amount will carry costs, the question of costs being with the judge. Hence the counsel for the plaintiff has no right to tell the jury, that, unless they should give damages for 5*l.*·5*s.*, in all probability the costs would be thrown upon the plaintiff.[2]

§ 4. In an action for fraud in the sale of a horse, the judge instructed the jury, that, in determining the damages, if they found a gross and wilful fraud, they were at liberty and it would be proper for them to give exemplary or vindictive damages, increased by taking into consideration the plaintiff's expenses in the suit. Held, the jury might have understood that they might properly add to the damages the entire amount of the plaintiff's expenses, without regard to the taxable costs to be recovered by him, and, since the verdict much exceeded the value of the horse, that they probably did so understand the charge; and a new trial was granted, unless the plaintiff would remit the taxable costs, or such part of the damages as would be equal to them.[3] So, in an action of trespass, if the wrongful act is neither wanton nor malicious, the jury are not at liberty to give more than actual damages; nor to take into consideration the expenses incurred by the plaintiff in the prosecution of his suit. Such expenses are no part of the natural and proximate consequences of the injury, and cannot be made the subject of averment in the declaration or of proof on the trial. A jury is allowed to take them into consideration in cases of wanton and malicious injury, as a known and actual incident of the injury, although not its natural consequence, only because the law furnishes no definite rule of damages in such a case. But where the injury is not malicious

[1] Per Ingraham, P. J., Black *v.* Camden, &c. 45 Barb. 41.

[2] Poole *v.* Whitcombe, 3 Fost. & Fin. 79. See Day *v.* Woodworth, 13 How. 363.

[3] Platt *v.* Brown, 30 Conn. 336.

or wanton, the law furnishes a definite rule of damages.[1] So, in an action for conversion, the plaintiff cannot recover as special damages the costs and expense of an unsuccessful suit against a person to whom the defendant had delivered the property.[2] So it is held that a counsel-fee, which the plaintiff may be required to pay his counsel in the cause, is not to be allowed by the jury in estimating the plaintiff's damages.[3] So the plaintiff, being in treaty with C for the purchase of the good-will of a business, was referred to B for the particulars of the returns of such business. The defendant, whom the plaintiff sent to B for such particulars, represented to the plaintiff that B had told him, that the returns were of a certain value, whereupon the plaintiff concluded his purchase. The value being afterwards found to be much less, the plaintiff, without further inquiry, sued C for a false representation, but failed, on the ground that no such representation had been made by either B or C. In an action against the defendant for false representation, held, that the plaintiff was not entitled to recover, as damages, the costs of the action against C, inasmuch as such were not the natural and proximate consequence of such false representation.[4] So A, professing to have authority from the owners of certain premises, granted a parol lease of them for seven years to B; and let him into possession. The owners, disavowing the authority of A, demanded possession from B; and, on his refusal, brought an ejectment against him. B, relying on a statement of A, that he had authority, and that the ejectment would not be persevered in, and also on the advice of his own attorney, defended the ejectment, but unsuccessfully, and was turned out. B having brought an action against A for this false assumption of authority, the jury found that A had acted *bonâ fide* and without fraud, and through a misapprehension that he had authority. Held, B was not entitled to recover the costs incurred in defending the ejectment.[5]

§ 5. But other cases hold a somewhat different doctrine. Exemplary damages may include reasonable counsel-fees.[6] Where malice is the gist of the action, and vindictive damages are recoverable, necessary and reasonable fees, paid to counsel in defending

1 St. Peter's, &c. *v.* Beach, 26 Conn. 355.
2 Wilson *v.* Mathews, 24 Barb. 295.
3 Welch *v.* North-eastern, &c., 12 Rich. 290. See Lincoln, &c., 23 Wend. 425.
4 Richardson *v.* Dunn, 8 C. B. (N. S.) 655.
5 Pow *v.* Davis, 1 Best & Smith, 220.
6 Roberts *v.* Mason, 10 Ohio (N. S.), 277.

against the wrongful act of the defendant, may be proved and considered by the jury in the assessment of damages.[1] So the jury, in a suit for fraud, may take into consideration the expenses of prosecuting the suit.[2] So, in trover by a party to a bailment, against a wrongful taker, he may recover the costs of a previous suit against himself.[3] So damages, if duly claimed in the declaration, are recoverable by the bailor, for time spent, and expenses, in searching for property wrongfully taken from the possession of the bailee.[4] So, in an action for negligence, the jury cannot take into consideration the probable expenses of conducting the suit, beyond the taxable costs and counsel-fees.[5] So in an action for flooding the plaintiff's land, a compensation to the plaintiff, for his trouble and expense in conducting his suit and establishing his right at law, is not recoverable.[6] So in an action for a nuisance upon the plaintiff's land, caused by the discharge of impure water, from the defendant's brewery into the plaintiff's clay-pits, through a drain dug by the defendant; the water having been complained of as a nuisance, and the Board of Health having ordered that one of the pits be filled up by the plaintiff; held, the expense of this operation should be included in the damages. "If filling up the pit was necessary to destroy the nuisance, the necessity having been caused by the defendant, he ought to be liable for the expense. It does not appear by the report, that any cheaper mode could have been adopted, and there being an order from the Board of Health to fill it up, it should be presumed to have been necessary, unless the contrary had been shown."[7]

[1] Marshall *v.* Betner, 17 Ala. 832.

[2] Ives *v.* Carter, 24 Conn. 392. See Linsley *v.* Bushnell, 15 ib. 225.

[3] Pritchard *v.* Blick, 1 F. & F. 404.

[4] Bennet *v.* Lockwood, 20 Wend. 223.

[5] Lincoln *v.* Saratoga, &c., 23 ib. 425.

[6] Good *v.* Mylin, 8 Barr, 51; overruling Wilt *v.* Vickers, 8 Watts, 235, and Rogers *v.* Fales, 5 Barr, 159.

[7] Shaw *v.* Cummiskey, 7 Pick. 73; per Parker, C. J., ib. 78.

CHAPTER XVI.

INJURIES RESULTING IN DEATH.

§ 1. CONTRARY to the rule of the common law, it is now very generally provided by statute, that, for an injury resulting in the death of the party injured, his official or natural representatives may maintain an action, and recover damages for the benefit of his family or heirs at law. The statutes on the subject contain very diverse provisions, but in their construction substantially similar principles have been adopted. If not originating in, or, as is probably sometimes the case, restricted to, accidents caused by *railroads*, they have, as might naturally have been expected, been chiefly called into practical exercise in cases of that description.[1]

§ 2. It is held, that in case of death, not instantaneous, caused by the fault of a railroad, the administrator may recover *punitive* damages.[2] But the term *punitive* damages, in a statute allowing a civil action by the personal representative of one killed by the wilful neglect of another, does not exclude the idea of damages for compensation. The damages are allowed as compensation for the loss sustained, but the jury are permitted to give exemplary damages on account of the nature of the injury.[3]

§ 2 *a*. In an action by a widow against a railroad company for negligence, by which her husband was killed, exemplary damages cannot be recovered, unless such negligence was wilful. Nor damages for the loss to his children.[4]

§ 3. Where a person is killed by the act of another, under such circumstances that the deceased, had he survived, could have maintained an action for the injury, an action can be maintained

[1] See Pym *v*. Great, &c. 4 Best & Smith, 396.

[2] Murphy *v*. N. Y. &c. 29 Conn. 496; Bowler *v*. Lane, 3 Met. (Ky.) 311.

[3] Chiles *v*. Drake, 2 Met. (Ky.) 146.

[4] Pennsylvania, &c. *v*. Ogier, 35 Penn. 60.

under 9 & 10 Vict. ch. 93, §§ 1, 2, for the benefit of the surviving relatives, in respect of an injury arising from a pecuniary loss occasioned by the death, although the same pecuniary loss would not have resulted to the deceased had he lived. The loss of the benefit of a superior education, and the enjoyment of greater comforts and conveniences of life, is a pecuniary loss for which the wife and children of the person killed may maintain an action, where the income of the deceased wholly ceases with his death, or where the premature death prevents the deceased from having made the extra provision for his family which he might reasonably be expected to have made had he lived out his natural life.[1] So, in an action for causing death by negligence, the jury may properly be instructed, that the wife of the person killed would have been entitled to a support from him for life, and his child during minority.[2]

§ 4. Where, in an action by a father for injury resulting from the death of his son through the negligence of a railway company, it appeared that the son, who was twenty-seven years of age, and unmarried, but living away from his parents, had for the last seven or eight years been in the habit of visiting them once a fortnight, and of taking them on those occasions presents of tea, sugar, and other provisions, besides money, amounting in the whole to about £20 a year; held, the jury might infer that the father had such a reasonable expectation of pecuniary benefit from the continuance of his son's life, as to entitle him to recover damages under the statute; but not the expenses of the funeral or family mourning.[3]

§ 5. It is not error, in an action by a widow for an injury resulting in the death of her husband, for the court, after giving a correct instruction to the jury as to the measure of damages, to add, "much is left, and much must always be left, to your sound discretion." It must be intended, that this discretion is to be exercised within the limitation previously prescribed to them by the court.[4]

§ 5 *a*. In an action brought by children jointly for negligence in causing the death of their father, the measure of damages is

[1] Pym *v.* Great, &c. 8 Jur. 819, 31 Law J. Q. B. 249; 10 Weekly Rep. 737; 6 L. Times (N. S.), 537.

[2] Althof *v.* Wolf, 2 Hilt. 344.

[3] Dalton *v.* South-eastern, &c., 4 Jur. (N. S.) 711; Franklin *v.* S. E. Railway Co. 3 H. & N. 211; 4 Jur. (N. S.) 365.

[4] Pennsylvania, &c. *v.* Ogier, 35 Penn. 60.

the pecuniary value of his life.[1] There is error "in supposing that none but those who can show some actual damage are entitled to recover. If such were to be the rule, we should have the indecent spectacle of an investigation whether the loss of a parent or child was or was not in fact an advantage rather than a loss; for, certainly, if none be allowed to recover but such as are able to show a pecuniary loss, the defendants would, with great apparent reason at least, be entitled to claim the right to prove the contrary, and to show peradventure that, by the death, the party suing may have succeeded to an estate, or, on the other hand, had been relieved from the burthen of maintenance. In case of the death of aged persons or helpless infants we might expect . . . to have the point discussed whether the death was an actual loss or gain. The law means not to open the door to anything so shocking. It treats the value of the life lost as a species of property, and gives it, where children sue, to them in the same proportions as the personal estate. . . . Hence the propriety of joining all the children."[2]

§ 5 *b*. But, in an action by the personal representative of a deceased person, to recover damages for his death under 9 & 10 Vict. ch. 93, the jury, in assessing the damages, are confined to injuries of which a pecuniary estimate can be made, in reference to a reasonable expectation of pecuniary benefit as of right or otherwise from the continuance of the life, and cannot take into consideration the mental suffering occasioned to the survivors.[3] So, in an action by a widow against a railroad company, for the killing of her infant son, by the negligence of an agent, the jury cannot consider, besides the actual pecuniary loss to the plaintiff, occasioned by the death, such other circumstances as have injuriously affected the plaintiff in person, in peace of mind, and in happiness.[4] So, in an action by a woman against a railroad corporation, for personal injuries occasioned to her by their engine, the death of her husband by the same cause, or the fact that she has children dependent upon her for support, is not admissible in evidence to increase the damages.[5]

§ 6. In an action, under the New York Statutes of 1847 and

[1] North, &c. *v.* Robinson, 44 Penn. 175.

[2] Per Thompson, J., ib. 178.

[3] Blake *v.* The Midland, &c. 10 Eng. L. & Eq. 437; Franklin *v.* South-eastern, &c. 3 Hurl. & Nor. 211; Dalton *v.* Same, 4 C. B. (N. S.) 296.

[4] Ohio, &c. *v.* Tindall, 13 Ind. 366.

[5] Shaw *v.* Boston, &c. 8 Gray, 45.

1849, for the death of a child, caused by negligence, damages cannot be allowed for the wrong done to, or the pain suffered by, the child, or the grief and anguish of the parents. Their interest is wholly pecuniary.[1] So, in an action against a railroad company by a husband, for causing the death of his wife, under the same statutes, damages cannot be allowed for loss of her society or for his mental suffering.[2] So, in an action, under the Pennsylvania statute of 1855, by a widow against a railroad for causing the death of her husband, the judge charged the jury: "The question of damages is for you; should you feel it necessary to examine that question, let fair and exact justice be your guide, and your own good sense will determine it." Held, the jury should have been instructed, that the measure of damages was the plaintiff's pecuniary loss, and that no allowance was to be made as a *solatium* for wounded feelings, or as vindictive damages.[3]

§ 7. Where a wife is killed by the negligence of a railroad, leaving children, in an action by the husband, as administrator, the value of her earnings, and the probable increase of the children's estate, upon his death, by means of such earnings, cannot make a part of the damages. Otherwise with the loss to the children of maternal nurture and education, which is a pecuniary injury within the statute.[4] In such action, the husband cannot recover for the value of the wife's services to him, and evidence of such value is inadmissible.[5]

§ 8. In a suit, brought by a husband and father for the death of his wife, resulting from the defendant's negligence, an expectancy of the children in the earnings of their mother's personal labor cannot be considered in the damages, since this became at once the father's property, and the children could only take them as next of kin, in the remote contingency of his continuing to own them and dying intestate in their lifetime. Though, if she had been a widow engaged in a profitable business, with a probability of acquiring and leaving wealth, her children might perhaps claim damages for being deprived of their probable succession. In such case, the death is a ground for damages by her children, under the statute; the word "pecuniary" not being confined to

[1] Lehman *v.* Brooklyn, 29 Barb. 234.
[2] Green *v.* Hudson, &c. 32 ib. 25.
[3] Pennsylvania, &c. *v.* Vandever, 36 Penn. 298.
[4] Tilley *v.* Hudson, &c. 24 N. Y. (10 Smith), 471.
[5] Dickins *v.* New York, &c. 23 ib. (9 Smith), 158.

cases of loss of money or property. And the damages should not be nominal merely. The plaintiff may show the habitual occupation and employment of the deceased, for the purpose of showing her general capacity and relation to her family.[1]

§ 9. Where a child, by A, his next friend, recovered in an action for injury from a horse and died nine days after the trial, and judgment was signed by A; held, no ground of new trial, although the damages were presumably given in the expectation that the child would live; and that proceedings should not be stayed.[2]

§ 10. In case of death from negligence, the amount received from a life-policy is not to be deducted from the damages.[6]

[1] Tilley v. Hudson, &c. 24 N. Y. (10 Smith) 471.

[2] Kramer v. Waymark, Law Rep. 1 Exch. 241; Amn. Law Rev. Oct. 1866, p. 121. See Sts. 17 Car. 2, ch. 8, § 1; 15 & 16 Vict. ch. 76.

[3] Althof v. Wolf, 2 Hilt. 344.

CHAPTER XVII.

HUSBAND AND WIFE; PARENT AND CHILD; SEDUCTION; ABDUCTION.

§ 1. In an action for seduction of a wife, damages may be given with reference to the happy relation of husband and wife, and the relation of friendship or obligation between the plaintiff and defendant; the provision for children of the marriage; and, in general, the facts connected with the intercourse between the guilty parties. Letters of the husband and wife, and her letters to the defendant and to third persons, are admitted as evidence of the feeling which subsisted between the husband and wife.[1]

§ 2. In an action for breach of promise, accompanied by seduction, damages may be given for the altered social position of the plaintiff in relation to her home and family through the defendant's conduct.[2]

§ 3. In an action by a father for seduction of his daughter, damages to the plaintiff's feelings may be recovered, though not specially alleged in the declaration; being a natural consequence of the principal injury.[3]

§ 4. In an action for abduction of a child, the plaintiff may recover for reasonable expenses in pursuit of the child, without proving malice.[4]

[1] Duke of Norfolk *v.* Germaine, 12 How. St. Tr. 927; Bull. N. P. 27; James *v.* Biddington, 6 C. & P. 589; 2 Greenl. Ev. § 55, p. 43; Jones *v.* Thompson, 6 C. & P. 415.

[2] Berry *v.* Da Costa, Law Rep. 1 C. P. 331 (Eng.) Amn. Law Rev. Oct. 1866, p. 121.

[3] Phillips *v.* Hoyle, 4 Gray, 568.

[4] Rice *v.* Nickerson, 9 Allen, 478.

CHAPTER XVIII.

MARINE TORTS.

§ 1. THE damages for injuries done *upon the water* often turn upon somewhat peculiar considerations, more especially in admiralty, and demand a brief separate notice.

§ 2. In an action against the master of a vessel, for breaking up the voyage and disposing of the vessel, the expense of bringing home the vessel, from a port to which the master has wrongfully navigated her, is a legal element of damages. So are reasonable damages for breaking up the voyage; but not conjectural or possible profits of a whaling voyage.[1]

§ 3. And in general the probable profits of a voyage are not a fit measure of damages in cases of marine torts.[2]

§ 4. If the vessel and cargo are lost, the true measure is their actual value, with interest. If they have been restored, demurrage has generally been allowed for the vessel, and interest on the value of the cargo. If they have been sold, the gross amount of the sales, with interest; and if the sale was under disadvantageous circumstances, or not at the place of the destination of the property, sometimes an addition of ten per cent.[3]

§ 5. The whole of the freight due, or to grow due, for and during the voyage which may be in prosecution or contracted for at the time, is liable for loss or damage by collision.[4]

§ 6. In a case of collision, no vessel having been hired to supply the place of the libellant's, he is entitled in damages to interest, at the rate of six per cent. upon the value of his vessel before the collision, until she was repaired and fitted to resume her trips.

[1] Brown *v.* Smith, 12 Cush. 366.

[2] The Amiable Nancy, 3 Wheat. 546; La Amistad, &c. 5 ib. 385; 13 La. An. 564.

[3] The Apollon, 9 ib. 362.

[4] The Benares, 1 Eng. L. & Eq. 637.

Although there is no settled general rule, as to whether anything or how much should be allowed.[1]

§ 7. In an action for negligent collision between a schooner and a steamboat, the towage costs of materials and repairs, to make the former as good as before, and her expenses while undergoing repairs, are the elements of damage. The remote or consequential damages, growing out of the supposed loss of profits, should not be considered.[2]

§ 8. Where a steamboat is hired for towing, and both vessels are under the direction of a licensed pilot; the owner of the steamboat is not entitled to damages on account of injury sustained in the course of the navigation, and not caused by undue negligence of the pilot.[3]

§ 9. For injury from collision to an old barge, of peculiar structure and capacity for usefulness, and therefore not having any established market value in the port where the collision occurs, the damages may be predicated upon the cost of repairing her.[4] (*a*)

§ 10. Upon condemnation of a vessel and cargo, the damages should be computed at six per cent. on the amount of the appraised value of the cargo (which had been delivered to the claimant on bail), including interest from the date of the decree of condemnation in the court below.[5]

§ 11. An American brig was unlawfully captured by three British privateers, and sent to Nassau. One of the privateers previously put on board of her sundry valuable goods, to be carried to Nassau. The British captain libelled for his goods; but the owners of the brig recovered damages out of the goods, and the rest were adjudged to be restored.[6]

§ 12. The commander of a ship of war of the United States, in obeying his instructions from the President, acts at his peril; and,

[1] The Rhode Island, 2 Blatch. Ct. 113.

[2] Minor *v.* Picayune, 13 La. An. 564.

[3] Reeves *v.* The Constitution, Gilpin, 579.

[4] The Granite, 3 Wall. 310.

[5] The Diana, 3 Wheat. 58.

[6] British Consul *v.* Thompson, Bee, 141.

(*a*) The defendants contracted to receive the plaintiff's ship into their dock at a certain time, and she was brought to the dock in ballast on a stormy day, but, by reason of an accident to the dock, could not be let in, was anchored by the captain outside the gates, and at the turn of the tide grounded on a sand-bank. In an action for the damage done, the jury could not agree whether the ship could have been taken to a safe place, but acquitted the captain of negligence. The judge having ordered a verdict for the plaintiff, held, there should be a new trial. Wilson *v.* Newport, &c. Law Rep. 1 Exch. 177; Amn. Law Rev. Oct. 1866, p. 164.

if those instructions are not strictly warranted by law, he is answerable in damages to any person injured.[1]

§ 13. The owners of a privateer are not liable, in case of a marine trespass upon neutral property, for exemplary damages, but only for the actual loss or injury sustained.[2]

§ 14. Trover lies against a ship-owner for a sale, by the master, of goods, at a place short of their port of destination, under circumstances not inconsistent with the general scope of the authority conferred upon the master by the owner.[3]

§ 15. A cargo of salt was shipped by the plaintiff at Liverpool for Calcutta, under a bill of lading making the same deliverable to A & Co., on payment of freight there "as per charter-party." The ship sustained damage in quitting the harbor at Liverpool, and ultimately became so leaky that the master was compelled to run for Bahia, where, finding the state of the ship such as to render her incapable of continuing the voyage, and being unable to forward the salt to its destination, he sold it by public auction, remitting the proceeds to his owner, who tendered the amount, after making deductions for general average and expenses, to the plaintiffs. Held, the master and owner were jointly liable for the cost price of the salt, and the sum which the plaintiff had paid on account of freight.[4]

[1] Little *v.* Barreme, 2 Cranch, 170.

[2] The Amiable Nancy, 3 Wheat. 546.

[3] Ewbank *v.* Nutting, 7 Com. B. 797.

[4] Ibid.

CHAPTER XIX.

MISCELLANEOUS POINTS; JOINT AND SEVERAL LIABILITY; DOUBLE OR TREBLE DAMAGES; REMITTITUR; EXCESSIVE DAMAGES.

§ 1. A FEW miscellaneous points relating to damages will close our view of that important subject.

§ 2. When a trespass is found by the jury to have been committed severally by the defendants, who plead severally, the damages ought to be severed; but if joint, the damages must be joint, although the defendants plead severally.[1]

§ 3. All torts are joint and several. In trespass against two, the jury cannot sever the damages, but they may find one guilty and acquit the other.[2]

§ 4. A plaintiff, in an action for violation of a patent right, may recover damages against one of two defendants, although the evidence given did not apply to both.[3]

§ 5. In an action against several, if one pleads to issue, and another is defaulted, damages must be assessed against both, at the same time, by the jury who try the issue.[4] In a joint action against several, if the jury sever the damages, the plaintiff must elect, and may take judgment against all jointly for the higher damages; and if the amount of the several damages exceeds the damages laid in the writ, it will not vitiate the judgment, if the plaintiff take judgment only for damages not exceeding those laid in the writ.[5]

§ 6. In an action for false imprisonment against two, where sev-

[1] Kennebec Purchase *v.* Boulton, 4 Mass. 419; Tyrrell *v.* Lockhart, 3 Blackf. 136; 1 ib. 409.

[2] Ridge *v.* Wilson, 1 Blackf. 409; Reutgen *v.* Kanowrs, 1 Wash. C. C. 168.

[3] 1 Wash. C. C. 168.

[4] Van Shaick *v.* Trotter, 6 Cow. 599; Wells *v.* Reynolds, 3 Scam. 191.

[5] Dougherty *v.* Dorsey, 4 Bibb, 207; Bell *v.* Morrison, 27 Miss. 68; Beal *v.* Finch, 1 Kern. 128; Stone *v.* Matherby, 3 Mon. 136.

eral damages are given, the plaintiff may cure the irregularity by entering a *nol. pros.* against one, and taking judgment against the other.[1]

§ 6 *a.* In trespass *de bon. aspor.* against several persons, damages can be assessed only for the joint acts of all, though defaulted by agreement.[2]

§ 7. In Illinois, where one defendant makes no defence, and the other defendant submits the cause as to him to a jury, the jury should assess damages against both.[3]

§ 8. Where an injury was done by two dogs, together, belonging to several owners, each owner is liable only for the damage done by his own dog.[4] Mr. Justice Wilde remarks: "This decision seems to be conformable to the principles of justice, and according to the true construction of the statute, by which the owner of any dog is made liable for the damage done by his own dog, and not by the dog of another. And by separate actions the party injured would have a full indemnity; for the recovery in an action against one owner would be no bar to an action against another. There may be some difficulty in ascertaining the quantum of damage done by the dog of each, but the difficulty cannot be great. If it could be proved what damage was done by one dog, and what by the other, there would be no difficulty, and, on failure of such proof, each owner might be liable for an equal share of the damage, if it should appear that the dogs were of equal power to do mischief, and there were no circumstances to render it probable that greater damage was done by one dog than by the other. But whatever the difficulty may be, it can be no reason why one man should be liable for the mischief done by the dog of another." [5]

§ 9. Where, in an action of tort against two jointly in fault, the jury or a referee severs the damages, and the plaintiff enters a judgment against all for the larger amount, the judgment will not be reversed because a *remittitur* of the lesser amount is not formally entered on the record. The entry of such a judgment, *per se*, remits all claim to the lesser amount.[6]

§ 10. Trespass is the proper action for recovering the *treble*

[1] Holly *v.* Mix, 3 Wend. 350.
[2] Folger *v.* Fields, 12 Cush. 93.
[3] Wells *v.* Reynolds, 3 Scam. 191.
[4] Buddington *v.* Shearer, 20 Pick. 477.
[5] Ib. 479.
[6] O'Shea *v.* Kirker, 4 Bosw. 120.

damages given by the provincial act of George II. ch. 4, for pulling down an uninhabited house.[1]

§ 10 *a.* The allowance of treble damages by statute does not affect the principle, that damages in an action of trespass are to indemnify the plaintiff for what he has actually suffered, taking into consideration all the circumstances. Therefore where A, having obtained a verdict and judgment of restitution, in a process for forcible entry and detainer against B, brought trespass to recover damages, sustained by reason of his being kept out of possession of the premises for the time intervening between the entry and the restitution; and on the trial B offered in evidence, for the purpose of repelling A's claim for damages, the record of a judgment in his favor against A, in a summary process to recover possession of the premises, in connection with evidence that the acts complained of were done by B, by virtue of this judgment, under a claim of right: it was held, that such evidence was admissible.[2]

§ 11. In actions founded on the Missouri statute, entitled "an act to prevent certain trespasses," the jury can only assess single damages; and when a proper case is made out for treble damages, they can only be given by the court. Where the petition also contains counts at common law, the court is not authorized to treble the damages assessed by the jury in a general verdict.[3]

§ 12. In Pennsylvania, treble damages may be recovered for cutting timber on another's land, and converting it, in an action of trespass *qu. claus. et de bon. aspor.*, as well as in trover, or trespass *de bon. aspor.* It is only necessary to prove that it was cut "without the owner's consent." [4]

§ 13. To authorize treble damages and costs, the count must be upon the statute which provides for such damages, and the jury must find for the plaintiff generally, and assess the single value *in terms*. Otherwise the court will intend that the jury found treble damages, or that the defendant brought himself within the provisos of the act.[5]

§ 14. The certificate of a judge will not be received, to entitle to treble damages and costs, in trespass on a statute.[6]

§ 15. Damages will not be doubled in an action for malicious

[1] Prescott *v.* Tufts, 4 Mass. 146. See Pierce *v.* Spring, 15 ib. 489.

[2] Bateman *v.* Goodyear, 12 Conn. 575.

[3] Brewster *v.* Link, 28 Mis. 147.

[4] O'Reilly *v.* Shadle, 33 Penn. 489.

[5] Benton *v.* Dale, 1 Cow. 160; Livingston *v.* Platner, ib. 175; Brown *v.* Bristol, ib. 176; Morrison *v.* Gross, 1 Browne, 1.

[6] Benton *v.* Dale, 1 Cow. 160.

prosecution, unless the (Penn.) act is recited, and the injury laid contrary to such act.[1]

§ 16. In Missouri, where a general verdict has been rendered for damages to property, without specifying the value of the property, the court are not warranted in giving treble damages found.[2]

§ 17. No action lies on Massachusetts Stat. 1841, ch. 125, to recover double damage sustained by reason of the neglect of a railroad to comply with an order of the county commissioners, requiring them to construct and maintain embankments, &c., for the benefit of the owner of land through which their road is laid out; unless the time within which such structures are to be made is prescribed in the order.[3]

§ 18. It is the general rule, that damages cannot be recovered beyond the amount claimed or alleged in the writ and declaration. Thus in trespass for taking goods, where the declaration alleges them to be of a certain value, the damages, so far as they relate to the goods, are to be restricted to this value.[4]

§ 19. The rule, that a plaintiff cannot recover more damages than he has claimed in his declaration, applies to an appeal from a justice's court.[5]

§ 20. It is no objection to a verdict, that it is for more than the amount indorsed on the writ, if it correspond with the amount claimed in the declaration.[6]

§ 21. In New Jersey, damages may be awarded, over and above the amount laid, in a sum equal to the costs of suit.[7]

§ 22. It is the general rule, that, where the damages assessed by the jury exceed those claimed in the writ, it is error, for which judgment will be reversed; but a *remittitur* may be entered for the excess, and judgment taken for the sum in the writ.[8]

§ 23. In Illinois, a judgment exceeding the *ad damnum* is erroneous; but the Supreme Court will not order a *remittitur*, but re-

1 Morrison *v.* Gross, 1 Browne, 1.

2 Herron *v.* Homback, 24 Mis. 492.

3 Keith *v.* Cheshire, &c. 1 Gray, 614.

4 Treat *v.* Barber, 7 Conn. 274.

5 Fish *v.* Dodge, 4 Denio, 311; Pleasants *v.* Bank, &c. 3 Eng. 456.

6 Williams *v.* Williams, 11 S. & M. 393.

7 Allen *v.* Smith, 7 Halst. 159.

8 Campbell *v.* Hancock, 7 Humph. 75; Roberts *v.* Smith, 1 Morris, 417; Griffin *v.* Witherspoon, 8 Geo. 113; Butler *v.* Collins, 12 Cal. 457; Hahn *v.* Sweazea, 29 Mis. 199; Durrell *v.* Carver, 9 Ohio (N. S.), 72; Garber *v.* Morrison, 5 Clarke, 476; Lester *v.* French, 6 Wis. 580; 3 Har. & J. 543; Fowlkes *v.* Webber, 8 Humph. 530; M'Whorter *v.* Sayre, 2 Stew. 225; Raney *v.* M'Rae, 14 Geo. 589; Pierce *v.* Wood, 3 Fost. 519; Hoyt *v.* Reed, 16 Mis. 294; Lewis *v.* Cooke, 1 Har. & M'Hen. 159; Lambert *v.* Blackman, 1 Blackf. 59; Fury *v.* Stone, 2 Dale, 184.

mand the case, to give the plaintiff opportunity to amend. But the court will not order such *remittitur* on error.[1]

§ 24. It is not error to render judgment for an amount exceeding the *ad damnum*, after the action, together with other claims of the plaintiff against the defendant, has been referred to arbitrators under a rule of court.[2]

§ 26. If after judgment, but during the same term, the plaintiff tenders a *remittitur* of a part of the verdict, the court may strike out the judgment, and enter a judgment for the amount of the damages laid in the declaration. If, however, judgment is entered on the verdict, no release or other act of the plaintiff can give validity to it, but it will be reversed as erroneous; and the law, in that respect, is not altered by the (Maryland) act of 1809, ch. 153. But, under that act, and the act of 1811, ch. 161, where judgment was entered on such a verdict, the Court of Appeals permitted the plaintiff to release the excess, and enter such release on record; and they amended the record by entering a judgment for the damages laid in the declaration.[3]

§ 26. In the case of damages deemed excessive, it is held proper to adopt, in actions of tort, the practice, sometimes pursued in actions of contract, of allowing the defendant to remit a part of the damages, instead of ordering a new trial absolutely. In such a case, the motion for a new trial may be denied, if, within a time appointed by the court, a stipulation is given by the defendant to reduce the damages to a sum deemed by the court to be reasonable; and if such a stipulation is not given, a new trial may be awarded, with costs.[4]

§ 27. In a late case, in New Hampshire, the following distinctions are taken. Where the verdict is for a sum larger than the *ad damnum*, the difficulty may always be remedied by entering a *remittitur* for the excess. The *ad damnum* may be amended after verdict, when it is apparent from the declaration itself that it was left blank, or too small a sum inserted through mistake or inadvertence only; and if there has been a full and fair trial on the merits, which appear from the declaration, without any knowledge by either party of the defect, judgment may be rendered, after amendment, without a new trial. If it does not appear that the

1 Pickering *v.* Pulsifer, 4 Gilm. 79.

2 Day *v.* Berkshire, &c. 1 Gray, 420.

3 Harris *v.* Jaffrey, 3 Har. & J. 543. See 1 Morr. 417.

4 Collins *v.* Albany, &c. 12 Barb. 492.

defendant had no knowledge of the defect, the amendment may be made, but a new trial must be granted, to give him an opportunity to contest the enlarged demand. But in actions sounding in damages only, where the plaintiff deliberately estimates the injury to himself, and there is only a difference in judgment between the jury and him, as to the nature and aggravation of the injury; no amendment increasing the *ad damnum* to cover the verdict will be allowed, and the only remedy for an excessive verdict is by a *remittitur*. Yet the court, in their discretion, may permit the *ad damnum* to be increased in any case after a full and fair trial, upon the claim of an appeal or review by the defendant.[1]

§ 28. The amount of damages awarded by a jury is a very frequent ground of application for *new trial*. Indeed this is the form, in which a large proportion of the rules stated in the foregoing pages have come up for discussion and adjudication. It is foreign from the plan of the present work, to do more than present a very brief view of *excessive damages*, as a cause for setting aside a verdict.

§ 29. A new trial may be granted for excessive damages; but in general this is a ground which courts regard with great caution. More especially in the case of personal torts.[2] Where there is no certain measure of damages, to justify a new trial on this ground, it is held, that there must be evidence of prejudice, passion, or corruption in the jury; or evidence compelling the conviction, that they acted under the influence of a perverted judgment;[3] — and these requisitions are applied with peculiar strictness to applications for a second new trial.[4]

§ 30. In England, the court will not set aside a verdict as against the weight of evidence, when the damages are under 20*l*.[5]

§ 31. The jury may find greater damages than the alleged value of the property, not exceeding the *ad damnum*.[6]

1 Taylor *v.* Jones, 42 N. H. 25.

2 Cook *v.* Hill, 3 Sandf. 341; Gilbert *v.* Burtenshaw, Cowp. 230; Smith *v.* Woodfine, 1 Com. B. (N. S.) 661.

3 Treanor *v.* Donahoe, 9 Cush. 228; Collins *v.* Albany, &c. 12 Barb. 492; Goodall *v.* Thurman, 1 Head, 209; Wells *v.* Sawyer, 21 Mis. 354; Payne *v.* The Pacific, &c. 1 Cal. 33; Clapp *v.* Hudson, &c. 19 Barb. 461.

4 Chambers *v.* Robinson, 1 Str. 691; Clerk *v.* Udall, 2 Salk. 649; Macon, &c. *v.* Winn, 26 Geo. 250.

5 Tarlington *v.* Spencer, 4 Hurl. & Nor. 859.

6 Terrell *v.* McKinny, 26 Geo. 447.

§ 32. Under special circumstances, damages may greatly exceed the price for which the property unlawfully taken was sold. As where, in trover for machinery in a factory, damages were given to three times the amount which it brought at the sheriff's sale.[1]

§ 32 *a*. "A person who has acquired the possession of goods, and who puts it out of the power of the owner to show the quality and value of the property by any artifice or concealment, may be held liable for the value of the best quality of such goods." [2]

§ 33. It is the prevailing rule, that a new trial will not be granted for excessive damages, where the presiding judge is satisfied with the verdict; though his dissatisfaction is not regarded as conclusive against it.[3]

§ 34. It is held, in a late case, that, in an action for a personal injury arising from indisputable negligence, the injury being permanent, and recovery apparently hopeless, the court will not reduce the damages if the judge is not dissatisfied with the verdict.[4]

§ 35. It is a strong consideration against the objection to a verdict of excessive damages, that the defendant had it in his power to prove the circumstances by which the amount should be regulated, while the plaintiff was necessarily unable to do it. As in an action for violation of a patent; the damages depending upon the amount of the defendant's manufacture and sales.[5]

§ 36. In a late English case, Lord Campbell suggested the point as a doubtful one, whether a verdict against two defendants could be set aside, on the ground that the damages were excessive as to one of them only, or whether, on the other hand, as claimed for the plaintiff, "the measure of damages ought to be the sum which ought to be awarded against the most guilty." [6]

§ 36 *a*. It is held in New York, that, when the damages given are wholly unwarranted by the evidence, the Court of Common Pleas has power, on appeal, instead of reversing the judgment, to make such abatement as appears reasonable, and suffer the plaintiff to retain judgment for the residue, if he so elects.[7]

[1] Ayer *v.* Bartlett, 9 Pick. 156.

[2] Per Bell, J., Bailey *v.* Shaw, 4 Fost. 301.

[3] Bennett *v.* Alcock, 2 T. R. 166; Tullidge *v.* Wade, 3 Wils. 18; Redshaw *v.* Brooks, 2 ib. 405; Britton *v.* South, &c. 3 H. & N. 963; Duberley *v.* Gunning, 4 T. R. 651.

[4] Britton *v.* S. Wales, &c. 27 L. J. Exch. 355.

[5] Stephens *v.* Felt, 2 Blatch. 37.

[6] Gregory *v.* Slowman, 1 Ell. & Bl. 369.

[7] Lamotte *v.* Archer, 4 E. D. Smith, 46. See Fitzgerald *v.* Boulat, 13 La. An. 116; Jones *v.* Pereira, ib. 102.

§ 37. Where the amount of damages is matter of *computation*, as in most cases of debt or contract, it is held a ground of new trial, that the damages are *too small*. And the same ground has been sometimes recognized, for the same reason, in actions for *tort*. As where trespass is brought for entering a house and taking property, and the jury find for the plaintiff less than the value of the property.[1] So where, in an action for injury by negligence, the jury found a verdict for the plaintiff with 6*d*. damages, though it appeared he had paid 4*l*. 10*s*. for medical attendance rendered necessary by the injury.[2] And a new trial has been granted for the same cause in actions relating to waste, libel, slander, assault, and injury upon a railroad.[3]

§ 38. But, on the other hand, it was held no ground for a new trial, in an action for assault and false imprisonment, that the plaintiff had incurred an expense of 7*l*. 14*s*. in procuring his discharge from custody, and the jury awarded him only a farthing.[4] So where, in an action against a bailee for injury to and destruction of goods, the jury returned a verdict for the plaintiff, with nominal damages; held, it was no ground for a new trial, that, according to the evidence, the damage, if any, must have been more than nominal, and that there was uncontradicted evidence of a loss of goods to the extent of 2*l*.[5] So a new trial was refused in an action of trespass, for taking the plaintiff before a magistrate upon an unfounded charge of felony, though a question of character was involved, and the verdict was for only a farthing damages.[6] And the fault of the plaintiff may prevent a new trial for small damages; as where very great bodily injury was sustained in being run over by a dray, the plaintiff having been in fault, though less so than the defendant, and the verdict being for fifty dollars.[7]

§ 39. If the jury find that the plaintiff is not entitled to damages, erroneous instructions as to their amount furnish no ground of new trial.[8]

[1] Porteous *v*. Hazel, Harper, 332.

[2] Tedd *v*. Douglas, 5 Jur. (N. S.) 1029, C. P.; 5 C. B. (N. S.) 895.

[3] Weeding *v*. Mason, 2 C. B. (N. S.) 382; English *v*. Clerry, 3 Hill (S. C.), 279; Levi *v*. Milne, 4 Bing. 195; Rixey *v*. Ward, 3 Rand. 52; Bacot *v*. Keith, 2 Bay, 466; Robbins *v*. The Hudson, &c. 7 Bosw. 1.

[4] Bradlaugh *v*. Edwards, 11 C. B. (N. S.) 377.

[5] Mostyn *v*. Coles, 7 H. & N. 872; 31 L. J. Exch. 151.

[6] Apps *v*. Day, 26 Eng. L. & Eq. 335.

[7] Flanders *v*. Meath, 27 Geo. 358.

[8] Pope *v*. Machias, &c. 52 Maine, 535.

§ 40. Under an ordinance of a city, requiring a committee of the city council, upon laying out a drain, to report the names of land-owners, with the amount of damages allowed each; with reference to the validity of the proceedings, a report of the names of all abutters, not mentioning any damages, is a sufficient award that no one is entitled to damages. It might be, that they all waived their claims to damages; or, if not, then any party would have his legal remedy, as upon an award that he was not entitled to damages.[1]

§ 41. Unless it appears that a bill of exceptions reports all the evidence relating to damages, the court above will not review the assessment of the jury, for want of evidence of actual or special damages.[2]

[1] Hildreth *v.* Lowell, 11 Gray, 345.

[2] M'Intyre *v.* Park, 11 Gray, 102.

APPENDIX.

FORMS AND PRECEDENTS OF DECLARATIONS AND PLEAS IN ACTIONS FOR TORTS.

The following forms, though not always *complete*, are sanctioned by the cases to which they respectively refer, and in which the sufficiency of the pleadings was the direct point of decision. The cases are mostly recent, and may sometimes turn in part upon local statutes. The statutory law, however, in simplifying, as it has done so extensively, the rules and forms of pleading, has everywhere proceeded upon substantially the same basis. Hence the forms, and the cases which accredit them, are believed to be of universal applicability, and reasonably safe guides for the practitioner under the same or similar circumstances. (*a*)

TORT AND CONTRACT. FRAUDULENT SALE.

The plaintiff bought of the defendant for (naming the sum), being a sound price, (naming the number) hogs, and said hogs had the disease of cholera. And the defendant represented said hogs to be sound and healthy, knowing such representations to be untrue. And the plaintiff bought said hogs relying upon said representations, and unable by reasonable diligence to ascertain that they were false. — 22 Ind. 257.

FRAUDULENT PURCHASE.

The plaintiff sold and delivered the defendant goods to the amount of, &c., on a credit of six months. And the defendant

(*a*) The incidental requisites of pleading — such as name, number, time, and place, and the formal introductory and closing averments — are of course to be added, unless, as is now often done, dispensed with by express statute. And the *citations* will fail of their chief purpose, if in actual practice they do not lead out of *abundant caution*, to an inspection of the entire forms as set out in the Reports.

was insolvent at the time of said sale, and purchased the goods without any intent to pay for them and with the intent to defraud the plaintiff of their value, and by reason of said fraud the defendant became liable to pay for the goods immediately upon their delivery. — 27 Barb. 652. (While this form of *declaring* is doubtless sufficient, there may be more doubt as to the rule of law upon which the action is founded.)

INDORSEE AGAINST FRAUDULENT INDORSER OF NOTE.

The defendant, with intent to deceive the plaintiff, falsely represented that said, &c. (the maker of the note), was solvent, and, relying on said representation, the plaintiff accepted said note. — 35 Mis. 483.

FALSE REPRESENTATION AS TO A MORTGAGE.

The defendant represented that said mortgage was good, and a valid security for payment of said note, and the plaintiff supposed and verily believed, at the time he bought the same as aforesaid, the said mortgage to be good, and that it was a valid and sufficient security. — 18 Wis. 196.

FALSE RECOMMENDATIONS.

The plaintiff purchased of the defendant a note against one (A) whom the defendant affirmed to be a person of good credit, the defendant well knowing said affirmation to be false; and the defendant was in fact poor, and the note was of no value, whereby the defendant deceived and defrauded the plaintiff. — 8 Fost. 118.

The defendant (a director of a bank) falsely and fraudulently represented, that the stock of said bank was worth par, when in truth said stock was worthless; the defendant knowing that said stock was not worth par, and making said representation with intent to induce the plaintiff to purchase said stock. — 3 Bosw. 346.

MISCELLANEOUS CASES OF FALSE REPRESENTATION.

The defendant, employed as architect by A and others to superintend the building of a church, falsely and fraudulently represented and pretended that he was authorized by A to order, and did order, stone of the plaintiffs for the building of said church, for and on account of, and to be charged to A; and the plaintiffs, relying on that representation, and believing that the defendant had authority from A to order the stone on his account, delivered the same, and the same was used in the building of the church; whereas, in truth and in fact, the defendant was not, as he well knew, authorized so to order the said stone. And, A refusing to pay for the stone, the plaintiffs, trusting in the defendant's representation, sued A for the price, and failed in their action, and had to pay A's costs, and also the costs incurred by their own attorneys. — 37 Eng. L. & Eq. 275.

The defendants falsely and fraudulently deceived the plaintiff in this, that they, as brokers of the plaintiff, employed by him to purchase oil, with the fraudulent intention of deceiving and injuring the plaintiff, falsely represented to him that they had "purchased for him twenty-five tuns of palm oil," to arrive by the, &c., at the price of, &c., per tun; whereas in fact the defendants purchased the oil on the terms that the said twenty-five tuns were sold, and would be delivered to the plaintiff after, and subject to, the prior delivery of eight hundred tuns of palm oil from the said vessel. And said vessel arrived with less than eight hundred tuns, in consequence whereof said twenty-five tuns were not delivered to the plaintiff. (Special damages.) — 20 Eng. L. & Eq. 467.

The defendants having brought a bill for the foreclosure of a mortgage executed to them by the plaintiff, to secure a note, it was agreed between the plaintiff and defendants, before the decree thereon, that the time for redeeming should be limited to the first Monday of January, 1851; but the defendants procured a decree thereon, that it should be redeemed previous to said day, namely, on or before the first *day* of January, 1851. And after said decree was passed, the defendants falsely and fraudulently, and for the purpose of preventing the plaintiff from redeeming within the time so limited, represented to the plaintiff, and thereby induced him to believe, that the time so limited was the first Monday of said January. And under said belief, and under an agreement between the plaintiff and the defendants, made after said first day of January, that the plaintiff might redeem on said first Monday of January, the plaintiff omitted to redeem until after said first day of January, but was prepared and offered to the defendants to do so on said first Monday, and on that day tendered to the defendants the amount due, which they refused to receive; and by means thereof he was foreclosed, and, in order to have the foreclosure opened, and to obtain the privilege of redeeming, was obliged to, and did, bring his application therefor to said court, on which he was allowed to redeem; and, in consequence of said wrongful conduct of the defendants, he was, in the prosecution of said application, subjected to great expense, trouble, vexation, and loss of time. (The formal preamble, time, amounts, &c., are to be added.) — 23 Conn. 134.

PLEAS OF FRAUD AND MISREPRESENTATION.

To an action upon a note made to a railroad corporation. Said note was given for a subscription to stock in said corporation, and through misrepresentations of one, &c., as to the amount of stock taken and the time when said railroad would be finished, said misrepresentations being made by authority of the plaintiffs, and known by them to be false. — 31 Ill. 490. (But see the case.)

To an action upon a written instrument. Said writing was obtained from the defendants by fraud, covin, and misrepresentation of the plaintiff. — 2 Met. (Ky.) 584.

To an action on a note given for the price of land. The plaintiff falsely and fraudulently represented, that there was on the land sufficient material to build a barn (describing the dimensions, quality, &c.), being lumber of the value of, &c., whereas the material and lumber actually on the land was worth only, &c., and the defendant was obliged to expend, &c., in addition to the sum last named, for the purpose of building said barn. — 14 Cal. 112.

To an action on a note for goods. Said note was given for the last instalment on a stock of goods, purchased by the defendants from the plaintiff, the plaintiff representing said stock to be worth $3500, and that it would invoice that sum or more. And the defendants were ignorant of the amount and value of said stock, and requested of the plaintiff an invoice, but the plaintiff said he had no time to make it. And the purchase was made upon said representation, the plaintiff knowing the same to be false. And said goods invoiced and amounted only to the sum of $1500. — 22 Ind. 233.

DECLARATIONS, ETC., FOR NEGLIGENCE. — INJURIES TO LAND, ETC.

The reservoir of the defendants, by reason of some fault in its construction, or some carelessness or mismanagement on the part of the defendants, broke away, &c. — 10 Cal. 413.

The defendant wrongfully and improperly, and without leaving any proper or sufficient pillars or supports, worked coal-mines under and contiguous to the close of the plaintiff, and dug for and got and moved the coals, minerals, earth, and soil of and in said mines, whereby the soil and surface of said close sank in, cracked, swagged, and gave way. — 1 Eng. L. & Eq. 241.

The defendant, *contriving and maliciously intending* to injure and aggrieve the plaintiff, dug up the soil of a contiguous lot, whereby the foundation wall of the plaintiff's house was injured, &c. — 17 John. 92.

A messuage and land, the reversion whereof belonged to the plaintiff, were supported by the land adjoining; yet the defendant wrongfully and negligently dug and made excavations in the land adjoining, without sufficiently shoring the messuage and land, and thereby deprived them of their support, whereby they sunk and were injured. — 4 Hurl. & N. 153.

INJURIES TO AND BY ANIMALS.

The plaintiff's animal (describing it) being upon the track of the defendants' railroad, was there negligently and carelessly run over and killed by their train. — 35 N. H. 356.

The defendant wrongfully and knowingly kept a horse accustomed to bite mankind. — 10 Cush. 509.

COLLISIONS BY LAND AND WATER.

The defendant drove his cart against the plaintiff's horse with force and violence, by and through the mere negligence, inattention, and want of proper care of the defendant. — 2 N. Rep. 117.

The defendant run down the plaintiff's ship, by the negligence and unskilfulness of the defendant in managing his vessel. — 8 T. R. 188.

COLLECTION OF DEBTS.

The defendant undertook for and with the plaintiff to collect a judgment against, &c., and promised out of the proceeds of said judgment, when collected, to pay the plaintiff, &c., but has failed and omitted to do so from mere neglect. — 25 Ala. 246.

The defendant did obtain judgment for the plaintiff on said note and accounts, and did, without the consent of the plaintiff, and contrary to his express directions, undertake to settle and adjust such claims with said A, and did not follow the instructions of the plaintiff; but so carelessly and negligently conducted the said trust, by taking the note of said A payable to himself for the amount of the judgment and execution recovered against said A, that the said debt has never been paid or collected, and the plaintiff has wholly lost the attachment, &c. — 2 Cush. 316.

ANSWER OR PLEA TO A DECLARATION AGAINST SHIP-OWNERS FOR NEGLIGENTLY AND CARELESSLY STOWING, ETC.

Salt-cake was a corrosive substance, rotting casks and other substances being in contact with it, which the plaintiffs knew, but which the defendants, without any default on their part, did not know, and could not be reasonably expected to know, until after the happening of the damage. And it was the duty of the plaintiffs to have informed the defendants of the destructive nature of salt-cake, in order to its proper and safe stowage by them. But the plaintiffs did not so inform the defendants, or ascertain that they were so informed, but, on the contrary, negligently delivered the salt-cake to the defendants in bulk, and thereby and otherwise represented to the defendants and induced them to believe, and they did reasonably believe, that the said salt-cake might be placed in contact with casks, &c. And, under this reasonable belief, and induced as aforesaid, the defendants stowed the said salt-cake in contact with and between and amongst casks of salt provisions, being, as they reasonably believed, a safe and proper mode of stowing the same, and afterwards, and without default of the defendants, the said salt-cake corroded, rotted, and destroyed the said casks, and the hoops thereof, and the brine therefrom damaged the salt-cake, and caused the default in the delivery thereof complained of in the declaration. — 5 C. B. (N. S.) 149.

Answer to an action for damages from falling into a ditch, which the defendants were alleged to have left open, without any fault or want of care on the part of the plaintiff. The defendant denies that the plaintiff, without any fault or want of care on his part, did fall therein. — 18 N. Y. 119.

Answer to an action for injury caused by a shaft. The defendants admit that the shaft was not sufficiently fenced, but allege that the plaintiff, contrary to the express command of the defendants, and knowing that it was dangerous to meddle with the shaft, took hold of it and set it in motion, whereby, and not by reason of the negligence of the defendants, the plaintiff was injured. — 3 Allen, 382.

ASSAULT AND BATTERY.

The defendant, on, &c., drove a coach over the wife and bruised her, by reason whereof the husband laid out divers sums of money for her cure, *et alia enormia*, &c. — 11 Mod. 264.

Plea, in trespass for assaulting and turning the plaintiff out of a police-office. Two of the defendants, being justices of the peace, were assembled in a police-office to adjudicate upon an information, and were proceeding to hear and determine the same, when the plaintiff (being an attorney) entered with the informer, not as his friend or as a spectator, but for the avowed purpose of acting as his attorney and advocate; and as such, without the leave and against the will of the justices, was taking notes of the evidence of a witness, and acting and taking part in the proceedings, as an attorney or advocate on behalf of the informer; and the defendants stated to the plaintiff, that it was not their practice to suffer any person to appear and take part in any proceedings before them as an attorney or advocate, and requested him to desist from so doing; and, although they were willing to permit the plaintiff to remain in the office as one of the public, yet he would not thus desist, but asserted his right to be present, and to take such part; and unlawfully, and against the will of the justices, continued in the office, taking part and acting as aforesaid, in contempt of the justices; whereupon, by order of the above two defendants, the other defendants turned the plaintiff out of the office. — 2 B. & Ad. 663.

Plea to an action for assault and battery. The defendants gently laid hands on the plaintiff to arrest him for felony, and did no more injury than was necessary in effecting the arrest. — 7 Dana, 453.

To an action of trespass *quare clausum*, and for an assault and battery. The plaintiff had felled a tree across a navigable stream, down which the defendants were conducting a boat, and, to enable them to proceed, it was necessary to remove the obstruction; and the plaintiff stood upon it with an axe, threatening to resist the removal; and they therefore gently laid hands upon him, &c. — 7 Dana, 428.

The public had a prescriptive right to navigate the stream, but the plaintiff obstructed it; and the defendants attempted to remove the obstruction, and, the plaintiff having assaulted them, they, in self-defence, necessarily beat and wounded him a little, using only such force as was necessary to remove the obstruction. — Ibid.

Action for assault on board a vessel. Plea, as to the assaulting, beating, and ill-treating the plaintiff. The defendant was the captain of a vessel, on board of which the plaintiff and others were passengers, and the plaintiff made a great noise, disturbance, and affray on board said vessel, and was then fighting with another person, whose name was to the defendant unknown, and was striving to beat and wound said person; wherefore the defendant, as such captain, to preserve peace and order, and prevent the beating and wounding of such person, gently laid his hands upon the plaintiff, which was the trespass complained of. — 2 Eng. L. & Eq. 201. (But this plea was held no answer to a charge in the declaration of knocking down and prostrating the plaintiff.)

DECLARATIONS, ETC., FOR FALSE IMPRISONMENT.

The defendants, A and B, A acting as attorney for B, recovered a judgment against the plaintiff for 30*l.* 7*s.* 4*d.*, and the plaintiff paid and satisfied to (B) the debt recovered, except 15*s.* 8*d.*, and the defendants sued out a *ca. sa.* upon the judgment, and wrongfully and maliciously, and without any reasonable or probable cause, indorsed the writ with directions to levy 5*l.* 14*s.* 8*d.* and interest, and 1*l.* 7*s.* for the costs of execution. And the plaintiff tendered and offered to pay to the defendants 3*l.* 8*s.*, which was sufficient to pay and discharge all that was recoverable against the plaintiff upon the judgment and writ, together with the costs of the writ of execution and all other legal and incidental expenses; and the defendants wrongfully and maliciously, and without any reasonable or probable cause, procured the sheriff to arrest the plaintiff and detain him until he paid 7*l.* 6*s.* 9*d.*; whereas the sum of 3*l.* 8*s.*, and no more, was due, &c. — 10 C. B. (N. S.) 592.

The defendant caused the plaintiff to be arrested and imprisoned without reasonable or probable cause, on a false and malicious charge of felony. — 27 L. J. Exch. 315; 3 H. & N. 950.

The plaintiff was, after he was taken, during his detention, and before his discharge, able and willing and offered to pay, and always afterwards during his detention was willing to pay, and was finally discharged from imprisonment upon paying (a sum smaller than that insisted on). And the plaintiff, by reason of the premises, was necessarily put to and incurred divers costs and expenses in and about obtaining his discharge. — 2 C. B. (N. S.) 467.

PLEAS, ETC.

If the plaintiff was arrested on two writs, as alleged, he was rightfully arrested, because the first action was discontinued by reason of his representations and notice given him of the discontinuance, before the commencement of the second action. — 6 Gray, 233.

The plaintiff attempted forcibly to break and enter the messuage or public-house of the defendant without leave; whereupon he resisted such entrance; and because the plaintiff behaved himself violently and created a disturbance in the street, by which means a mob was assembled, and the defendant's business interrupted, and his customers annoyed, and because the plaintiff threatened to continue such violent conduct, and to renew his attempts and efforts to get into the house; and because no request or entreaty of the defendant to the plaintiff to abstain from and abandon his attempts and efforts was complied with; the defendant, in order to preserve the peace, and to secure himself from a renewal of such attempts and efforts, gave him in charge to a constable, to be carried before a justice of the peace. (Held, good, after verdict.) — 1 M. & W. 516.

The defendant was possessed of a shop, and carried on the business of a baker therein, and the plaintiff had been in the shop making a great noise and disturbance, and abused the defendant, and disturbed him in the peaceable possession of his shop, in breach of the king's peace, and thereby obstructed the defendant in the exercise of his business. And the plaintiff went out of the shop into the public street in front of it, and continued there to make a great noise and disturbance, and to abuse the defendant, and thereby caused a great concourse of persons to assemble, and so disturbed the defendant in the possession of his shop, and obstructed his business, in breach of the peace (and thereby caused a great riot and disturbance). And the defendant requested him to desist and depart, but he refused; whereupon the defendant, in order to preserve the peace, sent for certain policemen, and requested them to remove the plaintiff. And they requested the plaintiff to cease making such noise and disturbance, &c., but he refused, and continued making such noise, riot, and disturbance, &c.; whereupon the defendant, in order to preserve the peace, charged them with the plaintiff, and he was taken to a station-house, and thence before a magistrate, who admonished and discharged him. — 2 M. & W. 477.

The plaintiff disturbed a congregation while the minister was performing the rites of burial, and the defendant *manus mollitur imposuit* to prevent such disturbance. — 1 Mod. 168.

The defendant was a constable, and a felony had been committed, and a reasonable suspicion and belief existed that the plaintiff was guilty of said felony. And one A and others informed the defendant that the plaintiff was guilty of said felony. (State briefly the facts upon which the informant's knowledge or belief was founded.) And, for the purpose of carrying the plaintiff before some justice of the peace to be dealt with, the defendant arrested him. — 6 Blackf. 406.

The act complained of was an arrest of the plaintiff, under a warrant issued at the instance of the defendant, who was city attorney of Utica, for the violation, by the plaintiff, of an ordinance made by the common council. — 2 Hill, 296.

Action against the Speaker of the House of Commons for forcibly, and with the assistance of armed soldiers, breaking into the messuage of the plaintiff (the outer door being shut and fastened), arresting him, taking him to the Tower of London, and imprisoning him there.

Defence. A parliament was held, which was sitting during the period of the trespasses complained of; and the plaintiff was a member of the House of Commons; and the House having resolved, "That a certain letter, &c., in Cobbett's Weekly Register, was a libellous and scandalous paper, reflecting on the just rights and privileges of the House; and that the plaintiff, who had admitted that the said letter, &c., was printed by his authority, had been thereby guilty of a breach of the privileges of that House;" and having ordered that for his said offence he should be committed to the Tower, and that the Speaker should issue his warrant accordingly: — the defendant, as Speaker, in execution of the said order, issued his warrant to the sergeant-at-arms, to whom the execution of such warrant belonged, to arrest the plaintiff, and commit him to the custody of the Lieutenant of the Tower, to receive and detain the plaintiff in custody during the pleasure of the House; by virtue of which first warrant the sergeant-at-arms went to the messuage of the plaintiff, where he then was, to execute it; and, because the outer door was fastened, and he could not enter, after audible notification of his purpose, and demand made of admission, he, by the assistance of the said soldiers, broke and entered the plaintiff's messuage, and arrested and conveyed him to the Tower, where he was received and detained in custody, under the other warrant, by the Lieutenant of the Tower. — 14 E. 1.

Action against the sergeant-at-arms, charged with the execution of such warrant.

Defence. Upon the plaintiff's refusing to submit to the arrest, and shutting the outer door against the sergeant, who had demanded admission for the purpose, and declaring that the warrant was illegal, and that he would only submit to superior force; and a large mob having assembled before the plaintiff's house, and in the streets adjoining, so that the sergeant could not arrest and convey the plaintiff to the Tower without danger to himself and his ordinary assistants, if at all, by the mere aid of the civil power; the sergeant thereupon called in aid a large military force; and, after breaking into the plaintiff's house, placed a competent number of the military therein, for the purpose of securing a safe and convenient passage to conduct the plaintiff out of the house into a carriage in waiting, and thence conducted him with a large military escort to the Tower, using at the same time every personal courtesy to his prisoner consistent with the due execution of his duty; which, however, would not safely admit of delay in the execution of such warrant. — 14 E. 163.

Trespass for assault and false imprisonment.

Plea. The plaintiff, just before the time when, &c., without leave of the defendant, at an unreasonable hour at night, entered into the defendant's dwelling-house, and, with force and arms, made a great disturbance, and insulted and abused the defendant therein, and disturbed him in the peaceable possession thereof in breach of the peace; whereupon the defendant requested the plaintiff to cease his noise and disturbance, and depart from out the dwelling-house, which the plaintiff reluctantly did, and threatened the defendant that he would rap at the door till the defendant delivered up a certain book. And the plaintiff did stand at the door, on the defendant's premises, rapping violently, illegally, and wrongfully against it, for two hours, and during that time insulted the defendant, and disturbed him in the possession of his dwelling-house, in further breach of the peace; whereupon the defendant requested the plaintiff to cease his noise and disturbance, and depart off the defendant's premises; which the plaintiff refused to do, and continued knocking, &c., and threatened the defendant to continue the noise and disturbance until he should deliver the book. The defendant then sent for a constable for the purpose of taking the plaintiff into custody, and thereby preventing him from further disturbing the defendant; and the plaintiff, having ascertained that he was about to be given into custody, ceased the rapping, which he had violently, &c., continued up to that period, and ran and escaped off and from the defendant's premises; when the defendant immediately pursued the plaintiff, and overtook him near the dwelling-house, and thereupon the defendant, it being necessary, in order to preserve the peace and prevent the plaintiff from continuing to disturb the order and tranquillity of the dwelling-house, and from continuing to make the noise and disturbance at the dwelling-house during the whole night, gave charge of the plaintiff to the constable, who had in his hands a legal warrant to arrest the plaintiff for the acts aforesaid, and who saw and witnessed the same, and requested the constable to take the plaintiff into custody, carry him before a justice to answer the premises, and to be dealt with according to law; and the constable gently laid hands on the plaintiff for the cause aforesaid, and took him into custody in order to carry him before a justice, to be there dealt with, &c. — 2 Ad. & Ell. (N. S.) 375.

Trespass for assault and false imprisonment and taking the plaintiff to a police-station.

Plea. The defendant was possessed of a dwelling-house, and the plaintiff entered the dwelling-house, and then and there insulted, assaulted, abused, and ill-treated the defendant and his servants in the dwelling-house, and greatly disturbed them in the peaceable possession thereof, in breach of the peace; whereupon the defendant requested the plaintiff to cease his disturbance, and to depart from and out of the house; which the plaintiff refused to do, and continued in the house, making the said disturbance and affray therein. And thereupon the defendant, in order to preserve the peace and restore good order in the house, gave charge of the plaintiff to a certain policeman, and requested the policeman to take the plaintiff into his custody, to be dealt with according to law; and the policeman, at such request of the defendant, gently laid his hands on the plaintiff, for the cause aforesaid, and took him into custody. — Cr. Mees. & R. 756.

Declaration for slander.

The plaintiff was a salaried superintendent of police at L., and it was his duty, as such, to conduct himself temperately and with decency and propriety, while on duty, and to hinder and repress indecent and disorderly conduct in the police-office. And the defendant, intending to injure the plaintiff in his office, and cause it to be believed that he had misconducted himself as such superintendent, and cause him to be dismissed from his office, in a discourse which he had concerning the plaintiff as such superintendent, and concerning the plaintiff's conduct in his office (specially setting forth how the words were connected with the office), falsely, &c., spoke and published concerning the plaintiff, and concerning him as such superintendent, and concerning his conduct in his office, the false, &c., words: "I" (meaning the defendant) "saw a letter two or three days since, regarding an officer of the L. police force" (meaning the plaintiff), "who" (meaning the plaintiff) "had been guilty of conduct unfit for publication." — 6 Ad. & Ell. (N. S.) 7.

The plaintiff was editor of a newspaper called the Massachusetts Cataract, and the defendant (adding a *colloquium*) published a false and malicious libel of and concerning the plaintiff, and his violations of the seventh commandment of Scripture, as follows: "To the editor of the Massachusetts Cataract. Can you" (meaning the plaintiff) "break every commandment in the decalogue and still go unwhipped of justice? Can you" (meaning the plaintiff) "be guilty of breaking the seventh commandment, and cover that noisy and licentious affair? Can you" (meaning the plaintiff) "recollect the tenth commandment, which says thou shalt not covet thy neighbor's wife? If you" (meaning the plaintiff) "recollect this commandment, can you" (meaning the plaintiff) "put your hand upon your heart and say you" (meaning the plaintiff) "have a clear conscience on this subject? Is not conscience a little unquiet? Does it not say hush, be still? It wont do to reveal the things of the prison-house; those things said and done in secret places." Meaning thereby, that the plaintiff had committed the crime of adultery, and that his conscience accused him of this crime. And by said words the defendant accused the plaintiff of the crime of adultery. — 11 Met. 473.

The discourse of the defendant was had, concerning a trial between the plaintiff and the defendant before a certain justice of the peace, &c., and concerning an oath the plaintiff took on said trial before said justice in proving his account. — 2 Humph. 434.

A was murdered, and the plaintiff was concerned in it, and had a hand in it; meaning that the plaintiff aided and assisted in the commission of the murder. — 10 N. H. 52.

The defendant publicly, falsely, and maliciously accused the plaintiff of the crime of larceny, in words spoken of and concerning the plaintiff substantially as follows: "He is a thief." — 14 Gray, 221.

He (the plaintiff) acknowledged that he swore to a lie about the money, and had taken seventy-five dollars out of, &c., more than he ought to; he acknowledged to me that he swore falsely in the trial with, &c.; and that he swore falsely in reference to the money, and that he never let, &c., have any money as he swore he did, and that he must go to State-prison. — 33 Verm. 182.

In a conversation of and concerning the plaintiff as a physician, &c., "The bitters that Dr. A gave to B caused his death; there was poison enough in them to kill ten men." — 22 Ind. 184.

MALICIOUS PROSECUTION.

The plaintiff was arrested, entered into recognizance, and was afterwards therefrom and thereof discharged and acquitted, and the prosecution was wholly ended and determined. — Cheves, 9.

The defendant, falsely and maliciously, and without probable cause, made affidavit in the Court of Exchequer, that the plaintiff was indebted to the Queen in a sum named, and was in embarrassed circumstances, and that the debt was in danger; by means whereof the defendant, maliciously and without probable cause, caused a commission to issue and an inquisition thereon to be taken, whereby it was found that the plaintiff was indebted to the Queen in the sum named; and the defendant afterwards, falsely, maliciously, and without probable cause, procured a writ of extent to be issued and delivered to the sheriff, under which the plaintiff's goods were seized, which writ of extent was afterwards superseded in the Court of Exchequer, and the said writ of extent was then and is ended; whereas the plaintiff was indebted only in a small portion of the sum named, and was not in embarrassed circumstances, and the debt was not in danger, as the defendant knew; and the plaintiff thereby suffered great damage, from loss of credit, by a creditor's selling the plaintiff's property under a power of sale given as a security, and another creditor's making an affidavit and giving notice to make the plaintiff a bankrupt. — 4 Ad. & Ell. (N. S.) 481.

The defendant falsely and maliciously made an affidavit, &c., and upon said affidavit falsely and maliciously caused and procured the plaintiff to be arrested, and imprisoned for ten days, at the expiration of which, the plaintiff, in order to procure his release and discharge, was forced to and did pay to said defendant a large sum of money, to wit, &c., and was thereupon discharged and released, &c. — 19 Ala. 760.

The defendant, upon a writ of *ca. sa.*, properly issued at his instance, for a large amount, but a great part of which had been afterwards satisfied, falsely and maliciously, and without any reasonable or probable cause, procured the sheriff to issue a warrant, to take and keep the plaintiff, &c., and falsely and maliciously, and without any reasonable or probable cause, procured the warrant to be indorsed to levy the larger amount, whereupon the plaintiff was taken and detained for four weeks, and suffered in his business and credit. — 26 Eng. L. & Eq. 200.

The defendant took and distrained the growing crops, &c., of the plaintiff, under color and as in the name of distress for rent, which crops, &c., were sufficient to have satisfied the arrears of rent and costs; and although the defendant might, under the said distress, have satisfied the said arrears, &c., yet he wrongfully and vexatiously made a second distress on the said growing crops, for the same arrears, and wrongfully kept and withheld the said crops, &c., from the plaintiff for a long time, &c. — 4 Ad. & Ell. (N. S.) 123.

The defendant falsely and maliciously, and without any reasonable or probable cause, charged the plaintiff with having feloniously stolen a certain horse of the defendant's. — 8 Blackf. 37.

The defendant falsely, &c., before a certain justice of the peace (naming him), charged the plaintiff with having wilfully and maliciously set on fire and burned a certain district school-house (naming the district, township, and county). — 6 Blackf. 295.

Declaration in case, for wrongfully suing out an attachment.

Plea. The attachment was not sued out wrongfully, maliciously, or vexatiously, or without reasonable or probable cause. — 20 Ala. 527.

NUISANCE.

The plaintiff was lawfully possessed of a certain close (describing the same), and the defendant, well knowing the premises wrongfully and injuriously kept and continued a building projecting and overhanging the plaintiff's said close, and before then wrongfully erected and built, projecting as aforesaid, for a long space of time. — 7 Allen, 431. (Held, a declaration for nuisance.)

The defendant, being possessed of a messuage adjoining a garden of the plaintiff, erected a cornice upon his messuage, projecting over the garden, by means whereof rain-water flowed from the cornice into the garden, and damaged the same, and the plaintiff has been incommoded in the possession and enjoyment of his garden. — 1 Com. B. 828.

The plaintiffs were possessed of a vault adjoining certain walls, and which was of right supported in part by parts of the adjoining walls; and were of right entitled that their vault should be so supported; and there were foundations belonging to the vault which the plaintiffs ought to enjoy. Yet the defendant wrongfully removed the wall adjoining the plaintiff's vault, without taking proper precautions to prevent them from giving way; *per quod* the plaintiffs' vault was damaged by the fall of some materials, which otherwise would not have hurt it (and special loss ensued). — 3 Bing. N. 334.

The plaintiff, before and at the time of committing the grievance alleged, was navigating his barges, laden with goods, along a public navigable creek, and the defendant wrongfully moored a barge across, &c., and kept the same so moored, from thence hitherto, and thereby obstructed the public navigable creek, and prevented the plaintiff from navigating his barges so laden; *per quod* the plaintiff was obliged to convey his goods a great distance over land, and thereby put to trouble and expense. — 4 M. & S. 101.

Trespass against the mayor, councilmen, and constable of a town, individually, for pulling down the plaintiff's house.

Defence. The corporation passed an ordinance, declaring the house a nuisance, it being unoccupied by the plaintiff or a tenant, but used by others in such manner as to endanger the town by fire, and also to make it offensive to the citizens and endanger their lives, and providing that, if the plaintiff did not within a specified time after notice abate the nuisance, the constable should proceed to do so. — 18 Ark. 252.

Defence for shooting the plaintiff's dog. Said dog attacked him, and was accustomed to attack and bite mankind. — 1 C. & P. 104.

Trespass for killing a mastiff.

Defence. He ran violently upon the defendant's dog, and bit him; and the defendant could not otherwise separate the mastiff from his dog. — 1 Saun. 83.

WATERCOURSE.

The plaintiff was owner of a mill a short distance from one occupied by the defendant on the same stream, and the defendant wilfully, and with intent to injure the plaintiff, frequently shut down his gates, so as to accumulate a large head of water, and then raised them, by which means an immense volume of water ran with great force against the plaintiff's dam, and swept it away. — 13 Ired. 50.

The defendants built dams, &c., whereby they kept back the water, and also opened gates, whereby mud washed out with the water, and filled the plaintiff's ditches, and rendered the water worthless. — 14 Cal. 25.

Lights, &c. The grievances complained of were occasioned by the defendant's pulling down a house and erecting another in its place, which he did with the acquiescence and consent of the plaintiff, and on the faith of such acquiescence and consent he incurred expenses.

Replication.

The plaintiff acquiesced and consented, &c., on the faith of false representations of the defendant; that is, that the grievances complained of would not result from his works. — 7 Jur. (N. S.) 1247.

FRAUD.

The plaintiff was a printer of silk goods, and had delivered to the defendant a lot of such goods, in which were woven fabrics of silk, printed by the plaintiff with a design for the ornamenting of them, which had been published by the plaintiff to the defendant and others; and the plaintiff was about to print other fabrics of silk with the same design, and to publish the same in the way of his trade for gain; of all which the defendant had notice; but the defendant, contriving to deceive, injure, and defraud the plaintiff, and induce him to desist from printing more with the design, and to deprive him of the gains he would have made, and to cheat him of the benefit of the design, and to acquire the same for the sole benefit of the defendant, and to put the plaintiff to expense; falsely, fraudulently, and deceitfully represented to the plaintiff that in the lot there was a copy of a registered pattern,[1] and that, the parties, &c., having asked the defendant for the printer, the defendant was obliged to give the plaintiff's name; and the parties intended to proceed against the plaintiff by injunction and order through the Court of Chancery; whereas, in truth, no such design, or design resembling it, had been registered according to the statutes aforesaid; and there were no parties interested in the design; nor had any parties asked the defendant for the printer; nor had the defendant given them the plaintiff's name; nor did any parties intend to proceed against the plaintiff by injunction, &c., as the defendant, at the time of making the representation, knew; by means of which representation the plaintiff, believing it to be true, was induced to travel a long distance for the purpose

[1] See Stats. 5 & 6 Vict. ch. 100, 6 & 7 Vict. ch. 65.

of inquiring into the matters represented, and satisfying the supposed parties, as it was reasonable for him to do under the circumstances; and was induced to abstain from further printing with the design, which he had orders to do, and from selling silk handkerchiefs printed with the design; and the defendant, by means of the premises, enjoyed the benefit of the design to the exclusion of the plaintiff, and printed with the design, and sold, for his profit, silk handkerchiefs, and took the profits, without the competition of the plaintiff, and to his exclusion. — 9 Ad. & Ell. (N. S.) 197.

CONVERSION.

Trover for a bedstead.

Plea. The plaintiff heretofore recovered a judgment in trover for the same identical bedstead, against A (describing the judgment). And the conversion by A, for which that action was brought, was a conversion not later in point of time than the conversion declared on, and, before this conversion, A, being possessed of the bedstead, sold it to the defendant, who paid him for the same, and received it under such sale; and the taking under such sale was the conversion declared on. — 3 Com. B. 266.

Trover for timber.

Plea. The defendant was possessed of a close, and was digging a saw-pit therein, and because the goods were put and placed on the close by the plaintiff, without leave or license, and were so buried therein by the plaintiff, that the defendant could not make the saw-pit without a little cutting and destroying the said goods, the defendant did necessarily a little cut and destroy them. — 20 Eng. L. & Eq. 445.

Trover by an assignee.

Plea. Before the insolvent petitioned for his discharge, the defendant sold and delivered to him divers, &c., being the same as those mentioned in the declaration, for £150, on the terms that the defendant might at any time, until payment of the price, take and retain the horses and harnesses as a pledge and security for such part of the price as should remain unpaid, until payment thereof. And at the time of the alleged conversion, £22, part of such price, remained due. And after the plaintiff became possessed as assignee, the defendant took the said horses and harnesses into his possession as such pledge and security, &c.; which is the conversion in the declaration mentioned. — 2 M. & W. 395.

TRESPASS.

The defendant broke and entered the plaintiff's dwelling-house in, &c., being the same dwelling-house occupied by the plaintiff, with force and arms, and did then and there imprison the plaintiff for the space of one hour, without any legal or probable cause. — 13 Met. 144.

The defendant on, &c., broke and entered the plaintiff's close, and ejected him therefrom, and kept and continued him so ejected from thence hitherto, whereby the plaintiff, during all that time, lost the use and benefit of said close. — 6 Gratt. 144.

Trespass *qu. cl.*

Plea. From time immemorial there hath been and still is a public port partly within said manor, and also in a river which has been a public and common navigable river from time immemorial; and there is, in that part of the port which is within the manor, a certain ancient work or erection, belonging to the said port, necessary for the preservation of the same for the safety and convenience of the ships resorting thereto. And this work being damaged and in decay at the said times when, &c., it became necessary that the said work should be immediately repaired. And neither the plaintiff, nor any other person bound to make said repairs, though duly notified to make the same, did nor would repair the same, but wholly neglected so to do; wherefore the defendants, after a reasonable time for repairing had elapsed, and having occasion to use said port, entered and repaired. — 3 D. & R. 556.

PUBLIC OFFICERS.

The plaintiffs were rated to a church-rate, &c., and were summoned before the defendants (justices of the peace) to answer a complaint that they had refused to pay it. And the plaintiff, duly attended, and in good faith, &c., disputing and intending to dis pute the validity of the said rate, upon the hearing gave to the defendants, then being and acting as such justices as aforesaid, notice that they disputed the validity of the rate, and required the defendants, as such justices, to forbear from and not to give judgment in respect of the matter of the complaint. And there was no evidence given, to or before the defendants, that the plaintiffs did not in good faith dispute the validity of said rate, or that they did not in good faith give such notice to the defendants as aforesaid; yet the defendants, disregarding said notice, and assuming to act as justices when they well knew that they had not jurisdiction to make any order upon the matter of the complaint, made an order for payment of said amount of said rate, together with a sum, &c., for costs. — 8 Jur. (N. S.) 482.

Declaration against a sheriff. Although the defendant could have levied of goods of the debtor within his bailiwick the moneys indorsed on the writ, yet the defendant, disregarding his duty, did not levy of the said goods the moneys or any part thereof; and the defendant, further disregarding his duty, falsely returned, &c. — 2 Eng. L. & Eq. 260.

The defendant (a sheriff) duly committed (A, an execution-debtor of the plaintiff), as sheriff, to the jail of the county of, &c., and the term of the defendant's office expired, and (B) was elected and duly qualified as sheriff in place of the defendant; and the defendant was duly served with a certificate of the clerk of the county, that (B) had qualified and given the security required by law. And the defendant did not, within ten days after such service, deliver to the new sheriff (A), then in the defendant's custody on said execution, and confined within the jail liberties. — 4 Bosw. 649.

Trespass for assault and false imprisonment.

Plea. The defendant was a justice of the peace; and a felony had been committed, and there was reasonable ground for suspicion that the plaintiff was guilty of said felony (stating particularly what the ground was), and, in consequence thereof, the defendant ordered the plaintiff to be arrested. — 5 Blackf. 406.

Trover for horses.

Plea. A judgment was recovered at, &c., against J. F. for, &c., and the defendant, an officer, seized them under an execution against J. F., the same being the goods and chattels of the said J. F., and liable to be seized and taken as aforesaid, and not being the property of the said plaintiff. — 1 M. & W. 682.

Trespass for breaking and entering the plaintiff's close and stable, and taking away two horses.

Plea. An execution against A was delivered to the sheriff, &c.; and the horses belonged to the execution-debtor, and were subject to the execution; and the sheriff by virtue of the execution, and the defendants by his command, broke and entered into the close and stable, and took the horses, &c.

Replication. The horses did not belong to the execution-debtor, but to the plaintiff. — 4 Blackf. 16.

Trespass for breaking and spoiling a lock, bolt, and staple appertaining and fixed to the outer door of the plaintiff's dwelling-house, and wherewith the same was fastened.

Plea. A *fi. fa.*, &c., issued against the plaintiff, and was delivered to the defendant, being a sheriff, &c.; by virtue whereof the defendant, then lawfully being in a room of the dwelling-house occupied by D as tenant to the plaintiff, peaceably entered into the residue of the dwelling-house, through the door communicating between the room and the residue, the same being then open, to take in execution the plaintiff's goods then in the dwelling-house, and did take them; and, because the outer door was shut and fastened with the lock, bolt, and staple, so that the defendant could not carry away the goods or execute the writ without opening the outer door, nor open the door without breaking the lock, &c.; and because neither the plaintiff nor any other on his behalf was in the dwelling-house, so that the defendant could request the plaintiff or such other to open the outer door, the defendant, for the purposes aforesaid, did open the outer door, and, in so doing, did necessarily break, &c., the locks, &c., doing no unnecessary damage. — 7 Ad. & Ell. 827.

Action for the recovery of specific personal property and damages for its detention.

Answer. The property was seized by the defendant as sheriff, on an execution, &c., against one J. R. And a trial of the right of property of J. H. R. thereto was had under the statute, before the justice and jury, which resulted in a verdict and judgment in favor of the claimant, J. H. R. And within three days after said trial, the plaintiff in execution executed an undertaking to the said J. H. R., in strict compliance with § 428 of the Code, and delivered the same to the defendant, as sheriff, and it was by him tendered to the claimant, who declined to receive it, and thereupon brought the present suit, said property being still in the possession of the defendant as such sheriff.—12 Ohio (N. S.) 105.

Action for assault and battery, committed on an officer by one whom he was attempting to arrest on a warrant.

Rejoinder. The plaintiff, at the time, &c., did not acquaint or give notice to the defendant that a warrant had been issued, or that he had any warrant, or process, &c., nor did the defendant know that any warrant had been issued, or that the plaintiff had any warrant or process.—2 Hill, 86.

JOINT PARTIES.

Action against A and B.

A was indebted to the plaintiff, &c. And A and B confederated and conspired together, to prevent the plaintiff from obtaining security for, or payment of, his debt; and, in pursuance of such purpose and intention, and in order to enable A to take the poor debtor's oath, the defendants caused his property to be removed from his own custody and possession into the possession of B, by whom the same or the proceeds thereof were kept secreted from attachment, both parties knowing that the debt had not been paid. And the plaintiff sued out a writ against A to recover the debt, and caused his body to be arrested. And A took the poor debtor's oath and was discharged from arrest; and the plaintiff entered the suit, &c., and recovered a judgment, &c., which remains wholly unpaid.—3 Cush. 145.

Action on the case against ten defendants.

Before and at the time of the grievances complained of, the defendants were proprietors of a stage-coach for the conveyance of passengers for hire from A to B, and they received the plaintiff as an outside passenger, to be safely conveyed thereon from A to

B, for hire; and by reason thereof they ought to have safely conveyed him accordingly; but they conducted themselves so carelessly in this behalf, that by and through the carelessness, unskilfulness, and default of themselves and their servants, the coach was overset; by means whereof the plaintiff was hurt, and sustained other injuries. — 6 Moo. 141.

CORPORATIONS.

Action by the N. Joint Stock Company, bankers and brokers, for money lent to purchase shares in the company.

Plea. The directors had in their annual reports falsely represented their affairs to be flourishing, whereas the company was insolvent; and paid large dividends, whereas such dividends were paid out of the capital; and A, their manager, falsely representing the said shares to be of great value, induced the defendant to purchase them, and at the same time, on the part of the company, offered to advance the money, and promised that the company would hold the shares for him until they could be sold at a profit, without his being called upon for the price; and he, relying on such representations, accepted the shares, which A accordingly bought and paid for, and still possessed. — 32 Eng. L. & Eq. 1.

Action for calls against a shareholder of a joint stock company.

Plea. The defendant was induced to become a shareholder by the fraud of the plaintiffs (setting out the particulars). And the defendant repudiated the contract by, &c., and has done nothing under it to make him liable as a shareholder. — 37 Eng. L. & Eq. 56.

RAILROADS.

The defendants did carelessly and negligently run over, &c. — 23 Ind. 133.

The plaintiff was injured by reason of the defendants' negligent management of the cars and engines of a railroad in Jersey city, of which the defendants then had possession. — 1 Dutch. 381.

The defendants were the owners of a certain railroad, running through the towns of W. and P., and of certain cars for the conveyance of passengers upon that road. And on, &c., the defendants were the owners of, and were running and propelling, upon said road, a certain train of passenger cars, for a certain reasonable reward paid to the defendants. — 21 Conn. 557.

Action for land damages.

Plea. The defendants entered upon the land under (statute and section), before the expiration of the prescribed period for exercising their compulsory powers; and having so entered, and being lawfully in possession, they, after the expiration of the prescribed period, continued in possession, and, in the due and lawful exercise of the powers of the said act, committed the alleged grievances. — 4 Eng. L. & Eq. 223.

TOWNS, ETC. — DEFECTIVE HIGHWAYS, ETC.

The plaintiff and his child were thrown from his wagon with great force and violence, and he and the child greatly injured and damaged thereby (briefly describing the injuries). — 35 N. H. 530.

The plaintiff, on August 27, 1831, at Chelmsford, was travelling on a highway in Chelmsford, which highway the town are and were on said day by law bound to keep in repair, on a part of the highway leading from the dwelling-house of I. S. to the stone guide-post near the Middlesex Turnpike in Chelmsford, being within said town of Chelmsford; and the highway within such limits was defective and in want of repair; and the plaintiff, being so travelling as aforesaid, at the time and place aforesaid, sustained the injuries complained of in consequence of such defect and want of repair. — 16 Pick. 128.

The defendants were incorporated, &c., for the purpose of building a bridge, &c., and by virtue of their charter erected a public bridge, and were bound to keep it in repair. And the plaintiff had a legal right to pass said bridge. (Notice of the defect — nature of the defect — statutory liability.) — 16 Pick. 541.

MASTER AND SERVANT.

The defendants were possessed of a certain cart and horse, which was being driven by and under the care and direction of their servant at the time of the grievance complained of; and whilst the plaintiff was crossing a certain street, &c., the defendants, by their servant, so negligently and improperly drove and directed the said cart and horse along the said street, that the plaintiff was knocked down and injured. — 13 Com. B. 237.

One J. W. had contracted with the plaintiff to sing, during a certain term (describing it), at his theatre, and not elsewhere, without the plaintiff's consent, and the defendant during the term maliciously enticed and procured J. W. to depart from her said contract, against the will of the plaintiff, whereby J. W. refused to sing for the plaintiff at his theatre during the whole of the term. And J. W. had been hired by the plaintiff as, and was, his dramatic artiste, for a certain term (describing it), and the defendant maliciously enticed and procured her to depart from her said employment during the said term. (Special damage.) — 20 Eng. L. & Eq. 168.

ATTORNEYS.

Action against attorneys for negligence and unskilfulness.

They conducted the suit so negligently and unskilfully, in not having a certain writ of attachment, affidavit, and declara tion, before then prepared by them in said action, prepared, drawn up, and filed, and made out according to the laws of said State and rules of said court, that the said plaintiff, by the said neglect of, &c., was hindered and prevented from recovering judgment, &c., and was forced and compelled to release and dismiss the levy of said writ of attachment. (Or) by reason whereof the said plaintiff has been prevented from recovering her demand, &c. (Or) the defendants, through want of care and skill, did dismiss the levy of a certain writ of attachment, before that time levied on the property of the defendants therein, and did dismiss, relinquish, and release all liens which had attached or accrued by virtue of said levy, &c., and by means of the unskilful management of the defendants, the plaintiff lost her said demand, and the means of recovering and collecting the same. — 21 Ala. 647.

HUSBAND, ETC.

Declaration, by husband and wife, for a personal injury to the wife (after stating the nature and extent of the injury). By means of such injury, she became sick, and was prevented from attending to her necessary affairs, and the plaintiffs were thereby forced to, and did, necessarily expend two hundred dollars in endeavoring to effect a cure. — 21 Conn. 557.

Action by husband and wife for injury to a right, belonging to her and appurtenant to her land, to take water from a reservoir of the defendant.

Declaration (in substance). The wife owned the land; the plaintiffs owned and possessed the right to take the water, as owners and possessors of the land; and by the wrongful act of the defendant the plaintiffs were deprived of the use of the water. — 25 Conn. 510.

The defendant unlawfully and unjustly persuaded, procured, and enticed the wife to continue absent, &c., by means of which persuasion she did continue absent, &c., whereby the plaintiff lost the company and society of his wife.— Willes, 577.

BAILMENT.

The defendants had the loading of a hogshead of the plaintiff, for a certain reward to be paid to one of them, and a certain other reward to the other two, and the defendants so negligently conducted themselves in the loading, &c., that the hogshead was damaged. — 3 E. 62.

The defendant was an oil-broker, and the plaintiffs, licensed crushers, retained him as such, to sell and deliver for them thirty tuns of linseed oil, according to the contracts of sale, to purchasers, for commission and reward to the defendant in that behalf; which retainer he accepted; and he, as such broker, in pursuance of the retainer, made a contract between the plaintiffs and A, by which the plaintiffs sold to A, and he bought of them, the thirty tuns, at the price, &c., to be delivered by parcels at a certain place and times, each parcel to be paid for in ready money. And the plaintiffs consigned two of the parcels to the defendant, and he delivered them to A on payment; and, after the making of the contract, and in pursuance thereof and of the retainer, the plaintiffs consigned to the defendant, as such broker, the residue of the thirty tuns, to be delivered by him to A on payment. And the oil arrived, &c., of which the defendant had notice, and took upon himself the delivery according to the contract; and thereupon it became and was the defendant's duty, as such broker as aforesaid, to use all reasonable care that the oil should not be delivered to A or any other person, without the price being paid to the defendant according to contract; yet the defendant, not regarding such duty, did not use reasonable care, &c., that the oil should not be delivered, &c., without the price being paid, but neglected and refused so to do, and so negligently and carelessly behaved in the premises, that, by the defendant's mere carelessness and negligence, the last-mentioned oil was delivered to B and C, without the price being paid by A or any person to the defendant, by reason whereof, and of A having become bankrupt and unable to pay, the plaintiffs lost the said oil, and the price thereof, &c. — 3 Ad. & Ell. (N. S.) 511; 2 Gale & Dav. 793.

CARRIERS.

Declaration against a common carrier of passengers for refusing to carry. The plaintiff offered, or was ready and willing, to pay the fare, &c. — 5 Mich. 520.

It was the duty of the defendants safely to carry and deliver, &c., but they did not deliver, &c., within a reasonable time, although a reasonable time for the delivery has elapsed. — 5 Man. & Gran. 551.

LANDLORD, ETC.

The plaintiff was reversioner of a house, &c., then occupied by his tenant, A; and the defendant was in the occupation of a close near to the house, &c., in which was a watercourse. And the defendant, by reason of his possession of the close, ought to have scoured, &c., to prevent the water from being obstructed, and from running out of the watercourse unto, into, and under the house, &c. But the defendant permitted the watercourse to be obstructed, so that the water was penned back, and ran into and damaged the house, to the injury of the plaintiff's reversion.

Plea. A wall, parcel of the plaintiff's premises, was situate near the watercourse and the defendant's close. And said A (or the owners and occupiers of the plaintiff's premises for the time being) was bound to repair said wall, but neglected so to do. And, by reason of the wall's being, through the neglect of, &c., ruinous, &c., part of the wall, near to the watercourse, fell down, and rubbish, &c., being part of the materials, fell into the watercourse, and the same was thereby choked up; and the water, for a short time, unavoidably was penned back, &c., and ran out, as in the declaration mentioned. And the defendant, in a reasonable time after he had notice that the watercourse was so choked up, &c., and before action brought, cleansed out the same, so that the water flowed as it ought to do. — 6 Mis. 592.

(The defendant), knowing that a certain house, &c., was in such a ruinous and dangerous state as to be dangerous to enter, occupy, or dwell in, and knowing that the state of the house was unknown to the plaintiff, by agreement in writing demised the said house to the plaintiff, and the plaintiff agreed to take the same at a certain rent, the plaintiff having previously proposed to take said house for the purpose of immediately occupying and dwelling in the same. And the plaintiff did not agree to put said house in repair before he commenced to occupy the same, and was induced, by his belief of the soundness of the house, to enter into such agreement to take said house. And the defendant falsely represented to the plaintiff, before the making of said agreement, that said house was in a safe and suitable condition for occupancy. And the plaintiff commenced to dwell in said house without notice of its said state, and so continued to the knowledge of the defendant. And the defendant neglected his duty in not giving the plaintiff notice the said house was in said state before entering into said agreement and before the plaintiff commenced occupying the same. And shortly after the plaintiff commenced occupying the same, said house fell down, whereby — (special damage). — 2 Eng. L. & Eq. 318.

INJURIES CAUSING DEATH.

A railroad engine, by the negligence of the servants of (the defendants) in managing the same, was run upon (the intestate), whereby he was killed. — 30 Conn. 184.

(The defendant's) horse, while being driven and trained by him, in a public place or thoroughfare in the city of Dublin, to the annoyance of great numbers of passengers, and among others of (the deceased), contrary to the provisions of the Dublin Police Act (5 Vict. session 2, ch. 24, § 14), by the negligence of (the defendant), ran against and injured (the deceased), whereby, as the necessary result and consequence of the aforesaid illegal act of (the defendant), (the deceased) shortly afterwards died. — 9 Ir. Com. L. Rep. 9.

MISCELLANEOUS.

The plaintiff had bought of C and son certain goods (for a sum mentioned), which the defendant had lent the plaintiff on his personal credit, without agreement for any lien on them in respect thereof, which sum the plaintiff paid to C and son, who accepted it in payment for the goods ; yet the defendant, falsely and wrongfully pretending that he was entitled to such lien, and had a right of preventing delivery to the plaintiff till the said loan should be repaid, wrongfully and maliciously, and without any reasonable or probable cause in that behalf, but under color of the said pretended lien, ordered C and son not to deliver the said goods to the plaintiff, but to keep them till they received further orders ; in consequence whereof C and son refused to deliver them to him. — Tyr. & Gran. 118.

The defendant received from the plaintiff money to the amount of, &c., and gave his receipt therefor to the plaintiff, specifying that certain land, to wit, &c., was to be entered therewith. And the plaintiff, relying on the assurance of the defendant, conveyed said land to, &c., for whose use this action is brought ; and since that time one, &c., has entered the land. — 3 Clarke (Iowa), 447.

The rooms of the plaintiff were furnished with gas-pipes and fixtures, which were connected with the main pipes of the defendants. And the defendants contracted with the plaintiff to supply his rooms with gas until reasonable notice of intention to withhold or withdraw the same. And the defendants had for some time, and until the injury hereafter alleged, supplied him with gas, for which he had paid them, as agreed. And the plaintiff was ready and willing to pay the defendants for a continued supply, upon which he was dependent for the lighting of his rooms, and which he desired the defendants to furnish. And it became and was the duty of the defendants to continue to supply him with gas, but they maliciously and wantonly shut off the gas, and refused to supply him; by means of which he was deprived of the means of lighting his rooms with gas, and put to great expense in procuring other means of lighting them. — 30 Conn. 521.

INDEX.

A.

B.

D.

E.

F.

G.

H.

M.

N.

O.

P.

R.

T.